THE ECONOMICS OF DEVELOPMENT AND DISTRIBUTION

WILLIAM LOEHR
University of Denver

JOHN P. POWELSON
University of Colorado, Boulder

HARCOURT BRACE JOVANOVICH, INC.

New York   San Diego   Chicago   San Francisco   Atlanta
London   Sydney   Toronto

318932

Printed in the United States of America
Library of Congress Catalog Card Number: 80-84070
ISBN: 0-15-518905-0

PREFACE

This book is addressed to students (in the broad sense of the word) who, having mastered basic principles of economics, wish to understand how a society lifts itself from penury to affluence, how equitable distributions of income and wealth are defined, and how they come about. These students might be upper-level undergraduates, graduates, professors, or professional economists. Since students rapidly become professionals, and some professionals are (like us) perennial students, the distinctions among them become blurred.

We define development as sustained material well-being, which can occur only with distributions tending toward equality. The study of development includes how institutions and relationships to sustain development are formed and nurtured, and how they sometimes erode for lack of care. We identify units of development, which are not always nation-states. Sometimes they are groups within states, sometimes groupings of states. The comparative development of subnational units implies a study of income distribution.

Some students may wish no more than to understand the process of development. It is to these students that this book is addressed. Others may also wish to become practitioners, such as foreign-aid administrators, economic advisers to governments, or part of the staff of development ministries or international lending agencies. Since we question whether the goals of practitioners are always compatible with maximum development, we consider them to be a subject of inquiry rather than a learning target. This is not a how-to-do-it book, but a why-did-it-or-did-it-not-happen book.

We write this book because we are not happy with the ways development has been taught for the past quarter-century. We believe that development texts have overemphasized macro-approaches such as growth theory and production functions while paying insufficient attention to institutions and the history of development. In addition, we feel the time has come to draw together the lessons emerging from a large number of micro-development studies, now widely scattered, but which in the aggregate provide new and valuable insights.

We can best describe this book in two distinct ways: How we prepared to write it and how we finally organized it. The former consisted of the following steps. First, we selected a number of conventional topics, such as growth models, development planning, income distribution, employment, technology, agrarian reform, and development policy, along with the theories and research of social scientists outside economics. We examined the literature in all these fields for overall insights.

We found the fields disorganized. Sociologists, anthropologists, social psychologists, and political scientists not only paid little attention to economists, but paid even less attention to each other; economists in turn paid little heed to any of them. Within economics, macro-growth theory seemed miles apart from the micro-studies of population, employment, and the like. Even technology meant something different when studied by macro- and micro-economists respectively.

We then read in economic and political history. The lessons of the past appeared to us revealing but little related to conventional interpretations of the present. In total disarray, we asked ourselves: How can all this scattered information be brought together into some consistent pattern?

It was then that we decided that present ways were inadequate and that we had better think of new ones. Rigorous, mathematical approaches were richly developed, but they told us much about only a small portion of the field. By and large, the concepts of development seemed to us primarily intuitional, and less than rigorously definable. Once we had swallowed that pill, we were ready to put the book together.

The core of our approach lies in three development paths (personal, sociopolitical, and economic), set forth in Chapter 1, plus five historical propositions that are not revealed until Chapter 15 (except for being previewed in this preface). In Chapter 2, we take our bow to growth theory, economic models, and planning. We pay less attention to the first two than do most textbooks, and we criticize conventional approaches to the third. This chapter is necessarily more technical than the rest of the book. Students who wish to be less technical may skip portions of it (indicated in a footnote at the beginning of the chapter).

In Chapter 3, we explore the offerings of the noneconomic social scientists, in an attempt to integrate their offerings with the work of economists.

In Chapter 4 (Part II), we turn to the plight of the poor. We are concerned for these people. Why is a large part of the world's population—from thirty to sixty percent, depending on how you measure it—malnourished or underfed, underclothed, and underhoused? Why do they die early? What, if anything, can be done about it? Most development economists believe that certain policies will alleviate poverty and that it is the government's task to identify such policies and implement them. We are not so sure. We consider government (for the most part) to be a contending party, which will help the poor if it is to the government's interest to do so, but which will not help otherwise. More than that, government is many contending parties, vying with one another. Only the poor themselves can alleviate their poverty, and only as their productivity is increased, by themselves or by others. (This is what history tells us.)

In Chapter 5, we evaluate different measures of income distribution and suggest a new measure of growth and distribution. In Chapter 6, we question whether income distribution improves or worsens with development. Some economists have argued the latter, but we believe they are mistaken. They have relied too heavily on cross-sectional comparisons of dubious validity. Our interpretation of the evidence is that economic growth not only enhances the positions of the poor but often increases their relative shares as well.

In Part III, we take up a number of development topics, generally the same as those found in conventional texts: employment and unemployment, technology, population, human capital (nutrition, health, and education), agriculture and agrarian reform, rural and urban development, migration, imperialism, multinational corporations, proposals for a New International Economic Order, dependency theory, and government and economic policy. For each of these topics, we believe we have an approach that varies somewhat from the conventional and that will therefore be controversial. For example, we see population control, agrarian reform, and other social reforms coming only when fundamental relationships between poor and rich are already changed—in other words, such reforms follow, rather than lead. We find that third-world governments have, for the most part, planned ineffectively and inefficiently, often harming development more than they have helped it. We suggest that the proposed New International Economic Order would, if adopted, have the opposite effect from that intended: It would transfer income and wealth from the poor to the rich, not vice versa. This is not a neutral book, and we do not expect our colleagues and students to agree with all of it. But we trust it will stimulate debate.

In Part IV, we turn to history, both past and present. We formulate five propositions for Europe, and then we ask whether they also apply to less-developed countries today. The propositions are these:

1. The history of Europe is one of protracted struggle for liberalism: freedom from serfdom, from monopoly, from crippling controls, from privilege, and for freedom of trade. The struggle has not yet ended.
2. Less-advantaged socio-economic groups in Europe have levered their power upward, by making strategic alliances with more powerful groups that were contending with one another and shifting those alliances when it was to their advantage to do so. The leverage of power, not the power itself, has been the secret of income distributions becoming more equal than before. Social pluralism has been an important factor.
3. The introduction of more complex means of production required institutions of trust, which were formulated slowly, painfully, and erratically, along benefit-cost principles.
4. Europe's economic development depended on the elimination of endemic warfare.

5. Development was also associated with a shift, among the rulers, away from a propensity for power and toward a propensity for material wealth.

Since these propositions are accompanied by clarifications and qualifications in Chapter 15, the reader is asked not to judge them at this point. In Chapter 16 we survey a number of less-developed countries today, questioning whether the propositions also apply to them.

In compiling a list of references for this book, we debated whether it would be useful to present a bibliography at the end of each chapter, for topical convenience, or to present all references at the end of the text for completeness. We decided to list at the end of each chapter only the references cited in that chapter and to publish our larger bibliography separately and by subtopics. See Powelson, J.P., *A Select Bibliography on Economic Development, with Annotations*, Boulder, Colorado, Westview Press, 1979.

Our responsibility as authors is equally shared. Each of us originally composed half of the chapters, but each carefully read, commented on, and sometimes revised the other half. Others provided assistance in one way or another. We are indebted to our students, in the University of Denver and the University of Colorado, for their many useful suggestions as they used the manuscript in graduate seminars. In particular, research done by Mark Bykowsky, Valerie Solheim, and Richard Stock has become part of the text. Stephen Fisher-Galati and Frank Hsiao, colleagues at the University of Colorado, have reviewed chapters in their specialized areas. Bruce Herrick and Geoffrey Hainsworth, as well as reviewers unknown to us, read the entire manuscript and made helpful comments. For all of these, we offer the usual qualification of "it goes without saying that . . . ." (Therefore, we do not say it.)

We also thank Velma Shanahan, Barbara Kuiper, and Catherine Kearns for helping us organize materials, Angela Gill for typing the entire manuscript several times, and Zeke Little and Michael Greenstein for assisting with computer calculations. Robin Powelson helped with the proofreading, and Judy Powelson enlightened her father on the fundamentals of astrophysics (see Prologue and Epilogue).

WILLIAM LOEHR

JOHN P. POWELSON

Denver and Boulder, Colorado

CONTENTS

PART TWO
WHO ARE THE POOR?

PART THREE
FACTORS OF ECONOMIC DEVELOPMENT

7. Unemployment   151

8. Technology   167

9. Population   193

PART FOUR
A NEW LOOK AT ECONOMIC DEVELOPMENT

A PERSPECTIVE
ON ECONOMIC
DEVELOPMENT

The fundamental value held by Renaissance Humanism, as taught by Petrarch and Erasmus, is that each person has an individual will. If this is so, then at least some part of human behavior has no outside explanation whatsoever. If this too is accepted, then there are limits to econometric models, which explain behavior only in empirical terms. From this point on, it is not a great leap to suggest that the watershed decisions leading toward or away from economic development have been made, and continue to be made, by key individuals whose motivations cannot be fathomed.

This idea, which underlies the philosophy of this book, does not deny the scientific nature of economics. Much remains that is logical and explainable. Indeed, the key decisions may be such a small proportion of the total that economic methodology, explaining the rest, lies among our most powerful ways of predicting human response. All we must remember is that this methodology is not everything.

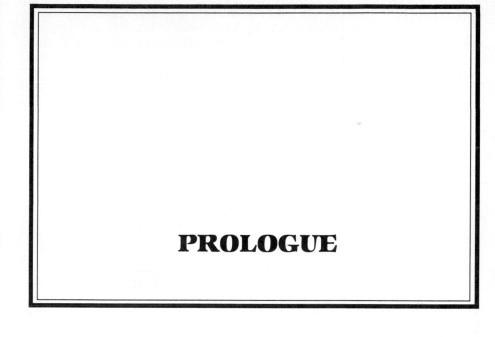

PROLOGUE

Economic development is to the economist what astrophysics is to the physicist: the evolution of a universe, how it began (if it ever did), how it came to be where it is, and where it is going, to the extent we can project.

Apart from the difference in subject matter, we see two major contrasts between economic development and astrophysics. The first is in how economists behave (compared to physicists), while the second lies in the nature of economics (compared to physics).

In the first (behavior), economists have been more modest than physicists. Indeed (as Winston Churchill said of his political opponent), we have much to be modest about. We have no big bang theory, for we have paid little attention to how economies began. We distinguish between economic historians and development economists. Why? With some notable exceptions (for example, Gerschenkron, Tuma, and Rostow), there has not been much communication between them. Why not?

Students of economic development are so caught up in what is happening *now*, or at most in the past two centuries, that we rarely look back at how it evolved. Pick up any book on today's less developed countries (LDCs); rarely will you find mention that all the current experiments in credit, agricultural extension, land reform, and redistribution of income were tried by the Chinese before the twelfth century and that many of them were tried in medieval Europe or even the Roman Empire. Surely a knowledge of these outcomes would be helpful in avoiding mistakes today.

Instead, however, the models for economic development are derived principally from the world depression of the 1930s. Their initial purpose was to help restore a prosperity shattered by insufficient demand in more developed countries (MDCs); their prescription was an increase in investment or government spending. But in LDCs half a century later, the problem is not insufficient demand, and government expenditures will not automatically lead to more employment and output, for the requisite institutions are not always there.

When astrophysicists look "out there," they examine whatever they find. If a strange phenomenon erupts, they do not first ask whether it is chemistry or physics, to decide whether they will ignore it because it belongs to other scientists. They do have models, but in the last quarter century they have done a fundamental turnabout, dropping the stationary-universe model in favor of the big bang. Economists, who have defined some variables as economic and others as ones to be ignored, are not so disposed to a fundamental change in models.

The second difference, in the nature of the two fields, is only to degree. As astrophysicists go farther out into the universe, they discover that concepts once thought to be clear become ambiguous: time, distance, and direction, for example. It is the same with economic development, *but much more so.* Yet we economists, in trying to be as rigorous as physicists, have (unlike them) confined ourselves to variables relatively close, hence clearly defined. Thus factor quantities, technology, and elasticities explain gross national product. These independent variables are clear bordered, either because by nature they are quantifiable or (more often) because economists have agreed on arbitrary distinctions.

But suppose one goes on to inquire, "What causes investment to be what it is? or elasticities?" And if one further asks, "What causes whatever that is to be what it is?" And if one carries the inquiry far out into space, one very early crosses the threshold beyond which lie only vague-bordered sets.

A *vague-bordered set* (some call it a "fuzzy set") has at least one element that is clearly within it, but at least one other element might be put either in that set or in another set by different observers. Alaric in the fifth century clearly belonged to the set of Visigoths, while the emperor he opposed, Honorius, was clearly of the Roman set. But because of intermarriages, physical moving, and defections, some were not clearly Visigoths or Romans but were surely one or the other. "Hard" subject matters are those that deal primarily in clear-bordered sets; "soft" subject matters deal mainly in vague-bordered sets.

Sets in physics tend to be clear bordered because of physical properties on which agreement is easy. In economics, by contrast, sets are almost never clear bordered until elements of different physical properties are put together by agreement. An electron contains physical properties identical to those of all other electrons; the set of "all electrons in the universe" is clearly distinguished from the set of "all protons." But "soil in Gujarat" and "iron in Minnesota" are assembled in the set "land as a factor of production" only by agreement for convenience. Such sets tend to become "frozen," and it then becomes difficult to change them when the convenience changes. It seems as though economists believe that economics can become a hard science simply by agreement and that there is virtue in so doing. In our approach to development in this book, we challenge both beliefs.

To our minds, therefore, development economists are not enough like astrophysicists in ways we should be (examining all forces affecting our universe), while trying to be like physicists in ways we should not be (by pretending our field is harder than it is by nature).

But wait! Have we not exaggerated? No, we have not, but we have told only the underside of the story. The other side is more hopeful. Working outside the models of economic growth, economists have studied specific subtopics of development, transcending the earlier confines of "economic." Unfortunately, their works have not been adequately integrated into overall models of growth and/or development.

Most of these studies are topic-specific and location-specific, such as "income distribution in Brazil" or "choice of technology in the diamond mines of Sierra Leone" or "poverty in Djakarta." It is difficult to generalize from such studies, for each location and each time has its own peculiarities. An enormous number of such studies must be done before commonalities can be perceived.

But an enormous number *is* being done. Furthermore, the time and place differences are turning out to be not so fearful, and social scientists *are* seeing commonalities. Reviews of the literature are proliferating, so that nonsubspecialists can start to put the whole together.

Historically, there is at least one similarity between our approach and that of physics, which is illustrated in the following story. Greek philosophers such as Aristotle, Democritus, and Epicurus had much to say about astrophysics. Epicurus deduced that the universe was infinite in time and space. Now, how could he deduce that in the fourth century B.C., lacking the prerequisites that leave even present-day scientists uncertain? He did not just guess; he applied his intuition to his observations. Indeed, he thought he had proved it.

Although he did not know it, Epicurus's contribution lay in framing the concept, not in solving it. Yet he could hardly have framed it at all, had he not had some intuitive idea about it, based on his observations, however unscientific. As rigorous tools were fashioned over the centuries, his ideas were put to test. Each test, of course, led to new enigmas.

By the same token, when we ask questions about development, successively into more remote tiers, we uncover enigmas for which contemporary tools are inadequate. At present, our rigorous tools apply (in macroeconomics) primarily to the "close-up" relationships defined in production functions and (in microeconomics) to many statistically-isolated studies that are explanatory only when taken together. Let us hope that in the future we are able to develop rigorous tools to treat these interrelationships, along with others constantly unfolding. In the meantime, observation-*cum*-intuition is all we have. We applaud its use, even though the results (like those of Epicurus) may be wrong. For only in discovering that they are wrong do we come upon what is right.

We do not agree with those who would confine development studies to statistically-provable relationships, for we believe they have not told the whole story. Yet observation-*cum*-intuition has had a bad press in the development literature. It is called "speculative" and "journalistic," both pejorative words. Rather, we believe intuition should be used, but it is important to distinguish between what is rigorously shown and what is intuition. All economists use intuition. Those who deny it make implicit assumptions that they fail to recognize. We prefer to put those assumptions out into the open.

Thus we mark the direction of the present book. We believe growth models have revealed most of what they can, until the rest of the field catches up. We believe history has been grossly ignored. We believe economists have pretended we are not intuitive, when really we are. We therefore examine the growth models rather briefly, explaining only the earlier, basic ones; we review the literature on microstudies in a number of subfields; we expand on history; and we offer a set of propositions which appear to us reasonable but which can be neither proved nor disproved.

In sum, let development economists explore our universe more widely. But let us treasure our identity as well. We are a *soft* science, which does not imply a lack of worth. Economic development is soft by its nature; it is worthy because it affects us vitally. Let us not seek to be what we are not, and let us respect ourselves for being what we are.

(To be continued in the Epilogue, on the assumption that the book has been read in between.)

INTRODUCTION

1

THE PROCESS OF ECONOMIC DEVELOPMENT

Who are the poor? In Part 2—where we ask the question—we find that 40% of the world's population is hungry, ill-clad, and poorly housed, and perhaps another 20% is malnourished as well. The concern of this book lies with these people, whether they are in poor or rich nations. Economic development, with its product equitably[1] distributed, is (we believe) the way to alleviate this human malfunctioning.

More and more, the study of economic development is evolving away from the *macro* and toward the *micro*. The tendency in the early 1950s toward *macro* explanations was a logical outcome of the Keynesian revolution and of relationships that were thereby established—or thought to be established—among saving, investment, government expenditures, foreign trade, and other determinants of the gross national product. Policies that had been successful (for the moment) in promoting full employment and economic growth in more developed countries (MDCs) were expected to have similar effects in less developed countries (LDCs). Hence the task of development was conceptualized within the same framework. But in the more than quarter century that has followed, both the obstinacy of underdevelopment and the large number of

---

[1]Already we encounter a gap in the English language. "Equal" is an absolute. Either two quantities are equal or they are not; we cannot speak of "more equal" or "less equal." "Equitable," on the other hand, means "fair." But what is fair is a matter of opinion; equality may not be equitable. Often in this book we will discuss policies for bringing income "closer to equality," but since that phrase is cumbersome we will usually substitute the term "more equitable." Thus we imply that income distribution in every country is farther away from equality than we would deem fair. In Chapter 5, we will suggest an objective measure of this subjective value.

micro studies done have begun to reveal the monumental complexity of the problem, and how little we know about it.

It is almost in order to say, "Let us make a fresh start. Let us cast aside the growth models of the last four decades and take a completely new look at the evidence, with no prejudice about the relevance of variables or structures." To do so to an extreme would be foolhardy. Useful devices may be put into new perspective, but they need not be invented again. Nevertheless, we should approach them with the same degree of skepticism that we accord any variables or structures vying for attention as growth-explainers.

The spirit of the present book is therefore the following. Economic development is the process by which a society (however defined) achieves greater material wealth and more equitable distribution of wealth among its members. The participation of all groups (however defined) in both the production and decision-making arenas is a goal in its own right, except for those whose omission is either by necessity or by social agreement, such as the aged, the infirm, and children. This definition of development—broader than most, and not yet precise—already exposes us to a number of variables not usually encompassed in an economic study. Yet we believe this departure is consistent with the new trends toward the *micro*, by which greater attention is focused on the individual, on rural areas and agriculture, on the distribution of income, and on the sociopolitical forces affecting them.

Just as the study of development is itself evolving, so also is the appropriateness of the methodology. When Joseph Schumpeter wrote his *Theory of Economic Development* (1911), it was not necessary to define the prime variables precisely. No one could count Schumpeter's entrepreneurs, for both they and managers constituted vague-bordered sets (for a definition, see the prologue). With the emergence of Harrod-Domar models and their descendants, precision became a fetish, and those who erred have been criticized for the "conjectural" nature of their analyses. Now the swing is again in the other direction, in that the new variables of concern—unemployment, rural development, the educated individuals—all are imprecisely defined.

In our "almost new" look, we carry this trend a bit further. The principles of development, as stipulated above, have been more or less achieved (mostly less) by all societies at all times in history. We believe that insights into development are therefore to be gained by an examination of history from its beginning; that what has happened before will happen again; and that cause and effect can be deduced from the many differing policies, and many differing degrees of success, of societies extant or extinct. Since history repeats itself a bit differently every time, however, relationships become a matter of interpretation and not of mathematical precision.

In development, the nation-state is the usual unit of measurement. Thus, gross *national* or *domestic* product, population, employment, and other data usually relate to the state. The farther back one goes in history, however, the less relevant the nation-state becomes, and the more appropriate other groupings become as units. And if one starts from an early century, and moves forward without prejudice into the era of nation-states, even then it is not at all clear that the new unit becomes the most significant for measuring development. In its favor are the facts that the national government holds political and military power, is capable of policy with wide-ranging effects, and sometimes combines homogeneous groups of (say) similar ethnic or linguistic background. The most compelling argument, perhaps, is that data are more available for the nation-state than for any other unit. But access to data is at best a questionable criterion for forming a theory.

Against adopting the nation-state as the prime unit for measuring development is the fact that elements of subnational or supernational groupings may hold more in common, in terms of mutual interests, or capacity to cooperate, or ability to influence other units, than do nation-states. A fundamental assumption of modern policy models is that the government of the nation-state is both the appropriate and the competent authority for determining the well-being of its constituents. In many cases, this assumption is absurd. Often the government is itself a conglomeration of contending parties rather than the arbiter.

The choice of the nation-state as the unit for development underlies the current discussion on compatibility between development and distribution. Should a nation attempt to maximize its growth first, and *then*, through transfer payments, see that the pie is equitably divided? Or should it promote equitable distribution along with growth? The trade-off between growth and equity is the subject of many learned discussions (Adelman and Morris, 1973; Okun, 1975; Ahluwahlia, 1976; and others). It would be just as logical to ask—although few do—whether there is a trade-off for the world as a whole, or for Europe, or for Africa, or for the state of Uttar Pradesh, or for the inhabitants of an urban slum.

Our search through history quickly reveals that large-scale, institutionalized redistributions occur only in industrialized countries. In preindustrial eras, such transfer payments are rarely made. They have emerged in MDCs only as recipient classes have achieved sufficient political or economic clout to impose a redistribution ethic upon the nation's social morality. Rather than debate the "nation-state-biased" question of trade-off, development theorists might more fruitfully examine the extent to which a group must develop economically (or politically) to be able to command transfer payments in its favor.

Our historical perspective, therefore, leads us to new units and new relationships among them. We define as a unit of development any recognizable set of people capable of acting cooperatively to improve their own material well-being or that of others. The individual (who causes his or her own resources to cooperate) is such a set. Other sets may be members of a municipality, a secret society, a tribe, a commune, a province, a nation-state, a continent, or even the world. Governments are units distinct from their constituents. Units may be subsets of other units.

Our task is to determine the conditions for development of a unit. To what extent is a unit capable of self-development, in a given environment? Or, to what extent must it change its environment (behavior of other units)? To what extent does the development of a unit depend on or conflict with the simultaneous development of other units? What arrangements (institutions) must emerge for units to cooperate to their mutual advantage? And so on.

We quickly confess that we have not answered the above or similar questions. Indeed, we have not even listed them exhaustively. On the contrary, the nature of the questions and their answers depends on the performance of a monumental number of *micro* studies, of which many more need to be done. We are ourselves doing some (and will report on them in Chapter 12), but we cannot even define all of them. Furthermore, we are unable to divorce ourselves from the nation-state as much as we would like, because it is the unit selected by others whose work we review.

Let us now outline a *process* of economic development, which we believe can be sustained empirically through the comparative experiences of a number of countries, described in Chapters 15 and 16. Our defense depends on certain historical events being judged as similar even though they occur at different times and places, with other events being judged as different.

Our development process is more a description than a theory, since causality is not necessarily implied. There is a succession of steps. At each one, critical individuals decide whether to take the next step or a different one. Their decisions are often based on stimuli extraneous to the preceding steps, and their visions of future steps are cloudy. Therefore, continued development is never assured. It occurs, lapses, and may be reversed—at any time, even in the most industrialized states. Nor does development "begin" at any point. Rather, all its elements are found in all societies at all times, but to varying degrees, and in no society are they maximized.

The process occurs along three paths: personal, political or institutional, and economic. Although analytically separable, the paths intertwine. Resistance increases along one path if the other two do not keep pace.

PERSONAL DEVELOPMENT

Personal development contains four elements, of which the first three are future vision, time preference (or time discount), and risk.

FUTURE VISION

Future vision is the ability to predict the probability function of one's own situation over some stated interval in the future, given alternative choices to be made now. It differs with respect to categories. For example, it may be easier to predict the probability of staying healthy with nutritious foods than the probability of success in the stock market. Anyone's future vision tends to be well developed in familiar categories. The Fante living on the Gold Coast in the seventeenth century may have assessed very well the probability of being captured as slaves if they ventured onto the trade routes toward the interior; a king's son may perceive quite clearly the probability of succeeding his father.

The personal development to which we refer, therefore, relates to the adaptability of future vision to new situations as the environment changes—especially with respect to economic development. Forecasting the profit and loss statement of a firm requires a different kind of vision from predicting the probability of a raid from a neighboring tribe. The individual must perceive how a stimulus from him or her will affect the behavior of others. The inexperience in so doing often leads (say) a central government to believe it has greater authority over local communities than it can exercise in practice, or policymakers not to understand the ways in which imposed restrictions can be resisted and offset.

TIME PREFERENCE

Time preference implies that some degree of future vision is already developed. Someone with the required future vision compares the probability of gaining X amount in a specified future, as opposed to having Y amount now (presumably, $Y < X$), and reaches a rational choice based on his or her time preference.

RISK

Risk refers to the objective probability function that X will occur. This may differ from the subjective probability of one's future vision. We are assuming here that such a function exists for future events, though the individual may have an imperfect vision of it.

INTERIM SUMMARY

Thus, risk refers to the objective probability of future events; future vision refers to the individual's greater or lesser ability to predict that probability, category by category; and time preference refers to the choices made on the basis of his or her predictions. We have not defined personal development in the traditional way, which would include education, skills, and work habits. While we feel these factors are important, we are more concerned with the variables determining individual choice on whether to opt for education, increased skills, or better work habits. Of course, that choice depends on availability, and knowledge about availability, but it also depends on the three elements just discussed.

POWER VERSUS MATERIALISM

The fourth element, propensity for power versus propensity for materialism, is more complex. In early societies, the desire to control the actions and decisions of others appears to dominate the desire for material wealth, at least among individuals able to make social choices. But as development occurs, the balance seems to shift to the latter. Generalizations on this element must be made with the greatest of caution, however, since either power or material gain may be desired as a means of achieving the other.

In feudal societies, the prospect of material gain must have appeared limited to most. The rich already enjoyed all the physical comforts their society could provide; any further need for resources arose mainly from war. The poor, on the other hand, had little prospect of improving their material situation no matter what they did. Among the rich, power and extension of domain were therefore the principal driving forces, and the poor filled the granaries that made conquest possible. This generalization is supported by the historical chronicles, literature, ballads, court reports, and parliamentary debates, which centered on conquest, rank and title, and land disputes, rather than on production.

Thresholds in the shift from the desire for power to the desire for material gain can be pinpointed in various societies. In English history, the period of Henry VII through Elizabeth I (1485-1603) emerged as production-oriented, compared with the period of dynastic struggles (Hundred Years War and Wars of the Roses) which immediately preceded it (1337-1485). In Japan, there was a significant shift after the Meiji restoration (1868). As such shifts occur, the first three elements of personal development become reoriented. Risk refers increasingly to the market and factory, and less to the battlefield. Future vision relates to the gaining of resources rather than power, and to gaining them by production rather than plunder. Time preference is also expressed increasingly with respect to goods and services as opposed to power. New methods, new channels, new institutions—sometimes very complex ones—must be organized and understood.

Propensity for power implies more than crude lust for control over others, however. Some units in some eras apparently believe that little of importance will happen unless they themselves control the processes. Other units in other eras, by contrast, are more prone to "let go," having faith that others will respond in nonthreatening ways. Roman dominance of the Mediterranean crept in from Rome's fear that she would not be secure unless she first controlled the Etruscans, then the Latins and the Italians, the Carthaginians, the Macedonians, the Seleucids and the Egyptians, the Greeks, and finally the Gauls. But all this was not enough, for the Persians, the Germans, and the Huns still threatened. Rome's fears were well grounded, for they were reciprocated by the others. No society at that time could conceive of equal, independent trading in a world made mutually secure.

The power network pervaded every level. Roman government relationships with allies, provinces, and client kingdoms, and Rome's international wars, were paralleled by personal relationships among patrons, clients, and slaves, and by family feuds. After a terrible period in which the whole system collapsed, European development had to be reconstituted through a gradual, painstaking decentralization of power, which we will describe in Chapter 15. Institutions were slowly formed to define and protect the balance, along with the rights and obligations of the decentralized units toward one another.

In what will doubtless be the most controversial proposition of this book, we include in propensity for power the belief of most LDC governments today, that development will occur only if it is primarily controlled by them. By contrast, the People's Republic of China has largely "let go," in that much power is decentralized among communes and their subunits (Chapter 16).

Propensity for power is also manifest in an unwillingness to countenance desired reforms if undertaken by another group. In the 1960s, the reformist APRA party in Peru united with the right wing to deny funds for agrarian reform to the centrist government of President Belaunde (de Onis, NYT, 5-21-80). In the early eighties, El Salvador's Marxist parties have been waging war against a military government that was undertaking the most radical agrarian reform in the country's history (Riding, NYT, 3-23-80). Bad faith is usually charged to such a "wrong" party, but often (as in these two cases) no opportunity is given to demonstrate faith of any kind.

Where we refer to "propensity for power" versus "propensity for material wealth," therefore, we do not mean the pure lust for control versus the desire for goods (although that may be a part). Rather, we encompass a total system of personal relationships, in which material wealth is believed to be most efficiently created in an atmosphere either of centralized control or of free, equal bargaining power.[2] Our choice of terms stems from our perception of a historical relationship, that as the balance swings from the former to the latter, so also does the desire for control give way to the desire for affluence.

Thus all four elements of personal development apply to any development unit, not just to the individual. And just as some persons grasp the implications of change more quickly than others, some societies are able to adapt more easily than others. This may occur, for example, because a society possesses a greater proportion of individuals with "advanced" traits.

Changes in all four elements may be contagious; alternatively, individuals possessing similar characteristics with respect to the four elements may band together, helping one another. Nothing in the present discussion should imply that differences are racial. Historically, the differences cut across racial lines and are apparently cultural. But the reasons why some development units adapt more rapidly than others need to be explored further than they have been. Disparities in income and wealth might be more readily explained thereby.

ILLUSTRATIONS OF FOUR-ELEMENT PERSONAL DEVELOPMENT

Some areas in which four element personal development might be evaluated are as follows: adoption of the scientific ethic, degree of understanding one's capabilities, proper assessment of the value and use of resources, and confrontation versus compromise.

The scientific ethic

Early societies rely heavily on magical explanations of physical phenomena. Over time, not only may science replace magic to explain "known" phenomena, but explanations of the unknown may be sought more and more by scientific methods. Adoption of the scientific ethic therefore includes the belief that one is capable of controlling one's environment. Persons with high future vision, low time discount, and high willingness to take risk, with respect to material production as opposed to power, may be more likely to perceive the value of scientific research than those with opposite qualities.

---

[2]Since centralized control may be either private (as in large companies) or public (as in national governments rather than local), our distinction does not correspond to the one between socialism and capitalism.

Understanding one's own capabilities

Each development unit must learn its capacity to affect the behavior of other units. Businesses learn how to influence customers; banks learn how to improve borrowing and repayment capacities of clients; governments learn which laws are enforceable and which can be evaded. Wrong guesses can be expensive, and are especially so when national development plans fail to yield expected results. Overcentralization is apt to occur where governments believe they have greater control over local communities than they do in fact, or where company presidents overestimate their influence over sales and production managers. Opportunities are lost if business managers do not assess correctly the relationships between increased costs (for example, for quality control) and increased revenues. Economic efficiency is sacrificed if government monopolies are incorrectly believed to pass economies of scale on to consumers while in reality they mainly dispense favors.

Proper assessment of the value and use of resources

Each development unit must stay approximately within its current budget, adjusted for its capacity to borrow and repay. History is replete with kings, nobles, businesses, presidents, and governments unable (or unwilling) to assess these capacities properly. Production and distribution become disturbed if all units in a given geographical area base their demands on the presumption that their society can produce much more than it truly can. Even the most advanced societies function only somewhat efficiently in this respect. If the sum of the demands of the people upon a government is far in excess of the resources available, through either taxes or borrowing, the resulting discontent is apt to lead to work stoppages or tax refusals. The supply of and demand for public goods does not reach an automatic equilibrium similar to that of private goods, which may be equilibrated in the market. By the same token, the sums of wage demands and price expectations must be roughly within the realistic capabilities of the society to supply. Development units in newly developing economies do not always have the experience or the discipline to make appropriate judgments; the course of development becomes itself a trial-and-error learning experience.

Confrontation versus compromise

Europe's ability to compromise was learned on the battlefield (Chapter 15). For the most part, the medieval wars were "winner-take-all" affairs; one of the notable exceptions occurred when Louis IX of France felt it a Christian duty to compromise with Henry III of England even though he had defeated him. On some occasions, to be sure, impasse led to the division of territory among combatants. But beheadings were also common, and by and large the defeated were given little quarter. By the seventeenth century, however, the nature of warfare had changed. In the wars of Louis XIV, for example, European monarchs became more and more aware that total warfare led to exhaustion; optimization therefore required compromise.

An analogous lesson lies in economic development. Those who believe that optimization for one development unit requires the "total defeat" of another (as in class warfare) are analogues of medieval European monarchs. They also ignore the empirical evidence that successful development units trade strongly with one another and are therefore dependent on one another's success, not failure. It is probably no coincidence that the European ability to compromise coincided with the gradual ending of endemic warfare, and that this in turn was associated with the previously mentioned English watershed of 1485 (as well as the French watershed at the time of their revolution and the Italian and German watersheds at the times of their unifications). It may also be no co-incidence that the confrontation politics currently being played with respect to southern African majority rule, Middle Eastern settlements, and guerrilla de-mands on governments (and government demands on guerrillas) in Colombia, Argentina, Chile, and Uruguay occur in conjunction with endemic warfare, retarded development, and poor prospects for improved income distribution.

We can carry the idea further, into vastly unexplored territory, but we warn that it becomes overly speculative. Business conflicts settled by confrontation may lead to non-Pareto-optimal moves,[3] such as more and more costly strikes, and hence less productive efficiency. Since this suggestion cannot be sustained, nor correlated with development (for the data have not been assembled), we mention it only as a possibility. In our historical analysis (again to be defended in Chapters 15 and 16), we find some relationship between greater ability to compromise (and less confrontation) on the one hand, and successful devel-opment with equitable distribution on the other. Once again, these situations derive from enhanced future vision, lower time discount, and greater affinity toward risk, with respect to material affairs.

POLITICAL AND INSTITUTIONAL DEVELOPMENT

Let us divide any preindustrial society (or development unit greater than the individual) into four basic categories: kings who claim divine right (or similar heads of state); nobility, who both advise the kings and derive their power from them; producers and traders; and laborers who possess no means of production other than themselves. In feudal times, large landowners belong to the nobility, and at all times, free farmers without serfs belong to the producers and traders. The last group may be either farm or handicraft workers, with or without skills.

In an early society, where war is endemic, kings and nobility demand goods and services from traders and laborers, and give them protection in exchange. Innovations occur in all historical eras, and knowledge of them is spread by warfare and occupation. But there are two basic limitations upon innovations during an era of constant warfare. First, they cannot achieve a scale larger than can be supplied by the relevant political unit, since potential enemy units will not normally cooperate. Second, they must not be so expensive or so obvious as to suffer high risk of loss through warfare. Sometimes warfare (as in medieval Europe) had very little impact on the farmers whose fields were overrun. The invading hordes would help themselves to current output, move on, and the

---

[3]A Pareto-optimal move is one in which no party loses, while some or all parties gain.

farmers would continue as before. More frequently, however, warfare would leave total destruction in its wake, and the decision to invest had to take that risk into account.

Development requires a set of arrangements for the protection of property, for the stipulation of obligations of one unit to another, and for the enforcement of promises. Early on, these arrangements are *ad hoc*, or else they are not made at all. Development requires their institutionalization.

The first institutionalization takes place historically between kings and nobles, without much reference to merchants, craftsmen, and workers. Thus the Sung Emperor called his nobles together on his accession (960 A.D.), parceled out the estates, and accepted their tacit agreement not to attack him. Thus King John acceded to Magna Carta in England (1215); thus the Ottoman sultans defined the rights and duties of the Janissaries. The same occurred when the King of Spain granted *encomiendas* to his generals and when kings and emperors of countless African states sought accommodations with their chief councilors. The relationships between kings and nobles, earlier defined by warfare and treachery, therefore shift over to formal definitions of rights and obligations.

Only after the kings and nobles have reached agreement with each other does history repeat itself for producers and traders vis-à-vis the upper groups— while all three groups continue to ignore the workers. There are two requisites for increased political and economic leverage for producers and traders. One is that kings and nobility must already be shifting their relative propensities away from power and toward material gain. Only then will they value the services of producers and traders sufficiently to reward them. The other requisite is that producers and traders must not be overly abundant. They first gain economic leverage by producing what kings and nobles want. Then, by combining into guilds or other associations, they gain political leverage as well. In the process they create new institutions—such as city-states, markets that are militarily protected, freedom of pricing—that enhance their status vis-à-vis the upper classes.

The last to achieve leverage is the working class. In England their advance had scarcely begun before the early nineteenth century, and their political representation was not complete until the twentieth. Universal compulsory education is a sign of workers' leverage; in most LDCs, it has not been achieved today. It is not the workers' lack of skills that is responsible for their position, but their numerical abundance. Even without skills, European workers advanced their position (temporarily) when their numbers were decreased by the Black Plague in the fourteenth century.

BALANCE OF LEVERAGE

Success in the political process depends on a relative *balance of leverage* among all four groups, or rather among all development units (for kings and nobles may disappear, and other units may form). *Economic leverage* is the ability to produce goods and services that other units want, and the ability to withhold them. Ability to produce stems from skills and resources; ability to withhold is (usually) inversely proportional to numbers. *Political leverage* is the ability to manipulate the governmental system in one's favor.

Economic and political leverage cannot be measured objectively, but quantification can be agreed on (if it is needed) by taking the average of subjective assessments by different observers. For most purposes, however, a general idea is sufficient, and agreement on this can easily be obtained. For example, some senators have more political leverage (influence over their colleagues' votes) than others, and we usually agree on who they are. Skilled artisans (because of their scarcity) have more economic leverage than unskilled laborers, and we similarly agree on their identity.

We did not choose the term "balance of power" for two reasons. First, it has been preempted by the process of international relations emerging among nation-states in Europe from the sixteenth to the nineteenth centuries. But second (and more important), "power" carries the implication of weight or force, while a "lever" is an instrument for increasing one's power. Economic and political leverage are ways of influencing others (perhaps more powerful, perhaps not) to exert their force in one's favor.

Leverage works as follows. Suppose there are two groups, A and B (who might be kings and nobles), each of which has power measured at 500 units. Another group, C (who could be the bourgeoisie), has only 100 units of power. Groups A and B are fierce rivals, but because their power is equal, neither can prevail over the other. So one of them (say, A) makes an alliance with C; their joint power (now 600) is sufficient to defeat B. As compensation, C may demand more reward from A than it could have obtained by direct use of its power of only 100. It has therefore *leveraged* its power. The arrangement may continue for awhile, but eventually B may make a better offer, and the alliance will shift. By repeated shifts, C may leverage its power until it becomes on a par with A and B.

Economic alliances are contracts to buy, sell, employ or be employed; they also include mergers and other methods of economic integration. Political alliances are groupings to achieve legislative or other non-economic objectives; they range from loose coalitions to political parties or fealty oaths. Short-term alliances have the advantage of fluidity, but well-conceived longer-term alliances may bring greater leverage. Leverage is gained from the ability to shift alliances, plus a knowledge of how to do so advantageously. Normally, a unit will balance its own leverages from different alliances, in proportion to the costs of obtaining them, in much the same way marginal utilities are balanced in proportion to prices. The discounted values of expected gains must be taken into account in long-term alliances. Leverage is thus a marginal concept, in contrast to power, which is a total concept. Leverage has the added value of enabling a unit to use the power of other units to its advantage.

Merely shifting alliances will not tend toward balancing leverages among groups, however. Indeed, it may concentrate them further. So we add another proposition. The more backward a region, the more underutilized is the economic potential of its poor, relative to its rich, either because of ignorance (within both groups) or because controls (such as in feudalism) inhibit shifts in alliances. Increased freedom from inhibiting forces and greater knowledge for the community as a whole will thus increase the leverages of the poor. Since these kinds of gains are themselves achieved by leverage, the process is cumulative. We refer to it, hereafter, as *tendency toward balance of leverage.* But it is neither automatic nor equilibrium-seeking; it may be reversed at any time; and equality of leverage is not its final object.

Now, economic development requires a reasonable degree of efficiency. Efficiency is the capacity to maximize production with a given set of resources. Since no society is perfectly efficient (totally maximizing), perfect efficiency is not a requisite for development. On the other hand, a society that wastes all its resources (is totally inefficient) does not develop. Thus some level of efficiency is essential to development. No one has yet defined this threshold; this deficiency is one among the many in our present knowledge. We may assume, however, that the greater the degree of efficiency, the greater the probability of development.

We shall now propose that the degree of efficiency in a society depends on the degree of balance of leverage. If *A* and *B* monopolize resources between them, and *C* does not use its leverage, production may be inefficient because of monopoly. But if *C* exercises its leverage for a more equitable distribution of resources, the monopoly may be broken. Now, suppose there are many groups *(A, B, C, D, . . .)*, all using their leverages through shifting alliances. There will be a tendency toward new alliances that produce a more efficient allocation of resources, simply because these alliances have a greater payoff than others. Conversely, a failure to spread leverage widely, or to permit new alliances freely, leads to monopolistic outcomes with their well-known inefficiencies. From this, it follows that the more closely a society approaches pluralism and balance of leverage, the greater the probability of economic development.

In the rest of this book (and especially in Chapters 15 and 16), we will defend this proposition. The distinction is not between market and nonmarket economies, or between socialism and capitalism, but between pluralism and balance of leverage on the one hand and their absence on the other. The market is one alternative institution for promoting efficient use of resources, *provided* sufficient pluralism and balance of leverage exist already. A market economy that is too centralized (too much leverage residing in the government) or too monopolized by a few individuals or companies may be a slow developer. Similarly, a decentralized socialist economy (such as the People's Republic of China) may develop rapidly; indeed, we later suggest (Chapter 16) that the pluralist-leverage model is today operating in the People's Republic of China as well as in Taiwan.

As a balance of leverage emerges, there must be institutional arrangements to preserve it. Institutions perform two functions. First, by enforcing contracts, they preserve trust among individuals who must cooperate. The division of labor is possible only if each participant is assured that others will perform according to their promises. Second, institutions provide channels through which acts of cooperation may be repeated, without having to be negotiated each time (wages paid regularly, money supplied according to certain principles, and so on).

Of course, institutions exist at all stages of economic growth. But the institutions that are necessary to maintain a balance of leverage are different from those that previously maintained the imbalance. For example, feudalism gives way to different provisions for land tenure and use, and different divisions of political responsibility.

Let us now turn to the relationships among institutional growth, violence, the power ethic, and economic development.

THE DECLINE OF ENDEMIC VIOLENCE

In both Europe and the Far East, endemic violence declined before the industrial revolution. We hypothesize that this decline is a requisite for industrial advance. In England before the sixteenth century, and in continental Europe before the eighteenth, war was virtually continuous; only thereafter did prolonged periods of peace ensue. In China, the same change occurred about the middle of the twentieth century. It is today occurring, at different rates, in other LDCs.

In this context, it is important to distinguish endemic violence from institutionalized warfare. Quincy Wright (1964: 641–646) has shown no decline in warfare over time; indeed, the number of participants and major battles is greater in the period 1900–1941 than in any previous period of history. There is, however, a difference. Before (say) 1485 in English history, every person was required to take into account the probability of a sudden despoliation of his capital, at any time, through an act of violence on the part of a neighbor. Economic activity occurred despite this threat. But it was not until the threat of violence *as a daily occurrence* had been removed that scientific advances culminated in the industrial revolution. The industrial revolution, and succeeding population growth, made life itself dependent on a widespread network of commercial and production relationships, which would have been impossible under the threat of endemic violence found in the fifteenth century and earlier. One may also make the conjecture that endemic violence in many LDCs today plays a role in the slowness with which these countries form appropriate commercial and financial networks.

The overall relationship that we see between prolonged periods of peace and economic development is difficult to define. Was development retarded by violence itself, or by the propensity for power that caused violence? Surely a continued state of violence is not conducive to trust, cooperation, and division of labor. However, scientific advance occurs despite warfare and perhaps even because of it. Discoveries such as the magnitude of the earth's circumference, the value of pi, the water clock, the water mill, and the steam engine occurred in Egypt and other Hellenistic kingdoms during their periods of internecine warfare in the first three centuries B.C. Scientific advance in China continued after each dynastic overthrow, almsot where it had left off earlier. Furthermore, institutions are not necessarily destroyed by warfare. The development of parliamentary government and the court system in England continued throughout the Hundred Years War and the Wars of the Roses. Finally, modern nations have recovered very rapidly from the world wars of the twentieth century; economic development was hardly dealt a blow.

Yet the pace of development is seriously retarded while violence is in progress, and development may be halted altogether if the violence is endemic. This endemic violence correlates so closely with the dominance of the power ethic that it is difficult to decide which causes the other. It is perhaps not necessary to decide. Instead, we shall hypothesize that institutions of trust and cooperation may develop before the decline of violence and the power ethic—indeed, they may cause that decline—and such was the case in Europe and the Far East. The same drama is now being repeated in many remaining LDCs, though the balance remains precarious.

We now encounter a new problem. We have hypothesized that endemic violence contradicts economic development, and that reforms may promote it. So we must ask: Is reform possible without violence? We define "reform" as an abrupt change in the structural relationship of one unit to another, especially with respect to the political process, access to institutions, or the distribution of income and wealth. Sometimes reforms are brought about through violence, and at such times one must analyze the situation for a net (positive or negative) effect. Many believe that the rich and powerful will not give up their privileges without a fight and that peaceful reform is therefore impossible.

History tells us the opposite. Time and again, both power and resources have been yielded peacefully (Chapter 11). The task, therefore, is to discover under which conditions reform occurs with violence and under which conditions it occurs without, and what the long-term effects are for each. Our general hypothesis—to be illustrated later—is that the development process itself shifts leverage in such a way that those units that must yield power and resources become archaic in the normal course of events. For example, the growth of industry shifts leverage away from aristocratic landowners and toward industrial units, which perceive the need for agrarian reform in order to feed urban workers adequately. Reforms achieved by violence (or other means), when the necessary leverage shift has not occurred, do not last.

Shifts of this nature are more likely if the relevant society has already developed a set of institutions that operate routinely to deprive some units (different ones each time) in favor of others as the needs of development demand, and if all units (including the ones deprived) would suffer if the institutions themselves were impaired. Such are the institutions of transfer payments that evolve in industrial societies. Individuals become willing to be taxed, provided they perceive the tax system in general as functioning in their interest.

PARALLEL GOVERNMENTS

Institutional development is no easy task. Only to a limited degree can institutions coerce people into keeping promises they would not have kept otherwise. Those that are designed solely to do so (*coercive institutions* as opposed to *institutions of trust*) are apt to be overthrown. In order to nurture the growth of delicate institutions, development units sometimes institute two layers, which might supplement or even duplicate each other. Either is able to serve as fallback in case the other fails.

The parallel governments in medieval Europe were the monarchy or feudal princedom on the one hand and the Church on the other (Chapter 15). Possessing a complete set of public officials, law courts, and taxation systems, as well as instruments for punishment (excommunication) and for limiting warfare ("Peace of God" and "Truce of God"), the church transcended the boundaries of kingdoms and princedoms; it served to unify Europe. No one can determine the degree to which the church contributed to the mutual respect that underlay the willingness of medieval capitalists to entrust their money to shipowners venturing into unknown lands. Nor can one guess the extent to which religious authority facilitated the growth of cities, or of the Champagne and other fairs, or of laws and traditions that began to safeguard commerce in the twelfth and thirteenth centuries. That it played a strong role, however, is indisputable.

Islam played a similar role in the Arab world, as it spread through North Africa and Spain from the eighth to the fifteenth centuries. Koranic law (shariah), more than the customs of Ottoman viceroys, Berber chiefs, or the sultan of Morocco, determined the limits for fair play. The rules were taught by religious authorities (ulama) more than by kings and chiefs. The same held true as Islam spread across the Sahara through the jihads of the Fulani, to the sultanate of Sokoto, and from the east to Bornu, providing all with a common basis for negotiating the terms of east-west trade (to Cairo via Darfur) and north-south trade (across the territory of the Tuaregs).

The modern counterpart of the church is the political party. In one-party states, which are common among LDCs, the political party plays a backup role to the government. In Mexico, the Institutional Revolutionary Party both dispenses "revolutionary" ideology and reconciles antagonistic interests. Often these reconcilements take place behind closed doors (as in the selection of the presidential candidate), since it is necessary to present a common front to the public. The degree of governmental decentralization in China (Chapter 16) is possible only because party cadres, vertically integrated, infuse a set of common beliefs and practices among the units at different hierarchical levels. Where this integration is not achieved, the coincidence of decentralization (balanced leverage) and institutional stability is not possible (such as in Brazil, where there is insufficient political leverage in the northeast, and in India, where effective agrarian reform is elusive).

One may surmise from European history that the political role of one of the parallel governments will decline as broad-based institutions develop for the other. But we do not have enough experience to know whether this is a universal occurrence, and the Far East provides little clue. The sessho-kampaku-Emperor (and later the shogun-Emperor) relationships in Japan were at best imperfect parallel governments. Though one might revive as the other failed (as in the Meiji restoration of 1868), the Emperor as figurehead did little to backstop the shogun during the latter's centuries of prime power.

Parallel governments have frequently conflicted with primary government (for example, in the investiture controversies of medieval Europe and the religious wars of later centuries). In fact, sometimes a formal government cannot implement laws and procedures because a powerful informal government supplants it (as in Trujillo's Dominican Republic, 1948–1960; Somoza's Nicaragua, 1952–1979; and Khomeini's Iran, 1979), but this is not the kind of parallel government we have in mind. The difference between an integrative and a destructive parallel government lies in degree and in personal restraint by the principal officers. On balance, parallel governments such as the church in medieval Europe and one-party systems in present-day LDCs appear to integrate. But their exact nature, role, and duration, as well as the reasons for their ultimate demise, have not been sufficiently explored.

ECONOMIC DEVELOPMENT

As we finally come to economic development, we propose alternative paths— classical and dualistic. Each is a polar construct, and neither is found anywhere in its pure form.

THE CLASSICAL PATH

The classical path runs roughly as follows. Each geographic unit starts out as a producer of agricultural goods for the most part, though fortunate ones also possess mineral resources. This generalization does not exclude the possibility of specialized services, such as those of the military, the witch doctor, or the king, that are dependent on agriculture. Occurring almost as early as the development of agriculture is the development of commerce. All societies have at all times traded with neighbors, and some societies currently labeled "primitive" had developed trade routes a quarter of the way around the world. The belief among modern development theorists (for example, Fei and Ranis, 1964) that the first capital comes from agriculture is almost a tautology. Virtually everywhere, the principal amassing of wealth that made development possible has come from commerce, or the risky venture of carrying goods, through hostile territory, from where they are cheap to where they are valuable.

For reasons that are still obscure (and that may differ among units and among theorists), at some point the successful unit increases its productivity substantially through technological innovation and saving of resources. The latter may be supplemented by inflows of capital from other units. This new capital is then combined with land and labor in ways that reflect the relative scarcity and abundance of each of the three factors. Capital becomes widely spread (through lending institutions) and invested in small-scale farms and small-scale industry. These investments are made in such a way that marginal revenue products are more or less equated (although the equalities may be neither measured nor known). Hence, returns are close to being maximized. The sizes of productive units increase as factors of production become scarce relative to output, and as economies of scale are achieved, but the equation of marginal revenue products continues.

Tariffs are low, relatively uniform, and *ad valorem* in the classical path. The only reason for tariffs at all is to recognize an "infant economy" (not "infant industry"), devoid of infrastructure and external economies. Promotion of some tariff-protected industry makes investment in infrastructure worthwhile on a social-return basis.[4] A low ceiling on protection encourages selection of comparative-advantage industries.

The allocation of resources between production for use within the unit and production for sale to other units is determined by a system of exchange, such as the market, in which individual utilities are equated at the margin. The same system determines the particular goods and the amount of investment capital to be acquired from other units.

A neutral monetary system, either unitary or with different currencies linked by exchange rates (cowrie shells, beads, pounds sterling, dollars), operates in such a way as to facilitate the natural balance of a unit's transactions with other units. The money supply remains at a relatively constant percentage (say, 20%) of gross domestic product per year, thus assuring relative price stability. As output increases, money increases *pari passu*. Increments in the money supply are offered for productive activity, either by private companies (banks) or by government (or a central bank), at competitive interest rates.

Governments (whether local, national or worldwide) tax according to principles of equity, raising sufficient revenue to provide public goods justified by their social marginal profitability, including the maintenance of public order and defense. Other social services, such as health, are offered because they are ethically desirable, or they provide security, or they promote economic growth which redounds to the benefit of all.

Innovation is encouraged, first by public policy and then (it is hoped) by a developing entrepreneurial spirit among the people. Government planners at all levels devote considerable attention to innovation, through technical assistance to farms and industry. The amount and direction of interunit technical assistance is determined by the social marginal profitability of the expected results, discounted for risk.

Structural reforms come about as the social need for them becomes evident. If feudal agriculture is inefficient, then feudal farms are divided and sold to (more efficient) small-scale farmers, with the aid of mortgages offered by the government or by banks. The increased earnings must be sufficient to amortize these mortgages. If the banking system is not adequate to meet the needs of small-scale farms and businesses, it becomes so as the advantages of lending in that sector become evident.

Inequity in the distribution of income may occur in the early stages of growth for three reasons. First, wealth (especially land) may be inequitably distributed from an earlier era, and holders of it would have *prima facie* advantage. Second, entrepreneurial genius may be scarce. Either wealth or entrepreneurial capacity would thus be a scarce factor that could command rent. Finally, labor starts out as illiterate, undisciplined, and unaccustomed to modern work methods. There is no clear-cut evidence, however, that these three conditions deteriorate the absolute income of the poor. In most preindustrial societies, in-

---

[4] The infant economy argument is based on social return, whereas the infant industry argument is based on private return. In the most efficient systems, where future vision, discount, and risk are developed, maximum efficiency requires the future flows of *discounted* individual returns to be maximized without tariff protection.

equity is probably as severe as it possibly can be, given the need of the lower classes to survive.

As progress along the growth path occurs, all three of these conditions are ameliorated. Wealth belonging to those who do not use it well is either lost (through taxation or misinvestment) or loaned to others who would use it well, and who demand their share of the proceeds. Entrepreneurial capacity increases with experience. Through proper educational institutions, and through experience working in factories, laborers become educated and disciplined. Over time, the productivity of labor is increased through more and more capital investment. The age of abundant labor gradually gives way to the age of labor scarcity and abundant capital. Rising marginal productivities of labor increase the share of wage-earners from (say) 40% to 60% of gross product, at the same time decreasing inequities in income distribution.

The classical path should not be confused with a market economy. We have stipulated a set of relationships among units (or sectors), but we have not indicated the institutional framework through which these relationships are realized. That framework may be the market (and was, in most of history), but it might also be a set of decentralized government institutions, or some combination of the two.

The classical path implies that the development of one unit is enhanced by the development of its neighbors. It is here that we part company with the Marxists, who would argue that capitalist development is possible only with the subjection of one group by another. To Marxists, Pareto-optimal moves are the exception rather than the rule.

Our model suggests that many structural reforms may be Pareto-optimal, but not initially. For example, before reform, the elites (kings and nobles) may have achieved a local maximum in their social welfare function. A greater global maximum exists, but only if these elites decrease their welfare first. This situation was described by William J. Baumol (1964: 359). Possibly the elites will sight the global maximum if their future vision is sufficiently well developed. More likely, they will be maneuvered into it, as in the pattern for agrarian reform mentioned previously.

The final defense of the thesis of mutual advantage, however, lies in trade and investment history. For the most part, the MDCs trade with and invest in one another. The LDCs that have made the most progress, with one major exception, are those that have traded more or less freely with the MDCs and received their investment. Even the exception, China, is now changing its policy and is becoming pro-trade and pro-investment. Income distribution in MDCs is more equitable (on the average) than it is in LDCs, and we believe this came about because the different development units saw mutual advantage in increasing the income of the poor.

THE DUALISTIC PATH

There are two kinds of dualism. *Economic dualism* is a state of wide discrepancies in income and wealth: a few very rich people living side-by-side with a mass of poor, and little in between. *Technological dualism* is a state of widely disparate production functions, with one small group of enterprises using technologies (for example, modern, capital-intensive) significantly different from those of the much larger group (for example, traditional, labor-intensive). Some argue that economic growth alone causes dualism of both kinds.

Economic dualism

Those who make this argument with respect to economic dualism usually assume as a starting point some kind of "traditional society" (Rostow, 1961; Adelman and Morris, 1973; Lewis, 1955; and Fei and Ranis, 1964), in which income and wealth are divided in a relatively egalitarian fashion. The opportunity for increased wealth is seized by some more readily than by others—because of their previous position or status, or their superior knowledge, or other chance circumstances—and disparities widen.

Unfortunately, this interpretation collapses history unduly. To us, "traditional" refers to very early societies (of which a few still exist), land-abundant and clan-organized, the kind described by Marshall D. Sahlins (1972) in *Stone Age Economics*. Sahlins dubs them "the original affluent society," in that their needs were few, supplied by about five hours of labor per day. Resources were wasted or not cared for, since they could easily be replaced; family goods were pooled, and successful hunters and gatherers shared with those in want.

The communalism of traditional societies, however, seems to depend on land abundance, migration or nomadism, and slash-and-burn agriculture. As soon as population growth makes land scarce, these societies form larger political units, dependent on chiefs and hierarchies to rationalize production. The chiefs then become wealthier than the rest. Inequalities in Mayan civilization are described by William L. Rathje (1970), for example.

The next stage is imperialism, with some tribes conquering others and exacting tribute or enslaving them. Among the earliest empires were the Shang of China, Egypt in Arabia and the Upper Nile, and the Assyrian, all of which began about 1500 B.C. In 200 B.C. the Chinese began their occupation of Vietnam, which continued for a millennium, and at about that time Cambodia conquered the Kingdom of Champa (now southern Vietnam). Although imperialism was common in the Far East, the imperialism of the Romans, Byzantines, and Franks are perhaps better known to Westerners. Later imperialisms included the tribal imperialism that existed in much of sub-Saharan Africa at the time the Arabs "discovered" it (*c.* 800–1200 A.D.) and the expansion of Islam (from the seventh century on).

In sum, for at least a millennium before the industrial revolution, and in many parts of the world longer, "traditional" societies had long since given way to imperialism. These imperialisms engendered sharp inequalities in income and wealth. Dominant units covered vast expanses of territory. They conquered frequently, often despoiling their victims totally. Within kingdoms and principalities, the disparities between nobility and commoners became extreme.

This general description applies to the early Chinese dynasties (of which Han, T'ang, and Sung are closest to ideal constructs), to the ancient Mediterranean world (for example, Egypt, Rome, and Greece), to the many kingdoms and empires of Africa from the tenth to the nineteenth centuries (Ghana, Mali,

Songhay, Sokoto, Bornu-Kanem, Kongo, Lunda, Bunyoro, Buganda, Nyamwezi, and Zulu, to name only a few), to the Mauryan and Mughal empires of India, and to the Mayan and Inca civilizations in the Americas. The expansions of the Vikings, Goths, Huns, Mongols, Arabs, Ottomans, and Mamluks also fit into this pattern.

Carlo M. Cipolla (1976: 10–12) has assembled a large number of estimates, both contemporary and recent, of income distribution in fifteenth-century Europe, showing a pattern not unlike that of LDCs today. Herlihy (1967) and Fiumi (1972) reported respectively that in Pistoia, Tuscany, 10% of the population owned 59% of the wealth while 70% owned 14%, and in Volterra, Tuscany, 7% owned 58% while 72% owned only 11%. De Roover (1966) examined the tax rolls of Florence for 1457 and classified families as rich (10%), very poor (50%), near beggars (20%), and beggars (10%). From data collected by King (1936), Cipolla went on to calculate the gini coefficient for families in England at .551. (For the significance and methodology of the gini index, see Chapter 5.)

If inequality was as great as possible in preindustrial societies, consistent with survival of a poor, laboring class, then it is impossible for the rich to extract *more* from the poor, absolutely, as a result of industrialization. But *relative* inequality may widen. Suppose a society's wealth is 100 units, of which 80 are held by 20% of the people and 20 by 80%. If the wealth increases to 120 units, and the entire increment goes to the richest 20%, they will then hold 83% (100/120), compared with 80% earlier. In absolute terms, the poor are neither better nor worse off than before.

There is some (inconclusive) evidence that even *relative* disparities in income and wealth may not widen with growth (Chapter 6). Even if they do, however, this observation tells us little, for it is already obvious that some grow faster than others, both for the world as a whole and within countries. Measures of relative dualism take on significance only in connection with normative analysis, such as in a theory of exploitation, in which it is argued that the poor *ought* to share more equitably in growth than they have. Those who make such propositions must defend some "ideal" path, stipulating the degree to which dualism is expected to increase or decrease (or remain relatively as it is).

It is because we have no such proposition that we prefer to treat the poor as a different development unit from the rich. The question is changed only slightly, to one of whether (and to what extent) development occurs for the poor, and whether it is impeded, enhanced, or unaffected by the development of the rich.

Technological dualism

Those who underwent the industrial revolution early experienced less technological dualism than those who entered it late. There were fewer choices of technology on the shelf in the eighteenth century; new technologies had to be invented more than borrowed. Choices were based on abundance or scarcity of factors required, in accordance with the classical path. That these choices led more or less to full employment is expressed in the economic theory of the day, which did not recognize unemployment as chronic. Today's LDCs, however, have the option between labor-using technology and the labor-saving technology developed by MDCs in response to their growing labor scarcity. Their frequent choice of the latter intensifies technological dualism. Whether technological dualism is cost-effective (optimal) is seriously debated. We will later examine that debate (Chapter 8) and conclude that for the most part, it is not.

More properly speaking, the dualistic "path" is a *set* of paths deviating from the classical. At various points in growth (often early), critical individuals opt for deviant paths. Each choice in some way or another promotes economic or technological dualism, or both. Europe and the Far East have wandered down dualistic paths many times. But they always have returned to the classical. It is, of course, still possible that at some point in the future they will deviate so far that they cannot return.

We will examine dualistic policies in Chapter 14. In brief, they are all those policies (price, wage, and exchange controls; quantitative restrictions; creation of monopolies not justified by scale; and nonneutral money and inflation) that cause deviations from the classical path. Such policies may be followed in a market or a nonmarket economy, under capitalism or socialism, just as classical policies are also neutral to political system. Dualistic policies have been followed, more or less, by virtually every society since ancient times.

We now ask why.

PROPENSITY FOR POWER

The ability to manipulate the money supply, to grant or deny import permits, to select prices for a wide range of goods, to say that certain goods cannot be produced or bought, and to determine what taxes must be paid is akin to the power that feudal lords held over their serfs. It conveys a sense of exhilaration, which is valued for itself. Similarly, the ability to vest subordinate officials with such power is a patronage instrument akin to the subinfeudation process of medieval times.

High propensity for power may pervade the petty as well as the high bureaucracy. Clifton Barton (1974) writes of this in the erstwhile Republic of (South) Vietnam:

> The requirements which the businessman faces are complex and oft-times contradictory. They result in some cases from decrees, in others from legislation and in still others from internal regulations of bureaucratic organizations. They come forth in an endless stream and change frequently in a manner which renders it difficult to know what the current regulations are, which are still in force, and which may have been superseded . . .

Barton observes that the ability to cope with business requirements depends on getting along with the petty officials, through friendship, kinship, or bribery. While it is possible that the system was set up for personal gain (corruption), the sense of power over others is also a likely explanation.

The harassment of small-scale businesses by local officials is well known but little researched. The five-year development plan of Kenya, for 1974–78 (Kenya, 1974: 294), reports that the competitive strength of small-scale industries has been severely limited by this harassment. "Indeed," it goes on, "there has been some counter-productive harassment of these enterprises, which will be promptly ended."

Barton hypothesizes that petty government regulation is a cause of dualism. The smallest firms, which are not considered important, generally escape it. Their owners are often illiterate and therefore unable to comply with complex regulations. Once a firm expands to a certain size, however, its operations become visible. It is then that the bureaucrat attempts to regulate and control the business. The middle-sized firm is apt to succumb, for it does not possess the skills, and only by chance may it have the connections, to deal with the petty bureaucracy. A much larger firm, with (say) 100 or more employees, may have specialists capable of expediting permits and resolving obstacles. For these reasons, Barton suggests that there may be a growth barrier which only a few firms can hurdle. Therefore, instead of becoming larger, small-scale entrepreneurs may tend to distribute their ventures, keeping them small (say, five or fewer employees) but intermixed, with flows of funds from one to another. Thus the permission-giver and tax-collector will ignore them. If this is an accurate portrayal, then this gap in size of business may be the delimitation between the traditional and the modern sector. From now on, we will refer to any thus-caused absence of a middle group of businesses as the *Barton gap*.

DISDAIN FOR THE POOR

Counterpart to the propensity for power is disdain for the poor. It has a long history. It underlies the caste system in India, which predates the Christian era, and similar systems in other countries. Throughout most of Chinese and Japanese history, craftsmen were looked upon as inferiors. Mao Tse-tung, in his final years, denounced Confucianism because its respect for scholarship and birth implied a denigration of the common person. Emperor Augustus believed it necessary to diminish the economic and political participation of the poor in the affairs of Rome, and he introduced grain doles and entertainment to keep them "contented." The derision showered on the poor in medieval Europe is reflected in Richard II's speech of "conciliation" after the Peasant's Revolt (1381): "Villeins ye are, and villeins ye shall remain." Michael Romanov put the lower Russian peasants under the tutelage of the nobility. In the Thermidorian Reaction of the French Revolution (1974), the Convention turned toward "men of substance," because it feared that rule by the *sans-culottes*, artisans, and shopkeepers would bring about chaos. In the Ottoman Empire, the term "Turk" was applied derisively to the masses. African kingdoms, from their earliest discovery by European explorers until the colonial period, displayed many examples of hierarchy, with privileges denied the poor. The radicals in France (1848) opposed universal suffrage because they thought the masses, ignorant of their best interests, would vote conservative. (As it turned out, they did!) Literacy qualifications for voting in many countries today reflect this same distrust. In Bolivia (as well as in other Andean countries), the term *indio*, deemed to be one of disrespect, was virtually abandoned after the Revolution of 1953, in favor of *campesino* (peasant).

Continental Europe in the latter part of the eighteenth century was ruled by the so-called "enlightened despots." Only France was an exception, where the kings were despotic but hardly enlightened. Among the "enlightened" were Frederick the Great of Prussia, Catherine the Great of Russia, Maria Theresa of Austria, Charles III of Naples, and Joseph I of Portugal. They were hard-working, and they promoted scientific farming and justice. While they had in common a love for the poor, they also shared an abiding contempt for their capabilities. They justified their absolutism by the assumption that all good things had to be done by the monarch, perhaps with the aid of the nobility.

The movement for universal suffrage and compulsory education in Britain, fought primarily during the nineteenth century, was severely slowed by the pervasive belief (even among the poor themselves) in the need for noble patronage. The extreme of this feeling was reflected in the opposition of the Adullamites to reform (1866), in which both the moral and intellectual competence of workers as a group were debated in the halls of Parliament, an event that strikes us today as rather curious.

It has not always been this way, and once again our search for general principles is confounded by the exceptions. The poor received a high degree of respect in the early days of the Roman republic, when popular assemblies and tribunes, with powers similar to those of the senate and magistrates, were set up to pass laws for them and defend them. Although these have a tinge of paternalism, they did reflect a respect lacking in later ages. Islam has always held that the lowliest person can rise to be among the greatest, and slaves in Ottoman and other Muslim countries have indeed so risen (for example, the Mamluks). All such cases, however, appear to be historically isolated examples.

The same disdain is widely observed in LDCs today. Within the past decade, Mexico (Reynolds, 1970: 153–60) and Brazil (LAER, 1977: 106) have opted for greater promotion of large-scale rather than small-scale agriculture and of labor-avoiding technology in industry. One of the principal arguments for capital-intensive development (sometimes called "the colonialist argument") is that the labor-intensive alternative is more costly because of absenteeism, lack of discipline, willful or careless damage inflicted by workers on their tools, and a backward-sloping labor supply curve (Myrdal, 1968: 977). The slender capacities of small-scale farmers for good management is a widely-supported argument against agrarian reform, although Barraclough (1973: 25) argues that it is the larger landholders who are less efficient. In its five-year economic plan (Kenya, 1974: 498), the government of Kenya promised a policy "to develop the effectiveness of local authorities," while pointing out that "in general, administrative and financial efficiency in local government leaves much to be desired." In many countries where decentralization is an ideological principle (for example, Zambia, Tanzania, Nigeria, and the Philippines), local planning is *de facto* undertaken by officials of the central government who have been dispatched to the districts. By contrast, in the countries of East Asia now undergoing industrial revolution, decentralized decision making in rural areas has become accomplished fact (Chapter 16).

CONCLUSION

Three decades ago, it was widely believed that economic development or its absence could be explained primarily by the presence or lack of capital. A number of models and theories of economic growth (to be examined in Chapter 2) were based on this presumption. Since that time, a large number of *micro* studies, covering a wide range of topics—such as technology, employment, motivations, and income distribution—have broadened our knowledge. These same studies have also revealed the complexity of the problem and the vastness of our ignorance.

The present book is written in the belief that the development model must be broadened and areas of ignorance defined. We have "started afresh" in the sense of not accepting, *prima facie*, the parameters stipulated by economists as the major explainers of growth, though we do not deny them either.

We suggest three intertwining paths of development: one personal, one political and institutional, and one economic. The personal path includes development in four dimensions: future vision, time preference, willingness to take risk, and propensity toward power versus propensity toward material gain. The reference points for the first three become redefined as the individual shifts on the propensity axis, from power to material gain. The progress of societies may be explained by the personal progress of leading individuals along these paths.

The politico-institutional path refers to the development of institutions that ensure the fulfillment of economic promises made by individuals and that help to routinize transactions. The institutions also maintain a certain balance of political and economic leverage among component groups, for without this balance the decisions taken on the economic path will not be appropriate.

The economic path is divided into classical and dualistic, the latter consisting of a variety of deviations from the former. We find that successful countries have followed the classical path, for the most part; when they have deviated, they have generally returned.

We do not, as yet, see any causal relationship on the paths. Hence they are described as a process and not as a theory of development. There are thresholds and cumulative effects, but there are also unexplained reversals. It would appear that watersheds occur with decisions by critical individuals. Why two individuals, when faced with similar sets of circumstances, make very different choices is one of the mysteries belonging to our vast amount of ignorance.

BIBLIOGRAPHY

Adelman, Irma, and Morris, Cynthia, 1973:
Economic Growth and Social Equity in Developing Countries, Stanford, California, Stanford University Press.
Ahluwalia, Montek S., 1976:
"Income Distribution and Development: Some Stylized Facts," *American Economic Review*, Vol. 66, No. 2, May.
Barraclough, Solon, 1973:
Agrarian Structure in Latin America, Lexington, Mass., Lexington Books (D.C. Heath).
Barton, Clifton, 1974:
Problems and Prospects of Small Industries in the Republic of Vietnam, Saigon, Industrial Development Bank of Saigon, December.
Baumol, William, J., 1964:
"External Economies and Second-Order Optimality Conditions," *American Economic Review*, Vol. LIV, No. 4, Part I, June.
Cipolla, Carlo M., 1976:
Before the Industrial Revolution, London, Methuen and Co.
de Onis, Juan, NYT 5-21-80:
"Peru's New Chief Won by Shrewd Use of Military Issue," *New York Times*.
De Roover, Raymond A., 1966:
The Rise and Decline of the Medici Bank, 1397–1494, New York, W. W. Norton, 1966.
Fei, John C. H., and Ranis, Gustav, 1964:
Development of the Surplus Economy, New Haven, Yale University Press.
Fiumi, E., 1972:
"Popolazione, società ed economia volterrana dal catasto del 1428–29," *Rassegna volterrana*, vols. 36–39.
Herlihy, David, 1967:
Medieval and Renaissance Pistoia, New Haven, Yale University Press.
Kenya, 1974:
Government of Kenya, *Economic Development Plan, 1974–78*, Nairobi, Government Printing Office.
King, G., 1936:
"Natural and Political Observations," in Barnett, G. E., ed., *Two Tracts by Gregory King*, Baltimore, Johns Hopkins University Press.
LAER (*Latin American Economic Review*), 1977:
"Brazil's New Inflation Moves Evade Rural Sector Problems," July 15.
Lewis, W. Arthur, 1955:
The Theory of Economic Growth, Homewood, Illinois, Irwin.
Myrdal, Gunnar, 1968:
Asian Drama: An Inquiry into the Poverty of Nations, New York, Twentieth Century Fund.
Okun, Arthur M., 1975:
Equality and Efficiency: The Big Trade-Off, Washington, D.C. Brookings Institution.

Rathje, William L., 1970:
   "Sociopolitical Implications of Lowland Maya Burials: Methodology and Tentative Hypotheses," *World Archeology*, Vol. 1, No. 3, February.
Reynolds, Clark W., 1970:
   The Mexican Economy: Twentieth Century Structure and Growth, New Haven, Yale University Press.
Riding, Alan, NYT 3-23-80:
   "El Salvador's Junta Unable to Halt the Killing," *New York Times*.
Rostow, W. W., 1961:
   The Stages of Economic Growth, New York, Cambridge University Press.
Sahlins, Marshall D., 1972:
   Stone Age Economics, Chicago, Aldine.
Schumpeter, Joseph A., 1911:
   The Theory of Economic Development, translated by Redvers Opie, Cambridge, Massachusetts, Harvard University Press, 1936.
Wright, Quincy, 1964:
   A Study of War, Chicago, University of Chicago Press.

2

GROWTH
MODELS AND
DEVELOPMENT
PLANNING[1]

*Theology sank into a branch of dialectic; whatever would not fit in
with a logical formula was cast aside as useless. But average
human nature does not take kindly to a syllogism, and theology
had ceased to have any appreciable influence on popular religion.*

"JANSENISM," AN EIGHTEENTH-CENTURY
RELIGIOUS MOVEMENT, *ENCYCLOPEDIA BRITANNICA*, 1968, V. 12:874.

Most people know what economic *growth* is: the increase in gross domestic
(or national) product.[2] Economic *development*, on the other hand, is
economic growth *plus* a variety of other elements, sometimes tangible and
sometimes not, the selection of which depends on the author. These elements
often include income distribution, human capital formation (however it may
be defined and/or measured), institutional change, political stability, and so
on. The lack of a definition for development, let alone a theory of it, is one

---

[1]This chapter is more technical than any other in the book. While it will not be difficult for
students who have mastered calculus, it may present a challenge for others. The latter may wish
to read only the first section (up to "The Keynesian Heritage"), then skip to page 44 ("Planning
From Above"), reading from there until the end. They may then continue to Chapter 3 with no loss
in continuity.

[2]Even at this elementary stage, there is disagreement over terms and their content. Gross national
product (GNP) is the final product of national factors of production, whether they operate at home
or abroad. Gross domestic product (GDP) is the final product for a given territory. If labor or capital
from Country A is put to work in Country B, the output associated with the resulting wages or
interest is gross *national* product of Country A but gross *domestic* product of Country B. The
distinction probably carries greater political significance than economic significance.

of the inadequacies of contemporary economics, to which we alluded in Chapter 1.

Rather than coming to grips with development, contemporary growth models circumvent it. They hold that the amount of GDP is determined by the quantities of inputs and the level of technology. In a physical sense, this is so. It is like stating that if one combines iron, coal, and other minerals in certain processes, the result will be steel. But it avoids the questions of why a society wants steel, where the capital comes from, how steel technology is diffused, who is able (or allowed) to build a steel mill, how the steel is marketed, and how the proceeds are shared among people of different income brackets. If the study is economic *development*, the latter kinds of questions may be more interesting than the shape of the production function.

One major defect in this steel-model analogy is that steel production is replicable. With only minor changes because of climate, identical steel mills can function almost anywhere in the inhabited world. By the same token, physical scientists usually call their experiments valid if they are replicable at different times and in different places. In economic growth models, however, one finds that the parameters change from time to time and from place to place. The same model structure may be applied to Pakistan in 1950 and to Sweden in 1980, but some of the parameters (such as the marginal substitutability of capital for labor or the consumption function) will differ in the two cases. And if statistically significant parameters can be found for one country over a given period (say, 20 years)—and this is not always the case—the usefulness of those parameters in projections even within the same country may still be an open question. While such an exercise may help us estimate the amount of capital needed in a development plan, it nevertheless tells us little about why the parameters are what they are, and why they differ from those of other countries. Information about the latter questions may be the most interesting in an overall understanding of development.

Economics, therefore, is deficient in development theory. What there is of it is sketchy, and the offerings of other social sciences (Chapter 3) do not integrate well with economics. To understand better the curious dichotomy between growth and development, we turn now to a description of growth models.

THE KEYNESIAN HERITAGE

Contemporary growth models owe their origin to three individuals more than anyone else: John Maynard Keynes, Roy Harrod, and Evsey Domar. But Keynes was concerned primarily with unemployment and depression, not with growth. In his explanation of unemployment (which we do not treat here), he developed a set of relations that others later expanded into the national income and product accounts. These accounts are a system, or network, of relationships among such items as gross domestic product, consumption, investment, saving, exports, and imports. The network, which is shown in simplified version in Table 2–1, is such that a change in any one quantity perforce changes at least

TABLE 2–1

Simplified Version of Gross Domestic Product Accounts
(with fictitious figures)

	Producing		Households		Government		International		Saving and Investment	
	Dr.	Cr.	Dr.	Cr.	Dr.	Cr.	Dr.	Cr.	Dr.	Cr.
F = Factor payments	80			80						
Tb = Business taxes	5					5				
Sb = Business saving	15									15
C = Personal consumption		72	72							
G = Government expenditure		10			10					
Id = Domestic investment		25							25	
X = Exports		12					12			
M = Imports (− in prod.)		−19						19		
Tp = Personal taxes			6			6				
Sp = Personal saving			2							2
Sg = Government saving					1					1
If = Foreign investment							7			7
Totals	100	100	80	80	11	11	19	19	25	25
	GDI	GDP								

one other; this mechanical fact sets the stage for hypotheses about cause and effect.

In Table 2–1, we show a country whose GDP is 100, the sum of the credit column for the producing sector. The first four items in that column (C, G, Id, and X) contain domestically-produced components and imported components; hence imports (M) must be subtracted in arriving at GDP. Gross domestic product is defined as being equal to gross domestic income (GDI), which in turn is divided into F, Tb, and Sb, shown in the debit column for the producing sector. The economy is then divided into three sectors: households, government, and international. Household and government incomes are shown as credits; expenses and saving (residual) are considered debits. The international sector, which represents counterpart transactions for foreigners (all who reside *outside* the given country), reflects the amount the rest of the world has bought (this country's exports) or sold (this country's imports); the balance (*If*) is the extent to which the rest of the world has supplied capital to the present country (which we presume in Table 2–1 to be in deficit by 7). The saving and investment account demonstrates that this country has invested 25 (Id), debit, which has been financed by the saving and foreign investment shown in the credit column. Each of the five accounts balances internally (that is, debits and credits are equal). By the same token, every line balances externally (shows equal debits and credits affecting different accounts).

All the national accounts (GDP or GNP) of all countries, summarized in the *Yearbook of National Accounts* (United Nations) are in some way adaptations of Table 2–1. All growth models are also derived from the identities implied by this table. For example, the GDP identity—GDP = C + G + Id + X − M —is simply the credit column in the producing account. The Keynesian saving/investment identity represents nothing more than the equality of debits and credits in the saving and investment account.

The simplest growth model is, in fact, a *contraction* of Table 2–1. If we assume only two sectors (producing and households), then the credit column of the producing account reduces to:

$$Y = C + I$$

where we use Y instead of GDP (because it is simpler) and I instead of Id (because, having assumed no foreign investment, we need not distinguish between Id and If).

Keynes (1935), and later Hansen (1953), assumed a linear functional relationship between C and Y. Thus the marginal propensity to save (MPS), or the proportion of increased income that households save, does not vary much in the short run. If C = f(Y), then the amount of Y can be controlled by variations in I.

Table 2–2 is a simplified version of Table 2–1, in which the government and international sectors are omitted. In reading this table, suppose that GDP = 100 units per "day" (a period of indeterminate length) and that each day households spend 80% of their income of the preceding "day," while (inde-

TABLE 2–2
Further-Simplified Version of GDP Accounts
(with fictitious figures)

		Producing		Households		Saving and Investment	
		DR.	CR.	DR.	CR.	DR.	CR.
F =	Factor payments	100			100		
C =	Personal consumption		80	80			
I =	Domestic investment		20			20	
SP =	Personal saving			20			20
	Totals	100	100	100	100	20	20

pendently of household decisions) businesses invest 20 units each day. The situation in Table 2–2 would be repeated day after day, a condition known as static equilibrium.

Suppose that on a given day, investment increases to 30 units (in real terms) and remains at that level thereafter. Households still spend 80% of their income of the *preceding* day; we therefore have the figures of Table 2–3. This process approaches an asymptote (day ∞), in which static equilibrium is restored, with $Y = 150$, $C = 120$, and of course $I = 30$ (set exogenously). Because Keynes was dealing with depression, he was assuming that unemployed factors of production would be available to produce the increased Y. The *multiplier* (the ratio of the increase in total Y to the initial disturbing increment) equals the inverse of the ratio of leakage, or percentage of income saved. In the present case, the marginal propensity to save is 20%, or one-fifth; hence the multiplier is 5 (the initial increment of 10 leads to a total increase in Y of 50).

TABLE 2–3
Illustration of Keynesian Multiplier

	Y	C	I
Initial equilibrium	100	80	20
Day of disturbance	110	80	30
Next day	118	88	30
Next day	124	94	30
Next day	129	99	30
Day ∞	150	120	30

HARROD-DOMAR GROWTH MODELS

The modern generation of growth models stems from Harrod (1939) and Domar (1946). Writing independently, they produced similar models, so we shall explain .them together. They start with the Keynesian assumption that the level of I determines Y and that increments of I therefore determine increments of Y. But Domar pointed out that Keynes analyzed the demand side only. Because of his assumption of unemployment, he assumed that the economy always had the capacity to produce an increment of Y. Suppose (asked Domar) full employment had already been reached, but there was still an increment in I. He reasoned that I not only generates demand (the Keynesian multiplier), it also increases supply, because additional capital would improve the economy's productive capacity. Would there be—Domar asked—a rate of growth in I that would increase the capacity to produce by exactly the same amount as the increase in demand for final product?

Domar found that the "warranted" rate of growth (Harrod's term) equaled the marginal propensity to save (s) divided by the incremental capital/output ratio (k), which is the ratio between an increment in capital (a one-time amount) and the increment in output (an indefinite flow, continuing period after period).

We now take Y as equal to the amount of GDP *demanded*, while we let Q equal the amount *supplied* and K equal the amount of capital possessed by the community. Then I represents the increment in K (that is, $I \equiv \Delta K$), whereas the increment in investment (from one period to the next) is symbolized by ΔI.

Let us first illustrate that the warranted rate of growth (in I or Y) equals s divided by k; later we will explain why this is so. In Table 2–4, we assume the same starting equilibrium as in Table 2–2 and the same s ($= 0.20$); we add the assumption that $k = 4/1$. The warranted rate of growth is therefore $0.20/4 = 0.05$.

The Keynesian model (Table 2–3) is one of *comparative statics*; an initial equilibrium is disturbed, a new equilibrium is reached, and then there is no more change until a new disturbance is introduced. In Table 2–4, this com-

TABLE 2–4
Expansion Path of the Harrod-Domar Growth Model
with $s = 0.20$, $k = 4/1$, and Rate of Growth of Investment = 5%

	Y = Q	C	I
Beginning	100.00	80.00	20.00
Next day (1)	105.00	84.00	21.00
Next day (2)	110.25	88.20	22.05
Next day (3)	115.75	92.60	23.15

And so on and on.

parative-static process is worked out *on a single line*. On every line entitled "next day," the increment in Y is five times the increment in I; thus the Keynesian process has jumped immediately to the new static equilibrium. The growth in Q, on the other hand, depends on I *of the preceding day*. Thus Q for the next day (1) is 5 greater than Q of the beginning day because I on the beginning day is 20, which calls for an increment in output of ¼ of its value (since $k = 4/1$). All other lines are worked out similarly.

The relationships are summed up in the following equations:

$$\Delta I/s \ = \ \Delta Y \text{ in which } s = \text{marginal propensity to save}$$
(and the multiplier is its inverse)

$$I/k \ = \ \Delta Q \text{ in which } k = \text{incremental capital-output}$$
ratio (also known as ICOR)

The equilibrium conditions require that $Y = Q$ and that for every day

$$\Delta Y = \Delta Q$$

Thus, if the equilibrium conditions are fulfilled, then

$$\Delta I/s = I/k$$

or

$$\Delta I/I = s/k$$

Therefore, the rate of growth of *investment* equals s/k. The rate of growth of output must be the same as that for investment, since k, which equals $\Delta K/\Delta Q$, is constant from day to day.[3]

In the Harrod-Domar models, every day represents an equilibrium. Because the successive equilibrium values depend on time, the model is dynamic.

---

[3]Our noncalculus explanation has required discrete leaps from one "day" to the next. That these events could occur continuously is demonstrated as follows (Domar, 1946):

Capital/output ratio: $dQ/dt = I/k$ (where t = time period)   (1)

Multiplier: $dY/dt = \dfrac{dI/dt}{s}$ (2)

Initial equilibrium requirement: $Q = Y$ (3)
Maintenance of equilibrium requirement: $dQ/dt = dY/dt$ (4)
Substituting (1) and (2) into (4) gives

$$I/k \ = \ \frac{dI/dt}{s} \quad\quad (5)$$

Equation (5) is a differential equation, whose solution is

$$I = I(0)e^{(s/k)t} \quad\quad (6)$$

so that s/k is the warranted rate of growth.

THE RAZOR'S EDGE

The constant rate of increase in investment ($\Delta I/I$) is exogenous. No parameter in Table 2–4 determines that the actual rate *must* be 5%; rather, *if* the rate is 5%, supply will equal demand each day forevermore. Let us now presume the same parameters ($s = 0.20$ and $k = 4$), but a rate of growth in investment of 4%, or less than the warranted rate of 5%. The result will be that supply exceeds demand. Just to explicate the model, we assume that producers add the excess to their inventories and continue to produce all they can. We let ΔU be the increment of unsold inventories, and we obtain the figures shown in Table 2–5.

Each day, the income of the community is Q (not Y), since factors of production are paid for the total amount produced (not the total demanded). We are assuming that I increases at 4% per day regardless of what is happening in the other columns. By the Keynesian multiplier, the consumption of any day (Y) equals .8 of Q for the same day. The amount supplied (Q) for any day equals Q of the preceding day plus I of the preceding day divided by k. But unsold inventories (ΔU) increase every day. Since producers could hardly be expected to keep the rate of investment at 4% in the face of increasing unsold inventories, ΔI would doubtless fall. Thus a rate of investment increase (here 4%) that is less than the warranted rate (here 5%) causes the former rate to fall, and it would continue to fall until investment increase approaches zero. Conversely, if we assume a rate of increase greater than the warranted rate (say, 6%), the excess of demand over supply would call for further increases in investment, forever. Harrod-Domar models are therefore unstable, in that disequilibrium leads to further imbalances, in the same direction. Only if the rate of growth is exactly the warranted rate will equilibrated growth continue on "the razor's edge."

SOLOW AND NEOCLASSICAL GROWTH THEORY

The "razor's edge" condition hardly represents reality. Solow (1956) has suggested that the Harrod-Domar model need not be abandoned because of this, but simply revised to make the assumptions more realistic. The model assumes a constant k but says nothing about the amount of labor. If labor is substituted for capital, Solow reasoned, the amount of capital per unit of output will decline; if capital is substituted for labor, it will increase. Thus, he suggested, k is variable.

Solow's analysis is based on neoclassical production functions. As a special case, we may use the Cobb-Douglas production function (Douglas, 1948), which appears as follows:

$$Y = aK^{\alpha}L^{\beta} \tag{2.1}$$

where

Y = the total output or income
a = a constant reflecting technology

TABLE 2–5
Expansion Path of the Harrod-Domar Growth Model
with $s = 0.20$, $k = 4/1$, and Rate of Growth of Investment = 4%

	Q	ΔU	Y	C	I
Beginning	100.00		100.00	80.00	20.00
Next day (1)	105.00	0.20	104.80	84.00	20.80
Next day (2)	110.20	0.41	109.79	88.16	21.63
Next day (3)	115.61	0.62	114.99	92.49	22.50
Next day (4)	121.24	0.85	120.39	96.99	23.40
Next day (6)	127.09	1.08	126.01	101.67	24.34
Next day (7)	133.18	1.33	131.85	106.54	25.31

K = the amount of capital
L = the amount of labor
α = the elasticity of Y with respect to K
β = the elasticity of Y with respect to L

In logarithmic form, this function becomes

$$\ln Y = \ln a + \alpha \ln K + \beta \ln L$$

When this equation is differentiated with respect to t (for time), it becomes

$$(1/Y)\,(dY/dt) = \alpha\,(1/K)\,(dK/dt) + \beta\,(1/L)\,(dL/dt) \qquad (2.2)$$

The left-hand member of this equation is the rate of growth of output. The first term of the right-hand member represents the elasticity of output with respect to capital (α) times the rate of growth of capital, while the second term is the elasticity of output with respect to labor (β) times the rate of growth of the labor force.

It has also been shown that the elasticity of output with respect to any factor of production may be interpreted as that factor's percentage contribution to total output. For example:

$$\alpha = \frac{dY/Y}{dK/K} = \left(\frac{dY}{dK} \cdot K\right)\Big/ Y \qquad (2.3)$$

where labor is held constant. Under marginal productivity theory, each factor earns the amount of its marginal product (dY/dK for capital with labor held constant). If this is multiplied by the amount of the factor (K), the result is the total factor share, or $dY/dK \cdot K$. The relative factor share is this amount divided by Y, which is the same as right-hand member of (2.3). This relationship also applies for labor (L).

If the right-hand member of (2.3) is substituted for α in (2.2), and similarly if $\left(\dfrac{dY}{dL} \cdot L \right) \Big/ Y$ is substituted for B, then that equation states that *the rate of growth of output is equal to the relative contribution of capital (to output) times the rate of growth of capital, plus the relative contribution of labor (to output) times the rate of growth of labor.*

By applying the Solow "correction," we may therefore conclude that the equilibrium growth of output is determined by the rates of growth of capital and labor. If we further assume that capital and labor are substitutable for each other, nothing in the above relationship would imply the same instability found in the Harrod-Domar model. This breakthrough marks the beginning of what is generally known as *neoclassical growth theory.*

We have also moved away from relying on the capital-output ratio, with its vague assumption of appropriate changes in the labor force, and are instead using marginal productivities, which possess more attractive theoretical properties.

UNDERSTANDING THE RATE OF GROWTH

Kindleberger and Herrick (1977: 59–60) reply as follows to the question, "Why study growth models?"

> Growth models force us to focus on the most basic elements of the growth process: the factor inputs, their relation to output and to each other, and to the role of technological progress. By stripping the process down to these fundamentals, we get a clarity of vision that the myriad details of the real world obscure. And more: in their mathematical purity, growth models deal quantitatively and in a unified fashion with a process that more frequently than not seems intellectually overwhelming.

We do not dispute this assessment. We add, however, that growth models represent a specific level of understanding only, and possibly not the most enlightening one. Numerous empirical studies testify to the relatively stable relationship between inputs and technology on the one hand and output on the other, given the time and the place. If this relationship is what one wishes to study, then growth models supply a convenient framework. If, on the other hand, one wishes to study why *the entire system of relationships* is or is not moving, or why it is moving at a specific rate and not another, then a knowledge of only the interaction among the elements may not be rewarding.

As long as these limitations are understood, growth models may clarify growth. When applied to planning, unfortunately, they are frequently misused. For example, a growth model may imply that a given aggregate investment will mechanically yield a calculated increment in output. Suppose, in some country, that the gross domestic product *(Y)*, the capital supply *(K)*, and the labor force *(L)* have been counted; suppose aggregate elasticities of output with respect to capital and labor (α and β respectively) have been estimated by econometric methods; suppose the rate of growth of the labor force $(1/L)$ (dL/dt) is known from extrapolations of demographic data; and, finally, suppose all this information is entered into equation (2.2). Only two unknowns are left: dY/dt and dK/dt. If a desired rate of growth $(1/Y)$ (dY/dt) is arbitrarily stipulated, then one can solve for the capital growth rate $(1/K)$ (dK/dt). But the impression that the amount of capital growth thus determined can in fact yield the specified output growth might be erroneous, for such factors as the institutional framework (banks and businesses), entrepreneurial attitudes and risk willingness, and appropriate social stability may still be missing. The errors of this reasoning from models, *ceteris paribus*, are perhaps obvious—yet they are precisely what happens in much development planning.

THE DESIRED RATE OF GROWTH

Some economists have used growth models to estimate the effects of diverting GDP away from consumption and into investment. "What is the most *desirable* rate of growth?" they ask. The answer is not always, "The more, the better." Growth has a cost, and this cost must be compared to benefits. Many have reasoned that the ultimate objective of development is consumption, and although investment diverts resources away from present consumption, it causes increased consumption in the future. The best way to deploy resources over time periods, they say, is to invest what is necessary to maximize the sum of present per capita consumption plus the discounted values of all future streams of per capita consumption.

Phelps (1961) reasoned that maximum discounted per capita consumption would be achieved if the rate of growth of labor (and so of Y under balanced growth) were equal to the rate of profit earned by society. He assumed constant returns to scale. Assuming a fixed rate of growth of labor (or population) over the years, Phelps reasoned that each possible saving rate would be associated with a unique balanced-growth path, and so a unique per capita consumption. Furthermore, these paths would not cross each other over time. Therefore, we may choose that saving rate which maximizes the per capita consumption at all times. This rate turns out to equal capital's percentage share of output. Societies following this pattern, Phelps reasoned, would be in a theoretical "golden age," applying the "golden rule" that each generation would invest for the benefit of future generations the ratio (I/Y) it would have had previous generations invest on its behalf.

But simply maximizing the discounted consumption stream will not close the gap between LDCs and MDCs. Aspirations to do that will require sacrifices on the part of earlier generations, so that the consumption of their grandchildren will be greater than on any "golden rule" path. It might be argued that Japan modernized along these lines. For many generations (roughly 1868–1941), Japanese peasants and workers toiled at very low wages, exporting at very low prices those goods that other nations did not care to produce (such as trinkets and dishware). By the time the Japanese shifted to newly-developed comparative advantages (automobiles and electronics, for example), they had built up a supply of capital capable of sustaining a consumption level completely unknown to previous generations.

In explaining growth of this type, Feldman (explained in Stewart, 1977: 141–145) has prepared a model that divides investment into two parts: that which produces new capital goods and that which produces consumption goods. If all investment were used to produce more capital, then (in the extreme) consumption would never increase. If (at the other extreme) all investment were used to produce consumption goods, then present investment would have no leverage on future output. Between these two extremes, Feldman argues, the greater the percentage of investment devoted to producing capital, the greater will be the *ultimate* consumption. If a very tiny, but fixed, proportion of investment is devoted to consumption goods, the remaining investment will grow exponentially, becoming so large that even the tiny proportion of invest-ment devoted to consumption will *ultimately* produce more consumption goods than would have been possible had a greater fixed proportion been devoted to consumption over the earlier years. The tradeoff, of course, is in time.

The Feldman model provided mathematical justification for the previously developed "big push" theories of economic growth (Rosenstein-Rodan, 1943, and Gerschenkron, 1962), as well as for plans based on this philosophy (such as the early Indian Five-Year Plans). Those who would not join Feldman to the extreme may be attracted to the "turnpike theory" of growth (Rand Corporation, 1949, and Dorfman, Samuelson, and Solow, 1958), which implies that you can travel faster via the turnpike (a la Feldman), but you can get off at any exit. Thus it would be possible to make a big push temporarily, then revert to a "golden age" path at any point.

PLANNING FROM ABOVE

Growth models have been widely used in economic planning. We dub this approach one of "planning from above," because normally the aggregate growth rates and capital requirements are first worked out by central authorities and then passed down to sectoral working parties (manufacturing, agriculture, and education, for example), which must formulate their plans to fit.

The *mechanics* of planning are rarely discussed in books and journals, yet they are perhaps crucial to the outcome. Because of gaps in the literature, the following discussion of planning mechanisms is based primarily on our own experience and informal conversations with planners in many countries and in the United Nations Industrial Development Organization.

Planning in Kenya is more or less representative of planning in many coun-tries. The first writing of the plan is the responsibility of the Permanent Secretary in the Ministry of Planning. Underneath him, a macro-economic unit provides the aggregate models and (in conjunction with the unit's counterpart in the Finance Ministry) projects government budgets over the plan period. A working party is established for each sector (manufacturing, agriculture, education, health, employment, public works, retail trade, and the like), with each party being staffed by professionals from the relevant operating ministry (for example, Agriculture, Education, or Commerce and Industry) and from the Ministry of Planning.

The aggregate growth rate is projected at the start by the macro-unit, along with capital availabilities based on savings functions and estimates of inflows from abroad. Government revenues over the five-year period are projected on the basis of prior experiences, proposed changes in tax laws, and borrowing policies. These are divided into recurrent and development budgets, and the latter are allocated among activities according to government policy (for example, to promote agriculture). All this information is provided to the working parties. Armed with certain expectations about growth, about the various markets, and about availability of government funds for development projects, the working parties estimate the sectoral growth rates. By trial and error (and negotiation), these are fitted into the overall growth rate, which might also be revised in light of the sectoral forecasts.

After overall and sectoral growth rates are decided, and after government budget allocations are made to the ministries, the working parties prepare lists of projects and priorities. A project unit in the Ministry of Planning coordinates these and makes recommendations for inclusion in the final government budget.

With modifications depending on country, the planning-from-above model is widely used. Virtually all such plans depend on econometric models, on which macro-economic policy is based. These models have been widely discussed in the literature. They present the following features:

1. Imagine an expanded Table 2–1, in which each item becomes a category divided into component items (factor payments divided into wages, interest, and profit; exports divided into products or product-types; and so on). The lists of component items may be made as long as one pleases, subject to data availability. In addition, GDP is broken down into value added per sector. This expanded table provides a set of identities, based on the equality of debit and credit columns for each sector. (The saving and investment account is not a separate identity, for its columns are the algebraic sums of the columns of the other sectors.)

2. A set of parameters is estimated by econometric methods, based on the data for a number of prior years. These parameters include static relationships such as the consumption function (other examples are the import function and the tax function), which can be applied to dynamic models in the way we applied the Keynesian consumption function to the dynamic Harrod-Domar models (Table 2–4). Other parameters represent growth features, such as the elasticity of output with respect to capital and/or labor. Written as differentials or exponents, these make the model dynamic.

3. A further set of stochastic equations, going beyond the variables in Table 2–1, is also estimated by econometric methods. Employment is not a "national product" variable (that is, not a component part of a category in Table 2–1). Nor is money supply within the "national product" system. Yet both employment and money supply may be related to output. Introduction of

the money supply implies price equations in those models where inflation is taken into account. (It is not generally necessary to introduce inflation, however, because projections are often made in constant prices. This is done when it is believed that inflation is neutral or absent, or when its effects cannot be estimated reasonably.)

4. As a result of parts 1, 2, and 3 above, a set of equations emerges, some of which are identities and some of which are stochastic. The system is now set up for some base period, and base-period data are entered. Ordinarily, this period will be the last year before the plan commences. In case that year is not considered representative (for example, there was a drought, or a series of strikes, or a severe depression), either the data may be adjusted (based on extrapolations of trends), or a different year may be chosen, or an average of prior years may be used. (The same problem is encountered in selecting base periods for index numbers.) Data must be complete for the base period.

5. The projection of subsequent years now begins. For every variable, there is either a growth rate (already determined); or a dependency relationship (mathematically expressed) upon some other variable, either of the present or a preceding year; or neither of these. The first two kinds of variables are *endogenous* and the third is *exogenous*. Since the model is usually expressed in continuous form, values dependent on the present year will be expressed linearly and those dependent on preceding years will be expressed as differentials. If the number of exogenous variables were equal to the number of equations, the system would be determinate. This condition occurs rarely, however; in practice, the exogenous variables usually exceed the number of equations, so the system up to this point is normally indeterminate.

6. A number of policy variables is now entered, equal to the excess of exogenous variables over the number of equations. For example, the interest rate may be policy-entered and the growth of investment made dependent on it (as well as on other variables, such as the exchange rate). Imports may be made dependent on consumption and investment, with an additional dependency on exchange rates and tariff levels. Different taxes may be included with their potential effects on consumption and investment, possibly broken down into industries or other kinds of goods.

7. The non-policy exogenous variables (sometimes called "irrelevant variables"), which remain as unknowns, have now been made equal to the number of equations, so the system is soluble. As long as there is at least one growth parameter, or one variable whose growth rate is influenced by policy, the system is dynamic. The computer can then calculate values of all variables for all years into the indefinite future. Naturally, planners confine their vision to the near future (say, a maximum of five years), and they tend to attribute more reliability to their projections for the first year or two than to those for later years. Some planners suggest a repetition of the process every year (a "rolling plan"), such that at the end of the first year, the estimates for years 2, 3, 4, and 5 are revised (with new parameters), and a sixth year is added. Thus the plan would always look five years into the future, with early years deemed "firm" and later years deemed "indicative."

8. Planners tend to "play" with the model by introducing alternative policies, so that they can show the politicians what the effects of different decisions will be. In principle, the politicians make their choices, and the practitioners prepare the plan accordingly.

CRITICISM OF "PLANNING FROM ABOVE"

We propose that "planning from above" contains certain inherent defects.

FIRST: The key proposition of "planning from above" is that the macro-exercise is done *first*, and sectoral planners depend on its results. The agricultural expert, for example, is not free to determine the extent to which his or her sector can progress independently of what is happening to other sectors. This constraint is justified by the proposition that the demand for foodstuffs depends on the nation's aggregate income. Suppose, however, that the planners for separate sectors independently decide that sectoral value added will be such that (unbeknownst to them) the sum will be greater (or less) than the GDP estimated by the macro-model. If a trial-and-error process follows, in which GDP estimates are negotiated between the sectoral experts and the macro-planners, then the estimates of the latter would at least be constrained by the former group. But such a process is usually too brief, and often the central planners have greater clout than the sectoral working parties. Also, the plan preparation is long and tedious, and civil servants at the top planning level are rarely willing to go through it a second time. In most cases (we understand informally), the word of the macro-planners is final, and the sectoral planners must conform.

SECOND: The exercise itself contributes to centralization. It concentrates power in the presidency (or the planning board, or the finance ministry), thus enhancing leverage of the central government over local communities or other development units. In principle, there is no reason why this should be so, and the world sports some notable exceptions, such as the People's Republic of China (Chapter 16). In practice, however, the planning operation often creates a sense of power in central-government officials, which becomes a self-fulfilling prophesy. Usually the parliament plays little role, being asked simply to approve or disapprove the plan when it is in final shape. And, for planning efficiency, the parliament should *not* play a role, since the political haggling might abort the entire process. Yet the result is usually that the power of the president and cabinet over the national resources is strengthened, at the expense of parliament, local authorities, and private groups (trade unions, professional associations, political parties, and so on). If the central government is a contending unit, rather than the impartial arbiter, the planning process may not only cause imbalance of national economic and political leverage, but also (through patronage) a less equitable distribution of income.

THIRD: Macro-economic models have become extraordinarily sophisticated and complicated. Most LDCs do not possess the technical capacity to produce them in a sophisticated manner, so this task often falls to the World Bank. Some years ago, the Bank began to insist that all borrowing countries prepare national plans, a not unreasonable proposition at the time. In a perverse application of Parkinson's law, however, the models accompanying these plans have grown in sophistication to meet the capacity of the Bank's technicians to produce them; they are not often based on an objective assessment of the capacities of LDC officials to understand and use them. We suggest (again from our informal conversations) that senior planning officials in developing countries tend to pay attention to models that they can understand themselves or whose underlying logic is clear, and not to models whose outcome must be explained to them by their own specialized subordinates or by foreign technicians. For the Bank on the one hand to foster labor-intensive technology, rural development, and smallness of scale in the general economy, and on the other hand to propose the most capital-intensive, electronically operated planning models to LDC officials, may well be the major paradox of the planning world.

FOURTH: The more complicated the model becomes, the greater the picture of pseudoreality it presents. The major argument *for* economic models is that reality is so complex that it cannot be grasped intuitively. Often a country will start with relatively simple models, but each year discover some way to "improve" them, in the belief that if logic shows that intuition is wrong, then more logic will show that it is "wronger." We suggest, on the contrary, that a point of entropy will be encountered, where the estimating errors of large numbers of variables become so compounded that the overall result may be less accurate than that of a simpler model. Although standard errors, t-scores, and R^2 estimates are usually shown in the appendix, where the equations are set forth, the significance of these to the planning official may not be fully explicated in the text of the plan.

FIFTH: Perhaps most important of all, planning from above tends to be quantitative-biased, and thus tends to ignore the kinds of personal and institutional variables that we have suggested in Chapter 1 to be the historically derived determinants of economic development. Human resources and institutions cannot be expressed in monetary terms. Although qualitative estimates do appear in plan chapters, they do not occupy what we feel is their deserved central position.

PLANNING FROM BELOW[4]

It has often been suggested that planning should start from local communities and build upward. This direction has been tried in many countries. The principal objection is that rural people "do not know how to plan." It is argued that they tend to envisage planning as a gift-list from the government, rather

---

[4]Our proposed model for "planning from below" has been described in greater detail (see Powelson, 1979).

Tanzania plan in 1976 was delayed by six months (Chapter 16) because the sum of local-plan costs so greatly exceeded what the government could afford that the exercise had to be virtually redone in the capital city.

If it is true that rural people do not know how to plan, the central government has two options: do the planning for them or teach them to plan (and in the meantime, have either no plan or a very simple one prepared by communities). The second option may be difficult to accept when governments face both the World Bank mandate and the existence of their well-entrenched planning departments. The decision they do take may also reflect the degree of their "disdain for the poor," which we discussed in Chapter 1.

We propose a reversal of the usual procedure. No econometric model need be prepared, and no parameters estimated, until the planning operation is well along its way. Sectoral working parties would have no instructions whatsoever from the macro-planning unit. In case local communities truly do not know how to plan, the central government might provide them with whatever expertise it can. The working party for agriculture would project output (under average weather conditions) for a five-year period, *crop by crop, location by location*, based on whatever assumptions it can make about technologies to be used and credit and extension services to be offered. Not yet knowing the government budget, the working party might make alternative estimates based on current or past budgets, and give its recommendations. If it wishes to ask for (say) an increased budget for extension services, it would justify the increase in terms of expected output. Agricultural technicians would thus estimate both the value added by agriculture and the amount of investment in the agricultural sector. They need not know anything about capital-output ratios, elasticity of output to capital, or marginal productivity of capital. All they need to do is to determine what new machinery and buildings will be required for the output increase they project, where these will be obtained, and how they will be financed.

The same would apply for any other sector. The industrial working party would project output in whatever degree of disaggregation (ISIC levels) it could, based on sample surveys of individual firms (both private and government). The projected output and investment of these firms would then be used as a guide by the working party to propose changes in policy. The educational working party would deal with numbers of pupils and needs of schools at every academic level. The result of this entire exercise would be two lists: values added and investment by sectors. The sum of the values added would be the first guess at projected gross domestic product, and the sum of the investments would be the first approximation of gross domestic investment.

In the meantime—and without yet communicating their results to the working parties—the macro-unit would project the resource availabilities of the economy: government revenues according to source, investment according to type, and labor force according to skills. These projections, however, would be built up from below by consultation with bankers, financiers, foreign-aid agencies, and international institutions, as well as from census data and extrapolations, category by category. By the time the working parties make their reports, the macro-economists would be able to determine whether the sums of their projections (GDP and investment) fall within a realistic range of the economy's total capabilities.

The major difference between this proposal and current general practice is that we suggest depending on trial and error, successive approximations, and negotiations, whereas the planning-from-above model depends on the simultaneous solution of a set of equations. Our proposed method has an aura of crudeness and uncertainty; the mathematical models present the aura of precision and definiteness. Those who argue for the latter point out that in fact, supply and demand are solved simultaneously in the real world—a truism with which we of course agree. But the general philosophy behind planning from above is that there exists a set of technical experts capable of understanding and manipulating the economy as a whole. Our observation is that there is no such set of experts; rather, the economy seems to function as the sum of individual decisions made by vast numbers of people with only partial knowledge. We therefore believe that a summary view of the economy is apt to be more useful if it, too, is prepared in this way.

One final point: It is unlikely that the sums of the projections of the working parties will be exactly equal to the macro-unit's estimate of aggregate capabilities. How should this difference be reconciled? If the working party sum falls short of the macro-economic estimates, then the central planning unit might ask the working parties to reconsider, for the excess aggregate capacity must exist within the sectors (assuming the macro-unit has guessed correctly). If, on the other hand, the working-party sum exceeds the estimates of the macro-planners, then the first question is whether certain policies can increase aggregate national capacities. For example, higher interest rates might induce more saving; training or selective importation of foreign skills might improve manpower availabilities; exchange depreciation might improve the ability to export; and so on.

Once again, we have a difference in philosophy. The planning-from-above models breed the belief that policy, by being complex, can bring about complex, simultaneous solutions. They therefore become biased toward central government control, through a large number of instruments, including exchange control, price and wage controls, taxes, interest rates, credit controls, import/export policies, and sometimes domestic production policies. Paradoxically, the World Bank often uses complex models to urge governments to simplify their controls and liberalize the economy. Our suggestion, by contrast, is that models developed by negotiating and reconciling the observations of many individuals with differing views are more likely to yield the kinds of economic policies necessary to promote balanced-leverage growth.

CONCLUSION

Growth models have evolved out of Keynesian economics, and therefore they possess a Keynesian-type structure, which relates gross domestic product to its component parts (consumption, government expenditures, investment, and exports less imports) and other variables within the national accounting system. Often models are abbreviated to concentrate on output, consumption, and investment. They are useful in understanding the sacrifices necessary for greater growth rates, as well as the concept of an optimal rate of growth.

Keynesian-Harrod-Domar models originated in a world where unemployment was caused by inadequacy of aggregate demand; where the provision of capital would increase output in fairly predictable amounts; where institutions (banking systems, accounting systems, markets) would allocate resources efficiently; and where perverse economic policies would not be expected to negate the flow of investment into its appropriate sectors. None of these conditions is widespread in the less-developed world.

When these models are applied to policy and planning, therefore, they present certain pitfalls. Paradoxically, mainstream economics is in a phase where simplicity is stressed in everything except the instruments of economists themselves. Planning models have taken on a sophistication that involves the simultaneous solution of the effects of various policies. Even though economists often use these models to persuade politicians to simplify and liberalize the economy, the process of model making itself may sustain belief in the capacity of the central government for control. If the government is in fact not an impartial arbiter but a contending party for the nation's resources, the total impact may be one of further centralization and greater inequity in distribution.

In order to counteract these tendencies, we propose a simplified model of planning from below, in which aggregate data are compiled, not as the result of macro-economic exercises, but as the sum of decisions by decentralized groups, each with partial knowledge. Projections of aggregate output and investment would be the result of negotiations among sectoral representatives and macro-planners. At the same time, policies would be negotiated to help develop the aggregate capacity to achieve the sum of sectoral projections.

BIBLIOGRAPHY

Domar, Evsey D., 1946:
    "Capital Expansion, Rate of Growth, and Employment," *Econometrica*, Vol. 14. Reprinted in Domar, 1957: *Essays in the Theory of Economic Growth*, New York, Oxford.
Dorfman, Robert; Samuelson, Paul; and Solow, Robert, 1958:
    Linear Programming and Economic Analysis, New York, McGraw-Hill.
Douglas, Paul H., 1948:
    "Are There Laws of Production?" *American Economic Review*, Vol. 38, March.
Gerschenkron, Alexander, 1962:
    Economic Backwardness in Historical Perspective, Cambridge, Mass., Belknap Press (Harvard University Press).
Hansen, Alvin, H., 1953:
    A Guide to Keynes, New York, McGraw-Hill.
Harrod, Roy F., 1939:
    "An Essay in Dynamic Theory," *Economic Journal*, Vol. 49, pp. 468–475.
Keynes, John Maynard, 1935:
    The General Theory of Employment, Interest, and Money, New York, Harcourt, Brace, and Co.

Kindleberger, Charles, and Herrick, Bruce, 1977:
  Economic Development, New York, McGraw-Hill.
Phelps, Edmund, 1961:
  "The Golden Rule of Accumulation," *American Economic Review*, September.
Powelson, John P., 1979:
  "Planning from Below with an Intermediate-Technology Model," *Cultures et Developpement* (University of Louvain, Belgium), Vol. XI, No. 3.
Rand Corporation, 1949:
  Market Mechanizations and Maximization, Part III, Santa Monica, California.
Rosenstein-Rodan, Paul N., 1943:
  "Problems of Industrialization of Europe and South-Eastern Europe," *Economic Journal*, June-September. Reprinted in Meier, Gerald, *Leading Issues in Economic Development*, Third Edition, New York, Oxford, 1976, pp. 632–636.
Solow, Robert M., 1956:
  "A Contribution to the Theory of Growth," *Quarterly Journal of Economics*, February.
Stewart, Frances, 1977:
  Technology and Underdevelopment, Boulder, Colorado, Westview Press.

3

SOCIO-POLITICAL DEVELOPMENT

The totalistic approach of (early sociological theories) soon had to be abandoned; before it could progress, sociology had largely to give up the quest for over-all patterns and "ultimate" causes of change. Although in general this reaction was well justified, possibly it was overdone by sociologists moving to the other extreme, avoiding not only the study of history in its broadest sense, the inquiry into the study of change of all times, but also the changes of specific societies at particular times. Hopefully, the concepts and tools recently developed will serve as the building stones of a new theory of change that is not only grand, but also testable, and one which when tested will be found true.

ETZIONI AND ETZIONI (1964:8–9).

By introducing personal and socio-political development as two of the paths of economic development, we invade the fields of our fellow social scientists: sociologists, anthropologists, social psychologists, and political scientists. We owe it to them and to us to find out how useful their literature will be to us. The answer is, "not very." They have been operating largely without concern for us, and we without concern for them; as a result, the gap has become so wide that we must almost return to the beginning before we can bridge it.

Yet because their research *may* be vital to us, we should examine it. In surveying the contributions of "other" social scientists, we find such an abundant platter that it is impossible, in one chapter, to taste it all. We therefore select those items that appear to us to be the most relevant to economic development. Our choices fall into four types.

First comes social theory, addressed primarily by sociologists but amply supplemented by anthropologists. It includes the structural-functional views of societies (Parsons, 1951; Merton, 1957; and others). In an earlier work (Powelson, 1972: 227–35), we commented on the closeness of social growth models to economic ones, in that both depend on parameters distinguishing structures on the one hand and the functioning of societies within these structures on the other.

Second, there is theory of history. Both sociologists and historians have sought common trends in the developments of societies (Comte, 1877; Durkheim, 1893; and Toynbee, 1946). The nineteenth century saw the popularity of chauvinistic theories, which compared earlier societies with primitive biological species, while our own species was considered the ultimate in evolution (Spencer, 1892). At the risk of some unpleasantness, we find a little of that also in Rostow (1956), in that "take off" appears a bit primitive and the "age of mass consumption" an ultimate. Both the first and second types of studies are excellently summarized in a book of readings (Etzioni and Etzioni, 1964), and except for Toynbee we leave them at that.

Third is political theory. Here alone there is plentiful choice; even tasting all of them may bring indigestion. We therefore confine ourselves to political stability. In Chapter 1, we suggested that continuity of institutions might correlate positively with economic growth. We will defend this proposition in the present chapter, in light of the findings of political scientists.

Fourth, the dessert platter contains a variety of research on modernization. It leads us to the trichotomy of who is responsible for poverty: the poor themselves for being "nonmodern?" Powerful people who exploit the poor? Or social institutions? We prefer not to join the debate, for we believe not only that all three forces are at work, but that they are closely intercorrelated. Weightings therefore reflect personal preferences, and ours are no better than those of others.

In the present chapter we will first review Toynbee's theory of history, in which we find elements corresponding to the development process outlined in Chapter 1. Next, we will look at the relationship between political stability and economic growth. Finally, we will sample the theories of modernization, and we will say a few words about the trichotomy.

TOYNBEE'S THEORY OF HISTORY

Unlike sociologists, development economists have not been greatly concerned with reductionism. How far "down" do we keep on asking "why?" We have seen that in growth models, macroeconomists derive parameters by an econometric examination of behavior in prior years. They sometimes speculate on why the parameters are what they are, and hypotheses may be offered. But it is not the custom to examine the hypotheses "downward" into the realms of "other" social scientists.

Toynbee carries his reductionism to a point where the question becomes no longer answerable. He proposes that civilizations grow out of challenges by the environment: climates become difficult for life, or blows or pressures are inflicted from outside. Whether a civilization will grow or not depends, in part, on how constructively the people respond. Sometimes successful response is out of their hands. Certain potential civilizations (such as the Vikings or the Western Celts) encountered challenges too difficult for anyone to meet; thus there is a "golden mean" of challenge (enough and not too much). Successful response provokes further challenge; growth therefore depends on continued responses. Toynbee does not address the question of why, when two civilizations are faced with roughly the same challenges, one responds creatively while the other does not.

Growth originates with creative individuals, or small minorities, who discover ways to face the challenge. These ways may occur in art, religion, industrial inventiveness, agricultural experimentation, physical movement, and a host of other areas. The creative minority must not only discover for itself, but it must convert the rest of society to the new way of life. The process is lengthy. Both individuals and minorities often withdraw from society for a period of time, then return. (Examples include Buddha and Christ.)

Toynbee speculates that the origins of Mediterranean civilizations lie in the desiccation of the Sahara, which caused some peoples to turn southward and some northward. The latter faced more new challenges (climate, sea barriers) than the former, and it was in response to these that trading and inventing social orders evolved.

Civilizations break down, according to Toynbee, when the creative minority fails to respond with creative power. It then becomes a dominant minority, and other groups—who had previously followed by mimesis—withdraw their allegiance. Toynbee lists the following reasons for failure: (1) the mechanical nature of mimesis (leaders become influenced by the mechanical nature of their followers and cease to lead), (2) the failure to establish new institutions called for by new times ("new wine in old bottles"), (3) selfidolization, when the self is ephemeral, (4) idolization of institutions, when they too are ephemeral, (5) idolization of techniques, also ephemeral, (6) suicide through military ventures, and (6) the intoxication of victory.

Toynbee suggests that the breakdown of Roman civilization began with the Peloponnesian Wars (fifth century B.C.). Faced with the challenge of population growth, which had previously been met by colonization, Athens and Sparta now turned upon each other, setting in motion the sequence by which the decay of Greco-Roman civilization began. Subsequent decisions (Alexander's conquests, Punic Wars, Roman civil and social wars, the establishment of the Empire, the growth of the universal church, and attacks by barbarian war bands) rounded out the process and planted the seeds for Western Christendom.

Our objective here is not to evaluate Toynbee's work, but rather to point out how we have been influenced by it. First, economic development (like the growth of civilizations) depends on *unexplainable* decisions made by individuals (and creative minorities). By this, we mean that others (at other times and places), faced with similar challenges, will make different decisions, thus de-

laying or aborting development. Of course theoreticians prefer to have explanations, but sometimes it is not necessary to explain a decision; to identify it
may be enough. Our own *process* (as opposed to theory) of economic development explicates three coinciding paths, as described in Chapter 1. We do not
know why some societies opt to deviate from these paths, any more than
Toynbee was able to explain why some civilizations have responded creatively
to challenges and others have not.

Second, since no two civilizations followed identical paths, the similarities
that Toynbee has seen among them are judgmental. Other social scientists (for
example, Geyl and Sorokin, 1949) have disagreed with him. Likewise, developing
countries do not follow identical paths, and our sightings of similarity are also
judgmental. We invite disagreement. Our arguments lie in the case studies, just
as Toynbee's were supported by his illustrations.

POLITICAL STABILITY

We have also been influenced by Huntington (1968), who writes (p. 1) that
"the differences between democracy and dictatorship are less than the differences between those countries whose politics embodies consensus, community,
legitimacy, organization, effectiveness, stability, and those countries whose
politics is deficient in these qualities." Our process of economic development
(Chapter 1) depends on these selfsame qualities and similarly does not relate
to whether a society is a democracy or a dictatorship, or whether it is socialist
or capitalist.

Numerous studies, which Huntington (1968: 40–59) reviews,[1] show negative
correlations between modernization variables (such as GNP *per capita*, literacy,
and school attendance) on the one hand and political violence on the other.
But Huntington makes an assertion that appears to us to go beyond the evidence.
He states that the movement is U-shaped; that violence is found *less* in poor
countries, *more* in middle-group (modernizing) countries, and once again *less*
in more modern countries. "If poor countries appear to be unstable," he says,
"it is not because they are poor, but because they are trying to be rich" (p. 41).
He supports this hypothesis by citing instances where the *degree* of violence has
been accentuated as modernization proceeds.

We find two problems with this reasoning. First, it is difficult to measure
the degree of violence. Is not the dropping of an atomic bomb perhaps the
greatest degree of violence that humankind has ever perpetrated, and was that
not done by one of the most modern powers? But more, Huntington's analysis
is cross-sectional, not longitudinal. He suggests that if most data do not currently
support his U-shaped hypothesis, it is because "by the 1960s every backward
nation was a modernizing nation" (p. 41) and therefore had passed the "traditional" stage of little violence.

---

[1]Feierabend and Nesvold, 1963; Russett, 1964; Tanter, 1965; U.S. Department of Defense and
Ried, 1965; LeVine and Campbell, 1966; and Tanter and Midlarsky, 1967.

We find this reasoning to be antihistoric. It is analogous to the supposition of economists, which we criticized in Chapter 1, that societies jumped from "traditional" (egalitarian) to "modern." But for more than a millennium prior to the industrial revolution, European societies were, more than not, both antiegalitarian and warlike. Relative peace was generally limited to small units, such as family and clan, in which cooperation was recognized as essential to social goals (mainly obtaining food and shelter). *It is only with industrialization that such cooperation becomes essential on a large scale.* And it is not the degree of violence, however measured, but its endemic (persistent) nature that hinders industrialization. Europe and the Far East stand as historic examples that endemic violence had to be overcome before an industrial revolution could occur.

We respect Huntington's review of the violence-modernization literature, as well as his emphasis on legitimacy, institutionalization, and cooperation as essentials of modernization (which corresponds with our own analysis). We agree also that modernization may provoke violence, for it provokes conflict. But we would like to add one point: The need to overcome violence (for economic development) varies directly with the degree of social differentiation (including division of labor), which in turn implies a need for the various units to collaborate (the production function becomes increasingly complex). It is for these reasons that violence, often endemic in preindustrial societies, must be controlled in modern societies. The great mystery is why some people, historically, have grasped this truth earlier than others when faced with similar Rubicons.

MODERNIZATION

What follows is a tray of offerings by social scientists on the process of modernization. It is difficult to fit these studies into any integrated theory, but one cannot ignore them either. We will first present them (in separate sections) and then (in our conclusion) judge the extent to which some of the contributions may be useful in an understanding of the economics of development and distribution.

ANOMIE AND THE CULTURE OF POVERTY

Anomie (literally, "normlessness") signifies "the absence of an institutionally grounded and ideologically legitimated sense of substantive limits in society and the personality" (LaCapra, 1976). The concept was used by Durkheim (1893) in a theory of suicide, and other sociologists have written of it as a persistent quality in all societies, to a greater or lesser degree.

The concept of *anomie* may apply to an individual or to a society. In an individual, it occurs because of displacement. Teenagers who rebel against their parents, who run away to become "street people," become removed from the social structures that used to contain them. Those constraints, however, served a purpose—that of limiting individual choice so that meaningful decisions could be made. Afflicted with anomie, a person loses his behavioral norms and feels lost and powerless over himself and/or over his society or both.

An entire society may be afflicted with anomie if its norms and traditions are destroyed or made meaningless by natural disaster, invasion by an enemy, or occupation by a colonial power. Without mentioning anomie, Huxley (1939) writes poignantly of the history of a Kikuyu family in Kenya and how its sons were affected by the onset of colonialism, with ensuing destruction of Kikuyu ways of life and attraction of Nairobi as a great city.

Certainly Lewis's (1961) culture of poverty is closely related to anomie. Among the lowest strata of social groupings, Lewis observed certain common characteristics that seemed to perpetuate themselves (thus constituting a culture) and therefore to perpetuate poverty. The culture of poverty, he wrote, "does not include primitive peoples whose backwardness is the result of their isolation and undeveloped technology and whose society for the most part is not class stratified. Such peoples have a relatively integrated, satisfying, and self-sufficient culture . . . The culture of poverty would apply only to those who are at the very bottom of the social scale, the poorest workers, the poorest peasants, plantation laborers, and that large heterogeneous mass of small artisans and tradesmen usually referred to as the lumpen proletariat" (1961, xxv). Among such groups, Lewis found "remarkable similarities in family structure, interpersonal relations, time orientations, value systems, spending patterns, and the sense of community in lower-class settlements in London, Glasgow, Paris, Harlem, and Mexico City" (1961, xxv). The characteristics of the culture include conditions imposed upon the poor by the wider culture as well as purely personal traits. Among the former would be low level of education and literacy and crowded living conditions. An intermediate set of factors would be the failure of the poor to participate in national institutions that might have provided them with economic betterment. Such institutions include labor unions, political parties, social security, and medical care (even free care offered by the Mexican government).[2]

Those of Lewis's critics who imply that he finds poverty to be the *fault* of the poor are not correct, for he states that the cultural traits may be imposed by a system of institutions for which the poor are not responsible. At the same time, however, Lewis points out that it is not clear how much effort the poor *might have made* to overcome their situation.

---

[2]The economic traits of the culture include "constant struggle for survival, unemployment and underemployment, low wages, a miscellany of unskilled occupations, child labor, the absence of savings, a chronic shortage of cash, the absence of food reserves in the home, the pattern of frequent buying of small quantities of food many times a day as the need arises, the pawning of personal goods, borrowing from local money lenders at usurious rates of interest, spontaneous informal credit devices *(tandas)* organized by neighbors, and the use of second-hand clothing and furniture" (1961, xxvi). The personal traits include "a high incidence of alcoholism, frequent use of physical violence in the training of children, a trend toward mother-centered families, . . . a strong predisposition to authoritarianism, . . . present time orientation with relatively little ability to defer gratification and plan for the future, a sense of resignation and fatalism . . ." Lewis sums up the heterogeneous nature of these traits and their various causes as "attempts at local solutions for problems not met by existing institutions and agencies because the people are not eligible for them, cannot afford them, or are suspicious of them."

"TRADITIONAL" TO "MODERN" MAN

Ours is an age of "evolution fever" among social scientists. Gone are the days of Spengler (1926), who believed that social systems moved in cycles and that each cycle ended just about where it had started. We are now in the age of Toynbee (1946), to whom society was progressing somewhere, even if it did move cyclically along the way. In this belief, we follow also in the traditions of Comte (1877), Weber (1947), Toennies (1957), and Parsons (1961).

Just as economists have believed there are laws of development that move societies inexorably from low to high income, so also sociologists have argued that after crossing a threshold, traditional society changes inexorably to modern. We will challenge the beliefs of both economists and sociologists on these scores, but first it is necessary to review the literature.

The contrast between "traditional" and "modern" man is forcefully made by Inkeles and Smith (1974: 75–6) in their characterizations of two Pakistani, named Ahmadullah (who represents traditional man) and Nuril (who is modern). Nuril "communicated a strong sense of personal efficacy" and "felt that the outcome of things depended very much on himself," while Ahmadullah "was relatively passive, even fatalistic, and very much dependent on outside forces, above all on the intervention of God." Nuril believed he could influence laws and public decisions; Ahmadullah would say, "I can't do anything, I am just an ordinary man."

Inkeles and Smith developed various indices of overall modernity (OM), based on their ratings of respondents on three perspectives: analytical, topical, and behavioral. They first analyzed modern man, showing him to be open, future oriented, confident, and valuing technical skills.[3] The second covers attitudes toward religion, family, social stratification, women's rights, birth control, and a number of other issues. The third covers his political activity, mathematical ability, consumption, verbal fluency, use of media, and other characteristics.

---

[3]The analytical perspective includes the following characteristics of modern man (pp. 19–25 *passim*). He is open to new experiences and is ready for social change. He has "a disposition to form or hold opinions on a large number of the issues arising not only in his immediate environment, but also outside of it." He uses a variety of sources of information, which extend beyond his immediate social group. He is "oriented to the present or the future rather than to the past . . . he would more readily accept fixed schedules as something appropriate, or possibly even desirable . . . The modern individual believes that man can learn how to exert considerable control over his environment." He is "oriented toward long-term planning, both in public affairs and in his private personal life." He has "confidence that his world is calculable, and that people and institutions around him can be relied upon to meet their obligations." He values technical skill and accepts it "as a valid basis for distributing rewards." His aspirations, both educational and occupational, include "formal education and schooling in skills such as reading, writing, and arithmetic," as opposed to traditional man, who "might see modern learning and science as an intrusion into a sacred realm which should be left a mystery or approached only through religion." Modern man is aware of, and respects, the dignity of others. He grasps the logic of underlying decision-making in industrial production. He favors "universalistic rules applied equally to all, rather than feeling it more appropriate that one should favor friends and relatives and in other ways rely mainly on personal influence." He is optimistic rather than fatalistic.

To determine whether OM is a worldwide phenomenon, Inkeles and Smith performed their tests (through surveys) in eight countries: Argentina, Chile, East Pakistan (now Bangladesh), India, Israel, Nigeria, Greece, and the United Kingdom. They did indeed discover that respondents strong in the analytical model had certain opinions with respect to the topical perspective and that they behaved in certain ways according to the behavioral perspective. The OM measurements then became a combined index incorporating ratings in all three perspectives.

Inkeles and Smith decided upon ten groups of independent (causal) variables, as follows: personal and family characteristics (age, religion, ethnicity, etc.), origin (rural or urban), residence, socio-economic level, education, intelligence and skill, occupational characteristics, factory characteristics (if subject worked in a factory), information-media exposure (newspaper, radio, movie, etc.), and work-behavior scales (leadership, work stability, workmanship, and others).

In every one of the eight countries, formal education correlated most highly with OM, ranging from .41 in East Pakistan to .60 in Argentina, with all data significant at the .001 level or better. Months of factory experience correlated next most highly (from .11 in India to .36 in Chile, again all significant at the .001 level or better). Objective skill, mass-media exposure, and the number of factory benefits followed, in that order. Lesser degrees of correlation, and some lessening of statistical significance, applied to the remaining variables, which ranked in the following order: years of urban experience since age 15, urbanism of residence, modernity of home-school setting, father's education, and consumer goods possessed.

Using the techniques of path analysis, the authors then discovered that indirect influences operated on OM via education. In the early stages, these were ethnicity and religion, and father's education, which influenced the availability of other opportunities. At the point the respondents left school, half of their eventual OM score had been determined, on the average (though with fairly wide dispersion). The eventual outcome "depended largely on the interaction between the stage at which the men left school and the nature and extent of their later contact with modernizing institutions" (p. 285).

Inkeles and Smith are optimistic about the prospects of modernizing traditional people, for they conclude that it is possible for anyone, at any age, to alter his attitudes. They do not, however, go quite so far as their predecessors, Deutsch (1961) and Lerner (1963), who strongly implied that the *process* of modernization, once set into motion, becomes irreversible. Deutsch wrote of a growing tendency in many countries (for which he compiled social indicators) for individuals to become socially mobilized and therefore to participate in politics. His indicators included exposure to mass media, voting participation, literacy, change of residence or occupation, linguistic and political assimilation, and income growth, among others. But he did not have a theory of the cause-effect manner in which the process would unfold.

Deutsch found that social mobilization was a requisite for growing national income, but that the former could occur for a long time before significant income changes were noted. Lerner, on the other hand, believed that economic events were causes. He cited a Turkish village that remained traditional until Ankara grew to encompass it; only thereafter were the inhabitants swirled on to the modernization path. Lerner measured modernization on the basis of urbanization, literacy, media participation, and political participation. Only when a new factor—*empathy*—had been achieved, however, would the process be culminated and become irreversible.

> For the true Transitional is defined, dynamically, by what he wants to become. What differentiates him from his Traditional peers is a different *latent structure* of aptitudes and attitudes . . . The aptitude is *empathy*— he "sees" things the others do not see, "lives" in a world populated by imaginings alien to the constrictive world of the others . . . The great gap is passed when a person begins to "have opinions"—particularly on matters which, according to his neighbors, "do not concern him." The empathic skill which makes this possible is not highly valued in the traditional community. There people are taught to handle the ego with minimum awareness of alternatives to current practices—in the technical sense, compulsively. The Constrictive Self is the approved personal style. Self-manipulation, continuous re-arrangement of the self-system to incorporate new experience, is regarded as unworthy of any person with "good character." (pp. 72–3).

FOSTER AND THE CONCEPT OF "LIMITED GOOD"

Lerner's "empathic lack" was perhaps a precursor to the concept of the "limited good." Foster (1965) wrote of the limited good as a cultural quality he found among the poor in the Mexican village of Tzintzuntzan; he felt this characteristic tended to perpetuate their poverty.

> . . . that broad areas of peasant behavior are patterned in such a fashion that peasants view their social, economic, and natural universes—their total environment—as one in which all the desired things in life, such as land, wealth, friendship and love, manliness and honor, respect and status, power and influence, security and safety, exist in finite quantity and are always in short supply, as far as the peasant is concerned. Not only do these and all other 'good things' exist in finite and limited quantities, but in addition there is no way directly within peasant power to increase the available quantities . . . it follows that an individual family can improve a position only at the expense of others. (pp. 304–05).

Such a concept of zero-sum game, Foster concluded, led to cultural restraints being placed upon those who would garner for themselves too much of the "good things." This, he declared, would explain pressure on more wealthy peasants to become patrons of religious or other festivals, where they would diffuse their savings among the rest of society. Those who behaved in entrepreneurial fashion, or who worked regularly and hard, would be ridiculed. The concept of the limited good is therefore a cultural rather than an individual characteristic. It restrains even those individuals who do not themselves hold the belief.

Foster's critics argue that all the phenomena he describes could be explained in ways other than by belief in the limited good; that Foster does not demonstrate that these characteristics are the sole province of peasant (or of poor) societies; and that even if the belief is strong, it does not preclude other, seemingly contradictory behavior that might not limit the poor in their search for material wealth (Stoller, 1977).

ENTREPRENEURSHIP

Ever since Schumpeter (1911), economists have associated growth with entrepreneurship. Unlike the qualities discussed in the preceding sections, entrepreneurship is not something that permeates, or needs to permeate, a society. It is necessary only that there be a certain (relatively small) number of entrepreneurs, sufficient to bring about innovations that cause new capital investment and ensuing employment. McClelland (1961) associated entrepreneurship with a psychological need for achievement, which when gratified would reflect a particular way of acquiring social recognition. While Hagen (1962) believed that a need for achievement would arise only over generations of deprivation and discrimination against a disadvantaged group, McClelland believed it could be inculcated by special training.

Such training was conducted experimentally by McClelland and Winter (1969) in India, with positive findings. Those who had been trained in achievement motivation worked longer hours, invested more capital, and had higher gross income after the training than before, or than did the control groups. The experiments were conducted with a minimum of cost and with small samples; they have not been widely replicated. One might question whether selection for the training course alone would explain the improvements of the participants. In a review of the McClelland-Winter report, Wilson (1970) found it "difficult to believe that these data are sufficient to permit the authors to draw some of their conclusions," though he felt that the findings would "justify further experimental efforts along these lines."

While awaiting further experiments, we content ourselves with the following comments. The idea that entrepreneurship depends on the need for achievement, which can be instilled, is intriguing. As we reflect on all the entrepreneurs who have emerged in history, however, we wonder whether the modern concept of the need for achievement could apply to them. The earliest entrepreneurs were in trading, in both the Far East and the Mediterranean. Wherever economic history has been written, entrepreneurs have been found. The tribes of Africa were very quick to adapt their economic enterprise to the needs of the Portuguese, and later the Europeans, for trade. They moved to new locations, shifted into hunting and crafts, became intermediaries, organized lengthy caravans, and divided the tasks tribally, with remarkable flexibility. Is it reasonable to suppose that the necessary entrepreneurial ability was evoked by many individual "needs for achievement"? Possibly "need for appreciation" is a more general term, encompassing the need for achievement and whatever other needs would be acceptable in different cultures. If so, what about the need for power, and the need for material wealth?

Closely associated with entrepreneurship is Weber's (1904) "Protestant ethic," or the thesis that religious dogma, initially associated with Protestantism, compelled its adherents to forgo earthly pleasures in order to accumulate capital and to produce. Other authors (including us: Powelson, 1965:19) have referred to a "capitalist ethic," since Weber's description did not seem to be confined to Protestantism. Hagen (1962) believed he found a similar "Catholic ethic" in Colombia.

In sum, McClelland's proposition shows some promise, but it has not been adequately investigated. It leaves us with some doubts about its applicability in different places and in different historical areas.

AMORAL FAMILISM

After studying a village of extreme poverty in southern Italy, which he identified only by the fictitious name Montegrano, Banfield (1958) coined the concept of "amoral familism" for its residents. An amoral familist will not "further the interest of the group or community except as it is to his private advantage to do so," and "only officials will concern themselves with public affairs, for only they are paid to do so."

Banfield modestly points out (p. 11) that his "intention is not to 'prove' anything, but rather to outline and illustrate a theory which may be rigorously tested by any who care to do so." Not many researchers, to our knowledge, have taken up his challenge. Furthermore, Banfield's assertions hint of the loose comments concerning LDCs that visitors (including economic technicians) make informally. They also hint of chauvinism, in their frequent comparisons with the United States. A reference to Toqueville appears on the first page of the introduction, and Chapter 1 begins with the following sentence: "Americans are used to a buzz of activity, having as its purpose, at least in part, the advancement of community welfare." Perhaps the climaxing criticism of Banfield is that the same observations might have been written by Adam Smith, but with a glow of approval.

Nevertheless, we must not dismiss Banfield lightly. Although his allusions to normative behavior and his lack of corroborative research do not sit well with social scientists, he offers a potential grain of enlightenment in support of those political theorists (Huntington, 1968) and sociologists (Durkheim, 1893; Weber, 1947; Parsons, 1949; Coser, 1956; Merton, 1957; and others) who have dealt with institutional development. *Certain institutions work to the disadvantage of every individual separately, but to the advantage of the collective unit.* Taxation, which damages the finances of every person taxed, nevertheless provides the finance for social benefits. The accompanying qualifications and limitations, such as differential participation in those benefits, are underscored by the many writers on the theory of public choice. While we recognize these limitations, we believe in the general validity of the statement. Economic development requires the legitimacy of a large number of such institutions, and individuals must recognize a net increase in their own welfare from them. Thus individual welfare gained from participation in the collectivity, minus welfare lost from private damage, must be positive in the minds of most constituents.

THE PRAETORIAN STATE

In an earlier work (Powelson, 1972), we proposed that institutions of economic growth evolve in response to laws of supply and demand. Demand is generated by awareness of the net welfare benefits to individuals. Supply is related to cost, which is a function of the expected net suffering, consequent to institutional formation, of groups with the political and economic clout to hinder it. Using concepts of this nature, Huntington (1968) has described the situation that occurs when demand for political institutions exceeds their supply. Such an imbalance, he claims, leads to the "praetorian society."

A praetorian state is one in which mediating, political institutions are underdeveloped, and therefore political functions are undertaken, secondarily, by a large number of other institutions with different primary functions. "Countries which have political armies also have political clergies, political universities, political bureaucracies, political labor unions, and political corporations" (p. 194).

> In a praetorian system social forces confront each other nakedly; no political institutions, no corps of professional political leaders are recognized or accepted as the legitimate intermediaries to moderate group conflict. Equally important, no agreement exists among the groups as to the legitimate and authoritative methods for resolving conflicts. (p. 196).

These institutions, Huntington suggests, required centuries to form in Western states. They were (we add) important influences in the decline of warfare, in the establishment of orderly procedures for economic interchange, and in the division of labor.

The classicial sociological text on institutional formation is doubtless that of Weber (1947), which suggests that policies in the process of formation usually rely first on charismatic leadership. The "routinization of charisma" is one of the features of institutionalization.

Perhaps the key to economic development would be acquired if we could understand the reasons for, and the sequence of, the formation of institutions. Unfortunately, at this point we reach "rock bottom," and further reductionism appears impossible. In the course of history, certain creative individuals, in varying positions of power and subject to varying pressures of others, perceived the need for institutions of conflict mediation. Among these were the founders of the tribunate in Rome and the forum in Greece; Kings John, Edward I, and Henry VII of England, along with later Prime Ministers Walpole, the two Pitts, Palmerston, Gladstone, and Disraeli; the early Prime Ministers of postwar Japan; Chou En-lai of China; Juarez and Obregón of Mexico; Saenz Peña of Argentina; and Nehru of India. Mostly, their reasons had little to do with economic development, and more to do with political survival. It was only as political survival encompassed divisions of power among kings, nobles, merchants, craftsmen, and finally laborers and farmers, that these institutions were recognized as being of great value in achieving economic objectives.

POSITIVISM

Many authors have referred to the transition from magical to logical thinking. The rational use of land in medieval Europe was delayed by the belief that forests were inhabited by witches and dragons. The transition from primarily magical to primarily scientific explanations has a long history in Europe, and no one knows how to define its beginning. Some historians cite Abelard (1200) as an early example, in his now-famous remark: "By doubting, we are led to inquiry, and by inquiry we are led to truth."

So many authors have touched on positivism, or its lack in LDCs today, that it is hard to select among them. For a variety, we draw on Bozeman (1976) for her studies of Africa, Myrdal (1968) for Asia, and Geiger (1967) for Latin America.

Bozeman argues that traditional values are currently in an upsurge in Africa, tending to stem the influx of values from the West. Literacy and nonliteracy are the chief distinguishing features, in three ways. First, certain mental processes, such as abstract intellectual activity, can evolve only in literate societies. The ability to write enables people to fix meanings, which in a nonliterate society remain fluid. Writing spans time and space, whereas the spoken work will be remembered differently by different listeners. Second, time is circular in nonliterate societies. The past, present, and future tend to be indistinguishable, and people believe they can communicate with the dead and the unborn as easily as with the living. In such a world, the boundary between natural and supernatural becomes blurred, and events, because they cannot be reasoned abstractly, become the result of magic and witchcraft. Third, nonliterate societies must be small or they will not endure, for communication over large areas is not easy. The universe is conceived as malevolent, and strangers—who may carry evil spirits—are to be distrusted.

Miskimin (1977: 102) writes analogously of Europe in the sixteenth century, in questioning how Jean Bodin could invent the quantity theory of money while also supporting bullionism. "The one position holds that the import of large quantities of bullion will cause domestic prices to rise, the other holds that domestic prices should be kept low so that large quantities of bullion may be imported." Miskimin suggests a possible explanation in that Bodin was also the author of *Démonamanie des Sorciers* (1580): one who believes in supernatural intervention need not reconcile contradictions. Only with systemic thinking (we add) may one properly analyze complex business or economic relationships; magic cuts the links within a system.

When the British colonized Africa, Bozeman continues, they thought that the tribes were as unified and organized as European states and that it was possible to make binding treaties with the chiefs. But the tribes turned out to be fluid as well as migratory; it was difficult to determine who was chief for a specific population or territory, and "promises" were not sacred. Disagreements among different tribes were settled by war or by raiding; thus there was endemic violence. Disagreements within a tribe, on the other hand, were settled by what the British called "customary courts," or local tribunals whose solutions were designed to placate the contending parties rather than to conform to prescribed forms of common or statutory law.

Bozeman's work is scholarly and well documented by illustrations and citations of other authors. Its relevance to our thesis lies in the fact that the characteristics of nonliterate societies do not change merely because their languages are put into writing. The major elements of African cultures remain largely prevalent today. Only a thin veneer of leaders, exposed to Western education or to colonial officials or businessmen, have adopted elements of positivism such as those embodied in economic planning or in the management of government budgets and monetary systems. Even here, it is not clear to what extent these leaders base their decisions on the new values. Oathing and cursing are known to be a part of political processes even in sophisticated Kenya. Certainly, however, the leaders of African countries understand that the tribespeople in rural areas and in urban slums are still governed mostly by traditional values. No doubt this understanding helps to convince them of the great social cost, and inordinate difficulties, they would encounter in any attempt to convert their peoples into robust societies of skilled managers, technicians, and disciplined laborers.

One who reads Myrdal can hardly help feeling depressed and pessimistic about the state of the economic and social development in the Southeast Asian countries he studied. Myrdal writes about a set of attitudes, values, and institutions inherited from colonial times that has developed a torpor and social inertia. He depicts Asian countries as "soft states," whose governments issue plans, pronouncements, and objectives that cannot possibly be fulfilled and demands on their citizens that they do not or could not enforce. Religion, he argues, has become the "emotional container" for an Asian way of life and work, which it has rigidified and made resistant to change.

Work attitude lies close to the heart of Asia's problem. Myrdal argues that

> the bulk of the labor force is imbedded in a climatic, social, cultural, and institutional matrix that not only tends to perpetuate present low levels of labor utilization, but also resists rapid and immediate adaptation to novel and unfamiliar ways of living and working. Idleness and low labor efficiency depend upon institutions, custom and tradition, attitudes toward work and

leisure—including taboos and inhibitions related to status and to the participation of women in work (p. 999).

He reports short hours on small-scale farms. In comparing South Asian agriculture with that of China, Japan, Europe, and the United States, Myrdal notes that the first three are labor-abundant, land-scarce areas, where land is intensively used, whereas the United States is land-abundant and labor-scarce, therefore with extensive agriculture. One would expect Asian countries to follow the pattern of the first group. Instead, they form a pattern of their own: extensive land use combined with a high man-land ratio, and low output per hectare.

In contrast to both Bozeman and Myrdal, Geiger emphasizes the political values of the elites in Latin America, though he finds that major elements of these were transmitted over time to Indians and mestizos. Dominant among these values is the *intentionalist ethic*, or the belief that intending to do something constitutes the moral equivalent of doing it. In the remainder of this book we will mention institutions formed with certain intentions, but whose performance has been thwarted by the contrary actions of the very groups that created them. Among these are the agrarian reforms of many countries, the Latin American Free Trade Area, the Economic Community of West African States, and the East African Community.

Geiger associates the intentionalist ethic with "millenial expectations" of redemption by divine grace rather than by one's own efforts. Here, however, he is not on solid ground, for the intentionalist ethic is almost universal, appearing in MDCs as well as LDCs, and certainly in societies where divine grace is less well esteemed than in the Catholic world. And even if the intentionalist ethic does appear to be less strong in MDCs (and we have not examined the evidence on this), it may only be that countervailing forces are better organized to require governments or other agencies to perform on their stated intentions.

The Bozeman, Myrdal, and Geiger analyses have the following in common: In differing ways they "explain" why large numbers of people in the less developed world have not embraced the positivist ethic. Whether it be because of beliefs in magic and witchcraft, or because of religious inhibitions and taboos, or because of the confusion of intent with action, there exist on today's earth millions of people who are not prepared to act on the basis of scientific explanations for economic and social phenomena, nor to believe that a complex network of cause-and-effect relationships, dependent on sets of individual actions, can bring about calculated changes in the physical or social matrix.

During the twentieth century, however, there has emerged within LDCs an elite governing corps which, by virtue of its wealth or position, or by being the mavericks of society, has become exposed to Western education and to Western ways of thought. The extent to which these elites have in fact developed the positivist ethic is still not clear. Virtually all of them intellectually accept the principle of economic planning and budgeting as a rational way to organize government and private economic activity. Often, however, the plans are statements of "intentions" that were never really intended. "Successful" plans are sometimes no more than projections of events that would have occurred anyway.

In some cases plans are prepared to satisfy international lending agencies, just as African tribes entered into "treaties" to satisfy the British. The number of national failures to balance the budget, to stem inflation, to keep debts within manageable capacity, or to cover international payments make it reasonable to doubt that planning, or other commitments to social and economic action, carry the same seriousness in most LDCs as they would in countries where the positivist ethic is more historically held.

INSTITUTIONS OF TRUST

Every market economy depends on trust. We define trust first as the ability to predict the behavior of others and second as the acceptance that that behavior will do no harm, and perhaps some good, to the subject. An *institution of trust* is any organization, or mode of behavior, that sustains trust among individuals. A department store that gains a reputation for quality products, low prices, and dependable service is an institution of trust. A customer will trust a salesperson whom he has never seen before, in the confidence that the institution will guarantee the behavior of its employees.

There are "costs of mistrust" in all economic societies. In MDCs they take the form of safe deposit boxes, cash registers, security guards, auditors, contract lawyers, and so on. Many of the same costs (such as security guards) are readily known in LDCs, but others (such as auditors) are often resisted, for reasons not always clear to Westerners. The decreased output from hiring only one's own relatives or tribesmen instead of more skilled market labor—a practice often criticized by Westerners—may in fact be simply a cost of mistrust (of nonrelatives).

Williams, Whyte, and Green (1966: 19–20) found startling differences between American college students (N = 2,975) on the one hand and Peruvian school boys (N = 1,833) and white-collar workers (N = 202) on the other when rated on a "faith-in-people" scale. In reply to the question of whether "most people can be trusted," 81% of the Americans said yes (19% no), while only 31% of the Peruvian school boys said yes (69% no), and 37% of the Peruvian white-collar workers said yes (60% no, 3% undecided). Similar comments were made in response to the statements, "These days a person really doesn't know whom he can count on," and "No one is going to care much what happens to you when you get right down to it." (Subjects were asked to agree, agree in part, or disagree). In all cases, the Americans showed themselves much more trusting than the Peruvians. After rating the white-collar workers according to the "faith-in-people" scale, and asking questions about their attitudes toward interpersonal relationships, the authors decided they had confirmed their hypothesis that "individuals who are high in interpersonal trust will expect and appreciate a leader-group climate which is democratic and participative as contrasted with those who are very low in interpersonal trust, who will anticipate a more authoritarian and nonparticipative climate and, therefore, will be satisfied with supervisors so long as they provide the structure in which work can be done."

Carroll (1971) found that factors of cohesion did not come spontaneously or voluntarily to Latin American peasants in cooperatives he studied. Rather, they were "last resorts," used when the survival of the group depended on them. He found distrust of others, as well as the concept of the limited good, to be a constraint.

Erasmus (1961) relates mistrust to an unwillingness among primitive societies to believe what has not been personally experienced; therefore, members tend not to learn from others or to believe that strangers will keep promises. He writes of "frequency interpretation" (a term borrowed from Reichenbach, 1951) defined as "a probability estimate based on inductive inference from experience" (p. 22). Frequency interpretation depends on casual observation; innovations must be spectacular to be accepted. Thus primitive societies may be unwilling to accept (for example) that drinking infected water leads to illness, since the delayed effect is not immediately linked to the cause, cannot be observed over and over, and is not "spectacular."

In a questionnaire study of one hundred businesses in former South Vietnam, Barton (1974) discovered that the ethnic Chinese had a better reputation among the general public for keeping their word and for producing quality output than did the ethnic Vietnamese. Barton attributed this difference to the set of business ethics that the Chinese had developed over many generations of trading. These ethics called for exposure of those who violated their trust, social stigma within their own community (which was close knit), and consequent business losses. Because their word was a contract, the Chinese were able to do business more simply than the Vietnamese, who tended to become bogged down in written contracts, invoices, and other protective mechanisms. A similar evolution in medieval Europe, from cumbersome formalities to simplicity of contract, will be discussed in Chapter 15.

If this finding could be extended to other ethnic minorities, such as Chinese elsewhere in Southeast Asia, or Asians in East Africa and Lebanese in West Africa, it might help to explain the apparently greater successes of these groups over indigenous entrepreneurs. However, except for Barton, we do not know of any research that would demonstrate whether or not this hypothesis is correct.

INSTITUTIONS OF TRUST VERSUS ENDEMIC WARFARE

Let us now, however, suppose that the formation of institutions of trust will in itself limit endemic warfare. Bozeman (1976) has argued that the desirability of extinguishing conflicts is a Western concept; in African societies, it is legitimate for conflicts to brew over long periods, and to be contained by periodic violent acts. Although Bozeman's distinction may be too stark (witness, for example, feuding in the United States), it nevertheless makes a point. Westerners are apt to believe that guerrilla warfare and terrorism are illegitimate as normal mechanisms of conflict resolution. If their illegitimacy were also accepted in the LDCs, they presumably would have been stopped long ago.

Duff and McCamant (1976: 42) make the culture-bias error of assuming that "violence . . . is a manifestation of social disintegration." This assertion might apply in the United States, but—as just discussed—in many African contexts violence is a normal, integrative method of resolving conflicts. It would, on the other hand, be appropriate to assert that violence is not consonant with a high-income, high-technology society, and therefore culture change is required (specifically, nonviolent cooperative techniques of conflict resolution must emerge) if traditional people are to join the modern sector.

ARE THE POOR PERCEPTIVE?

In Chapter 1, we noted that contemporary economic thought is swinging away from belief in the backward-sloping labor supply curve and the inability of peasants to perceive market forces. Indeed, "an impressive body of statistical evidence has accumulated which indicates that contrary to general belief, the private marketing systems in LDCs are, by and large, highly competitive and operate efficiently given the conditions in which they function. On the average, regional and seasonal price disparities are generally not greater than transport and storage costs" (Lele, 1972, in which fifteen different studies are cited).

Both Schultz (1964) and Reynolds (1975) have defended the "optimizing peasant." Hayami and Ruttan (1971) show that efficiency differences among farms in the same region in LDCs are no greater than in the United States. Reynolds concludes that deviations from optimizing behavior "are not explained by peculiarities in motivation. Rather, they stem from a variety of constraints on economic behavior," such as uncertainties, risk aversion associated with low income, and market imperfections. Taking such factors into account, Reynolds finds that the peasant in LDCs is generally "a shrewd fellow who has learned through experience to allocate efficiently and who is responsive to economic incentives *within his perceived opportunity set*" (p. 5; italics added).

We receive these studies with welcome relief. Surely the peasant has been maligned by those with the culture bias to depreciate him. However, we have two hesitations. First, we know historically that innovations have not always been adopted as rapidly as they might have been. The Romans knew about the water mill but did not use it widely. Cato (c. 160 B.C.) and Varro (c. 55 B.C.) wrote about agricultural methods used by the more scientific farmers of the day, and urged their adoption by others. When horses were gradually superseding oxen as draft animals in the Middle Ages, there was much discussion of their relative merits (oxen ate less and were stronger, but horses were faster). Benefit-cost analyses were done on horses versus oxen, but results were not agreed on widely; the British resisted the change, while the French proceeded with it.

Second, we observe, both historically and in modern times, that certain ethnic groups tend to engage in certain types of economic activity more than do others. Barring discrimination—we will return to it in a moment—one would expect the division of economic activity to fall randomly among ethnic groups in a given locality. But the Chinese in Southeast Asia, the Asians (from the Indian subcontinent) in East Africa, the Lebanese in West Africa, and the Germans in some areas of South America, for example, are known to engage in shopkeeping and small industry more than those indigenous to the area and often with greater success. More capital, better education, and discrimination in their favor during colonial times have been suggested as reasons. Perhaps so. Today, however, discrimination is often *against* them, yet their decision-making skills may seem superior to those of their immediate neighbors. Similar anomalies are noted historically. The ancient Romans made greater use of hoeing, weeding, plowing, and rational field organization than did the Greeks or the inhabitants of Asia Minor. Parain (1966: 129) reports that these differences have persisted over the centuries. "In Africa today the Kabyles, who have preserved many Roman traditions, are most particular about hoeing and weeding, whilst the Arabs, with their oriental habits, once they have sown the seed leave it until harvest." Others have noted the tendency in North Africa for Arabs to engage in nomadic cattle-raising, while the Berbers are more associated with small-scale farming.

All these differences can be explained as accidents of history, or as a result of different situational variables applying to each ethnic group. It has been suggested that the Jews specialized in money management in Europe because they were exempt from the Catholic Church constraints on usury. What cannot be explained is the persistence of ethnic specialization for decades and even centuries.

Obviously, there has been insufficient study of the matter; we are forced to rely on intuition and must do so with caution. We propose three *possible* explanations of the observation that different sets of people may respond differently to market signals. The first would be that cultural barriers interfere. Along with Lele, Reynolds, and the authors they cite, we reject this explanation, for the studies they review are numerous and convincing. A second reason (referred to previously by Reynolds) appears more reasonable: the uncertainties of marginal living and consequent risk aversion. This second reason may indeed be the cause of poor ratings on the first three variables in the "personal" path: high time discount, low risk taking, and clouded future vision. The third possible explanation is that people's perceptions differ depending on their familiarity with the type of stimulus. Here we are influenced by Erasmus' findings (discussed previously) about frequency interpretation in primitive peoples.

Most small-scale rural producers in LDCs do not keep accounts. Some researchers (e.g., Marris and Somerset, 1972) have suggested that accounts are not necessary for enterprises of that size. This does not appear to us to make sense. On the contrary, lack of literacy and numeracy may prevent rural producers from making fine-tuned distinctions to their advantage, although they may respond to those market signals that are very loud or very visible. Thus they may not be able to adequately recognize the fine-tuned signals because their "personal" qualities may not be highly developed in these areas.

In addition to lack of cash records and cost accounting, other deficiencies may be the unwillingness to advertise, to experiment, to merge with others, and to expand operations. On the social level they may include the unwillingness to pay taxes; to form political bodies, school boards, and cooperatives; and to provide the village infrastructure that is within rural means. We will return to this matter in Chapter 12.

We are, finally, ready to hazard that positivism, personal trust and institutions of trust, and time discount, future vision, and propensity for risk may be differently developed in different cultural groups. These groups may be peasants as opposed to factory workers, rural as opposed to urban people, or different ethnic groups. But we must keep in mind that we can go no farther than to hazard the suggestion. This area remains among the less explored, and therefore among the more mysterious, of economic development.

PUTTING IT ALL TOGETHER

In Table 3–1, we list the various ideas and authors we have reviewed in this chapter. Should (and how can) their ideas all be put together in a theory of economic development? There are several problems. First, on many (for example, anomie, culture of poverty, or limited good) there is scholarly disagreement on the validity of the proposition. Second, each represents a distinct subfield; authors refer to others who have written in the same subfield, but there is little intercommunication. Therefore, we do not know whether there

TABLE 3–1
Summary of Personal and Socio-Political Characteristics Covered in this Chapter

Topic	Author
A theory of history	Toynbee
Political stability	Huntington and others
Anomie	Durkheim
Culture of poverty	Lewis
Modernity	Inkeles and Smith, Deutsch, Lerner
Limited good	Foster
Entrepreneurship	McClelland, Hagen
Amoral familism	Banfield
Praetorian state	Huntington
Institutional development	Parsons, Merton, Coser
Positivism	
Illiteracy, circularity of time	Bozeman
Torpor and social inertia	Myrdal
Intentionalist ethic	Geiger
Lack of trust	Bozeman, Williams *et al*, Barton
Frequency interpretations	Erasmus
Violence	Huntington, Bozeman, Duff and McCamant
Perceptions of the poor	Schultz, Lele (economists)

is any correlation between (say) anomie and entrepreneurship. Third, despite an occasional mention of GNP, most of the authors make little reference to economic theories of development.

The questions are then: To what extent, if any, do the qualities listed in Table 3–1 affect the capacity of individuals (a) to make efficient decisions on the allocation of resources and (b) to be innovative? Our suggestion of the fourfold path of personal development—risk-taking, time discount, future vision, and propensity for materialism versus power—is intended as a channel for answering these questions. How do (for example) anomie, modernity rating, ideas on the limited good (and others) affect these four qualities in an individual?

We would sum up the state of affairs as follows. Toynbee supplies us with a theory of history into which our suggested process of development can fit. The path of personal development receives some support from the research of Inkeles and Smith, Deutsch, Lerner, Myrdal, Geiger, and Bozeman. However, the relationships are conjectural and tenuous. The path of politico-social development receives a bit more support from Huntington and the researchers he cites, especially in the negative correlation found between violence and economic growth.

Our attempt to explain the personal development path in terms of time discount, future vision, risk aversion, and propensities for power versus material wealth is perhaps typical of the tendency of some economists (including us) to reduce a variety of phenomena into a small number of variables for easy handling. All the modernity concepts of Inkeles and Smith could (we believe) be collapsed into the four characteristics we cite for the personal development path. The failure to develop trust and to form the institutions to preserve it, which Bozeman, Williams *et al*, and others observed, could also be explained in these terms. The intentionalist ethic noted by Geiger could be described as cloudy future vision.

The gap between economists and other social scientists lies first and foremost in the fact that each group has grossly neglected the other, neither learning the theories nor showing much sympathy for the propositions of the other. If this neglect were to be overcome, a second difficulty would be uncovered: that of reducing the wide, and often unconnected, variety of observations that other social scientists have made into a small number of agreed upon variables that represent them all. Our personal development path is suggestive only of the direction in which we believe we should start.

BIBLIOGRAPHY

Abelard, Peter, 1200:
   Sic et Non, Paris.
Banfield, Edward C., 1958:
   The Moral Basis of a Backward Society, New York, Free Press (Macmillan).
Barton, Clifton, 1974:
   Problems and Prospects of Small Industries in the Republic of Vietnam, Saigon, Industrial Development Bank of Saigon, December.

Bozeman, Adda B., 1976:
   Conflict in Africa, Princeton, N.J., Princeton University Press.
Carroll, Thomas, 1971:
   "Peasant Cooperation in Latin America," in Worsley, P. M., ed., *Two Blades of Grass*, Manchester, England, Manchester University Press.
Comte, Auguste, 1877:
   System of Positive Polity, London, Longmans, Green, and Co.
Coser, Lewis A., 1956:
   The Functions of Social Conflict, New York, Free Press (Macmillan).
Deutsch, Karl W., 1961:
   "Social Mobilization and Political Development," *American Political Science Review*, September.
Duff, Ernest, and McCamant, John, 1976:
   Violence and Repression in Latin America, New York, Free Press (Macmillan).
Durkheim, Emile, 1893:
   The Division of Labor in Society, translation, New York, Free Press (Macmillan), 1933.
Erasmus, Charles J., 1961:
   Man Takes Control, Minneapolis, University of Minnesota Press.
Etzioni, Amatia, and Etzioni, Eva, 1964:
   Social Change: Sources, Patterns, and Consequences, New York, Basic Books.
Feierabend, Ivo K. and Rosalind L. and Nesvold, Betty A., 1963:
   "Correlates of Political Stability," paper presented at annual meeting, American Political Science Association, September.
Foster, G. M., 1965:
   "Peasant Society and the Image of Limited Good," in Potter, J. M.; Diaz, M. N.; and Foster, G. M., eds., *Peasant Society: A Reader*, Boston, Massachusetts, Little, Brown, and Co.
Geiger, Theodore, 1967:
   The Conflicted Relationship: The West and the Transformation of Asia, Africa, and Latin America, New York, McGraw-Hill, for the Council on Foreign Relations.
Geyl, Pieter, and Sorokin, Pitrim, 1949:
   The Pattern of the Past: Can we Determine It?, Boston, Beacon Press.
Hagen, Everett, 1962:
   On the Theory of Social Change, Homewood, Illinois, The Dorsey Press.
Hayami, Y., and Ruttan, V. W., 1971:
   Agricultural Development: An International Perspective, Baltimore, Johns Hopkins.
Huntington, Samuel P., 1968:
   Political Order in Changing Societies, New Haven, Yale University Press.
Huxley, Elspeth, 1939:
   Red Strangers: A Story of Kenya, London, Chatto and Windus.
Inkeles, Alex, and Smith, David H., 1974:
   Becoming Modern: Individual Change in Six Developing Countries, Cambridge, Mass., Harvard University Press.
LaCapra, Dominique, 1976:
   Emile Durkheim: Sociologist and Philosopher, Ithaca, N.Y., Cornell University Press.
Lele, Uma, 1972:
   "Role of Credit and Marketing Functions in Agricultural Development," mimeographed paper presented at International Economic Association conference on "Agriculture in the Development of Low-Income Countries," Bad Gotesburg, Germany, August 26-September 4.
Lerner, Daniel, 1963:
   The Passing of Traditional Society: Modernizing the Middle East, New York, Free Press (Macmillan), 1963.

LeVine, Robert A., and Campbell, Donald T., 1966:
"Report on Preliminary Results of Cross-Cultural Study of Ethnocentrism," *Carnegie Corporation of New York Quality*, January.

Lewis, Oscar, 1961:
The Children of Sanchez, New York, Vintage Books (Random House).

Marris, Peter, and Somerset, Anthony, 1972:
The African Entrepreneur, New York, Africana Publishing Corp.

McClelland, David C., 1961:
The Achieving Society, Princeton, N.J., D. Van Nostrand Co.

McClelland, David C., and Winter, David, 1969:
Motivating Economic Achievement, London, Collier Macmillan.

Merton, Robert K., 1957:
Social Theory and Social Structure, New York, Free Press (Macmillan).

Miskimin, Harry A., 1977:
The Economy of Later Renaissance Europe: 1460–1600, New York, Cambridge University Press.

Myrdal, Gunnar, 1968:
Asian Drama: An Inquiry into the Poverty of Nations, in three volumes, New York, Pantheon (Random House).

Parain, Charles, 1966:
"The Evolution of Agricultural Technique," in Postan, M.M., ed., *The Cambridge Economic History of Europe*, Vol. 1, Cambridge, England, Cambridge University Press.

Parsons, Talcott, 1949:
Essays in Sociological Theory: Pure and Applied, New York, Free Press (Macmillan).

Parsons, Talcott, 1951:
The Social System, New York, Free Press (Macmillan).

Parsons, Talcott, 1961:
"Some Considerations on the Theory of Social Change," *Rural Sociology*, vol. XXVI, No. 3.

Powelson, John P., 1965:
Latin America: Today's Economic and Social Revolution, New York, McGraw-Hill.

Powelson, John P., 1972:
Institutions of Economic Growth, Princeton, N.J., Princeton University Press

Reichenbach, Hans, 1951:
The Rise of Scientific Philosophy, Berkeley, University of California Press.

Reynolds, Lloyd G., 1975:
Agriculture in Development Theory, New Haven, Yale University Press.

Rostow, W. W., 1956:
The Stages of Economic Growth, New York, Cambridge University Press; second edition, 1971.

Russett, Bruce M., 1964:
Handbook of Political and Social Indicators, New Haven, Yale University Press.

Schultz, T. W., 1964:
Transforming Traditional Agriculture, New Haven, Yale University Press.

Schumpeter, Joseph A., 1911:
The Theory of Economic Development, translated by Redvers Opie, Cambridge, Massachusetts, Harvard University Press, 1936.

Spencer, Herbert, 1892:
Sociology, New York, Appleton and Co.

Spengler, Oswald, 1926:
The Decline of the West, New York, Alfred A. Knopf, Inc.

Stoller, Irene, 1977:
"A Review and Critique of Foster's Image of Limited Good," in Loehr, William and

Powelson, John P., eds., *Economic Development, Poverty, and Income Distribution*, Boulder, Colorado, Westview Press.

Tanter, Raymond, and Midlarsky, Manus, 1967:
"A Theory of Revolution," *Journal of Conflict Resolution*, September.

Tanter, Raymond, 1965:
"Dimensions of Conflict Behavior within Nations, 1955–60: Turmoil and Internal War," *Papers, Peace Research Society*, No. 3.

Toennies, Ferdinand, 1957:
Community and Society: Gemeinschaft und Gesellschaft, translated and edited by Charles P. Loomis, East Lansing, Michigan, Michigan State University Press.

Toynbee, Arnold, 1946:
A Study of History, New York, Oxford, ten volumes; abridged into two volumes by D. C. Somervell, New York, Oxford, 1965.

U.S. Department of Defense and Reid, Escott, 1965:
The Future of the World Bank, Washington, D.C., World Bank.

Weber, Max, 1904:
The Protestant Ethic and the Spirit of Capitalism, translated by Talcott Parsons, New York, Scribners.

Weber, Max, 1947:
The Theory of Social and Economic Organization, New York, Oxford.

Williams, L. K.; Whyte, William F.; and Green, Charles S., 1966:
"Do Cultural Differences Affect Workers' Attitudes?" *Industrial Relations*, vol. 5, No. 3, May.

Wilson, C. Z., 1970:
Review of McClelland-Winter (1969), *Journal of Economic Literature*, December.

WHO ARE THE POOR?

4

WHO ARE THE POOR?

*Gulnar, India—Mohan Lal, a six-year-old boy with a shy smile
and a swollen abdomen, does not get enough to eat, and he
probably never has. The water he drinks is filthy, he has no clothes
at all and he has never seen a doctor, a toilet, a piece of soap or
an electric light bulb.*

*To the despair of the experts on development, this is the real
India—millions and millions of Mohan Lals in hundreds of
thousands of villages much like this one.*

BORDERS, *NEW YORK TIMES*, JANUARY 2, 1979

No one cares enough about the world's poor to keep statistics on them comparable in accuracy to those of gross domestic product. No one knows how many landless peasants are seeking seasonal work on other people's farms, or how many slaves there are, or how many people wander the streets and sleep under bridges or on public land.

Some would excuse this deficit by arguing that it is expensive to gather information on the poor, and—after all—statistics are selected by benefit-cost considerations, just as other economic products are. But the cost of gathering accurate data on GDP is also considerable, and no one (to our knowledge) has shown that it is less than that of gathering data on the poor.

There is, nevertheless, a ray of movement in the opposite direction. In a few countries, such as Kenya, data on the rural poor have been collected and systematized (Kenya, 1977). Indeed, enough governments and other sources have gathered such data that the International Labor Office (1974) has compiled a volume entitled *Household Income and Expenditure Statistics, 1960–72*, with information disaggregated according to income groups. Alas, the title is deceptive! Most countries have data for only one year within the thirteen mentioned, so it is not possible to make comparative studies either intertemporally or interspatially, or to aggregate. These operations are essential if a proper analysis is to be made.

The problem of Mohan Lal *is* the problem of development. Whereas the early postwar literature on development stressed the difference between rich and poor *nations*, more and more concern has been verbalized for the Mohan Lals, and the programs of international agencies have turned more and more toward absolute poverty. In this chapter, we use what data we have to obtain some wide-order guesses on the magnitude of absolute poverty.

In Table 4–1, we guess that about 1.65 billion people live in rural areas in the third world. Any Western visitor to these countries knows that only a very few rich people live in the countryside, so almost all of these one and two-thirds billion people are poor. They live in one-room huts, with the earth as their floor, without running water, and mostly without electricity. Another 260 million people inhabit the city slums. They also live in one-room huts, generally made from waste materials (sometimes from cardboard boxes), often not secure

TABLE 4–1
Rough-Order Guesses on
The Distribution of World Population

	(in millions)
In 1980 the world's population was approximately	4,550
From which we subtract China (because of insufficient data)	950
Leaving	3,600
From which we take away the more industrialized countries (Europe, North America, Oceania, Japan, and the USSR)	1,200
This leaves us, in the "third world" (or over half the people of the world)	2,400
Of which, we have in:	
Asia	1,600
Africa	450
Latin America	350

We examine Asia, Africa, and Latin America separately, as follows:

	Total	Asia	Africa	Latin America
The total population is	2,400	1,600	450	350
Of which, there are				
in rural areas	1,650	1,200	350	100
in urban areas	750	400	100	250
Of the latter, there are				
in urban slums	260	160	30	70

against the weather, usually crowded, and smelling of human excrement where toilets are lacking. Water might be delivered once or twice a week by truck, or there may be multifamily community water taps. More than 40 percent of the world's population lives at these levels of poverty.

What are the occupations of the poor, and how much do they earn? We know something about the former, and we are learning a bit about the latter. Most of the rural poor work on farms, though they supplement their incomes with handicrafts or services. Many of them own no land at all, but sell their labor by working on other people's farms. Some are in migratory tribes that range over wide areas, with shifting cultivation or cattle-herding. Many have a few acres from whch they feed their families, or they may sell some of their produce in the local market. Usually farming is a seasonal occupation, with the supplementary work occurring at times other than planting and harvesting.

Residents of urban slums are sometimes unemployed, but more often they work in services or handicrafts or peddling. Western economists have referred to these activities as the "informal sector" (or sometimes the "murky sector"), implying that they are substitutes for unemployment—for the *real* work is presumably found in modern factories. We will argue (Chapter 12), on the contrary, that the informal sector constitutes the backbone of economic development, for here lie the nascent activities of comparative advantage.

How much do the poor earn? Some guesses appear in Table 4–2. We emphasize that (like the percentage of population living in the slums) the figures are guesses, though educated ones. Table 4–2 divides the world for which we have data into MDCs and LDCs. The first column shows *per capita* GDP, which is the gross domestic product divided by the population, without regard to how income is distributed. On the basis of studies assembled by the World Bank, the next three columns show the percentages of GDP earned by three different segments of the population; these are divided according to income. The following three columns show the *per capita* income of the three segments, based on an application of the percentages of the earlier columns upon GDP. These figures must be considered guesses, however, because the World Bank percentages were calculated in different studies and for different years from the estimates of GDP. Also, many of them are based on small samples. The *per capita* GDP for a given bracket is a guess at the average for that bracket, but it does not tell us in which direction that average is moving. Nor does it tell us what percentage of the people are moving up and what percentage are moving down. Indeed, the average for a bracket *might* be increasing while the incomes of most people within the bracket are decreasing.

The Gini coefficient found in the final column is an index of concentration of income, whose calculation will be explained in Chapter 5. It is based on a scale of zero to one. If every income recipient in a country had exactly the same income as every other recipient, then the Gini for that country would be zero. If one person had all the income and the rest had nothing, then the Gini would be one. Thus a higher Gini means a greater concentration of income (in fewer people). The average Gini for the sample of MDCs selected is .3871, with a standard deviation of .064. For the LDCs selected, the average Gini is .5141, with a standard deviation of .098. (The difference between the means is significant at less than the .001 level. Thus income is more concentrated in LDCs than in MDCs, a point that will be further explained in Chapter 6.

In Table 4–2, we guess that the *per capita* income of the poorest 20 percent of the population in Benin is only $50 a year, and in Burma only $44, though in Argentina it is $498 (compared to $1,690 in the United States). In virtually all LDCs, *per capita* income of the poorest 20 percent is less than $500, and in most it is less than $100.

What does it mean—in terms of purchasing power in (say) the United States—that *per capita* income of the poorest 20 percent in some country is (say) $100? Our figures are based on gross domestic product. Since some of GDP is sifted off into taxes or depreciation and therefore not all of it goes into personal income, a *per capita* income of $100 may in reality correspond to a personal income of only $80. But it is the income per person, not per family. Suppose the average family size is seven (which is not unusual in the developing world); the mean family personal income might then be $560 (or 7 times $80). Larger families with more earners (say, at least ten years old) may earn more than smaller families, though large families with mostly dependents will be worse off than the mean. Since the poor usually have their own houses (albeit rudimentary), they spend their income mainly on food and occasionally on clothing. This is an oversimplification, since some of the poor also save, and they spend money on gifts and on religious and other types of festivals. But their *principal* purchase is food. Since fruits and vegetables are almost always lower priced in the less developed world than in the United States, it is likely that a family income of $560 will buy an amount of food that might cost (say) $1,000 in the United States or Europe. As a wild guess, therefore, one might multiply each *per capita* income by as much as 9 or 10 to arrive at a corresponding average family purchasing power (for food alone). This multiplier is, of course, of small comfort in (say) Sierra Leone, where we have guessed $11 for the *per capita* income of the 20 percent poorest.

Two new indices have recently been developed to assess the situation of the LDC poor. In the first, the World Bank has attempted to estimate the average percentage of "absolute poor" in LDCs. These are the ones whose income does not enable them to buy the minimum food, shelter, and clothing necessary for staying alive and in adequate health. Any such estimates are bound to be subjective. In general, the Bank draws its poverty line around $50 or $75 *per capita* in 1970 dollars. In order to provide international comparability, the Bank has drawn on the International Comparisons Project of Kravis *et al.* (1978), which has attempted to estimate international or "purchasing power parity" (PPP) dollars, in which exchange-rate distortions have been eliminated. In general, a *per capita* GNP of $200 in 1970 PPP dollars is taken as the internationally comparable poverty level.

Table 4–3 gives an idea of how *per capita* GDP in PPP dollars compares with the conventional measure by exchange rates. The higher the *per capita* GDP, the less the deviation (note how the deviation index, in the third column, declines as the *per capita* GDP rises). PPP dollars should not be thought of as family income; they take into account only the differences in purchasing power,

TABLE 4–2 (a)
Selected Information on Income Distribution
More-Developed Countries

Country	Per capita GNP ($), 1977	Percentage of GD Bottom 20%	Mid 60%	Top 20%	Per capita GDP ($) Bottom 20%	Mid 60%	Top 20%	Gini
Australia	7,290	7.1	54.0	38.9	2,526	6,404	13,839	.3185
Canada	8,350	6.7	53.3	40.0	2,878	7,632	17,182	.3333
Denmark	9,160	5.4	52.4	42.2	2,448	7,917	19,129	.3673
Finland	6,190	2.7	46.9	50.4	861	4,984	16,067	.4729
France	7,500	2.3	43.0	54.7	825	5,143	19,626	.5176
Germany (Federal Republic)	8,620	5.6	41.2	53.2	2,354	5,773	22,364	.4826
Israel	3,760	7.1	54.4	38.5	1,448	3,699	7,853	.3143
Japan	6,510	8.2	52.5	39.3	2,503	5,342	11,996	.3106
Netherlands	7,710	4.0	46.7	49.3	1,480	5,760	18,242	.4493
New Zealand	4,480	5.7	53.0	41.3	1,288	3,991	9,330	.3557
Norway	8,570	4.7	54.3	41.0	2,074	7,986	18,089	.3622
Spain	3,260	6.0	48.5	45.5	956	2,575	7,246	.3930
Sweden	9,340	5.2	50.7	44.1	2,463	8,005	20,888	.3872
United Kingdom	4,540	6.3	50.8	42.9	1,379	3,707	9,391	.3642
United States	8,750	3.9	50.4	45.7	1,690	7,282	19,808	.4171
Yugoslavia	2,100	6.6	52.0	41.4	670	1,759	4,202	.3474

We are indebted to Kenneth and Lawrence Powelson for calculation of this table.

TABLE 4-2 (b)
Selected Information on Income Distribution
Less-Developed Countries

Country	Per capita GNP ($), 1977	Percentage of GDP			Per capita GDP ($)			Gini
		Bottom 20%	Mid 60%	Top 20%	Bottom 20%	Mid 60%	Top 20%	
Argentina	1,870	5.1	41.0	53.9	498	1,335	5,266	.4895
Barbados	1,770	6.8	49.2	44.0	600	1,447	3,881	.3690
Benin	210	5.5	42.8	51.7	50	129	467	.4675
Brazil	1,410	2.8	29.9	67.3	201	714	4,821	.6465
Burma	140	6.5	48.8	44.7	44	109	300	.3806
Chile	1,250	4.8	39.4	55.8	339	928	3,944	.5065
Colombia	760	2.9	37.6	59.5	114	494	2,343	.5615
Costa Rica	1,390	5.4	44.2	50.4	401	1,096	3,748	.4445
Dominican Republic	840	4.3	41.4	54.3	193	619	2,435	.4928
Ecuador	820	1.8	26.2	72.0	76	367	3,024	.6626
Egypt	340	4.6	47.0	48.4	78	266	821	.4337
El Salvador	590	3.7	45.5	50.8	124	506	1,696	.4653
Gabon	3,190	3.2	29.3	67.5	831	2,536	17,527	.6439
Guyana	520	4.3	49.2	46.5	115	440	1,247	.4192
Honduras	420	2.5	36.9	60.6	57	282	1,388	.5658
India	160	5.1	40.8	54.1	41	110	436	.4878
Indonesia	320	6.8	41.2	52.0	117	236	894	.4625
Iraq	1,570	2.1	31.0	66.9	152[a]	746[a]	4,829[a]	.6288
Ivory Coast	770	3.9	37.6	58.5	168	541	2,525	.5342
Jamaica	1,060	2.2	36.6	61.2	171	942	4,751	.5766
Kenya	290	3.9	29.2	66.9	59	147	1,014	.6368
Korea (Republic)	980	9.9	52.9	37.2	477	849	1,791	.2718
Kuwait	12,690	8.0	38.0	54.0	4,674	7,400	31,548	.4700
Malawi	150	5.7	41.4	52.9	43	105	403	.4696
Mexico	1,160	4.2	32.6	63.2	246	637	3,706	.5827

Pakistan	200	8.4	50.1	41.5	83	165	410	.3299
Panama	1,200	4.6	48.0	47.4	292	1,017	3,016	.4258
Peru	720	2.2	22.4	75.4	84	286	2,892	.7582
Philippines	460	3.9	42.1	54.0	91	328	1,263	.4941
Senegal	380	3.2	34.3	62.5	59	211	1,152	.5874
Sierra Leone	200	1.1	36.1	62.8	11	121	629	.6117
South Africa	1,400	1.8	36.2	62.0	133	892	4,582	.5813
Sri Lanka	160	5.1	48.6	46.3	43	135	386	.4092
Tanzania	210	5.2	35.1	59.7	54	122	623	.5451
Thailand	430	5.7	36.8	57.5	124	266	1,246	.5103
Tunisia	840	4.2	40.3	55.5	177	567	2,343	.5019
Turkey	1,110	2.9	36.5	60.6	165	6,903	3,452	.5679
Uganda	—	6.2	47.2	46.6	104	265	784	.4007
Uruguay	1,450	3.0	43.5	53.5	219	1,057	3,901	.4968
Venezuela	2,630	2.7	31.9	65.4	356	1,401	8,615	.6223
Zambia	460	5.4	36.4	58.2	128	288	1,382	.5226

NOTES: Data for computing *per capita* gross domestic products were taken from World Bank, World Tables, Second Edition, 1980.

Data for income distribution (percentage of total income for each bracket) are from Jain, Shail, *Size Distribution of Income: A Compilation of Data*, Washington, D.C., The World Bank, 1975. In this volume Jain has compiled the Lorenz curve data and the Gini coefficients for a number of scattered studies of 81 countries. The Lorenz data are sometimes for total income recipients, sometimes for households, sometimes for total population, sometimes for workers, ard so on. Sometimes they are on a national basis, and sometimes they are regional (such as only rural or only urban.) They are also for different years. We have included in the table only those countries for which Jain has data on a national basis. Among the studies of each country, we selected one with data for income recipients; if there were none, we selected one for households; and if there were none of these, we selected one for population. Different selections yield different percentages. In applying proportional distributions for earlier years to later (1977) data, we assume that these distributions do not change much from one year to the next. Since the distributions vary widely in method and coverage as well as by years, we have labeled our figures "educated guesses," to be used only as rough-order magnitudes.

To obtain a rough guess of the total GDP for each income bracket, we applied the percentages from the Jain data to the GDP. This we divided by the number of population within that bracket (20% or 60% of the total population) to obtain a guess at the mean income of the bracket.

The Gini coefficients are as reported in Jain.

[a]Distribution data for Iraq are for 1976.

TABLE 4–3
Per Capita Gross Domestic Products of Selected Countries in Exchange-Rate Dollars and PPP Dollars, 1973

	Exchange-rate dollars	PPP dollars	Deviation index (3) = (2) ÷ (1)
	(1)	(2)	(3)
Kenya	184	379	2.06
India	129	394	3.06
Philippines	259	755	2.91
South Korea	366	904	2.47
Colombia	440	1,106	2.51
Malaysia	633	1,180	1.81
Iran	914	1,809	1.98
Hungary	1,619	2,793	1.72
Italy	2,525	2,913	1.15
Japan	3,738	3,962	1.06
United Kingdom	3,136	3,750	1.20
Netherlands	4,402	4,236	0.96
Belgium	4,618	4,663	1.01
France	4,777	4,709	0.99
Germany (Federal Republic)	5,535	4,791	0.87
United States	6,192	6,192	1.00

SOURCE: Kravis *et al.* (1978: 10). Reprinted by permission of the World Bank.

not the other differences between *per capita* GDP and family income that we have already mentioned.

The second measure, known as the "physical quality of life index" (PQLI), was developed by the Overseas Development Council (1977: 146–154), based on three indicators: life expectancy, infant mortality, and literacy. Each country is rated on each of these indicators on the basis of 1 to 100, with a grade of 100 being assigned to the country with the most favorable rating and a grade of 1 given to the country with the lowest rating. A simple average is taken of the three ratings. Table 4–4 shows how the PQLI has improved for a sample of LDCs and MDCs from the 1950s to the 1970s.

Table 4–5 summarizes the socio-economic situation of less developed countries in 1977, showing *per capita* GNP and its recent rates of growth, population, PQLI, and the percentage of absolute poor according to the World Bank's estimates. The poorest *region* is Africa south of the Sahara, with a PQLI of 27 and with 48 percent of the population in absolute poverty. In twenty-six low-income areas of that region, 59 percent of the population is in absolute poverty. The low-income countries of South Asia come next, with a higher PQLI (42) and a lower percentage of absolute poor (41 percent). With only a few exceptions, the PQLI rises and the percentage in absolute poverty falls as *per capita* GNP rises.

TABLE 4—4
Physical Quality of Life Index for Selected Countries, 1950s, 1960s, and 1970s

Country	1950s	1960s	1970s
Algeria	35	38	42
India	28	36	42
Egypt	32	41	45
Brazil	53	. . .	66
Sri Lanka	62	77	83
Poland	72	86	93
United States	92	94	97
France	87	94	97
Norway	. . .	. . .	99

SOURCE: Overseas Development Council (1977: 151). From *The United States and World Development: Agenda 1977* by John W. Sewell and the Staff of the Overseas Development Council. Copyright © 1977 by the Overseas Development Council. Reproduced by permission of Praeger Publishers.

The story of Mohan Lal is frightening, and nothing in these data would cause any feeling of relief. The total population of LDCs in Table 4—5 is 2,172 million, and of those, 32 percent, or 695 million, are in absolute poverty. This represents an enormous amount of suffering for the human conscience. The ray of hope for the future, which we detect in Tables 4—4 and 4—5, does nothing to help those who are currently afflicted. It is a ray of hope nonetheless. Table 4—4 shows the PQLI increasing over time for a representative sample of countries (both LDC and MDC). Table 4—5 shows that as *per capita* income increases, for the most part this PQLI also increases and the percentage of those in absolute poverty declines. Some years ago, GNP *per capita* was cited as the major index of growth and development, with the assumption that "all other things" would come in proportion. It is possible that this assumption was not far wrong.

Let us examine poverty further. How do the poor survive? In fact, many of them do not. Our information on people who die of hunger or malnutrition is sketchy. Data on deaths of young children are more firm, though they may be underestimated by failure to report. In the United States, 17.6 out of every 1,000 babies die before the age of one (1973 data). In Rwanda, the corresponding figure is 132.9 (1970), and in Egypt it is 97.9 (1973). Data for selected LDCs are found in Table 4—6. Historically, death may be a mercy. The large number who survive but who are perpetually malnourished or hungry, and whose lives are only a fraction as productive or satisfying as they might be, are perhaps the ones who suffer most.

It is reasonable to suppose that in those countries where the death rate is high among children, there is also a sizeable number of adults who die of starvation or malnutrition each year. What we do not know is how these death rates divide between the rich and the poor. If we can suppose that infant mortality in LDCs is considerably lower among the rich than among the poor, then obviously the rates for the poor are higher than the average for the country.

TABLE 4–5
The Socio-Economic Situation of LDCs in 1977

	per capita GNP 1977 ($)	Population (millions) 1977	per capita GNP growth rates (%) 1960–77	per capita GNP growth rates (%) 1970–77	Physical quality of life index	Absolute poor (%)
South Asia						
7 low-income countries	150	862	1.4	0.7	42	41
Africa south of the Sahara						
26 low-income countries	190	205	1.0	0.1	27	59
11 low-middle-income countries	440	121	2.4	3.0	27	27
Entire region	280	326	1.8	1.7	27	48
Far East						
1 low-income country	250	197	1.5	1.6	47	51
6 low-middle-income countries	580	142	4.6	5.4	71	18
2 upper-middle-income countries	1,470	22	6.2	6.2	66	<5
1 higher-income country	3,300	3	6.4	5.7	83	6
Entire region	480	363	3.8	4.3	60	32
North Africa and the Middle East						
2 low-income countries	320	47	2.6	3.8	40	—
4 low-middle-income countries	710	34	3.0	4.0	45	16
3 upper-middle-income countries	1,750	68	4.8	6.0	43	9
6 higher-income countries	6,150	16	6.7	4.0	36	8
Entire region	1,550	164	5.3	5.3	42	11

Central and Latin America						
1 low-income country	240	5	0.2	2.3	33	—
12 low-middle-income countries	760	92	1.9	2.4	65	12
9 upper-middle-income countries	1,340	223	3.1	3.5	72	8
2 higher-income countries	2,880	13	3.0	3.2	80	5
Entire region	1,230	333	2.9	3.3	70	9
Mediterranean						
4 upper-middle-income countries	1,470	74	4.7	4.9	67	7
3 higher-income countries	3,100	49	5.3	3.5	91	<5
Entire region	2,120	124	4.9	3.9	76	6
All less-developed countries						
38 low-income countries	180	1,316	1.4	1.0	40	45
33 low-middle-income countries	590	389	3.0	3.7	54	19
18 upper-middle-income countries	1,450	387	3.9	4.4	67	8
12 higher-income countries	3,660	81	5.6	3.9	79	5
Totals and averages	610	2,172	3.5	3.5	49	32
20 OECD countries (for comparison)	7,010	661	3.4	2.6	94	<5

SOURCE: OECD, 1979: 180–181. This source also gives the same data, country by country (not reproduced here). Reprinted by permission of OECD.

TABLE 4–6
Infant Mortality and Population per Physician in Selected Countries

COUNTRY	Deaths under 1 yr. old per 1,000 births		Population per physician	
	YEAR	NUMBER	YEAR	NUMBER
AFRICA				
Angola	1972	24.1	1971	10,730
Egypt	1973	97.9	1971	1,820
Ghana	1971	67.3	1971	12,390
Kenya	1970	55.0	1971	6,550
Liberia	1971	159.2	1969	10,450
Libya	1972	80.3	1971	1,500
Rwanda	1970	132.9	1971	57,120
LATIN AMERICA				
Chile	1972	78.0	1971	2,020
Colombia	1971	62.8	1969	2,160
Costa Rica	1973	44.8	1971	1,620
Cuba	1972	27.5	1968	1,150
Ecuador	1973	75.8	1970	2,930
Guatemala	1973	79.1	1971	4,430
Haiti	1972	25.8	1969	13,210
Mexico	1973	51.9	1970	1,440
Paraguay	1973	30.0	1970	2,340
Peru	1970	65.1	1969	1,920
Uruguay	1971	48.6	1971	920
Venezuela	1974	46.6	1971	1,060
ASIA				
India	1970	61.0	1970	4,800
Japan	1973	11.0	1971	860
Kuwait	1973	44.1	1971	1,120
Pakistan	1968	124.3	1970	3,800
Philippines	1972	37.9	1971	2,710
Thailand	1972	27.0	1971	7,250
EUROPE AND NORTH AMERICA				
Austria	1973	23.8	1971	530
Belgium	1973	17.0	1971	630
Canada	1973	15.5	1971	670
Germany (Democratic Republic)	1973	15.5	1971	610
Germany (Federal Republic)	1973	15.6	1971	560
France	1973	15.5	1971	720
Greece	1973	24.1	1971	600
Italy	1973	7.4	1971	540
Sweden	1974	9.2	1971	720
United Kingdom: England and Wales	1973	16.9	1971	790
United States	1973	17.6	1971	620

SOURCE: World Health Organization, (1976: 15–17; 1975: 47–50). Reprinted by permission.

The same applies to the number of physicians (Table 4–6). In the United States, there is one doctor for every 620 inhabitants (1971 data). In Rwanda, the corresponding number is 57,120 (1971), and in Egypt it is 1,820 (1971). In most LDCs, medical services are concentrated in urban areas, where they are more readily accessible to the rich than to the poor. Even with the best of statistical intentions, it would not be possible to determine how many persons there are per doctor in the lowest income stratum compared to the highest, for the same doctor may be available to both rich and poor, but with biased time allotments. Hours of doctor services consumed by the poorest 20% of the population (compared to other income levels) is a real number, but no one knows how much it is for any country.

A similar comment serves for education. While we know the percentage of total population enrolled in schools and universities of all levels, country by country, we do not know how enrollment is distributed among income groups. From 1960–61 to 1966–67, 14.0 percent of the world's population was in school, and by area the percentages were distributed as follows:

Africa	7.8
Asia	11.4
Northern America	24.5
Latin America	14.8
Europe	16.6
Oceania	20.7
USSR	17.6

(UNESCO, 1971)

The World Bank has provided data on education by country according to income group, which it derived from the *UNESCO Yearbook*, as follows (World Bank, 1976: 522–23):

Per Capita Income Group ($) 1970	ADJUSTED SCHOOL ENROLLMENT RATIO PRIMARY		SECONDARY	
	1960	1970	1960	1970
100 and below	24.1	38.0	2.8	6.9
101–200	40.2	48.2	5.7	8.8
201–375	71.2	85.8	12.8	23.3
376–1,000	107.5	109.7	52.2	69.4

Two observations are salient. The first is that in low-income countries, only a very small percentage reaches secondary school. But the second is that in all cases, for both primary and secondary education, the percentage increases both over time and according to income bracket. Once again, we are dealing with rich and poor *countries,* and it is not certain that the same observations can be made for rich and poor within a country. But it is not too far-fetched to believe that as a country's *per capita* GDP increases, the percentage of its population enrolled in schools also increases.

How can we tell whether the poor in a given country have enough to eat? Here we are asking about both calories and nutritional content. There are two ways of making estimates on calories. One is through a "food balance sheet."

It begins with the output of food, to which available inventories and imports are added. Whatever is not available for human consumption (for example, seed for next year, animal feed, and amounts wasted) is then subtracted. The remainder available can be compared with the nation's population times the minimum required calories as estimated by the United Nations. In a calculation of this nature, Mayer (1976) concluded that average caloric intake is insufficient for the general populations of Central America, western South America (except Chile), almost all of Africa (though not South Africa or Libya), Pakistan, India, and Indonesia. In most of the remaining LDCs, it is just about enough, and in virtually all the MDCs it is excessive (except Spain, where it is just sufficient). Of course, none of this says anything about how caloric intake is divided between rich and poor within countries. We can only assume that if it is insufficient for a country as a whole, then the poor are affected even more adversely.

The second way of estimating calories is to take information based on hospital records and other indicators of reported cases of hunger or malnutrition. On studies of this type, Mayer (1976: 44) writes as follows:

> Projections based on the results of 77 studies of nutritional status made among more than 200,000 preschool children in 45 countries of Asia, Africa, and Latin America place the total number of children suffering from some degree of protein-calorie malnutrition at 98.4 million. Percentages ranged from 5 to 37 in Latin America, from 7 to 73 in Africa, and from 15 to 80 in Asia (excluding China). These surveys, however, did not employ standardized procedures. In some of them clinical assessments were made and in others the children were measured against international weight tables. Thus, although the general indications of such studies are useful, figures derived from them are rough at best.

What about diseases that come from poor water? White (1977) reports that "there are over 1,200 million people in 91 of the developing countries who are estimated by WHO (1973) as not having access to safe water supplies, and must carry their daily supply home from springs, wells, rivers, ponds or ditches, some of which are contaminated all or part of the time . . . With rapidly growing population in both rural and urban situations, the health hazard from unprotected supplies is increasing, as is the absolute number of people drinking from such supplies."

What are the trends? Are hunger and malnutrition increasing, or decreasing? Once again, we can look at the overall agricultural statistics, but we have little information on how much of the increased output is going to the poor. The Food and Agriculture Organization estimates that because of increasing population, demand for food grew at a rate of 3.5 percent in LDCs compared to 2.5 percent in MDCs during the 1950s and 1960s (FAO, 1975: 9):

> In 22 developing countries the rate of growth of food production exceeded the Second Development Decade target of 4 percent per annum, while in 13 countries it was less than 2 percent during the period 1953–71. In 33 out of 86 developing countries for which data are available, food output grew faster than food demand; in 54 it grew faster than population . . .

However . . . (it was) not vigorous or effective enough, and this shows how tremendous is the strain put upon the agricultural sector in countries where population and general economic activity are both expanding rapidly.

The FAO goes on to estimate that "out of 97 developing countries, 61 had a deficit in food energy supplies in 1970. In the Far East and Africa, 25 and 30 percent, respectively, of the population are estimated to suffer from significant malnutrition. Altogether in the developing world (excluding the Asian centrally planned economies, for which insufficient information is available), malnutrition affects around 460 million people; a less conservative definition might give a much higher figure" (p. 10). Details appear in Table 4–7.

We observe that the World Bank estimated that the number of people in absolute poverty is 695 million (Table 4–5), but the FAO (Table 4–7) tells us that 462 million are below the protein/energy limit. Since absolute poverty represents the food-clothing-shelter limit, we can assume either that the World Bank has a more rigorous perspective on the limit than the FAO or that the differences in data are great. The large discrepancy between the two numbers illustrates a lesson in statistical data: they give us only *very rough* orders of magnitude.

In one sense, malnutrition is not a function of low income. Berg (1973) points out that although rich people eat better than poor, nevertheless the poor do not voluntarily improve their nutrition standards with an increment of income. Indeed, they have been highly resistant to efforts on the part of nu-

---

TABLE 4–7
Estimated Number of People
with Insufficient Protein/Energy
Supply, by Regions, 1970

Region	Population	Percentage below lower limit	Number below lower limit
	(THOUSAND MILLION)	(PERCENT)	(MILLIONS)
Developed regions	1.07	3	28
Developing regions (excluding Asian centrally planned economies)	1.75	25	434
Latin America	0.28	13	36
Far East	1.02	30	301
Near East	0.17	18	30
Africa	0.28	25	67
World (excluding Asian centrally planned economies)	2.83	16	462

SOURCE: FAO 1975: 22. Reprinted by permission of the Food and Agriculture Organization of the United Nations.

tritionists and other types of educators. Often their cultural imperatives, including taboos, prevent them from taking healthful food when it is available. Berg argues that the world's hungry have it within their physical power to alleviate their condition substantially. He cites educational programs through which the poor have learned new nutrition practices, but without adopting them. He also cites cases of public programs that have fallen afoul of black markets and corruption, preventing the food from going to those most in need.

In a more realistic sense, however, hunger and malnutrition can be solved only through increased agricultural output and more equitable distribution of income. Berg is convincing in his arguments that the culture changes sufficient to reduce wastage and misallocations in the use of food will not be made, except over a long period. Perhaps there is some threshold income beyond which people have enough so that malnutrition will be avoided even though some nonnutritious food is eaten. Surely this is the case for most people in MDCs. But if so, we have as yet no idea of what that threshold would be.

CONCLUSION

Two decades ago, development literature tended to stress the differences between rich and poor *nations;* the major task appeared to be that of national development. Many economists believed either that higher incomes would "trickle down" to the poor or that the poor would be taken care of through redistributive measures.

Faith that either of these would automatically occur appears to be ebbing. Some economists judge that the poor are not benefiting at all from economic growth, and others feel thay they are not receiving their "fair share." We find the evidence, one way or another, to be too sparse to make reasoned conclusions. Indeed, what evidence we have seems to point to gradual improvements in the positions of the poor, absolutely and maybe relatively as well. But this is small hope, and no ground for complacency. Instead, the burden of poverty is *overwhelming*, with 40 to 60 percent of the population of LDCs undernourished, underfed, and ill-protected from disease. Whether there is no improvement or slow improvement then becomes an extraneous question. The problem is one of *poverty*, not of nations as such, but of people within nations—not all people, but principally those in rural areas, or those migrating into urban slums.

This problem is manifold. It is one of providing access to resources for the poor and of increasing their human potential and their economic productivity. It is to the plight of these people that the rest of this book is addressed.

BIBLIOGRAPHY

Berg, Alan, 1973:
    The Nutrition Factor, Washington, D.C., Brookings.
Borders, William, NYT, 1-2-79:
    "Task Facing India," *New York Times*.

Food and Agriculture Organization, 1975:
    Food and Nutrition, Volume 1, No. 1.
International Labor Office, 1974:
    Household Income and Expenditure Statistics, Vols. I and II, Geneva.
Jain, Shail, 1975:
    Size Distribution of Income: A Compilation of Data, Washington D.C., World Bank.
Kenya, Government of, 1977:
    Integrated Rural Survey, 1974–75, Nairobi, Government Printing Office.
Kravis, Irving B; Heston, Alan; and Summers, Robert, 1978:
    International Comparisons of Real Product and Purchasing Power, Baltimore, MD.,
    Johns Hopkins University (for the World Bank).
Mayer, Jean, 1976:
    "The Dimensions of World Hunger," *Scientific American*, September.
OECD, 1979:
    Organization for Economic Cooperation and Development, *Development Coopera-
    tion, 1979 Review*, Paris.
Overseas Development Council, 1977:
    The United States and World Development, Agenda 1977, New York, Praeger.
UNESCO, 1971:
    Unesco Yearbook.
White, Anne U., 1977:
    "Water Supply and Income Distribution in Developing Countries," in Loehr, William,
    and Powelson, John P., eds. *Economic Development, Poverty, and Income Distri-
    bution*, Boulder, Colorado, Westview Press.
World Bank, 1976:
    World Tables 1976, Baltimore, Md., Johns Hopkins University Press.
World Bank, 1980:
    World Tables 1980, Baltimore, Md., Johns Hopkins University Press.
World Health Organization, 1973:
    "Community Water Supply and Sewage Disposal in Developing Countries," in *World
    Health Statistics Report 26.*
World Health Organization, 1975:
    World Health Statistics, Annual for 1971.
World Health Organization, 1976:
    World Health Statistics, Annual for 1973–76.

5

MEASUREMENT

Quantification, despite some limitations, has improved
our ability to describe large systems beyond the reach
of individual experience. It inevitably changes our
overall image of the larger system and by changing this
is likely to change our values.
KENNETH E. BOULDING

Dissatisfaction with gross domestic (or national) product as a single measure of development has led to suggestions for alternatives. We have already discussed the PQLI. Primarily with reference to MDCs, Nordhaus and Tobin (1973) have proposed an index of human welfare. Before the end of this chapter, we will propose an additional index: GAD, for growth and distribution. The more basic question, to which we now address ourselves briefly, is: When is a single measure useful, and when is it not?

We propose the following criteria on a commonsense basis. A single, composite measure of a complex phenomenon will help our understanding of that phenomenon under the following two circumstances.

The first is that in which all parts of the phenomenon, independently measurable, are functionally related, in such a way that the composite measure can serve as proxy. Suppose we are concerned about GDP, GDP per capita, distribution of income and wealth, education, and political stability, to name only a few measurable variables. Suppose we have found empirically that GDP per capita serves as a valid predictor of all the other variables, within acceptable levels of confidence. If so, then it becomes a valid single measure. One reason economists differ about GDP per capita is that they disagree not only on how functional relationships are specified, but on whether they exist.

The second circumstance occurs when trade-offs, either physical (objective) or subjective, can be specified among all component parts of a phenomenon. It is then possible to stipulate a single value for any possible combination of parts, and different combinations yielding the same value are taken as equal. The simplest examples are the isoquant, where different combinations of factors of production yield the same quantities of physical output, and the indifference curve, in which utility is deemed equal at different combinations of consumption inputs.

Let us liken the problem to that of a person selecting a career, deciding upon a graduate school, hiring an employee, or simply judging whether on balance Country X has performed "better" in development than Country Y. Many elements enter, but the final choice must be that one is superior to the others. This superiority may be expressed by a numerical rating that takes into account all possible tradeoffs.

In cases that are opposite to either of these two circumstances, a single indicator is not appropriate. The opposite of the first circumstance is clear. GDP per capita is not a good proxy for income distribution if (as we believe) wide variations in distribution may accompany any given level of GDP. But the opposite of the second circumstance is not so clear. It occurs only when it is not necessary to make a choice. If God wills that I be a farmer and not a physician, or vice versa, then there is no need for me to value one higher than the other. But with that observation, we would rule away almost the entire field of economics, which is one of choice. Consequently, it would seem that a single indicator is appropriate in most circumstances, for we cannot normally escape judging that one combination is better than another.

But we are uncomfortable with that conclusion, for two reasons. One is that single indicators are not well enough developed; there are always problems of measurement. The other is that different individuals assign different weights to the component parts of a phenomenon. Hence a single measure, suitable to one individual, may not help another. With GDP per capita, we think of a publishable measure that many will read and agree on: "More is better." With GAD, an index developed later in this chapter, we have a measure tailored to the subjective trade-offs of one individual. Only if there were widespread agreement on a welfare function would GAD become an acceptable index for many people.

PERCENTILE SHARES

A percentile-share distribution is a table that relates percentages of income to percentages of population. By "population" we do not necessarily mean all the people in the country, but alternatively all the income recipients, or all the households, or all the individuals in a certain region (such as rural or urban), and so on. We will discuss which population to choose after we have described the measure. To avoid confusion, hereafter we will refer to the "accounting unit" rather than to the statistical population.

Table 5–1 reflects the distribution of income by deciles for households in Brazil in 1970. The first decile represents the 10 percent of the population (of households) with the lowest incomes, the second decile is the 10 percent with the next lowest incomes, and so on to the tenth decile, which is the 10 percent with the highest incomes. If there had been absolute equality in Brazil in 1970, then each decile would have the same income, or 10 percent. If there had been absolute inequality (one person having all the income), then of course the first nine deciles would have zero income, and the tenth decile—which would contain the one lucky (or unlucky) person—would have 100 percent. In fact, however, the lowest-income 10 percent of the population (of households) received only 1.2 percent of total income and the next 10 percent had only 1.8 percent, while the top 10 percent received 45.5 percent. Brazil has one of the worst income distributions in the world.

THE GINI INDEX

Percentile shares are informative, but clumsy to present. The Gini index, on the other hand, is a single measure of relative poverty and the most frequently encountered in studies of income distribution. First employed by Gini in 1912, it is based on a curve fitted to percentile shares, which was developed by Lorenz in 1905, and, not surprisingly, named after him—the Lorenz curve. Figure 5–1 illustrates this curve and a Gini index that flows from it.

TABLE 5-1
Percentile Distributions for Households in Brazil, 1970

Population Decile	Percentage of Income
first	1.2
second	1.8
third	2.7
fourth	3.5
fifth	4.6
sixth	6.0
seventh	7.9
eighth	10.8
ninth	16.0
tenth	45.5
	100.0

SOURCE: Jain (1975)

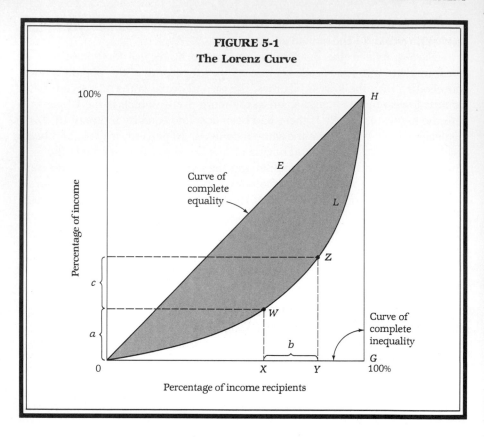

FIGURE 5-1

The Lorenz Curve

The vertical axis measures the percentage of income going to income recipients, who are arrayed in percentiles on the horizontal axis. Income recipients are ordered from the poorest to the richest, moving from left to right. Thus in Figure 5–1, OX percent of the population (the poorest group) receives a percent of the income, and so on, giving the Lorenz curve, L. Complete equality would occur only if a percent of the population received a percent of the income, as indicated by the curve of complete equality, E. The curve of perfect inequality is OGH, with a right angle at G. This curve represents the case where one person has 100 percent of the income.

The shaded area in the figure, enclosed by the theoretical line of equality, E, and the observed Lorenz curve, L, is known as the concentration area (or area of inequality). The Gini index is the ratio of this area to the total area under the line of equality. The simplest computation of the Gini proceeds by taking the sum of the areas under all trapezoids such as $WXYZ$ and subtracting this from the area under E to give the concentration area. The required ratio then follows.

Given the way income data are usually reported, the computation of the Gini index is simplified by calculating twice the concentration area and dividing this by twice the area under E (Bronfenbrenner, 1971). The area of a trapezoid such as $WXYZ$ (called T) is:

$$T = ab + \tfrac{1}{2}\,cb$$

Doubling this and rearranging for convenience, we have:

$$2T = 2ab + cb$$
$$2T = b(2a + c)$$
$$2T = b(a + [a + c])$$

Since twice the area under E is the area of the square, or 10,000, the Gini index, G, is given by:

$$G = \frac{10{,}000 - \sum_{i=1}^{n} b_i(a_i + [a_i + c_i])}{10{,}000}$$

where i refers to each income recipient category, of which there are n.

As an example, suppose we are given the income data of Table 5–2, which results in the Lorenz curve shown in Figure 5–2. Normally, censuses report the data in a form that will allow us to calculate the first two columns. The first column gives us the base of each trapezoid (b). The number a, is the cumulative percentage of income received by lower income groups. The amount $a + c$ is the cumulative percentage of income received by the group under consideration plus all preceding groups. Thus, column 4 shows $a + (a + c)$, which comes from summing the two previous numbers in column 3. For example, for the

TABLE 5-2
Worksheet for Calculating the Gini Index

Income bracket	1 Percentage of income recipients (b)	2 Percentage of income (c)	3 Cumulative percentage of income $(a + c)$	4 Paired sums $a + (a + c)$	5 Twice the trapezoid areas $b(a + [a+c])$
$5,000 and below	20	10	10	10	200
$5,000–$10,000	30	20	30	40	1,200
$10,000–$15,000	35	30	60	90	3,150
$15,000 and above	15	40	100	160	2,400
				Total =	6,950

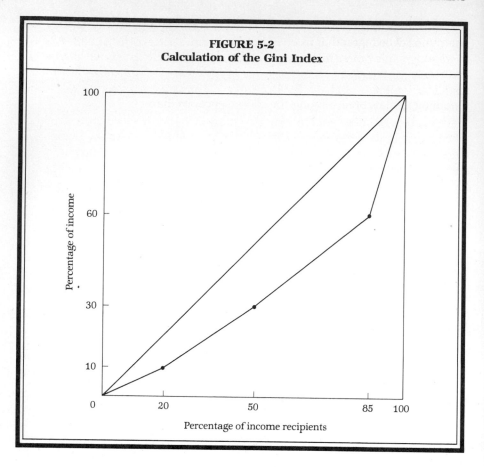

FIGURE 5-2
Calculation of the Gini Index

$5,000 to $10,000 income category, $a = 10$, $c = 20$, and $a + c = 30$. Finally, the sum of twice the trapezoid areas is shown in the last column, and:

$$G = \frac{10,000 - 6,950}{10,000} = .305$$

As with most of our measures of income distribution, the Gini index is not perfect. Three distinct problems immediately come to mind. First, no algebraic formula exists for the Lorenz curve, and thus a simple integration for the exact area under it is not possible. The computation as described above gives an approximation that understates the Gini, because each trapezoid includes a tiny area above the curve L. The fewer the income categories we have to work with, the larger is the underestimation. Comparative studies may give misleading results if we compare Gini indices based upon, say, three income categories in one country and 20 in another.

Second, the Gini index is insensitive to some changes in income distribution. In Figure 5–3, for example, we have depicted a shift from L_1 to L_2. It is entirely possible that this shift would go unnoticed if area A and area B were equal.

The Gini index does not always reflect what Roberti (1974) refers to as "non-unamimous" changes, that is, changes where some parts of society move closer to equality while others move away from it. Unambiguous readings on the Gini occur only for "unamimous" changes, which imply greater or lesser inequality for all. If we know that the Lorenz curves of two distributions do not cross, then the Gini is a good measure of comparison.

Third, the Gini does not give any indication of where the inequality lies, nor, when a distribution changes, where the change has taken place. In Figure 5–3, the shift from L_1 to L_2 shows more inequality in the lower income categories and less in the upper ones. If our intention is to examine the source of inequality, the Gini may be of limited help, whereas a table of percentile shares may be adequately revealing.

PROBLEMS OF MEASUREMENT

Up to this point, it may have seemed that measurement is straightforward, provided the data are available. One simply prepares a table of percentile shares and calculates the Gini index. But many undercurrents lurk. First, whose income

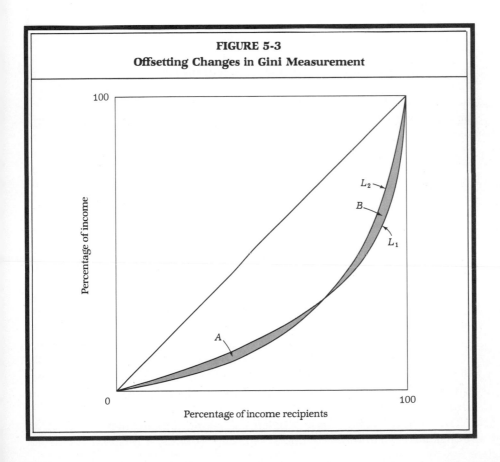

FIGURE 5-3
Offsetting Changes in Gini Measurement

100

Percentage of income

L_2

B

L_1

A

0

100

Percentage of income recipients

do we measure? That of all individuals? All income recipients? Families? If the latter, who belongs to an extended family in an African tribe, where incomes may be shared communally? Do we count a part-time college student with the same weight as a fifty-year-old business executive?

THE ACCOUNTING UNIT

Alternative accounting units would be (1) the individual (every member of the population), (2) the income recipient (excluding those individuals who receive no income), and (3) the family or household. For special studies, these units might be limited to, say, rural people, urban people, inhabitants of particular areas, members of particular professions, workers, and the like.

At first consideration, the *individual* might appear to be the relevant unit. But individuals include children and old people, who may not be gainfully employed. Would it be reasonable to give a country a high Gini (inequitable income distribution) just because it had a large number of old and young who were being supported by their families? Do we exclude them, accounting only for persons between certain ages (say, 15 to 65)? If so, the included ages are arbitrarily selected, and the logical limits might differ from country to country. Furthermore, some of the unemployed young and old might receive property income.

The next suggestion might be to exclude those who are earning no income at all; the inclusive category would be labeled *income recipients*. However, the income recipient is difficult to define. Since the data come from sample surveys, persons may be excluded if they do not fit the definitions of the survey, or if they have kinds of income not recorded by the census. Some might be excluded for cultural reasons. For example, men or women from certain racial groups may not be permitted to enter the labor force, and thus their incomes may not be observable to census takers.

Property income and earnings out of household activities (Kuznets, 1963) create further measurement problems. Property is often owned by family units, so income from it must be apportioned among family members. Household production, which often reaches significant proportions in LDCs, is usually a joint effort of family members and therefore cannot be attributed to specific individuals. In addition, redistributions that take place among extended family members create almost insurmountable obstacles in matching individuals with their true incomes.

Several authors—mostly from the West, where the nuclear family dominates—have recommended adoption of the *family* or *household* (Kuznets, 1963, and Bentzel, 1970) as the relevant unit. Presumably this unit determines choices about how income is to be earned and spent. Use of the family as a unit also provides closer correspondence between the measure of income distribution and the distribution of consumption. Finally, supplementary income earned by family activities can be added in and attributed to the true source of that income: family activity.

There are, however, some problems. Separate families may be "related" through income. In some countries, especially in LDCs, it is common practice for related people who dwell separately to support one another economically. Relatively high-income individuals in the city may still support parents, siblings, and other relatives who have remained in the countryside. Some households may appear to have no income at all if we ignore transfers from family members of different households. In some African tribes, a man may establish a separate domicile for each of two or more wives; the domiciles may be adjacent to each other or widely separated, sometimes in different towns.

In some countries, large families are deemed desirable because they provide more income-earners for the unit. Hackenberg (1977) found this to be so in the Philippines. In studying a sample of Mexican families, Weiskoff (1970) found that family size was directly related to income. In 1963, while the overall average family size was 5.8, the average for the lowest-income families was 4.8 and that for the wealthiest was 6.7, with an almost linear relationship in between. If size of family depends on income level, then the family makes a reasonable accounting unit.

One would expect that measurements based on the family would show greater equality than those based on the individual. Suppose families increase (or decrease) in size. Measurements based on the family might show some change, but measurements based on the individual would probably show greater change. The family becomes a less useful unit for cross-country comparisons of income distribution, since larger families in LDCs than in MDCs would mean that a given income must stretch over more people.

SHORT-RUN FLUCTUATIONS

Whatever the unit, measurement is complicated by short-run fluctuations. People may be temporarily unemployed, or alternatively enjoying extraordinary income, when a point-in-time survey is made. If these fluctuations occurred randomly among groups, leaving the overall distribution unaffected, the problem might not be serious. But short-run fluctuations may affect different groups in different ways. In MDCs business-cycle fluctuations are widely felt, but in LDCs income cycles relating to agricultural production may hit rural areas specifically. Some groups may be able to protect themselves better than others from short-run fluctuations, both within countries and in cross-country comparisons. Rich countries, and rich people within poor countries, probably protected themselves from the oil crisis much better than middle-income groups. The very poor, who never consumed much petroleum, were little affected.

SPOT-TIME VERSUS LIFETIME INCOME

Measurements of income distribution in a single year probably would show greater inequality than the measurements of lifetime income of the same subjects. Dich (1970) distinguishes between "horizontal" and "vertical" income distributions. The former express differences at a point in time, including those caused by short-run fluctuations and by age distribution. The latter express lifetime income. There is general agreement (Dich, 1970; Kuznets, 1963; and Stoikov, 1975) that the vertical distribution is more informative—though Morgan (1962) has claimed that short-run fluctuations have less impact on overall inequality than might at first appear to be the case.

Measurement of lifetime income, however, presents almost insurmountable problems. Longitudinal surveys would have to be conducted over long periods, and by the time the later data were collected, the earlier data would be out of date. Policymakers also could not wait for the information. Some analysts have constructed estimates of the present value of expected lifetime income (Fair, 1971), but these must be based on conjecture or on restrictive assumptions about the future. Expected growth and the accompanying changes would make such estimates more difficult in LDCs than in MDCs.

PRICING PROBLEMS

We are concerned not so much with income as with its purchasing power. In sharply dualistic economies, where prices are considerably lower in rural areas than in urban ones (but where goods available in the latter may be scarce in the former), incomes must be adjusted for purchasing power to make comparisons between the two. Rural to urban migration will affect these disparities, especially when urban earners spend some of their incomes in the city and send some back to their families in the countryside.

TAXATION AND PUBLIC GOODS

An individual's consumption is composed of private and public goods. The former must be paid for out of the person's income, but the latter are "free." Thus, if we are indeed interested in the distribution of consumption, we must adjust income to take public goods into account.

Public redistributive measures and provision of public goods can alter factor incomes from what they would be under the free market (Kuznets, 1963:2, and Dich, 1970:269). Over time, however, incomes may move back toward their original proportions. For example, a progressive tax might initially reduce post-tax income differentials among employees. As a result, however, pre-tax incomes may change, reinstating at least part of the original income differential. Suppose a higher-skilled employee receives three times the income of a lower-skilled employee, and a progressive income tax cuts the after-tax differential to 2:1. In response to relative marginal productivities, the pre-tax wages of skilled workers may move to more than 3:1, say to 3.5:1. Then the post-tax ratio might be, say, 2.5:1. Such adjustments are likely where people in different income groups have differing abilities to protect their incomes, or where the market has a strong tendency to maintain given differentials.

Similarly, public goods provided to the poor (such as health care and education) may make them more willing to accept lower wages. Thus, both a progressive tax and "free" benefits to the poor may cause inequities in nominal incomes to appear greater than they are in fact. These taxes and transfers affect a greater proportion of the incomes in MDCs (about 30 percent) than in LDCs (about 10 percent). We have already observed that Ginis for MDCs are, in general, lower than for LDCs. Because of their greater transfers, it may be that the real Ginis in MDCs should be even lower. Thus the "distribution gap" (greater equity in MDCs than in LDCs) may be even greater than it appears. This gap would, however, be narrowed by the fact that in many cases, public goods are provided preferentially to the rich (farm benefits to large farmers with more land, better education to urban than to rural dwellers, and so on).

ACCURACY OF MEASUREMENT

Since our main interest is poverty, we must continually ask ourselves whether or not our measures adequately reflect poverty levels. The many factors just discussed, which may create inaccurate linkages between income and poverty, must be accounted for whenever possible. Most of the data available on income distribution (in LDCs especially) do not deal with all these problems explicitly, and the picture of poverty may therefore be inaccurate.

Are these inaccuracies serious enough to prevent us from making correct statements about income distribution and poverty? We believe not. Studies on income distribution and development have reached surprisingly homogeneous conclusions, using a wide variety of data that vary in both coverage and quality. Some studies have "tried on" different data sets and have found that the conclusions reached are not overly sensitive to the differences among the sets. The Adelman and Morris (1973) study of inequality in 43 countries mixes income distribution data based on both households and total population. Twenty-one countries are represented by household data; 22 are represented by population. The fact that population data tend to show greater inequality than household data does not seem to have biased the Adelman and Morris results. They have rerun the same analyses using other distribution specifications and have come up with substantially similar conclusions each time.

Incomes of the poor in LDCs are so low that even major inaccuracies do not have a large impact upon measures of distribution. Under the most optimistic set of assumptions, the poorest groups still possess extremely low incomes, whether absolute or relative. If we were to wait for data that accurately reflect all our concerns, we would make no progress whatsoever.

We must, therefore, resort to what Ahluwalia (1976) calls "stylized facts"—information collected on various bases—for these constitute our current knowledge of income distribution in LDCs. There is always the danger, of course, that in the face of inadequate data we may be forced to interject value judgments. While this is to be avoided where possible, we will minimize our error by obtaining a clear understanding of what our measures tell us and what they do not. We must also make our value judgments as explicit as possible.

CHANGES IN INEQUALITY OVER TIME

Most studies of income distribution by country have been on a spot basis. Where two investigators have studied the same country in different years, they usually have examined different accounting units or used different methods, so their studies are not comparable. There have, however, been a few comparative studies by the same investigators, using the same units and the same methods for beginning and ending dates. These studies illustrate ways in which percentile distributions can be used jointly with Gini indices to illuminate developments over time.

Data from eight such studies are summarized in Table 5-3. The countries are listed in order of decreasing inequality (increasing Gini) in the second year of observation. It is easily seen how the ranking by Gini indices corresponds to the percentile distributions. If the share of the poorest 20 percent in the second year is taken alone, the ranking remains the same, except that Mexico and Colombia change places. If just the shares of the richest 10 percent are taken, the ranking also remains the same, except that Sri Lanka and Costa Rica switch places, as do Mexico and Brazil (by a narrow margin). No switches are necessary in the ranking of the middle group (20 to 60 percent).

Of the four countries whose Gini moved *toward* equality over time (South Korea, Taiwan, Sri Lanka, and Costa Rica), all showed an increased income share for the poorest 20 percent except Costa Rica. Even though the Gini for that country was declining at a rate of 1.7 percent per year, the share of the poorest 20 percent was also declining by 1.1 percent. In the other three countries, increased equity was achieved by an across-the-board, or "unamimous," redistribution. In Costa Rica, equity apparently increased through a redistribution away from the rich *and* the poor, in favor of the middle groups. The hypothetical shift from Lorenz curve L_1 to L_2 in Figure 5–3 might well illustrate the Costa Rican case.

Among countries whose Ginis show increasing inequality, in two countries— Mexico and Brazil—the shares of the poorest 20 percent improved despite the

TABLE 5-3
Inequality in Eight Countries

	Year of Observation		Gini Index		Share of the Poorest 20%		Share of the 20–60% Income Group		Share of the Richest 10%	
	(1)	(2)	YEAR 1	YEAR 2	YEAR 1	YEAR 2	YEAR 1	YEAR 2	YEAR 1	YEAR 2
South Korea	1968	1971	.30	.27	8.6	9.9	30.1	31.3	24.2	23.5
Taiwan	1953	1964	.56	.33	2.7	7.8	27.3	29.1	45.6	26.3
Sri Lanka	1963	1969	.46	.37	4.5	7.2	23.0	26.9	36.8	29.3
Costa Rica	1961	1971	.52	.44	6.0	5.4	17.6	23.0	37.0	24.4
India	1953	1960	.34	.47	8.0	4.0	32.0	23.0	28.0	36.0
Colombia	1962	1970	.48	.55	5.9	3.5	20.4	18.0	42.7	44.1
Mexico	1963	1968	.54	.59	3.5	3.8	17.5	15.6	42.0	52.2
Brazil	1960	1970	.59	.63	0.8	1.5	17.2	14.8	45.5	51.7

NOTE: All inequality data are calculated on the basis of households, with the exceptions of Brazil and Colombia, which are based on "economically active" populations.

SOURCE: Jain (1975). *Size Distribution of Income: Compilation of Data*, Baltimore, Md., Johns Hopkins University Press. Copyright © by The Johns Hopkins University Press.

highest inequality levels. In those countries, the shifts penalized the 20 to 60 percent income groups and benefited the upper and lower groups. Colombia and India demonstrate redistributions in favor of the rich. While India maintains a "middle" level of inequality, only slightly more than Costa Rica, it has performed worst of all. Its Gini rose at the greatest rate. Shares of the lowest and middle income groups fell at the most rapid rate, and the share of the rich rose fastest.

An interest in the poor is not always well served by aggregate inequality measures. Table 5–4 illustrates two hypothetical cases where the same shift causes *opposite* changes in the Gini index. In Case I there are only two income groups averaging $10 and $100, respectively. Case II has these two groups plus an additional, very wealthy class that averages $1,000. In both cases, 85 percent of the population is in the lowest income class. If we consider a Pareto optimal shift of 10 percent of the population from the $10 class to the $100 class in both cases, the Gini will rise in Case I and fall in Case II. Intuitively, this occurs because the transfer is to the wealthier class in Case I, thereby increasing the weight of the income differences between rich and poor. In Case II, the transfer is to the middle class, which reduces the weight of the difference between the extremely high incomes and the rest.

These examples demonstrate the additional insight gained by examining the Gini index and percentile shares together. Since percentile shares are direct inputs into the calculation of the Gini, an examination of them helps to explain why the Gini has changed as it has. The Gini has the advantage of providing a single index of rank, but the percentile shares show specific changes for specific income groups. Since our interest centers upon a specific group—the poor—we must seek the implications of changes in overall inequality for that group.

TABLE 5-4
Two Hypothetical Cases: Before and After

	Income-Bracket Average ($)	Percentage of Income Recipients	Gini
Case I:			
Before	10	85	.49
	100	15	
After	10	75	.52
	100	25	
Case II:			
Before	10	85	
	100	10	.79
	1,000	5	
After	10	75	
	100	20	.76
	1,000	5	

THE ARBITRARY CHOICE OF PERCENTILES

Because the choice of percentiles is arbitrary, artificial distinctions in the behavioral characteristics of members of each income group may inadvertently creep into the analysis. Also, comparisons among distributions, say between two countries, may be complicated by the arbitrary choice of percentile groups (Adelman and Morris, 1973). For example, among the countries just examined, the poorest 60 percent of income recipients in India are undoubtedly at a much lower income level than the poorest 60 percent in Mexico. Thus the problems of the poorest 60 percent of Indians, and policies aimed toward them, are likely to differ from the problems of the poorest 60 percent of Mexicans and appropriate policies there.

Percentile shares can be used to create new indices, dictated by the task at hand and the imagination of the researcher. Adelman and Morris (1973) found it useful to classify income recipients into the poorest 60 percent, middle 20 percent, and richest 5 percent, and to examine the income share of each. Oshima (1962, 1970) has created a measure he calls the "standard deviation of percentile shares." He reasons that equality implies that each percentage of the population receive the same percentage of income. Thus, if we were dealing with deciles, each decile could be expected to receive 10 percent of the income in a situation of complete equality. The measure he used is:

$$d = \frac{\sum_{i=1}^{10} |x_i - 10|}{10}$$

where x_i refers to the observed share of each decile, i. Thus d is simply the average of the deviations of each decile from equality. Oshima shows that this measure is easy to work with, avoids some of the bias contained in the Gini index, and has more intuitive and empirical appeal than measures that require squaring, logs, and so forth. But it has its shortcomings. Besides the fact that it is based on an arbitrary choice of deciles, it fails to reflect redistributions from one percentile group to another where both groups have either positive or negative deviations before and after the transfer.

IMPACT OF STRUCTURAL CHANGES
ON INCOME DISTRIBUTION

Structural changes such as agrarian reform or major population shifts may cause changes in income distribution. Kuznets (1963) recognized that intersectoral shifts that accompanied development were a cause of increased inequality. Oshima (1970) notes that shifts of economic activity from a rural to an urban focus explain changing income distribution better than growth itself. Observed inequalities in LDCs tend to be greater in the urban (industrial) sector than in the rural (agricultural) groups (Weisskoff, 1970, and Swamy, 1967).

Imagine a country with most of the people in the rural sector (relatively equal distribution) and a few in the cities (highly unequal). Then suppose there is a large migration from rural to urban areas, with the people taking on the characteristics of the latter as they move. Suppose further that the incomes of all migrants increase, but some more than others. It would appear that the migration, rather than the growth process per se, is the cause of greater inequality, unless the migration is taken as an indispensible part of growth. Dualism appears to be associated with *rapid* growth, in which the industrial sector grows more rapidly than the agricultural group (Adelman and Morris, 1973). Rapid population growth and rural-to-urban migration combine to ensure that income distribution becomes more unequal, overall.

Robinson (1976) noted how income inequality can be partially explained by rural to urban migration. An overall measure such as the Gini is a combination of two factors. One is a weighted average of the Ginis for the rural and urban sectors G_r and G_u, if each Gini were calculated separately. The other is the difference, D, between the average incomes of the two sectors, appropriately weighted. It is possible that $G_r = G_u < G_t$ (where G_t is the Gini for the total population). This would occur if the income distribution were the same in the two sectors, but the average urban income was higher than the rural.

In most cases, however, $G_r < G_u$, and D is substantial. In Brazil, for example, G_r was .55 in 1970 while G_u was .59. Meanwhile, average urban incomes were 4.3 times the incomes in rural areas. Since Brazil is about 60 percent urbanized, the weight placed upon G_u and upon the income difference between the two sectors is great, leading to an overall measure of $G_t = .63$ (Jain, 1975).

Inequality, therefore, is likely to move in three stages:

1. In the early stages of development, the primary weight within G_t is on G_r, but as development proceeds, increasing weight is placed upon G_u, which is usually greater than G_r. This also causes the significance of D to increase, and G_t rises.
2. Due to the heavier weight placed upon D as urbanization increases, G_t becomes greater than G_u. Dualism may also cause the absolute level of D to increase.
3. As society becomes increasingly urbanized, G_t falls and approaches G_u. Also, G_r is weighted less and less heavily and D falls in significance. An associated factor here would be a shortage of labor in rural areas, raising its marginal productivity along with rural incomes in general, thereby reducing the magnitude of D.

In a study of inequality in India, Swamy (1967) separated the increase in inequality into two parts: that attributable to intersectoral inequality *(D)* as opposed to intrasectoral inequality *(G_t or G_u)*. He found that changes in intrasectoral inequality (1951–1960) were small. No observable change took place in the agricultural sector, while the income distribution in the nonagricultural sector became slightly more unequal. Only 15 percent of the overall increase in inequality could be attributed to changes in the intrasectoral income distribution. The remaining 85 percent occurred as a result of the increased intersectoral inequality, that is, shifts in population from the low inequality (agricultural) to the higher inequality (nonagricultural) sector. Weisskoff (1970) also examined the shift from agriculture to nonagricultural economic activities and found overall inequality widening as a result.

POPULATION GROWTH AND INCOME INEQUALITY

Population growth rates have shown positive associations with inequality in cross-section studies (Ahluwalia, 1976). Paglin (1975) has shown that they can significantly affect aggregate measures of income distribution. Most countries have an age/income profile similar to that of the United States, shown by line *AB* in Figure 5–4. People generally start out and end their careers with much lower incomes than they have during middle age. Thus, a shift in the population age structure, such that the relative number of old or young people increases, would cause the Gini index to rise, indicating greater income inequality. This would be true despite the fact that lifetime income may remain the same for everyone.

Countries at the "middle" levels of economic development (around $500–$700 per capita annual income) tend to experience the most rapidly increasing populations. The typical path starts with a poor, primitive economy with high birth rates but high mortality rates as well (especially infant mortality), yielding a low net rate of population increase (on the order of 1.0–1.5 percent). As de-

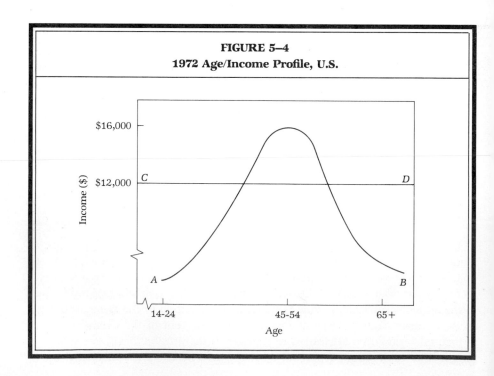

FIGURE 5–4
1972 Age/Income Profile, U.S.

velopment proceeds, mortality rates decline rapidly. With birth rates unaffected, net population growth rates accelerate to the 3–4 percent per annum range now being experienced by countries such as Brazil, Mexico, and the Philippines. The MDCs maintain low mortality rates, but they also have lower birth rates, reducing the overall population growth to about 1–1.5 percent.

As population growth rates accelerate, we expect the age distribution of the population to shift. Lower infant mortality rates put larger proportions of the population in the younger age groups. If life expectancy is also extended, increasingly large proportions of people are found in older age categories as well. Usually the former is greater than the latter.

The effect of a varying population growth rate on the Philippine and U.S. age distributions is shown in Table 5–5. By a change in the total fertility rate (TFR) and nothing else, the simulated proportion of the population in each age group changes substantially over the period 1970–1995. The proportion of the population in the 0 to 14-year-old age group in the United States rises from about 28 to 36 percent simply by raising the TFR from 2.3 to 4.0 gradually over the 25-year period. In the Philippines, cutting the 1970 TFR to 4.0 causes a reduction in the proportion of the population in the 0 to 14-year-old group from 47 to 39 percent. The variables required by these estimates are fertility

TABLE 5–5
Some Demographic Characteristics with Age Distribution by Percentages and Different Suppositions for Fertility Rate Between 1970 and 1995

	United States			Philippines		
	1 1970	2 1995	3 1995	1 1970	2 1995	3 1995
Total population						
(millions)	204.8	249.4	304.7	37.5	89.9	75.5
Growth rate						
(percent)	.76	.62	1.82	3.43	3.51	2.2
Total fertility						
rate*	2.3	2.3	4.0	6.7	6.7	4.0
Ages (percentage of						
population)						
0–14	28.3	25.1	35.6	46.9	47.3	39.4
15–24	19.8	15.1	15.4	19.3	19.3	21.0
25–34	12.3	14.5	11.9	14.8	13.3	15.8
35–44	11.3	15.5	12.7	8.6	8.7	10.3
45–54	11.4	11.5	9.4	4.0	5.6	6.7
55–64	9.1	7.7	6.3	3.9	3.4	4.0
65+	9.5	10.1	8.3	2.5	2.4	2.8

*Total fertility rate = live births per woman of child-bearing age (15–44 years).

Source: PLATO IV, a data bank and simulation program maintained at the University of Illinois. Reprinted by permission of Paul Handler, Director, Population Dynamics Group, University of Ill., Urbana, IL 61801.

rates, infant mortality, and life expectancy, combined with the original age distributions in the countries of concern.

Clearly, as population growth rates accelerate, and as greater proportions of the population appear in the younger and older portions of the age distribution, we should expect overall income inequality to become greater, all else equal. This is true even where the income distribution *within* any given age group remains unchanged, since in an overall measure we weight the income of each age group in proportion to its importance in the overall population. In effect, we end up weighting the incomes of low-income earners (the young and old) more heavily because there are more of them.

It is possible to construct an index that shows the degree of inequality due to the age/income profile separately from inequality due to everything else. Income recipients are grouped by age: the income share of the poorest age-group is recorded, then that of the next poorest, and so on until all income recipients are accounted for. A curve similar in shape to a Lorenz curve can then be constructed, and labeled P as in Figure 5–5. The area below the E line and above P is an indicator of inequality due only to the age/income profile. A standard Lorenz curve, labeled L in Figure 5–5, can also be constructed. The

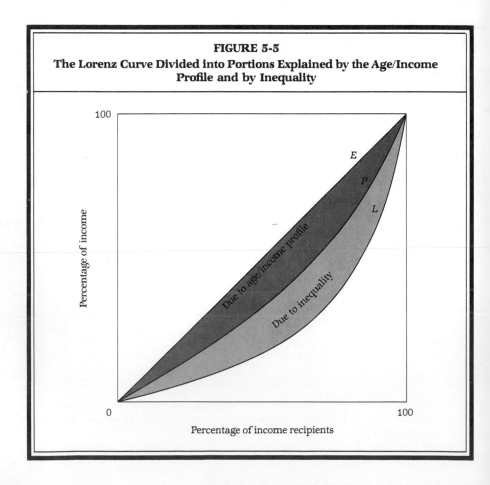

FIGURE 5-5

The Lorenz Curve Divided into Portions Explained by the Age/Income Profile and by Inequality

area between L and P is an indicator of inequality due to factors other than the age/income profile.

For the United States in 1972, Paglin shows that the degree of true inequality is sharply reduced by adjusting for the age/income profile. The Lorenz Gini for 1972 has a value of .359. The Paglin Gini shows a value of only .239, since the age Gini is .120. Apparently one-third of all inequality in the United States is due to the effect of the age/income profile. Furthermore, Paglin shows that while the Lorenz Gini dropped from .378 in 1947 only to .359 in 1972, giving rise to the popular notion that inequality has been about constant over this period, the Paglin Gini dropped from .303 to .239, a 21 percent reduction in inequality. The rise in the age Gini from .075 to .120, which accounts for the difference, is attributable to an increasing number of both young and old in the population, as well as an arching of the age/income profile due to extended periods of higher education among youth.

The Paglin results have clear implications for developing countries. Over the post-war period—and in some countries over the past decade—sharply reduced death rates and declining infant mortality have caused the proportions of young and old people to rise rapidly. It is entirely possible that the increasing inequality observed by many economists can be attributed to the changing age/income structure in developing countries, rather than to the adverse effects of economic growth per se.

When we compare population growth rates in the eight countries examined in Table 5–3, we note that increasing equity has in all cases been preceded by a peak in the population growth rate. Table 5–6 shows the population growth rate record in all eight countries. Comparing the periods of increasing equity in Table 5–3 with the peaks in population growth rates in Table 5–6, we find that increasing equity has occurred during or after a peak, while population growth was slowing. In all cases of increasing inequity, population growth rates were either rising or were at a peak.

TABLE 5–6
Population Growth Rates for Various Periods

	South Korea	Taiwan	Sri Lanka	Costa Rica	India	Colombia	Mexico	Brazil
1940		2.5	1.5	2.4	1.3	2.0	1.7	2.0
1950		3.0	2.2	3.0	2.1	2.5	3.0	2.6
1960	1.9	3.5	2.6	3.7	1.5	3.1	3.0	2.8
1970	2.4	3.3	2.3	3.4	2.1	3.3	3.3	2.8
1975	1.7	2.0	2.3	2.6	2.1	2.8	3.5	3.0

NOTE: Growth rates shown are compound rates over the period preceding the year indicated, that is, over each decade or over 1970–75.

SOURCE: The 1970–75 growth rates are from IMF *International Financial Statistics*. All others are from PLATO IV, a data bank and simulation program maintained at the University of Illinois.

AN INDEX OF GROWTH AND DISTRIBUTION

Our target is growth with equitable distribution. Whenever there is a dual target such as this, the problem of trade-off emerges. This problem occurs whether we believe trade-off is physically necessary or not. Some authors believe that maximum growth *requires* less equitable distribution along the way. Our interpretation of the evidence is that it probably does not. Nevertheless, there are policies that may enhance distribution more than growth and vice versa. Since policy implementation usually has a cost, we should in each case determine which of the two (growth or distribution) requires the greater marginal push.

On the surface, that problem may seem simple. We measure growth by increased GDP and distribution by the Gini coefficient in conjunction with percentile shares. We then make a choice based on our subjective view of welfare. Even if all the reservations expressed so far are resolved, further complications arise. We can explain these best by developing an index of growth and distribution (GAD index), which takes into account all the target choices.

Let us define the GAD index as follows:

$$\text{GAD} = Y\,[1 - W\,(a\,A + b\,R)(Y/Y_1)^c]$$

in which:

Y = gross domestic product per capita
W = weight to be placed on poverty, as opposed to growth
A = percentage of the population in absolute poverty (the poverty line must be stipulated)
a, b = weight placed on absolute versus relative poverty, such that
$\quad a + b = 1, 0 < a < 1,$ and $0 < b < 1$
R = measure of relative poverty, scaled from zero to one; a suggested measure would be $R = G - D$, in which G is an agreed-upon Gini index and D is the desired (or target) Gini[1]
Y_1 = that level of per capita GDP at which poverty (both relative and absolute) ought to be abolished
c = a modifying exponent, to allow a variety of standards for MDCs and LDCs

Thus the GAD index is based on GDP per capita. If there is no absolute poverty ($A = 0$), and if the desired Gini has been reached ($R = 0$), then GAD

---

[1]In principle, $A = f(R,Y)$. For example, if R remains unchanged while Y increases (that is, all incomes increase in proportion), then the percentage of population receiving incomes below the arbitrary poverty line will decrease. However, we are unable to take this relationship into account if the Gini is used as a basis for R. The Gini does not necessarily vary with the percentage of population in any income bracket. For example, if both the poor and the rich lose income relative to the middle, the Gini may remain unchanged. This defect applies to virtually any single-number measure of income distribution (such as those based on the standard deviation). If a more satisfactory measure of R should be developed, such that $A = f(R,Y)$ may be written explicitly, then the formula for GAD might be rewritten to omit A. Until then, we must be content with separate measures for A and R.

$= Y$. Where one or the other has not been achieved, GAD is "penalized" (made less than Y) by an amount that depends on W, the weight the policymaker places on poverty as opposed to income per capita.

The penalty is a function of $(aA + bR)$, which we refer to as the *poverty factor*. The subjective weights placed on absolute versus relative poverty (a, b) might appear deceptive, since A and R are different concepts. Therefore, $a = b = .5$ should not be interpreted as equal weighting. (There is no such thing as equal weighting.) The stipulation that $a + b = 1$ enables the poverty factor to vary from 0 to 1, a convenient range for intercountry or intertemporal comparisons.

Let us call Y/Y_1 the *income ratio*. Its use implies that the policymaker may be more lenient with LDCs than with MDCs. (If he will not, he sets c equal to 0). The penalty for a low-income country is reduced, because LDCs are "expected" to have inequalities; they should be given time to redress them. A country with a relatively high per capita income (Y), however, should have redressed them, so the penalty factor applies full force.

There is, however, no reason why the penalty mitigation should be exactly the same as the income ratio, or even a linear function of it. A policymaker more tolerant of LDCs would set c very high, thus reducing disproportionately the penalty for very low income countries.[2]

We do not propose an international set of standards for GAD or the regular publication of GAD indices by international agencies. Our purpose has been to demonstrate the extent to which the assessment of poverty is judgmental and to separate out the elements of judgment that might otherwise become blurred. The rational policymaker should have separate preferences for W, a (and therefore b), D, Y_1, and c. Policymakers with a given set of preferences might program GAD into their computers, and assess the progress of an individual country over time, or evaluate its spot comparison with other countries.

In order to present an idea of how GAD might work, we have calculated it for 49 countries (Table 5–7), using in the first two columns our own subjective preferences of $W = 3.0$, $a = b = .5$, $D = .30$, $Y_1 = \$7,500$, and $c = 0.4$. Two other estimates, based on other values for W and c, are shown in the final four columns. If W is reduced (so that less weight is put on poverty), it is necessary

---

[2]To see how this happens, suppose Y_1 is set at 4 and there are two LDCs, showing $Y = 1$ and $Y = 3$. The *penalty adjusting factor* (income ratio to the power c) would vary as c varies in the following way:

c	$(\frac{1}{4})^c$	$(\frac{3}{4})^c$
-1.0	4.00	1.33
-0.5	2.00	1.15
0	1.00	1.00
0.3	0.67	0.92
0.5	0.50	0.87
0.7	0.38	0.82
1.0	0.25	0.75
2.0	0.06	0.56
3.0	0.02	0.42

TABLE 5-7

GAD Indices, GDP per capita, Gini Coefficients, and Absolute Poverty Percentages for 49 Countries
(with $a = b = .5$, $D = .30$, and $Y_1 = \$7,500$)

Country	GAD $W = 3.0, c = 0.4$	GAD rank $W = 3.0, c = 0.4$	GDP per capita 1973	GDP per capita rank	Gini	Absolute Poverty Percentage	GAD $W = 1.0, c = 0.0$	GAD rank $W = 1.0, c = 0.0$	GAD $W = 5.0, c = 2.0$	GAD rank $W = 5.0, c = 2.0$
LATIN AMERICA										
Brazil	542.75	26	768.00	25	0.64	0.14	581.18	26	758.20	25
Colombia	351.79	35	440.00	33	0.56	0.15	348.59	35	438.42	33
Costa Rica	733.28	20	818.00	23	0.44	0.02	749.49	20	813.92	23
Dominican Republic	445.81	29	529.00	31	0.49	0.11	448.90	29	527.00	31
Ecuador	252.99	38	386.00	36	0.68	0.37	240.74	38	384.07	36
El Salvador	299.65	37	345.00	38	0.46	0.13	293.19	37	344.45	38
Guyana	357.68	34	396.00	35	0.41	0.09	354.57	34	395.42	35
Honduras	247.84	39	323.00	39	0.56	0.28	234.85	39	322.18	39
Jamaica	678.31	22	894.00	20	0.57	0.10	725.65	21	882.04	20
Mexico	679.97	21	883.00	21	0.58	0.07	723.75	22	871.96	21
Panama	839.49	17	938.00	18	0.42	0.03	862.58	18	932.10	18
Peru	396.45	32	617.00	27	0.75	0.18	417.33	31	610.24	27
Uruguay	827.60	18	970.00	17	0.49	0.02	862.42	19	961.00	17
ASIA										
Burma	69.54	49	82.00	49	0.38	0.53	56.71	49	81.98	49
India	96.72	47	118.00	47	0.48	0.44	80.66	47	117.95	47
Iraq	312.46	36	429.00	34	0.62	0.24	306.99	36	427.00	34
Korea	374.38	33	379.00	37	0.27	0.05	373.92	33	378.93	37
Lebanon	675.76	23	796.00	24	0.53	0.01	697.69	23	790.46	24
Pakistan	89.66	48	99.00	48	0.32	0.32	81.43	46	98.98	48
Philippines	228.70	40	262.00	40	0.49	0.13	219.54	40	261.74	40
Sri Lanka	176.11	43	209.00	43	0.40	0.33	163.10	43	208.82	43
Taiwan	625.81	24	660.00	26	0.28	0.10	629.87	24	658.83	26
Thailand	212.86	41	262.00	41	0.51	0.26	199.34	41	261.61	41
Turkey	432.46	30	543.00	29	0.56	0.12	437.68	30	540.23	29

TABLE 5–7 (con't)

Country	GAD $W = 3.0, c = 0.4$	GAD rank $W = 3.0, c = 0.4$	GDP per capita 1973	GDP per capita rank	Gini	Absolute Poverty Percentage	GAD $W = 1.0, c = 0.0$	GAD rank $W = 1.0, c = 0.0$	GAD $W = 5.0, c = 2.0$	GAD rank $W = 5.0, c = 2.0$
AFRICA										
Gabon	573.71	25	834.00	22	0.64	0.15	625.12	25	821.08	22
Ivory Coast	460.19	27	548.00	28	0.53	0.07	464.64	27	545.77	28
Senegal	203.07	42	253.00	42	0.58	0.22	188.43	42	252.63	42
Sierra Leone	134.00	44	179.00	44	0.61	0.43	112.17	45	178.80	44
South Africa	810.35	19	1129.00	16	0.58	0.12	902.46	16	1103.33	16
Tanzania	98.26	46	130.00	46	0.54	0.57	76.43	48	129.91	46
Tunisia	400.65	31	513.00	32	0.50	0.22	403.50	32	510.43	32
Uganda	129.19	45	143.00	45	0.40	0.21	120.57	44	142.95	45
Zambia	460.03	28	541.00	30	0.52	0.06	463.74	28	538.99	30
MORE DEVELOPED COUNTRIES										
Australia	4430.15	6	4553.00	8	0.31	0.00	4491.07	7	4456.41	6
Canada	5369.88	2	5620.00	3	0.33	0.00	5526.42	3	5357.29	1
Denmark	4957.03	4	5440.00	5	0.36	0.00	5256.94	4	4958.46	3
Finland	3007.13	12	3742.00	12	0.47	0.00	3418.50	12	3339.35	12
France	3565.16	11	4923.00	6	0.51	0.00	4387.37	8	3769.10	10
Germany (Federal Republic)	4235.97	7	5601.00	4	0.48	0.00	5089.62	5	4175.01	7
Israel	2822.20	13	2864.00	14	0.31	0.00	2843.52	14	2849.06	14
Japan	3719.55	9	3765.00	11	0.31	0.00	3745.04	11	3739.85	11
Netherlands	3605.40	10	4402.00	9	0.44	0.00	4073.39	9	3835.98	9
New Zealand	3771.00	8	4034.00	10	0.35	0.00	3921.65	10	3871.49	8
Norway	4491.26	5	4874.00	7	0.36	0.00	4722.41	6	4553.91	5
Spain	1864.75	15	2033.00	15	0.39	0.00	1938.46	15	1998.26	15
Sweden	5446.83	1	6198.00	1	0.38	0.00	5927.76	1	5275.24	2
United Kingdom	2791.59	14	2991.00	13	0.36	0.00	2894.98	13	2914.65	13
United States	5164.55	3	6166.00	2	0.41	0.00	5804.98	2	4945.92	4
Yugoslavia	875.46	16	903.00	19	0.34	0.00	881.59	17	901.44	19

SOURCE: GDP per capita measurements from International Financial Statistics; Gini coefficients from Jain (1975) and from Table 4–2; absolute poverty percentages from Chenery (1974:12).

also to reduce c (otherwise LDCs will be excused entirely). Similarly, if W is increased, c must also be increased in order for the results to make sense.

It is not surprising that GAD correlates with GDP ($r = .99$ in the first experiment). One who looks only at the correlation coefficients might conclude that GAD does not show independent information. Instead, however, GAD is intended to show the extent to which individual country ratings are penalized as a result of policymakers' preferences and tolerances of different income distributions. A policymaker accustomed to using GAD would find some meaning in the fact that Brazil is penalized $225 (from $768 to $543), while Taiwan's penalty is only $34 (from $660 to $626).

CONCLUSION

Dissatisfaction with GDP as a single measure of development has led to suggestions for alternatives, such as the PQLI or the Nordhaus-Tobin measure of welfare. But such alternatives embody the same, serious problem as GDP per capita. They assume that a widely-agreed-upon welfare function (set of trade-offs) exists, and therefore that a single, publishable index, serving as proxy for all the variables traded off, will present to all people a statement of welfare, quality of life, or other achievement. But the art of measurement is not sufficiently advanced (and probably cannot be) to yield an index that serves as a confident proxy. Furthermore, there is no agreement on trade-offs among the component parts of the single index.

With GDP per capita, we are led to believe we have no choice on objectives. More is better, and that's that! But the situation is more complex. When different individuals place different weights on absolute poverty, relative poverty, both measurements of poverty versus economic growth, and a host of other variables we have not included in the GAD index, then there is no widely-publishable index of maximization that will satisfy all. Our purpose in introducing GAD was not to supply an alternative to GDP per capita and Gini coefficients, but to demonstrate how subjective economic development is. Differing subjective trade-offs lead to different assessments of a maximand.

Early in the chapter, we concluded that single indices are useful. We now qualify that judgment. A single index is useful to an individual who knows his trade-offs, who may not trust his intuition sufficiently on a judgment he is required to make, and who therefore wishes to specify the trade-offs in mathematical form. He may also wish to play simulation games with his judgment and discover what decision he would make if his trade-offs were different. A single index is therefore also useful to a society with enough cohesion to provide widespread agreement on trade-offs.

Let us now return to the real world, which is not the world of GAD. Since our interest lies in growth and distribution, we must choose measures that reflect both. GDP per capita is doubtless the most convenient measure for growth alone. If we were able statistically to separate out any development unit we wished (rural areas, urban slums, remote tribes), then the product per capita for each of these separately might tell us all we wished to know. Being unable to do this, we must rely on certain measures of distribution.

All such measures have disadvantages and can only tell the story imperfectly. We find that the Gini index, combined with an examination of percentile shares of income, reflects our concern for poverty as well as, or better than, alternative measures. The PQLI and the percentage of absolute poverty (Chapter 4) round out our picture. Some other measures may be useful for specific analyses; these are described briefly in the appendix to this chapter.

APPENDIX

MEASURES OF INEQUALITY

One could easily survey dozens of measures of inequality. Clearly this can not be done in an appendix of this length and has nevertheless been done by others (Cowell, 1977; Stark, 1972; Bartels, 1977; and Ferguson, 1976). Our intention here is to indicate the general kinds of measures and the specialized uses to which they can be put. Three general types of measures will be introduced. First, some measures are not based upon any preconceived notion of the probability distribution of income, nor upon any social welfare function within which income plays a role. Second, some measures do stem from specific assumptions about the probability distribution of income. Third, assumptions about welfare functions lead to still another set of measures. In each case we will introduce measures that are used commonly and suggest that interested readers follow up on others in the citations.

Measures Not Based on Probability Distributions or Welfare Functions

The Gini index used in Chapter 5 is a measure falling in this category. The *coefficient of variation* is another commonly used measure of inequality and is defined as:

(1)
$$C = \frac{\sqrt{V}}{\bar{y}}$$

where V is the variance of income:

(2)
$$V = \frac{1}{n} \sum_{i=1}^{n} (\bar{y} - y_i)^2$$

The symbol $\bar{y}$ is the average income and the symbol y_i is the income of the individual i.

One might ask why V is not used in the first place. V has the undesirable property that should everyone's income be doubled, V would quadruple (Cowell, 1977:29), making a cross-section comparison almost impossible. The standardization in (1) avoids this problem.

There are some normative connotations in using C that analysts should be aware of. For example, assume two countries with the following properties:

$$\text{Country 1: } \bar{y} = 2000; \sqrt{V_1} = 1000$$
$$\text{Country 2: } \bar{y} = 400; \sqrt{V_2} = 200$$

Clearly C is the same in each. The implication is that C treats the more widely spread distribution in the richer country as equivalent to a more narrow spread in the poorer country. Another way of viewing this is that if $\sqrt{V}$ remains fixed but $\bar{y}$ increases, C indicates declining inequality (Oshima, 1970).

One should also be aware that in using C to evaluate income transfers, the effect of a transfer is independent of the level at which the transfer occurs (Atkinson, 1970). A transfer of $100 from a person with a $1500 income to one with a $1000 income would show the same change in the coefficient of variation as a $100 transfer from a person with $1 million to one with $500 less. In general, all equal transfers from persons with incomes of y_i to persons with incomes of $y_i - h$ are weighted the same.

Because of the squaring involved in calculating V, the effect of extremely high incomes can have a disproportionately great impact upon C. If one is interested in inequality due to extremes of wealth, C may be an acceptable measure. But interest in extremes of poverty would probably not be well served by C, since low incomes carry a small weight in the measure.

Other measures that are not based on assumptions about probability distributions or welfare functions include the mean deviation, equalization percentages, and mean differences, as well as several variations on the Gini coefficient. These are reviewed by Bartels (1977:16–35). For additional measures, refer to Theil (1967) and Herfindahl's index described by Cowell (1977:61).

Measures Based on Probability Distributions

It is well known that income distributions are skewed to the right and that the lognormal distribution often provides a convenient statistical "fit." If one can assume that incomes are lognormally distributed, then distributions can be compared by comparing the parameters of the distribution of the logs of income, that is, the mean, $\bar{Y}$, and variance, $\bar{V}$, where:

$$\bar{V} = \frac{1}{n} \sum_{i=1}^{n} [\log(\frac{y_i}{\bar{y}})]^2$$

The assumption of lognormality provides several useful characteristics in addition to an easily calculated measure of dispersion. The lognormal distribution itself possesses convenient statistical properties akin to those of the normal distribution (Aitchison and Brown, 1957). It can also be shown that certain random processes cause income distributions to become lognormal (Cowell, 1977:81, and Gibrat, 1957). Finally, in empirical work, the lognormal distribution usually fits data reasonably well. Indeed, no theoretical distribution fits most income distributions perfectly, but portions of the upper end of income distributions are frequently well represented by the lognormal. The lower end is the most difficult part to represent with theoretical distributions, the lognormal included.

As a measure of inequality, $\bar{V}$ has several useful qualities. Transfers at high income levels have little effect on $\bar{V}$, since the process of taking logs shrinks relative proportions.

Conversely, transfers at low income levels have a large effect. Unlike C, $\bar{V}$ treats equal transfers differently, depending upon where in the distribution they occur. A transfer of $100 from someone with $1500 to someone with $1000 will reduce $\bar{V}$ by more than the same transfer from a person richer than $1500 to a person $500 poorer.[3] If the assumption of lognormality is appropriate, then use of $\bar{V}$ will always cause one distribution to appear unambiguously more equal than another. The use of $\bar{V}$ for comparative purposes carries the implicit assumption that Lorenz curves do not cross, or that if they do cross, it is not relevant in assessing the overall distribution. This latter property may prove bothersome if Lorenz curves do cross and if the analysis needs to determine how inequality changes affect various income groups.

Ultimately, the productive use of $\bar{V}$ depends on whether distributions being compared are truly lognormal. Tests in developed countries have demonstrated the appropriateness of the use of the lognormal there. But some claim (Oshima, 1970) that the same conditions do not often hold in LDCs. If comparisons are made on the basis of $\bar{V}$, and the distributions being compared are not lognormal, then the comparisons are largely arbitrary.

The use of the lognormal distribution is explained fully in Cowell (1977:77–78). The Pareto curve, generating measures of inequality for only upper income groups, is described in Cowell (1977: 88–98) and Bronfenbrenner (1971: 44–45).

Measures Based on Welfare Functions

Infrequently are economists and others interested in income per se. Rather, it is the social welfare level implied by income that attracts attention. Since welfare is usually not directly measurable, income is taken as a proxy. However, if a social welfare function is known or can be reasonably assumed, inequality measures are straightforwardly derived from the parameters relating income to welfare. These measures have explicit normative properties, since the welfare function specifies how income, equality, and justice are interrelated in determining human wellbeing. The advantage of this approach is that once the form of the social welfare function is agreed upon, the student of inequality need only know the strength of society's aversion to inequality in order to produce a set of statistics that compare different distributions based on social preference.

The most well known measure using a predetermined social welfare function as a basis is Atkinson's (1970). His measure centers on the concept of a uniform level of income y', which if equally distributed would yield the same social welfare as the actual distribution, given the actual mean income $\bar{y}$. In its simplest form, the measure is:

$$A = 1 - \frac{y'}{\bar{y}}$$

The trick to actual measurement comes in determining y'. Clearly y' will differ for different degrees of inequality aversion held by society. Thus, an income inequality aversion factor (E) plays a major role in Atkinson's work. He assumes that if an individual's income increases by a given percentage, regardless of the person's position in the distribution, his weight in total welfare declines by E percent (Cowell, 1977: 45). The higher the E, the more rapid the decline in welfare weights applied to increments in income. Using an example from Cowell (1977: 45–46), consider two individuals, one with five times the income of the other. Call them R and P, respectively. If $E = 0$, we

---

[3]Unfortunately, at very high incomes $\bar{V}$ can show the perverse result that a transfer from a richer to a poorer person can cause $\bar{V}$ to *increase* rather than decrease (Cowell, 1977, Appendix 163).

apply no differences in weight to a person's position in the income distribution, and we would agree to a transfer of $1 from R only if it increased the income of P by the same amount. If $E = 1$, total welfare would be unchanged if $5 were taken from R in order to raise P's income by $1. If $E = 2$, $25 from R would be equivalent to a $1 increase for P. In general, for this pair of individuals, in order to raise the income of P by $1 we are willing to tax R by $5^E. Thus, to determine y' we must know E, and for each value of E there will be a different value for y' and for A.

The advantages and disadvantages of this approach are clear. If agreement can be reached on inequality aversion, inequality measures that reflect social preferences can be calculated. This would be a vast improvement over measures that simply describe the data and leave an interpretation open. With measures based on social welfare, the interpretation is already done by the time inequality is measured.

The obvious disadvantage of the social welfare approach is that rarely will agreement be forthcoming. Indeed, from a policy-making point of view, *disagreement* on weights such as E is the rule, with few exceptions. Measures that rely on the exception are not likely to be of much use in the formulation of public policy. They are of great use in academic quarters, however, for they force us to specify clearly what it is that income will tell us about welfare once we have measured the former.

Atkinson's is not the only formulation of an inequality measure based on social welfare. Dalton (1920) made an attempt similar to Atkinson's sixty years ago. Aigner and Heins (1967a, b) and Champernowne (1974) have made headway more recently. These efforts are compared by Bartels (1977) and Cowell (1977).

In summary, the uses to which the analysis is to be put determines the best inequality measure to use. The properties of different measures have been compared in several papers (see Champernowne, 1974, and Cowell, 1977). Interested readers will want to follow up on these before embarking on empirical work.

BIBLIOGRAPHY

Adelman, I. and Morris, C. T., 1973:
    Economic Growth and Social Equity in Developing Countries, Stanford, Stanford University Press.
Ahluwalia, M. S., 1976:
    "Inequality, Poverty and Development," *Journal of Development Economics*, Vol. 3, pp. 307–42, September.
Aigner, D. J. and Heins, A. J., 1967a:
    "On the Determinants of Income Inequality," *American Economic Review*, Vol. 57, 175–84.
Aigner, D. J. and Heins, A. J., 1967b:
    "A Social Welfare View of Measurement of Income Inequality," *Review of Income and Wealth*, 13, 12–25.
Aitchison, J. and Brown, J. A. C., 1957:
    The Lognormal Distribution, Cambridge, Cambridge University Press.
Atkinson, A. B., 1970:
    "On the Measurement of Inequality," *Journal of Economic Theory*, Vol. 2, pp. 244–63.
Bartels, C. P. A., 1977:
    Economic Aspects of Regional Welfare, Income Distribution and Unemployment, Leiden, Martinus Nijhoff.

Bentzel, R., 1970:
"The Social Significance of Income Distribution Statistics," *Review of Income and Wealth*, 16:3, pp. 253–64, September.

Bronfenbrenner, M., 1971:
Income Distribution Theory, Chicago, Aldine.

Champernowne, D. G., 1974:
"A Comparison of Measures of Inequality of Income Distributions," *Economic Journal*, 84:336, December, 787–816.

Chenery, H., et. al., 1974:
Redistribution With Growth, London, Oxford University Press.

Cowell, F. A., 1977:
Measuring Inequality, New York, John Wiley and Son.

Dalton, H., 1920:
"The Measurement of the Inequality of Incomes," *Economic Journal*, 30, pp. 348–61.

Dich, J. S., 1970:
"On the Possibility of Measuring the Distribution of Personal Income," *Review of Income and Wealth*, 16:3, pp. 265–72, September.

Fair, R. C., 1971:
"The Optimal Distribution of Income," *Quarterly Journal of Economics*, 85:4, pp. 551–79, November.

Ferguson, R. H., 1976:
"Some Techniques for Analyses of Income Distribution," Cornell University, Mimeo.

Gibrat, R., 1957:
"On Economic Inequality," *International Economic Papers*.

Gini, C., 1912:
Variabilita e Mulabilita, Bologna.

Hackenberg, R., 1977:
"Exports, Entrepreneurs and Equity," in Loehr and Powelson, eds., *Economic Development, Poverty and Income Distribution*, Boulder, Colo., Westview Press.

Jain, S., 1975:
Size Distribution of Income: Compilation of Data, Baltimore, Md., Johns Hopkins University Press.

Kuznets, S., 1963:
"Quantitative Aspects of the Economic Growth of Nations: Distribution of Income by Size," *Economic Development and Cultural Change*, 11:2, Part II, pp. 1–79, January.

Lorenz, M. O., 1905:
"Methods for Measuring Concentration of Wealth," *Journal of the American Statistical Association*, Vol. 9.

Morgan, J., 1962:
"The Anatomy of Income Distribution," *Review of Economics and Statistics*, 44:3, pp. 270–83, August.

Nordhaus, William D., and Tobin, James, 1973:
"Is Growth Obsolete?" from Moss, Milton, ed., *The Measurement of Economic and Social Performance*, Studies of Income and Wealth, Vol. 38, New York, National Bureau of Economic Research.

Oshima, H. T., 1970:
"Income Inequality and Economic Growth: The Post War Experience of Asian Countries," *Malayan Economic Review*, 15:2, pp. 7–41, October.

Oshima, H. T., 1962:
"The International Comparison of Size Distributions of Family Incomes with Special Reference to Asia," *Review of Economics and Statistics*, 44:4, pp. 439–45, November.

Paglin, M., 1975:
"The Measurement and Trend of Inequality: A Basic Revision," *American Economic Review*, 65:4, pp. 598–609, September.

Roberti, P., 1974:

"Income Distribution: A Time Series and Cross-Section Study," *Economic Journal*, 84:335, pp. 629–38, September.

Robinson, S., 1976:

"A Note on the U-Hypothesis Relating Income Inequality and Economic Development," *American Economic Review*, 66:3, pp. 437–40, June.

Stark, T., 1972:

"A Digression on the Statistical Measures of Inequality," *The Distribution of Personal Income in the United Kingdom 1949–1963*, Cambridge, Cambridge University Press.

Stoikov, V., 1975:

"How Misleading Are Income Distributions?" *Review of Income and Wealth*, 21:2, pp. 239–50, June.

Swamy, S., 1967:

"Structural Changes and the Distribution of Income by Size: The Case of India," *Review of Income and Wealth*, 13:2, pp. 155–73, June.

Theil, H., 1967:

Economics and Information Theory, Amsterdam, North Holland Publishing, Co.

Weisskoff, T., 1970:

"Income Distribution and Economic Growth in Puerto Rico, Argentina and Mexico," *Review of Income and Wealth*, 16:4, December.

6

INCOME DISTRIBUTION WITH DEVELOPMENT

To suppose that income distribution worsens with economic growth implies both that we know when growth begins and that income distribution was not askew earlier. We question both these assumptions.
THE AUTHORS

Does the very process of economic growth bring about increased inequality in income? Many recent studies have "shown" that it does (Adelman and Morris, 1973; Chenery et al., 1974; Kuznets, 1963; Paukert, 1973; and Roberti, 1974). In particular, these studies promote the proposition that the poorest segments of an LDC society may be hurt by economic growth.

In this chapter we review the major studies of growth and distribution and conclude that, on the contrary, no powerful statements can be made based on them. Then we examine a set of countries where distributional data are available at two points in time. These data give no support to the belief that as countries grow economically, the poor become poorer, either relatively or absolutely. Indeed, it would appear that growth and alleviation of poverty are not at all incompatible with each other.

THE HYPOTHESIS

The hypothesis of the inverted U—that inequality first increases, then declines with growth—has come to be widely accepted. It is supported by the propositions of Chapter 5, that inequalities widen because of rural-urban migration and population increase. But it is based on cross-section studies, and therein, we believe, lies its difficulty. We question whether the inverted U can be demonstrated by time-series analysis.

International comparisons of income distributions in LDCs began in earnest in the early 1960s, only 15 years or so behind the earliest studies on MDCs. Kravis (1960) compared income distribution cross-nationally and sought reasons why inequality appeared greater in LDCs than in MDCs. Oshima (1962) examined several LDCs, seeking explanations for the differing degrees of inequality among them.

Most of our early insights, however, were provided by Kuznets (1963); the other studies of the day tended to agree with him. But his data base was not precise. He referred (p. 12) to "synthetic estimates" rather than to precise readings, in which the ingenuity of the researcher adjusts for data deficiencies. He generated usable data on sixteen countries, nine of them LDCs. In classifying before-tax family income by quintiles, he made the following observations:

1. The income shares of the highest income groups in LDCs are significantly greater than the shares of the same groups in MDCs. This finding is consistent with that of Kravis (1960), who compared income distribution in ten countries with that of the United States. The top decile of families in LDCs, Kuznets found, received about 40–45 percent of the income (average 43 percent), while the same group in MDCs received about 30–35 percent (average 32 percent). Any bias is likely to be along lines that would understate the incomes of the upper decile in LDCs, because of a reluctance of upper-income persons to report their incomes accurately, for fear of taxes.
2. The shares of the lowest quintiles are about the same in MDCs and LDCs. The poorest 60 percent of families in MDCs received about 29–33 percent of the income, while in LDCs they received 25–32 percent. The poorest quintile received about 5 percent of the income in both types of countries.
3. It follows from (1) and (2) that there is greater equity in the middle-range incomes in LDCs than in MDCs, in the sense that the Lorenz curve would appear straighter for them in those areas. (If the curve takes a sharp swing upward at the end for LDCs, it must be relatively straighter in the middle.) Indeed, the entire scale is characterized by a fairly even distribution of income up to, but not including, the upper 5 or 10 percent of families. This would mean that middle-income groups are not much better off than lower-income groups. In MDCs, by contrast, the inequality starts much lower down and therefore does not become quite so extreme as in LDCs.

Kuznets believed his findings were caused by a greater concentration of property income and "participation" income among upper groups in LDCs. The former refers to income from interest, dividends, and rent, and the latter to the distribution of product and income among industries (participation of agriculture, participation of manufacturing, and so on). Property income would be more concentrated because fewer people save and because LDCs do not have the equalizing effects of tax legislation and mobility found in MDCs. Also, monopoly power is more easily maintained in LDCs, with their fragmented markets, than in MDCs. Kuznets observed greater differences in participation income in LDCs than in MDCs, particularly between agriculture and nonagriculture. He attributed these partly to differences in technology and partly to institutional forces (such as inputs and credit more easily available to nonagriculture).

Kuznets' findings on participation income are consistent with those of Oshima (1962), who showed that income distribution peaks at a lower level in agriculture than in nonagriculture (that is, the modal income is lower). Thus the form of the combined distribution, for the country as a whole, would be affected by the preponderance of agriculture in the economy.

All of these early works—Kuznets, Kravis, and Oshima—opened the way toward "blaming" income inequality on dualism. In Oshima's words (p. 442), "the major determinant of the dispersion of quintile shares between countries is the weight of the farm or rural sector in the total economy." Furthermore, within both the rural and urban sectors, inequality is largely influenced by the dispersion of assets—landholdings for rural and capital per worker for urban. The explanation that sharp dualism is associated with sharp income inequality will appear time and again in the literature.

In addition to these three studies (Kuznets, Kravis, and Oshima), done in the early 1960s, studies from the early 1970s gave support to the hypothesis of the inverted U. Paukert (1973) examined inequality data on 56 countries ranked in order of 1965 income per capita, lowest to highest. He found a sharp increase in inequality, measured by the Gini index, moving from the lowest per capita GDP countries to those in the $300–$500 range. As higher per capita income levels were approached, inequality became progressively less. All other major studies involving more than just a country or two (Adelman and Morris, 1973; Chenery et al., 1974; and Roberti, 1974) are similar to Paukert's, in that they rely on cross-section data and cannot be carried across time due to data limitations. They also reach similar conclusions about the inverted U.

Scattered evidence on individual countries, or comparisons of a few countries, have shown that those experiencing rapid rates of economic growth often suffer from increasing inequality. Fishlow (1972) and Wells (1974) point to the increasing inequality that accompanied rapid growth in Brazil in the late 1960s, and Arndt (1975) finds similar trends in Indonesia. Chenery et al. (1974) witnessed these trends in several countries; Weisskoff (1970) saw them in Argentina, Mexico, and Puerto Rico. Swamy (1967) observed them in India, though this case was not so clear cut (Kumar, 1974). Exceptions were found in South Korea and Taiwan, where both growth and movement toward income equity proceed apace (Ranis, 1977a, 1977b).

The inference drawn from most of these cross-section studies is that countries begin the development process with a population that is homogeneously poor. As development begins, a few people are able to seize upon new opportunities. Incomes increase for them, while the majority remain in the traditional state. Thus inequality increases as growth proceeds. As higher levels are reached, more and more find opportunities to leave the traditional sector and enter new activities; they raise their incomes and contribute to further growth. As the proportion of such sectoral migrants increases, inequality increases until those in the traditional sector become a minority. Thereafter, growth is accompanied by decreasing inequality.

But cross-sectional data have their pitfalls. The inverted U hypothesis must be interpreted *across countries* only. It does *not* say that as a poor country moves up the income scale it will become the way more developed countries are now. Only time-series data can do that.

Failure to appreciate this difficulty has led to misleading impressions. Adelman and Morris (1973:189) reach the "disturbing implication . . . that development is accompanied by an absolute as well as a relative decline in the average income of the very poor." Their analysis-of-variance technique groups cross-sections of countries by growth rates. Postulating that countries shift from low-growth status, where the share of the poor is high (in cross-section), to high-growth status, where shares of the poor are low, does not mean that those countries that shift instantaneously take on all the characteristics of the group of countries they have just joined (Cline, 1975:376–7). It is unfortunate that the Adelman and Morris statement has received so much uncritical reference in the development literature, especially when elsewhere in their otherwise excellent study, statistically significant relationships between incomes of the poor and growth were not found (Appendix C. 220–5). Other studies have shown that when data on absolute incomes of the poor were available, they did not correlate well with growth (Ahluwalia, 1974:14), and when different cross-sectional groups are examined, the share of the poor may or may not correlate well with per capita income levels.

DOES INCOME FLOW TO THE MIDDLE?

Some researchers have suggested that as growth proceeds, the shares of the richest *and* the poorest decline, in favor of those in the middle. In such a case, no generalization can be made of the Gini, which might increase, decrease, or remain the same. In studying six MDCs (Finland, the Netherlands, Norway, Sweden, the U.S., and the U.K.) in the post-war period, Roberti (1974) found that a time series of income shares showed:

1. Deciles below the mean income generally had higher probabilities of reducing their income shares than those above the mean.
2. Except for the top decile, all deciles above the mean gained or at least maintained their income share.
3. The top decile lost more than any other group. This erosion of the top decile's share, however, did not cause an accrual of income in the lowest deciles, but rather in the middle groups.

In an attempt to check upon the generality of his findings, Roberti examined the relationship between decile income shares and the level of GDP per capita for a sample of 24 MDCs and LDCs for which cross-sectional data are available. In general, GDP per capita is negatively related to both the top and bottom deciles' shares, positively related to the shares of the fourth through eighth deciles, and not related at all to the shares of the second and ninth deciles. Income would therefore tend to flow from both ends into the middle.

Roberti's findings are consistent with those of Berry (1974), in his study of Colombia. Since the requisite time series do not exist for Colombia, it was necessary to infer distributional changes from data on wages for groups of workers, together with information on occupational structure over time. Overall, from 1934/1935 to 1964 both the top decile and the lowest deciles experienced a slight reduction in their income shares. Meanwhile, gains accrued to the two deciles just below the top. Overall income distribution in Colombia became increasingly unequal from 1934/1935 until the mid-1950s, whereupon it improved somewhat, corresponding to the increasing share of income accruing to nonagricultural workers. The idea presented by Adelman-Morris (1973, 1974) that some poorer groups suffer an absolute deterioration in real income as growth proceeds receives some support from Berry's data. For example, real agricultural wages were below their 1935 level for almost the entire 1935 to 1964 period. Overall, however, there is little or no evidence that major income groups have suffered decreasing absolute incomes over substantial periods (Berry and Urrutia, 1976: 118–120).

A CROSS-SECTION AT TWO POINTS IN TIME

Time-series data on income distribution over many years do not exist for any developing country. For only two points in time, however, they have been compiled in Jain (1975). From her data, we have chosen (Table 6–1) all LDCs (non-Eastern European)[1] for which the initial and terminal years were based on the same income-recipient group. Where we had a choice of more than one group, we selected households. Moreover, in ten cases the data originate from the same or comparable sources.

The distributions for Bangladesh, Colombia, Taiwan, Peru, and Costa Rica are not from the same source for both years, and thus the comparability may be questioned. However, these data appear to be consistent with other available data in both magnitude and direction of change.[2] In the cases of Bangladesh, Pakistan, South Korea, and El Salvador, only very short periods (two to three years) are referred to, because comparable data for longer periods are not available. Normally such short-run changes would not be considered significant, since measurement errors or small transitory changes could account for re-

---

[1] Jain does present comparable data on Eastern European countries for two points in time. These were not considered here because their socialist characteristics tend to promote growth and equity in different ways from the more market-oriented countries examined here (Cromwell, 1977).

[2] Alamgir (1975) presents data for Bangladesh that show trends similar to the one we show here. For Colombia, other data listed in Jain (1975:24) indicate a similar increase in inequality, provided the same base is used (also see Berry, 1974). The trend toward greater equality in Taiwan has been noted by other writers (Ranis, 1977). In Peru, the deterioration in the share of the poorest groups, despite a slight tendency toward greater overall equity as seen in our data, has been noted by Webb (1977:42 and 94). Costa Rica is generally felt to be experiencing greater equality (Loehr, 1978).

TABLE 6-1
Inequality and Growth at Two Points in Time for 15 LDCs

	GDP Per Capita 1970 (U.S. $)[a]	Years for Which Ginis are Available		Gini		Share of the Poorest 20%		Share of the Richest 10%		Real Growth Rate in GDP Per Capita 1960–1970 (%)
		1	2	Year 1	Year 2	Year 1	Year 2	Year 1	Year 2	
Bangladesh[b]	89	1963	1966	.37	.34	6.9	7.9	28.7	26.7	1.2
India	92	1954	1964	.42	.47	7.0	5.5	34.9	38.9	1.5
Sri Lanka	93	1963	1973	.47	.35	4.5	7.3	36.9	28.0	2.2
Pakistan	151	1968	1970	.34	.33	8.2	8.4	27.3	26.3	3.4
South Korea	229	1968	1971	.30	.27	8.6	9.9	24.2	23.3	6.2
Philippines	230	1961	1971	.51	.49	4.2	3.9	40.3	37.1	1.0
El Salvador	290	1966	1969	.54	.47	3.2	3.7	41.3	33.0	2.6
Colombia[b]	320	1962	1970	.48	.56	5.8	3.5	39.2	44.1	1.9
Malaysia	347	1957	1970	.44	.52	5.8	3.8	34.8	41.1	2.8[c]
Taiwan[b]	348	1964	1972	.33	.28	7.8	8.8	26.1	22.4	6.2
Brazil	393	1960	1970	.60	.64	0.8	1.1	45.0	50.3	3.0
Peru[b]	423	1961	1970	.61	.59	2.6	1.8	49.6	45.1	2.3
Cost Rica[b]	508	1961	1971	.52	.44	5.7	5.4	44.0	34.2	2.8
Mexico	613	1963	1968	.58	.61	4.4	3.7	49.0	51.7	3.4
Panama	699	1960	1970	.50	.45	5.0	4.1	41.1	33.1	4.8

[a]At 1967–1969 average prices and exchange rates

[b]Gini indices not calculated by the same source

[c]For the period 1961–1970

SOURCE: GDP data are from World Tables 1976, published for the IBRD by Johns Hopkins Press, Baltimore. Reprinted by permission of the World Bank.

ported differences. In each case, however, the trends indicated by these short time-spans are consistent with other data reported in Jain and elsehwere.[3] Given other reports on these countries, we are confident that the data here represent at least the correct direction of change if not the precise magnitude.

One can easily verify that the cross-section of the 15 LDCs is consistent with other cross-sectional data sets in which comparative levels of inequality and GDP per capita have been examined. The Gini for the second time period is directly related to GDP per capita in 1970. In Figure 6-1 we have plotted these variables and drawn in the simple regression line relating the Gini index to GDP per capita. The regression equation:

$$\text{Gini} = .36 + .0003(\text{GDP per capita}) \quad R^2 = .22$$
$$(t = 1.93)$$

exhibits a positive slope, significantly nonzero at the .05 level.

In the LDC cross-section, inequality generally increases as one moves from low-income to higher-income countries. The share of the poor tends to decline throughout, and that of the rich tends to increase. The share of the poorest 20 percent of income recipients (hereinafter called "the poor") in the poorest LDCs (Bangladesh, India, Sri Lanka, and Pakistan) tends to be about 7 or 8 percent, whereas it ranges down to less than 3 percent in some of the richest LDCs (Brazil and Peru). The richest 10 percent of income recipients in the high-income LDCs receive about 35 to 50 percent of the total income, while in the poorest countries their share is around 30 percent. Thus, if viewed as a cross-section, this group of 15 LDCs is consistent with other cross-sections and conforms very well to the lower end of the inverted U.

Nevertheless, the full inverted U hypothesis cannot be tested with the data employed here. While the distributions for the LDCs do conform to the lower end of the inverted U, and those of MDCs to the upper end,[4] there is such a wide income gap between the richest and poorest countries that one would have to use considerable imagination to see a smooth decline in Gini indices for countries that might fill that gap. For example, if MDCs were placed on Figure 6–1 along with LDCs, the figure would be six pages wide with two blank pages between Panama and the United Kingdom. Furthermore, within MDCs, no correlation can be observed between inequality and GDP per capita, regardless of whether we look at shares of income groups or Gini indices. If there is something about the different GDP per capita levels that affects inequality among LDCs, the same forces are apparently not at work in MDCs.

The implication from other cross-section studies that growth implies increased inequality does not stand the test of time. For each of the countries examined, we calculated the change per year of the Gini and the income shares of the various groups. We then searched for correlations between these annual

---

[3]See Alamgir (1975) on Bangladesh and Pakistan and Ranis (1977b) on South Korea. Jain (1975:82–83) reports on several additional sources that indicate a slight egalitarian trend in Pakistan.

[4]Comparable data are available from Jain (1975) on inequality in 12 MDCs at two points in time.

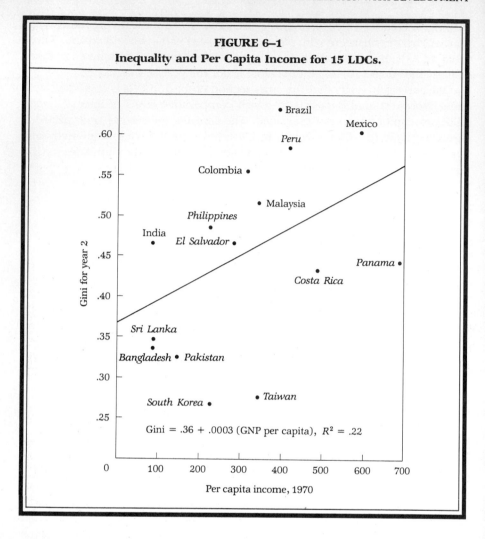

FIGURE 6–1

Inequality and Per Capita Income for 15 LDCs.

changes and GDP per capita growth rates. No statistically significant relationship was found between changes in the Gini coefficients and economic growth, nor between changes in the shares of the rich and growth. A mild relationship was found between growth and the share of the poor in LDCs, but this was *positive* rather than the negative one that most cross-section studies would lead one to expect.

In sum, there is no direct evidence that countries that grow rapidly are worse off in terms of equity than those growing slowly at a given level of development. Growth should be thought of as moving countries through different phases of development and inequality, without generating inequality in and of itself. The idea that as poor countries grow they will take on the distributional characteristics of the countries that are now richer must be put to rest.

A country-by-country examination of the data in Table 6–1 reveals the wide variety of experience found among developing countries. Among the 15 LDCs,

10 show falling Gini indices. While a declining Gini normally implies a larger share of income for the poor, in this case four countries—the Philippines, Peru, Costa Rica, and Panama—show decreasing shares for the poor under these circumstances. In fact, Peru's declining Gini accompanies a reduced share for the poorest 50 percent of income recipients, reflecting a decreasing inequality due to redistributions away from both the very rich and the poor and into upper middle income groups. Sri Lanka and Bangladesh also show lower income shares for the poorest 50 percent despite less inequality overall. Apparently this is a result of redistribution to the very poor from all other income groups, including those that are one step above the most extreme poverty. Conversely, Brazil shows an increasing share for the poor despite a rising Gini index. Clearly, one must carefully examine both aggregate measures and percentile shares to obtain an accurate idea of the changes.

While a simple cross-section of the countries shown here is consistent with the increasing inequity part of the inverted U hypothesis, the changes in inequality over time are not. The U hypothesis states that as a poor country reaches higher levels of GDP per capita, it will begin to show greater income inequality. In Figure 6–1 we have italicized those LDCs in our sample that are experiencing decreasing inequality. Among the seven countries below $300 per capita, only one, India, conforms to the U hypothesis: that is, it is moving from its current point upward to the right. All remaining countries contradict the hypothesis, since for them higher GDP per capita is associated with lower levels of overall inequality. Their movements would eventually bring them below the regression line.[5]

Among the higher-income LDCs (those above $300), four of the countries show increasing inequality and four show decreasing inequality. The former group is moving in a direction that will eventually place them above the regression line. The combined effect over time of the different movements in inequality as we see it here would be to cause a steepening of the line in future cross-section studies. It is perhaps this steepening that has recently given rise to the notion that growth causes inequality. As we have seen, however, the experience with inequality is varied and tends to appear differently in different settings. Furthermore, even when income distribution worsens, the poor do not necessarily suffer absolutely. They might still be better off if growth offsets the reduction in their income share.

The data in Table 6–1 refer only to income shares, not to absolute levels. To offer some measure of the latter, we have constructed an "income index" of the poorest 20 percent of the population by multiplying their share of income by the real GDP for each time period and dividing the result by 20 percent of the total population. This index appears in Columns 5 and 6 of Table 6–2. The annual rates of growth in the index are shown in Column 7.

---

[5]This argument remains unaffected even if we take a conservative course and assume that a change of a few points in the Gini index is not significant and that countries with such small changes can be considered to have unchanged inequality. This would affect Bangladesh, Pakistan, South Korea, the Philippines, Peru, and Mexico, where the Gini changed by .03 or less.

TABLE 6–2
Income Index for 15 LDCs

Countries	Years Covered 1	Years Covered 2	Population (thousands) year 1 (1)	Population (thousands) year 2 (2)	Total Real Income (millions of $)[a] year 1 (3)	Total Real Income (millions of $)[a] year 2 (4)	Income Index for the Poorest 20% year 1 (5)	Income Index for the Poorest 20% year 2 (6)	Annual Rate of Growth in Income Index (7)	Growth in per capita Income, year 1 to year 2 (8)
Bangladesh	1963	1966	58,400.0	63,300.0	4,750.4	5,477.9	28.1	34.2	6.8	2.1
India[b]	1954	1964	386,613.0	480,890.0	28,506.5	40,033.1	25.8	22.9	-1.2	1.2
Sri Lanka	1963	1973	10,582.0	13,522.2	814.9	1,231.2	16.9	33.2	7.0	1.7
Pakistan	1968	1970	58,510.0	62,640.0	8,056.1	9,486.3	56.4	63.6	6.2	4.9
South Korea	1968	1971	30,171.0	31,828.0	5,763.8	7,901.7	82.1	123.0	14.4	9.2
Philippines	1961	1971	28,175.0	37,919.0	5,990.1	9,110.4	44.6	46.8	0.5	1.2
El Salvador	1966	1969	3,012.0	3,324.0	828.1	940.8	44.0	52.4	6.0	1.0
Colombia	1962	1970	16,723.1	21,632.0	4,606.2	6,921.7	79.8	56.0	-4.3	1.9
Malaysia[c]	1961	1970	8,113.0	10,877.0	2,269.9	3,773.7	72.7	65.9	-1.1	2.4
Taiwan	1964	1972	12,070.0	15,130.0	2,857.5	6,256.0	92.3	181.9	8.8	7.2
Brazil	1960	1970	69,796.7	92,763.5	20,383.7	36,484.5	11.7	21.6	6.3	3.0
Peru	1961	1970	10,319.0	13,338.6	3,618.6	5,644.5	45.6	38.1	-2.0	2.1
Costa Rica	1961	1971	1,298.0	1,776.0	492.4	927.3	108.1	141.0	2.7	3.2
Mexico	1963	1968	39,871.0	47,267.0	18,707.3	27,340.8	103.2	107.0	0.7	4.3
Panama	1960	1970	1,096.6	1,434.4	465.6	1,001.7	106.4	143.2	3.0	5.1

[a]At 1967–1969 average prices and exchange rates

[b]Indian distribution data were for 1953–1955 and 1963–1965. Thus years for population and GDP are 1955 and 1965. Data for the 1955 GDP were not available in World Tables. However, the UN Yearbook of National Account Statistics 1968 reported that real growth in GDP for 1950–1960 was 3.5% per year, so GDP was estimated by extrapolating back to 1955 from the 1960 GDP level reported in World Tables 76.

[c]Malaysian data on GDP were available only for 1961; distribution data were for 1957–1970. The share of the poorest 20% declined from 5.8% of GDP in 1957 to 3.8% in 1970, so it was assumed that the decline was proportioned year to year and that the share of the poorest 20% was therefore 5.2% in 1961.

SOURCE: World Tables 1976 published for the World Bank by the Johns Hopkins University Press, Baltimore. Reprinted by permission of the World Bank.

The index does not represent per capita income within the income group, nor does it allow cross-section comparisons of absolute income levels. But the growth rate of the index may be a crude approximation of the rate at which per capita income is growing for the lowest 20 percent. The data are based on several different criteria, though they are always the same for a given country. Nine of the sets of data are based on household surveys, three cover economically active populations, two cover income recipients, and the remaining one covers the total population. Also, GDP is not entirely distributed as income to the groups mentioned. Major items such as depreciation and indirect taxes must be removed from the GDP before an adequate estimate of income can be made.

The income index is based on two assumptions. First, the proportion of GDP received as income by each group remains constant from one time period to the next, for each country. Second, the relationship between number of households, income recipients, and economically active people remains the same vis-à-vis the total population. These assumptions appear to be justified, in that the national income accounts for these countries, for years approximately the same as those listed for years 1 and 2, do not reveal any major changes in the proportional relationship bewteen GDP and other relevant variables. Similarly, household size and the proportion of economically active persons does not appear to have changed in relative terms. "Income recipient" is not normally reported in statistical sources and depends on the definition of the census takers. Where income recipient is the basis for the distributional data (India and Panama), the sources are the same, and therefore the likelihood of a consistent definition is high. Whether or not the proportion of income recipients within the total population has remained constant cannot be determined here.

The income index of Table 6–2 only evaluates the way income has changed between two points in time, given the above assumptions. It is in the category of "stylized facts" that Ahluwalia (1976) considers necessary to pursue analyses of income distribution, given inadequate data. It represents both factors necessary to make inferences about the absolute incomes of the poor—the size of the total income available and the share of that income accruing to the income groups in question.

Column 7 indicates that among the 15 countries, in only four have incomes of the poorest 20 percent failed to increase. India, Colombia, Malaysia, and Peru all suffer sharp declines in the shares of the poor, combined with rather sluggish economic growth. In Peru, there has been a slight movement toward greater overall equity, as measured by the Gini index, resulting from a redistribution in favor of the middle class.[6]

Our findings on the incomes of the poor in Colombia and Malaysia are consistent with those of Berry (1974) and Lee (1977), respectively. Both attribute declining incomes of the very poor to adverse shifts in internal terms of trade and to structural changes that excluded the poor from participating in economic development. Swamy's (1967) analysis of the Indian experience is also consistent. He shows that over roughly the same time period (1950–1960 compared to our 1954–1964), traditional agricultural productivity and income declined

---

[6]This is consistent with the evidence presented by Webb (1977).

slightly, and the income gap between the agricultural and nonagricultural sectors widened considerably.

Reductions in aggregate equity do not always signal a deterioration in the incomes of the poor. In Mexico, a noticeable rise in the Gini index and decline in the share of the poor seem to have been offset (barely) by the relatively rapid growth of the economy. Brazil's overall inequality worsened during the 1960s but not at the expense of the poor. As the Brazilian economy grew, the poor increased their share considerably, permitting them an income growth rate of more than twice the national average.[7]

The question asked most frequently is: Does growth help or hurt the poor? A simple regression of the growth rate in our income index for the poor, against the growth rate in per capita income for the two years indicated, is:

$$\text{Growth in the index} = -.975 + 1.35(\text{growth per capita income}) \quad R^2 = .42$$
$$(t = 3.07)[8]$$

Apparently growth is not harmful to the poor, as has been implied by some of the earlier literature. The countries in our group that are growing most rapidly, say 3.0 percent per year or better, all show a rise in the income index of the poor. For four of the seven countries in this situation (Pakistan, South Korea, Taiwan, and Brazil), the rise in the incomes of the poor exceeds that of the population at large. Three countries in the rapidly-growing category (Costa Rica, Mexico, and Panama) have experienced declining income shares for the poor. Growth has nevertheless offset those declines, allowing the poor to experience increased absolute income. Mexican poor seem to be barely holding their own, with an annual growth rate of only 0.7 percent in the income index, despite a very respectable growth of 4.3 percent in GDP per capita.

Experience among the more slowly-growing countries (under 2.5 percent per year) is more varied. The income index for the poor declined in four— India, Colombia, Malaysia, and Peru—with the sharpest decline (−4.3 percent per year) in Colombia. In Bangladesh, Sri Lanka, and El Salvador, the poor seem to have experienced considerable growth in their absolute incomes despite relatively slow growth overall. The data for El Salvador might be distorted, since year 2 for that country, 1969, is the one in which the "soccer war"[9] with Honduras occurred. Had it not been for that encounter, the overall growth rate for El Salvador would doubtless have been much higher. Sri Lanka is one of the few LDCs that has taken positive steps to raise the incomes of the poor even at the expense of growth (Loehr, 1978, and Lee, 1977).

These data are only rough indicators of what is likely to be happening to income levels within income groups. Nevertheless, the clear impression is that

---

[7]These conclusions, and our calculations, are similar to those of Fields (1977). He puts the growth of the poor at 5 percent per year, compared to our 6.3 percent. His figure is lower because his "poor" group comprises about 35 percent of the population, as opposed to our 20 percent.

[8]Statistically significant at less than the .025 level.

[9]A war which erupted over a soccer game, although its underlying causes were deeper.

there is a positive relationship between growth and absolute incomes of the poor.

Even the rather pessimistic assumption that the inverted U does hold over time for countries in a cross section below the turning point ($600 per capita, 1975) does not lead to the conclusion that growth injures the poor in any absolute sense. Ahluwalia, Carter, and Chenery (1979), as part of their work for the World Bank, have simulated absolute incomes of the poor for a sample of 36 countries on the assumption that the shares of income of various income groups in each country change over time in the same way they do in cross section. That is, each country is assumed to move parallel to the inverted U. Poverty is defined in terms of a specific dollar income,[10] and policies of growth and redistribution are compared as tools to reduce poverty. Projecting to the year 2000, they showed that an accelerated growth of 1 percent above the historical trend for each country had about the same effect on the number of persons below the poverty line as did a policy of redistribution of income.[11] The Ahluwalia, Carter, and Chenery study can be taken as a sort of lower estimate of the effect of growth on poverty, since it assumes that the inverted U holds for all LDCs despite the appearance of several countries in their sample where the reverse is actually the case. While their study is much too aggregate to devise policy for any specific country, it illustrates the dual nature of growth and redistribution and the powerful effect that both together can have on absolute poverty—even under pessimistic assumptions.

THE CORRELATES OF INEQUALITY

Empirical literature on income distribution in LDCs repeatedly homes in on given sets of explanatory variables. While the same ones do not all appear in all studies, there is enough overlap so that several areas for policy intervention can be identified. We will examine these factors more thoroughly later on, but let us take a quick look at them here.

Economic dualism, cited by early analysts and emphasized by Adelman and Morris (1973; 1974), occurs because growth begins in a narrow, modern sector. This sector is often oriented around an abundant natural resource or some specialized economic activity. Lewis (1954) described this kind of origin, and others (Kelly, Williamson, and Cheetham, 1972, and Paauw and Fei, 1973) described the process of dualism. The income share for the poorest 60 percent

---

[10]The poverty line was set at $200 PPP (Kravis) dollars per person. This corresponds to the income level of the 45th income percentile in India.

[11]The redistribution policy was one which assumed that 45 percent of the increment in GNP accrues to the bottom 60 percent of the population. This is higher than the proportion of GNP increment accruing to the poorest 60 percent of the population in Taiwan, Yugoslavia, and South Korea, the countries that have achieved the most enviable records of sustained growth and income redistribution in recent years. In these countries, between 30 and 40 percent of GNP growth has accrued to the poorest 60 percent of the population.

of the population declines sharply, while that of the top 5 percent increases (Adelman and Morris, 1973: 178). Apparently these changes are due to the enclave nature of many early growth efforts, which involve only a small part of the population. This effect wanes as higher development levels are reached and growth becomes more broadly based.

Dualism per se is normally not a policy variable, but a condition to be affected by policies in such areas as employment, technology, land tenure, and so on. Rather than discussing dualism specifically, we will usually turn to variables that affect it. Some of these will be policies to stimulate labor-intensive production, for both home consumption and exports. Other variables in this category are removal of market imperfections in credit, marketing and technological diffusion, and agrarian reform.

The concept of dualism plays a central role in the remainder of this book. Three broad economic forces play such a large role in the dualism theory that they are given separate chapters in part III. These are employment, technology, and agrarian reform.

Dualism aside, factors that affect income distribution may be placed into four broad categories: (1) *human resources*, (2) *population growth*, (3) *intersectoral shifts*, and (4) *public policy*.

(1) *Human resources* (Chapter 10) are a focus with high potential payoffs. Many studies have shown that basic education (either primary education or literacy) is related positively to the shares of the lowest income groups and that higher-level education (secondary education) has a similar effect on middle incomes (Adelman and Morris, 1973, and Ahluwalia, 1976). The upgrading of skills, combined with economic growth that is labor- and skill-intensive, will likely lead to greater equity. Presumably a shift from unskilled, low-paid labor to skilled, high-paid labor leads to both a reduction in wage differentials and an increase in the share of wages in total output (Ahluwalia, 1976: 21). Reliance on skill-intensive, high-employment industrialization has allowed South Korea and Taiwan to achieve increasingly equitable income distributions while growing rapidly.

Unlike other forms of capital, human capital is less prone to concentration. If income distribution is functionally related to capital concentration, then reliance on human capital rather than other forms is likely to stimulate greater equity. This is likely for several reasons (Ahluwalia, 1976):

(a) Unlike physical capital, an expansion of the amount of human capital involves dispersing the investment over a wide cross-section of the population.
(b) Whereas concentration of physical capital in a few hands is possible, there is a limit to the human capital that can be embodied in one person.
(c) Human capital cannot be bequeathed across generations.

(2) *Population growth* (Chapter 9) appears to be positively related to income inequality, but its role is so poorly understood that no strong statements can be made about it. Paglin (1975) has explained how population growth

rates can have a significant impact upon income distribution. Although he analyzed the U.S. economy, his work has relevance to the recent history of LDCs, as was mentioned in the preceding chapter. A wide-ranging set of variables related to population growth can also be expected to have some indirect influence on income distribution (Sirageldin, 1975). These generally have to do with the interaction of demographic variables with changing social and institutional forces or with changes in the labor force, aggregate savings, and so forth. Ahluwalia (1976) finds a significant inverse relationship between rate of population increase and the share of the poorest 40 percent of income recipients in LDCs. In a limited sample, we have also observed that improvements in equity were preceded by reductions in population growth rates (Loehr, 1978), while increases in inequality were not.

The lesson is clear for LDCs. Many have felt the medical revolution only recently, and population growth rates are high. In countries where population growth rates have recently accelerated, or where they are still accelerating, we should expect inequality to be increasing. In countries that have recently reduced population growth rates, we expect (and in South Korea and Taiwan we find) increasing equity. Changes in population growth rates can be felt only with a considerable lag, since it will take years for the children who are born today to become low-paid workers, sometime around the turn of the century.

(3) *Intersectoral shifts* accompanying economic development were recognized by Kuznets (1963) and Oshima (1970) as being cause for expecting increased inequality, as we have noted earlier in this chapter. Generally, rapid growth proceeds in a dualistic fashion, such that growth in the industrial sector (where inequality tends to be greater) is more rapid than growth in the agricultural sector (Adelman and Morris, 1973). In addition, rapid population growth and rural-to-urban migration occur. These factors alone are enough to ensure that, *ceteris paribus*, income distribution will become more unequal overall. Some attention will be paid to the relevance of migration to the inverted U-shaped relationship between economic growth and income inequality in Chapter 12.

If rural-to-urban migration is motivated by the expectation of higher wages in urban areas (Harris and Todaro, 1970, and Todaro, 1969), and if dualism creates even the perception of an income gap between the two, then migration, dualism, and income distribution are tightly linked (Chapter 12). Refinements of the expected income-gap model (Fields, 1975b, and Yap 1976) have led us to a greater understanding of the migration process, but much work remains to be done in devising policies that will creatively link migration and income distribution. Work with aggregate data (Ahluwalia, 1976:17) has already directed our attention to the significant statistical relationships between intersectoral shifts in economic activity and changes in income distribution.

(4) *Public policy* (Chapter 14) can have a direct impact on inequality. Most measures, however, are not designed specifically for any given effect on distribution. Rather, they are normally directed toward foreign trade, inflation, and other problems of priority interest to policymakers.

Studies of public policy and distribution fall into two very general categories. First, and by far the most often studied, is the effect of the fiscal system on distribution. Analyses of this type abound for almost all MDCs, and methods for delving into tax/expenditure incidence are well developed (Meiszkowski, 1969, and Blinder *et al.*, 1974). Second are the studies on the distributional impact of specific public programs, such as those in education, agriculture, and construction.

Studies of fiscal systems in LDCs generally show that these systems can be used to exert favorable redistributive pressures. Snodgrass (1974) indicates that progressivity within the Malaysian fiscal system has increased noticeably since 1958. McLure (1975) indicates that the fiscal system of Colombia exhibits mild progressivity overall. On the whole, surveys of general tax/expenditure incidence in LDCs (deWulf, 1974) indicate that the benefits received by upper-income groups are a smaller proportion of their incomes than are those received by low-income groups. Both conceptual and methodological problems, however, throw serious doubt on the adequacy of these studies in determining whether or not public policy is "pro-poor." Usually what is measured is the amount of public expenditure on, for example, teachers and irrigation projects, rather than the value of the education to those being taught and the marginal value of agricultural products to farmers. Since the recipients of public benefits at the low end of the income scale rarely have any say in what the quantity or quality of services to them will be, we cannot say that their evaluation of the services will correspond to that of public officials.

Many public expenditures provide public goods and services that make it difficult to evaluate the incidence of benefits. There are no generally accepted ways of allocating benefits, so assumptions about their value must be used only as rules of thumb. Some assume that all persons benefit equally (since they consume equally); others assume that benefits are received in proportion to income or wealth or that benefits are valued in some impressionistic way. The proportion of public goods in most government budgets is large, and the assumptions as to how benefits are to be assigned largely determine the outcomes of benefit-distribution studies (deWulf, 1974: 22).

Students of tax/expenditure incidence are further thwarted by poor quality data. The excellent study of Krzyzaniak and Ozmucur (1972) is a good illustration. Their analysis of the incidence of taxes in Turkey resulted in estimates of tax burdens for 35 income categories and demonstrated that, under varying assumptions, Turkish taxes overall are probably proportional. However, the number of adjustments that were needed to make the data comparable, and to force them into a format that allowed a study of this type, introduces the possibility of a wide range of errors.

Studies of specific public policies generally show that benefits to lower-income recipients amount to a larger portion of their incomes than do benefits to higher-income people. Studies cited by deWulf (1974: 23), however, indicate that because of prior extreme inequality, the absolute benefits to upper-income groups are far in excess of those accruing to the poor. Colombian data on education, for example, show that the lowest-income classes receive benefits equivalent to 13.1 percent of their incomes and that the highest-income group receives as little as 0.8 percent. But when measured in absolute terms, the latter group receives over six times the educational benefit to the poor. Fields' (1975a) study of higher education in Kenya indicates that there is a "systematic process operating against the poor," tending to perpetuate inequities.

Stabilization policies seem to have been associated with sharply increased inequality. Arndt (1975) has analyzed the stabilization and growth policies of post-Sukarno Indonesia (after 1966). With per capita income growing at a rapid 4% per year, ever-larger shares were accruing to only the upper-income groups. While the poorest-income groups lost part of their relative shares, it is Arndt's judgment that they were at least holding their own in absolute terms. The severe stabilization program in Brazil, begun in 1964, also resulted in rapid economic growth and a deterioration in economic equity (Wells, 1974). The data presented by Wells (1974, Table 8) indicate that the poorest decile of the working population could not possibly have been holding its own on an absolute scale, since its relative share dropped by over 40 percent. Informal reports from Chile are that current trends (1980) are mostly along Brazilian lines. Unfortunately, the cases cited present such a mixture of economic and political confusion that few clear economic forces can be observed.

Where data permit, simulation exercises help determine the impact of specific programs on income distribution. Weisskoff's (1973) study of growth in Puerto Rico, in which he plotted the path of employment and income distribution, probably could not be done in many developing countries because of data limitations. Via simulation, Thirsk (1972) examines the Colombian policy of subsidizing the mechanization of agriculture. He sets forth the changes in income distribution that result from changes in relative prices of productive factors. He shows that withdrawing the subsidy improves income distribution (by increasing labor intensity and decreasing the income share of capital owners). Furthermore, it increases GDP through a more efficient allocation of resources.

Occasionally, reference will be made in the literature to policies designed to improve income distribution as part of overall development strategy. Development plans are replete with statements about combining distributional objectives with other development goals such as growth and export expansion. Often, however, no analytical framework ties distribution to other considerations. One cannot easily see whether or not the multiple objectives are consistent with one another, or—if there are trade-offs among them—what the trade-offs are. In the Chilean case, for example, Foxley and Muñoz (1974) indicate that the Allende government's objectives for 1970–76 of increasing economic growth and employment, plus reducing foreign indebtedness, were not consistent given internal savings propensities. Their evaluation could be applied more generally. "The way to promote a sustained redistribution effort must . . . make direct redistributive efforts compatible with the savings and investment efforts, and also with an increase in efficiency . . ." (Foxley and Muñoz, 1974:29).

Overall studies of specific policies or sets of policies usually do not single out the specific groups that benefit or pay the cost. It is insufficient merely to indicate income classes that will feel some impact, since each class consists of a variety of people with different behavioral patterns. More information on specific functional groups, such as small farmers, shopkeepers, skilled labor, or entrepreneurs, is needed. These often span several income categories. Nevertheless, all are tied into a set of economic activities that eventually determine what the overall income distribution will be. Since people in each of these groups operate in a slightly different economic area, their motivations and needs will differ. Therefore, studies must be designed to understand these specific needs so that policies can be derived to meet them effectively. We will return to this problem in Chapter 12.

CONCLUSION

Both research and theory on development and income distribution are embryonic. Any hypothesis on their relationship is still conjecture, and specific, parametric tests are not yet possible. Nevertheless, there has been a rushing flow of information over the past two decades, and the field is rapidly developing.

For those who must make decisions, and policy, it is necessary to form some opinion. Although unproved, the opinion must be based on the available empirical evidence. Other researchers have concluded that the gap between rich and poor is widening, at least relatively if not absolutely. The evidence we have reviewed in the present chapter, however, leads us to the belief that probably it is not doing either.

How can this be? Is it not "obvious" that development proceeds unevenly, and some people acquire its fruits before others, with a transitory imbalance as the result? That depends on the state of society when measurement begins. The development literature often refers to a "traditional society," with a romantic view of clanspeople and tribespeople living as happy families, with income relatively well distributed.

There is no doubt that the monetary value and the real value of the gap widen as development proceeds. If a society's income ranges from $100 to $1 million, then the richest earns $999,900 more than the poorest. If the range is from $100 to $1,000, the richest earns only $900 more. But *on a relative basis* (measured by the Gini or percentile distributions), the proposition of the inverted U depends on the assumption of relative equality in the "traditional" society. In Chapter 1, we have argued that while such a "traditional" society may have existed in Neolithic times, and while a few such scattered societies still exist, nevertheless gross inequality has been the experience of the preindustrial milennium for most of the world.

Whether the hypothesis of the inverted U stands or falls therefore depends on whether this already-great inequality becomes greater or less with growth. It appears to us that when the broad, historical perspective is studied, inequality becomes less, even progressively less as growth proceeds. In that sense, equitable distribution is not only compatible with growth, it depends on it.

BIBLIOGRAPHY

Adelman, I., and Morris, C. T., 1973:
   Economic Growth and Social Equity in Developing Countries, Stanford, Stanford University Press.
Adelman, I., and Morris, C. T., 1974:
   "Who Benefits from Economic Development?" in Organization for Economic Co-operation and Development, *Planning, Income Distribution, Private Foreign Investment*, pp. 49–82, Paris.
Ahluwalia, M. S., 1974:
   "Income Inequality: Some Dimensions of the Problem," in Chenery *et al*, 1974.
Ahluwalia, M. S., 1976:
   "Inequality, Poverty and Development," *Journal of Development Economics*, Vol. 3, No. 4.
Ahluwalia, M. S.; Carter, N. G.; and Chenery, H. B., 1979:
   "Growth and Poverty in Developing Countries," *Journal of Development Economics*, 6, pp. 299–341.
Alamgir, M., 1975:
   "Poverty, Inequality and Social Welfare: Measurement, Evidence and Policies," *Bangladesh Development Studies*, 3:2, pp. 153–80, April.
Arndt, H. W., 1975:
   "Development and Equality: The Indonesian Case," *World Development*, 3:2 and 3, pp. 77–90, February/March.
Berry, A., 1974:
   "Changing Income Distribution Under Development: Colombia," *Review of Income and Wealth*, 20:3, pp. 289–316, September.
Berry, A., and Urrutia, M., 1976:
   Income Distribution in Colombia, New Haven, Conn, Yale University Press.
Blinder, A. S., *et al.*, 1974:
   The Economics of Public Finance, Washington, The Brookings Institution.
Chenery, H., *et al.*, 1974:
   Redistribution With Growth, London, Oxford University Press.
Cline, W. R., 1975:
   "Distribution and Development: A Survey of Literature," *Journal of Development Economics*, 1:4, pp. 359–400, February.
Cromwell, J., 1977:
   "The Size Distribution of Income: An International Comparison," *Review of Income and Wealth*, 23:3, pp. 291–308, September.
de Wulf, L., 1974:
   "Do Public Expenditures Reduce Inequality?" *Finance and Development*, pp. 20–23, September.
Fields, G., 1975a:
   "Higher Education and Income Distribution in a Less Developed Country," *Oxford Economic Papers*, 27:2, pp. 245–59, July.
Fields, G., 1975b:
   "Rural-Urban Migration, Urban Unemployment and Underemployment and Job-Search Activity in LDCs," *Journal of Development Economics*, No. 2: pp. 165–187.
Fields, G. S., 1977:
   "Who Benefits from Economic Development? A Reexamination of Brazilian Growth in the 1960s," *American Economic Review*, 67:4, pp. 570–82, September.
Fishlow, A., 1972:
   "Brazilian Size Distribution of Income," *American Economic Review*, Vol. LXII No. 2, pp. 391–402, May.
Foxley, A., and Muñoz, O., 1974:
   "Income Redistribution, Economic Growth and Social Structure: The Case of Chile," *Oxford Bulletin of Economics and Statistics*, 36 (1), pp. 21–44.

Harris, J. R., and Todaro, M. P., 1970:
"Migration, Unemployment and Development: A Two Sector Analysis," *American Economic Review*, Vol. LIX, No. 1, pp. 126–142, March.

Jain, S., 1975:
Size Distribution of Income: Compilation of Data, Baltimore, Md., Johns Hopkins University Press.

Kelly, A.; Williamson, J. G., and Cheetham, R. J., 1972:
Dualistic Economic Development, Chicago, Ill., University of Chicago Press.

Kravis, I. B., 1960:
"International Differences in the Distribution of Income," *Review of Economics and Statistics*, Vol. XLII No. 4, pp. 408–416, November.

Kumar, D., 1974:
"Changes in Income Distribution and Poverty in India: A Review of the Literature," *World Development*, Vol. 2, pp. 31–41.

Kuznets, S., 1963:
"Quantitative Aspects of the Economic Growth of Nations: Distribution of Income by Size," *Economic Development and Cultural Change*, 11:2, Part II, pp. 1–79, January.

Krzyzaniak, M., and Ozmucur, S., 1972:
"The Distribution of Income and the Short Run Burden of Taxes in Turkey, 1968," Program of Development Studies, Rice University, Houston, Texas, Paper No. 28, p. 40, Fall.

Lee, E., 1977:
"Development and Income Distribution: A Case Study of Sri Lanka and Malaysia," *World Development*, 5:4, pp. 279–89.

Lewis, W. A., 1954:
"Economic Development with Unlimited Supplies of Labor," *The Manchester School*, May.

Loehr, W., 1977:
"Economic Underdevelopment and Income Distribution: A Survey of the Literature," in Loehr and Powelson, eds., *Economic Development, Poverty, and Income Distribution*, Boulder, Colo., Westview Press.

Loehr, W., 1978:
"Economic Growth, Policy and Income Distribution," in Kamrany, ed., *The New Economics of the Less Developed Countries*, Boulder, Colo., Westview Press.

McLure, Jr., C. E., 1975:
"The Incidence of Colombian Taxes: 1970," *Economic Development and Cultural Change*, 24:1, pp. 155–183, October.

Meiszkowski, P., 1969:
"Tax Incidence Theory: The Effects of Taxes on the Distribution of Income," *Journal of Economic Literature*, 7:4, pp. 1,103–124, December.

Oshima, H. T., 1970:
"Income Inequality and Economic Growth: The Postwar Experience of Asian Countries," *Malayan Economic Review*, XV (2), pp. 7–41, October.

Oshima, H. T., 1962:
"The International Comparison of Size Distribution of Family Incomes with Special Reference to Asia," *Review of Economics and Statistics*, Vol. XLIV, No. 4, pp. 439–445, November.

Paauw, D. S., and Fei, J. C. H., 1973:
The Transition in Open Dualistic Economies, New Haven, Conn., Yale University Press.

Paglin, M., 1975:
"the Measurement and Trend of Inequality: A Basic Revision," *American Economic Review*, 65:4, pp. 598–609, September.

Paukert, F., 1973:
"Income Distribution at Different Levels of Development: A Survey of Evidence," *International Labor Review*, 108: 2–3, pp. 97–126, August/September.

Ranis, G., 1977a:
"Growth and Distribution: Trade-Off or Complements," in Loehr and Powelson, eds., *Economic Development, Poverty and Income Distribution*, pp. 41–59, Boulder, Colo., Westview Press.

Ranis, G., 1977b:
"Development and the Distribution of Income: Some Counter-Evidence," *Challenge*, 20:4, pp. 55–56, September/October.

Roberti, P., 1974:
"Income Distribution: A Time-Series and a Cross-Section Study," *Economic Journal*, 84:335, pp. 629–638, September.

Sirageldin, I. A., 1975:
"The Demographic Aspects of Income Distribution," in W. C. Robinson, ed., *Population and Development Planning*, pp. 153–187, New York, the Population Council.

Snodgrass, D. R., 1974:
"The Fiscal System as an Income Redistributor in West Malaysia," *Public Finance*, 29:1, pp. 56–75.

Swamy, S., 1967:
"Structural Change in the Distribution of Income by Size: The Case of India," *Review of Income and Wealth*, 13:2, pp. 155–173, June.

Thirsk, Wayne R., 1972:
"Income Distribution, Efficiency and the Experience of Colombian Farm Mechanization," Program of Development Studies, Rice University, Houston, Texas, Paper No. 33, p. 54, Fall.

Todaro, M. P., 1969:
"A Model of Labor Migration and Urban Unemployment in Less Developed Countries," *American Economic Review*, Vol. LIX, No. 1, pp. 138–148, March.

Webb, R. C., 1977:
Government Policy and the Distribution of Income in Peru, 1963–73, Cambridge, Mass., Harvard University Press.

Weisskoff, R., 1970:
"Income Distribution and Economic Growth in Puerto Rico, Argentina and Mexico," *Review of Income and Wealth*, 16:4.

Wells, J., 1974:
"Distribution of Earnings, Growth and the Structure of Demand in Brazil during the 1960s," *World Development*, 2:1, pp. 9–24.

Yap, L., 1976:
"Internal Migration and Economic Development in Brazil," Quarterly Journal of Economics Vol. XL, No. 1, pp. 119–137, February.

FACTORS
OF
ECONOMIC
DEVELOPMENT

UNEMPLOYMENT

*. . . strategies pursued by most developing countries have not
produced the wide distribution of benefits some thought would
follow naturally from the attainment of reasonable rates of
growth. One of those benefits—the opportunity to earn a living—
has turned out to be particularly elusive to growing numbers
of people.*

EDWARDS (1974:1)

Mass unemployment has become so visible and so poignant in the cities
of less developed countries that economists and politicians cannot avoid
seeking its causes and its alleviation. Naturally, they wonder whether income
distribution would be improved if only the unemployed were put to work. This
euphoric hope, however, is fading almost as rapidly as it rose—not because
unemployment is so great but because it is so complex, so elusive in concept,
and so intertwined with more fundamental ills of development that it cannot
be leveraged as an individual problem. Furthermore, simple arithmetic tells us
that merely putting the unemployed to work, with wages equal to present
marginal productivity, would hardly put a dent in current inequitable distributions.

OPEN VERSUS DISGUISED UNEMPLOYMENT

Open unemployment refers to those persons who are seeking wage-employment in a business establishment, in a government office, or in personal service. They would work specific hours and receive specific pay. In most LDCs, the openly employed are a small minority of the work force. In Kenya, for example, only about 1 million hold such jobs, out of a population of about 12 million (*Economic Survey*, 1979:46), compared to approximately 5 million who are self-employed (or family-employed), in farms or handicraft or service activities.

The openly unemployed are found mostly in cities. Usually, they were not born there, but migrated from rural areas. We will return to their living conditions and their prospects in Chapter 12; for now let it suffice to say that their problem is serious. But to put them to work in government-financed jobs, such as occurred in the United States during the great depression, would only open the floodgates to more rural to urban migration, and the cost would explode far beyond the government's power to tax or to borrow.

The 1950s and 1960s saw a heated (and we now believe sterile) debate as to whether the rural poor were "underemployed." Models originating with Lewis (1954) aimed toward eventual elimination of unemployment by investing as rapidly as possible in the "modern sector," drawing "surplus labor" (with zero marginal productivity) from the traditional sector at an institutionally fixed wage, slightly above subsistence level. Profits, presumed to be mostly reinvested, would assume an ever-expanding share of total output. Whether or not it is accurate, the Lewis model nevertheless has had a major impact on development theory and policy. Policies based on it were hardly equity- or employment-oriented, for growth depended on continued unemployment and an increasing share for the owners of capital. One might even argue (Jarvis, 1974) that the unemployment and poor income distribution in LDCs has not been a result of policy failure, but rather of its outstanding success, in terms of Lewis' dualistic growth path!

A debate over whether or not there existed zero marginal productivity of rural labor centered around the zero. Some (Haberler, 1957, and Viner, 1957) argued that zero marginal productivity is nonsense, for it would imply that work is desirable over leisure. Others would rejoin that work indeed has a social and personal value per se, for unemployment is demoralizing, and that therefore people work even when marginal productivity is zero. The debate cooled with the realization that the border between zero and low marginal productivity is both vague and uninteresting. *Low* productivity is the real problem, to which attention should be shifted.

In a strict sense, zero marginal productivity does not apply to the present case anyway. The concept of marginal productivity relates to a given technology and therefore to a given production function. Once technology is changed, a different function is implied. The withdrawal of a single person from a family farm, with no change in output, implies that the others are doing something differently; hence it is a different technology. It is the picayunity of this point, we believe, that makes the debate sterile.

The problem becomes more acute because of the difficulty in specifying who is employed and who is not in a preindustrial, rural society (Ndegwa and Powelson, 1973:2). Not only does everyone appear to be doing something, but the delineation between production and consumption is not clear. A woman works the half acre behind her hut, brings the produce into the kitchen hut where she cooks it, then assembles her family to eat it. All these activities keep life going, and the persons concerned may not see them separately as production and consumption. In an extended-family or tribal setting, work and incomes are shared, in ways that are traditionally determined. Work (if it could be defined) does not necessarily relate to income, and the very concept of employment as an income determinant becomes meaningless. Unemployment has been called a luxury (Myrdal, 1968), available only to those who can afford it. We are tempted to say—but do not go quite that far—that employment and income distribution are concepts that arose out of Western, industrialized societies, and that completely different concepts need to be defined for the problems of rural societies in LDCs.

Whatever the reasons or the concepts, the arena has shifted away from unemployment as such, and toward the causes of low productivity among the rural and urban poor. The International Labor Organization (ILO), with its series of studies on unemployment in LDCs, has been a major force in this intellectual shift. Other international agencies, including the World Bank and the Food and Agriculture Organization, as well as national foreign aid programs and the Ford Foundation (Edwards, 1974), have affected the new direction.

Table 7–1 provides some idea of magnitude. It includes ILO estimates of open unemployment and underemployment, both total and urban, among major world areas of LDCs. Total unemployment in LDCs would appear to be

---

TABLE 7–1.
Estimates of Unemployment and Underemployment in Developing Countries by Region, 1975
(in millions)

Region	Unemployment				Underemployment				Total			
	TOTAL		URBAN		TOTAL		URBAN		TOTAL		URBAN	
	NO.	%	NO.	%	NO.	%	NO.	%	NO.	%	NO.	%
Asia[a]	18	3.9	6	6.9	168	36.4	20	23.2	186	40.3	26	30.1
Africa	10	7.1	3	10.8	53	37.9	7	25.1	63	45.0	10	35.9
Latin America	5	5.1	5	6.5	28	28.9	14	22.8	33	34.0	19	29.3
Oceania	—	—	—	—	1	49.0	—	—	1	49.0	—	—
Total	33	4.7	14	8.0	250	35.7	41	23.3	283	40.4	55	31.3

[a]Excluding China and other centrally-planned economies.

SOURCE: ILO Bureau of Statistics, as reported in ILO, *Employment Growth and Basic Needs* (Geneva, 1976), p. 18.

no greater, as percentages of the labor force, than in MDCs. The percentages in urban areas are higher than the totals, because rural open unemployment is negligible. The actual percentages may be even higher than the ILO estimates, judging from the great visibility of unemployment in cities of LDCs—people sleeping in the parks, congregating in the markets, or walking the pavement. (Admittedly, however, unemployment is probably more visible in LDCs than in MDCs.) In addition, national estimates (on which ILO data must ultimately be based) are not highly reliable, and they tend to be underestimated for political reasons. To summarize, the ILO figures on open unemployment may well be too low, but they are the only overall data we have.

The measurement of underemployment is even more risky than that of open unemployment because of the conceptual difficulties mentioned before. When zero marginal productivity is taken as only the limiting extreme, then the number of persons who may be "removed" with negligible effect on output becomes confounded by a range of low marginal productivities, in which the dividing point between "low/zero" and "some" becomes obscured. However the ILO may have based its perceptions, underemployment (or low productivity) still affects a far greater percentage of the labor force than open unemployment, and it affects rural areas more heavily than urban. Total unemployment and underemployment for all LDCs is estimated at 40 percent of the labor force. Some specific urban areas show unemployment much higher than the ILO estimates—up to 10 or 20 percent, and even 40 percent among 15 to 24 year olds (Edwards, 1974).

Population increase compounds the problem. The LDC labor force grew by 1.6 percent per year during the 1950s, by 2.0 percent in the 1960s, and by 2.3 percent in the 1970s (Edwards, 1974). If the rate were frozen at the latter percentage (which it no doubt will not be), the labor force would double in 30 years.

UNEMPLOYMENT AND INCOME DISTRIBUTION

To put the openly unemployed to work would materially reduce absolute poverty. This would occur even if nothing were done for the flood of rural-to-urban migrants that would fill the newly-created vacuum. The ILO studies on various countries demonstrate this point persuasively. Despite this fact, *the national distribution of income would be little affected.*

Neoclassical economic theory sees a rise in employment occurring simultaneously with increased wage rates and a shift in income shares toward labor (for a survey, see Bronfenbrenner, 1971, or Johnson, 1973). In many LDCs, labor typically earns some 40 percent of the gross domestic product, compared to about 70 percent in MDCs. However, neoclassical theory depends on the relative scarcity of labor to achieve this result. Where labor is not scarce, the shift would not occur.

Indeed, the distribution of nonwage income primarily explains (statistically) the maldistribution of income in LDCs. McLure (1972) shows that in Panama, "property income is sufficiently large and sufficiently inequitably distributed to explain a large part of overall income distribution." The lowest third of wage-earners receives about 10 percent of the labor income, while the upper 10 percent receives about one third. Thus the remaining 57 percent of labor income goes to about 57 percent of the wage-earners (in the middle brackets). But the nonlabor income shares of the upper 2.2 percent of the population are as high as 44 percent, while the bottom 50 percent receives only 7 percent. Similar distributions were found by Webb (1972) for Peru, where the wealthiest 1 percent receives about 80 percent of property income but only 10 percent of labor income. Thus "a major share of property income accrues to a few hundred families" (p. 6). Since nonlabor income is usually a high percentage of the total (up to 40 percent of the national income in Panama), one should not expect a great change in inequality simply by putting more people to work (Jarvis, 1974).

Although empirical work is scanty, what there is of it would confirm this hypothesis. Weisskoff (1973) simulated 1963 levels of final demand in Puerto Rico as if 1953 technology (more labor-intensive) had been used. Total employment would have almost doubled over the period, instead of increasing by only 10 percent. But instead of improving, income distribution would merely have remained as it was in 1953 (Gini = .43). In actuality, distribution became more concentrated (1963 Gini = .47). Thorbecke and Sengupta (1972) simulated two potential paths of economic growth for Colombia to 1980, one more labor-intensive than the other. Assumptions of both high employment (3.3 percent increase per year) and low employment (2.8 percent) yielded the same income distribution.

These findings are consistent with those of Adelman and Morris (1973), who report that the distribution of income is more equitable in socialist countries than in capitalist. The reason is clearly that in socialist countries, property income does not accrue to the private sector. Outside of this fact, however, socialist LDCs have some of the same problems of open unemployment, underemployment, and low productivity as capitalist LDCs. We can therefore see the problem in its two faces. An increase in employment per se would not greatly improve distribution, while the abolition of property income, which would improve distribution, would not, per se, resolve unemployment and low productivity.

EMPLOYMENT VERSUS PRODUCTIVITY

In earlier chapters, we have stressed that the only way to improve income distribution permanently is to increase the productivity of the poor. Let us carry this point further. Within any country, income distribution depends on three basic categories:

(1) the income-earning capacity of each sector, which in turn depends on:
   (a) ownership of or access to productive assets
   (b) human capabilities
(2) the supply of public goods, and their distribution among sectors
(3) redistributions within the tax system

The roots of the income distribution problem lie in the first category, both (a) and (b), since these forces alone deal with the primary distribution of earned income. The other two categories constitute redistributions, or transfer payments, which are ephemeral or unreliable in most LDCs.

Within the first category, the subheadings—access to resources and human capabilities—are not clearly separate. Providing new assets to low-productivity people has often been the first policy response by economists to the problem of distribution. But it is more often suggested than implemented, and when implemented, the capacity of the poor to utilize such income-earning assets is often limited. In the chapter on rural development (Chapter 12), we will suggest that the most effective use of resources to ameliorate income distribution would be through increasing their availability to small-scale rural producers, both farm and nonfarm. But this provision would have to be accompanied by increased learning and an attitudinal change on the part of the poor, through which they would improve their management capabilities (Myrdal, 1968). The literature is rife with examples of assets that have been provided to the poor (agricultural credit, fertilizers, tools, small loans) and that were not used as intended. We thus link subheadings (a) and (b) of the first of the three categories enumerated above.

We will also argue (in Chapter 12) that access to resources does not depend on the magnanimity of others (such as a benevolent despot), but on (a) the capability of the poor to use existing financial institutions and (b) saving by the poor in conjunction with investment opportunities they perceive. Some of these activities can be economically undertaken only by cooperative, community action, but others can be achieved by the individual. Whichever the direction taken, they are all part of the human capabilities that must be combined to provide employment at higher levels of productivity.

Our purpose thus far has been to present the complexity of the unemployment problem. The references to other chapters (earlier and later) reflect its pervasive linkage to other development components. In sum, merely providing jobs for the openly unemployed is not enough. The problem, which is low productivity, permeates the rural as well as the nonmodern urban sector. In part it is one of resources, but even this is a minor element. The "solution"—if that is the appropriate word—lies in providing work opportunities *with increased productivity* potential. Our own studies (as well as those of others) lead us to the belief that saving in rural areas depends on perceived opportunities more than it does on the interest rate or level of income. When the opportunities are perceived, the saving is adequate to create the needed employment and incomes.

THE ELASTICITY OF EMPLOYMENT

Employment in LDCs is not increasing, percentagewise, as much as output. Overall, it is probably increasing by no more than the labor force itself (hence no reduction in unemployment), and in many countries by less (hence worsening unemployment). Edwards (1974) has provided data for Latin America (1960–1969) on the elasticity of employment with respect to output. These data are recapitulated in Table 7–2, which indicates that for such major sectors as agriculture, mining, manufacturing, and transport, each 1 percent increase in output is associated with an increase of .4 to .6 percent in employment.

The elasticity of 1.0 for miscellaneous services implies no increase in productivity. If 10 percent more people are employed, there is only an increase of 10 percent in output. Both the miscellaneous and unspecified sectors are largely residual. They are the source of employment for the millions who cannot otherwise find jobs and who are willing to do almost anything to stay alive. For want of unemployment insurance, the urban unemployed are often found here. They shine shoes, collect and sell discarded materials, run errands, hawk vegetables and clothing, or beg and steal. Hence it is difficult to distinguish them, statistically, from the unemployed. The elasticity of 1.1 in the unspecified sector implies even a decline in productivity, possibly because the urban unemployed engage in activities that are increasingly marginal.

By the same token, those sectors with an elasticity of less than unity reflect an increase in the productivity of labor. The reasons fall into two general classes. One is the improvement in management and labor capabilities, such that output increases in greater proportion than both labor and capital (that is, the productivity of *all* factors of production increases). The other is that more capital per worker may be supplied, such that the productivity of labor (but not necessarily of capital) increases. The former class reflects increased efficiency, and one can hardly fault it. The latter class, however, may reflect the displacement of labor by capital. We will return to this possibility in the following chapter

TABLE 7–2
Elasticities of Employment with Respect to Output in Latin America, 1960–1969

Sector	Elasticity: $\dfrac{\text{\% change in employment}}{\text{\% change in output}}$
Agriculture	0.4
Mining	0.5
Manufacturing	0.4
Construction	0.8
Transport and Public Utilities	0.6
Commerce and Finance	0.8
Miscellaneous Services	1.0
Unspecified (Services)	1.1
Aggregate Output	0.6

SOURCE: Edwards (1974), p. 15.

(on technology), where we raise the question of whether unemployment is exacerbated by the choice of "inappropriate" technology.

Whatever the cause of low elasticity, it supplies us with some interesting arithmetic. In recent years, the population and work force in Kenya have been increasing by a bit more than 3 percent per year (Government of Kenya, *Economic plan, 1974–78)*, while gross domestic product has increased by slightly over 7 percent. Increases in productivity of labor have kept employment from increasing by more than the labor force; hence there is zero net impact on the unemployment backlog. The Kenya data are not atypical of LDCs; in many countries, the net progress in reducing unemployment is simply zero.

The problem is more acute because in most countries, the urban labor force is increasing by more than the employment availabilities in the modern sector. A little arithmetic will simulate its magnitude. Suppose our objective is to absorb all such new labor into manufacturing, construction, and transport and public utilities, whose elasticity of employment with respect to output is (say) 0.6. It is not unreasonable to assume an urban labor force growing at 8 percent, where 3 percent is through natural growth and 5 percent is from migration from rural areas. Output in these sectors must expand by 13.3 percent if the increment in labor is to be accommodated. If we assume an incremental capital-output ratio of 4 and also assume that the three sectors contribute 30 percent of gross domestic product (both realistic approximations for LDCs), then investment of 16 percent of GDP is needed just to "stand still" on unemployment.

A few countries have achieved this percentage, but it is not general. Furthermore, our model does not take into account the increased rural-to-urban migration that would result from the increased investment, and it does not address rural employment problems. Clearly the problems of unemployment cannot be solved by simply expanding the activity of the "modern," urban sector using standard technology.

Morawetz (1974:491) confirmed this general conclusion in a survey of the implications of industrialization in LDCs. "A manufacturing sector employing 20 percent of the labor force would need to increase employment by 15 percent per year merely to absorb the increment in a total work force growing at an annual rate of 3 percent. The required rate of increase of manufacturing output is even greater than 15 percent if increases in labor productivity are taken into account." Out of 68 LDCs that he surveyed in Asia, Africa, and Latin America, in only eight did manufacturing account for more than 20 percent of the labor force and in only three did the growth rate in manufacturing exceed 15 percent per year. "In the light of these orders of magnitude," he concluded, "the contribution of the industrial sector to employment over the last decade has been disappointing in many developing economies" (p. 496).

Only through radical changes in technology, with far greater emphasis on employment than before, can there be any hope of alleviating the problem. Such changes could occur through the use of more labor-intensive methods in producing the same set of goods now demanded, or by changing the composition of goods now demanded to those whose production methods require more labor and relatively less capital, or by some combination of the two.

IS THERE AN EMPLOYMENT-OUTPUT TRADE-OFF?

Arithmetic and data such as the above have led some economists to question whether full employment is technologically consistent with maximum output. Neoclassical theory permits no such conflict, so long as labor and capital are substitutable and the market is free. The price of the unemployed factor (say, labor) will fall, causing it to replace the scarcer factor (say, capital). Provided aggregate demand is adequate (under Keynesian conditions), relative price movements will cause each factor to be fully employed.

This condition is demonstrated by the familiar Edgworth box diagram, which is reproduced for convenience in Figure 7–1(a). Those who wish an explanation are referred to any textbook in microeconomics (for example, Mansfield, 1979: 427–31). Position C, on the contract line, is more efficient than position A, because all labor and capital are employed. The relative prices of labor and capital are determined by the slopes of the two isoquants at their common point of tangency C. If we remove the assumption of factor substitutability and take the opposite extreme (zero elasticity of factor substitution), then unemployment is possible, as in Figure 7–1(b). The isoquants are now rectangular, and unless their tips happen to coincide (a rare condition), no unique contract curve is possible. Consider the amounts of production represented by isoquants ABC for product 1 and DEF for product 2. In this case B is the most efficient point for product 1 and E is most efficient for product 2, and GI labor is left unemployed. The labor-capital ratio is not affected by relative factor prices. A host of straight lines could be drawn through E, the slope of each representing a different relative price combination for capital and labor. For product 2 the labor-capital ratio is represented by the slope of the ray from the origin O_2 to the point of production E on isoquant DEF. The amount of unemployed labor for each combination of products 1 and 2 would be represented by the distance between the lines representing their labor-capital ratios. Only at point P do the corners of a pair of isoquants happen to meet, and only there is there full employment.

Let us consider three ways for production to change: by an increase in capital, by a change in technology, or by a shift in demand. An increase in capital increases the size of the box. In Figure 7–1(c) we represent this by an expansion in the horizontal direction by the amount O_2O_2'. The isoquant map for product 2 now emanates from O_2'. Continuing the assumption of zero factor substitutability, the points of maximum efficiency for product 2 for each level of production now fall along the ray $O_2'E'$, which represents the same labor-capital ratio as in the preceding example. Assuming that product 1 is unaffected, output for product 2 is expanded and unemployment is reduced. Production can now take place on isoquant $D'E'F$. This represents greater output than DEF since it is further from its origin (O_2') than DEF is from O_2. Unemployment is reduced to GI'.

A neutral technological improvement (unchanged labor-capital ratio) is represented by a general shift in the isoquant map back toward the origin; vertical or horizontal shifts occur depending on whether the innovation is labor- or capital-saving. If, for example, there is a labor-saving innovation in product 2,

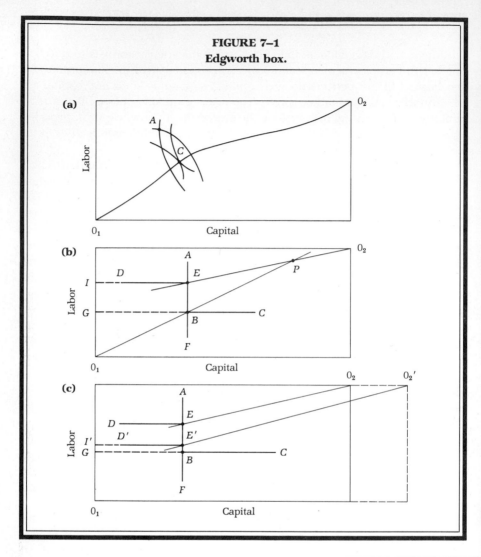

FIGURE 7–1
Edgworth box.

the same amount of output formerly represented by isoquant *DEF* may now be represented by isoquant *D'E'F* in Figure 7–1(d). If the output mix remains the same, unemployment is increased from *BE* to *BE'*. The labor-capital ratio for product 2 will drop and be represented by the slope of a line from O_2 to *E'* (not drawn). The distance between the rays O_2E' and O_1B increases, and therefore so does unemployment at any output combination.

Let us now consider different degrees of factor substitutability across industries. In the situation described by Figure 7–1(e), no factor substitutability is possible for product 1; therefore the labor-capital ratio is fixed along the ray O_1BB'. The industry that produces product 2 may be considered the "rest of the economy," where factor substitutability is possible and the isoquants are therefore of the "normal" shape. Let us assume that we are at *B*. Industry 2

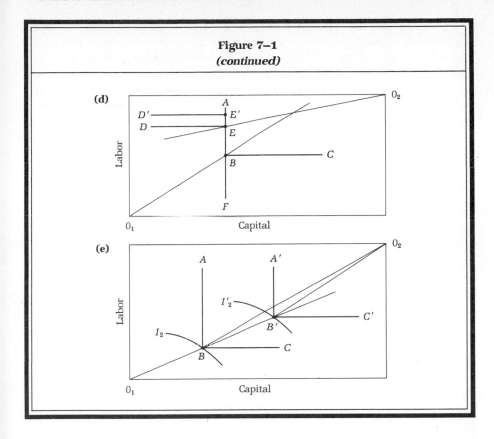

Figure 7–1
(continued)

(d)

(e)

is producing the output represented by isoquant I_2 with a labor-capital ratio represented by the slope of the ray O_2B. Assume now that there is an expansion in the production of 1 to isoquant $A'B'C'$ and that therefore there is a change in the product mix. Production of 1 expands and production of 2 contracts.

Several important points flow from this example. First, unemployment is not possible, since we have introduced at least one activity where labor-capital substitution is possible. Second, all the adjustment in the model is thrown off on to the activity where factor substitution is possible. For example, at point B the relative factor prices in industry 1 are indeterminate, but in industry 2 they are determined by the slope of I_2 at B. After a change of product mix to B', factor prices in activity 1 are still not observable, but the labor-capital ratio in industry 2 has risen, and the relative price of labor has declined. Third, we have drawn diagram 7–1(e) in such a way that industry 1 has a labor-capital ratio lower than that in the overall economy. This is sufficient to force industry 2 (the remainder of the economy) to be labor-intensive, no matter what the configuration of its "normally-shaped" isoquants. In general, any shift in demand or public policy favoring those items that are capital-intensive will intensify labor use in the rest of the economy and lower the rewards to labor relative to capital. Wages in the expanding industry may or may not decline, since labor use is not determined by relative factor prices over a broad range.

In sum, in the neoclassical model an increase in capital *must* bring about an increase in employment (regardless of factor substitutability), but a new technology may not do so if factors are not substitutable. It is the latter case that gives rise to a potential employment-output trade-off. Furthermore, if factor substitution is not the same everywhere, it is the sector or sectors where substitution is possible that bear the brunt of adjustment when the product mix changes. Increases in the production of goods with rigid factor proportions will cause relative changes in factor rewards and therefore changes in income distribution in other sectors.

Whether the nontrade-off situation of Figures 7–1(a) and 7–1(c) dominates the trade-off situation of Figure 7–1(d) is a matter for empirical investigation, on which we will report in the next chapter. Although recent microstudies show that the nontrade-off may be more common than the trade-off, nevertheless if there are particular products in high demand, where elasticity of substitition is low, then a trade-off may occur, or the nontrade-off may occur only with a shift in income distribution.

In a now-classical article on the "factor-proportions" problem, Eckaus (1955) pointed out that a seemingly labor-intensive method may in fact be more capital intensive when both working and fixed capital are taken into account. For example, the extra time required to complete a given product on a hand loom (seemingly labor intensive) may make it more capital intensive than a machine loom, since yarn is tied up. The case for no trade-off, on the other hand, is exemplified by "capital stretching," which occurs when the addition of laborers to given quantities of machinery increases output. Ranis (1973) shows how capital stretching played a significant role in the twentieth-century development of Japan, Taiwan, and South Korea.

If there is a trade-off between employment and output, there may also be a trade-off between present and future employment. The selection of increased output at any given time will imply the possibility of increased investment (if saving is a positive function of income); the increased investment may provide more employment opportunities in the future (if we still assume low elasticity of factor substitution). Those who argue for greater investment or greater present output on the basis of these possibilities should, however, take into account society's time preference (Stewart and Streeten, 1971). Discounting should apply to employment just as it does to output. It may be that the discounted value of more future employment is less than the value of the present employment with which it is compared.

Whether trade-off is possible, therefore, depends on factor substitutability and choice of product. If a society chooses to produce those goods for which labor and capital must be applied in fixed (or almost fixed) proportions, it is likely to run into the trade-off. If, on the other hand, it concentrates on those goods with high factor substitutability, then full employment is compatible with maximum output.

In a study of the petrochemical industry in Colombia, Morawetz (1975) demonstrated the high employment gains possible from a change in output composition. Between 1957 and 1965, over $100 million was invested in the Colombian petrochemical industry. Simultaneously, employment in that sector decreased by 290 persons. Comparing the investment in petrochemicals with investments that could have been made in the more labor-intensive clothing, footwear, and wooden furniture industries, one finds that the employment could have been directly expanded by 47,500 jobs—more than one-fifth of Colombian industrial employment! Indirectly, the $100 million in petrochemicals generated fewer than 1,000 jobs in related sectors. A similar investment in clothing, footwear, and wooden furniture would have indirectly created 102,000, 56,000, and 49,000 jobs, respectively, in related activities (Morawetz, 1975: 99–101).

Thus industry may have the dual disadvantage of being overly capital intensive compared to the alternatives and of possessing little possibility for factor substitution. Input prices may make little difference in determining the employment generated. Furthermore, there is much evidence that both traditional and nontraditional exports of LDCs tend to be labor intensive (Krueger, 1978, Watanabe, 1972, and Morawetz, 1974). In particular, Japan, Taiwan, South Korea, Hong Kong, and Singapore have promoted "outward oriented" (export-inducing) policies, as opposed to import substitution industrialization. These countries have been more successful than most LDCs in solving their unemployment problems. It would follow that virtually *any* LDC might alleviate unemployment if it would liberalize its trading and other policies, allow the rich to buy their luxury goods elsewhere, and promote production of traditional and export goods within its own territory. However, a tendency to rely too heavily on manufactured exports, with the possible neglect of traditional exports, is not likely to have much impact on employment. The manufacturing base in most LDCs is so small that the growth required to increase employment would be unrealistic for most LDCs (Tyler, 1976).

INCOME DISTRIBUTION AND EMPLOYMENT

Earlier, we showed that increased employment, per se, will not greatly alleviate the maldistribution of income. Let us now turn the question around. If income redistribution were to occur first (through, say, tax and fiscal measures), would employment be enhanced? Some have suggested that this would be so, simply because the poor consume more labor-intensive goods than the rich.

The few empirical studies available indicate that unemployment relief is not a likely outcome of income redistribution. Tokman (1974 and 1975) has investigated this point with considerable care in Ecuador, Peru, and Venezuela. He finds that the industrial goods likely to be in increased demand due to income redistribution are not the most labor intensive. Ballentine and Soligo (1978) examine the second-round effects of a redistribution of 10 percent of income from the richest 6 percent of the work force to the poorest 70 percent in Colombia. Through input-output analysis, the changes in demands of different income groups can be traced. The results indicate that ". . . not only is there no substantial shift in factor earnings toward the poor . . . but in fact the factor earnings of the rich rise more than those of the poor" (p. 701). This is due to a decline in labor income caused by a drop in employment. The most striking decline in employment was felt by nonagricultural wage earners, who derive 48 percent of their income from the sale of their services to the rich.

In assessing this evidence, considerable caution must be exercised, and a modified view of the trade-off between employment and output may be called for. The concept of aggregate output depends on prices. Apples and oranges can be added only if they are first weighted by their prices; the sum is the monetary value of fruit. If apples and oranges do not bear the same unit price, and we shift output from one to the other (keeping the total amount of fruit constant), we will change the aggregate monetary value, thus having "increased" or "decreased" our output. But the shift may not have much operational sense, if (for example) apples and oranges should provide equal nutrition or have other attractive features in common.

This applies to a shift in output from goods consumed by the rich to those consumed by the poor. Redistribution of income away from the rich causes the demand for goods consumed by the rich to decline and the demand for goods consumed by the poor to increase. Therefore, prices of "poor" goods will rise relative to those of "rich" goods. In assessing pre- and post-redistribution conditions, the set of prices used must become explicit, because it is entirely possible that the post-redistribution output can be shown to have risen or fallen depending on the set of prices used.

The concept of maximum output is unequivocal only when there is but one product. As soon as there are two or more, maximum output depends on the price weights assigned to each. The concept of increased output is unequivocal only when one or more products are increased and none is reduced. As soon as other combinations are admitted, the concept becomes ambiguous, as does the idea of a trade-off. No society, therefore, should be hesitant to change an output mix because the monetary value of the new may be less than that of the old. All social values should be examined, including the value of employment. If greater employment is considered a desirable object along with apples and oranges, then it becomes simply one of the products, and the concept of trade-off passes into further obscurity.

CONCLUSION

We have now discovered how deeply rooted the unemployment problem is. It cannot be solved simply by providing jobs for the openly unemployed. One-third of the total labor force in developing countries may be underemployed; most of these are in the agricultural sector. Therefore, to be of greatest benefit any program aimed at the employment problem will attack both open unemployment and underemployment. The roots of the problem extend to the kinds of technology selected and the composition of goods and services to be produced, imported, and exported. Thus, the problem impinges on the entire gamut of policies at the disposal of government.

Evidence indicates that a push for greater employment will probably have little effect on an income redistribution, and vice versa, all else being equal.

What is important is to consider other changes that could take place simultaneously and to try to capture a view of the interacting effects of all variables. For example, Tokman's (1975) study of Ecuador shows that an income redistribution *alone* will have only a mildly bouyant effect on employment. But if the redistribution is accompanied by technological change that promotes more labor-intensive methods, employment could rise by up to 18 percent. For maximum effect, attention must also be focused on channeling demand toward labor-intensive goods.

A trade-off between employment and output may make employment-oriented policies not only difficult, but unwise. Whether or not a trade-off exists remains an open question; both supporting and contradictory evidence can be found. The existence of a trade-off depends on the context. In some countries at some points in time, there may well be an output cost involved in employment programs. But there are enough counter examples to indicate that it is possible to devise programs that are both growth- and employment-oriented.

We have not said all that should be said about unemployment, for we cannot at this point. We must first assess the available shelf of technologies (Chapter 8), consider human potentials and education (Chapter 10), and evaluate alternative government policies (Chapter 14).

BIBLIOGRAPHY

Adelman, Irma and Morris, Cynthia Taft, 1973:
   Economic Growth and Social Equity in Developing Countries, Stanford University Press.
Ballentine, J. G. and Soligo, R., 1978:
   "Consumption and Earnings Patterns and Income Distribution," *Economic Development and Cultural Change*, 26:4 (July) 693–708.
Bronfenbrenner, M., 1971:
   Income Distribution Theory, (Chicago, Aldine Atherton).
Eckaus, Richard S., 1955:
   "The Factor Proportions Problem in Underdeveloped Areas," *American Economic Review*, September.
Edwards, E. O., ed., 1974:
   Employment in Developing Nations, Columbia University Press, New York.
Haberler, Gottfried, 1957:
   "Critical Observations on Some Current Notions in the Theory of Economic Development," *L'Industria*, November, No. 2, pp. 3–5.
Jarvis, L. S., 1974:
   "The Limited Value of Employment Policies for Income Inequality," in Edwards, ed., *op. cit.*, pp. 165–80.
Johnson, H. G., 1973:
   The Theory of Income Distribution, Gray-Mills Publishing, Ltd., London.
Kenya, Government of, 1974:
   Economic Plan, 1974–78, Nairobi.
Krueger, A. O., 1978:
   "Alternative Trade Strategies and Employment in LDCs," *American Economic Review* 68:2 (May) 270–74.

Lewis, W. A., 1954:
"Economic Development with Unlimited Supplies of Labor," *The Manchester School*, May.

Mansfield, E., 1979:
Micro-Economics: Theory and Applications, Third Edition, W. W. Norton Co.

McLure, Jr., L. E., 1972:
The Distribution of Income and Tax Incidence in Panama, 1969, Program of Development Studies, Paper No. 36, Rice University, Houston, Texas.

Mingo, J. J., 1974:
"Capital Importation and Sectoral Development: A Model Applied to Postwar Puerto Rico," American Economic Review, Vol. LXIV, No. 3, June.

Morawetz, D., 1974:
"Employment Implications of Industrialization in Developing Countries: A Survey," *Economic Journal* 84:335 (September).

Morawetz, D., 1975:
"Import Substitution, Employment and Foreign Exchange in Colombia: No Cheers for Petrochemicals," in Timmer *et. al. The Choice of Technology in Developing Countries*, Harvard University Press, Cambridge.

Myrdal, G., 1968:
Asian Drama: An Inquiry into the Poverty of Nations, Twentieth Century Fund, New York.

Ndegwa, Philip, and Powelson, John P., eds. 1973:
Employment in Africa: Some Critical Issues, Geneva, International Labor Office.

Ranis, Gustav, 1973:
"Industrial Sector Labor Absorption," *Economic Development and Cultural Change*, 21:3 (April), also Yale University Economic Growth Center, paper #193, New Haven.

Stewart, Frances and Streeten, P., 1971:
"Conflicts Between Output and Employment Objectives in Developing Countries," Oxford Economic Papers, 23:2, July.

Thorbecke, E. and Sengupta, J. K., 1972:
"A Consistency Framework for Employment, Output and Income Distribution Projections Applied to Colombia," Washington: IBRD.

Tokman, V. E., 1974:
"Distribution of Income, Technology and Employment: An Analysis of the Industrial Sectors of Ecuador, Peru, and Venezuela," *World Development*, Vol. 2.

Tokman, V. E., 1975:
"Income Distribution, Technology and Employment in Developing Countries: An Application to Ecuador," *Journal of Development Economics*, Vol. 2.

Tyler, W. G., 1976:
"Manufactured Exports and Employment Creation in Developing Countries: Some Empirical Evidence," *Economic Development and Cultural Change* 24:2 (January) 355–73.

Viner, Jacob, 1957:
"Some Reflections in the Concept of Disguised Unemployment," *Contribuicoes a Analise do Desenvolvimento Economico*, Libraria Agit Editora, Rio de Janiero.

Watanabe, S., 1972:
"Exports and Employment: The Case of the Republic of Korea," *International Labor Review* 106:6 (December).

Webb, R. C., 1972:
"The Distribution of Income in Peru," Research Program in Economic Development Discussion Paper No. 26, Princeton: Woodrow Wilson School.

Weisskoff, R., 1973:
"A Multi-Sector Simulation Model of Employment, Growth and Income Distribution in Puerto Rico," Economic Growth Center Discussion Paper No. 174, Yale University, New Haven.

8

TECHNOLOGY

*There is no more reason to consider capital a constraint on
economic growth than skilled labor, fertile land, or any other
factor of production. All are scarce, and the task is both to
increase them and to do the best with what we have. To presume
that technology somehow "explains" all growth not attributable to
factor increments is to supply one sweeping answer to the mystery
of growth. But the subject is not simple,
and the answer is not sweeping.*

THE AUTHORS

Even if full employment would not materially affect the distribution of
income, it is a worthy object in its own right. The unemployment problem
now leads us directly to technology. If more labor-intensive (as opposed to
capital-intensive) techniques were used in LDCs, would there be enough jobs
for all who want them? Why is there a tendency toward capital-intensive techniques, anyway?

Not only does unemployment lead us to technology, but almost every question
in economic development does also. Bruton (1967) compiled empirical evidence
from numerous studies on technology and concluded that an increased quantity
of physical inputs (capital and same-quality labor) rarely accounts for more
than half the increase in gross domestic product. Thurow (1971) reached a
similar conclusion. The remainder of the increase must be assigned to productivity increases, which take the form of better management capabilities or
new techniques of production.

We think of technology in two senses: *embodied* and *disembodied*. Embodied technical change occurs when new machines and processes, combining with other factors of production, raise the productivity of those factors. Disembodied progress, on the other hand, refers to the unexplained increment cited by Bruton, Thurow, and others. An entire set of potential forces and new processes promotes greater efficiency in the use of resources, such as more highly skilled labor, reorganization of plant layout, improved accounting for inventories and cash receipts, firmer labor discipline, and so on. The technology is disembodied in that one cannot point to a new machine or other visible input that causes the increased output. Disembodied technical progress is generally measured with some standard production function, such as the Cobb-Douglas or CES. The production function measures the output increments due to increased inputs; output in excess of this is due to disembodied technical change.

Technical change becomes so intermixed with fundamental forces of change that it is impossible to extricate it from the process of development itself. These fundamental forces include increased income (and thus greater demand for agricultural and industrial products), new investment deployed differently from before, urbanization, shifts in political power from a land-based aristocracy to an urban, manufacturing elite, a changing role of international trade, and more. Schiavo-Campo and Singer (1970) refer to the "virtuous circle" of technological change, which leads via increased demand to further improvements in technology.

Historical experience sheds light on the functioning of this virtuous circle. Rosenberg (1970) shows how changing consumer demand, and malleable public tastes, assisted the Anglo-American transition from handicraft to highly specialized machines. Postwar experiences of Japan and West Germany illustrate growth-induced technological progress (Caves and Uekusa, 1976, Dennison and Chung, 1976, and Patrick and Rosovsky, 1976). The exceptional productivity growth in Korea and Taiwan during the same period demonstrates how developing countries can benefit from technological change.

In the present chapter, we address six hotly-debated questions with respect to technology, as follows:

FIRST, to what extent are capital and labor interchangeable? How do we measure their interchangeability? If physical laws over which we have no power were to dictate no substitutability, then of course the matter would be ended. But we know they do not. However, we also know that there are some processes (such as throwing a man to the moon) that can be performed by machine and not by any number of laborers. So we must examine where, between the extremes, a unit may function.

SECOND, if—as we have suggested earlier—capital-intensive methods are now being used where labor-intensive methods would be possible, what is the reason? Are they "naturally" cheaper, or "artificially" cheaper? They are naturally cheaper if purely market forces rule in their favor. They are artificially cheaper if governmentally-induced price distortions cause their adoption. Are these alleged distortions caused (as some have suggested) by policies of import-substitution industrialization (ISI)? Or, are capital-intensive methods selected for reasons other than relative prices (such as bureaucratic or political reasons)?

THIRD, when answers to the first two questions are taken into account, how do we determine the "appropriate" technology for a given situation?

FOURTH, how is technology obtained? We assume that producers in LDCs do not need to "invent the wheel." If more advanced technology is available in MDCs, how can it be most readily transferred? Through direct purchase? Through multinational corporations? Through foreign aid programs?

FIFTH, is MDC technology too expensive? Many from LDCs argue that the marginal cost of technology is zero, because it is already possessed by foreigners who, they say, would lose nothing by giving it away. Therefore, world economic welfare would be maximized if it were transferred without charge. It is not free, they aver, only because it is held—through patents, secrets, or other restrictions—by monopolists. Is this indeed so?

SIXTH, to what extent is technology developed in MDCs applicable to LDCs anyway? MDC technology was developed in situations where labor is scarce and capital abundant. Is obsolete technology, perhaps forgotten in MDCs, now appropriate for LDCs? Alternatively, should appropriate technology for LDCs be sought through research and development (R & D) on the site?

DEFINITIONS

Before turning to these questions, we must set forth some definitions. First, a *technique* is a way of doing something, such as producing a good or service. It has many dimensions, both physical (engineering or architectural, for example) and economic. The former are spelled out in precise designs. The latter, derived from the former with the application of prices, can be described as the amounts and values of productive inputs. In the simplest case, with only two productive inputs, the technique could be represented by K/L, the capital-labor ratio.

As generally used in economic literature, *technology* is the entire set of techniques that are or may be used for a given output. Again for the simplest (capital-labor) case, alternative technologies may be represented by isoquants.

Stewart (1977:2) has criticized these definitions as being narrow. She has suggested, rather, that it is not appropriate to speak of the technology for a product, since the "product" is not primarily a good or a service but a way to satisfy a need. Where two goods could alternatively satisfy the same need, they become part of the technology, instead of the final product. She believes technology should be conceived with respect to need satisfaction and should be defined according to the following characteristics: product type, product nature, scale of production, material inputs, labor input (skilled and unskilled separately), managerial input, and investment requirements. A variation in any of these items would represent a change of technology.

We do not disagree with Stewart, for we see many ways of defining technology. Clearly, definition of the product should take place first—and the product may be either satisfaction of a need or a specified good or service. Once the product is defined, there are many ways in which the inputs may be specified. Stewart's "product type" and "product nature" can refer to any intermediate product needed as input for the final product, however it may have been defined. In the present chapter, we use a two-input model for convenience (because isoquants can be drawn). Whatever we say about the two-input model could be expanded to a multi-input model.

World technology, or the *technology shelf* (Stewart, 1977:21, and Ranis, 1973:392), consists of all technologies that have ever existed. Some have become obsolete for engineering reasons, such as when a new technology requires less of *all* inputs. Others are no longer used for economic reasons, which may occur, for example, if the cost of labor increases relative to the cost of capital. The former group are not optimal anywhere in the world, but the latter—now obsolete in MDCs—might be optimal in LDCs, where labor remains abundant and capital is scarce.

By the same token, innovations may be economically suboptimal because they are "before their time." For example, diesel locomotives were known in the nineteenth century, but they did not (as yet) replace steam locomotives because coal cost so much less than diesel fuel. Similarly, technology now used in MDCs may not yet be economically optimal in LDCs. Its use *anyway* (for reasons of prestige or politics), may be a cause of unemployment.

The term *intermediate technology* has been coined (Schumacher, 1974) to apply to all those techniques that have become economically unfeasible in MDCs but may still be feasible in LDCs because of their abundance of labor and scarcity of capital. It may also include technology newly-invented through R & D in LDCs, which is adapted to these same conditions (labor abundance and capital shortage). While we honor the thought behind this term, we do not use it because it seems to imply universality, in that some technology is considered "advanced," regardless of time and place, and other technology is "less advanced." This distinction should apply only to technology that has been rendered obsolete for engineering rather than economic reasons. We therefore prefer the term *appropriate* technology, which may imply a time/space differential. What is appropriate in one time or place may not be appropriate in another.

Appropriate technology is simply efficient technology. It is the set of techniques that minimizes the social cost of pursuing objectives. It may (if one wishes) be further narrowed to socially-approved objectives. The term "social cost" implies that some costs may be paid by someone other than the producer. For example, a highway may have been built by the government, from which a private farmer takes benefit. The amortization and maintenance of that highway must be taken into account in the social cost of the farmer's output.

In specifying appropriate technology, one must value social costs at their *shadow prices*. A shadow price is one that reflects the true relative scarcity of a factor of production. It would be the market price in a perfectly competitive and free market. In many cases, however, the market price is distorted by private monopolies, government price controls, or other restrictions or taxes. Often the assessment of a shadow price is a matter of judgment, in which honest differences of opinion are possible.

For analyzing the unemployment problem, we need a measure of *labor-*

intensiveness. This concept is elusive, and it is defined in different ways by different authors. We will use the simplest definition, that of the ratio of labor to capital *(L/K)*. *Capital-intensiveness* is therefore the inverse ratio *(K/L)*. Bhalla (1975:19) has pointed out that this definition "leaves out of account efficiency considerations which are better examined through input-output coefficients, for example, labor-output ratios *(L/O)*, capital-output ratios *(K/O)*, or the share of wages in value added." Some have used the capital-output ratio as a measure of capital-intensiveness; for example, industries with high capital-output ratios would be deemed more capital-intensive than those with low ratios. Such a definition appears to us inappropriate for two reasons. One is that it says nothing about other factors of production, such as the amount of labor used. The other is that the capital-output ratio is measured over time and therefore reports the result of other changes, including utilization of plant capacity (which may vary with demand), improved methods with no change of capital stock, or extension or contraction of working hours.

The term "labor-intensiveness" makes no sense except by comparison. No technology is labor-intensive or capital-intensive per se. Rather, one technology can only be more labor-intensive than another, if *L/K* for the former exceeds *L/K* for the latter. By extension, a product may be more labor-intensive than another if its production technology requires a higher *L/K* than does that of the other.

Labor-capital ratios (and their inverses) must also be interpreted with caution. Variations in their empirical measurements can be caused by variations in capacity utilization across industries. Both *K* and *L* are normally taken as homogeneous inputs when the ratio is specified; in fact, they are heterogeneous. Skilled labor is a form of human capital, but investment in education is normally measured as an increase in *L* and not in *K*. Bhalla (1964) has even shown that an industry or technique could be both capital- and labor-intensive, compared to a second industry or technique, if one measurement is made by the capital-labor ratio and another by the capital-output ratio.[1] In sum, there is no pure indicator of labor-intensiveness.[2] But policy decisions on technology must be made, and a working definition is therefore needed.

THE CHOICE OF TECHNOLOGY

Many technologies in LDCs have not been appropriate. The literature is rife with examples of choices that are not efficient by private calculations, let alone social. Pickett *et al.* (1974) found that the sugar and footwear industries in

---

[1]With constant returns to scale, K/L and K/O can be expected to rise together. With increasing costs, firms farther out along a ray from the origin of an isoquant map have the same K/L as firms closer to the origin, but they have a lower K/O. Therefore, the firms farther out will appear less capital-intensive because of the scale of production, not because labor is more intensively used.

[2]Bhalla's (1975) rankings of industries in Brazil and Mexico use four indices of labor intensiveness: L/O, K/O, K/L, and the wage share in value added. The ranking order of industries differs, often considerably, according to the measure chosen.

Ghana and Ethiopia would have shown improved private and social benefit/cost ratios had less capital-intensive techniques been chosen. Morawetz (1975) showed that the technology chosen for petrochemicals in Colombia fared worse than available alternatives in employment creation, foreign exchange earnings, international cost competitiveness, and linkages with the rest of the economy. Wells (1975) studied 43 industrial plants in Indonesia in six different industries. He compared their technologies with labor-intensive alternatives and concluded that:

> At any reasonable set of capital costs that a firm in Indonesia might face, the economics of the situation point to the conclusion that the choice of capital-intensive technology requires an investment per worker saved that is far beyond that which would be consistent with the actual wages paid . . . In spite of the fact that the capital costs involved in the capital-intensive technology generally far exceeded any possible wage savings, such investments were frequent and were being contemplated by many firms now using less automated techniques (pp. 76–77).

Further examples have been cited by other authors (for example, Cooper and Kaplinsky, 1975, and Stewart, 1977).

In standard microeconomic theory, differences in technique are viewed as responses to differences in the relative prices of productive factors. In Figure 8–1, for example, with only two productive inputs of homogeneous capital and labor, the technique chosen to produce a given quantity of output, represented by the isoquant II, depends on the price of capital relative to the price of labor.[3] In a capital-rich, labor-scarce country, a relatively high price of capital, depicted by the slope of line CL, would dictate that production take place at P. The technique chosen at P can be described by the ray from the origin, OA, the slope of which is the capital-labor ratio. A capital-poor, labor-rich country with relatively cheaper labor (more expensive capital), such as that shown by the slope of line C_1L_1, would be most efficient producing at Q, with technique OB.

In theory, we would expect low-wage, capital-poor countries to produce with more labor-intensive techniques such as OB, rather than with capital-intensive techniques such as OA, found in high-wage, capital-rich countries. In practice, we often find this not to be the case. We simply do not observe the kinds of techniques within an industry that we would expect given the wide differences in relative capital and labor abundance across countries. Even casual observation turns up repeated attempts to use the "best-practice" techniques, saving labor even in labor-abundant countries (Pickett et al., 1974:210).

What explains the choice of techniques such as OA in capital-poor countries rather than OB, which after all would be expected to raise both profits and employment? First is a technological explanation. The range of techniques, and therefore technology, may be described by the isoquant II. However, if only one technique is known, and that technique is described by OA, then the technology is described by the isoquant $I'PI'$. In that case, there would be no choice of

---

[3]The argument here follows that of Pickett et al., 1974.

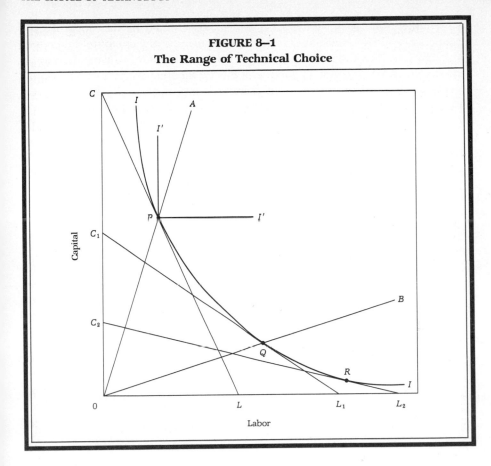

FIGURE 8–1
The Range of Technical Choice

technology, and relative factor prices would become irrelevant. Either technique *OA* is chosen (when it is at least as profitable as other kinds of investment), or the good is not produced.

Second, an economic explanation of why productive techniques in developing countries tend to be more capital-intensive than expected is that prices are distorted. Overvalued exchange rates, artificially high wages, restrictive hiring regulations, interest subsidies, and a host of other factors are accused of lowering the price of capital and raising that of labor such that more capital-intensive techniques become most profitable (Chapter 14). However, in practice we rarely, if ever, find that the relative prices of labor and capital in LDCs are the same as in MDCs. Capital still tends to be more expensive and labor is still cheaper in LDCs, no matter what distortions are operative. Thus, factor price distortions *alone* do not explain why techniques chosen in LDCs would be the same as in MDCs.

Factor market distortions can, however, explain why techniques chosen may be more capital-intensive than would otherwise be the case. Shadow prices of capital relative to labor might be represented by the slope of C_2L_2 in Figure 8–1 in a country with distorted market prices, represented by the slope of C_1L_1. Production will take place at Q rather than R, using a higher capital-labor ratio than that which would maximize social efficiency. Point R is the most desirable production point, Q is not so good, and P is by far the least efficient. Although P is least desirable from a social point of view, it seems to be a frequent outcome. To understand the selection of appropriate techniques, therefore, the starting place must be at P. We must examine the reasons for the choice of P as a point of production, rather than the production point that would come about through a search for maximum private profits given whatever distortions exist (that is, Q). We must also understand the impact of distortions leading to point Q rather than to the optimum point R.

ARE CAPITAL AND LABOR SUBSTITUTABLE?

In the early postwar years, capital and labor were believed to be not substitutable for each other in a large number of operations. It was thought that for most cases, there was one and only one "modern" production function; a given amount of capital would require so much labor and no more, and vice versa for a given amount of labor. If capital-labor substitutability is low, then relative price changes do not determine relative factor intensity.

Most estimates of the elasticity of substitution between capital and labor suggest considerable range for substitution between factors. An elasticity of substitution (s) equal to zero would result if no substitutability existed between factors, a situation normally depicted by right-angled isoquants such as $I'PI'$ in Figure 8–1. Values of s approach infinity as factors become perfect substitutes. The normal line of economic inquiry has been to see whether $s > 0$, for if it is, then changes in relative prices can affect factor intensity. Most empirical studies reveal that $s > 0$ and that price policy is therefore a legitimate variable affecting technological choice.

How can elasticity be measured empirically? On what evidence do we base our suggestion that substitutability in LDCs is greater than was supposed a quarter of a century ago? At once we discover that a seemingly simple question is extraordinarily complex. Indeed, the matter can never be proved; any assertion is an opinion based on the weight of evidence as assessed by the investigator.

There are millions upon millions of firms that might be investigated; small and large, rural and urban, producing thousands upon thousands of individual items. Do we draw a random sample from all of them, from all countries? Or do we stratify the sample according to type of enterprise? If so, what classifications do we use, and how do we weight them? Since we are always comparing a "might-have-been" (what ratio of factors might have been used had relative prices been different), we have three choices, for each of the millions of firms. First, we might ask the managers what decisions they would have made under other price conditions. But we don't know whether they will answer correctly. Far better (is it not?) to verify how they *have* behaved. Second, we may compare two similar firms that have faced different price conditions. But no two firms are exactly alike, and if they are very similar, they probably face similar prices. Third, we could make comparisons over time: How do a single firm's decisions change as factor prices change? This method is reasonable if we can hold all other influences constant, but of course we cannot. Indeed, there is no "surefire" way.

To "solve" the problems of millions upon millions of firms, investigators have aggregated, some more than others. Almost all studies are at a two-digit ISIC (international standard industrial classification) level, which is more aggregative than (say) the three-digit level. Thus a wide range of activities will be treated as one, becoming the average for many individual firms that may face varying degrees of factor substitutability. For example, sugar processing may be done in several ways, the vacuum-pan process being only one. Studies using a two-digit classification would include sugar production in the food category, thus hiding whatever factor substitutability might come from switching from the vacuum-pan process to another process. Pickett *et al.* (1974:211) point out that the vacuum-pan method can be subdivided twelve ways, each of which can be further broken down into six subprocesses. In all, there are potentially more than 311,000 ways in which vacuum-pan sugar can be produced, if each combination of subprocesses is taken as one. Even if interdependence of subprocesses eliminated 80 percent of those ways, there would still be 60,000 alternative techniques for making sugar!

Final products are often composed of several intermediate goods, each of which may be an independent process with capital-labor substitution possibilities. In the construction industry, for example, goods such as bricks, wood products, and fixtures can be produced with a range of capital-labor ratios. The choice of one input over another (for example, wood over brick) may affect the labor-intensiveness of the final product.

Ideally, studies of factor intensity should involve separate measures of the numerator and denominator of the ratio K/L (or L/K). Both the heterogeneity of labor, and the difficulty in defining and measuring capital, make these difficult. In most LDCs, there is no satisfactory measure of the amount of capital invested by industry. What data can be found are often distorted by evasive income-tax reporting. Therefore, many economists have relied on standard production functions, such as CES (constant elasticity of substitution).[4] The Cobb-Douglas function cannot be used because its design presupposes a specific elasticity of substitution (unity). The CES function possesses well-known limitations, all of which derive from the fact that it was invented for mathematical convenience, and the real production functions of individual firms may in fact be something quite different. While most economists are content to use CES functions and other inadequate measures of substitutability, O'Herlihy (1972) argues that the limitations are such as to void completely the results shown from most studies.

We are ready to accept the empirical findings for three reasons. First, we must make *some* judgment on substitutability. Practical policy-making, as well as an academic understanding of development, require it. Second, the large

---

[4]These functions are normally explained in textbooks on mathematical economics; see, for example, Chiang (1974:407, 419). The origins of Cobb-Douglas are explained in Douglas (1934), and those of CES are in Arrow, Chenery, Minhas, and Solow (1961).

numbers of processes for making specific products, plus the choices of different intermediate inputs, seem intuitively to lead to possibilities of substitution. It is hard to believe that all such choices would have the same K/L ratio for any final product. But third, and most important of all, the empirical studies point overwhelmingly in one direction: that elasticity is greater than zero. Errors due to data and method limitations ought to fall randomly; we see no reason for systematic bias.

Fourteen studies surveyed by Morawetz (1976) estimate elasticity of substitution (s) to exceed zero in all cases. In five of these cases, s was one or better.[5] Daniels (1969), Humphries (1976), and Bruton (1976) all made similar estimates with similar results. If all these studies are taken together, s tends to be nonzero, mostly between .5 and 1, and in about a third of the cases greater than 1. Gaude (1975) compiled evidence based on a large number of cross-sectional and time-series studies. Although he concluded that s is a measure of doubtful validity, nevertheless the studies reviewed showed overwhelmingly that $s > 0$. As we consider these studies jointly with others (Pickett et al., 1974, Timmer et al., 1975, and Bhalla, 1975), as well as with comments by Morawetz (1974) and Acharya (1974), we find a preponderance of evidence that there is considerable room in LDCs for capital-labor substitution, and that the more labor-intensive production process is apt to be more efficient.[6]

Technological dualism—which we introduced in an earlier chapter—implies two widely-distinct technologies existing side-by-side: the traditional, labor-intensive technology and the modern, capital-intensive one. Firm in our belief that labor and capital are substitutable for each other over a wide range of potential technologies, we must now ask why a modern, capital-intensive technology is chosen, for the modern sector, in the face of labor abundance and capital scarcity? If we could answer that question, we would understand why dualism occurs.

Potential explanations fall into four categories, but no hypothesis can be proved. We list them as follows, and then discuss them in turn:

(1) Prices are distorted by the government, either for political reasons or through ignorance, thereby inducing the modern sector to adopt capital-intensive methods.

(2) Centralized planning, common to LDCs, may *as a process* be biased toward capital-intensive methods. There is a common tendency to overestimate capital availabilities, and by the time the truth is perceived, government

---

[5]The value $s = 1$ is a convenient reference point. Under neoclassical assumptions, if $s < 1$, a decrease in the price of one factor will increase its intensity but decrease its share in total output (Morawetz, 1976). Thus, with $s < 1$, a decrease in wages would cause a decline in the total share of income paid to labor, even though employment would increase. The result could be the paradox of greater employment combined with greater inequality in income distribution.

[6]An exception to the superiority of the labor-intensive alternative was found in Kenya, where the ILO reported that of two processes available in the metal container industry, the automated, capital-intensive technique was most efficient given market prices. The shadow price of labor would have to be "very low" before the semiautomatic, labor-intensive technique could be considered more efficient (ILO, 1972: 371–82).

enterprises may be locked into processes already chosen. Bureaucratic inertia prevents the revision of earlier decisions.

(3) Capital-intensive methods may be less risky than labor-intensive ones.

(4) Engineering criteria may dominate economic criteria. Decision-makers might seek the technology producing the "best" product (for example, a four-lane, divided highway) though the increment of superiority may not justify the cost.

DO PRICES MATTER?

Some economists have suggested that government policies, intended to promote investment for development, or to cause substitution for imports, have resulted in an artificial lowering of the price of capital relative to that of labor.

In the late 1940s and early 1950s, it was widely believed that economic development was a "natural" process, impelled by natural laws. Rather than examine forces that would cause development, the literature emphasized what might prevent it. If development was not occurring, it was because something was standing in its way—not because essential requisites were not being met. The principal bottleneck was believed to be capital. Thus the way to promote investment would be to lower its price.

Belief in the bottleneck of capital was strengthened by three currents of events. The first was the postwar recovery of Europe. European countries, whose capital had been destroyed by bombing, were being restored by massive infusions from the United States as well as by domestic saving. Other requisites (such as managerial capacities, skills, and entrepreneurship) had not been destroyed in the war as capital had. Somehow, it was felt that the miracle of restoring Europe by capital injections could be translated into development for LDCs. The second current was Keynesian economic thought, with its strategic role for capital. Under Keynesian equations, the level of national income is determined (via the multiplier) by the amount of spending. Even before World War II, it was recognized that Keynes referred only to the demand for gross national product. But supply of output was also believed to be determined by the amount of capital. It remained for Harrod (1939) and Domar (1946) to spell out the exact functions. With both demand and supply of national output allegedly depending on capital, it was easy to believe that any difficulties in increasing output must be explained by lack of capital. The third current was the history of MDCs, in which economic development was often equated with the growth of capital, for new plants and infrastructures always were accompanied by growth.

With this thinking embedded in the minds of politicians and economists alike, it is not difficult to understand that policies encouraging the accumulation of capital were formed. Since it was believed that capital—and especially modern machines—could only be obtained from the MDCs, these policies promoted the import of capital goods. High duties were placed on consumer goods (to encourage "infant industries"), lower duties were placed on intermediate products, and very low or no duties were put on capital goods. In addition, LDC currencies tended to be overvalued, possibly because of a conscious effort to make capital imports cheaper, and possibly as the residues of inflations where (for political pride or other reasons) currency depreciations did not keep pace with price rises. In any event, the result was the same: imports were promoted and exports were penalized. The latter were, of course, goods in which LDCs had comparative advantage because of their labor-intensive technologies and the national abundances of labor.

Such measures to encourage investment had the effect of lowering the price of capital relative to that of labor. Two other currents accentuated this distortion. First, labor unions began to seek both minimum wage legislation and higher rates of pay in general. Political independence and growing nationalism strengthened unionism, especially where the employers were multinational corporations, and it was believed that higher rates of pay were one way of retaining the revenues of these entreprises in the LDCs. Second, as development planners wondered which types of new production to encourage, it was only natural to think of goods that had previously been imported, for which the market had been proved. Import-substitution industrialization (ISI) thus became widespread among LDCs. If a domestic manufacturer was willing to produce such substitutes, or if the government saw the possibility of initiating a public enterprise (often known as a parastatal company[7]), either the activity would be protected by high tariffs or the import would be partially or entirely excluded. Such goods were often capital-intensive, for the comparative advantage lay in MDCs.

Thus the quest for investment, the power of unions, and ISI have probably all caused the price of capital to fall relative to labor. And if capital and labor are substitutable over a wide range, as we believe they are, one might suppose that these distortions would cause the selection of capital-intensive rather than labor-intensive technologies.

While this seems intuitively logical, we nevertheless confront one objection. Many have argued that producers in LDCs are not price-sensitive. The theory of the rectangular isoquant was first presented not only from the supply side, but from the demand side as well. Two decades ago, it was believed that producers in LDCs had fixed notions of the productive processes they wanted. Modern manufacturers would insist on the latest engineering model, while small-scale rural producers were presumably too ignorant to sense and follow the signals of the market.

Research of the past 20 years demonstrates that this supposition is false. Della Valle (1975) showed that although U.S. producers in the minerals industry (copper and aluminum) are more responsive to price changes than producers in LDCs, both adjust capital-labor ratios to some extent. Stewart's (1975) study of cement block production in Kenya shows that in rural areas, where labor is cheaper, manual techniques are used more frequently than they are in the cities. Schultz (1964) and others supply a large number of examples of price-responsiveness among "tradition-bound" peasants. Further evidence of price-

---

[7]A parastatal company is one owned by the government, usually reporting to a ministry, but which is managed autonomously. Such companies are widely employed in LDCs.

sensitivity is presented by Nerlove (1967) and Sicat (1968). Williamson and Sicat (1968) showed how the K/L ratio changed after the Philippine peso had been decontrolled. There is much evidence also that small-scale rural producers in LDCs use labor-intensive techniques (Bruton, 1976, and Marsden, 1969). Since capital subsidies do not generally reach them, and restrictive labor legislation does not easily bind them, they face relatively cheap labor and expensive capital. Helleiner (1975) cites studies that point to the same conclusion for agriculture. Winston (1974) has described as "terribly stringent" those conditions that would be necessary to support the notion that "factor prices don't matter." Mason (1971), after studying manufacturing firms in nine different industries in the Philippines and Mexico, concluded that:

> The major contributing element to the rapid capital deepening and relatively low rates of labor absorption in developing countries is factor market price distortions. There are sound *a priori* arguments for rejecting real technical fixity as the main difficulty. Empirical evidence indicates too that elasticities of substitution are greater than zero and that entrepreneurs do alter capital to labor ratios when relative factor prices change.

BUREAUCRACY

Most technological choice is made through some sort of organization—governmental or private—and is therefore affected by the structure of that organization and its mode of operation. Organization theorists (Thomas, 1975, and Simon, 1976) have suggested that organizations tend to "satisfice" rather than optimize. To avoid risks, they stick to established procedures rather than make continual reorganizations to face new situations.

Satisfactory rather than optimal solutions occur because the latter cannot be readily identified. Organizations often operate under pressure of time and lack full information on alternatives. Waterston (1969) has pointed to the small number of potential projects from which planning agencies choose. Furthermore, with multiple objectives (full employment, output growth, product improvement, and so on) but no clear trade-off among them, policy-makers often have no standard for optimality. They "muddle through" with choices that seem satisfactory to all, but that may not be optimal from any point of view.

But why should this lead to a bias toward capital-intensiveness? Timmer (1975) suggests that there is a human tendency to overestimate the amount of capital available for a project, and that by the time "reality dawns," the project initiator is already "locked in" to the original choice of technology. It usually can be scaled down, but rarely abandoned. He cites the case of fishery planners in Indonesia, who recommended that 100 vessels be acquired, to increase output by 10 percent annually. As it turned out, there was capital for only ten vessels, with an increase in annual output of 1 percent. By the time this limit was discovered, it was "bureaucratically" too late to reconsider the more favorable alternative: with the same capital, the existing fleet might have been improved, with an increase in output of 8 percent.

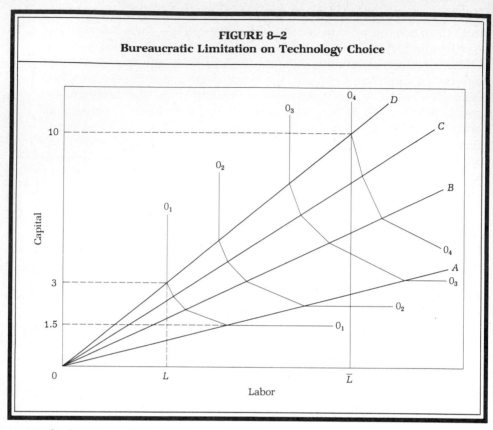

FIGURE 8–2
Bureaucratic Limitation on Technology Choice

NOTE: This figure is modeled after Timmer's (1975:7).

Figure 8–2 outlines the situation facing the sectoral planner, with capital on the vertical axis and labor on the horizontal. Let $\bar{L}$ represent full employment. Four techniques are known, each with a different K/L ratio, represented by the four rays from the origin. Each isoquant (of which there would be an infinite number) represents a different level of output. Maximization of output *and* employment therefore depends on the amount of capital available to the sector. If that is only 1.5 units, then maximization of both calls for technique A, the most labor-intensive. If 10 units of capital are available, then technique D meets the dual objectives.

Suppose 10 units of capital were originally projected, and technique D was therefore selected. Later, however, it became clear that only three units would be available. By then, the sectoral planners do not have the time to reconsider all techniques, for the national plan has a deadline for presentation to parliament. Furthermore, only technique D has been written into the plan, so the central planners do not know of alternatives. In recommending technique D, sectoral planners have had to make the case to central planners that it is the best choice. They have had to put their professional reputations behind it; abandoning it now may appear as indecision. The "easiest way" is to retain technique D, but to scale it back, from isoquant O_4 to O_1.[8] Thus only OL of labor is employed, leaving $L\overline{L}$ without jobs. More output *and* employment would have resulted if a shift had been made from technique D to technique B, given three units of capital. Alternatively, the same level of output (O_1) could have been achieved with half as much capital *and* greater employment generated had a shift occurred to technique A.

RISK AVOIDANCE

Risk avoidance might be classified as a bureaucratic reason for capital-intensive selections if it can be shown (as many believe) that organizational decision-makers are less risk-prone than individuals. In a "satisficing" world, an executive may be judged more by his ability to avoid errors than to achieve successes. Of course, an outstanding innovator will be rewarded, but his personal risk is great. Those who want only to "hang tight" will not select new technologies.

But why should someone "hanging tight" be biased toward capital-intensive choices, when the traditional technologies in LDCs are labor-intensive ones? It may be because machines are often more reliable than people. Thomas (1975) writes of a decision in East Pakistan in favor of capital-intensive technology for tubewells even though the labor-intensive alternative was more profitable in both private and social terms. But the latter would have required a large number of local contractors, who would have used local materials and unskilled labor. The capital-intensive technique used foreign contractors, which the World Bank and other project supporters believed were more likely to stick to a schedule and meet technical specifications, even though pilot projects had shown the labor-intensive wells to be on a par with the higher-cost ones. Furthermore, the labor-intensive choice would have enjoyed some additional advantages. The drilling operation could have been more easily moved from place to place and thus would have benefited more regions, and it would have had stronger linkages with other labor-intensive sectors. The choice made is but one of many examples of lack of trust—or "disdain for the poor"—which we have emphasized in earlier chapters. In short, *economic development* (which includes the training and utilization of people) *is risky, and risk avoiders who focus only on the expected value of growth may find it convenient to avoid development.*

One way to reduce risk is to pursue ventures where as many critical variables as possible fall under an organization's control. In the tubewell example, it was probably easier to direct and control the foreign contractor, using 160 drilling rigs employing two men each, than it would have been to oversee the hundreds of rigs employing two eight-man shifts per day, which would have been needed with the labor-intensive alternative.

Organizational concern over risk and control of operations is a sharp deterrent to the adaptation of the older techniques that have been used in MDCs

---

[8]Thomas (1975) reports that even the World Bank receives requests for capital from aid recipients for a specific technique, with no mention of alternatives considered. In Pakistan tubewells, three alternatives were considered, but when the request for funds arrived at the World Bank, only the one technique chosen by local planners was mentioned.

in the past. This is especially true where this technology is available only in the form of second-hand machinery and equipment. A study (Cooper and Kaplinsky, 1975) of second-hand jute processing equipment in Kenya revealed that while the cost of used machinery was much lower than that of new, costs associated with transportation, installation, and repair were much higher. In addition, the used machines generally required more labor and working capital than new ones would have, and they operated at a much lower proportion of designed capacity. Most of the additional costs associated with used equipment are not easily calculated and to a large extent are unknown beforehand, while the costs and scale of output of new equipment are easily determined and fairly accurate. Additionally, the second-hand machinery required greater skill in operation and maintenance, creating problems of control in production that were not significant with new equipment. The question of whether second-hand machinery is appropriate or not is an empirical one,[9] but the extra risk and element of uncertainty are likely to bias decision-makers in favor of less risky new equipment, objective profitability notwithstanding.

A few personal anecdotes will illustrate the lack of trust in unskilled workers. When a government official in one LDC was asked why electric signals were being installed on the roundabouts (traffic circles) of the capital city rather than using policemen, he replied that policemen on the four intersections of one roundabout would not be able to coordinate their signals. When a suggestion was made to another official that house-to-house delivery of mail might be a useful, profitable, and employment-providing service (as opposed to collection in post office boxes), he responded by saying that the deliverers could not be trusted not to steal letters or their contents. Control was easier when the workers were supervised in a central location.

Market risk may also cause a bias toward capital-intensive technology. Although little research has been done, it may be that firms prefer to maintain excess capacity and higher inventories in periods of uncertainty (Bhalla, 1975:317). Wells (1975) suggests that capital-intensive plants allow greater flexibility for managers to respond to unforeseen demand fluctuations or to cope with liquidity crises.

Wells (1975:79–80) also found that firms tend toward capital-intensity as they become more monopolistic. Competitors will vary in their risk-willingness; the one who assumes the most risk selects the labor-intensive technology and forces others to follow suit. But monopolies do not have the same constraint.

ENGINEERING VERSUS
ECONOMIC CONSIDERATIONS

Economists are often at the mercy of engineers. Only after engineering data have been gathered does the isoquant map take shape and a rational economic choice become possible. If the engineer fails to find or invent certain tech-

---

[9]The Cooper and Kaplinsky (1975) study found no general consistency: some used looms were superior to new ones, others were not. Pack (1975, 1978) found that used spinning equipment is efficient, given relative factor prices in most LDCs, even when substantial modification and repair are required.

niques, they do not become part of the economic calculus. Right-angled isoquants may result from insufficient communication between the engineer and the economist.

We will not join the popular debate on the values of engineers, about whether they "prefer" to cover the world with concrete or to construct the most complicated machine imaginable. But we do emphasize the differing functions of engineers and economists, as well as the difference between technical and economic efficiency. The economist tries to minimize cost, while the engineer's task is to maximize output per unit of scarce input, or to design the technically-best product with only secondary regard to cost. Engineering data will be expressed in "output per acre" or "per machine" or "per unit of raw material."

In principle, there should be no conflict. The scarce input on which the engineer wishes to economize should be the same as the most costly which the economist would prefer to minimize. In fact, however, their different backgrounds, in both education and experience, may lead to differing emphases. This will be the case especially if the engineer is from an MDC, where factor proportions are different and different "inefficiencies" are therefore sought.

The literature provides several illustrations of engineering predominance in the interchange with economists. Wells (1975:84) reported that both foreign and Indonesian firms tended to accept the single technology proposed by engineers, without doing economic studies of alternatives.[10] Rather, a single technology is subjected to economic rate-of-return calculations, and if the rate is acceptable, the investment is made. In many of the studies already cited, such as those for sugar and footwear in Ghana and Ethiopia (Pickett, Forsyth, and McBain, 1974, and Bhalla, 1975), the choices for capital-intensive technology were made by engineers who acted within only broad economic constraints. So long as private profits justified the projects, they would be accepted despite the possibility of greater profits with more appropriate technology.

Sometimes the quality of the product is a factor. Baron's (1975) study of sugar production in India found that capital-intensive methods were chosen so that quality would be comparable to that of competing sugars in the export market. While this was so, nevertheless very little of the sugar was in fact exported. In many rural areas, the craving for sweetness is satisfied by jaggery or low-quality sugar, which may even be healthier than refined sugar. But only the most refined will be consumed by urban elites—an example of how demand may be affected by the quest for engineering perfection.

FACTOR INTENSITY IN GOVERNMENT PROJECTS

It has often been suggested that governments can influence the L/K ratio by selecting labor-intensive methods for projects under their direct control. While lip service is given to this thought in many development plans, there is little

---

[10]Private firms are not the only entities to act in accord with engineering interests. International aid agencies also recommend capital-intensive techniques, in part because they are "modern" and in part because they are easier to control. An ILO (1972:142) study of Kenya mentions that the World Bank provided funds for 65 tractor-mounted rotary grass cutters for trimming the edges of highways. Traditionally this is done by gang labor using a specially-curved knife.

evidence that governments (other than the People's Republic of China) have taken it seriously.

Road-building would appear to be an opportune activity for this choice. The preparation of a roadbed, grading and drainage, can be done by a bulldozer with one operator or by picks and shovels with many laborers. One of the authors was invited to visit an experimental, labor-intensive road being constructed in Vihiga, Kenya, in 1973, by the United States foreign aid program (USAID). For almost a kilometer, the road was covered with laborers, one wherever one would fit, working with hand tools. The supervisor (an American from USAID) explained that he paid the minimum wage (5 shillings per day) and at that wage he could have hired many times the number for which he had jobs. The project was financially viable, though borderline, when compared with the alternative, capital-intensive cost. At an appropriate shadow price of labor, the labor-intensive technology would have been clearly attractive. One major obstacle, we were told, was that local chiefs were impatient with the length of time needed. "Why not bring in the bulldozer," they would ask, "and get it done with?"

Studies of labor-intensiveness in road-building show mixed results, if market prices are used (Irvin, 1975, and Edmonds and Hussain, 1976). The Irvin study, sponsored by the International Labor Organization, showed that *at market prices*, capital-intensive techniques are preferred, but that major cost savings would be possible with labor-intensive techniques at appropriate shadow prices. Rossow (1976) reviewed a number of case studies and concluded that results are mixed (sometimes favoring one technology, sometimes another) at market prices. Once again, however, shadow prices would shift the balance to labor-intensiveness. Burns (1975) has argued that it is difficult to provide a good local road system with labor-intensive technology unless there is decentralized local government and costs are therefore supplied by local finance. The chiefs who want to have "the bulldozer and get it done with" might think differently if they were required to raise the cost by taxing their constituents.

In sum, there appears to be much opportunity, but little interest, for government-financed projects to use labor-intensive methods.

THE TRANSFER OF TECHNOLOGY[11]

Curiously, the literature decrying capital intensity in LDCs emanates primarily from the MDCs. A quick review of the authors cited in earlier parts of this chapter will reveal that their names are primarily Anglo-European. When one travels in LDC circles, one finds a totally different concern: how to obtain technology from the MDCs as inexpensively as possible.

The present authors—possibly because of our own Anglo-European background—believe that the most effective route to development, full employment, and equitable distribution of income lies in the creation of new technology

---

[11]Much of the material for the present section was compiled by Mark Bykowsky, in a graduate seminar on economic development at the University of Colorado.

within the LDCs or in the adaptation of imported technology to suit LDC conditions and relative factor availabilities. Both of these would require much greater local R & D. We tend to cite studies showing that technology is time- and place-specific. For example, in early American history, European technology carried to the United States was adapted to the availability of wood rather than coal as a principal fuel. The Japanese have also borrowed much technology, but their success doubtless lies in their selection of labor-intensive techniques, some of them obsolete in more capital-intensive countries, and in their adaptation of other techniques to labor-abundant conditions. Pack and Todaro (1969) have argued in favor of domestic capital-goods industries for LDCs because they tend to be labor-intensive, adapt technology to local conditions, and provide on-the-job skills.

For economists and politicians in LDCs, however, the thrust is much different. In the Declaration for a New International Economic Order (United Nations, 1974), they have urged that institutions be established for the easier and cheaper identification and transfer of technology from MDCs to LDCs. They argue that much modern technology is held by large monopolies in MDCs, which make it available to LDCs only at excessive prices or unacceptable terms.

The major costs of technology transfer, they point out, fall into five categories: (1) costs to use patents, licenses, and trademarks, (2) payments for technical experts to provide information in pre-investment, investment, and operations stages, (3) payments for imports of capital with "embodied" techniques, (4) hidden costs levied by multinational corporations through overpricing of inputs or underpricing of exports from subsidiary to parent, and (5) profit remittances by multinational corporations. A United Nations Conference on Trade and Development (UNCTAD 1971:14) study to estimate these costs showed that technology payments by LDCs averaged in the neighborhood of 5 to 7 percent of exports and ranged up to 14.7 percent (Pakistan, 1965–70) and 15.9 percent (Mexico, 1968). These same costs often amounted to ½ percent to ¾ percent of gross domestic product. The study also showed that during the 1950s and 1960s these payments were increasing at very high rates, many of them in the neighborhood of 40 or 50 percent yearly (p. 16).

LDC governments consider themselves to be in a weak bargaining position for technology. First, they point out that the purveyors are largely monopolies or oligopolies. Second, they assert that the recipients are less sophisticated than the sellers, dependent on the latter for advice on what they should buy. They cite the property rights and secrecy that characterize the market for technology. The monopolistic nature of this market is argued by UNCTAD (1971:4) in a citation of the high percentages of costs paid to a single country to obtain information on technology for a particular sector. These percentages can be extremely high, often in the neighborhood of 99 percent.

The patent system has come under particular attack. Vaitsos (1972) argues that most of the patents in LDCs are in fact held by foreigners, and in particular by multinational corporations. Often they are used to confine production to the home country (MDC), and the LDC is not allowed to buy a license at any price. UNCTAD (1971:31) reports that 45 percent of Chilean patents were held by foreigners in 1937 and 78 percent in 1967. The study also reports (p. 40) that only 10 of the 3,513 patents outstanding in Colombia in 1970 were actually used for production, the rest presumably being to protect monopolistic producers in other countries. Similarly, from a sample of 4,872 patents granted between 1960 and 1970 in major industrial sectors in Peru, only 54 were reported to have been exploited. Studies performed in Chile, Argentina, and Tanzania show similar results, and an analysis for Mexico yielded use-rates in the neighborhood of 5 to 10 percent. The strong presumption implied in the UNCTAD study is that these low percentages result from attempts to preserve foreign monopolies. In fact, however, there are many unused patents in MDCs as well—patents on inventions that turned out to be market-unfeasible because costs were too high or demand too low.

Licensing arrangements for patents have also been restrictive. Licensees may be required to buy certain inputs from the patent-owner, or they may not be permitted to sell in certain markets (for example, export markets reserved for the patent-owner). Out of 247 contracts studied by UNCTAD (1971:12) for four Latin American countries, 200 carried total prohibition of exports and 12 more permitted exports only in certain areas.

MDC negotiators in international conferences (such as at UNCTAD or the United Nations itself) are often perplexed by these "complaints" from LDCs. The Declaration of the New International Economic Order implies that new institutional arrangements are required to deal with the situation—arrangements that might limit international patenting, for example. The Andean bloc, for one, has banded together to prohibit certain restrictive clauses in international licensing within their countries. But the patent system holds a long and honored tradition in MDCs, having been hammered out through historical compromises between their libertarian tradition and the need to reward invention. Most MDC negotiators believe the solution lies not in new institutional arrangements, but in increasing sophistication on the part of LDC producers, so that they are able to bargain as effectively as their counterparts in MDCs. The solution is also believed to lie in more R & D within LDCs, resulting in a shift in emphasis from the purchase of foreign technology to the creation of their own technology and to the adaptation of what they import.

CONCLUSION

Let us return to the six hotly-debated questions at the beginning of the chapter. We have discovered that none of them can be answered definitively; no "proof" can be achieved for any. Rather, each answer is judgmental, depending on the weight that the observer assigns to variables that have been empirically researched. But we believe that the preponderance of evidence makes the following judgments reasonable.

FIRST, capital and labor are interchangeable over wide areas within LDCs. Any government that is serious about solving unemployment should make a special effort to use labor-intensive techniques. But labor-intensive techniques are risky and require great attention to training, management, and attitudinal change. They therefore bring us to the heart of development, as opposed to mere growth.

SECOND, capital-intensive methods are widely used in LDCs because they are "artificially cheaper" as a result of price distortions attributable to government regulations and bureaucratic centralization. Many economists stop with these explanations, but we shall go one step further. Control over prices, and the form of bureaucracy, are choices freely made by governments. So why are such distorted selections actually made? In part, it would seem that governments "fell into" them, because of the early belief in capital and the development bottleneck. In part also, it is because of an unwillingness to assume the risks of labor-intensive development and because of a lack of trust in (and even disdain for) the poorer elements of society and their abilities to participate in modern economic activity.

THIRD, an appropriate technology is an efficient one, which takes into account relative availabilities of factors of production and is judged on the basis of shadow prices.

FOURTH, more advanced technology may be transferred from MDCs to LDCs in a number of ways, all of which are in current use. No new institutional procedure is necessary, though increased sophistication, obtained through education and experience, would help the ability of LDC managers to bargain. Above all, new technology must be created, through R & D within LDCs, and almost all technology that is acquired from abroad should be adapted to local conditions.

FIFTH, whether MDC technology is or is not too expensive is a question not likely to be resolved. The very nature of new technology development implies monopolistic control, since diffusion is both naturally slow and restrained by patent and other legislation that is not likely to be changed. These are among the "facts of life" that producers—in MDCs as well as LDCs—must face. The resolution lies once again in developing one's own technology, or one's own adaptations, and in more sophisticated international bargaining.

SIXTH, there is indeed much technology from MDCs that is useful to LDCs. In Chapter 15, we will point out how technological diffusion over the centuries has engendered much of the world's growth—from China and the Arab world to Europe, from Europe to America, and so on. Much of it was transmitted by skilled persons moving from advanced to less advanced countries, although some was also acquired by apprentices from the latter to the former countries. Nothing essential has changed in the modern world. Most technology transmitted from one area to another has had to pass the test of market feasibility, and sometimes obsolete technology passes better than modern. Adaptation of technology also has a long history, and that lesson is not apt to change.

Studies of technology and its choice are deficient in many respects. All inputs must be examined, not just homogeneous capital and labor. The full range of different kinds of capital and labor skills, as well as different intermediate and raw material inputs, must be considered in the choice of appropriate technology.

The assumption that capital is the scarce input may not be valid; more often, it will turn out to be skilled labor.

Small-scale producers, whether farmers or nonagricultural, have largely been ignored by policy-makers. Yet there is evidence that they are able to mobilize resources and to take risks, and that they respond to market incentives. We have not stressed this important arena in the present chapter, for we will discuss it at length in Chapter 12. In Chapter 11, we will examine the critical question of how labor-intensive agriculture ought to be.

The problems considered here cry out for microstudies. Aggregative analysis has given us some insight into capital-labor substitutability and the effect of relative prices on factor proportions. But these studies are of little use in specific policy analyses, since they require equally specific information about incentives and trade-offs. Almost any choice of technology requires that detailed studies be conducted *a priori*. If there is to be a "next wave" of technology research, it could best be devoted to more case studies of important industries in LDCs.

BIBLIOGRAPHY

Acharya, S. N., 1974:
"Fiscal/Financial Intervention, Factor Prices and Factor Proportions: A Review of Issues," IBRD, Bank Staff Working Paper No. 183 (Washington: IBRD), p. 72.

Arrow, K. J.; Chenery, H. G.; Minhas, B. S.; and Solow, R. M., 1961:
"Capital-Labor Substitution and Economic Efficiency," *The Review of Economics and Statistics*, Vol. XLIII, #3, August.

Baron, C. G., 1975:
"Sugar Processing Techniques in India," in Bhalla (ed.) *Technology and Employment in Industry* (Geneva: ILO), pp. 175–202.

Bhalla, A. S., 1964:
"Investment Allocation and Technological Choice: A Case of Cotton Spinning Techniques," *Economic Journal* Vol. LXXIV, No. 295 (September).

Bhalla, A. S., (ed.) 1975:
Technology and Employment in Industry: A Case Study Approach (Geneva: ILO).

Bruton, H. J., 1967:
"Employment, Productivity and Income Distribution," in A. Cairncross and M. Puri (eds.) *Employment, Income Distribution and Development Strategy: Problems of the Developing Countries* (New York: Holmes & Meier Publishers), pp. 71–89.

Burns, Robert E., 1975:
"The Current Controversy over Low-Cost Road Construction in Developing Countries," Xerox paper presented at First Conference on Highway Planning and Project Evaluation, Addis Ababa, January 1976.

Carr, M., 1976:
Economically Appropriate Technologies for Developing Countries: An Annotated Bibliography, London: Intermediate Technology Group.

Caves, Richard and Uekusa, Masu, 1976:
Industrial Organization in Japan, Washington, D.C., Brookings.

Chaing, Alpha, 1974:
Fundamental Methods of Mathematical Economics, revised, New York, McGraw-Hill.

Cooper, C. and Kaplinsky, R., 1975:
"Second-Hand Equipment in Developing Countries: Jute Processing Machinery in

Kenya," in Bhalla (ed.) *Technology and Employment in Industry* (Geneva: ILO), ch. 5.

Daniels, M. R., 1969:
"Differences in Efficiency Among Industries in Developing Countries," *American Economic Review* Vol. LIX, No. 1, (March).

Della Valle, P., 1975:
"Productivity and Employment in the Copper and Aluminum Industries in Developing Countries," *American Economic Review*, Vol. LIX, No. 1, (March).

Denison, Edward F. and Chung, William K., 1976:
How Japan's Economy Grew so Fast: The Sources of Post-war Expansion, Washington, D.C., Brookings.

Domar, Evsey, 1946:
"Capital Expansion, Rate of Growth, and Employment," *Econometrica*, Vol. 14, April, pp. 137–47, reprinted in Domar, *Essays in the Theory of Economic Growth*, New York, Oxford, 1957, pp. 70–82.

Douglas, Paul, 1934:
The Theory of Wages, New York, Macmillan.

Edmunds, G. A., and Hussain, M. I., 1976:
"Labor Intensive Road Construction: A discussion of the critical issues," ditto paper, Technology and Employment Branch, World Employment Program, International Labor Organization.

Gaude, J., 1975:
"Capital-Labor Substitution Possibilities: A Review of Empirical Evidence," in Bhalla (ed.), *op. cit.*, pp. 35–58.

Harrod, Roy F., 1939:
"An Essay in Dynamic Theory," *The Economic Journal*, Vol. 49, (March), pp. 14–33.

Helleiner, Gerald K., 1975:
"Smallholder Decision Making: Tropical African Evidence," in Reynolds, Lloyd, ed., *Agriculture in Development Theory*, New Haven, Yale University Press, pp. 27–52.

Humphries, J., 1976:
"Causes of Growth," *Economic Development and Cultural Change* 24:2 (January), pp. 339–53.

ILO, 1972:
Employment, Incomes and Equality: A Strategy for Increasing Productive Employment in Kenya (Geneva: ILO).

Irvin, G., 1975:
Roads and Redistribution, International Labor Organization, Geneva.

Marsden, K., 1969:
"Towards a Synthesis of Economic Growth and Social Equity," *International Labor Review* (November).

Mason, R. H., 1971:
The Transfer of Technology and the Factor Proportions Problem: The Philippines and Mexico, New York, The United Nations Institute for Training and Research Report No. 10.

Morawetz, D., 1974:
"Employment Implications of Industrialization in Developing Countries: A Survey," *Economic Journal* 84:335 (September), pp. 491–542.

Morawetz, D., 1975:
"Import Substitution, Employment and Foreign Exchange in Colombia: No Cheers for Petrochemicals," in Timmer *et al.*, *The Choice of Technology in Developing Countries*, *op. cit.*, pp. 95–107.

Morawetz, D., 1976:
"Elasticities of Substitution in Industry: What We Learn from Econometric Estimates," *World Development* 4:1, pp. 11–15.

Nerlove, Marc, 1967:
"Recent Empirical Studies of the CES and Related Production Functions," in *The*

Theory and Empirical Analysis of Production, Studies in Income and Wealth, New York, National Bureau of Economic Research.

O'Herlihy, C. St. J., 1972:
"Capital/Labor Substitution and the Developing Countries," *Bulletin of the Oxford University Institute of Economics and Statistics*, Vol. 34, pp. 269–80.

Pack, H. and Todaro, M., 1969:
"Technology Transfer, Labor Absorption and Economic Development," *Oxford Economic Papers* 21:3 (November), pp. 395–403.

Pack, H., 1975:
"The Choice of Technique and Employment in the Textile Industry," in Bhalla (ed.) *Technology and Employment in Industry* (Geneva: ILO), pp. 153–73.

Pack, H., 1978:
"The Optimality of Used Equipment: Calculations for the Cotton Textile Industry," *Economic Development and Cultural Change* 26:2 (January), pp. 307–25.

Patrick, Hugh and Rosovsky, Henry, eds., 1976:
Asia's New Giant: How the Japanese Economy Works, Washington, D.C., Brookings.

Pickett, J., Forsyth, D. J. C., and McBain, N. S., 1974:
"The Choice of Technology, Economic Efficiency and Employment in Developing Countries," in Edwards (ed.) *Employment in Developing Nations, op. cit.*, pp. 209–21.

Ranis, Gustav, 1973:
"Industrial Sector Labor Absorption," *Economic Development and Cultural Change*, 21:3 (April), also Yale University Economic Growth Center, paper #193, New Haven.

Rosenberg, Nathan, 1970:
"Economic Development and the Transfer of Technology: Some Historical Notes," *Technology and Culture* (October), pp. 550–75.

Rossow, Janet, 1976:
"Labor-Capital Substitution in Highway Construction: A Review of Some Case Studies," Xerox paper presented at First Conference on Highway Planning and Project Evaluation, Addis Ababa, January.

Schiavo-Campo, S. and Singer, H. W., 1970:
Perspectives of Economic Development (Boston: Houghton Mifflin).

Schultz, T. W., 1964:
Transforming Traditional Agriculture, New Haven, Yale University Press.

Schumacher, E. F., 1974:
Small Is Beautiful: Economics as if People Mattered, New York: Harper and Row.

Sicat, G., 1968:
Industrial Production Functions in the Philippines, Discussion Paper No. 68–18, Institute of Economic Development and Research, University of the Philippines.

Simon, Herbert A., 1976:
Administrative Behavior: A Study of Decision-Making Processes in Administrative Organization, New York, Free Press (Macmillan).

Stewart, F., 1975:
"Manufacture of Cement Blocks in Kenya," in Bhalla (ed.) *Technology and Employment in Industry* (Geneva: ILO), pp. 203–40.

Stewart, F., 1977:
Technology and Underdevelopment, Boulder, Colorado, Westview Press.

Timmer, C. P., et. al., 1975:
The Choice of Technology in Developing Countries: Some Cautionary Tales (Cambridge: Harvard Center for International Affairs).

Thomas, J. W., 1975:
"The Choice of Technology for Irrigation Tubewells in East Pakistan: Analysis of a Development Policy Design," in Timmer *et al.*, *The Choice of Technology in Developing Countries*, *op. cit.*

Thurow, Lester C., 1971:
"Research, Technical Progress and Economic Growth," *Technology Review* (March), pp. 44–52.

United Nations, 1974:
  Declaration of a New International Economic Order, Sixth Special Session of General Assembly, Supplement No. 1 (A/9559), 9 April–2 May.
United Nations Conference on Trade and Development (UNCTAD), 1971:
  Transfer of Technology, Report by the Secretariat.
Vaitsos, Constantino, 1972:
  "Patents Revisited: Their Functions in Developing Countries," *Journal of Development Studies*, Vol. 9.
Waterston, A., 1969:
  "An Operational Approach to Development Planning" *International Development Review* (September), pp. 6–12.
Wells, L. T., 1975:
  Economic Man and Engineering Man: Choice of Technology in a Low-Wage Country," in Timmer *et al., op. cit.,* pp. 69–93.
Williamson, J. G. and Sicat, G., 1968:
  Technical Change and Resource Allocation in Philippine Manufacturing, 1957–65, Discussion Paper No. 68–21, Institute of Economic Development and Research, University of the Philippines.
Winston, G. C., 1974:
  "Factor Substitution, Ex Ante and Ex Post," *Journal of Development Economics* 1:2 (September), pp. 145–63.

9

POPULATION

*(Dr. Herman Kahn) expects world population growth to peak in
the next five years and world economic growth to reach its height
a few years later, with both gradually stabilizing in the 22nd
century at a level of unprecedented affluence.*
CRITTENDEN, *NEW YORK TIMES*, MAY 5, 1976

*Birth control pills are "ruining" the girls of Kenya, the National
Assembly was told yesterday.*
*In a bitter attack on Government spending on "the Pill," an
Assistant Minister declared:*
*"Some of our women taking these pills are now producing kids
with four legs."*
*Mr. M—W—, an Assistant Minister for Agriculture, added: "Some
of these pills that our girls are taking are ruining them. Some of
them are bearing kids with nuts in their heads—kids that you
cannot teach anything."*
DAILY NATION, NAIROBI, MAY 24, 1974

"Take care of the people, and population will take care of itself."
SLOGAN AT THE BUCHAREST POPULATION CONFERENCE, 1974

World population in the 1960s was growing faster than ever before in history, at about 2 percent per year. Not only did over two-thirds of this population live in LDCs, but the rates of growth were highest there, at about 2.4 percent per year. At a compound annual rate of 2.4 percent, a population will double in about thirty years. In the 1970s, the world growth rate slowed somewhat, to 1.9 percent, while that of LDCs remained at 2.4 percent during the first half of the decade, and then (1975–1977) appeared to decline to 2.3 percent (USDC 1978:15).

In the meantime, the rate of growth in food production is only slightly ahead of that of population. At a World Food Council (UN agency) meeting in Mexico in 1978, it was announced that food output had slowed during the seventies, to about 2.4 percent per year, compared to 2.8 percent in the sixties. "Four per cent is the increase that experts think would be necessary for major progress in eradicating hunger and malnutrition" (Rensenberger, 1978:5).

Not only does rapid population growth threaten malnutrition and starvation, but there are other demographic effects as well. *Demographic investment* is needed—in schools, health facilities, urban infrastructure, and other areas—just to supply new arrivals with the per capita benefits the present population enjoys. A growing population has a greater percentage in lower-age groups than a stable population and thus a higher dependency ratio (persons not working to persons working). Even if the growth rate in fertility slows to zero, population itself will grow for many years to come because of *demographic momentum.* Those born while the rate is positive will only later move into the reproductive period.

All these ominous forces have led many to believe that family planning should be officially promoted in LDCs. Although the term is neutral in content (people may plan for large as well as for small families), the hope is that such planning would lead to limiting births. Against this opinion is a strong current, felt especially in LDCs, that population growth should be left alone. First, it is said to be dependent on income. Only as its income rises will a family decide to control births. Second, poor families often increase their incomes by having more children, who become earners. Consequently, it is said, family limitation would harm the poor. Third, children are their parents' social security. In very-low-income countries, where infant mortality is high, families must have many children to ensure that some survive until working age; risk-averters may overestimate the number necessary. Finally, there is the philosophical point that birth prevention is immoral, for it deprives a potential human being of life. "How do you know that the people whose births you would prevent are not the very ones with the genius to solve the population problem?" (The question was put to one of the authors at a symposium in Caracas, Venezuela). Many assert that family planning is a "plot" on the part of MDC governments to keep LDCs in a subordinate state, because—it is believed—strength depends on numbers (Mamdani, 1972).

We shall examine these questions in the present chapter. First, we will seek an historical perspective. How has world population behaved since the beginning of historic time? Second, we will examine the situation in LDCs today. Third, we will turn to the question of *optimal population.* Is there, in some economic *or* philosophical sense, an optimal population for a society? How rapidly *should* a population grow? From this question, we are led into *macro*-studies, with their intercountry comparisons of aggregates. Fourth, we will look at the abundance of *micro*-research from recent years to seek the correlates of population growth. We will find that these scattered bits of information, drawn from many similar studies, are revealing, but many more must be done to confirm general impressions now emerging. Finally, we will look briefly at population effects on the growth of income and its distribution.

HISTORY OF POPULATION GROWTH

Before humans grew their own food (about 8,000 B.C.), world population was only five to ten million (Ohlin, 1965, and Clark, 1968). As the ancients learned not only agriculture, but also how to breed cattle, to irrigate, and to employ other techniques, their numbers grew, reaching 256 million the year Emperor Augustus died (14 A.D.), as is shown in Table 9–1. From then on, it took about 1600 years for world population to almost double: it reached 470 million in 1650. This increase averages only 0.043 percent annually, but it resulted from many ups (with prosperity and peace) and downs (with wars, famines, and plagues). Thereafter, population doubled again in only 200 years, to slightly over one billion in 1850. It took only 80 years to double once more (to two billion in 1930) and only 45 years for the next doubling (to almost four billion by 1975). At the present rate of growth, population would double again by 2012. These estimates are subject to margins of error that increase the earlier one goes. Early data are based on archeological finds and behavioral indicators, on whose interpretations experts disagree. But they are the best data we have, and perhaps all we need.

TABLE 9–1
World Population
A.D. **14 to 1975**

	A.D. 14	1000	1200	1500	1750	1900	1975
World Total	256	280	384	427	731	1668	3967
Asia excluding the USSR	184	172	242	225	478	985	2253
(of which, China)	(73)	(60)	(123)	(100)	(207)	(500)	(839)
Europe, excluding the USSR	37	32	45	62	102	284	476
USSR	8	12	12	12	34	127	255
Africa	23	50	61	85	100	122	401
North America				1	2	81	237
South and Central America	3	13	23	40	13	63	324
Oceania	1	1	1	2	2	6	21

SOURCE: Clark (1968:64,108), Durand (1977:256), and UN Demographic Yearbook (1975).

Prior to industrialization, population was subject to wide fluctuations, long periods of stagnation, other periods of rapid growth (but always less than 1 percent per year), and sudden declines. Figure 9–1 shows how the Chinese fared over the centuries, with sharp drop-offs during invasions and periods of internal warfare, and rapid growth (as much as 0.8 percent per year) during periods of prosperity (such as the early Han, T'ang, Northern Sung, Ming, and early Ch'ing dynasties). Also evident are periods of stagnation and slight decline.

In Europe, population declined along with the Roman Empire (Figure 9–2); it began to increase as the Franks consolidated their empire (0.2 percent per year, 600 to 800) and continued to rise until approximately 1250. Cipolla (1976) suggests that before the fourteenth century, the dispersal of people checked the spread of the plague. Gradually, however, the growth of cities, with their unsanitary conditions, increased the dangers to health. North and Thomas

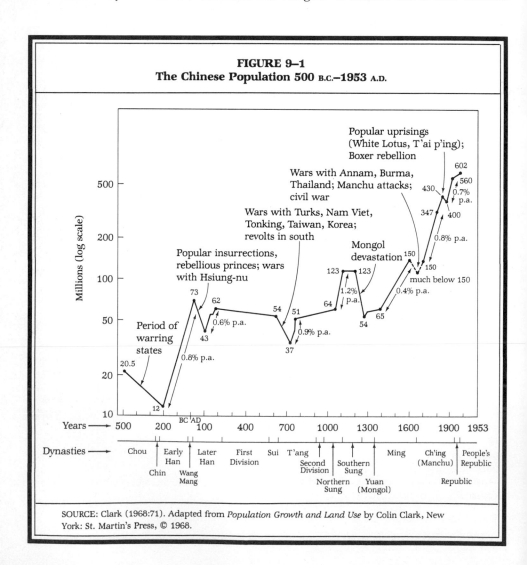

FIGURE 9–1
The Chinese Population 500 B.C.–1953 A.D.

SOURCE: Clark (1968:71). Adapted from *Population Growth and Land Use* by Colin Clark, New York: St. Martin's Press, © 1968.

FIGURE 9–2
Population Estimates of Europe

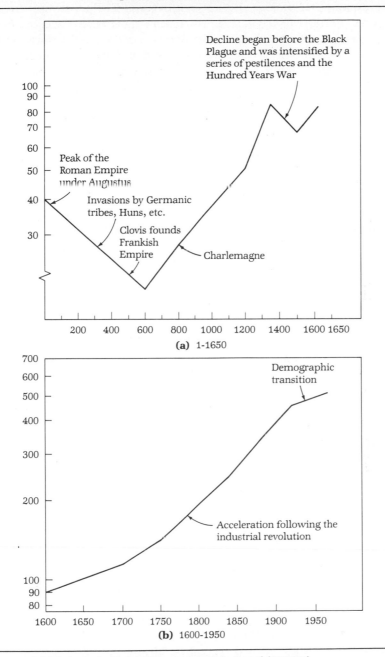

Decline began before the Black Plague and was intensified by a series of pestilences and the Hundred Years War

Peak of the Roman Empire under Augustus

Invasions by Germanic tribes, Huns, etc.

Clovis founds Frankish Empire

Charlemagne

(a) 1-1650

Demographic transition

Acceleration following the industrial revolution

(b) 1600-1950

SOURCE: (a) Estimates by Clark (1968), reported also in Durand (1977:270).
(b) Estimates by Willcox (1940) and Bennett (1954), reported also in Durand (1977:271).
Adapted with the permission of the Population Council from "Historical Estimates of World Population: An Evaluation," by John D. Durand, *Population and Development Review* 3, no. 3 (September 1977): Figure 3A (p. 270) and Figure 3B (p. 271).

(1973) suggest that by the end of the thirteenth century, Europe was overpopulated, given its technology. Diminishing returns had already set in, and a Malthusian specter was appearing. The Black Plague (1348) was but one of a series of pestilences attendant on the almost continuous warfare (Hundred Years War, Wars of the Roses), which caused the decline to continue until approximately 1500. From 1500 on, however, Europe's population again grew, and steadily. Growth accelerated after the industrial revolution (Figure 9–2b).

The European and North American population increases of the nineteenth century are associated with the decline in the death rate caused by medical advances such as smallpox vaccinations and by better sanitation and improved health facilities. These increased life expectancy from 35 years or less in the eighteenth century to 70 years or more today (Coale, 1974:48).

In all countries, the decline in the death rate has, with some lag, been followed by a decline in the birth rate. In France, the two rates fell almost simultaneously, early in the nineteenth century. Therefore, French population growth was modest: 0.53 percent per year from 1800 to 1830 and 0.31 percent from 1830 to 1870, compared with the British rate of 1.46 percent and 1.18 percent, respectively, for the same periods (Clark, 1968:106–7). British increases fell off thereafter, to 0.5 percent in 1910 to 1920; they have remained in the same neighborhood in all decades since. The Japanese population, relatively stagnant until the Meiji restoration (1868), thereafter took a sharp upturn, but began to taper off about 1920 (Clark, 1968:68).

The drop in death rates, with the subsequent drop in birth rates, has come to be known as the *demographic transition*. Many theories have been advanced to explain the time lag. All relate to changes in perceptions about the value of children. Some refer to decreased need of children for old-age security; some to the substitution of quality (healthier, better-educated children) for quantity; and some to the more satisfying occupations for parents, as alternatives to raising children.

Coale (1974:49) has depicted the demographic transition as shown in Figure 9–3. Before the transition, the birth rate is constant, while the death rate varies (with epidemics and wars). As transition begins, the death rate falls. After a time lag, the birth rate also falls. Thereafter, the death rate is constant, while the birth rate varies (for example, the "baby boom" of World War II).

POPULATION IN LDCs TODAY

Table 9–2 shows that only Europe, Northern America, and Oceania experienced the demographic transition at the end of the nineteenth century and in the early twentieth. For these areas, population growth rates peaked in the half-century from 1850 to 1900 and declined thereafter. Meanwhile, the rates for the rest of the world continued to rise.

In LDCs, declining mortality rates were responsible for the increase in population, sometimes with spectacular results. In Sri Lanka, the antimalarial campaign of 1946–1947 was credited with reducing death rates from 20 to 14 per thousand in only one year. Life expectancy has been greatly extended in

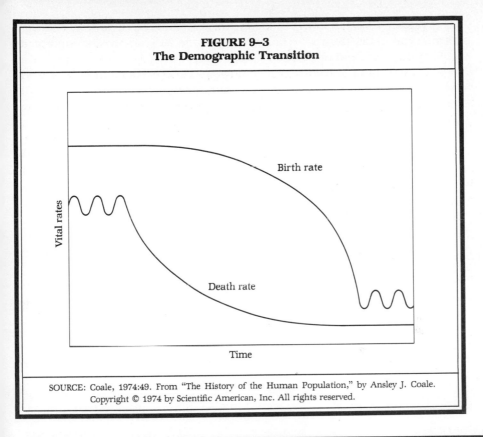

FIGURE 9–3
The Demographic Transition

SOURCE: Coale, 1974:49. From "The History of the Human Population," by Ansley J. Coale. Copyright © 1974 by Scientific American, Inc. All rights reserved.

TABLE 9–2
Population Growth Rates
Average Annual Percentage Since 1650

	1650–1700	1700–1750	1750–1800	1800–1850	1850–1900	1900–1950	Current rate (1975–1977)
World total	0.43	0.26	0.44	0.51	0.64	0.90	1.90
Asia excluding the USSR	0.61	0.29	0.46	0.43	0.42	0.83	2.16
Europe and Asiatic USSR	0.31	0.39	0.58	0.71	0.87	0.60	0.58
Africa	–0–	–0–	– 0.11	0.11	0.47	1.24	2.83
Northern America	–0–*	1.40*	2.22	2.10	2.30	1.45	0.81
Southern America	–0–	0.16	1.10	1.11	1.30	1.91	2.63
Oceania	–0–	–0–	–0–	–0–	2.22	1.56	1.30

*These figures are based on Clark's (rounded) estimate of 1 million in each of 1650 and 1700, 2 million by 1750, and 6 million by 1800. U.S. Historical Statistics show the population of the U.S. growing at 3.03 percent from 1790 to 1800.

SOURCE: Clark (1968:64) for 1650–1750, Hauser (1971:106) for 1750–1900, and estimates by Carr-Saunders (1963) and United Nations for 1950. Current rate is from U.S.D.C. (1978:15).

many LDCs: in Mexico from 36 to 60 years during the three decades ending in 1964, and in India from 27 years in the 1920s to 32 years in 1945, and on up to 50 years today. Infant mortality has declined abruptly.

Today's LDCs differ from MDCs of 150 years ago in that a far more substantial medical revolution has occurred. MDC mortality rates declined but slowly in the nineteenth century, as medical technology was laboriously improved. But the advances of the last two centuries are suddenly available to LDCs now. As a result, their population is growing at greater rates than was ever the case in MDCs. Table 9–2 shows European population growth rates at 0.71 percent during the first half of the nineteenth century and at 0.87 percent during the second half. Several European countries reached more than 1.0 percent, but they rarely exceeded 1.5 percent. By contrast, Table 9–3 shows the world as a whole growing at 2.0 percent in 1965–1970, with Africa now growing at 2.8 percent.

Figure 9–4 compares growth rates of the fifty largest countries in 1966 and

TABLE 9–3
World Population by Continent
and Development Category, 1950–1979

Average annual rate of growth (percent)					
	1975-1979	1970-1975	1965-1970	1960-1965	1955-1960	1950-1955
WORLD	1.7	1.9	2.0	2.0	2.0	1.8
More developed	0.7	0.9	1.0	1.2	1.3	1.3
Less developed	2.1	2.4	2.4	2.3	2.3	2.1
AFRICA[a]	2.9	2.7	2.6	2.5	2.3	2.1
ASIA	1.9	2.2	2.3	2.1	2.2	2.0
More developed	1.4[c]	1.6	1.5	1.4	1.4	1.7
Less developed	2.2[c]	2.3	2.3	2.2	2.2	2.0
LATIN AMERICA[a]	2.4	2.6	2.7	2.8	2.8	2.6
NORTHERN AMERICA[b]	0.8	0.9	1.1	1.5	1.8	1.8
EUROPE AND SOVIET UNION[b]	0.6	0.7	0.8	1.1	1.1	1.1
OCEANIA	1.1	1.9	1.9	2.2	2.3	2.4
More developed	1.0[c]	1.7	1.8	2.1	2.2	2.3
Less developed	2.4[c]	2.5	2.6	2.7	2.6	2.6
Excluding the People's Republic of China:						
WORLD	1.8[c]	1.9	1.9	1.9	1.9	1.7
Less developed	2.4[c]	2.4	2.5	2.4	2.3	2.1
ASIA	2.2[c]	2.2	2.3	2.2	2.1	1.9
Less developed	2.3[c]	2.3	2.4	2.3	2.2	1.9

[a]Less developed
[b]More developed
[c]1975–1977

SOURCE: USDC (1978:15 and 1980:9).

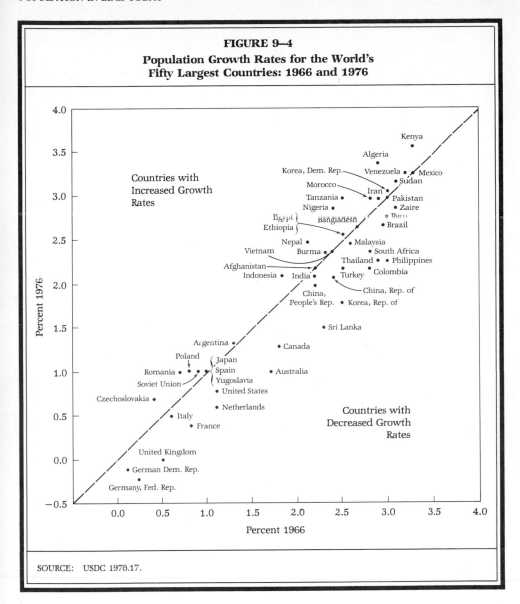

FIGURE 9—4

**Population Growth Rates for the World's
Fifty Largest Countries: 1966 and 1976**

SOURCE: USDC 1978.17.

1976. Countries growing at the highest rates (toward the upper right corner of the figure) are primarily LDCs; slower-growth countries (lower left corner) are mostly MDCs. But LDCs differ in the direction of the growth rate. Some (below the diagonal line) have decreasing rates, while others (above the line) have increasing ones. The rates for Kenya, Algeria, and Venezuela are well above 3.0 percent and are increasing.

Only a decade ago, predictions pointed almost universally toward continued increases in the growth rates of LDCs. The medical revolution has not yet spent itself, and countries with growth rates of less than 3 percent were expected to raise them as mortality declined further. These were the prospects for the "population explosion," grimly Mathusian. Policymakers in MDCs began to talk of *triage*, suggesting that the neediest countries might be abandoned so that scarce food supplies might be saved for those for whom there was some hope (Green, 1975). Berg felt it necessary to plead (1975) that potential expansion of food supplies might give the world more time.

· In the early seventies, new evidence began to appear. Kirk (1971) reported that the demographic transition in LDCs was already occurring, and with a much shorter lag than the MDCs had experienced 80 years ago. He showed (Table 9–5) that birth rates for many LDCs were already declining in the mid-sixties. His principal conclusions were as follows (p. 145):

1. A growing number of countries have been entering the demographic transition on the natality side since World War II, after a lapse of some 25 years in which no major country entered this transition.
2. Once a sustained reduction of the birth rate has begun, it proceeds at a much more rapid pace than it did historically in Europe and among Europeans overseas.
3. The "new" countries may reduce birth rates quite rapidly, despite initially higher levels than existed historically in western Europe.

Supporting evidence soon came from other sources. The Population Reference Bureau found (NYT, 4–29–76) the world birth rate declining from 34 per thousand in 1965 to 30 per thousand in 1974 and predicted that it might go as low as 20 per thousand in another ten years. It reported that population programs had had a "marked effect" in the three most populous LDCs: China, India, and Indonesia. Significant results had also been achieved in South Korea, Taiwan, Hong Kong, Cuba, Costa Rica, and Jamaica. By 1978, the Worldwatch Institute announced a "wary optimism" on birth rates in LDCs (NYT, 2–5–78), and demographers Ong Tsui and Bogue of the University of Chicago announced (AP, 1978) that "if recent trends continue, the world population crisis appears resolvable."

In 1978, the U.S. Department of Commerce published a major report, compiling the recent demographic estimates for all countries and regions of the world for which information was available (USDC, 1978); our Tables 9–3 and 9–4, and Figure 9–4, are taken from this report. It presents what we cited in the first paragraph of this chapter, that the world rate of population growth declined from 2.0 percent in 1965–1970 to 1.9 percent in 1975–1977. Unfortunately, the major components of that decline are in MDCs (Table 9–5), whose demographic transition apparently continues. But Asia and Latin America also show declines for the first time in this century. In 1980, the officials of Sichuan, the most populous province of China, announced that their population growth rate has been reduced to 0.6 percent per year (Butterfield, 1980). Only Africa's rate remains high, and it is increasing.

No one should assume from these reports that the "population explosion"

TABLE 9-4
World Population by Continent
and Development Category, 1950–1977

	Midyear population (millions)						
REGION	1977	1975	1970	1965	1960	1955	1950
WORLD	4,258	4,100	3,722	3,371	3,058	2,770	2,526
More developed	1,154	1,137	1,087	1,037	975	913	855
Less developed	3,103	2,963	2,634	2,335	2,082	1,856	1,671
AFRICA[a]	431	407	356	313	277	247	222
ASIA	2,486	2,382	2,133	1,903	1,710	1,534	1,387
More developed	160	156	143	133	124	116	106
Less developed	2,326	2,227	1,990	1,769	1,586	1,418	1,281
LATIN AMERICA[a]	342	324	284	249	216	189	166
NORTHERN AMERICA[b]	240	236	226	214	199	182	166
EUROPE AND THE SOVIET UNION[b]	737	729	702	675	640	604	573
OCEANIA	22	21	19	18	16	14	13
More developed	17	17	15	14	13	11	10
Less developed	5	4	4	3	3	3	2
Excluding the People's Republic of China:							
WORLD	3,275	3,157	2,875	2,617	2,375	2,159	1,978
Less developed	2,121	2,020	1,788	1,581	1,399	1,246	1,123
ASIA	1,504	1,439	1,286	1,149	1,027	924	839
Less developed	1,344	1,284	1,143	1,015	903	808	733

[a]Less developed.
[b]More developed.

SOURCE: USDC (1978:15).

has been solved or that it will automatically heal itself. On the contrary, the patient is still critical, still requires intensive care. There is some evidence that unremitting efforts in family planning, in the face of official discouragement, are in part responsible for the turnabout, though no one can be sure. Most serious of all, population itself will increase for at least another 30 or 40 years because of demographic momentum.

Demographic momentum is illustrated in the age structure diagrams of Figure 9–5. Like that of most LDCs, the population of Mexico is young, with the greatest numbers among the lower blocks of the pyramid, in contrast (say) to Sweden, whose population is more evenly spaced over age groups. Even if Mexico should reduce its birth rate per couple to equal its mortality rate, the advancing of lower age groups into reproductive years (pyramidal blocks moving upward) would increase the number of parents for many years to come,

TABLE 9–5
Birth Rates for All Less Developed Areas of over 500,000 Population Designated by the United Nations as Having "Virtually Complete" Vital Statistics, 1950–1969

	Average Birth Rate				Latest Birth Rate	
	1950–54	1955–59	1960–64	1965[a]	Year	Rate[b]
LATIN AMERICAN						
REGION	33.7	35.9	34.8	31.9	1967	30.9
Chile	49.1	49.1	44.8	40.0	1968	37.7
Costa Rica	49.0	49.3	48.6	44.4	1969	41.9
El Salvador	51.3	48.7	47.7	44.0	1968	42.5
Guatemala	42.9	43.6	42.0	38.2	1968	35.1
Guyana	34.8	39.2	40.3	37.0	1968	34.3
Jamaica	44.9	45.9	46.0	43.7	1969	42.2
Mexico	37.5	39.8	40.6	38.6	1969	38.0
Panama	36.6	33.7	31.2	26.7	1969	24.5
Puerto Rico	37.7	38.3	36.9	29.0	1968	27.4
Trinidad and Tobago						
NEAR EAST						
Israel	32.5	27.9	25.5	25.5	1969	26.1
Jordan	45.0	40.1	45.9	48.0	1966	47.8
Tunisia[c]	30.8	39.9	42.8	42.7	1968	40.4
ASIA						
Ceylon	38.5	36.6	34.9	32.2	1968	31.8
China (Taiwan)	45.9	42.8	37.1	29.7	1969	25.6
Hong Kong	34.2	36.3	32.8	24.2	1969	20.7
Malaysia (West)	44.1	44.4	40.3	36.4	1967	35.3
Ryukyus	35.5	29.2	24.0	21.4	1969	21.5
Singapore	45.5	42.8	35.6	27.0	1969	22.2
OTHER						
Albania	38.9	41.8	40.1	34.9	1968	35.6
Fiji	40.0	40.7	39.2	33.8	1968	30.2
Mauritius	46.2	41.0	38.9	31.8	1969	27.2

[a]Average from 1965 through the latest year, indicated in the next column.

[b]The most recent figures are usually provisional and are subject to later adjustment.

[c]Registered births. As corrected for underregistration, the average for 1961–64 is 49.1; the average for 1965–68 is 45.4; and the 1968 figure is 43 (7).

SOURCE: United Nations, *Monthly Bulletin of Statistics*, New York, July 1970; also cited in Kirk (1971:128). Copyright, United Nations, 1970. Reproduced by permission.

thus increasing the population. It has been estimated that even if world fertility rates should decline to replacement levels per couple in 1980–1985 (an extremely unlikely event), world population would eventually expand by 75 to 125 percent of 1970 levels and LDCs as a whole would expand by 90 percent (Teitelbaum, 1974:749). A more realistic fertility decline to replacement levels by 2000 would

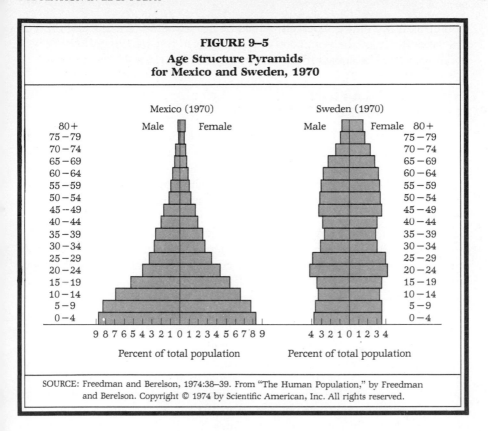

FIGURE 9–5

**Age Structure Pyramids
for Mexico and Sweden, 1970**

Mexico (1970)

Sweden (1970)

9 8 7 6 5 4 3 2 1 0 1 2 3 4 5 6 7 8 9

Percent of total population

4 3 2 1 0 1 2 3 4

Percent of total population

SOURCE: Freedman and Berelson, 1974:38–39. From "The Human Population," by Freedman and Berelson. Copyright © 1974 by Scientific American, Inc. All rights reserved.

imply an eventually stable population more than double the 1970 figure for such large countries as Bangladesh, Nigeria, Mexico, and the Philippines.

Increments of this order will require major demographic investment. The United Nations has estimated that in a "typical" LDC, 4 percent of national income must be spent for every 1 percent of population growth just to maintain the per capita levels of capital and to provide constant-productivity employment for increments in the labor force (ILO, 1973). Thus investment of about 12 percent of GDP would be required for a "typical" LDC whose population is growing at 3 percent per year. Rarely can an LDC save 20 percent of its GDP, and even if one does, then at this rate of population growth, two-thirds of the investment would go toward maintaining the status quo. There may be an illusion of progress: new schools, hospitals, factories, and a greater GDP. More jobs might even be available, but they might absorb only the increments in the labor force, leaving the hard-core unemployment unattended.

Walsh (1971, cited in ILO, 1973) has estimated demographic investment for Jamaica. Starting with 1970, he contrasts an unchanging fertility rate with one that would decline to replacement levels by 2000. The investment needed for a constant per capita income for 1975–1980 would be 14.8 percent of GDP under the high fertility assumption and 11.4 percent under the low. By 2000, 15.4 percent of GDP would be needed to maintain income levels under the high assumption, but only 2.2 percent would be needed under the low assumption. The labor force of the year 2000 is already born, but the capital with which it can work can be substantially affected by fertility rates.

OPTIMUM POPULATION AND OPTIMAL RATE OF GROWTH

Many economists have pondered whether a theoretical optimum can be found for both the amount of population and its rate of growth, such that optimal postulates can be applied to any specific situation. These economists have in mind some *other* optimum (or maximum) to which population may be related. For example, one may wish to maximize the discounted stream of per capita income into the indefinite future.

The concept was originated independently by Cannan (1888) and Wicksell (1909). Each referred to an optimal population at a given moment of time, other things (such as overhead capital, conditions of trade, and technology) being equal. The possibility that these determinants would shift caused Robinson (1956:343) to dub optimality a "will-o'-the-wisp," particularly so because population changes might themselves feed back upon the independent variables (Pitchford, 1974:87–88).

Samuelson (1958, 1975, 1976), who would maximize the per capita consumption stream, notes that an increased rate of population growth reduces consumption because of the need for demographic investment. It is therefore a negative force. On the other hand, an increased growth rate will improve consumption for retired persons, by providing more working-age individuals to support them. Samuelson thus calculates the optimal rate as something in between, "which maximizes per capita lifetime utility of consumptions" (1976:516). Along the same vein, Simon (1977) projects a model which argues that moderate rates of population growth have positive effects on the standard of living, superior to that of either a stationary or a very fast rate.

An optimum *population* (as opposed to *growth rate*) is presumably the number of people that leads to a present maximum of whatever is being maximized: per capita income, military strength, corruption income of government officials, or what have you. The population curve increases in the lower ranges, as the value of the maximand rises with increasing returns to (population) scale. As population becomes "excessive," with diminishing returns, the curve falls. Obviously, there is a maximum point in between. As technology, capital, and other complementary factors accumulate over time, the entire curve shifts, probably to the right (as world population increases). But the size of the earth could be the limiting factor that would ultimately slow down the increase in optimum population.

Besides the interrelatedness of variables mentioned by Robinson, critics point to a lack of agreement on the maximand. Indeed, there may be several maximands, in which case a welfare trade-off is required. Not only does the conceptual problem become complex, but the optimal size of growth rate selected may be so different from prevailing ones that the concept of optimum loses significance in LDC planning and in other decisions.

POPULATION GROWTH MODELS

Of greater potential use are macro-models of population growth, which can determine the impacts of many exogenous and endogenous variables simultaneously. Indeed, such models have frequently been integrated into economic growth models of the types discussed in Chapter 2. They are of two sorts: those in which population is taken as exogenous and those in which it is endogenous. In the pure Malthusian model, population growth is exogenous; it expands at its own, geometrically-progressing pace, constrained only by limited resources.

Population may be made endogenous in a Malthusian-type model, however, if its growth depends on income. Leibenstein (1957) and Nelson (1956) pioneered this type of model.[1] Perhaps the best-known model is that of Coale and Hoover (1958), in which positive rates of growth imply more dependents, who consume but do not (in their early years) produce. Since any growth in population increases the dependency ratio, it follows that the greater the growth rate, the lower the increase in "adult-equivalent" consumption over time. Coale and Hoover made a high-fertility (HF) and a low-fertility (LF) assumption. In the short run (15 years), total product grew more slowly under HF than under LF, but in the long run (50 years), the order was reversed. Even so, per capita income declined, because the population growth more than offset the increases.

Kelley (1974:40–44) suggests that a number of independent variables should be considered as affecting the population growth rate and that the interdependent (simultaneous) nature of household decisions should be recognized, on such matters as family size, saving, expenditure allocations, and workforce participation. But, he goes on, most of these presumed interrelationships are unresearched. For example, he says the conventional wisdom that children reduce a family's saving is not necessarily true. But "hard evidence on the relationship between family size and household saving rates is almost non-existent" (p. 41).

An extraordinarily complex, and ambitious, set of models was published by Correa (1975); variables include fertility, mortality, morbidity, intelligence, labor productivity, per capita output, birth control programs, health care conditions, nutrition, educational spending, and crime rates. Much empirical evidence is cited, but basically the models are simulation exercises. In such models, the effects of varying the independent variables (as if in a laboratory) are traced through.

By a cross-section study of 82 countries in four regions (with 1968 data), Hazledine and Moreland (1977) have prepared a macro-model of development and growth, in which they conclude that current income per capita does indeed determine changes in population, either directly or indirectly through the infant mortality rate and the percentage of the population living in rural areas. The relationships, however, differ significantly for the different world regions and particularly between LDC and MDC regions. For LDCs, they find some evidence for the Malthusian low-level equilibrium trap (in which increasing populations and low incomes are mutually reinforcing).

---

[1]Leibenstein also wrote a review of the literature in the field (Leibenstein, 1974).

How does one assess such information? And what is the use of macro-models? As in Chapter 2 (on planning), we find them interesting analytically, but deficient for providing a synoptic picture of population events. First, the recent evidence that LDCs are indeed reducing their birth rates appears to contradict the Hazledine-Moreland projections of the low-level equilibrium trap. A likely explanation lies in the deceptive nature of cross-section data, as opposed to time series, which we have already encountered on the question of income distribution during growth (Chapter 6). If the demographic transition becomes compressed over time, as Kirk (1971) has suggested, this fact would not be picked up by the cross-section analyses of Hazledine and Moreland. Second, most of the relationships between suspected independent variables on the one hand and birth and death rates on the other have not been adequately investigated (except perhaps that between the medical revolution and mortality). How do we assess a high R^2 in an empirical exercise, when we know of variables not included or when (from other evidence) we doubt the values of the parameters? (A rhetorical question.) Third, many macro-models are simulation exercises. They show the upper and lower limits of population growth, and related variables, *given* the assumptions of the model-maker. ("Gloom-in-gloom-out".) How can we evaluate the realism of assumptions? (Another rhetorical question.)

In criticizing macro-indicators, Birdsall (1977:81) argues that "cross-section analysis . . . does not necessarily mirror what has occurred within countries or what will occur over time. . . . One multivariate analysis that estimated *trends* in fertility as a function of *trends* in several socioeconomic indicators within groups of countries indicated no particular relationship between changes in fertility and the indicators (Janowitz, 1973). And several historical studies of the fertility decline in parts of eighteenth and nineteenth century Europe have led scholars to conclude that no particular indicator or set of indicators was related to changes in birth rates there." The implication is that correlates differ in different countries, not only in their direct effects but in the ways they intercombine; only a large number of micro-studies could sort them out. "Macro-determinants," she goes on, "cannot elucidate the specific mechanisms through which changes in gross indicators over time, or differences in gross indicators across countries, influence the fertility behavior of individuals."

AN ECONOMIC THEORY OF FERTILITY

Economists have attempted to treat decisions on fertility in a manner consistent with other areas of economic behavior (Becker, 1960). For a family, the decision to have children can be viewed as a constrained optimization problem where children enter the family utility function as a form of durable goods, along with other consumption items. Utility is then maximized subject to the constraints of income, wealth, and time, especially time spent by the mother.[2] As a durable good, children can be assumed to imply certain costs, but to yield benefits, either in the form of "psychological income" to parents or monetary income

[2]Mathematical detals are worked out fully by Willis (1973); also see Lindert (1978:43–57).

through work in later life. Thus, fertility would become a function of income, costs associated with child rearing, wealth, time, and tastes, including tastes for consumption of goods and services other than the enjoyment of children.

Over time, family formation takes on aspects of a stock adjustment model. Given family characteristics, a desired family size is determined. Fertility is then adjusted to create a family of the desired size. Births are simply the flow required to adjust the stock of children. This adjustment (Repetto, 1979:15–16) is determined, first, by the number of children currently alive, perhaps along with some of their personal characteristics such as sex. Community and/or household factors affecting child survival probabilities could be used to form an idea of the expected family size at points in the future should no new births take place. Second, stock adjustment will be determined by the number of children demanded. Third, the speed and efficiency with which fertility can be controlled will eventually determine the rate at which the stock can be adjusted.

Economic models tend to center on the second point above, the demand for children. One would expect that, *ceteris paribus*, increases in income would have a positive effect on fertility unless children are an "inferior" good, which there is no reason to believe. As income increases, however, the *cetera* are not *paria*, and several factors that can have a negative impact on fertility come into play. The costs involved in child rearing can rise with income if families feel they must spend more on the children they already have. Becker (1960) distinguishes between the mere quantity of children and their quality, where children of higher quality enjoy better nutrition and health care, education, recreational possibilities, and so on. If, as income rises, parents demand children of higher quality, the cost of raising children rises, and the effect of the increased cost can more than offset the positive influence of higher income. It is Becker's (1960:215) suspicion that the "quantity" elasticity of demand with respect to income is positive but small, while the "quality" elasticity is positive and high. Thus, on balance, increased income would decrease desired family size because of the negative effect of increased cost.

The cost of child rearing may also rise for reasons independent of quality considerations. As economic development occurs generally, and income rises, economic opportunities for women improve. Time spent in child rearing rather than as an economically active member of the labor force raises the opportunity cost of the former. The higher the educational levels of women, the greater is this opportunity cost (Cochrane, 1979). Higher levels of education also reduce the cost of understanding and obtaining birth control products. Additionally, development is likely to bring with it minimum educational requirements for children, as well as urban residence (rather than rural), where costs of food and shelter tend to be higher. Increased family income may reduce the need for the benefits of old-age support from one's offspring, and public social security programs may substitute for them in any event. The income earned by children may cease to be important to family support, and their participation in the labor force may be sharply limited by child labor laws anyway.

The rate at which fertility responds to income and cost changes can differ. Many of the factors mentioned in the previous paragraph, all tending to reduce fertility, are likely to affect desired family size only with a lag. Pure income effects (positive) will be felt first, then the impact (negative) of increased cost or preference for higher quality children will be felt. Perhaps for this reason, empirical work (Simon, 1977:353–63, and Repetto, 1979) has revealed that increased income tends to have a short-run positive effect on fertility, but that in the longer run, fertility tends to decline.

Convincing evidence has recently been presented by Repetto (1979) that the negative fertility response to increased income is greatest among lower-income families (also see Simon, 1977:364–75). The effect becomes smaller as one moves up the income ladder. At high income levels, fertility may respond positively to income increases, as costs become of little relevance and there is a greater positive wealth effect.

Economists and sociologists have many complementary interests that as yet have not been fully explored. Economists tend to stress the costs and benefits of children, and these studies are only beginning to bear the fruit of empirical testing. Sociologists dwell more upon the formation of preferences for families of certain sizes (Repetto, 1979). As development proceeds, people's concern for the future sharpens along with their belief in the efficacy of individual effort. A host of positivist forces can take hold. It is our expectation that increased cooperation across social science disciplines will improve upon our currently all-too-dim demographic view of LDCs.

AN OVERALL JUDGMENT

We seek an overall judgment on demographic events in LDCs. We do not expect mathematical precision, but we do want something more than intuition alone. Models with large numbers of variables and complex interrelationships suffer three disadvantages. First (a temporary one, we hope), most of the parameters are unresearched. Second, and more serious, different sets of independent variables may substitute for one another—being equally effective or ineffective on the birth rate—in different countries, as Hazledine and Moreland pointed out. Third, more independent variables mean fewer degrees of freedom. Some statistical techniques that combine unlike data (such as cross-section data with time-series data) increase their degrees of freedom, but the statistical significance thereby calculated must be accepted with some (indeterminate number) of grains of salt.

We therefore turn to an assembly of seemingly isolated sets of relationships, which have been brought out by both macro-model investigations and micro-type research. We then combine this statistical evidence with our own intuition, to judge such questions as whether population growth rates do respond (negatively) to per capita income and whether rich people tend to control births more than poor. A related question is whether maldistribution of income will cause the poor to grow in large numbers relative to the rich within countries, and whether therefore the Malthusian trap may apply differentially to them, as opposed to the rich. For policy purposes, it would be helpful also to have some idea as to whether family planning programs work.

STUDIES OF POPULATION CORRELATES

Fortunately, we are assisted by excellent review articles by Cassen (1976) and Birdsall (1977). They cite the principal conclusions of the growing abundance of micro-studies, as well as those of some macro-studies directed toward specific relationships. All the findings are tentative to some degree, although some are reasonably firm. As in so many other factors affecting economic development, once again we must reach opinions based on insufficient information.

FIRST, Leff (1969) found that the dependency burden does affect saving negatively. However, he used cross-section data (from 74 LDCs and MDCs), a method we have already criticized. He also discovered that the correlation is reduced if certain atypical countries are deleted. He found that governments able to impose higher taxes (because of higher incomes) have done so, regardless of the dependency burden. Our own intuition tells us to accept tentatively that population growth may adversely affect savings, but that there are likely to be exceptions, and we should be prepared to change our minds when new (time-series) information becomes available.

SECOND, a decline in fertility will not occur unless there has been a prior decline in mortality. This finding stands on more sold ground, having been confirmed by large numbers of historical and current studies (Carvalho, 1974, Demeny, 1968, and Gray, 1974, as well as the history of all European countries). No threshold has been discovered, however, and no exact parameter can be specified.

THIRD, children in large families are likely to suffer in a number of ways, relative to those in small families. They are more likely to be malnourished (Wray, 1971, and Gopalan, 1969), to be physically smaller (Terhune, 1975), and possibly even to be less intelligent (Zajonc, 1976). Although a generalization based on the particulars of any of these studies would be "heroic," nevertheless in the aggregate they point toward the probability of some disadvantages to children in large families, if only in that the burden of deprivation falls heavily on them.

FOURTH, the more educated the parents, the less likely they are to have large numbers of children. A continuous relationship supporting this is found in studies within countries (Botswana, 1972, Kenya, 1966, Knodel and Prachuabmoh, 1974, Turkey, 1970, and United Kingdom, 1976), as well as internationally and interregionally (Cochrane, 1979). This finding is therefore reasonably firm. Reasons for it, however, are speculative. Perhaps better-educated parents prefer more education for their children, the cost of which they can afford more easily if there are fewer children. Some suggest that better-educated parents, with greater earning and saving capacity, are less in need of children as old-age security. Lewis's "culture of poverty" (Chapter 3) might be consistent with the proposition that better-educated people show more concern for the welfare of their children, though some would take this suggestion as a show of cultural arrogance.

Birdsall (1977:87) reports that education of the mother correlates closely and negatively with birth rate. Her presumption is that educated mothers have greater access to birth control methods; that their age at marriage may be greater; and that they are more likely to take employment rather than to rear children, since they may enjoy higher earning power and therefore the opportunity cost of children is higher. Several studies show that female labor-force participation correlates negatively with fertility only in high-prestige jobs in the modern sector.

FIFTH, overpopulation has unfortunate ecological consequences. Eckholm (1976) found that growing populations are stripping the land of its fertility and resources in wide areas of Africa, Asia, and Latin America. Overgrazing and overcultivation of marginal lands have increased the amount of desert, especially in the Sahel. In Chapter 11 (on agrarian reform), we will find that nomadic populations probably make more efficient use of marginal lands than they would as settled farmers. It is when the balance is upset by declining mortality, and nomads become increasingly settled, that the land suffers. Forests disappear as they are taken for firewood and as new trees are given insufficient time to grow; erosion, flooding, and silting of rivers follow (Cassen, 1976:807). Irrigated lands lose productivity through water-logging and salinity. The impact of growing populations on the limited totality of earth resources—minerals as well as land—became a focus of the United Nations conference on environment in Nairobi in 1975 (Mohr, 4–20–75). Much controversy but little solid evidence surrounds these wider concerns, valid though they may prove in the long run. The impact of population growth on cities will be discussed in Chapter 12.

SIXTH, family planning may not be very effective in persuading parents to adopt birth control, but given proper organization, it may assist them in implementing the decision, once taken.[3] In many countries, it has not realized its potential. These are very loose judgments, however; others might easily infer something else, given the same information.

There is no way of conclusively separating the effects of family planning from other events, such as development itself. Writing for the World Bank, Cuca and Pierce (1978) emphasize how difficult it is to obtain randomization and well-matched comparison groups, and how some researchers have been forced to use proxy variables (knowledge, attitude, practice) instead of fertility. The question is not whether family planning correlates (negatively) with fertility—in some programs it does and in some it doesn't—but rather which kinds of programs are more effective than others. The researchers found that use of the mass media augments awareness, but there is no evidence of the degree to which awareness translates into decreased fertility. An integrated health approach may have a synergistic relationship to family planning, in which some program structures are more effective than others. Results of intensive campaigns have been mixed; payments to acceptors have immediate results, but

---

[3]For an excellent and concise summary of positions for and against population control, see Teitelbaum (1974:750–53).

no one knows the long-term effect (except, of course, for irreversible sterilization). Inundation, or the easy availability of cheap contraceptives (usually condoms), generally results in increased sales, but no one knows about effective usage.

Selective successes are reported for particular countries. A combination of government and private family-planning services in Colombia is credited with helping to reduce the number of children a woman is expected to bear in her lifetime from seven in 1960–1964 to four in 1977 (deOnis, 1977). Planned Parenthood reports similar results for Costa Rica, Chile, Jamaica, and Puerto Rico. They also reveal that about 20 percent of the 80 million women of fertile age in Latin America are using contraceptives—while, of course, a whopping 80 percent are not.

A survey taken in Costa Rica (Waisamen and Dunlak, 1966:48) finds significant overall receptivity, which is even greater among the following groups of people: those who are younger and better educated, those who use the mass media, those knowledgeable about reproductive processes, those satisfied with personal life conditions, those less committed to religious conformity, innovative people, and those with high educational aspirations for their children.

Indonesia, with the fifth largest population in the world (after China, India, the Soviet Union, and the United States), is generally credited with an exceptionally successful official program, supported by the World Bank, United Nations agencies, and U.S. foreign aid. Fertility has declined from 44 per thousand in 1970 to 34 per thousand in 1977 (Kamm, NYT, 5–14–78). Of course, no one can prove any cause-effect relationship. Nag (1978), of the Population Council in New York, believes a high latent demand for contraceptive services in Bali and East Java existed before the program began, in part because of the high proportion of women working outside the home.

Among the most successful in reducing the birth rate are certain Far Eastern countries previously identified as successful in economic growth and greater equity in the distribution of income and wealth. Although the population growth rate of the People's Republic of China increased from 1.9 percent in 1950 (perhaps low because of war aftermath) to 2.4 percent in 1955–1957, it declined to 2.0 percent by 1974–1976 (these and the following data are from USDC, 1978). The rate for Taiwan fell from 3.3 percent in 1950 to 2.1 percent in 1976. For South Korea the rate rose from a wartime low (0.1 percent in 1950) to 3.3 percent in 1959–1960, but then dropped to 1.8 percent (1975–1976). (In North Korea, however, the rate has remained high, at around 3.1 percent.) In Japan, the rate fell from 1.6 percent in 1950 to 1.0 percent in 1976. All these countries that have exhibited falling rates have had strong family planning programs, but the other successes they have enjoyed may have been equally responsible.

One testimony to the effectiveness of family planning is the report (NYT, 3–13–79) that the birth rate among blacks in Zimbabwe, already the highest in Africa, soared when family-planning clinics were closed because of wartime financial stringencies.

The southern cone of Latin America is also a "success" area, but here the cause can be neither family planning nor economic progress. Argentina's population growth rate fell from 2.0 percent in 1950 to 1.3 percent in 1974–1976; Chile's fell from 2.6 percent to 1.6 percent in the same period; and Uruguay's fell from 1.3 percent to 0.6 percent. No one knows why. Unfortunately, the same successes are not evident in much of the rest of Latin America.

Alongside these examples of success are some that are less so. In 1976, the Government of India began to penalize its citizens if they would not thereafter limit their families to two children. Government employees would not be promoted, and "a couple's access to almost the entire range of government assistance—from government jobs and housing to loans, medical care, schools, and drinking water" would be cut off (NYT, 2–26–76). Birth control services were offered ubiquitously; sterilization was encouraged and, some charged, imposed through high pressure on those too ignorant to resist. More than anything else, the downfall of the Indira Gandhi government in 1977 is credited to this campaign (she was reelected in 1979, however). Family planning was severely set back, because the successor government had to proceed very cautiously.

Voluntary campaigns in some other countries have shown limited, if any, success. In 1974, the Population Institute of the University of the Philippines announced fewer enlisters in the family planning program, although the birth rate had been cut five percent in the four years since the program had started (NYT, 12–15–74). Because of the personal convictions of President Ne Win, Burma is the only Asian country offering official opposition to family planning, with the import of contraceptives banned (Lelyveld, 1974).

Freedman and Berelson (1976) have assessed family planning programs the world over, grading them according to "program effort" and "social setting," and have measured performance by the percentage of married women of fertile age who have used contraceptives as clients of the program (Cassen, 1976:796). This performance, they find, varies positively with both measures. Furthermore, "they find a considerable proportion of acceptors among disadvantaged socioeconomic groups in at least three countries (Indonesia, South Korea, Taiwan)" (Cassen, 1976:796–97). They also find an overall relationship between national birth rates and proportions of contraceptive users.

Some family planning studies have compared the costs and benefits of averting a single birth and, by extension, any number of births (if a linear relationship is assumed). The cost is usually that of the family planning services; benefits are the demographic investment and the consumption saved, less the lifetime marginal product of the potential person. But the assumptions of these studies, especially with respect to benefits, are too difficult to assess. The whole concept is often out of line with community values, or it treads on community sensibilities, and therefore cannot be put to any useful purpose.

POPULATION, PER CAPITA INCOME, AND INCOME DISTRIBUTION

When plotted on coordinate axes, the growth rates of GDP and population scatter widely (Chesnais and Sauvy, 1973, Conlisk and Huddle, 1969, Easterlin, 1967, Kuznets, 1965, and Thirwall, 1972). There may therefore be no relationship. But there may also be a double-reverse relationship: population growth may increase GDP growth rates, which in turn reduce population growth, so that the two rates cancel each other. We cannot tell whether one of these is the case, or whether there is something else. On the other hand, greater growth rates in income per capita are usually associated with lesser population growth rates. However, the two are so intertwined with other demographic variables that no one can isolate causes and effects (Hazledine and Moreland, 1977:253–62, and Cassen, 1976:806).

There is much evidence that low-income people in LDCs prefer large families and that it is to their economic advantage to have them. Mamdani (1973) found this to be so for a small village in India. In studying the bazaar economy in Davao, Philippines, Hackenberg (1973) discovered that families with an extra worker could open up another retail store. They probably did not add to aggregate retail services, but instead appropriated for themselves a greater share of the total. Thus they demonstrated Samuelson's (1980) fallacy of composition, that what is good for every individual separately may be detrimental, in the aggregate, for the community.

The impact of population growth on income distribution is also complex. First, it may set in motion changes in the socioeconomic framework. An increased number of poor workers may cause reduction in their wages; an increased number of farmers may cause an increase in their land rents. There is much historical evidence of changes in the proportions paid by sharecroppers to their landlords as land and labor became expensive or scarce, relative to each other (the increase in farm wages after the Black Plague, 1348, for example). But more subtly, an increased population may set up mobility from occupation to occupation, or from rural areas to urban, and these different sectors may have different levels of living.

We might secure a better purchase on income distribution if we knew whether the poor population was growing more rapidly than the rich. There are scattered indications that this is so, though population censuses in LDCs do not normally reveal much about income-brackets. One case where data are available indicates that the poor (black people) are growing more rapidly than the rich (white people) in South Africa. Citations such as those of Mamdani (1973) and Hackenberg (1973), as well as the earlier-mentioned evidence relating levels of education to fertility, lead us indirectly to believe that in most LDCs, the poor are growing at a more rapid rate than the rich. If this is so, then income distribution probably becomes more inequitable the more rapid the population growth—not only because of the sheer numbers, but also because of the Hackenberg effect cited above and, in general, the working of the marginal productivity theory of wages.

Second, there is a purely mechanical effect. Those entering the labor force in their teens and twenties generally command lower incomes than more experienced workers in their forties and fifties, and the latter may have higher incomes than retired people in their seventies and eighties. Paglin (1975), Peek (1974), and others refer to the age-income profiles we discussed in Chapter 5. Profiles for Mexico and the United States appear in Table 9–6. In Mexico, peak income is reached during ages 50 to 59, while in the United States it occurs

TABLE 9–6
Age-Income Profiles, United States and Mexico

UNITED STATES		MEXICO	
Age of family head (years)	Average Annual Family Income, 1972 (US$)	Age of family head (years)	Average Annual Family Income, 1972 (US$)
14–24	7,892	under 24	1,421
25–34	11,699	25–29	1,594
35–44	14,394	30–34	1,776
45–54	15,690	35–39	1,787
55–64	13,757	40–44	2,179
over 64	8,356	45–49	2,158
		50–59	2,306
		60 +	2,044

SOURCE: Paglin (1975), Banco de Mexico (1974, Table II–4). Reprinted by permission of the American Economic Association and Fondo de Cultura Económica.

between 45 and 54. In countries where population growth rates accelerate and greater proportions of people are in lower-age groups, income inequality would increase, other things being equal. It would increase all the more if decreased mortality rates stretched the senior brackets. But these biases are statistical only, for lifetime expected earnings of any age group are not affected.

The "age-income profile" bias might be overcome statistically if income comparisons over time were disaggregated into age groups. Paglin (1975) has done this for the United States, but we know of no one who has done similar work for LDCs.

In sum, the impact of population growth on income and its distribution is so complex and so lacking in hard data that little can be said without major qualifications. Within these qualifications, however, our scattered evidence is that population growth takes place more rapidly in lower income groups. Although an individual family may gain, on balance, by another pair of hands, in the aggregate more rapid growth probably harms the poor, because of the marginal productivity effect—even after adjustment for the age-income-profile bias.

CONCLUSION

Since the dawn of settled agriculture and cattle breeding, populations have increased with prosperity and peace and declined with famine, pestilence, and war. Until the seventeenth century, the net result was slow overall growth, coupled with migrations into open land. From the eighteenth century onward, European and American populations grew at an increasing rate, along with technological progress in both the economy and medicine. These growth rates began to taper in the latter part of the nineteenth century and (with some interruptions) have continued to do so during the twentieth.

The medical revolution did not extend to LDCs generally until the twentieth century. When it did, population growth rates spurted to heights never before seen. Whereas rates for European countries were at a maximum of about 1.5 percent in the nineteenth century, many of today's LDCs have reached 3.0 percent or more, and some are even approaching 4.0 percent.

We can never be sure that a present route will exactly follow a similar one from the past. This admonition is needed even more when the starting point is a different place: at higher population growth rates; during a "sudden" rather than a "slow" medical revolution; when there is little cross-sectional correlation between population and prosperity; and when international migration potential is almost exhausted. Despite these differences, there is already some indication that the demographic transition in LDCs has started. The unresolved issues are: whether it will continue, how long it will take, and what damage may be done in the meantime. Unfortunately, history is of little use to us here, for now the difference in starting points assumes its meaning.

There is much resistance to family planning in LDCs, because (it is argued) large families help the poor. There is some evidence that for individual families this is true, although the aggregate effect on the poor is negative. The case against family planning is also argued on the basis of human values and sensibilities, and a few believe that family planning is a plot on the part of MDC governments to make LDCs servile by reducing their numerical strength. The latter argument is fallacious. The evidence, both historical and current, is overwhelming that supernumeraries weaken, rather than strengthen, an economic and political entity.

Family planning has had a mixed experience in LDCs, and no one can assess its direct relationship to the increasing demographic transition. There is strong evidence that it has been successful in some countries. Only a few successful cases, of course, are necessary to demonstrate its potential. One researcher, who evaluated family planning programs according to their quality, discovered that the performance of higher-quality programs was greater than that of lower and that there is a loose correlation between quality of program and decline in fertility. Evidence that family planning programs persuade couples to reduce their fertility when otherwise they would not do so (or even when they are wavering) is hard to come by. The numbers of success relationships recorded would, however, support the intuitive belief that they help couples to implement such a decision.

Despite the mixed response of LDCs to family planning programs, one should not regard lightly the LDC slogan with which we began this chapter: "Take care of the people, and population will take care of itself." The point may have been overstated for political impact, but it remains nonetheless: that improved living standards, rising incomes, and greater equality are negatively related to fertility.

So long as growth rates are positive, population will of course continue to grow, and because of demographic momentum it will grow for a long time. The approach by those who are concerned must be one of continued vigilance, improvement in quality of family planning programs, and sustained economic development. It must also be one of adaptation to, and provision for, the larger populations which over the next fifty years cannot be avoided.

We continue, therefore, to be sobered by the following news (Reinhold, 1979):

> Despite widespread signs that the world population growth rate has finally started to decline, the Census Bureau reported today that the population could be expected to increase by about 50 percent, reaching 6.35 billion by the year 2000.
>
> If the projected increase of 2.26 billion people between 1975 and the year 2000 holds true, the population rise for just a quarter of a century would be equal to the entire world population increase from the time of Christ until about 1950. About 90 percent of the growth would occur in poorer countries inhabited by black, brown and yellow-skinned peoples . . .

BIBLIOGRAPHY

Associated Press Report, 10–18–78:
"Population Time Bomb Defused by Birth Control," Associated Press news report.
Banco de Mexico, 1974:
La Distribución del Ingreso en México, Mexico, Fondo de Cultura Económica.
Becker, G. S., 1960:
"An Economic Analysis of Fertility," in National Bureau of Economic Research, *Demographic and Economic Change in Developed Countries*, Princeton, N.J., Princeton University Press, 209–231.
Bennett, M. K., 1954:
The World's Food, New York, Harper and Brothers.
Berg, Alan, 6–15–75:
"The Trouble with Triage," *New York Times Magazine*.
Birdsall, Nancy, 1977:
"Analytical Approaches to the Relationship of Population Growth and Development," *Population and Development Review*, 3:1 and 2, March/June, 63–102.
Botswana, 1972:
Report on the Population Census, 1971, Gabarone, Central Statistical Office.
Butterfield, Fox, 1–29–80:
"Chinese Area Claims It Curbs Population," *New York Times*.
Cannan, E., 1888:
Elementary Political Economy, London.
Carr-Saunders, Alexander M., 1963:
World Population: Past Growth and Present Trends, Oxford, Clarendon Press.
Carvalho, J. A. M., 1974:
"Regional Trends in Fertility and Mortality in Brazil," *Population Studies*, November.
Cassen, Robert H., 1976:
"Population and Development: A Survey," *World Development*, Vol. 4, No. 10–11, October–November.
Chesnais, J. S., and Sauvy, A., 1973:
"Progrès économique et accroissement de la population; une expérience commentée," *Population*, July–October.
Cipolla, Carlo, 1976:
Before the Industrial Revolution: European Society and Economy, 1000–1700, London, Methuen and Company.
Clark, Colin, 1968:
Population Growth and Land Use, New York, St. Martin's Press.

Coale, Ansley J., 1974:
"The History of the Human Population," *Scientific American*, September.
Coale, Ansley J., and Hoover, E. M., 1958:
Population Growth and Economic Development in Low-Income Countries, Princeton, N.J., Princeton University Press.
Cochrane, S. H., 1979:
Fertility and Education: What Do We Really Know? World Bank Staff Occasional Paper No. 26, Baltimore, Md., Johns Hopkins University Press.
Conlisk, J., and Huddle, D., 1969:
"Allocating Foreign Aid: An Appraisal of a Self-Help Model," *Journal of Development Studies*, July.
Correa, Hector, 1975:
Population, Health, Nutrition, and Development: Theory and Development: Theory and Planning, Lexington, Mass., Heath, Lexington Books.
Crittenden, Ann, 5–5–76:
"Khan Sees Hope for World's Poor," *New York Times.*
Cuca, Roberto, and Pierce, Catherine S., 1978:
Experiments in Family Planning: Lessons from the Developing World, Baltimore, Md., Johns Hopkins, for the World Bank.
Daily Nation, 5–24–74:
"The Pill Blamed for Freak Babies," Nairobi.
Demeny, P., 1968:
"Early Fertility Decline in Austria-Hungary; a lesson in demographic transition, *Daedalus*, Spring, reprinted in Glass and Revelle.
dcOnis, Juan, 1977:
"Birth Control in Latin America Making Little Headway as Population Pressures Grow," *New York Times*, June 20.
Durand, John, 1977:
"Historical Estimates of World Population: An Evaluation," *Population and Development Review*, September.
Easterlin, R., 1967:
"Effects of Population Growth on the Economic Development of Developing Countries," *Annals of the American Academy of Political and Social Science*, January.
Eckholm, Erik P., 1976:
Losing Ground: Environmental Stress and World Food Prospects, New York, W. W. Norton.
Freedman, R., and Berelson, B. 1974:
"The Human Population," *Scientific American*, September, pp. 38–9.
Freedman, R., and Berelson, B., 1976:
"The Record of Family Planning Programmes," *Studies in Family Planning*, Vol. 7, No. 1, January.
Glass, D. V., and Revelle, R., 1972:
Population and Social Change, London, Edward Arnold.
Gopalan, C., 1969:
"Observations of Some Epidemiological Factors of Protein-Calorie Malnutrition," in A. Von Muralt, ed., *Protein-Calorie Malnutrition*, New York.
Gray, R. H., 1974:
"The Decline in Mortality in Ceylon and the Demographic Effects of Malaria Control," *Population Studies*, July.
Green, Wade, 1–5–75:
"Triage: Who Shall be Fed, and Who Shall Starve?" *New York Times Magazine.*
Hackenberg, Robert A., 1973:
A Developing City in a Dual Economy: Economic and Demographic Trends in Davao City, Philippines, 1972, Davao City, Davao Action Information Center.
Hazledine, T., and Moreland, R. S., 1977:
"Population and Economic Growth: A World Cross-Section Study," *Review of Economics and Statistics*, 59:3, August, 253–63.

Hauser, Philip M., 1971:
"World Population: Retrospect and Prospect," in U.S. National Academy of Sciences, *Rapid Population Growth: Consequences and Policy Implications*, Baltimore, Md., Johns Hopkins University Press.

ILO, 1973:
Population and Labor, International Labor Office, Geneva.

Janowitz, Barbara S., 1973:
"An Econometric Analysis of Trends in Fertility Rates," *Journal of Development Studies*, April.

Kamm, Henry, 5–14–78:
"Birth Control Program Succeeds in Cutting Indonesian Growth Rate," *New York Times*.

Kelley, Allen C., 1974:
"The Role of Population Models of Economic Growth," *American Economic Review*, Vol. 64, No. 2, May.

Kenya, 1966:
Population Census, 1962, Nairobi, Ministry of Economic Planning and Development.

Kirk, Dudley, 1971:
"A New Demographic Transition?" in National Academy of Sciences, *Rapid Population Growth: Consequences and Policy Implications*, Baltimore, Md., Johns Hopkins University Press.

Knodel, J., and Prachuabmoh, V., 1974:
"Demographic Aspects of Fertility in Thailand," *Population Studies*, November.

Kuznets, Simon, 1965:
"Demographic Aspects of Modern Economic Growth," *World Population Conference*, Belgrade.

Leff, Nathaniel, 1969:
"Dependency Rates and Savings Rates," *American Economic Review*, Vol. 59, No. 5, December.

Leibenstein, Harvey, 1957:
A Theory of Economic-Demographic Development, Princeton, N. J., Princeton University Press.

Leibenstein, Harvey, 1974:
"An Interpretation of the Economic Theory of Fertility: Promising Path or Blind Alley?" *Journal of Economic Literature*, Vol. 12, No. 2, June.

Lelyveld, Joseph, 11–5–74:
"Burmese Leader Resists Birth Control Programs," *New York Times*.

Lindert, P. H., 1978:
Fertility and Scarcity in America, Princeton, N.J., Princeton University Press.

Mamdani, Mahmood, 1973:
The Myth of Population Control: Family, Caste, and Class in an Indian Village, New York, Monthly Review Press.

Mohr, Charles P., 4–20–75:
"Tampering with Nature Perils Health, U.N. Environment Unit's Report Warns," *New York Times*.

Nag, Moni, 5–25–78:
"Birth Control: An Indonesian Success Story," *New York Times*.

Nelson, Richard, 1956:
"A Theory of the Low-Level Equilibrium Trap in Underdeveloped Countries," *American Economic Review*, December.

New York Times, 12–15–74:
"Manila Set Back on Birth Control," *New York Times*.

New York Times, 11–2–75:
"Burmese Leader Resists Birth Control," *New York Times*.

New York Times, 2–26–76:
"Delhi to Penalize Couples for Not Limiting Births," *New York Times*.

New York Times, 4–29–76:
    "World Birth Rate Down for Decade," *New York Times.*
New York Times, 2–5–78:
    "Food and Population: Wary Optimism," *New York Times.*
New York Times, 3–13–79:
    "Decades of Black Gains Being Wiped Out by Guerrilla War," *New York Times.*
North, Douglas, and Thomas, 1973:
    The Rise of the Western World: A New Economic History, New York, Cambridge University Press.
Ohlin, Goran, 1965:
    Presentation at World Population Conference.
Paglin, M., 1975:
    "The Measurement and Trend in Inequality: A Basic Revision," *American Economic Review*, September.
Peek, P., 1974:
    "Household Savings and Demographic Change in the Philippines," *Malayan Economic Review*, 19:2, October, 86–104.
Pitchford, J. D., 1974:
    Population in Economic Growth, Amsterdam, North-Holland Publishing Company.
Reinhold, Robert, 2–26–79:
    "50% Rise in World Population Forecast by Year 2000," *New York Times.*
Rensenberger, Royce, 7–16–78:
    "Lag in World Food Output Renews Fear of Famine," *New York Times.*
Repetto, R., 1979:
    Economic Equality and Fertility in Developing Countries, Baltimore, Md., Johns Hopkins University Press.
Robinson, Joan R., 1956:
    The Accumulation of Capital, New York, Macmillan.
Samuelson, Paul A., 1958:
    "An Exact Consumption-Loan Model of Interest With or Without the Social Contrivance of Money," *Journal of Political Economy*, December.
Samuelson, Paul A., 1975:
    "The Optimum Growth Rate for Population," *International Economic Review*, October.
Samuelson, Paul A., 1976:
    "The Optimum Growth Rate for Population: Agreement and Evaluations," *International Economic Review*, June.
Samuelson, Paul A., 1980:
    Principles of Economics, Eleventh Edition, New York McGraw-Hill.
Simon, Julian L., 1977:
    The Economics of Population Growth, Princeton, N.J., Princeton University Press.
Teitelbaum, Michael S., 1976:
    "Comment," *World Development*, 4:10 and 11, October/November, 831–35.
Teitelbaum, Michael S., 1974:
    "Population and Development: Is a Consensus Possible?" *Foreign Affairs*, July.
Terhune, Kenneth, 1975:
    Review of the Actual and Expected Consequences of Family Size, U.S. National Institute of Health (Dept. of Health, Education and Welfare), Washington, D.C., U.S. Government Printing Office.
Thirwall, A. P., 1972:
    "A Cross-Section Study of Population Growth and the Growth of Output and *Per Capita* Income in a Production Function Framework," *Manchester School*, December.
Turkey, 1970:
    Census of Population 1970: Sampling Results, Ankara, State Institute of Statistics.

United Kingdom, 1976:
   Bangladesh Retrospective Survey of Fertility and Mortality, London, Ministry of
   Overseas Development.
USDC (United States Department of Commerce), 1978:
   World Population 1977, Washington, D.C.
USDC (United States Department of Commerce), 1980:
   *International Population Dynamics, 1950–79: Demographic Estimates for Countries
   with a Population of 5 Million of More*, Washington, D.C.
Waisamen, F. B., and Dunlak, Jerome J., 1966:
   A Survey of Attitudes Related to Costa Rican Population Dynamics, San José, Costa
   Rica, American International Association for Economic and Social Development
   (Apartado 1587, San José).
Walsh, B. T., 1971:
   Economic Development and Population Control: A Fifty-Year Projection for Jamaica,
   New York, Praeger.
Wicksell, Knut, 1909:
   The Theory of Population, its Composition and Changes, Stockholm, Albert Bonniers
   Forlag.
Willcox, Walter F., 1940:
   Studies in American Demography, Ithaca, N.Y., Russell.
Willis, R. J., 1973:
   "A New Approach to the Economic Theory of Fertility," *Journal of Political Economy*,
   81:2, Part II, March/April, 514–64.
Wray, Joe D., 1971:
   "Population Pressure on Families: Family Size and Child Sparing," in National
   Academy of Sciences.
Zajonc, R. B., 1976:
   "Family Configuration and Intelligence," *Science*, April.

10

HUMAN CAPITAL, NUTRITION, HEALTH, AND EDUCATION

*On a wall of the school of medicine at Mexico National University,
students have painted a seemingly obvious message for a country
in which half the population receives no medical attention: "We
demand the right to work. Medicine for the people."*

*Yet every year, thousands of newly-graduated doctors, whose
education has cost the country millions of dollars, are unable to
find work. And among those who are granted residencies in
Government hospitals or who have enough capital to establish
their own practices, most remain in the urban centers of
Mexico City, Guadalajara, and Monterrey.*

(RIDING, *NEW YORK TIMES*, MARCH 3, 1979).

Along with physical capital, investment in human beings—in their health, well-being, and education—is widely considered a key to economic growth. Chronic illness and ignorance are a drag on all sectors of an economy because of the labor and skills that are lost. It is sometimes suggested that greater attention to health and education would improve the distribution of income.

Unfortunately, the record is disappointing. In health, potential payoffs have not been realized. The marginal economic contribution of healthy people (as opposed to ill) has been estimated at many times the cost to make them healthy—yet chronic illness continues where its elimination is feasible and cheap. Education, on the other hand, often receives high priority in LDCs, being first in the budget of some countries and second only to military in the budgets of many others. But the tendency is to subsidize the rich, by emphasizing secondary schools and universities, while slighting the poor, who are more in need of the basic literacy and numeracy taught in primary grades.

Many studies in production functions reveal that a large part of output increments cannot be explained by the increase in physical inputs alone (Schiavo-Campo and Singer, 1970). About one-half of the "residual" must be caused by human endeavor, in improved technology, organization, labor discipline, and health. (For a survey of these and other studies of human capital, see Mincer, 1970.)

In the present chapter, we will first consider health and nutrition, and then education. Although each of these has a consumption value, in that it is desired for its own sake, we will concentrate only on the quantifiable economic consequences of investment in these areas. At the end of the chapter, we will examine some of the historical parameters of education.

HEALTH AND NUTRITION

Poor health and nutrition damage the economy in three ways. First, they withdraw labor, through absenteeism and premature death. Second, they waste current resources, in that it is often more costly to cure a person than to keep him healthy in the first place. Third, they reduce labor productivity, in that ill people may work at a slow pace. We will consider these in turn.

REDUCTION IN AVAILABLE LABOR

Not only does absenteeism lead to direct loss of labor, but skilled labor cannot easily be replaced. Often losses are substantial. Berg (1967) estimated that the Philippines suffered an annual loss of $11 million due to beriberi, including production loss from absenteeism, medical costs for ill workers, loss from premature death, and burial costs. Beriberi can be simply treated by introducing thiamin into traditional diets—a clear case of preventive cost being a tiny fraction of losses suffered. A tuberculosis program in South Korea (World Bank, 1975) returned $150 for every dollar spent, through increased working life and decreased absenteeism.

Not only is life itself prolonged by adequate health care, but *working* life is likely to be increased. The loss of working life can be costly in the case of skilled labor, since job training and experience are wasted.

WASTE OF RESOURCES

Enteric diseases are among the most prevalent health problems in LDCs. Dysentery is probably the leading cause of death in Paraguay, Guatemala, El Salvador, and Pakistan (World Bank, 1975), and it may be in other countries as well. Common among infants and small children, it is debilitating when not fatal. Enteric diseases generally impair the body's ability to absorb nutrients.

A study in Panama showed that the value of excess food consumed to offset losses from enteric disease is worth about $10 per person per year.

Most health expenditures in LDCs have been curative rather than preventative. Similarly, most health aid from foreign donors has been for formal health facilities, such as hospitals, health centers, and training of doctors and nurses.

Poor health conditions are often associated with wider failures in the use of resources. In many areas of Africa, sleeping sickness has made potential agricultural land uninhabitable, and in Africa, Asia, and Latin America, particularly resistant strains of malaria have prevented the maximum use of large land areas. In some cases, the potential for tourism as well as agriculture suffers. Furthermore, diseases affecting animals (such as hoof-and-mouth) diminish export potential.

REDUCTION IN LABOR PRODUCTIVITY

Many cases are on record of poor health reducing a laborer's capacity to work hard or to concentrate. In Indonesia, the World Bank (1975) found that 85 percent of workers in construction and rubber were infected with hookworm. Of these, 45 percent had associated anemia, on account of iron deficiencies. Iron supplements for 60 days, at a cost of 13¢ per day per worker, increased their productivity by about 19 percent—yielding a benefit-cost ratio of 280:1.

When construction of the Pan-American Highway fell behind schedule, inefficiencies in the deployment of capital and materials were first suspected. When some firms began providing three balanced meals per day for workers, however, productivity went up 200 percent (Berg, 1967).

Children in LDCs are often mentally retarded because of inadequate nutrition (Berg, 1973). Selowsky and Taylor (1973) calculated the income forgone by Chilean adults who were mentally retarded as children, compared to normal adults. Their study was in two parts. First, they regressed the IQs (intelligence quotients) of a sample of children from a Santiago slum on a number of potential explanatory variables, several of which represented family background, such as parents' education and parents' IQs. They found that in general, a 10 percent increase in a child's weight was associated with a 5 to 6.5 percent increase in IQ, while there was no statistical relationship to the socioeconomic variables.

Second, they constructed a measure of reduced productivity from nutritionally-induced mental retardation in a sample of 91 construction workers. These workers were of similar socioeconomic background to the children; indeed, they were in the type of occupation the children could be expected to enter later on. The workers' incomes were found to correlate with their IQs (a 10 percent increase in IQ led to a 6 to 7 percent increase in income), but they did not correlate with amount of schooling. Besides IQ, the major explanatory variable found to be significant was age.

By putting the two studies together, the authors estimated that adequate nutrition would increase the children's IQ from an average of 72 to the 90–95 range. If the IQs were raised to 87, if children entered the work force at 15, and if a discount rate of 10 percent is taken, the present value of future income increments was estimated, at age 2, to be $250 to $400. Thus an expenditure within that range for increased nutrients, from birth to two years, would have been "economically profitable," not to mention all the enjoyment the individual would have achieved from a normal life. Furthermore, these estimates might be on the low side, because the greater productivity of future schooling might further enhance earning capacity.

Most of the nutritional supplements could be acquired at low cost. Protein available for human use could be doubled by adding lysine (or other amino acids) to certain food products during milling and processing. Alternatively, research might produce grains with high lysine content and therefore increased proteins. Berg (1967) referred to a strain of corn with double protein availability because of extra-high lysine content.

Inadequate diet during a period of breast-feeding can cause both mother and child to suffer malnutrition. In the Mekong River basin, pregnant or lactating women are not allowed, by local custom, to eat meats, some fish, and some vegetables. Women in that area typically spend one-third of their years between 15 and 45 either lactating or pregnant. Inadequate diet causes mothers and children to suffer from beriberi and other diseases, which may well be the cause of mental retardation.

Breast-feeding is a form of nonmarket production. If a new mother decides instead to enter the labor market, she must spend part of her earned income on dietary supplements if she wishes to provide the infant with the same level of nutrition he or she would have enjoyed from breast-feeding. Hence her "real income" is less than her nominal income, by about 50 percent according to some estimates (Reutlinger and Selowsky, 1976).

A recent tendency away from breast-feeding in LDCs is cause for concern. We do not know how widespread this tendency is, for we know of no measures of it. However, it can be assumed from the fact that, at an earlier date, the lack of prepared infant formulas made breast-feeding mandatory, while their availability now has caused many women to adopt them. In a hearing before a U.S. Senate subcommittee on health, a doctor from Jamaica "estimated that about 10 million cases of malnutrition and diarrhea in poor countries were attributable to inadequate bottle-feeding" (NYT, 5–24–78). Not only are improper supplements used, but often the water with which they are mixed is not pure, nor adequately boiled.

It is, perhaps, only natural to fault the producers of infant formulas for the unfortunate results. Some have charged that their advertising (and distribution of free samples in hospitals) has induced mothers to shift from breast-feeding; a world-wide protest boycott of Nestlé products was initiated in Europe and the United States in the mid-seventies. The companies reply that their products are essential to mothers who lack sufficient milk for breast-feeding or who wish to work. Furthermore, they argue, they do not attempt to persuade other mothers and even print admonitions on the labels affirming the superiority of breast-feeding.

Obviously, an ethical question is involved, in which the interests of inadequate breast-feeders and working women must be weighed against the protection of mothers too ignorant to read the labels. In October, 1979, the World Health Organization and UNICEF recommended a ban on all sales promotion of breastmilk substitutes in LDCs, to which major producers subscribed (Nestlé news release, November 15, 1979, which stated that Nestlé had abandoned consumer advertising and other promotional efforts in LDCs in July, 1978).

But who would enforce such a ban in the future? Governments of LDCs? An international agency supervising multinational corporations? Governments of MDCs where parent companies are located? Questions of paternalism and infringement of sovereignty abound. Our belief—for whatever it is worth—is that the only successful efforts will lie in the education of the mothers, and then only with a time lag. Once again, it would appear that escape from ignorance is the only reliable defense.

NUTRITION, INCOME DISTRIBUTION, AND SIZE OF FAMILIES

The following generalizations are probably valid: that malnutrition affects the poor far more than it does the rich, that families tend to be larger among the poor than among the rich, and that, for any given income level in which malnutrition occurs, children in large-size families suffer more, both from malnutrition and from disease, than those in small-size families.

Overall estimates of calorie availability, for countries as well as for larger geographical areas, tend—by the nature of averages—to obscure the number of malnourished. Such estimates are usually derived by computing the number of calories produced in the region and subtracting the requirements (the daily requirement of an individual, multiplied by the number of people); the difference is the surplus or deficit. It is easy to be misled by the supposition that surpluses in one country (or area, or income group) offset the deficits of another. A 1960 family budget survey of Brazil found that average daily consumption was around 2,566 calories. An adequate intake is defined by United Nations agencies as being about 3,000 calories per day for a man and 2,200 for a woman; if the population is half male and half female, the average requirement would be 2,600. Thus Brazil in 1960 was very close. If the same data are analyzed by income group, however, it turns out that 44 percent of the Brazilian population at that time was calorie deficient. Data by Reutlinger and Selowsky (1976:25) show that calorie availability varies positively with income in the cross-section of LDCs that they studied.

The relationship between family size and malnutrition has been demonstrated in several studies. Wray (1971) found that the probability of malnourishment in preschool children in Calendaria, Colombia, was .38 in families with four or fewer children, but .44 in those with five or more (significant difference at the .05 level). Similarly, in Thailand the probability was .42 in families of three or fewer, and .58 in families of four or more. Given a certain family income level, there is less money (and therefore food) per person in large families. When family size correlates negatively with income, however, it is impossible (and maybe not necessary) to distinguish the primary causal force.

Infectious diseases are likely to hit larger families harder than smaller ones, both because malnutrition reduces resistance and because of increased probability of infection. Table 10–1, from a survey in Cleveland, Ohio, in 1964, illustrates the rising probability in families where children were not malnourished.

From all the above, one would expect also that mortality is related to family size. Table 10–2 refers to a study of 11 Punjab villages during 1955–1958. Column 2 shows deaths per thousand infants (up to one year) by parity of mother, shown in column 1. Column 3 records second-year mortality. A parity of one indicates that the child that has died is the first. Thus (row 1) mothers having their first child see that child die in the first or second year more frequently than those having their second or third child (rows 2 and 3). From that point on, however, both infant- and second-year mortality increase with parity, and presumably with family size.

Any estimates of the rate of growth of income and/or agricultural output that will be necessary to overcome malnutrition are bound to be games in numbers, since such a large number of uncertainties must be taken into account: income distribution, cultural changes necessary to accept better nutrition, education of family heads, and so on. A commonly-used number calls for a 4 percent annual increase in agricultural production to provide the basic minimum for poor people while continuing to meet the increasing demands of the richer brackets. One never knows if this is the right number, only that increases not now expected are necessary. Realistic estimates of the potential expansion in food supplies, therefore, would probably show that no substantial reduction in malnutrition in LDCs can be expected over the next 20 years, given present rates of population growth.

EDUCATION AND INCOME DISTRIBUTION

The conventional wisdom proclaims that more education in LDCs would be an income-leveling force. Yet surprisingly little is known empirically about that question. Our own review of what is known would lead us to believe that education expenditures, far from leveling, have aggravated the maldistribution. This need not be the case, however. An *appropriate* allocation of resources might alternatively supply a schooling system that helps the poor.

Even in MDCs there is little agreement among studies of income and education. Over the past 15 years, the "human capital" school has emerged, with the proposition that differences in education are a prime explanation of differences in income. Mincer (1976) finds that in the United States, one-half the dispersion of earnings among male workers (adjusted for length of work year) is explained by different levels of formal schooling, experience, and on-the-job training. Employing different techniques, Taubman (1976) found instead that intelligence and other personal factors, such as family background and "attitudes," were the primary explanations and that education works indirectly

TABLE 10-1
Incidence of Infectious Diseases by Family Size
(Cleveland, Ohio, 1964)

Family Size	Illness/year/person
3	.97
4	1.18
5	1.53
6	1.89
7	1.89
8	2.11

SOURCE: Wray (1971). Reproduced from *Rapid Population Growth*, 1971, with the permission of the National Academy of Sciences, Washington, D.C.

through them. Gintis (1971) suggests that education does not increase productivity directly, but only through the discipline and acculturation to a modern work environment that it induces. Berg (1970) and Arrow (1973) view education as a screening device. Contributing little to productivity, it nevertheless enables those with greatest ability and talent to rise to high-productivity positions. Jencks (1972) found no statistical relationship between education, intelligence, or family background on the one hand and income differentials on the other.

All of these studies employed relatively sophisticated data, of a kind not generally found in LDCs. Once we drop below the level of aggregate, country-wide data for LDCs, only a few bits of evidence, widely scattered, apply directly to the relation between education and income.

In turning to the scant information that exists, let us see what we can do with aggregate data. In Table 10-3, we present cross-sectional data on GDP

TABLE 10-2
Mortality Among Children by Family Size
(Punjab, 1955-1958)

Parity	Infant Mortality (deaths/1000)	Second-Year Mortality (deaths/1000)
1	172	76
2	117	16
3	145	24
4	124	92
5	172	96
6	164	77
7-12	206	95

SOURCE: Wray (1971). Reproduced from *Rapid Population Growth*, 1971, with the permission of the National Academy of Sciences, Washington, D.C.

TABLE 10–3
Literacy Rates and Inequality

	GDP Per Capita, 1973	Predicted Literacy Rates, 1970	Actual Literacy Rates, 1970	Educational Effort (EE) (3)–(2)	Gini
	(1)	(2)	(3)	(4)	(5)
Argentina	1647	93	93	0	.49
Barbados	891	70	97	27	.37
Brazil	768	66	68	2	.65
Burma	82	46	70	24	.38
Chile	1749	96	90	−6	.51
Colombia	440	56	74	18	.56
Costa Rica	818	70	89	19	.44
Dominican Republic	529	59	51	−8	.49
Ecuador	386	55	68	13	.68
Egypt	260	51	40	−11	.43
El Salvador	345	53	58	5	.46
Honduras	323	53	52	−1	.56
India	118	47	36	−11	.49
Indonesia	131	47	56	9	.46
Iraq	429	56	26	−30	.63
Ivory Coast	548	60	20	−40	.53
Jamaica	894	70	86	16	.58
Kenya	186	49	30	−19	.63
South Korea	379	54	91	35	.27
Lebanon	796	67	69	2	.54
Mexico	883	70	84	14	.58
Panama	938	71	82	11	.43
Peru	617	62	72	10	.76
Philippines	262	51	72	21	.49
Senegal	253	51	10	−41	.59
Sierra Leone	179	48	15	−33	.61
Sri Lanka	209	49	85	36	.41
Taiwan	421	56	73	17	.30
Tunisia	513	58	55	−3	.50
Turkey	543	59	55	−4	.57
Uruguay	970	72	91	19	.50
Venezuela	1572	90	77	−13	.62
Zambia	541	59	43	−16	.52

SOURCE: Jain (1975); World Bank, *World Tables 1976.*

per capita (1973), literacy, and Gini coefficients for 33 LDCs. By regressing literacy rates[1] on GDP per capita, we arrive at the following equation:

$$\text{Literacy rate} = 43.1 + .03Y \qquad R^2 = .32 \qquad (\text{significance} < .05)$$
$$N = 33$$

---

[1]The literacy rate is only a proxy for education in general. It may not reflect specialized educational efforts such as efforts in business management, home economics, agricultural technology, or other vocational training. On the other hand, these kinds of programs can only be mastered by literate audiences. If a single measure of educational effort is taken, literacy is probably as good as any other.

On the basis of this equation, we enter predicted literacy rates in column 2 of Table 10–3. By subtracting predicted from actual literacy rates (column 3), we arrive at an index of "educational effort" (EE), in column 4, which may be positive or negative.

We do not regress the Gini on the literacy rate, because we have already discovered (Chapter 6) a positive relationship between GDP per capita and Gini in LDCs. Since there is also a positive relationship between GDP per capita and literacy, it would follow that any relationship between Gini and literacy might reflect only the influence of GDP per capita; in short, we might again measure the inverted U. Instead, we remove the influence of GDP per capita by comparing the predicted literacy rate with the actual rate.

Next, we regress the Gini coefficient on the EE index, and we arrive at the following equation:

$$\text{Gini} = .521 - .0025(EE) \qquad R^2 = .22 \qquad (\text{significance} < .05)$$
$$N = 33$$

Our exercise suggests the possibility that greater educational effort may be associated with improved distribution of income. The relationship, however, seems to be slightly nonlinear. If we rerun the regression of the Gini on the EE index, using only those countries where EE > 0, then the relationship is stronger than for the group as a whole:

$$\text{Gini} = .621 - .0078(EE) \qquad R^2 = .35 \qquad (\text{significance} < .05)$$
$$N = 18$$

Both regression lines are drawn on the scatter diagram shown in Figure 10–1.

Similar cross-section results have been found by Ahluwalia (1976). Also using the literacy rate as a measure of the stock of educational capital, he found a

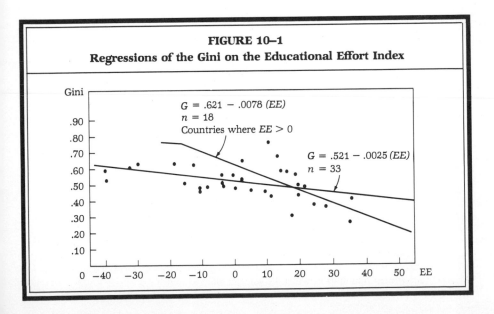

FIGURE 10–1
Regressions of the Gini on the Educational Effort Index

positive correlation between it and the income share of the poorest 60 percent of income recipients. In addition, secondary school enrollments were found to correlate positively with the share of middle-income groups. In each case, the expanding share of the lower-income groups occurred at the expense of the upper 20 percent.

Despite the happy inferences that might be drawn from these exercises, other evidence causes us to be wary. Warnings against drawing time-series inferences from cross-sectional data are sprinkled throughout this book. A positive association between educational effort and distributional equity in cross section does not imply directly that when education is expanded, equity is promoted. The studies that we cite below—again not enough for very positive statements—nevertheless suggest that it is the quality of education that counts, not the expansion alone.

Two main features of education are likely to determine its distributional impact. First is the effect upon income and/or social mobility. Caste, race, and other factors may limit mobility despite income gains.[2] Second is the way in which education is made available—the extent of coverage, who pays for it, and who is subsidized by it. Two separate but related questions are:

(1) Is inequality in schooling reduced by expanding education? This inequality might be measured by a coefficient expressing various percentages of the population that have achieved certain levels of education (but we know of no one who has calculated such a coefficient).
(2) Do less-educated groups ("the poor") receive greater (or less) return for the lower investment in their education than that received by the higher-educated groups ("the rich")? This question, applicable to average returns, might also be asked for marginal returns.

Despite the lack of direct answers to these questions, scattered evidence would indicate that educational development proceeds in ways that do not promote equity. Teachers assigned to rural areas, where the proportion of students coming from poorer families is highest, are often paid less than their urban counterparts. The larger size and greater visibility of urban schools often evokes a disproportionate amount of public financial support. Some countries rely on boarding schools for secondary education, and these are often located in cities. Rural families who send their children to these schools must bear the cost of supporting them away from home, which is likely to be a higher proportion of their income than in the case of richer, urban families.

The rate of return on primary education—which is often the only education for the poor—is usually believed to be high, for no other reason than that literacy is the common ground for income achievement. However, the value of a given level of education depends on its supply as well as its demand. If there are only a few literate people, the return may indeed be high. But the burgeoning of primary education in LDCs causes the supply of literates to be no longer

---

[2]One of the authors is reminded of a South African acquaintance of Asian descent who owned a block of apartment buildings in which he was not allowed to live.

"rationed" (Jallade, 1976) in many countries. The lowered marginal productivity resulting from greater quantity may mean that the return on primary education is less than that on more advanced levels.

In some LDCs (for example, Kenya), both minimum wages and educational requirements for specific jobs are set by government. Employment in scarce, high-minimum-wage positions may be rationed by educational requirements that exceed the actual skill requirements of the job. Sometimes the requirements set by government are different (more classical, less vocational) from the skills needed in practice. All such cases increase the demand for lower-level education, if only to meet the requirements for entry into the next level higher. This phenomenon has prompted Todaro (1977:247) to make the ironic observation that the more unprofitable a given amount of education becomes, the greater the demand for it!

The net return from education for the poor is sometimes reduced, relative to that for the rich, by special circumstances of the poor. The opportunity cost of sending children to school, relative to family income, is often greater for the poor than for the rich, particularly when children are called away at peak labor periods such as planting and harvesting. If we assume a diminishing marginal utility of family income (and the same function for every family), then a dollar's worth of child-income lost to the poor family is worth more than the same amount forgone by the rich. Not only that, but the children of the rich may not work at all. Finally, the marginal value of education to the rich child is likely to be higher than to the poor because the former can combine it with other assets such as land, financial capital, social position, and family connections, which are not enjoyed by the poor.

All of the above is theoretical. Let us now turn to the bits of empirical evidence, which do indicate lower returns for the poor in many places. Bhagwati (1973) has found higher opportunity costs and lower returns for children from poor families in India. Fields (1975) shows the same for Kenya. Hoerr (1973) found that in Malaysia, the return to primary education—which is almost universal—is far below that to secondary education, which is enjoyed by only about one-third of eligible children. He suggests (p. 260) that rapid expansion of secondary education will reduce its return substantially in the near future. Staff and Tullock (1973) and Stiglitz (1973) found that even in MDCs, the educational system perpetuates inequalitites in ways described here.

TAXES AND SUBSIDIES IN EDUCATION

Investment in education automatically implies large amounts of taxation and public expenditure. Advantages or disadvantages for different income groups can be affected by the ways in which these are managed. Unfortunately, in most countries, the systems have not been designed with distribution in mind.

In the early postwar period, it was widely believed that the educational pyramid needed to be stretched at the top. Harbison (1959) stressed the need for top-level management in industrializing economies. Skilled manpower and high-level technicians might be acquired cheaply, it was argued, by advancing more primary school graduates into secondary school and more secondary school graduates into the university, rather than by increasing the pyramid symmetrically, with more starters at the base.

Over time, massive demand for education at lower levels has led to a proliferation of primary schools. More and more, it was suggested that the pyramid could not support a heavier top unless the base was widened as well. But the intellectual bias for the upper levels has remained. As the *numbers* of primary schools have increased, the weight of spending has remained at the top. Quality seems to be valued more at the university than at the lower levels. Using a sample of twenty MDCs and ten LDCs, Harbison (1977) found that LDCs send a smaller proportion of student-aged population through the higher levels, but spend a greater proportion of GDP on them. The per-student expense in proportion to GDP in LDCs is up to four times as great as in MDCs for secondary school students and two to ten times as great for university students.

In some countries, school fees at lower levels effectively eliminate children from poor families. In Kenya, secondary school fees are approximately equal to per capita annual income. Primary school fees are less, but families who send at least one child through secondary school ordinarily send more than one to primary school. At the university level, on the other hand, students are not only exempt from fees, payments for books, and other direct expenses, they are given a living allowance as well. Only students from relatively rich families can withstand the financial rigors of all the lower levels; these are, of course, the very students who are subsidized at the higher levels (Fields, 1975). The political power of university students (they may strike or riot or provide intellectual leadership for antigovernment factions) may explain, in part, this favored status.

Few studies of the incidence of taxation and educational expenditure have been as extensive as that of Jallade (1974) on Colombia. He found that, on balance, the Colombian system does redistribute income from rich to poor, though the effect is different by sector and by level. The urban poor receive benefits equal to three times their tax payments, while the rural poor just "break even." The urban rich are taxed more heavily in proportion to benefits received than are their rural counterparts. (This is in part due to the large role of locally-determined taxes and expenditures.) Primary education redistributes income from the richest 13 percent of families to the poorest 87 percent. At secondary and higher levels, however, subsidies accrue to middle-income groups, paid for by taxes on both the rich and the poor. Jallade (1974:70) fears, however, that the regressive return from education (that is, greater for the rich) may more than offset the progressive nature of the tax-expenditure system.

EDUCATION FOR DEVELOPMENT

Not only may educational systems perpetuate inequity, they may also be incompatible with maximum growth. In most LDCs, formal education is oriented toward ever-greater amounts of education (Bhagwati, 1973, and Harbison, 1977). The subject matter at each level is directed more toward pushing the student to the next level than to attending to the skills needed by students who will leave school at any given level. While education may be an escape from "a life sentence in traditional agriculture" (Harbison, 1977:129), few from poor families are likely to advance far enough to acquire the credentials for high-paid, modern-sector occupations.

Some authors have suggested that LDCs may have overinvested in education regardless of level (Edwards, 1975). Hoerr (1973) found that the social rates of return in both primary and university education were less than the return for capital invested in other sectors. The *private* return, however, is so high that demand continues to be strong. But in the Philippines, rapid advances in middle- and higher-educational levels in the late 1960s, accompanied by low rates of overall growth, were felt to have reduced the real incomes of the better-educated as a group (Berry, 1978).

Yet education *may* provide potential for both greater growth and increased equity, if attention is paid to special development needs. As Ahluwalia (1974) points out, choosing among the various views on education requires judgment more than it requires reliance on the general findings of research, most of which was done in MDCs. Each LDC presents special circumstances, with educational traditions and social structures demanding unique efforts. The question is not whether education *per se* is desirable, but how to ensure that it is the right kind and that it is available to all income groups. In many countries, a reassessment would show not only an overemphasis on higher education (Harbison, 1977), but also an outstanding need for nontraditional measures to raise productivity directly—especially vocational and on-the-job training.

AN HISTORICAL VIEW OF EDUCATION

Western tradition holds science and education as values in their own right: education should be free of influence by state and religion, and judgment should combine empiricism with rationality. According to these beliefs, only those who are educated in this manner will be capable of harnessing nature to help the world escape Malthusian poverty.

We join and support this tradition. At the same time, we recognize it as an historical exception. In all societies, education has not been an end in itself, but a means to preserve the culture or the religion or the state. Where dominant elites believe this preservation requires segmentized learning, controlled access, and traditional as opposed to scientific approaches, and where there is no effective opposition, education tends to "bottle up" rather than promote the escape from poverty.

Nor is the Western tradition an exception to the overall principle. It did not come about because Westerners "saw the light" independently of their cultures. Rather, the encouragement of free inquiry is a way to preserve the set of values that arose from the Reformation of Luther and Calvin, the Enlightenment of Locke, the Naturalism of Rousseau, and above all, the Industrial Revolution of England and (later on) of Western Europe. The scientific ethic—as we will call this tradition—is therefore of recent ascendancy in Europe (though its origin was centuries ago).

Nor did this ethic develop evenly over Europe. Peter the Great introduced it into Russia, and Catherine carried it on. But a single dynasty with "enlightened despotic" tendencies could not nurture it as well as the many competing philosophical schools with which Western Europe was blessed. It received setbacks in the Napoleonic era, and Parliamentary debates over reforms in England reflect much conservative opposition in the nineteenth century.

The ethic also entered the Far East and is the foundation of current economic successes there. The Dutch introduced Western science into Japan even during the Tokugawa closure; Western studies became increasingly popular after the Meiji restoration. The present Chinese push toward Westernization reflects a new comprehension that economic development is incompatible with an ideologically-closed educational system (Chapter 16). Western scientific principles have more or less penetrated LDCs—we referred to this in the section on magic versus science in Chapter 3—and the extent to which they are implemented will doubtless be the telling force distinguishing successful LDCs over the next half century.

No one should suppose that the scientific ethic is permanently entrenched in the Western world. Some argue that scientists are the new elites in education and that the system must be made more "average." Thus the populist impulse that once promoted science may now encumber it. The excesses of industrialization occasionally engender reactions, in the form of astrology, religious cults that deny the value of education, or "returns" to Eastern religions with their emphases on intuition, induction, and contemplation, as opposed to science, deduction, and experiment. Appropriate balances must always be sought, and they may not be the right ones. No state is permanent; none escapes vulnerability.

EDUCATION FOR PRESERVATION OF CULTURE

From the ancient world on down to the Renaissance, the Church and the army were the principal agencies for perpetuating cultures and protecting them from attack. Quite naturally, the task of education was assigned to religious and military elites, who taught their replacements. No learning was needed for the masses, whose station was to till the soil under the supervision of their patrons. In Medieval Europe, the military learned chivalry and horsemanship, as well as poetry and the arts; monks needed to read, write, and count. Little had changed, in principle, from the ancient Egyptian and Mesopotamian schools for soldiers and scribes.

Of course, there were exceptions. The Koran prescribes education for all, and some Muslim societies have tried to comply. But it is usually religious education, conducted by religious authorities (the *ulema*). King Asoka of the Mauryan Empire (Northern India, *c.* 327 B.C.) believed strongly in human equality, down to universal education. Buddhists made several attempts to open learning (primarily religious) to all, though they ran counter to secular authorities—especially in Han China. Athens departed from the strictly-military orientation for which Sparta was notorious, but of course its educational democracy did not apply to aliens or slaves. By and large, however, these movements were only exceptions; none carried over to modern times.

Education for preservation of culture has usually emphasized moral character. In ancient China, Confucianism, along with other great schools of philosophy, taught reverence for elders, which would hardly be an upsetting social force. In China, as in many other societies, training for the civil service was the principal function of schools. In virtually all ancient and medieval societies, religion or philosophy supplied those values whose common acceptance made interpersonal trust possible. Thus grew the belief—no doubt correct in the preindustrial world—that social cohesion required either a common moral code (China) or a universal religion (Islam or Christianity). This belief not only fused education with the church, it may also have delayed the emergence of independent, scientific inquiry.

EDUCATION AND SCIENCE

In China, the link between science and education has persisted from early times, though both were periodically overthrown by foreign invasions and violent dynastic successions. In ancient Greece and Rome, science and mathematics were taught at academies for sons of the elite, while technology-based inventions (for irrigation, sailing, and agriculture) were developed outside of formal education. The Hellenistic Age (323–30 B.C.) saw significant inventions such as seige engines, the water clock, the water mill, and sewerage and water systems. Gupta and Harsa in India (fourth to eighth centuries A.D.) saw an age of universities, with advances in science and mathematics, such as the development of zero and of decimals. There was also vocational training down to the village level.

For all its emphasis on religion, Muslim education was widespread and popular. Its aim was to synthesize the study of the Koran and secular knowledge. Perhaps (and perhaps not) it was this synthesis that led to its scientific base. The Umayyad caliphate (661–750 A.D.) preserved in Syria the scientific advances of the Hellenistic world; the Abassid caliphate (750–1100 A.D.) advanced them, with astronomical tables, trigonometrical tables, and a geographic encyclopedia. No one knows why the Arabs served as such a vital link over time; perhaps it was because they were also a link over space, transmitting Chinese science to the West. Also, it remains a mystery why the Arabs did not make better use of science themselves, bringing the industrial revolution to the Mediterranean and Northern Africa, where commerce also flourished. We suspect that the wars of the Ottomans, which ruptured relationships with Europe, may explain this at least in part, but no one can be sure. At any rate, the link over time was vital, for the Arabs transmitted to Europe the basic technology on which, centuries later, the agricultural and industrial revolutions were founded.

In Europe, however, the link between education and science is a modern one. Given the religious and cultural bases for schools, Medieval Europe did not ordinarily conceive of them as locales for developing science. New technology came from craftsmen and independent inventors.

The move toward science-based education did not occur suddenly. It is foreshadowed by Abelard's words in the twelfth century: "By doubting we are led to inquiry, and by inquiry we perceive the truth." But it swelled during the age of Humanism, succored by philosophers such as Erasmus, who wished to combine the humaneness of religion with the potential of science.

It is not possible to disaggregate the mutual reinforcements of humanism, nationalism, the industrial revolution, science-based schools, and universal primary education, though we have listed them in roughly the order they appeared in Europe. For development with equity, we are concerned with the last one, and we will now consider how, and when, it came about.

UNIVERSAL PRIMARY EDUCATION

We have already seen that education for the poor occurred from time to time when some benevolent ruler willed it. It might also have been offered by some religious group as a matter of charity. But always these efforts developed slowly, and often they ended as the regime changed or as new religious authorities lost interest.

With the rise of cities in Europe in the eleventh and twelfth centuries, however, the parameters began to change. Not only did apprentices and artisans need to read and count, but unhealthy people were recognized as a menace, since so many diseases were contagious. Public funds became allocated for both medical services and elementary schools for the poor.

> Florence was in the vanguard of Europe in the fourteenth century. During the fifteenth and sixteenth centuries, one city after another followed her example, but the diffusion of elementary education among the masses remained typically an urban characteristic. In the Protestant countries the Reformation succeeded in spreading the rudiments of reading and writing among the rural population but in Catholic countries, the bulk of the peasants remained illiterate until the modern era. (Cipolla, 1976:92).

Literacy and numeracy for all—rural and urban alike—came when they were needed to support the dominant cultural trend. This was so despite the fact that every one of the movements toward universal schooling was propelled by religious and/or philosophical pioneers, such as the Wilberforces and the Quakers, who would reform because it was right and moral to do so. For most, however, morality was born only after the custom was established.

As we question the bias in LDCs toward secondary and higher education, we note that the same bias existed in all MDCs right down to the twentieth century. Universal, free, compulsory primary education—which prevents parents from denying literacy and numeracy to their children—was virtually unknown in Europe and the United States when the nineteenth century dawned. By the early twentieth century, it was found in all countries, and most citizens would not dream of not having it. Primary education also became widespread in Latin America, though it was not universal and not always available to the Indians.

The initiation of education for the poor in Europe was part of a broader movement, directly associated with the industrial revolution. Literate workers were needed for the factories. With the advancement of scientific agriculture, which could be taught only by the written word, they were also needed on the farm. There was nothing left for illiterates to do. Since they could not be left to starve, they had to be taught.

THE LDCs IN HISTORICAL PERSPECTIVE

It has often been charged that the colonial powers were negligent and discriminatory in their failure to promote indigenous education in Asia and Africa. Indeed, they were both. The British in particular, eager for all colonies to be self-financing, left education largely to the missionaries. But in so doing, they were only transmitting to the colonies the laissez-faire principles they were also applying at home. State-supported primary education appeared in many colonies simultaneously with, and sometimes before, its appearance in Britain. It did not become compulsory or free, however, as it did in Britain from the 1860s to 1890s. So long as industry and farms were not modernized and scientifically based, there was not the same need for popular literacy as in the home country, and popular education would have been a fiscal drain which, the colonial powers reasoned, would probably not be "appreciated" anyway.

Similar attitudes prevalent among governments of LDCs may explain the modern tension. On the one hand, pressure from below has led to a great increase in primary schools, though often they are of poor quality and starved for funds. On the other hand, dualism—with its emphasis on modern, capital-intensive industry and agriculture—requires the technical skills taught in higher institutions. Until the dominant culture (that of the decision-makers) swings in favor of technology requiring only literacy and numeracy, the present dilemma will continue.

It may be that decisions emphasizing technological dualism and high-skill education are *economically* optimal. Just as in the many historical eras in which it made sense to leave the poor ignorant, the social cost today of raising the poor to more productive levels may be greater than the perceived yield.

A missionary teacher in the desert area of Northern Kenya (among the Turkana people) told[3] of a student in a construction class who could not comprehend the use of a T-square. The teacher reflected that this student had never seen a right angle in his life; no construction in his area was rectangular. Another teacher commented on the difficulty of instilling into students the concepts of spatial relationships. A student learning to multiply, say, 18 × 35 could not envisage the product as being a space 20 units as big as 35 (or 700) from which two units were subtracted (therefore 630). Such perception would have enabled him to arrive immediately at the answer, as opposed to the painstaking application of rules learned by rote and not understood.

Most education ministries know how much it costs to teach a child the necessary skills to pass a sixth grade examination. What they do not know is

---

[3]This occurred in a conversation with one of the authors, 1974.

the cost to raise a child to given degrees of functional literacy, so that he has the minimal spatial and literary perceptions to perform specific tasks in the most efficient way. This question has always been answered intuitively, and the answers may not be right.

CONCLUSION

We have brought out certain empirical material in this chapter, and then we have raised questions whose answers can never be definite. Empirical exercise points to the high probability that investment in preventive health care (most of which would concern the environment: clean water and adequate sewage) would have an extremely high economic payoff, quite apart from the human satisfaction it would bring. It also points to the fiscal importance of education in LDCs (relative to other budgetary lines) and to the relative weight on secondary schools and universities compared to primary and vocational schools, just as in MDCs before them. The questions are: Why do not development units in LDCs (governments at all levels and ordinary people) make the appropriate investments in health? Does the relative emphasis on higher education reinforce technological dualism and the maldistribution of income? Would not a shift toward better-quality primary and vocational education yield greater opportunities for the poor, in both quantity and quality of employment? If so, why does the shift not occur?

When answers can only be speculative, but they are needed for understanding as well as for policy making, then speculation becomes legitimate. We suggest that the situation on health stems from either faulty future vision or high time discounts. It is hard to attribute it to unwillingness to take risk, since the empirical results have already been demonstrated with very high probability. High time discount seems to be the most likely explanation. Although the payoffs have been discounted back to a present value, nevertheless they always occur sometime in the distant future. Often the next election is the politician's relevant time horizon. His constituents may be more inclined to reward him for curing illness than for maintaining health—another case of faulty vision.

For education, we have questioned whether overall expenditures are too high, as well as whether they are allocated to the "right" places. It would seem that shifts in relative funding toward primary and vocational schools would most promote opportunities for the poor. But this judgment is more complex, more susceptible to error, and more likely to bring about disagreement than the one concerning health. Primary and vocational education have blossomed in MDCs only in the last century or so. Throughout history, education has reinforced dominant cultural values, such as religious and military values. Only in technologically-oriented societies are universal literacy and free inquiry valued. Only as skilled labor has become scarce has the need for vocational proficiency been grasped by the authorities. The growing scarcity of skilled labor in LDCs, the redundancy of unskilled labor, and the growing concern for technological capabilities perhaps augur well for a shift in these countries as well.

BIBLIOGRAPHY

Ahluwalia, M. S., 1974:
"The Scope for Policy Intervention," in Chenery *et al*, *Redistribution With Growth*, New York, Oxford University Press, 73–90.

Ahluwalia, M. S., 1976:
"Inequality, Poverty and Development," Washington: IBRD, mimeo, April.

Arrow, K. J., 1973:
"Higher Education as a Filter," *Journal of Public Economics*, Vol. 2.

Berg, A., 1967:
"Malnutrition and National Development," *Foreign Affairs*, October.

Berg, A., 1973:
The Nutrition Factor, Washington, D.C., The Brookings Institution.

Berg, I., 1970:
Education, Jobs: The Great Training Robbery, New York, Praeger.

Berry, A., 1978:
"Income and Consumption Distribution Trends in the Philippines, 1950–1970," *Review of Income and Wealth*. 24:3, September, 313–31.

Bhagwati, J., 1973:
"Education, Class Structure and Income Equality," *World Development*, 1:5, May, 21–36.

Cipolla, Carlo M., 1976:
Before the Industrial Revolution: European Society and Economy, 1000–1700, London, Methuen and Co.

Edwards, E. O., 1975:
"Investment in Education in Developing Nations: Policy Responses When Private and Social Signals Conflict," *World Development*, 3:1, January, 41–45.

Fields, G. S., 1975:
"Higher Education and Income Distribution in a Less-Developed Country," *Oxford Economic Papers*, 27:2, July, 245–59.

Gintis, H., 1971:
"Education, Technology and the Characteristics of Worker Productivity," *American Economic Review*, 61:2, May, 266–79.

Harbison, F. H., 1959:
Lecture (unrecorded) at the Institute for International Development, School for Advanced International Studies, Johns Hopkins University, Washington, D.C.

Harbison, F. H., 1977:
"The Education-Income Connection," in C. R. Frank and R. C. Webb, eds., *Income Distribution and Growth in the Less-Developed Countries*, Washington, Brookings Institution., 127–58.

Hoerr, C., 1973:
"Education, Income and Equity in Malaysia," *Economic Development and Cultural Change*, 21:2, January.

Jain, Shail, 1975:
Size Distribution of Income: A Compilation of Data, Washington, D.C. World Bank.

Jallade, J., 1974:
Public Expenditures on Education and Income Distribution in Colombia, World Bank Staff Occasional Paper Number 18, Baltimore: Johns Hopkins University Press.

Jallade, J., 1976:
"Education Finance and Income Distribution," *World Development*, 4:5, 435–43.

Jencks, C., *et al*, 1972:
Inequality, New York, Basic Books.

Maddison, A., 1975:
"Education, Inequality and Life Chances: The Major Policy Issues," in OECD, *Education, Inequality and Life Chances*, Paris, OECD, 12–30.

Mincer, J., 1970:
   "The Distribution of Labor Incomes: A Survey with Special Reference to the Human Capital Approach," *Journal of Economic Literature*, 8:1, March, 1–26.
Mincer, J., 1976:
   "Progress in Human Capital Analyses of the Distribution of Earnings," in A. B. Atkinson, ed., *The Personal Distribution of Incomes*, London, George Allen and Unwin, 136–92.
Nestlé News Release, 11–15–79:
   "Nestle Endorses World Health Organization Guidelines on Infant Food Marketing," White Plains, N.Y., Nestlé Corporation.
NYT, 5–24–78:
   "Formula for Infants in Third World Opposed," *New York Times.*
Republic of China (Taiwan), 1975 and 1976:
   Statistical Yearbook, Taipei, Council for Economic Planning.
Reutlinger, S., and Selowsky, M., 1976:
   Malnutrition and Poverty, Baltimore, Johns Hopkins University Press for the World Bank.
Riding, Alan, 3–9–79:
   "Mexicans Lack Health Care, but Doctors Can't Find Work," *New York Times.*
Schiavo-Campo, S., and Singer, A. W., 1970:
   Perspectives of Economic Development, Boston, Houghton Mifflin.
Selowsky, M., and Taylor, L., 1973:
   "The Economics of Malnourished Children: An Example of Disinvestment in Human Capital," *Economic Development and Cultural Change*, 22, October, 17–30.
Staff, R. J., and Tullock, G., 1973:
   "Education and Equality," *Annals*, 409, September, 125–34.
Stiglitz, J. E., 1973:
   "Education and Inequality," *Annals*, 409, September, 135–45.
Taubman, P., 1976:
   "Personal Characteristics and the Distribution of Earnings," in A. B. Atkinson, ed., *The Personal Distribution of Incomes*, London, George Allen and Unwin, 193–226.
Todaro, M. P., 1977:
   Economic Development in the Third World, New York, Longman.
Tuma, Elias H., 1965:
   Twenty-Six Centuries of Agrarian Reform, Berkeley, University of California Press.
World Bank, 1975:
   Assault on World Poverty, Baltimore: Johns Hopkins University Press.
World Bank, 1976:
   World Tables, 1976, Baltimore, Johns Hopkins University Press.
Wray, J. D., 1971:
   "Population Pressure on Families: Family Size and Child Spacing," in National Academy of Sciences, *Rapid Population Growth*, Baltimore, Johns Hopkins University Press, 403–61.

11

AGRICULTURE AND AGRARIAN REFORM

The zamindars *and* jagirdars *were walking hand in hand;*
They laughed like anything to see such quantities of land.
If all of this should be reformed,
Oh God, we would be damned!
APOLOGIES TO LEWIS CARROLL

In the declining days of the Roman Empire, droves of peasants sought protection *(patrocinium)* from powerful lords against despoliation, banditry, taxation, and relentless regulations from Rome and Constantinople. Some were already landless. Those who owned land yielded it to new masters. Both worked as virtual slaves, for under Roman law, no farmer might change his residence.

They were not driven by scarcity of land; indeed, the fifth-century wars had depopulated many regions, creating vacuums which Roman emperors filled even with barbarians. Rather, the origins of Western feudalism lay in the absence of effective alternative government.

Feudalism is not generally associated with the Roman Empire, since the full-blown system of seigneurial-vassal relationships grew later, out of the Frankish-Carolingian conquest of Europe. While Roman central government lasted, the emperor and his Caesars dominated political life, and towns were the focus of commercial activity. But the Franks, unlike the Romans, could not control their vast domains centrally. Instead, *patrocinium* grew into feudalism, which be-came—as it has always been—not just a system of land tenure, but a complex of politico-social relationships defining the status, economic activity, *corvée* labor, and other obligations of all who lived on fiefs. Defense was an overriding feature.

Feudalism appeared in China long before it did in the West. It was a feature of the Shang dynasty (1520–1030 B.C.). It yielded to individual ownership, with *corvée* labor and land taxes paid directly to the emperor, by the later years of the Chou dynasty (1028–250 B.C.). It was destroyed and recreated many times in the dynastic cycles that followed, as new emperors would confiscate land from their enemies and allocate it among their friends. Fiscal and regulatory oppression, as well as the need for defense, forced the peasants (as in Roman times) to ally themselves with influential nobles.

This same feudalism is coming to an end only in the latter part of the twentieth century, as a direct result of economic development of the third world. Remnants of European feudalism can be found today in southern Europe, especially Spain and Portugal. Feudalism in China ended only with the agrarian reforms of the early 1950s. Feudal estates with distinct similarities to the Frankish and Chinese estates still exist in Ecuador and Colombia and have been abolished only recently in Peru, Bolivia, and Chile. India, Pakistan, and Bangladesh possess versions of the same system, and its displacement is only now in process in Middle Eastern and North African countries (including Ethiopia). Many economists judge that feudalism is a prime cause of today's dualism and agricultural stagnation.

In order to know how feudalism will end, it is necessary to understand how it began and what purposes have sustained it. It is also necessary to know why it developed in some regions and not in others.

Some authors have associated modern-day feudalism with colonialism. Surely the British fostered it in India, where their tax-collection systems elevated local *zamindars* and *jagirdars* to positions of power and ultimately ownership; surely the French launched feudal estates in Algeria and Tunisia, with their land confiscations from "rebellious" natives and settlements of loyal French nationals. Ottoman sultans allocated conquered land to Janissaries and Mamluks, and the Spaniards relied on feudalism to administer their territories in the Americas.

But colonialism does not explain feudalism completely, for it developed in some countries that were not colonized (for example, China and Japan). The Incas possessed a feudal hierarchy which the Spaniards simply took over. The absence of feudalism in subsaharan Africa[1] and in several southeast Asian countries also shows that it was not an inevitable consequence of colonialism.

Let us offer a hypothesis. Feudalism occurs in agrarian societies where mobility (such as by horse) is sufficient for conquests over large areas, but not for effective central control. That is, the empire is larger than optimal size for economic efficiency. A further requisite is that agriculture must be sufficiently advanced to require a more subtle administration than brute force; thus slavery becomes no longer practical. It was in this latter point that Carolingian feudalism differed from the Roman slave *latifundia*. Sometimes, however, slavery

---

[1]Some might define as feudal the Tutsi-Hutu relationship in Burundi, or the Portuguese *prazos* of the Shire Highlands in the seventeenth and eighteenth centuries. But the former appears to us to involve too indefinite a set of obligations, while the latter were too far removed from the Portueguese feudalism to which they were formally linked. Also, we are not considering Ethiopia a part of subsaharan Africa.

shades into feudalism, as it did in early Japan, in the Ottoman Empire, and even in the Roman Empire.

Feudalism may not have arisen south of the Sahara because slavery lasted, *de facto*, right up to the era of intense colonialism (the end of the nineteenth century). Also, the territories of the Ghana, Mali, and Songhay empires were miniscule compared to the extent of suzerainty claimed by the Romans, Franks, or Ottomans in their times. Migratory conquests, such as those by Germanic tribes and Huns in Europe, Mongols in Arabia, the Fulani *jihads* in West Africa, the *mwata yamvo* of the Lunda in Central Africa, and the *mfekane* of the Zulus, did not lead to sufficiently advanced agriculture to require feudal organization. Slavery and tributary states were sufficient. The same Mongols stepped into a feudal empire when they conquered the agriculturally more advanced Southern Sung dynasty of China, however.

This sketch of the beginnings of feudalism is much too brief. But we must devote most of our attention to the other end of history, where we suggest that the demise of feudalism stems from a further development of the forces that caused it to rise. Effective national states emerge; economies of scale cause the size previously determined by conquest to become more efficient than before (though not necessarily optimal). Efficiency also requires a different distribution of functions between central and local administrations, to which the feudal estate is not appropriate. The growth of manufacturing requires more efficient food production than feudal structures, with their lack of incentives, can apply. Political power and social prestige slips away from the landed aristocracy and abides more in industry and the cities. Whereas earlier, land (and in migratory societies, cattle) was the primordial symbol of investment and prestige, in industrial societies it ceases to hold either of these places and vies with financial instruments as one of the many forms of preserving wealth. Choices among investments are then made according to marginal returns, more than for power or prestige.

These are the overall parameters that determine the time and place for agrarian reform. Subject to them, we must examine the detailed ways by which individual reforms are implemented: violent or nonviolent, legal or illegal, and publicly or privately supported (extension services, credit) in varying degrees. While a choice among these methods may determine the precise year or type of reform, only the overall parameters determine whether or not it will occur within a given generation. If a reform comes before it is "ready," it is likely to be reversed or offset.

In this chapter, we will first distinguish a few types of tenure systems in current and historic use. Then we will survey the systems currently in use throughout the third world, along with a few recent reforms.[2] Next we will

---

[2]The presentation of reforms in the present chapter is necessarily curtailed. The most comprehensive descriptions we know of, covering agrarian reforms the world over, are in King (1977); also of interest is Tuma (1965). The United Nations produces an annual report on *Progress in Agrarian Reforms*. Writing in elementary style, Querol (1974) is very informative on Asia. Barraclough (1973) outlines the situation for Latin America. Finally, a wealth of research on individual reforms has been done by the Land Tenure Center, University of Wisconsin, through which many detailed reports are available.

examine those bottlenecks in agricultural development whose resolution, many experts believe, can be secured only through tenure reform. After that, we will compare the salient features of recent reforms to seek reasons why some have been more successful than others. Finally, we will evaluate the prospects both for further reform and for its occurrence without violence. Here again, we will find that history has something to tell us.

TENURE SYSTEMS

Let us distinguish six categories, each of which has many subdivisions and variations, and all of which coexist today.

PASTORAL (NOMADIC) TENURE

A tribe holds customary rights, which it may have to defend from time to time, to a territory over which it roams seasonally. Nomadic tribes often graze cattle, living in tents or temporary shelters, and move on when grasses are seasonally exhausted.

CUSTOMARY (TRIBAL OR CLAN) TENURE

The chief holds the land in trusteeship for the community. Usufruct is allocated by the chief, usually according to established principles, and may be reallocated as necessary. Village or common lands are available to all members, generally for grazing. Sometimes different people are granted different rights (to dwell, hunt, farm, or fell timber) to the same land.

FEUDAL TENURE

The lord dominates the land and has wide-ranging rights over the tenants, sometimes including the right to their personal property or even to their lives. In exchange for cultivating the lord's lands, and other services, the tenants receive his protection against enemies and other contributions to their well-being. Tenants may fall into different categories such as serfs and villeins, according to their degrees of freedom. In some Latin American countries, a hierarchy has been customary, with low-level tenants obligated to higher-level tenants, on a scale that may have several tiers. The feudal lord in turn owes allegiance to the central government or king.

TENANCY

The owner lets his land out in exchange for payments in cash or in kind. Sharecropping is included in this type. Tenancy usually implies the legal right of the tenant to leave. But if he has no alternative opportunities, and if his tenancy therefore holds a capital value that he cannot sell, the distinction between it and feudal tenure may become blurred. Sometimes the law provides for security of tenure, but in some jurisdictions it may be differentially enforced, or extra-legal pressures may be used to dispossess the tenants.

FEE SIMPLE

This is the dominant system in Europe and North America. The owner has full right of possession, subject to community strictures such as the use to which the land may be put (zoning) and subject to condemnation with fair compensation for community purposes such as roads or parks. Lands are surveyed and titles publicly recorded. Because fee-simple lands may be leased, there is some overlap between this type of tenure and tenancy. Corporate tenure (such as for plantation farming) may be a form of fee-simple ownership.

COLLECTIVE TENURE

The land is owned by some government agency (central or local) or by individuals who have agreed (voluntarily or not) to combine their individual holdings into a cooperative. It is used in ways determined by the collectivity.

Historically, there has been a tendency for tenure to evolve from the first four types into the last two. But pastoral tenure persists in many pockets, such as Scandinavia, the Middle East, central Asia, and northern Africa. Agronomists are now coming to the opinion that pastoral tenure is the most economical way to use marginal lands and that (especially with population pressure) its further reduction will slow. Tribal tenure also exists on all continents, including within the United States, but it predominates in Africa.

ILLUSTRATIONS OF TENURE SYSTEMS AND RECENT REFORMS

The Carolingian and Chinese feudal systems made a profound impact on the modern world. From the Mediterranean, feudalism spread north to Europe and east to Asia Minor. The Moslems carried it beyond the Caucasus and into the Indian subcontinent. On the way, they met the Mongol hordes, who—although principally nomadic—found the system compatible with what they had known in East Asia. The Arabs extended feudalism westward, reinforcing it in North Africa and Spain. The Slavs carried it into Kievan Russia. The Sahara, however, was an impenetrable barrier in the south. Even though Moslem traders and religion established themselves on its southern fringes, local tenure habits prevailed there. The Chinese system also reached its geographical limit to the south; it did not penetrate what are now Burma, Thailand, Malaysia, Viet Nam, and Indonesia, although Chinese hegemony did. By the time the New World was settled, feudalism had already died in Northern Europe, but not in Spain and Portugal. These countries transferred it to Central and South America, where they found it compatible (in the Andes at léast) with existing Indian tenure systems.

MEXICO, PERU, AND CHILE

Thus the *hacienda* system (Spanish-type feudalism) took root in Mexico, in Central America (except Costa Rica), and in the Andean countries of Venezuela, Colombia, Ecuador, Peru, Bolivia, and (in a modified form) Chile. The Portuguese brought it to Northeast Brazil, where it was fostered in the sugar/slave plantations of the Dutch in the mid-seventeenth century. It did not develop in Uruguay, Argentina, or Southern Brazil, where extensive landholdings were allocated to ranchers by emphyteusis and other means, or to Paraguay, where the large holdings are in timber. Nor did it spread to the thinly-populated center of South America.

The demise of the *hacienda* system began in Mexico at approximately the turn of the twentieth century. It was associated with three events. First, the growth of steel and other industries around Monterrey provided new jobs for migrant workers. Second, new railways brought trains slow enough so that *hacienda* deserters could jump aboard and go to Monterrey or otherwise look for work in the expanding mines. Third, a financial panic in New York (1907) reduced the assets of many *hacienda*-owners, and an unseasonal freeze in Northern Mexico (1909) reduced their working capital. The Mexican revolution (1910–1920) was not begun over the land question, but the bankruptcy of the *haciendas* and their losses of *peons* suited its purpose. Before the revolution ended, land reform had become its principal rallying cry.

Sixty years later, the *hacienda* is gone, farms are smaller, and both output and productivity have increased greatly. Clark Reynolds (1970:96) estimates that real crop production was growing at 0.6 percent per year during the Diaz regime (1886–1910), at 1.1 percent from 1910 to 1940 (despite the ravages of revolution), and at 6.3 percent from 1940 to 1960. UNECLA (1973:440) puts the increases at 3.6 percent per year from 1961 to 1971. A spate of independent studies cited by King (1977), and principally that of Dovring (1970), have confirmed this progress. Using a Cobb-Douglas production function, Reynolds (p. 124) found that for a 4.5 percent annual increase in output (1929–1959), 3.2 percent was "explained" by an increase in inputs and 1.3 percent by a residual, which presumably would represent improved productivity. Both input and productivity increases have therefore been high by LDC standards.

Nevertheless, in what can be construed as a case of "disdain for the poor," the government has channeled its major resources not into the small farms of the Central Valley, but into large-scale irrigation schemes in the Northwest. The profits from these have gone primarily to the middle-sized farms (significantly smaller than the old *haciendas*, however), with educated, middle-income owners. Reynolds (1970:103) found that in the decade of the 1950s alone, crop production in the Northwest states (Sonora and Sinaloa) increased by 192 percent, compared to 64 percent for the country as a whole. Productivity increase in the same states, however, was the lowest in the country, measuring only 0.2

percent per year (Cobb-Douglas residual) for 1952–1959, compared to 1.3 percent for the country as a whole. The highest productivity gains occurred in the Gulf area, where physical investment was minimal.

The implication of this observation is that while the agrarian reform may have been an essential ingredient for productivity increase, the results did not particularly favor the poor. Despite the miraculous transformation of the Northwest desert, capital might have yielded more had it been invested in small-scale, labor-intensive farming elsewhere in the country.

Reforms in other parts of Latin America are more recent than that of Mexico, but already a similar pattern is emerging. The *hacienda* system was abolished in Peru in 1968, with the Velazco military takeover. Both *haciendas* in the *sierra* (highlands) and plantations on the coast were converted into cooperatives, with the former *peons* as members. The agricultural production index declined from 110 in 1967 to 106 in 1968, increased to 113 in 1969 (the year of the reform), and then increased to 122 in 1970 and on to 123 in 1971 (1961–1965 = 100) (UNECLA 1973:563). Thus output did not decrease after the reform, but (like the early years after the Mexican reform) its increase was slow.

Still, the Peruvian reform seems not to have helped the very poor. Rather, it may conform to a pattern more generally observed by Berry (1972), who divides the farm population into three parts: large landowners, small-scale farmers, and landless peasants. If a reform distributes large holdings among tenants and sharecroppers, excluding the landless "outsiders," the welfare of these, the poorest, may deteriorate. In Peru, the "outsiders" were not only the landless but also *minifundio* owners who had been accustomed to working part-time on *haciendas*. After the reform, their exclusion led to considerable unrest and threats that they might invade the government-sponsored cooperatives. Fitzgerald (1976:17) observes that 30 percent of the Peruvian work force is rural, earning only 8.8 percent of the national income, with an output index of only 102 in 1972 (1960 = 100).

The Chilean reform (1967; accelerated after 1970 by the Popular Unity government) was designed, in part, to remedy a gross inefficiency in food production. Although Chile possesses one of the most fertile basins in Latin America, her agricultural output has increased very slowly over the years, and even declined by 5 percent per capita from 1948 to 1963 (Barraclough, 1973:141) as the country shifted from being a net exporter to a net importer of foods. Many lands that could have been used for intensive truck farming or fruit orchards were instead left idle or were put into extensive cattle raising.

Early in the reform, cracks opened in the Popular Unity coalition. Whereas the government had specified that farms of less than 80 hectares would not be expropriated, the extreme leftists encouraged workers to take over all farms. Violent seizures ensued in the early seventies, and both investment and plantings declined (Chapter 16). Although agricultural production did increase by 5 percent from 1970 to 1971, and by 1.5 percent the next year, it declined by 10 percent from 1972 to 1973 (Barraclough, 1973:11). Agricultural imports increased from $166 million per year (average 1965–1970) to $230 million (1970–1971) and on to $400 million (1971–1972) and $666 million (1972–1973) (Collarte, 1974:3). The decreases in output had many causes, including not only the violence of the expropriations, but also the monumental management problem of transforming an entire institutional structure within two years. In addition, balance-of-payments deficits made the import of essential inputs difficult. Also among the problems was the discontent of "insiders" (former *hacienda peons*) in the face of the government's admittance of *afuerinos* (landless peasants and *minifundio* owners) into full participation in settlements and state farms.

After the overthrow of the Popular Unity government (1973), the military *junta* reversed the trend toward state farms. Land that had been illegally expropriated (22.9 percent of the total expropriations) was returned to the former owners. The remaining 77.1 percent was not returned, but was scheduled to be divided up and registered in the names of the settlers (Stanfield, 1976:2). The major change was that parcels awarded to new owners were much larger than planned when the reform law was passed (1967), with fewer beneficiaries.[3]

Although the *hacienda* system appeared to be gone forever, the *afuerinos* would be left out (just as in Peru). It is too early to tell whether reform will overcome the previous stagnation in Chilean agriculture, but there are also no signs that it will cause an increase in the welfare of the very poor.

PEOPLE'S REPUBLIC OF CHINA, TAIWAN, JAPAN, AND INDIA

In the first three of these countries, agrarian reform has occurred together with increases in both farm output and productivity; decision-making has been decentralized (prices and production are largely in the hands of the farmers themselves, or—as in China—in their local organizations); equity in income distribution has been greatly improved; and absolute poverty has been reduced. In India, while production and productivity have increased comparably to China, equity has not. Private landlords with large holdings remain the dominant force in agriculture. Although formal feudalism may be eroding, tenancy (its second cousin) continues to be strong and absolute poverty abounds.

We do not have the space to review all Asian agrarian reforms. However, the "success" comments for the first three might be extended to both South and North Korea and probably to Viet Nam as well (King, 1977:219–251), while the "failure" comments for India would apply also to Pakistan and Bangladesh.

---

[3]No titles were given during the Allende years. The 1967 law (passed during the Frei administration and unalterable by Allende because of Congressional opposition) provided for state farms for experiment and demonstration as well as providing for cooperatives. Although the intention was that there should be only a few state farms, no number was specified. In a conversation in 1972, the Director of the Agrarian Reform Corporation told one of the authors that the Allende government planned to make the state farm the basic entity throughout the country: owned by government, farmed cooperatively. After the 1973 coup, the Pinochet government decided to grant titles; how many and to whom became a major question. The decision to award considerably larger plots than originally intended revoked the land rights of many peasants who had belonged to the private *fundo* before Allende and who had been incorporated into the cooperative under Allende. *Afuerinos* who had also been incorporated were similarly dispossessed. The nature of the reform was therefore changed, but the fact of a major land redistribution remains.

The situation is different in Burma, Thailand, and Malaysia, where feudalism did not take hold. In the Philippines, agrarian reform has had considerable success (Querol, 1974) but has been slow because of politically-connected resistance and exemption of farms producing sugar.

Modern agrarian reform in China began even before 1949, as the Red Army occupied more and more of the land. They executed landlords, abolished tenancy, and divided farmlands among the peasantry. After their 1949 victory, they did away with feudalism and tenancy throughout the mainland, in favor of peasant ownership, by 1952. From the beginning, the Chinese leadership was divided between immediate collectivization (favored by Mao Tse-tung) and a period of peasant ownership followed by collectivization when it was required for mechanization (favored by Liu Shao-chi) (Chao, 1970). While the discussion continued, collectivization occurred in stages: first with "mutual-aid teams" (combinations of farms), then with collective farming. By the end of 1955, over 60 percent of China's 110 million farm households had pooled their land (MacFarquhar, 1974:15). In April, 1958, the first commune was formed out of 27 collectives, and by the end of the year more than 90 percent of Chinese peasants had been brought into communes.

More than all the others, the Chinese agrarian reform can be understood (we believe) only in the context of the overall development of the People's Republic; therefore we leave details (including data and sources) to Chapter 16, where P.R. China is taken up as a case study. The overall picture is the following. Chinese planning is decentralized, taking place on all levels (central government, communes, and subdivisions of the communes, as well as production brigades and teams). Each commune is told (by the central planners) how much grain and other products it is expected to deliver to the cities, and at what price, but the technology of production is left to local authorities. Local authorities also determine what goods will be produced for local consumption and what their prices will be. Prices are not determined in a free market, but the fact that they are set *locally* both distinguishes them from the centrally-controlled prices in most LDCs and (we believe) makes for reasonable satisfaction of local needs and efficiency in resource allocation. Incomes are also distributed according to local decisions (of communes, brigades, and team members). All decisions to save and invest are made similarly.

The fact that saving and investment is determined locally has proved to be a strong incentive for using labor-intensive methods. Lands have been reclaimed, terracing installed, giant mounds of earth moved by hand labor. We do not know whether the Chinese are "fully" employed (as opposed to underemployed). Some observers believe they are not. However, the massive unemployment of other LDCs is clearly not a problem for China (nor for Taiwan, Japan, or North and South Korea); there appears always to be work in rural areas for those who wish it.

Agricultural output in China has increased by an average of 2.7 percent per year during the period 1949–78, a record that is neither exceptionally good nor poor by LDC comparisons. But agriculture has been upset by two massive political crises: the Great Leap Forward (1959–1960) and the Great Cultural Revolution (1967). With relative calm in the 1970s, output increases have been much greater—for example, 4.5 percent per year from 1974 to 1978–which *is* high by comparison with progress in most LDCs.

We do not have Lorenz curve or Gini data for China. But the fact that most Chinese are still on the land, that they have been relieved of heavy payments (about 40 percent of their crops) to feudal landlords, that their output has increased substantially since 1962, that production and distribution decisions are in the hands of the peasantry (except for quantities and prices of output to be delivered to the government and the amount of agricultural tax), and that terms of trade are improving for farmers—all these indicators would lead one to believe that income distribution in China is among the more equitable.

The Nationalist government of China had not been interested in agrarian reform before its defeat and exile to Taiwan in 1949. Thereafter, partly under pressure from the United States, partly influenced by examples on the mainland and in Japan, and partly because of the political ease of expropriating Japanese-owned lands, it instituted a series of acts that first reduced tenant rents, then sold public land, and finally (1953) expropriated with compensation all tenanted land above three *chia* (equal to 2.874 hectares), for sale to tenants. The government then offered a variety of services, including technical assistance, credits, access to inputs, and instruction in farm management. Marketing cooperatives were formed, and the government provided roads and other parts of the infrastructure.

Several authors (Ladejinsky, 1964, Jacoby, 1966, and Manzhuber, 1970) have argued that Taiwan's agrarian reform was Pareto-optimal, in that all parties (landlords, tenants, government, and consumers) gained—except for former Japanese owners, of course. Landlords were compensated with government bonds and stock in government corporations; presumably they went into business in an economy made prosperous by (among other things) the agrarian reform.

Smith (1972) studied how the landlords had in fact fared. Most, he discovered, not only did not participate actively in business, but soon spent the proceeds of their bonds, primarily for consumption. Almost all sold their government stocks in the first few years, at an average price of $7.325, compared to the issue value (par) of $10. They predicted well, for the few who held them until 1969 would have been able to sell for an average of only $11.38, representing an annual return of 0.9 percent compared to annual inflation of 6.1 percent (a real loss of 5.2 percent per year). Hence the Taiwanese reform, like all other successful reforms, was confiscatory toward landlords.

All other parties gained, however. Chao (1972) reports that output had increased to 124.9 in 1960 (1953 = 100), an annual average of 3.2 percent, while productivity stood at 103.8. The increases do not appear extraordinary, but they are greater than those in Japan or P.R. China during the comparable period after reform.

In 1962, a ten-year consolidation program was mapped out by the government, in which farmers combined plots in order to use inputs more efficiently. More infrastructure (feeder roads, irrigation ditches, drainage canals, bridges, and culverts) began to be built by the farmers themselves (Querol, 1974:78–79). Farm output during the 1960s was increasing by about 3.7 percent per year, and in 1974 the index stood at 3.23 times the amount for 1949, while the number of farm households had increased by 41 percent (Republic of China, 1975:80, 92). This would imply an increase in labor productivity (on a household basis) of 165 percent over the 25-year period.

Japanese agrarian reform began with the Meiji restoration of 1868. The great estates of feudal lords were confiscated and distributed among the peasantry. Output increased and proceeds were invested in industry. However, successful farmers bought out less successful ones, and by World War II land concentration was again considered "great" (even though over 99 percent of the farms were less than five hectares), and tenancy had again become widespread.

The reform of 1946 was imposed on Japan by the American conquerors, who feared the militarism and political influence of the gentry. All tenanted land, as well as resident-owned land in excess of one *cho* (.991 hectares),[4] was purchased by the government and sold to tenants or others. Because payment was in bonds and heavy inflation ensued, real compensation was negligible. Although the average size of farms could not decline by much, the tenancy status changed decisively. Owner-cultivators increased from 31.2 to 61.8 percent of all farm units between 1941 and 1950, while part-tenant part-owner cultivators decreased from 20.0 to 6.7 percent and tenants from 27.7 to 5.0 percent (Doré, 1959:176).

Extension services have been subsidized by the government but provided by local prefectures. Farmers have formed cooperatives for purchase of inputs, provision of marketing services, education, and mutual assistance. The emphasis has been on local communities organizing their own services, and the response has been high.

Agricultural output since the reform has increased by about 3 to 4 percent per year (King, 1977:199), which is a "decent" rate by international standards but considerably less than Japan's 10 percent for industry. Labor productivity has increased by about 4.75 percent per year, while land productivity is also on the rise. The number of households employed primarily in agriculture declined by 55 percent from 1955 to 1974 (Statistical Yearbook, 1976:93); the others have mostly been released for industry, where unemployment is among the lowest in the world (Patrick and Rosovsky, 1976:24).

In sum, Japanese farmers set their own prices, make their own decisions about production, and have organized themselves for common services. Their productivity and output have increased. But farming is still poor competition for employment in modern industry, where labor is scarce (United Nations, 1976:81).

In contrast to the successes of East Asia, agrarian reform has little affected the poorer farmers of South Asia. When the British East India Company first arrived in India (1600), they found a tenure system in which no one owned the land. Rather, land was tied to a complex set of obligations and privileges related to birth, status, and caste. The system differed in details according to place, but the following is typical: Some individuals *(ryots)* cultivated the land, and others *(zamindars)* collected tribute from them (although a few *zamindars*

---

[4]In Hokkaido, where farms were larger, the limit was four *cho*.

cultivated their own land). All in turn paid taxes to higher *zamindars*, to princes, or to an emperor. In some areas, *jagirdars* had received land privileges (not grants), known as *jagirs*, often as rewards for military service. No arrangement was secure, for all privileges could be withdrawn. Periodic rebellions and wars might dispossess any or all groups.

The British hoped to turn the *zamindars* and *jagirdars* into efficient estate managers and the *ryots* into "sturdy yeomen." But when the restraints of the customary system were removed, some officials became more aggressive, more knowledgeable, more shifty than others, and commercial agriculture, which had existed earlier, expanded, providing opportunities for extortion from the ignorant. Moneylenders arose, and properties were lost through debt. Landholding was thus highly concentrated at the time of Indian independence (1947).

The Indian government set forth an outline for reform, but implementation (under the constitution) had to be left to the states, where landowners are politically prominent and powerful. While intermediaries have been successfully abolished, and rents have been reduced, ceilings on ownership have not been effective. Court cases tend to drag on for years, and every delaying tactic is tried. More than 20 years after the "reform," 72 percent of agricultural holdings were still (1976) smaller than two hectares and accounted for only 20 percent of agricultural land, while holdings of above eight hectares accounted for 5 percent of the total number and occupied 36 percent of the land (United Nations, 1976:66).

Services have also been inequitably distributed. The Small Farmers' Development Agency, which provides subsidized credit for land improvements and irrigation, excludes the lowest stratum because they do not own the necessary minimum. Thus, large investments in irrigation have been utilized only to a fraction of their potential. As a result, the "green revolution," which introduced new, high-yielding varieties of plants, has brought marked increases in productivity for large landowners with sufficient water resources, but has done little for the peasants, who remain passive, unorganized, and inarticulate. King (1977:287) reports that the abolition of *zamindaris* brought "no notable increase in agricultural productivity" and "no change in peasants-to-land ratio." For most, "the annual land tax remained what it had been under the *zamindars*; the government had merely replaced the *zamindar* as the tax collector."

Agricultural output has increased at an average of over three percent per year since independence (Bardhan, 1971:6; GOI, 1975:165). This is a respectable showing, approximately equal to that of P.R. China (though it is less than in Taiwan, Japan, and North or South Korea). India's growth rate has been steady compared with wide fluctuations in P.R. China resulting from political convulsions. However, overall productivity has risen by less than 1 percent per year; thus the increased output is explained mainly by a heavy increase in the number of cultivators: from 49 million in 1950–1951 to 78 million in 1970–1971 (GOI, 1957:272, and GOI, 1975:292), or an annual average rate of 2.35 percent.

By all the measures we have suggested (peasant access to land and other resources, decision-making over inputs and prices, and increases in productivity, output, and income of small farms as opposed to large), the East Asian reforms have been successful and the South Asian (typified by the Indian) have not been. Three possible reasons suggest themselves. The first is that the green revolution, with its high-yielding seed varieties, irrigation, and fertilizers, was pushed heavily in India and Pakistan and that it demanded skilled management, which (being scarce) was more economically utilized over large estates. Irrigation could more easily be coordinated in such estates than over many small farms. But this reason does not stand up, for—with adequate governmental support—a green revolution was undertaken on small farms in the Chinese-Japanese-Korean countries, through extension and management services and through greater commitment to working out complex irrigation patterns. In Luzon Island, Philippines, where water is plentiful and irrigation easy, a green revolution in rice crops on small farms has also been successful. The second reason is that either the governments in South Asia did not want to take the trouble of reform or they believed that agricultural innovations would be more risky if undertaken by many peasant managers than by the large landowners (disdain for the poor). Finally, the third reason is that local landowners remained powerful in South Asia, whereas they had been outmaneuvered in East Asia.

But none of these reasons is an ultimate; each requires another "why?" Stepping back into a broader (historical) perspective, we note that the countries of East Asia have a longer tradition in science and scholarship and in reliance on small-scale initiative than do those of South Asia. The green revolution has affected P.R. China, Korea, Taiwan, and Japan in the context of small farming; there appears not to have been a prejudice that small-scale farmers could not "do the job." Finally, the East Asian countries were applying to agriculture policies similar to those being applied to business: smallness of scale, labor-intensive technology, and export orientation. Thus the two groups of countries differed in patterns affecting the *total economy*; hence agriculture does not have its explanation *sui generis*.

LAND REFORM WITHOUT VIOLENCE?

In Chapter 1, we proposed that endemic violence is a significant obstacle to economic development. There is, however, a conventional wisdom that the rich will never give up their possessions without fighting. "Neither income nor asset ownership is relinquished without a fight, any more than is political power or military control" (Clark Reynolds, 1970:30).[5] If this is true, then it would be necessary to calculate some trade-off between the damage done by violence and the benefits of reform.

Fortunately, there is no trade-off, for the conventional wisdom is wrong. Many times in history, substantial assets have been transferred from the rich to the poor without violence. Solon, archon of Athens in 594 B.C., abolished the system of *hektemeroi*, by which serfs were required to pay one-sixth of their

---

[5]It is not clear whether Reynolds meant a violent fight or not, though the comment was made in the context of the Mexican Revolution.

crops to landowners; without violence, he took estates from the rich and gave them to the poor; and Attica became a land of free peasants. Similar reforms were undertaken in Rome, by Tiberius and Gaius Gracchus in 133 B.C. and thereafter, with no civil war. There were sporadic uprisings, and Tiberius was murdered, but these related to a broader scope of events than the reforms per se. Emperor Wang Mang of China confiscated many landed estates (9 A.D.) and turned them over to the State. In the early part of the T'ang dynasty, the emperors passed land equalization laws (618–624 A.D.), legislating maximum sizes of farms and causing land to be taken from the rich. Again in the early part of the Ming dynasty (1368 *et ff.* A.D.) great landed estates were confiscated, divided up, and rented out. Taxes were remitted to peasants, and other efforts were made to assist them. The Japanese reforms after the Meiji restoration (1868) also occurred without war.

The abolition of slavery also meant taking "property" from the rich, as in Britain and South Africa in 1833, and in the remaining countries of Europe and all of the Americas during the nineteenth century. Only in the United States was it accompanied by violence.

In addition, modern agrarian reforms have taken place without violence. Beginning in 1962, the Shah of Iran began the "white revolution" (so-called because it was to be bloodless), in which he voluntarily distributed all his own estates among the poor, compelling the nobility and religious leaders to do the same with much of theirs. The reaction against this was one of the factors leading to the Shah's abdication in 1979; the ensuing violence, however, was associated with a broader set of events than the agrarian reform (Chapter 16). In Egypt, the reform of 1952 required that no farm be larger than 200 feddans (1 feddan = 1.04 acre), a size subsequently whittled down to 100 and then to 50 feddans (Abdel-Fadil, 1975). In Peru, a bloodless coup d'etat (1968) led to the expropriation of all large farms, as we have already seen in this chapter. There appears to be much informal belief that the Pinochet government of Chile (post-1973) reversed the bloodless agrarian reform of the Popular Unity years and returned all farms to former owners. We have seen earlier in this chapter that this is only partially so.

When reforms occur within the context of endemic violence—that is, where violence is the accepted, normal means of resolving disputes—then it is difficult to state categorically that *anything* of importance occurs without violence. The events that we have singled out occurred without a direct, warlike reaction on the part of the deprived. There is no doubt that they were pressured or coerced. Our task, therefore, is to identify the common situations in which the ability is gained nonviolently to pressure or coerce for agrarian reform.

Some of the reforms mentioned above were quickly reversed. Wang Mang is often depicted as some kind of historical devil, who wanted himself to benefit from landholdings absorbed by the State. His reforms were quickly nullified. The impacts of the ancient Greek and Roman reforms lasted many years, but all of them were dissipated as, over the centuries, the decline of civilization itself gave rise to new land concentrations. Furthermore, land concentrations have remained after the modern reforms in Iran and Egypt; we list them because substantial redistribution did occur.

The conditions for reform appear to have been that new economic parameters made the old system obsolete. Slavery ended because the system had become inefficient. Workers could be more easily controlled and disciplined, and productive efficiency was greater, with free hiring and wage incentives (Chapter 15). This lesson was learned in the middle ages; it had to be relearned in the nineteenth century.

We will see, in the next section, that nonfeudal forms of agriculture (whether socialist or capitalist) are historically associated with greater efficiency than feudal forms. The major successful reforms appear to arise from the need for a growing supply of foodstuffs to growing industry and thus from a shift in political power as industry becomes dominant.

Other parameters may, however, determine the time and place. Indian agrarian reform has been delayed by decentralized decision-making and by the political power of landlords within the context of state governments. It has probably also been delayed by the green revolution, which has made it possible to supply sufficient foodstuffs to urban areas even with inefficient agriculture. It would seem that only when the "pinch is on" (as in Egypt, Chile, and Peru) will the pertinent authorities swing in the direction of reform.

PRODUCTIVITY: SMALL VERSUS LARGE

In assessing the need for agrarian reform, economists ask the following question: *Will agricultural output be increased in most LDCs if large farms are partitioned into small ones and if tenure is vested in peasant cultivators?*

Some countries now have more than two decades of experience with agrarian reforms in which large farms have been so partitioned. But the experience is mixed. Based on Taiwan, Korea, Japan, and Sri Lanka, one must vote for "success" (although the "large" farms in the first three were hardly large in the Latin American sense). Based on Cuba and Chile, the answer is "not likely." In Mexico, it would be "yes for some, no for others." In many cases where partitional reform laws have been passed, they have not been fully implemented. If we look back a century and a half to the experience of Britain and France, the answer is "no": consolidation, not partition, leads to agricultural efficiency. Because macro-empirical studies tell us little, therefore, we turn to micro-empirical studies, to see if they form the basis for a theory.

Over the past 30 years, an abundance of micro-studies have been done. Each of these has covered a limited territory for a limited period, and only recently have generalists been able to observe tendencies by aggregating them. Although the following points are not accepted by everyone, we believe the weight of evidence now substantiates them.

FIRST, there is very little free land left in the world. A hasty glance at a population map might "reveal" vast expanses of unused territory in central South America, western Zambia, central Zaire, on the fringes of the Sahara, or in the northern parts of South Asian countries. In fact, however, virtually all this land is already occupied to the extent of its economic capability; most

of it suffers some deficiency of soil or climate that would make it difficult to cultivate further. If rural population growth is to be accommodated on farms, agriculture must be more labor-intensive than it now is in
most places.

SECOND, in most LDCs population pressure is so high that the optimal amount
of labor to be combined with land has already been exceeded. Although the
marginal product of labor is still positive, each new person to join the population, while another reaches work-force age, would tend to cause a decrease
in per capita output. So far, in LDCs the world over, such decreases have
been slightly more than offset by productivity increases. In most LDCs, therefore, agricultural output per capita is growing, though very slowly.

THIRD, agricultural output in most LDCs could be increased by a transfer of
labor from small-scale to large-scale farms. On the former, the marginal
product of labor is low and that of land high, while on the latter (except
plantation farms) the opposite holds true. In less technical terms, small-
scale plots are already cultivated so intensively that another laborer would
add little output; but if all laborers working on a given small plot were
awarded a tiny increase in their land, they could do wonders with it. On the
other hand, new land added to large-scale farms might go to waste, while
more laborers could be fruitfully used.

This situation has been found primarily in Asia and Latin America, where
large farms (relative to small ones) are in greater abundance than in Africa.
The situation was examined for seven Latin American countries by the Inter-
American Committee for Agricultural Development, whose studies have been
summarized by Barraclough (1973). Lele (1972) reports that existing evidence is "overwhelming that under traditional technology, where input of
labor is much more important than that of capital, small farms have a
higher yield than do large farms.[6]

FOURTH, government assistance to agriculture, including credit, technical advice, easy access to fertilizers and other inputs, subsidies, and infrastructure
such as irrigation, has (in nonsocialist countries) benefited large-scale, rich
farmers more than small-scale, poor ones.[7] The fruits of the green revolution,
with higher-yielding seeds and superior methods, have also been enjoyed
differentially by the rich, since these benefits have depended on the possession
of land and control over irrigation.

FIFTH, markets in LDCs respond quickly to changes in supply, demand, and
prices. Lele (1972) reports that "an impressive body of statistical evidence
has accumulated which indicates that contrary to general belief, the private
marketing systems in LDCs are, by and large, highly competitive and operate
efficiently given the conditions in which they function." She cites 15 studies
that support this position.

---

[6]Her conclusion is supported by Bhagwati and Chakravarty (1969), Khusro (1964), Mazudar
(1965), Rao (1968), and Rudra (1968). Lloyd Reynolds (1975:4) also confirms this assertion, by
reference to a number of studies.

[7]This fact is brought out in a large number of studies, of which the following are only a few:
Abercrombie (1967), Adams and Coward (1972), Jain (1971), Lele (1972), United Nations (1970),
Jodha (1971), B. P. Rao (1970), and C. H. H. Rao (1970).

SIXTH, both labor and land productivity on small-scale farms in Asia, Africa, and Latin America is significantly lower than on farms of any size in Europe, North America, and Japan. Low productivity is probably not explained primarily by the inefficiency of small-scale farms (given existing conditions and technology), by low-quality management, nor by an unwillingness of farmers to adopt technology already known elsewhere, although all these may contribute. Rather, the major deficiency appears to lie in insufficient research and insufficient dissemination of locally-generated knowledge. Seeds, fertilizing and weeding methods, and insect control appear to be very location-specific, such that methods used in MDCs cannot be readily transferred to LDCs. "Programs designed to transplant modern technology have continuously come up against the realization that the technology offered had little or no advantage over the old or traditional methods, given the economic, soil, and climate conditions facing producers" (Evenson, 1975:192).

These six observations do not immediately answer the question concerning small versus large farms. Indeed, it is not at all clear that agrarian reform *necessarily* increases agricultural productivity, and this fact no doubt explains, at least in part, the mixture of the empirical results.

Our own conclusions are the following. Scientific farming, high productivity, and appropriate distribution of its fruits among the peasantry can be achieved— and have been achieved—with virtually any system of land tenure. This occurrence seems, rather, to be an integral part of a wider context, in which productive efficiency is increasing over a broad range: in manufacturing, services, government and other sectors.

It is because feudalism does not integrate easily with these other developments that it becomes the least likely form of tenure to achieve scientific farming and equitable distribution. Testimony for this observation comes from its decline all over the world, but only alongside industrialization, broadening of markets, and improved income distribution in the secondary and tertiary sectors of the economy. The greater productivity of labor on large-scale as opposed to small-scale farms calls for a transfer of workers from the latter to the former. The experience of the reforms we have cited shows, we believe, that this transfer is most likely to be achieved, politically, with the expropriation of large-scale farms and their division into small-scale farms. In both modern and ancient history, we find that such expropriation must be at least partially confiscatory, and that it may occur with or without violence.

MECHANIZATION AND SMALL-SCALE FARMING

A frequently-heard argument for *not* dividing the land is that small-scale farms cannot appropriately take advantage of mechanization. Proponents of agrarian reform favoring this argument tend to suggest cooperatives and state farms, instead of small, individual plots. A more basic question is: Should LDCs use mechanized means of agriculture at all? Or, is not labor-intensive technology the most appropriate in countries where labor is the abundant resource?

The arguments in favor of labor-intensive technology are as follows. Except for a few specialized tasks, such as drilling deep wells and removing stumps, there is virtually nothing a machine can do in agriculture that human labor, with rudimentary tools, cannot do. Agriculture is thus not like industry. For example, no amount of labor could throw a person to the moon. But men and women with hoes and shovels can plough, plant, weed, spread insecticides, and harvest, provided there are enough of them. Therefore, if laborers are abundant and have no alternative opportunities, it is better to employ them rather than machines.

Furthermore, economies of scale in agriculture have not been proved in any statistical sense. Indeed, comparing large and small farms introduces so many variations in choice of crops, production techniques, tenure arrangements, and so forth that comparability is largely destroyed. Nothing in the research literature would indicate that economies of scale in LDC agriculture are significant. Hence mechanization should not be cited as a reason for large-scale farming.

The argument in favor of mechanization is that rural unemployment or underemployment in LDCs is a myth. The demand for labor must be counted in its most intensive season: the harvest, which is usually a period of labor shortage. To some extent, it is possible to move labor about seasonally. In Argentina, a significant amount of migratory labor converges on Tucumán at sugar harvest, goes south to Mendoza for the grape harvest, and disperses through the rest of the country for other crops. In countries where harvests are concentrated into short periods, however, it is impossible to mobilize enough labor, and it is necessary to resort to tractors. Once these tractors have been purchased, of course, they may be used throughout the year. The result is a surplus of labor in non-harvest months.

How is this labor employed? Hymer and Resnick (1969) reported significant non-farm activity, referring to it as the production of "Z-goods." Such labor is available for handicrafts, services, and trading. The problem, therefore, is in finding an optimal year-round allocation of labor and in determining the kinds of mechanization that would complement it.

In some countries, small-scale (garden-type) tractors are used extensively. These tractors are gradually replacing the *carabao* as the principal source of power in Philippine rice fields; they are used on communes in China. The International Labor Organization, which has studied technology in LDCs extensively, has concluded that *selective* mechanization can lead to *both* higher output and employment for LDC farmers. This recommendation appears in a number of ILO country reports on employment.

Every case is *sui generis*, and the only blanket generalization is that the efficiency of mechanization depends on whether the correct machines have been selected and whether the overall, year-round use of labor, in agriculture and nonagriculture, is efficiently organized.

Let us pause briefly for one more argument against small-scale farming. It is often suggested that management capabilities are in short supply and that more economical use of skilled managers requires that they be concentrated on large farms. We believe the abundance of micro-studies, cited by Lloyd

Reynolds (1977) and Helleiner (1975) and discussed in Chapter 4, shows that this is not so. Management may always be improved, and extension services are always needed. But by and large, management is not the principal constraint.

DOES THE "FAULT" LIE WITH THE PEASANT OR WITH THE GOVERNMENT?

The peasant and the government have both been blamed for the low productivity of agriculture in LDCs or for the failure of agrarian reform. If we assume that the principal problem is indeed inadequate research and development and the low level of scientific technology and its distribution, it is possible to find ways in which both peasants and government are "at fault." In so doing, however, we are led to the sterile nature of the question itself.

Those who would fault the peasants draw on the types of personal limitations and lack of overall modernity cited in Chapter 3 (for example, Bozeman, Myrdal, Foster, Lewis, and Inkeles and Smith). A study (Sri Lanka, 1973) of "small-holdings in the coconut triangle" found that "some of the small-holders were of the opinion that it was not necessary to manure the grass" (p. 10), that there was "a lack of motivation and discipline for optimum cultivations" (p. 15), and that "smallholdings on coconut lands display poor standards of husbandry; they can be improved by enlightened cultivating practices, diversification, intercropping, and livestock keeping" (p. 17).

Other studies have referred to lack of initiative or innovation. Smith, Stanfield, and Brown (1974) showed how Chilean farmers (*asentados*), after the agrarian reform, stayed with the vegetable cultivation, which they had been familiar with, rather than deal with the complex marketing processes of other crops.

Myrdal's *Asian Drama* (1968) is a monumental work based on careful statistical analysis and the accumulation of information from a large number of micro-studies of Asian agriculture and industry. On the basis of these studies, Myrdal generalizes as follows (p. 508):

> In short, the more efficient production of plantation crops takes place on the larger estates, mostly controlled by Europeans, whereas *the least efficient is found on small-scale native holdings* (italics added).

Those who would fault the government point to inadequate credit facilities, extension services, infrastructure such as electricity and farm-to-market roads, or to discriminatory price and tax policies. In a work entitled *Nigeria's Neglected Rural Majority*, Olatunbosun (1975) reports on a number of failures due not only to government negligence, but also to inefficiency. He cites the perverse effects of marketing boards, which have manipulated the terms of trade against small-scale farmers. Writing of marketing boards in all West African countries, Bauer (1954, reprinted 1972:405) concluded that "the terms of trade of the producers were depressed far below what they would have been without this system and well below those of their principal competitors." We will return to this point in Chapter 14.

In the eyes of many authors, government policy has been biased in favor of export crops, to earn foreign exchange to finance the imports of a modern urban sector. Suggesting that African hunger is politically inspired, Lofchie (1975:551–567) argues that lands capable of production for indigenous consumption have been diverted to exports for this reason. The American Friends Service Committee (1976:9) has made the same case with respect to strawberries and tomatoes exported from Northwest Mexico to the United States. Many more such instances, unresearched, are heard in political disquisitions, where it is hinted that multinational companies have used "modern" national land laws and their superior weight to deprive ingenuous peasants of their traditional land heritage (in the Philippines, Liberia, and Central America, for example).

We have examined much of this literature, listened to many of the conversations, and have come to the following belief. There is, indeed, in many LDCs, a bias against small-scale agriculture and favoring large-scale, export-oriented agriculture. In some cases, land is directly taken by the knowledgeable and powerful from the poor and ingenuous. None of these cases (that we know of) has been researched in a social-science sort of way. However, we are familiar with the manner in which Liberian land was originally seized by colonizers at the point of a gun; we even know who pointed it—Lieutenant R. F. Stockton of the U.S. Navy (Fyfe, 1976:191). We are aware of the similar ways in which the Dutch duped the Khoi and the San into yielding their lands in southern Africa, and how the British outmaneuvred the Kikuyu, Masai, and the Zulu, although the latter yielded only after a bloody war. The unresearched conversations about powerful governments and corporations doing the same today, by people "close to the scene," appear convincing to us, and we will believe them until there is evidence to the contrary.

In some cases, therefore, traditionally tribal land, heretofore growing food for local consumption, is being diverted into export crops, by unsavory methods. We cannot countenance this at all. But to extend this situation, as some authors have done (such as Lofchie, 1975, and the American Friends Service Committee, 1976), to suggest that *other* lands devoted to export crops should be reconverted into lands for producing domestic crops, seems to be counterproductive. We have already cited Clark Reynolds (1970) as showing that resources can be more effectively used in the Central Valley and Gulf coast of Mexico than in the Northwest. With appropriate policies, therefore, Mexico could "have its cake and eat it, too." Land and resources for export crops and for indigenous crops are often not competing, and the fact that exports are favored does not mean that if they were not, the supply of indigenous food would suddenly increase.

In most cases, peasants are not so put upon that they are unable to find *any* ways to improve their own welfare. Indeed, investigations of peasant management capabilities affirms that in many countries, they are moving toward optimization. The key lies, perhaps, in the phrase *"within his perceived opportunity set,"* in the quotation from Lloyd Reynolds on page 70. What the peasant can do most is to expand his "perceived opportunity set."

Often a nudge from outside agencies is helpful. In the Philippines, the International Institute of Rural Reconstruction (a nongovernment agency visited by one of the authors in 1978–1979) is teaching farmers the rudiments of scientific experimentation: how to apply different methods of weed control, insect control, or new seeds to sample fields; how to set up a control field; and how to compare results. Learning to experiment is perhaps something the farmer could do by himself, or by imitating his neighbors. In India, a simple, inexpensive system of training, along with visits by the Israeli who devised it (Daniel Benor), has won the plaudits of the President of the World Bank for its amazing results (Rowen, 1978).

There is no doubt, on the other hand, that official intervention is helpful and that government research (as exemplified by the green revolution) can spread new, locally-adapted techniques. In addition, the government can provide extension services, infrastructure, and credit. Much heat has been generated in shouting these facts, but the literature sheds little light on the conditions that will motivate the government itself to take any action.

CONCLUSION

Agriculture is the basis for most LDC economies. In all but a few countries, it employs the bulk of the people, is the principal resource, and supplies the basis for local consumption. In most LDCs, farms could probably produce much more than they do now. The reasons why they fall short are complex; they include lack of management capabilities, apathy at all levels, inefficient or inadequate organization of complementary resources and services, and lack of indigenous research and development. We believe the latter, as well as insufficient diffusion of its results, is the single, crucial element to which most attention should be devoted.

In a physical sense, the type of land structure is unimportant; there are small private farms, large private farms, cooperatives or collectives, tenancy, and feudalism. Given complementary institutions and pressures, any one of these would be capable of producing maximum output and egalitarian distribution of income. Historically, however, feudalism has failed to do so, not because of its inherent qualities, but because it has existed within a wider framework in which the distribution of power and privilege, wealth and income, has not been conducive to demanding maximum output from farms.

Successful agrarian reforms have occurred in those two areas (Europe and East Asia) that we have already designated as having achieved, or of currently achieving, economic growth with equitable distribution of income. We define as successful reforms those in which access to land is open to peasants; where decisions over prices and products are vested in the peasants; where the terms of trade are not turned heavily against the peasants through manipulation of prices, taxes, or monopoly rents; and where peasants are not discriminated against in the provisions of credit, fertilizers, and other inputs. We believe it is no coincidence that these countries are the same ones that we have identified as, by and large, having adopted, or coming to adopt, the classical path toward development outlined in Chapter 1, with its export orientation and tendencies toward decentralization and/or liberalism.

Thus reform does not come for its sake alone, or for the sake of justice. It comes when it is demanded in a broader complex of production and trade, affecting both the nation and the international markets. Feudalism originated with the need for defense and in conjunction with socio-political frameworks in eras when cooperation, division of labor, and trade were limited. It has survived only as long as those limitations have lasted. When they end, so also does feudalism.

BIBLIOGRAPHY

Abdel-Fadil, Mahmoud, 1975:
>   *Development, Income Distribution, and Social Change in Rural Egypt*, New York, Cambridge University Press.

Abercrombie, K. C., 1967:
>   "Incomes and Their Distribution in Agriculture and the Rest of the Economy," *Monthly Bulletin of Agricultural Economics and Statistics*, Vol. 16, No. 6, June.

Adams, Dale W., and Coward, E. W., 1972:
>   *Small-Farmer Development Strategies: A Seminar Report*, New York, Agricultural Development Council, July.

American Friends Service Committee, 1976:
>   *The United States and Latin America Today*, Philadelphia, Pa., AFSC.

Bardhan, Pranab, 1971:
>   "Indian Agriculture: An Analysis of Recent Performance," in Chen, Kuan-I and Uppal, J. S., *Comparative Development of India and China*, New York, Free Press (Macmillan).

Barraclough, Solon, ed., 1973:
>   *Agrarian Structure in Latin America*, Lexington, Mass., Lexington Books (D.C. Heath).

Barraclough, S., 1974:
>   "The State of Chilean Agriculture Before the Coup," *L.T.C. Newsletter*, January/March.

Bauer, Peter T., 1954, reprinted 1972:
>   *Dissent on Development*, Cambridge, Mass., Harvard University Press.

Berry, R. Albert, 1972:
>   *Land Reform and the Agricultural Income Distribution*, Center Paper No. 184, New Haven, Yale University, Economic Growth Center.

Bhagwati, J. N., and Chakravarty, S., 1969:
>   "Contributions to Indian Economic Analysis," Supplement to *American Economic Review*, Vol. 59, No. 4, September.

Chao, Kang, 1970:
>   *Agricultural Production in Communist China, 1949–1965*, Madison, University of Wisconsin Press.

Chao, Kang, 1972:
>   "Economic Effects of Land Reforms in Taiwan, Japan, and Mainland China: A Comparative Study," LTC No. 80, Madison, Land Tenure Center, University of Wisconsin.

Collarte, Juan Carlos, 1974:
>   "New Agricultural Policies in Chile," *LTC Newsletter*, Madison, Land Tenure Center, University of Wisconsin, October–December.

Doré, R. P., 1959:
  Land Reform in Japan, New York, Oxford University Press.
Dovring, Folke, 1970:
  "Land Reform and Productivity in Mexico," *Land Economics*, August.
Evenson, Robert, 1975:
  "Technology Generation in Agriculture," in Reynolds, Lloyd, ed., *Agriculture in Development Theory*, New Haven, Yale University Press.
Fitzgerald, E. V. K., 1976:
  The State and Economic Development: Peru Since 1968, New York, Cambridge University Press.
Fyfe, Christopher, 1976:
  "Freed-Slave Colonies in West Africa," in Flint, John E., ed., *Cambridge History of Africa*, New York, Cambridge University Press.
GOI, 1957, 1975, 1978:
  Statistical Yearbook, Government of India, New Delhi.
Helleiner, Gerald K., 1975:
  "Smallholder Decision Making: Tropical African Evidence," in Reynolds, Lloyd, ed., *Agriculture in Development Theory*, New Haven, Yale University Press.
Hymer, Stephen, and Resnick, Stephen, 1969:
  "A Model of an Agrarian Economy with Nonagricultural Activities," *American Economic Review*, Vol. 49, No. 4, September.
Jacoby, Neil, 1966:
  U.S. Aid to Taiwan, New York, Praeger.
Jain, H. C., 1971:
  "Growth and Recent Trends in Institutional Credit in India," *Indian Journal of Agricultural Economics*, Vol. 26, No. 4, October–December.
Jodha, N. S., 1971:
  "Land-Based Credit Policies and Investment Prospects for Small Farmers," *Economic and Political Weekly*, Review of Agriculture, Vol. 6, No. 39, September.
Khurso, A. M., 1964:
  "Returns to Scale in Indian Agriculture," *Indian Journal of Agricultural Economics*, Vol. 19, October–December.
King, Russell, 1977:
  Land Reform: A World Survey, Boulder, Colorado, Westview Press.
Ladejinsky, Wolf, 1964:
  "Agrarian Reform in Asia," *Foreign Affairs*, April.
Lele, Uma, 1972:
  "Role of Credit and Marketing Functions in Agricultural Development," paper presented at International Economic Association Conference on "Agriculture in the Development of Low Income Countries," Bad Gotesburg, Germany, September 4.
Lofchie, Michael F., 1975:
  "Political and Economic Origins of African Hunger," *Journal of Modern African Studies*, Vol. 13, No. 4.
MacFarquhar, Roderick, 1974:
  The Origins of the Cultural Revolution, New York, Columbia University Press.
Manzhuber, Albert, 1970:
  "The Economic Development of Taiwan," *Industry of Free China*, Vol. 33, No. 4, May.
Mazumdar, D., 1965:
  "Farm Size and Productivity," *Economica*, May.
Myrdal, Gunnar, 1968:
  Asian Drama, New York, Pantheon (Random House).
Olatunbosun, Dupe, 1975:
  Nigeria's Neglected Rural Majority, Ibadan, Oxford University Press.
Patrick, Hugh, and Rosovsky, Henry, eds., 1976:
  Asia's New Giant: How the Japanese Economy Works, Washington, Brookings Institution.

Querol, Mariano N., 1974:
  Land Reform in Asia, Manila, Solidaridad Publishing House.
Rao, A. P., 1968:
  "Size of Holding and Productivity," *Economic and Political Weekly*, November 11.
Rao, Bodepudi Prasada, 1970:
  "The Economics of Agricultural Credit Use in Southern Brazil," Ph.D. thesis, Ohio State University.
Rao, C. H. Hanumantha, 1970:
  "Farm Size and Credit Policy," *Economic and Political Weekly*, Review of Agriculture, Vol. 5, No. 52, December.
Republic of China (Taiwan), 1975:
  Statistical Yearbook, Taipei, Council for Economic Planning.
Reynolds, Clark, 1970:
  The Mexican Economy: Twentieth Century Structure and Growth, New Haven, Yale University Press.
Reynolds, Lloyd, ed., 1975:
  Agriculture in Development Theory, New Haven, Yale University Press.
Reynolds, Lloyd G., (1977):
  Image and Reality in Economic Development, New Haven, Yale University Press.
Rowan, Hobart, 11–12–78.
  "Poorest of Poor's Crop Yield Soars," *Washington Post.*
Rudra, A., 1968:
  "Farm Size and Yield per Acre," *Economic and Political Weekly*, July 19.
Smith, Stephen M.; Stanfield, David; and Brown, Marion, 1974:
  "Some Consequences for Production and Factor Use of the Chilean Agrarian Reform," *LTC Newsletter*, Madison, Land Tenure Center, University of Wisconsin, October–December.
Smith, Theodore Reynolds, 1972:
  East Asian Agrarian Reform: Japan, Republic of Korea, Taiwan, and the Philippines, Hartford, Connecticut, John C. Lincoln Institute, Research Monograph No. II. (The date 1972 is inferred; the publication bears no date).
Sri Lanka, 1973:
  Smallholdings in the Coconut Triangle, Colombo, Agrarian Research and Training Institute.
Stanfield, David, 1976:
  "The Chilean Agrarian Reform, 1975," *LTC Newsletter*, Madison, Land Tenure Center, University of Wisconsin, April–June.
Statistical Yearbook 1976:
  Government of Japan.
Tuma, Elias H., 1965:
  Twenty-Six Centuries of Agrarian Reform, Berkeley, University of California Press.
UNECLA, 1977:
  Economic Survey of Latin America, 1976, United Nations, Economic Commission for Latin America, Santiago, Chile, and New York.
UNECLA, 1973:
  Statistical Yearbook for Latin America, United Nations Economic Commission for Latin America, Santiago, Chile, and New York.
United Nations, 1970:
  Progress in Land Reform, Fifth Report, New York, E/4769ST/SOA/94, Sales no. E.70.IV.5.
United Nations, 1976:
  Progress in Land Reform: Sixth Report, New York, ST/ESA/32, Sales No. E.76.IV.5.

12

RURAL AND URBAN DEVELOPMENT

Between the tenth and twelfth centuries, the population of Italy rose approximately twofold, reaching a total variously assessed at 7,000,000 to 9,000,000 inhabitants ... Most spectacular was the increase, unparalleled elsewhere, in the size of urban population which, although in no place ever so dense as that of ancient Rome, in many towns rose from a mere 5,000 or 6,000 souls to 30,000 or more, and in some to over 50,000 (Bologna, Palermo), 90,000 (Florence), and even 100,000 (Milan, Venice, and possibly Genoa) ... The principal cause, as monastic and other evidence shows, was a vast spontaneous movement of rural emigration ...
JONES (1971: 344–5)

If current population trends continue for the next quarter century, cities like Bogota, Manila, Karachi and Jakarta will triple in size. Lagos, with a current population of 2.1 million, will quadruple. Some cities, with populations already over 10 million, will double in size in the next ten years. London and Tokyo, in contrast, will grow less than one per cent ... Nearly all the new urban population, half of which will be rural emigrants and half native-born, will be poor. Slums and illegal shantytowns that surround Third World cities will balloon ...
DeYOUNG, *WASHINGTON POST*, FEBRUARY 6, 1977.

Rapid population growth brings many imbalances, among them between urban and rural areas. Industry and opportunity well up in cities, which become magnets for rural people. The number that flock to the cities far outweighs the available jobs and housing. Even with this heavy outmigration, however, rural population continues to grow—at perhaps 2 percent per year (World Bank, 1975:5), though rates vary from place to place. The cities, of course, grow faster, at perhaps 5 percent per year (World Bank, 1972:3), though some reach 7 percent and a few even 10 percent or more. At an annual rate of 5 percent, a population will double in 14 years; at 7 percent, it will double in 10 years.

The burden on the cities is enormous. Because adequate houses cannot be built rapidly enough, and the immigrants could not afford them anyway, enormous slums spring forth: huts of wood and metal scraps, occasionally of cardboard, sometimes jammed one against another. They often lack water, sanitation, or garbage collection, and sometimes electricity. Garbage and refuse are strewn in pathways among them, and flies and vermin are attracted. Disease follows. In some cities, such as Rio de Janeiro, the municipal government provides water taps or central toilets, while in others, such as La Paz, Bolivia, water is delivered by tank truck, for which the residents must line up with cans.

The slums are not planned by linear programs to minimize the distance between home and work. Instead, the new people tax the transport system. If they do find jobs, they may spend two to four hours daily in crowded, polluting buses. Not enough schools are built, nor are they in locations convenient to the slums. The areas are not always properly drained; they may become rutted and muddy during a rainy season.

The urban problem is not separate from the rural. It is not possible to determine how much of the migration is "pushed" and how much is "pulled." Push factors include land shortage with growing population and declining rural opportunities. Pull factors are "city lights" and higher-income possibilities.

That push factors are strong is undeniable. "Of the population in developing countries considered to be in either absolute or relative poverty," the World Bank (1975:4) writes, "more than 80 percent are estimated to live in rural areas. Agriculture is the principal occupation of the rural poor. These people are found in roughly equal proportions in densely populated zones (over 300 persons per square kilometer) and sparsely populated zones (less than 150 persons per square kilometer). Thus, poverty is found in the highly productive irrigated areas of Asia, as well as in the adverse conditions of the Sahel, northeast Brazil, the Andean Altiplano and the dry zones of India."

Empirical studies have made it quite clear that migrants are pulled to urban areas in response to increased-earnings opportunities that the cities provide over the countryside.[1] Reynolds (1977:82) cites studies in Zambia, Rhodesia, Ghana, Malawi, Colombia, and Brazil which show that migration varies in-

---

[1]The "bright city lights" and other cultural explanations have not fared well under empirical testing (see Fields, 1975, and the authors that he cites).

versely with income potential in rural areas and positively with that potential in cities. Papenek (1975:8) reports that even in such lowly occupations as collecting cigarette butts and wastepaper, real incomes in cities can be as much as three times what they are in rural areas. The incomes of the "urban poor" in Jakarta, Papanek goes on, may be over ten times the incomes of the "rural poor" (p. 9).

MODELS OF RURAL-TO-URBAN MIGRATION

The earliest of the modern models were suggested by Lewis (1954) and Fei and Ranis (1961 and 1964). They envisaged development as a process in which "surplus" labor would be released by agriculture into industry. While such models make sense intuitively—because early economies are agrarian and later ones are urban and industrial—nevertheless the historical complexities of the migration pattern make us wonder about their usefulness. Rural population *increased* in England throughout the industrial revolution, right up to 1851 at least (Ashton, 1948: 61, and Pollard, 1978: 105–115). As the English moved to the cities, the Irish and Scottish filled the English countryside. Furthermore, migration from the agrarian South to the industrial North did not occur in quantities that might be expected from the models, and there was much reverse (urban to rural) movement, as well as much new industry in rural areas. Similar patterns occurred in continental Europe during the nineteenth century. Historically, therefore, the idea of a linear movement from rural to urban is much too simple.

The Lewis-Fei-Ranis (L-F-R) models are not specifically addressed to migration. They are overall development models, designed to show how an agrarian society becomes transformed into an industrial one. They assume agriculture as the initial source of both human and industrial capital. Growing population reduces the marginal productivity of rural labor to (or close to) zero; by the same token, opportunities for rural investment become exhausted. Capital and labor both flow to the cities, in response to new industrial opportunities. The movement continues until labor scarcity raises marginal productivities in both city and country, after which resources are allocated according to classical principles.

Todaro (1969, 1976a) has criticized these models for their imprecision and also substituted his own. He points out (Todaro, 1976a:23–24) that L-F-R models make three erroneous assumptions: that the rate of migration is proportional to that of urban capital formation, that there is surplus labor in rural areas and full employment in urban, and that urban wages remain low and constant until all rural surplus labor is absorbed.

By contrast, Todaro suggests that a rural laborer will decide to migrate if the discounted value of his expected lifetime stream of earnings in the city exceeds the same discounted stream in his home area by more than the cost of moving. To simplify, we assume that incomes and their determinants do not change over a person's life. Once the basic model is understood, this assumption can be easily removed. Suppose a potential migrant can stay in peasant agriculture with an income of Y_r or move to the city and *possibly* earn a greater income, Y_u. If he takes the latter choice, however, he runs the risk of being unemployed, with an income of zero. Let us designate the objective probability of his finding urban employment as P. Let us suppose that he will migrate only if the expected value of his urban income equals or exceeds his assured rural income, or only if:

$$PY_u \geqq Y_r \tag{1}$$

If he is a risk-averter, such that he prefers an assured income to an equal expected income with risk, then the decision to migrate requires that PY_u be greater than Y_r by some factor that takes into account his aversion to risk.

Again to simplify, let us assume that all potential migrants are not risk-averters and that all will migrate under the conditions of (1). Then, given the values of Y_r and Y_u as they really are, there must be a critical P^* which equates them. Thus at any time:

$$P^*Y_u = Y_r \tag{2}$$

Migration will occur if $P > P^*$. By increasing the potential pool of unemployed in the city, however, migration reduces P. Thus migration will continue until P falls to equality with P^*. The equilibrium condition (indifference to migration) is therefore one of:

$$PY_u = Y_r \tag{3}$$

To illustrate, assume the equilibrium holds and that $P = P^* = .8$ while $Y_u = 5$ and $Y_r = 4$. For equilibrium to continue, the creation of each new job (paying an income of 5) would call forth $1/.8$ (= 1.25) new migrants; each of them would have .8 probability of receiving a job. At equilibrium, therefore, for every employed person in the cities there must be $1/P^*$ unemployed, and every job created at wage Y_u would call forth $1/P^*$ migrants. If this is so, job creation in the cities increases unemployment, by bringing in a greater number of migrants than the number of jobs created.[2]

Modifications of the Todaro model were made by Harris and Todaro (1970), Johnson (1971), Bhagwati and Srinivasan (1974), and others (see Todaro, 1976a,

---

[2]In the text we use simplified expressions to represent the incentive to migrate. A more complete statement would be:

$$V(0) = \int_{t=0}^{n} [p(t)Y_u(t) - Y_r(t)] e^{-it}dt - C(0)$$

where:

$\qquad$ $V(0)$ is the value of migrating in period 0

$\qquad$ $C(0)$ is the cost of migration

$\qquad$ $p(t)$ is the probability of securing an urban job at the going income level in period t

$\qquad$ $Y_u(t)$ is the average real urban income level in period t

for other citations). Noting that the Todaro formulation is too narrow in its assumption of only two occupations, Fields (1975) added the "murky" sector to the model. This sector, sometimes referred to illogically as the "traditional urban" sector, consists of a host of miscellaneous activities, such as shoeshining, errand running, and collecting discarded but usable materials. Presumably, few people aspire to murky-sector employment, but they accept it to earn subsistence while seeking the modern-sector job.

Modifications of the basic Todaro model, then, would have the potential migrant adding the expected income to be earned in the murky sector to the expected income from modern-sector employment, given the probability of unemployment. Also, nothing is certain, and one should assign some probability of earning a given income in the traditional rural area from which migrants come (Fields, 1975). Thus, migrants would base their decision to migrate on the comparison:

$$P_r Y_r \lessgtr P_m Y_m + P_u Y_u \text{ where } (P_m + P_u) \le 1 \tag{4}$$

The symbols P_r, P_m, and P_u refer to the probabilities of obtaining the rural income, Y_r, the murky-sector income, Y_m, and the modern-urban income, Y_u, respectively.

The status that one has in the city can also determine the probability of eventually gaining the modern-sector wage. If one becomes occupied in the murky sector, he presumably has less time to search for the modern-sector job or to obtain the necessary credentials for such a position. In that case, unemployment at zero wage might be preferred to murky-sector employment at a low wage. The expected value of a move to the city might be higher for a person who can withstand a period of unemployment if it raises the probability of eventually obtaining modern-sector employment.

$Y_r(t)$ is the average real rural income level in period t

i is the potential migrant's rate of discount

n is the number of periods in the migrant's planning horizon

Todaro suggests that the probability of employment, $p(t)$, is directly related to the probability, π, of the migrant having been randomly selected, from among persons like himself, in the present period t or some previous period. This probability in turn depends on the ratio of new job openings to the number of unemployed. Thus:

$$p(1) = \pi(1)$$

and

$$p(2) = \pi(1) + [1 - \pi(1)]\pi(2)$$

Therefore, in general:

$$p(x) = \pi(x - 1) + [1 - \pi(x - 1)]\pi(x) =$$

$$\pi(1) + \sum_{t=2}^{x} \pi(t) \prod_{s=1}^{t-1} [1 - \pi(s)]$$

where:

$\pi(t)$ is the ratio of new job openings to the number of unemployed in period t

EMPIRICAL PROBLEMS

Empirical research demonstrates overwhelmingly that income is the prime determinant of migration.[3] But what about the specific form postulated by Todaro: that expected lifetime earnings, discounted and subject to employment probabilities, pull the migrant from country to city? Some studies (for Tanzania, Kenya, and Venezuela) show that employment probability has independent statistical significance in a regression, and that "when the wage and probability variables are combined to form an 'expected' wage variable, the result is a definite improvement over the nominal wage rate in terms of the amount of variation explained" (Todaro, 1976a:69). Todaro calls these findings "preliminary support" for his thesis.

No direct testing of the Todaro model would appear possible, however, since the probability factor cannot be determined. Migrants are a fluctuating population, difficult to count even if a statistical office should set its mind to the task. Nor are unemployment data reasonably accurate for LDC cities, nor data on available job openings.

The most intractable part of the Todaro model empirically is the estimation of the probability of employment *in the mind of the potential migrant.* That evaluation probably includes the potential migrant's view of his capabilities and a consideration of his or her skills or "connections" as well as his or her impressions (and misimpressions) of job opportunities in the city. No one knows with certainty how these subjective probabilities are formed, for research on this factor has not been done, and rural residents surely do not think explicitly in terms of equations such as those just given.

In most of the empirical work on the Todaro model, the probability of obtaining the urban wage is represented by the employment rate. This rate, expressed as a decimal, is the probability that a person will be employed if people are randomly chosen from the labor force. It is clearly not the probability that a randomly chosen person will get a job if he enters the labor force. The employment rates in cities are probably related to the way in which rural people form subjective opinions of their job prospects, but many other factors (such as differential skills) enter simultaneously. Unemployment rates are therefore only the roughest of proxies for subjective evaluations of job probabilities and may become very inaccurate when other forces predominate. Only if all else remains equal and potential migrants take urban employment rates into account, however inaccurately, will subjective evaluations of the probability of employment change directly with employment rates.

---

[3]Yap (1975) has provided a review of the literature, cited also in Todaro (1976a). This includes studies of Ghana (Beals, Levy, and Moses, 1967), Kenya (Huntington, 1974), Tanzania (Barnum and Sabot, 1975), Colombia (Schultz, 1971), Brazil (Sahota, 1968), Venezuela (Levy and Wadycki, 1972a and b, 1973, 1974a and b), India (Greenwood, 1971a and b), and Egypt (Greenwood, 1969). Studies too recent for the Yap article are also cited by Todaro (1976a): Kenya (Knowles and Anker, 1975, and House and Rempel, 1976), Tunisia (Hay, 1974), Venezuela (Schultz, 1975), Costa Rica (Carvajal and Geithman, 1974), and Peru (Falaris, 1976).

UNEMPLOYMENT: VOLUNTARY OR FORCED?

In the Todaro model, unemployment is voluntary in the sense that each migrant had the option of staying home and sharing in the family income. Suppose, however, one goes to the city and does not find a job, either because his probability estimates were wrong or because he was unlucky.

In his first assessment, he assumes he must go to the city because searching on the spot gives him an advantage (Fields, 1975). He may even accept a murky-sector job with a lower wage than he was earning at home, as the price of the increased probability of finding a preferred urban job (that is, the probability increases as a result of being in the city). But suppose his information was incomplete. His subjective P may have reflected objective conditions of some months ago; in the meantime, the objective P may have dropped below P^*. He then is involuntarily unemployed (or involuntarily employed in the murky sector) in the sense that he would not have come, had he known the true probabilities. Thus a potential migrant might make the assessment:

$$P_r Y_r < P_u Y_u \tag{5}$$

where both Ps are subjective. Suppose P_u is greater than P^*_u, so he migrates. But after migrating, he finds that $P'_u < P^*_u$, where P'_u is his revised probability estimate. He wants to go back, but because he has cut ties, the objective probability P_r has dropped to P'_r, and $P'_r < P_r$. For some individuals, it may turn out that:

$$P'_r Y_r < P'_u Y_u < P_r Y_r \tag{6}$$

That is, expected urban income after migration is less than rural income was before, but the prospects of moving back are even less promising.

If technological change sends a message to the countryside that P has risen, then (with a lag) an unjustifiably great wave of migration may be evoked. Migrants become "stuck" in the city, in occupations they never would have contemplated; they would not have come had they had full, accurate, and timely information. None of the hypotheses in the previous paragraph has been tested empirically, but if urbanization breaks down traditional society (as some have claimed), some migrants will permanently have damaged their incomes and welfare.

In sum, by relying on urban employment rates as proxies for subjective probability, the Todaro model mistakenly implies that unemployment is voluntary. Attention as to how that probability is formed, and to time lags, will surely show that migrants make mistakes. Some, involuntarily unemployed, will permanently damage their income potential. To our knowledge, no empirical work has been done on these issues.

THE TODARO PARADOX

Suppose productivity increases in cities, but the supply is not matched by increased demand. Workers are laid off, but (because of union pressures) the remaining workers earn higher wages. By promoting the substitution of capital for labor (Chapter 8), these higher wages promote unemployment even in those industries where productivity has not increased. Thus the probability of modern-sector employment (P_u) declines while the wage (Y_u) rises. Whether the critical value $P_u Y_u$ rises or falls depends on the relative strength of each component. If Y_u rises faster than P_u declines, then increased migration is induced in the face of rising unemployment.

If, however, the government follows some job-creation policy, such as a public-works program or employment subsidies for private business, then P_u rises again. But we have already shown that increases in $P_u Y_u$ may bring in more migrants than the number of new jobs that are available. To test for this paradox, Todaro examined the data for 14 LDCs to determine the minimum elasticity of migration with respect to job probability for which the paradox would hold. He found it to be low. The implication is that policies to create urban employment may defeat themselves, by attracting more migrants than the number of jobs they create.

But it would be unfortunate if LDC policymakers should use the Todaro model as their pretext for ignoring urban unemployment. Like other macro-analysis, this model deals in aggregates, in a situation full of nuances and complexities. Different policies may be appropriate to different kinds of migrants. The Todaro model assumes only jobs at going wage rates. If employment could be subsidized, or menial public-service jobs offered, but only at lower-than-market wages, then the expectations of potential migrants might become less aroused. Like *triage*, it appears to us dangerous to propose *general* actions or nonactions based on aggregate parameters, whether of population or employment, when policies might instead be tailored to those local circumstances that the aggregates do not reflect.

Such policies, however, should minimize market distortions. In the late 1960s, the Government of Kenya introduced the "Tripartite Agreement" of labor, business, and government, in which businesses were required to increase employment by specific amounts, while unions conceded a wage freeze (ILO, 1972:91, and Fields, 1975). During the early seventies, the Popular Unity Government of Chile also required businesses to increase employment. Both schemes failed, because (we believe) they imposed quantitative obligations where economic incentives were not changed.

AN ALTERNATIVE MODEL

Aside from empirical difficulties, the principal objection to the Todaro model is that it is overly aggregative. It lumps all migrants together without regard to whether they are the well educated, upwardly mobile group or the poorest, menial-type workers. Surely the analytical framework could be applied to each group separately, but just as surely the parameter differences between groups would be enormous.

Sabel (1979) suggests an alternative hypothesis for menial-type migrants. He draws on empirical literature covering international migration to MDCs as well as literature from LDCs. He asks: Why do these workers do jobs that no one else will do? He finds naïve the supposition that their lack of skills, or discrimination against them, or their laziness, left them no other opportunity. Rather, he suggests that they originally migrate in order to earn a specific sum of money, then to return home with added capital to undertake specific opportunities that they had earlier perceived, such as shopkeeping, training for artisanry, or schooling for children. Many do in fact return, such as Italians in the United States after the turn of the century (data are cited) and Mexicans and Puerto Ricans in the United States today.

Bell (1972) and Nattras (1979) have documented similar behavior among migrants in Southern Africa. We ourselves found (Loehr and Powelson, 1979) that a number of small businessmen in rural Western Kenya obtained their original capital during temporary residence in Nairobi. Extension of this hypothesis to other parts of Africa might be supported by the fact that many migrants leave their families behind, often retaining land rights or ownership in tribal areas. In many African cultures, however, it is important to be buried on tribal land and to know where one's ancestors are.

The general format of the Todaro model could probably be used to analyze this phenomenon, but the post-migration rural income would have to be made a function of the specific urban activity carried out by the migrants. The model is far too aggregative to do this at present.

Many, Sabel suggests, discover that it takes longer to earn the desired sum than they had at first believed. They bring families; children grow up who are strangers to the "old country;" new roots extend. At that point, the migrant discovers he is indeed the "lowest of the low," and he looks for advancement through unionization or further training, for himself or his children. In this, some succeed and some do not. Those who fail, Sabel goes on, enter into a Lewis-type culture of poverty (see our Chapter 3), remaining marginal for life, little respected by themselves and their families.

It is just as difficult to test the Sabel hypothesis empirically in LDCs as it is the Todaro. But to us it rings no less useful if only for its recognition of diversity among migrants. We agree with Todaro (1976b:222) that "there is no strictly urban solution to the urban unemployment problem." Instead of erecting dikes on the perimeter of the city, policymakers must turn off the spigot at its source, by promoting rural development. Indeed, the main strength of the Todaro model is that it suggests balanced growth as a solution to the problem of urban immigration. But this would still not resolve the problem of those many who are in the city, have acculturated to the city, cannot succeed in the city, and will not return to the farm no matter how little policymakers do to help them in the city.

THE BAZAAR ECONOMY: ENGINE OF GROWTH?[4]

While Todaro wrote little about the informal sector as such, other authors have referred to it negatively. The slum dweller is depicted as a drain on the urban economy, parochial in his values, lacking credentials for productive work (Perl-

---

[4]This section was suggested by Valerie Solheim, student in the graduate seminar on economic development at the University of Colorado, who did the research for it.

man, 1976:152, Lubell, 1978:749, and Morse, 1961). Fields' term "murky" reflects this approach.

But let us take a step back, to question whether these economists have not been overly influenced by the values of industrialized societies, which assign virtue to modern employment. If we look at England in the eighteenth century, France in the nineteenth, and the small-producer segments of China and Japan today, do we not see a ferment that resembles the proliferation of economic activity in the informal urban sector in today's LDCs? We need a name for that sector, more appropriate than "traditional" (which it is not) or "informal" (which it is, but this is not its essential characteristic) or "murky" (which is pejorative). Let us call it by its oriental term, the bazaar economy.

Instead of a repository for the dregs, the bazaar economy may well be the main attraction for the migrant. Here he can have his own business or work in a family enterprise. If he takes a job in the formal sector for a while, it may be temporary, to gain capital for a bazaar enterprise. After years of study in Davao, Philippines, Hackenberg and Ramos (1979:411) find that "the bulk of employment in the informal sector . . . is economically efficient and profit-making, though small in scale and limited by simple technologies, little capital and lack of links with the other (formal) sector." Mazumdar (1976:659) found that "in a representative set of primate cities in Asia and Latin America the urban informal sector contained 50 to 70 percent of all employment in 1970."

The bazaar economy is distinguished from the formal sector in two ways. First, it is highly competitive, flexible, and dynamic. It is not "firm-centered" (Sethurman, 1976:80), but is composed of individuals or households, self-employed, who work irregular hours, negotiate their prices, and perform on a micro-scale. Second, it receives no subsidies or institutional help from the government. Its invisibility puts it on the low side of the Barton gap (defined in Chapter 1).

Several researchers have found that many inhabitants of the bazaar economy prefer it to the formal sector (Hackenberg and Ramos, 1979, Morse, 1961:62, and Mazumdar, 1976). Using a study by Webb, Mazumdar (1976) found that for certain occupations, earnings in the bazaar economy in Lima competed well with those in the formal sector, although the average was lower. Furthermore, because it is less distorted by government restrictions, the bazaar economy may well produce goods and services more satisfying to local needs, with more appropriate technology, than does the modern sector.

Is it perhaps possible that the migration models have unduly equated urbanization with the modern sector and depreciated the bazaar? Could this bias have warped our understanding of a "normal" process of development that has been occurring all along? Could it have influenced policy making away from urban improvements that might have attracted presumably-unemployable migrants? Could it have diverted the thinking of governments away from the infrastructre, credit, and other services so badly needed by the bazaar economy? Could it have turned factor prices in favor of the formal sector, thus stunting the bazaar? As we think of "shutting off the migration tap" by rural improvements, have we truly assessed the relative potentials of rural areas and the urban bazaar as generators of employment and higher income?

RURAL VERSUS URBAN VERSUS OVERALL INEQUALITY

For the most part, urban incomes in LDCs are less equitably distributed than rural. Table 12–1 shows higher Gini coefficients in urban than in rural areas for 14 out of 20 countries. In 4 of the cases where rural Ginis are greater than urban, the difference is so small as to be insignificant. (India, Indonesia, the Philippines, and Taiwan). Different populations and different years are examined; also, some data are for incomes and some are for consumption ex-

TABLE 12–1
Rural-Urban Income and Inequality Differences

Country	Year(s)	Type of Population Surveyed	Urban Gini	Rural Gini	Urban-to-Rural Income Ratio
Argentina[a]	1961	Households	.42	.51	1.31
Bangladesh	1966–67	Households	.40	.33	1.49
Brazil	1970	Economically Active Persons	.56	.45	2.81
Colombia	1970	Income Recipients	.55	.48	2.33
Costa Rica	1971	Households	.44[b]	.37	2.32
Cyprus	1966	Households	.32	.19	1.75
India	1967–68	Households	.46	.48	1.35
Indonesia	1969–70	Household Member Expenditures	.34	.35	1.19
South Korea	1971	Households	.34	.31	1.87
Malaysia	1970	Households	.50	.46	2.16
Mexico	1968	Family Expenditures	.44	.35	1.93
Pakistan	1966–67	Households	.39	.33	1.41
Panama[c]	1972	Income Recipients	.42	.35	1.91
Philippines	1971	Households	.46	.47	2.08
Sri Lanka	1973	Income Recipients	.40	.37	1.31
Taiwan[a]	1972	Households	.27	.29	1.22
Tanzania	1969	Household Expenditures	.33	.30	2.62
Thailand	1970	Households	.39	.45	2.45
Tunisia	1961	Household Member Expenditures	.42	.36	1.69
Uganda	1970	African male Employees	.40	.27	1.75

[a]Data refer to agricultural and nonagricultural incomes.

[b]San José metropolitan area.

[c]Data refer to metropolitan and nonmetropolitan areas.

penditures. However, in all cases where Jain (of the World Bank) was able to collect data in 1975, urban earnings substantially exceed rural, for equivalent income groups. The ratio of urban to rural incomes is reported in the final column. In every case, urban incomes are higher, and in 13 cases they are more than 150 percent of the rural level. In each of these cases, data were collected by the same individual or institution, at the same time, and with the same population (households, economically-active persons, and so on) for both rural and urban sectors.

In disaggregating inequality, it is necessary to weigh each sector by its share in country-wide personal income (or expenditures, or wealth). How and why were discussed in Chapter 5. Using Theil indices,[5] van Ginneken (1976) has calculated relative inequalities for the five countries shown in Table 12–2. Here, the inequality between urban and rural areas reflects mainly the difference in average incomes of the two sectors, while the inequality within areas reflects not only the inequality coefficient, but also the relative weight. As one might expect, the urban-inequality component is larger in the urbanized countries (Mexico and Tunisia), while the rural-inequality component is larger in the countries with greater rural population (Indonesia, Pakistan, and Tanzania). No generalization can be made about inequalities between urban and rural areas, which account for larger proportions of country-wide inequalities in Mexico, Tanzania, and Tunisia than in Indonesia and Pakistan.

Theoretical support for the inverted U might be deduced by the assumption that upon migration, an individual leaves the rural income stream in favor of the urban. If the inequality indices are otherwise unaffected, the migration would simply shift weight from the more-egalitarian rural to the less-egalitarian urban sector, thus increasing the national inequity. This movement might continue for a long time, for only as industrialization intensifies (and labor becomes scarce) would urban incomes move toward greater equity and rural-urban income gaps begin to close.

This "conventional wisdom" is vulnerable, however. Suppose a low-income-earner (relative to rural average) migrates, becoming a low-earner (or zero-earner) in the city. His exit will have increased the rural average income and improved rural equity; his entry into the city will have decreased the urban average income and increased urban inequity. In addition, the rural-urban differential will have been narrowed. Obviously, if he has the same income in the city as he had in the country, the national Gini index will be unaffected. One can invent scenarios that will show different results depending on the assumptions, but short of empirical investigation that has not yet been done, there is no way to predict any actual outcome.

KAKAMEGA

In order to understand migration and unemployment, it is necessary to know the dynamics of a community—where it stands, and where it is moving. Aggregate models, such as those of Todaro, may confirm or dispute the findings

---

[5]The Theil index is compared with other measures of income dispersion in Champernowne (1974); the Theil decomposition is explained in van Ginneken (1976:26, also his Appendix A).

TABLE 12-2
**Components of Country-Wide Inequalities of Households' Income or Expenditures,
as Measured by the Theil Index, for Five Countries**

COUNTRY	Inequalities				
	URBAN-RURAL	WITHIN URBAN	WITHIN RURAL	TOTAL	PERIOD
Indonesia, expenditures	2	22	76	100	1969–70
Java, expenditures	6	24	70	100	1969–70
Mexico, expenditures	30	54	17	100	1968
Mexico, income	30	55	15	100	1968
Pakistan, expenditures	8	44	48	100	1970–71
Pakistan, income	8	44	48	100	1970–71
Tanzania, expenditures	39	8	54	100	1969
Tunisia, expenditures	16	51	33	100	1964–68

SOURCE: van Ginneken (1976:27).

of micro-investigations, but nothing replaces the plodding research, by which it may be discovered (through samples) who the individuals are, what their expectations are, and where they conceive of themselves as moving (physically, economically, or socially). In Kenya, the *Integrated Rural Survey* (Government of Kenya, 1977b) has taken an initiative in this direction; few countries have achieved as much.

In Western Province, Kenya, 64 percent of heads of rural households have never attended school, 20 percent have achieved only fourth grade (standard 4), another 12.5 percent have achieved seventh or eighth grade, and 3.5 percent have had two years of secondary school or more. Of the total population, however, only 42 percent have never attended school at all—hence education is increasing as more of the young go to school. Seventy-three percent of household heads had no other employment than working their small farmholdings, 2.3 percent operate a second holding, 3.33 percent labor on someone else's holding, 5.54 percent do other rural labor, 8.21 percent are in teaching or other government employment, and 7.74 percent commute to jobs in a nearby city. With income groups by thousands of shillings (8 sh. = $1: 1975), the modal group is 2,000 to 2,999 shillings (or $250 to $375), which contains 29 percent of households. Only 3.5 percent of the households earn 8,000 shillings ($1,000) or more.

Western Province is the second most populous province of Kenya (after Central Province, where Nairobi is located). About 250 miles from the capital, it shares its western border with Uganda. Because of its fertile soil and abundant rainfall, its population is dense and growing; 56 percent is sixteen years old or less, while 22.5 percent is five and under. The province is cut by a two-lane tarmac highway from Kisumu (on Lake Victoria) to Kitale in the north, on the main road from Nairobi to Uganda. It is crisscrossed by secondary roads, a few of which are paved, but most of which are gravel. The majority of people live in one-room huts with earthen floors; the median farm plot is about 1.5

hectares, with only 10 percent having more than 5 hectares. Most families walk over paths and across fields to arrive at even a secondary road. One *senses* the density of population; *always*, in the daytime, the roads and paths are covered with people walking. There are three kinds of schools: government, *Harambee* (local initiative, government-aided), and missionary. Classified in another way, they are primary, secondary, and one vocational. Most residents of the province belong to the Abaluhya tribe. A Quaker mission at Kaimosi offers education of all kinds, plus a hospital. There is a government hospital at Kakamega, the provincial capital.

Table 12–3 shows the earnings of all of rural Kenya by farm size; the Western Province total and percentages appear in the final two columns. These data indicate that, roughly, households who save have incomes of 3,000 Kenya shillings (hereafter, K.Shs.), or about $375, or more. Those with lower income dissave. This table also describes the distribution of income in rural Kenya, since each holding may be taken as a household.

Western Province is dotted with towns and rural markets. A typical market area will contain perhaps 20 to 30 shops made of concrete blocks, each with one or two rooms, rectangular, total size approximately 30 by 15 feet, all painted white, all adjoining and in a row. Many shops duplicate one another, carrying a few staples, such as canned goods, matches, soap, tea, and cigarettes. Outside the shops there is likely to be an open field in which the village market assembles once or twice a week, with wares (principally vegetables, pottery, and textiles) sold by women sitting on the ground. There is, however, not a great deal of commerce in farm produce, for most families grow their own.

If we were truly to know the prospects for rural development in Western Province—whether young people will seek occupations within the province or whether population growth is driving them off the farm, into cities such as Kisumu, Nakuru, or Nairobi—it would be necessary first to interview many of them. We would also need to take a census of income-earning opportunities within the province, including recent trends, and to know the demographic structure, as well as the educational needs and opportunities. From this and similar information, it would be possible to sketch a moving profile, so that one might picture the demography and economy of the province, say, some ten years hence. If this were done for all provinces, then (we submit) a reasonable assessment of the migration pattern would emerge. Although some tentative starts have been made (the Kenya survey being among the more advanced), we know of no country in which a complete study is even contemplated.

We have ourselves made a humble incursion by examining a number of small businesses, mostly retailers, in the rural markets of Kakamega, the principal district in Western Province. All businesses in our sample were receiving management advice from Partnership for Productivity (PfP), an advisory service originated in 1970 with inspiration from an American religious group, but which has since been completely Kenyanized and secularized. Although the service has expanded since then, in 1977 (when we did our investigation), there were twelve Kenyan advisors, who had completed form four (tenth grade) and one year of vocational school at Kaimosi, as well as intensive in-service training by PfP. Although many of their business clients were illiterate, and none kept

TABLE 12–3
Income and Outlays by Farm Holding and Income Group, for Rural Kenya, with the Western Province Shown Separately, 1974–1975

	Negative Savings				Positive Savings					WESTERN PROVINCE	
	LESS THAN 0 K.SHS.	0–999 K.SHS.	1,000– 1,999 K.SHS.	2,000– 2,999 K.SHS.	3,000– 3,999 K.SHS.	4,000– 5,999 K.SHS.	6,000– 7,999 K.SHS.	8,000 K.SHS. AND OVER	TOTAL	TOTAL	PERCENT
Number of Holdings	98,982	175,057	332,813	204,972	174,002	200,501	117,919	179,176	1,483,422	254,618	
Farm Operating Surplus	(2,624)	128	649	1,327	1,933	2,944	4,239	7,865	2,081	1,186	47.55
Nonfarm Operating Surplus	(832)	87	170	250	409	572	421	1,390	354	126	5.05
Regular Employment	183	46	142	128	457	449	1,290	2,331	566	559	22.41
Casual Employment	155	116	217	350	222	266	439	281	252	165	6.62
Remittances from Relatives	241	159	261	389	390	443	404	322	324	407	16.32
Other Gifts	38	14	46	61	45	141	160	128	75	50	2.00
TOTAL HOUSEHOLD INCOME	(2,840)	551	1,485	2,505	3,456	4,815	6,953	12,317	3,652	2,494	100.00
TOTAL OUTLAYS	3,691	1,611	2,165	2,721	3,364	3,892	5,618	6,505	3,450	2,808	
CURRENT SAVINGS	(6,530)	(1,060)	(681)	(216)	93	923	1,335	5,812	202	(314)	

SOURCE: Government of Kenya, *Integrated Rural Survey, 1974–75*: 54–55.

books beyond simple cash registers, the PfP advisors attempted to reconstruct their balance sheets and profit and loss statements. Out of some 400 clients, they had accumulated over 100 sets of business records, which we would describe as fragments of financial information. We examined all of these, and in consultation with the PfP advisors, we concluded that 62 of the reconstructed financial statements were internally consistent and (in the opinions of the advisors) were reasonable representations of reality.

Our results are reported at length in an earlier article (Loehr and Powelson, 1979); they are summarized in Table 12–4. Table 12–5 outlines the demographic data collected with our sample. Although the sample was not random, we found 62 small-scale businesses, with an average life of five years (standard deviation, $s = 3.7$), that displayed the following features. Most enterprisers had begun with capital from their own savings, sometimes combined with loans from family and friends. Because they had the security of a hut and land on which to feed their families, the business income was additional to minimum needs. Average earnings on labor and capital were K.Sh. 13,631, or $1,704, although the variation was wide. This return was higher than (say) a job in urban-sector manufacturing, where the average earning was K.Sh. 7,200 (GOK, 1977a:46), even if such employment were available. Enterprisers drew money from the businesses, not on a regular basis (like a monthly salary), but for special occasions, such as school fees, weddings, and funerals. Nevertheless, the rate of reinvestment was high (56.2 percent of net earnings).

If average profit were reduced by K.Sh. 9,548 for estimated earnings of the owner and the family workers (based on going wage rates), and another K.Sh. 1,000 were taken off for depreciation, then it comes to K.Sh. 3,083, or 14.3 percent of net worth. This rate compares to a profit rate of 18 percent for grocery stores in the United States (Dun and Bradstreet, 1976); it is a reasonable rate of return both by international standards and in comparison with current interest rates in Kenya.

These quantitative data, as well as our interviews with PfP advisors and a few clients, led us to believe that if our information is representative, then immediate, perceived investment opportunities are the principal determinant of rural saving. *Of course* saving correlates positively with income (as the macro-models will tell us), and perhaps there is some stable function in the aggregate. But we do not know (by the aggregate models) whether greater income causes higher saving or vice versa, and whether the stable relationship will continue in the future. Without this knowledge, the macro-relationship is almost trivial. The real task is (1) to enlarge perceived opportunuties for local investment and (2) to increase the channels by which savers will transfer funds to investors, having faith that their funds will be invested wisely and honestly. The first is an area for immediate attention; the second will follow, because the demand for such institutions will emerge as opportunities of increasing complexity are perceived.

Economic planners often compare a situation that *is* with a situation that is *desired* and then determine the strategy for moving from the former to the latter. Less often do they take into account those trends currently in effect and how those trends can be modified. Intuitively, we sensed a certain *momentum*

TABLE 12–4
Clients of Partnership for Productivity
Kakamega, Kenya
Means, Standard Deviations, Maxima
and Minima for Financial Statements
(in Kenya shillings)

Profit and Loss Statement
Recent 12-month period (ending 1976 or 1977, according to the client)
$n = 64$ (see text)

	Mean		Standard Deviation	Minimum	Maximum
Sales	113,092		122,781	9,920	673,445
Less cost of goods sold	94,410		113,524	0	623,944
Gross margin on sales		18,682	17,712	2,002	107,097
Less expenses		5,051	7,527	498	52,847
Net profit		13,631	12,568	−334	56,160
Less drawings		5,974	8,254	0	55,405
Reinvested earnings		7,657	10,692	−20,137	47,280

Balance Sheet
Recent date in 1976 or 1977 (according to client)
$n = 62$ (see text)

Assets

	Mean		Standard Deviation	Minimum	Maximum
Current assets					
Cash	2,437		3,588	7	20,917
Receivables	796		1,299	0	8,050
Inventory	6,477		6,348	0	26,500
Total current assets		9,710	8,513	429	38,402
Fixed assets					
Furniture	1,346		1,770	0	8,000
Equipment	3,237		14,520	0	112,580
Vehicles	410		1,534	0	10,000
Buildings	9,193		18,073	0	80,000
Land	239		1,559	0	12,000
Other	8		69	0	540
Total fixed assets		14,433	23,783	0	112,580
Total assets		24,143	27,351	1,330	119,780

Liabilities and Net Worth

	Mean		Standard Deviation	Minimum	Maximum
Current liabilities					
Trade credits	637		2,126	0	13,785
Other credits	1,891		8,153	0	61,000
Total current liabilites		2,528	8,307	0	61,046
Long-term liabilites		0	0	0	0
Net worth					
Starting capital	10,517		18,608	4	87,905
Subsequent investments	2,355		7,477	0	47,000
Reinvested earnings	8,743		11,817	−2,976	1,745
Total net worth		21,615	23,765	830	99,617
Total liabilites and net worth		24,143	27,351	1,330	119,780

NOTE: One client had three separate profit and loss statements (for three businesses), but only one balance sheet. Hence $n = 64$ for profit and loss statements, but $n = 62$ for balance sheets.

TABLE 12–5
Demographic Information on Businesses Studied in Kakamega

	Total Group [a]n = 60–64	Petty Traders n = 39–42	Other Retailers n = 4–5	Service n = 14–15	Manu-facturers n = 2
Average age of clients	40	39	39	40	49.5
Percentage of male clients	84%	42%	100%	100%	100%
Average number of years of education	6.0	6.1	6.0	5.6	5.5
Percentage that have had vocational training	41%	37.5%	0%	57%	100%
Average number of years in business	5.1	4.4	3.6	6.9	7.5
Percentage that started the business themselves	92%	90%	100%	93%	100%
Average number of other businesses owned per client	.158	.171	.20	.07	.50
Percentage that own land	69%	62%	80%	80%	100%
Average number of acres owned	7.53	5.7	7.6	10.54	18.00
Percentage that have had previous businesses	25%	22.5%	40%	21%	50%
Average percentage of time spent in business (100% = full time)	84%	85%	65%	75%	100%
Average difficulty with keeping accounts, (3 = much, 2 = some, 1 = little)	1.7	1.6	1.8	1.9	1.0
Percentage that own their business premises	37.5%	35.7%	40%	33%	100%
Percentage that keep regular hours	89%	88%	80%	93%	100%
Percentage that have telephones	1.6%	2.4%	0%	0%	0%
Percentage that have electricity	12.5%	14.3%	20%	6.6%	0%
Average number of family workers (not counting the owner)	.587	.619	1.00	.467	0
Average number of nonfamily workers	.603	.262	0	1.60	1.50
Percentage that live on their business premises	26.6%	31.0%	0%	27%	0%
Percentage that own their own businesses	90.6%	90.5%	100%	87%	100%

[a]n varies because not all information was availuble for every respondent.

in Kakamega. Without more data, we cannot be confident of our senses, but they are all we have to rely on for the moment.

The momentum we see is the following. Population increase will create more and more supernumeraries on the already-small farms. The strong belief that education opens doors will lead villagers to seek more schooling for their children, forming more *Harambee* schools and seeking more government assistance. We discovered a weak correlation between vocational training and business earnings; more such education will be demanded. The government appears to be cognizant of this, and vocational schools will expand, according to the national economic plan.

Some of the more aggressive retailers will expand and put others out of business. Already a so-called "supermarket" exists in Kakamega town, though it carries few goods and is not at all comparable to the modern supermarket in Nairobi. But it, or another one, will grow. Others will sprout in the rural markets. The supernumeraries in retailing will either migrate to cities or seek training in service industries (tailoring, bicycle repair, automobile mechanics) or manufacturing (baking, food preserving and storage, textiles). It would be useful for local authorities to have rough ideas of trends in all these professions. But for the most part, they do not.

A SCHEMATIC MODEL

We have qualified our initiative in Kakamega as "humble." All we have accomplished is a reconstruction of the financial statements of a few, nonrandomly-selected rural businesses, most of which are retailers. If the rural-urban problem is to be understood, similar initiatives must be made with respect to all the boxes shown in Figure 12–1. We already know much about farming income and peripheral earnings of farms. We also know something of the earnings of employed people in both rural and urban areas, and we know how many persons pass through various levels of education. What we usually do not know is the income from rural retailing, wholesaling, services, and artisan-type manufacturing. Those who favor "intermediate technology" often point to these as activities that must be developed; yet we know very little about how they are faring *now*.

If information on numbers, incomes, and directions (increases or decreases over time) could be plugged into the schematic model of Figure 12–1, we would have a much firmer grip on the rural-urban problem. We now return to two observations made earlier, and repeatedly, throughout this book. The first is that "no one cares enough about the poor to compile relatively reliable information on them." Privileged problems receive privileged statistical attention; this fact has led to the collection of aggregate income and monetary data, but to insufficient information on the movements of the poor. The other observation is that the abundance of micro-studies currently being performed (but not yet in sufficient quantities) provides us with the major insights into economic development. If the schematic model of Figure 12–1 is ever to be filled out, it

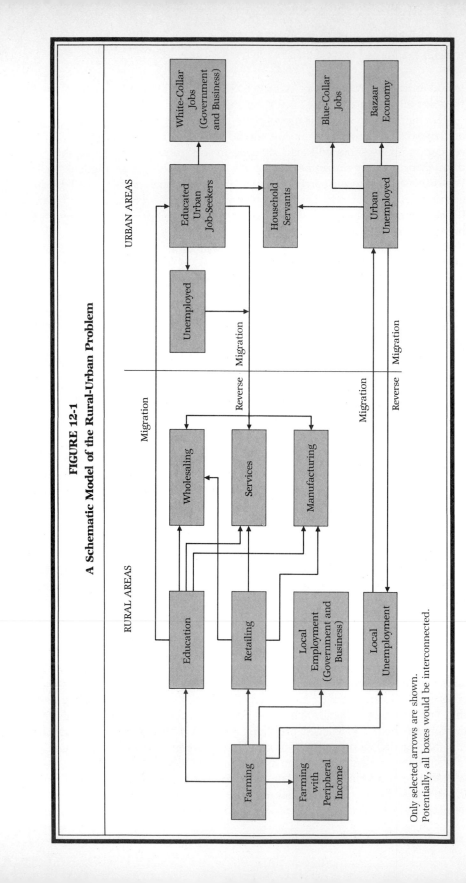

FIGURE 12-1

A Schematic Model of the Rural-Urban Problem

Only selected arrows are shown.
Potentially, all boxes would be interconnected.

will only be by way of a large number of micro-studies of each box separately. (Our own study of retailing in Kakamega covers only one box, and for only one district.)

CONCLUSION

Population growth and economic development create many imbalances, with the most serious being that between rural and urban areas. Urban populations have been increasing at very high rates, while rural ones have been growing more slowly. Gigantic slums are spawned in cities, and infrastructure (transportation, electricity, water, schools, and so on) cannot be built rapidly and adequately to serve the new people.

A number of aggregate studies show persuasively that the principal incentive for migration is economic. Rural earnings are much lower than urban, on the average, and income distribution is probably more skewed in the city than in the country. But the economic information is too highly aggregated, and the observation that people follow economic incentives is not solid enough to provide a basis for policy prescriptions.

Two opposite types of migrants have not been adequately distinguished: the poorest of the poor, who take menial tasks that no one else will perform, and the educated, who aspire to white-collar employment in business and government. Reviewing studies of migrants in the more developed world, Sabel has hypothesized that these poorest leave their homeland with the intention of earning a specific sum and then returning. Many do return. But unforeseen events (especially attitudes of children) delay others indefinitely in their new surroundings, where they may finally organize to protect their interests, or, failing that, join a Lewis-type culture of poverty.

Using aggregate models, Todaro has suggested that the discounted stream of lifetime expected earnings in urban compared to rural areas, minus the cost of migration, is the determining factor in the numbers of migrants. There is some statistical evidence confirming that expectations have something to do with the matter, but the precision of the theoretical model and the empirical tests that it has spawned do not provide a basis for analyzing the employment problems of specific migrant groups. When it comes down to a *true* explanation of migrant behavior (not merely a statistical explanation), we are still largely in the dark.

The Todaro models possess one potential danger. They suggest that urban job programs alone may be counterproductive, in that they will generate more migrants than they will employees, thus aggravating unemployment. We are reminded of the argument for *triage* (Chapter 9), in which well-meaning analysts would leave children to starve so as to discourage population growth. Our own attitude is that starving children should be fed. We are impatient with aggregate parameters that suggest a policy so crude that it might be reversed when the nuances of particular situations are taken into account. We feel the same way about urban unemployment, though we recognize—along with Todaro—that the urban problem cannot be divorced from the rural; the approach must be simultaneous.

Our own schematic model of the rural-urban problem is presented in Figure 12–1, where we attempt to delineate hypothetical flows of people in response to income incentives. We made a small approach to one box in that model, in one small area: rural retailers in Kakamega district, Western Province, Kenya. Our sample was nonrandom, since it was taken from only those who were able to compile the information (most retailers being illiterate and nonnumerate). It told us, however, that probably there are rural opportunities competing with urban ones and that rural people save (a matter confirmed by aggregate data from the Kenya Statistics Bureau). Even more important, it gave a weak indication that perceived, immediate investment opportunity is the principal motive for individual saving.

BIBLIOGRAPHY

Ashton, T. S., 1948:
  The Industrial Revolution, 1760–1830, London, Oxford University Press.
Barnum, H. N. and Sabot, R. H., 1975:
  Education, Employment Probabilities and Rural-urban Migration in Tanzania, Paper presented at the World Congress of the Econometric Society, Toronto, mimeographed.
Beals, R. E., Levy, M. B. and Moses, L. N., 1967:
  "Rationality and Migration in Ghana," *The Review of Economics and Statistics*, Nov. 1967, pp. 480–86, Cambridge, Mass., Harvard University Press.
Bell, R. T., 1972:
  "Migrant Labor: Theory and Policy," *South African Journal of Economics*, Vol. 40, No. 4, Dec., pp. 337–60.
Bhagwati, J. N. and Srinivasan, T. N., 1974:
  "On Reanalyzing the Harris-Todaro Model: Policy Rankings in the Case of Sector-specific Sticky Wages," *The American Economic Review*, June 1974, pp. 502–08, Menasha, Wis., American Economic Association.
Carvajal, M. J. and Geithman, D. T., 1974:
  "An Economic Analysis of Migration in Costa Rica," *Economic Development and Cultural Change*, Oct., 1974, pp. 105–22.
Champernowne, D. G., 1974:
  "A Comparison of Measures of Inequality of Income Distribution," *Economic Journal*, Vol. 84, No. 336, Dec. 1974, pp. 787–816.
DeYoung, Karen, 2–6–77:
  "Massive Third World Cities Forecast in Next 25 Years," *Washington Post.*
Dun and Bradstreet, 1976:
  Key Business Ratios, New York.
Falaris, E. M., 1976:
  The Determinants of Internal Migration in Peru: An Economic Analysis, Minneapolis, Minn., University of Minnesota, Department of Economics, Mimeographed.
Fei, J. and Ranis, G., 1964:
  Development of the Labor Surplus Economy, Homewood, Ill., Richard D. Irwin.
Fei, J. and Ranis, G., 1961:
  "A Theory of Economic Development," *The American Economic Review*, September, 1961, pp. 533–65.
Fields, G., 1975:
  "Rural-urban Migration, Urban Employment and Underemployment, and Job-

search Activity in LDCs," *Journal of Development Economics*, June 1975, pp. 165–87, Amsterdam, North-Holland Publishing Co.

Government of Kenya, 1977a:
Economic Survey 1976, Nairobi, Government Printing Office.

Government of Kenya, 1977b:
Integrated Rural Survey, 1974–1975, Nairobi, Government Printing Office.

Greenwood, M., 1969:
"The Determinants of Labor Migration in Egypt," *Journal of Regional Science*, August, pp. 283–90, Philadelphia, Regional Science Research Institute.

Greenwood, M., 1971a:
"An Analysis of the Determinants of Internal Labor Mobility in India," *Annals of Regional Science*, No. 1, pp. 137–51, Bellingham, Wash., Western Washington State College.

Greenwood, M., 1971b:
"A Regression Analysis of Migration to Urban Areas of a Less-developed Country: The Case of India," *Journal of Regional Science*, August, 1971, pp. 253–62.

Hackenberg, Robert, and Ramos, Gil, 1979:
"A Second Look at Urbanization, Industrialization, and Demographic Transition," EWPI Conference Memorandum: Research on intermediate cities of southeast Asia, typed.

Harris, J. and Todaro, M. P., 1970:
"Migration, Unemployment and Development: A Two-sector Analysis," *The American Economic Review*, March, pp. 126–42.

Hay, M. J., 1974:
An Economic Analysis of Rural-urban Migration in Tunisia, Minneapolis, Minn., University of Minnesota, unpublished Ph.D. dissertation.

Houghton, D. H., 1960:
"Men of Two Worlds: Some Aspects of Migratory Labour in South Africa," *The South African Journal of Economics*, October, pp. 177–90, Braamfontein, Economic Society of South Africa.

House, W. J., and Rempel, H., 1976:
"The Determinants of and Changes in the Structure of Wages and Employment in the Manufacturing Sector of the Kenyan Economy, 1967–1972," *Economic Development and Cultural Change*, March.

Huntington, H., 1974:
An Empirical Study of Ethnic Linkages in Kenyan Rural-urban Migration, Binghamton, NY, State University of New York, unpublished Ph.D. dissertation.

International Labour Office, 1972:
Employment, Incomes and Equality: A Strategy for Increasing Productive Employment in Kenya, Geneva.

Jain, Shail, 1975:
Size Distribution of Income: A Compilation of Data, Baltimore, Johns Hopkins Press.

Johnson, G., 1971:
"The Structure of Rural-urban Migration Models," *East African Economic Review*, June, pp. 21–8, Nairobi.

Jones, Philip, 1971:
"Medieval and Agrarian Society in its Prime: Italy," Postan, M. M., ed., *The Cambridge Economic History of Europe*, Vol. I, New York, Cambridge University Press.

Knowles, J. C., and Anker, R., 1975:
Economic Determinants of Demographic Behaviour in Kenya, Geneva, ILO, World Employment Programme paper for restricted distribution only, mineographed.

Levy, M. and Wadycki, W., 1972a:
"A Comparison of Young and Middle-aged Migration in Venezuela," *Annals of Regional Science*, No. 2, pp. 73–85.

Levy, M. and Wadycki, W., 1972b:
"Lifetime Versus One-year Migration in Venezuela," *Journal of Regional Science*, December 1972, pp. 407–15.

Levy, M. and Wadycki, W., 1973:

"The Influence of Family and Friends on Geographic Labor Mobility: An Internal Comparison," *The Review of Economics and Statistics*, May 1973, pp. 198–203.

Levy, M. and Wadycki, W., 1974a:

"Education and the Decision to Migrate: An Econometric Analysis of Migration in Venezuela," *Econometrica*, March, pp. 377–88, New Haven, Conn., Econometric Society.

Levy, M. and Wadycki, W., 1974b:

"What is the Opportunity Cost of Moving? Reconsideration of the Effects of Distance on Migration," *Economic Development and Cultural Change*, January, pp. 198–214.

Lewis, W. A., 1954:

"Economic Development with Unlimited Supplies of Labour," *The Manchester School of Economic and Social Studies*, May, pp. 139–91.

Loehr, W. and Powelson, J. P., 1979:

"An Accounting Analysis of Rural Business in Kenya," *Industry and Development*, No. IV, Vienna, United Nations Industrial Development Organization.

Lubell, Harold, 1978:

"Urban Development and Employment: The Third World Metropolis," *International Labor Review*, vol. 17, no. 6, November–December.

Mazumdar, Dipak, 1976:

"The Urban Informal Sector," *World Development*, August.

Morse, Richard M., 1961:

"Latin American Cities: Aspects of Function and Structure," *Comparative Studies in Society and History*, vol. 4.

Nattras, J., 1979:

"Poverty and Uneven Development in South Africa," presented at *Conference on Global Poverty in Perspective*, University of Southern California, Los Angeles, Feb. 1–2.

Papanek, G., 1975:

"The Poor of Jakarta," *Economic Development and Cultural Change*, Vol. 24, No. 1, October, pp. 1–28.

Perlman, Janice E., 1976:

The Myth of Marginality: Urban Poverty and Politics in Rio de Janeiro, Berkeley, University of California Press.

Pollard, Sidney, 1978:

"Labour in Great Britain," in Mathias, Peter, and Postan, M. M., ed., *The Cambridge Economic History of Europe*, Vol. VII, New York, Cambridge University Press.

Reynolds, L. G., 1977:

Image and Reality in Economic Development, New Haven, Conn., Yale University Press.

Sabel, Charles F., 1979:

"Marginal Workers in Industrial Society," *Challenge*, March–April.

Sahota, G. S., 1968:

"An Economic Analysis of Internal Migration in Brazil," *Journal of Political Economy*, March–April, pp. 218–45.

Schultz, T. P., 1971:

"Rural-urban Migration in Colombia," *The Review of Economics and Statistics*, May, pp. 157–63.

Schultz, T. P., 1975:

The Determinants of Internal Migration in Venezuela: An Application of the Polytomous Logistic Model, paper presented at the World Congress of the Econometric Society, Toronto.

Sethurman, S., 1976:

"The Urban Informal Sector: Concepts, Measurement, and Policy," *International Labor Review*, vol. 114, no. 3, November–December.

Todaro, M. P., 1969:
"A Model of Labor Migration and Urban Unemployment in Less Developed Countries," *The American Economic Review*, March, pp. 138–48.
Todaro, M. P., 1976a:
Internal Migration in Developing Countries, Geneva, International Labor Organization.
Todaro, M. P., 1976b:
"Urban Job Expansion, Induced Migration and Rising Unemployment: A Formulation and Simplified Empirical Testing for LDCs," *Journal of Development Economics*, September.
van Ginneken, W., 1976:
Rural and Urban Income Inequalities, Geneva, International Labor Organization.
World Bank, 1972:
Urbanization, Sector Policy Paper, Washington, D.C., World Bank.
World Bank, 1975:
Rural Development, Sector Policy Paper, Washington, D.C., World Bank.
Yap, L., 1975:
Internal Migration in Less Developed Countries: A Survey of the Literature, Washington, D.C., World Bank, Urban Poverty Task Force paper.

13

IMPERIALISM, MULTINATIONAL CORPORATIONS, AND THE NEW INTERNATIONAL ECONOMIC ORDER

I am poor because you are rich.
PRESIDENT JULIUS NYERERE (TANZANIA),
BEFORE THE UNITED NATIONS, 1975.

Simply and poignantly, President Nyerere's statement before the United Nations expresses a belief that is widely, intensely, and tenaciously held. The process by which MDCs have become rich is the same one by which LDCs stay poor. Furthermore, this process has become institutionalized; it is known variously as "neocolonialism" or "neoimperialism." Poor countries produce primary goods (minerals and foodstuffs) needed by the rich, but the rich control the channels of trade and therefore set the prices. The rich also manage the world's money supply, setting the terms by which international reserves are created. Capital and technology are monopolized by the rich.

Let us refer to this as the "terms-of-trade belief." Nyerere (1976) has elaborated on it, and we present scattered citations:

> In one world, in one state, when I am rich because you are poor, and you are rich because I am poor, the transfer of wealth from the rich to the poor is a matter of right; it is not an appropriate matter for charity . . . There is nothing accidental about this situation. At any one time there is a certain amount of wealth produced in the world. If one group of people grab an unfair share of it, there is less for the others . . . Tanzania cannot set its sisal prices to take account of the extra production costs. The price of our sisal fibre exports are set in Europe and North America . . . In 1965 I could buy a tractor by selling 17.25 tons of sisal. The price of the same model in

293

> 1972 needed 42 tons of sisal . . . In a so-called free market economy, eco-
> nomic power depends on wealth . . . wealth gives the rich the power of
> direct decision-making over the economies of the poor.

The terms-of-trade belief has not gone unchallenged. Critics fault Nyerere
for thinking of "a certain amount of wealth produced in this world" as if it
bubbled forth from a spring, untended by anyone, to be seized and monopolized
by beasts of prey. On the contrary, they say, the rich are rich because their
productivity is high, and the poor are poor for the opposite reason. Furthermore,
the poor were poor long before the wealthy became rich; therefore the enrich-
ment of some is not responsible for the immiseration of others.

The dichotomy will never be resolved. Furthermore, in the context in which
we view development—one in which advantages are gained through leverage—
it becomes inconsequential. Our own philosophy on this question, which we
believe is derived from a historical context, is summarized as follows.

FIRST, the MDCs are wealthy primarily because they utilize scientific methods
   and ideas and because their skills in social organization have facilitated ever-
   increasing cooperation among factors of production, hence they create economies of scale.

SECOND, limitations of scarcity and physics underlie the laws of economics.
   These limitations cannot be repealed by agreement, international or otherwise, but can only be modified by scientific advance.

THIRD, the rich have imposed on the poor in unconscionable ways. They have
   seized the lands of the poor, have enslaved the poor, have interfered with
   and sometimes destroyed their cultures, and have forced damaging changes
   in their social and governmental processes.

FOURTH, except in limited or temporary circumstances, the poor will not
   receive unrequited concessions from the rich. It does them little good to
   speak of "fairness" and "right," or to urge a restructuring of international
   institutions or changes in the world pricing system in ways that defy scarcity
   or physical constraints.

We predict that, over time, the poor nations will tire of seeking unrequited
concessions from the rich, in the name of fairness and right, and will turn
increasingly toward *Realökonomie*,[1] or the examination and use of leverage
that they possess now or can achieve in the future. An increase in their own
productivity is doubtless the most effective way of increasing international
leverage.

But they have not tired yet. In 1974, they introduced into the United Nations
a *Declaration on the Establishment of a New International Economic Order*
(NIEO), "based on equity, sovereign equality, interdependence, common interests and co-operation among all States, . . . which shall correct inequalities
and redress existing injustices, make it possible to eliminate the widening gap

---

[1] Our apologies to the Germans for coining a word in their language.

between the developed and the developing countries . . ." (United Nations, 1974a). The accompanying program calls for major, but as yet unspecified, changes in the world pricing system, new controls over multinational corporations and the transfer of technology, changes in the international monetary system and the management of debt, and changes in tariffs and trade restrictions. Other proposals are made as well, but these four appear to us to be the most pressing.[2] In the hope of specifying the contents of these changes, a series of meetings known as the North-South dialogues occurred in the mid-seventies. For the most part, they have been failures. Virtually no concessions have been made by MDC governments in any of the areas except tariffs, and here the LDC governments were so dissatisfied that many of them delayed signing the document on the trade agreements of 1979 (the Tokyo round). We shall take up these four points of NIEO in order, and then we will consider them jointly, to assess what has happened.

TERMS OF TRADE

In the broad sense in which we have used the expression, "terms of trade" refers to the entire set of mechanisms by which world prices are determined: the organizations (such as multinational corporations) that set prices, government interference with prices (through tariffs and other restrictions), and direct international pressures (such as insistence that some countries restrict exports). In this section, we will use "terms of trade" in its narrower sense, that of the relative prices of exports and imports (*commodity* or *barter* terms of trade), expressed by the following formula:

$$\text{Terms of trade} = \frac{P_x}{P_m} (100)$$

in which P_x is a price index of exports and P_m is a price index of imports. We are assuming the reader is already familiar with price indices and their various limitations.

Primary products (minerals and foodstuffs) dominate the exports of LDCs; in exchange, they receive manufactured goods, primarily from MDCs. The situation is not quite this clear-cut, however. Many LDCs export manufactured goods, and all of them import primary products. In monetary terms, in fact, the MDCs export more primary products than do the LDCs (though a more

---

[2]In addition to the four topics covered in this chapter, the NIEO asks for increased development assistance and other resources from MDCs on more advantageous terms, acceleration of the transfer of labor-intensive industries from MDCs to LDCs, and MDC acquiescence to LDC cartels. Shortly after proposing the NIEO, the LDCs introduced into the United Nations a resolution for a Charter of Economic Rights and Duties of States (United Nations, 1974b), which would affirm each country's sovereignty over its own resources and give them the right to resolve investment disputes each in its own way, by its own courts or other institutions. The United States, which opposed the declaration, argued that this provision would "deny the applicability of international law to investment disputes" (United States, 1975:50).

restricted definition of primary products might either reverse this balance or increase it). Despite these qualifications, the negotiating problem is one of primary products in exchange for manufactured goods. The NIEO calls for "rectifying and achieving satisfactory terms of trade" for LDCs.

For over 25 years, LDC economists and diplomats have argued that, over time, the prices of primary products decline in relation to those of manufactured goods; therefore, the terms of trade move against the LDCs. Some believe this is a secular trend, which has persisted for a century or more. This idea was initiated by Prebisch, writing in United Nations (1950) and reprinted as Prebisch (1962). Using data originally compiled by Schlote (1938) and Lewis (1952), Prebisch compared British export and import prices from 1876–1880 to 1936–1938 and showed that the terms of trade deteriorated for Britain's LDC trading partners from 100 to 64.1. When criticized for using depression years as a terminal period, he extended the study to 1946–1947, at which time the index stood at 68.7

To be credible in professional circles, such a proposition must have theoretical as well as empirial support. Prebisch argued theoretically as follows. The classical doctrine[3] provides that terms of trade will move against innovating countries, in this case against MDCs and therefore in favor of LDCs. Innovations taking the form of decreased costs will lead (competitively) to decreased prices of exports. The innovating country (MDC) does not lose thereby, but shares the gains of innovation with its customers (LDC). But, Prebisch argued, the advent of monopolies (in both labor unions and producers) changed the parameters. By withholding the products of innovation, monopolists in MDCs have kept the prices of their exports high, thus reserving the gains for themselves. Because producers of primary goods have remained competitive, gains from innovations on their side have been shared with MDCs. Thus (in real terms) the prices of primary products have been brought down over time, but those of manufactured goods have not. Hence the classifical doctrine is set aside: the terms of trade do move secularly against LDCs (according to Prebisch).

Prebisch has been criticized in both his empirical and theoretical analyses. The empirical criticisms fall into two classes. First, Ellsworth (1956) pointed out that from the 1870s until 1912, a revolution in transportation technology had greatly reduced the cost of overseas shipping. By using British data, of which imports are c.i.f. and exports are f.o.b., Prebisch included shipping costs in his calculations of declining British payments for imports, but not in his calculations for exports. If an adjustment is made for shipping, Ellsworth showed, the amount the British were paying for their primary-product imports decreased during the time period studied, while the amount the LDCs were receiving increased. Second, Prebisch used British data alone. Drawing in part on data from Kindleberger (1956), Bairoch (1975) showed that European or American export prices either did not rise as much as Prebisch had found in

---

[3]The classical doctrine is associated with Mill (1844); a concise treatment is found in Viner (1950:535–41). Nurkse (1961:122–23) also defends the classical doctrine by pointing out that "the terms of trade between crude and manufactured products are now just about back to where they were in 1928."

British prices, or might even have fallen. With freedom to purchase in the cheapest markets, the LDCs could surely have protected themselves.

In a study of European trade from 1870 to 1955, Kindleberger showed that the terms did not move against primary producers, but that they might have moved against LDCs. He thus emphasized that primary producers and LDCs are not conterminus. He theorized that during this period, LDCs might have been less able than MDCs to shift factors of production from less- to more-profitable occupations; hence they may have decreased their prices rather than their output in depressed markets. If this is the explanation, LDCs could increase their leverage by improving factor mobility; changes in the manner of determining prices would not be necessary.

Criticisms of Prebisch on theoretical grounds center on his argument that monopolists can keep their prices high, regardless of cost-saving innovations. This argument pays scant attention to the classical theory of monopoly. If monopolies can maximize their profits by selling more (as would be the usual case with declining marginal costs on account of innovation), they *must* lower their prices, for why would buyers take more if the price remains the same? In real terms, the only case in which innovating exporters would not lower their prices vis-à-vis foreigners would be the extreme one in which they (including their laborers and other compatriots) wish themselves to consume the entire increment from the innovation rather than exchange some of it (however little) for the products of other countries. Meier (1968) has worked out alternative scenarios with reciprocal-offer curves, while Powelson (1970) has argued that if monopolists (labor unions or producers) attempt to keep prices high in the face of innovation, the advantages will still be shared with the outside world through a depreciating exchange rate.

Prior to World War II, the paucity of data on terms of trade required special studies, such as those of Lewis, Prebisch, and Kindleberger. Since World War II, however, LDCs as well as MDCs have routinely published price indices for imports and exports, which the United Nations and other international agencies have assembled into indicators of the terms of trade. What do these data tell us of the last 30 years?

We believe they show overwhelmingly that there is no long-run trend, in one direction or another (Jaksch, 1977). We have ourselves (Powelson, 1978:36) spliced various indices of the United Nations to reflect terms of trade for LDCs (1938–1960) and for Latin America (1960–1972), which are duplicated in Figure 13–1. Data from the World Bank (1976:472) and the International Monetary Fund (1977a:11; 1977b:291) generally support the observation that no secular trend exists.

But prices of primary products do fluctuate widely, sometimes maintaining a direction (downward or upward) for a decade or more. The *biased* observer may select the years 1950–1954 as base. Primary-product prices were extraordinarily high in those years because of the Korean War and a series of frosts in coffee-producing countries. If the observer carries his series no farther than, say, the mid-sixties, he can proclaim that the terms of trade are "secularly" declining. This is precisely what Pinto and Kñackal (1973:80) have done, and the American Friends Service Committee (1976:9) has copied them. This time

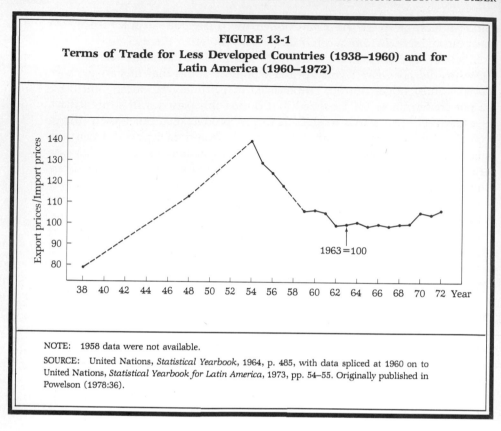

FIGURE 13-1

Terms of Trade for Less Developed Countries (1938–1960) and for Latin America (1960–1972)

NOTE: 1958 data were not available.

SOURCE: United Nations, *Statistical Yearbook*, 1964, p. 485, with data spliced at 1960 on to United Nations, *Statistical Yearbook for Latin America*, 1973, pp. 54–55. Originally published in Powelson (1978:36).

period has also been used in speeches before the United Nations Conferences on Trade and Development (UNCTAD), the North-South dialogues on commodity agreements, and other international meetings. Nyerere's citation of sisal prices from 1965 to 1972 is also a case of selective perception. Had he chosen coffee (another Tanzanian export) from 1969 to 1977, he would have seen its price rise by 825 percent, while the unit value of U.S. exports increased by only 150 percent, an improvement in terms of trade from 100 to 660 (International Monetary Fund, May 1978 and April 1979).

On the grounds that secular decline has deprived them of a just price for their exports, LDCs have proposed (in UNCTAD and in the North-South dialogues) that an international commodity fund support prices of primary products. Dialogue on this proposal, however, has confused two separate questions: the wide fluctuations in primary-product prices (which are to the advantage of no one) and the overall level of these prices. Discussions are usually couched in terms of "stabilization" rather than "support." But the negotiations themselves show that LDC governments will not accept the former without the latter, and hence the stalemate to date. An international support fund for commodities was agreed on, in general, by representatives of both MDCs and LDCs in 1980, but the exact arrangements have not been worked out.

Regardless of how the terms of trade have behaved historically, we are disturbed that the prices of primary products might be raised, artificially, to levels higher than the market trend, for three reasons.

FIRST, we deplore a development "mentality" based on monopolies and restrictions. State and parastatal enterprises in LDCs have not been noted for their innovativeness and competitiveness (we will have more to say on this in Chapter 14), and we suspect that worldwide monopolies designed to keep prices high would promote corruption and inefficiency more than they would new scientific technology.

SECOND, international agreements to raise commodity prices have been tried numerous times since the 1930s, and except for agreements on petroleum prices, none has ever worked over time. When at a given price, a willing buyer and a willing seller exist, and their transaction will harm no third parties, it is enormously difficult (and oppressive) to prevent it from occurring. The necessary organization and police force are not only costly, but they concentrate power in ways that the international community has to date found impractical or intolerable. Commodity agreements have failed primarily because they could not be enforced.

THIRD, and most important of all, *interference with the market tends to transfer income from the poor to the rich*, more than the other way around. OPEC (Organization of Petroleum Exporting Countries) is a case in point. This coalition has been able to maintain an oligopoly because of high inelasticity of demand for petroleum (due to its strategic industrial importance and a lack of inexpensive substitutes and because of the concentration of its production in a few countries. Both the MDCs and non-oil-producing LDCs (the NOPEC group) must pay higher prices as a result (Stern and Tims, 1975).

With their increased incomes, oil-exporting countries have increased their purchases from MDCs more than from LDCs, and surplus funds are mostly invested or deposited in MDCs. Thus, the balance-of-payments impact on MDCs has been within reasonable bounds. But the non-oil-producing LDCs must balance their accounts by cutting back on development expenditures and by borrowing heavily from MDCs. High cost has put chemical fertilizers out of reach for many LDC farmers. While the real impact (terms-of-trade loss measured in exports paid for imports) is not negligible for MDCs, nevertheless it is not nearly so great for them, relative to GDP, as it is for non-oil-producing LDCs. In terms of ability to pay, the primary suffering has therefore been by poor countries, and it has been severe. We have published the data supporting these observations earlier (Powelson, 1977b:10–26).

LDCs do not export primary products to the same degree; indeed, there are sizeable variations. In general, high-income LDCs would be the primary beneficiaries of higher raw-material prices (Weintraub, 1979). Also, if the price of copper were raised, the gainers would be Zambia, Chile, Peru, and Zaire. The poor in urban slums everywhere, who would have to pay more for copper piping and wiring, would be among the losers.

Thus, raising the level of commodity prices is not likely to have the worldwide equalizing effect that LDC diplomats have suggested. An estimate of world income distribution by Cline (1980), using data on internal country distributions compiled by Jain (1975) and "real" income derived by Kravis, Heston, and Summers (1978), allows us to determine which commodities have an equalizing effect when their prices are raised and which do not. A simulated fourfold price increase for "equalizing" commodities shows that world income distribution is affected hardly at all. The income share of the world's poorest 40 percent rises only from 4.148 to 4.275 percent. The world Gini coefficient remains at about .67.

Finally, we question how production restrictions will be shared by rich and poor within countries. In many coffee countries, some farms are large plantations, while others may be only a hectare or two. When reduced crops are called for, to support the artificially higher price, can one reasonably suppose that the reduction will fall primarily on the rich, or even be shared proportionately? Or will the poor farmer be the one to be left out?

MULTINATIONAL CORPORATIONS AND THE TRANSFER OF TECHNOLOGY

The NIEO calls for "an international code of conduct" for multinational corporations, which would prevent them from interfering with internal affairs or collaborating with racist or colonial regimes, eliminate restrictive business practices, assist the transfer of technology, and promote reinvestment of profits rather than their repatriation.

If any debate is more intense than that over the terms of trade, it is the one about multinational corporations (MNCs). In an earlier article (Powelson, 1977a), we have listed and commented on the charges commonly directed at MNCs. These charges are summarized (with our comments on their validity) in Table 13–1. More data appear in Tables 13–2 and 13–3.

Charge number 3 (Table 13–1), that repatriations exceed investments (see Table 13–2), represents an underlying misconception of economic processes.

TABLE 13–1
Summary of Charges Against Multinational Corporations and Comments on the Validity of These Charges

Charge	Comment on validity
1. MNCs move freely from country to country, settling where they receive the best of terms.	1. They do so move, but not always freely. They are constrained by costs, by naturally favorable or unfavorable locations, and by fixity of investment.
2. They pay low wages.	2. Their wages are lower than in their home countries, but they tend to pay up to 100 percent higher wages than those paid by corresponding national companies in host contries (ILO, 1976).

TABLE 13–1
(continued)

Charge	Comment on validity
3. They earn high profits, tending to repatriate them rather than reinvest in host countries.	3. Profit rates (Table 13–3) tend to be high for petroleum, medium high for other minerals, and not excessive for manufacturing. These are, of course, subjective judgments. MNCs do tend to repariate rather than reinvest, and in recent years repatriations have exceeded new investments (Table 13–2).
4. They use capital-intensive methods of production where labor-intensive methods would be more appropriate.	4. Empirical data are not clear-cut: sometimes MNCs are more capital-intensive, sometimes they are more labor-intensive.
5. They attempt to maximize global profits rather than profits in the host country; for example, they might suppress exports from a subsidiary in the host country so as not to interfere with markets of the parent company.	5. Probably valid in most cases, but the question is highly complex. Garnier *et al.* (1979) found a high degree of Mexican participation in decisions of MNC subsidiaries operating in Mexico.
6. They use artificial transfer prices for transactions between the subsidiaries and the parent company to cause profit to be "earned" in the country of least tax, or to evade exchange controls or profit-transmittal restrictions.	6. Probably valid, but little hard evidence is available.
7. They transfer technology to their subsidiaries only at high cost, sometimes withholding technology when to do so is to the advantage of the parent company.	7. Probably true, but once again, little hard evidence is available.
8. They tend to employ home-country nationals in high positions, being prejudiced against host-country nationals.	8. True at one time, but decreasingly so. In many countries, national legislation has forced increasing employment of host-country nationals; in Mexico, it is virtually 100 percent.
9. The greater sophistication and worldwide knowledge of MNC officials puts them at a bargaining advantage vis-à-vis LDC officials.	9. Clearly true at one time, but less and less so as LDC officials become more knowledgeable and sophisticated themselves.
10. MNCs tend to use domestic capital, thus failing to supply new capital to LDCs in need of it.	10. To a large extent this is true, but MNCs will seek capital where it is cheapest. If LDCs provide artificially-low interest rates to stimulate investment (Chapter 14), they can expect MNCs to borrow there.
11. MNCs transmit the culture of the home country, often undesirable, to LDCs (for example, drinking Coca Cola, bottle-feeding babies).	11. Doubtless true, but LDC nationals are free to accept or reject this cultural behavior. Any kind of international contact transmits culture, and we shudder at the prospect of "culture controls."
12. By their great power, MNCs bribe host-government officials and manipulate their legislation.	12. Doubtless true, but who should control them? LDC governments, with the power they obviously have to nationalize MNCs or limit them in other ways, certainly could control their illicit practices if they would decide to.

TABLE 13–2
U.S. Direct Investment Flows to LDCs, Compared to Transmitted Earnings,
1966–1975
(millions of dollars)

	All industries	Mining and Smelting	Petroleum	Manufacturing
1966 Investment flows(net)	499	83	−4	237
Repatriated earnings	1,946	373	1,229	132
Balance (flows less earnings)	−1,447	−290	−1,233	105
1967 Investment flows (net)	757	50	245	264
Repatriated earnings	2,171	398	1,382	168
Balance (flows less earnings)	−1,414	−348	−1,137	96
1968 Investment flows (net)	1,151	170	531	308
Repatriated earnings	2,430	418	1,580	203
Balance (flows less earnings)	−1,279	−248	−1,049	105
1969 Investment flows (net)	798	−35	309	286
Repatriated earnings	2,652	443	1,684	206
Balance (flows less earnings)	−1,854	−478	−1,375	80
1970 Investent flows (net)	984	109	458	157
Repatriated earnings	2,340	297	1,496	248
Balance (flows less earnings)	−1,356	−188	−1,038	−91
1971 Investment flows (net)	1,302	121	590	284
Repatriated earnings	2,712	232	1,895	258
Balance (flows less earnings)	−1,410	−111	−1,305	26
1972 Investment flows (net)	1,132	22	645	323
Repatriated earnings	3,079	177	2,213	289
Balance (flows less earnings)	−1,947	−155	−1,568	34
1973 Investment flows (net)	921	3	24	443
Repatriated earnings	4,729	267	3,595	353
Balance (flows less earnings)	−3,808	−264	−3,571	90
1974 Investment flows (net)	1,676	−252	−596	670
Repatriated earnings	12,556	401	10,700	421
Balance (flows less earnings)	−10,880	−653	−11,296	249
1975 Investment flows (net)	3,713	342	1,903	393
Repatriated earnings	4,540	147	2,747	447
Balance (flows less earnings)	−827	195	−844	−54

SOURCE: Calculated from U.S. Department of Commerce, *Revised Data on U.S. Direct Investment Abroad*, *1966–1974*, and *Survey of Current Business*, August 1976. Originally published in Powelson (1977a:421).

TABLE 13–3
Rate of Return on U.S. Direct Investment in LDCs, 1966–1975
(million of dollars)

	All industries	Mining and Smelting	Petroleum	Manufacturing
1966 Reinvested	.03	.01	.01	.06
Repatriated	.14	.23	.24	.04
Total earnings	.17	.24	.26	.09
1967 Reinvested	.02	.02	.01	.03
Repatriated	.15	.22	.26	.04
Total earnings	.17	.24	.27	.07
1968 Reinvested	.03	.01	.01	.05
Repatriated	.15	.21	.27	.05
Total earnings	.18	.22	.28	.10
1969 Reinvested	.02	.03	−.01	.06
Repatriated	.15	.22	.27	.04
Total earnings	.17	.26	.26	.10
1970 Reinvested	.03	.02	.01	.06
Repatriated	.12	.14	.23	.05
Total earnings	.15	.16	.24	.10
1971 Reinvested	.03	−.01	.01	.05
Repatriated	.13	.10	.26	.04
Total earnings	.16	.10	.27	.09
1972 Reinvested	.03	.01	.01	.06
Repatriated	.13	.08	.28	.04
Total earnings	.17	.09	.28	.11
1973 Reinvested	.06	.02	.06	.08
Repatriated	.19	.16	.43	.05
Total earnings	.25	.18	.48	.12
1974 Reinvested	.06	.02	.05	.08
Repatriated	.44	.22	1.30	.05
Total earnings	.51	.25	1.35	.13
1975 Renvested	.08	.02	.10	.08
Repatriated	.13	.07	.25	.04
Total earnings	.21	.09	.35	.13

SOURCE: Calculated from U.S. Department of Commerce, *Revised Data on U.S. Direct Investment Abroad, 1966–1974*, and *Survey of Current Business*, August 1976. Originally published in Powelson (1977a: 419).

Repatriated earnings should not be compared with new investment, but with the stock of capital, accumulated from previous investments, on which it has been earned. An investor who makes an annual deposit of $1 in a savings bank at 5 percent interest, and who withdraws his interest annually finds that at the end of the twentieth year he is withdrawing $1 in interest while continuing his annual investments of $1. In subsequent years, his interest withdrawals exceed his new deposits. But his earnings stem from his *previous* deposits, which become the basis of comparison. The legitimate question, therefore, is not the balance between withdrawals and current investment, but whether the rate of return on investment is "too high." This is an ethical concern, not an economic one, to which each reader may apply his own values. The best information we have, which may be inaccurate because book values do not always reflect real values of investment, is shown in Table 13–3. Returns on mining investments appear to us to be "high," though company managements insist they are offset by the uncompensated portion of expropriations. In manufacturing, MNCs appear to be content with lower rates of return, which do not greatly exceed their profit opportunities at home.

Critics of MNCs are often ambivalent about wages (charge number 2). Barnet and Müller (1974:170) criticize MNCs for paying *higher* wages than their local competitors, thus having "every incentive to buy more machines and to employ fewer workers." Later on (p. 312), the same authors fault MNCs for paying *lower* wages in LDCs than they do in their home territories. "Should not the wages in Detroit and Hong Kong be the same?" they ask.

We find much of the debate on MNCs to be sterile, taking place between those who will find reason to criticize the companies no matter what they do and those who will defend them no matter what crimes they commit. Some authors (such as Vernon, 1971) appear middle-of-the-road and objective. Reporting for the Harvard research project on MNCs, Vernon points out that their net balance-of-payment impact depends not only on repatriated earnings versus new investments, but also on the companies' exports and imports and their domestic production of goods that would otherwise have been imported. If one assumes that all goods produced by MNCs for local sales would have been imported otherwise, and that MNC exports would not otherwise have been made by national companies, then MNCs probably have a large, positive impact on their host countries' balance of payments. With the opposite assumptions, the balance would be slightly negative. The most likely probability (a subjective judgment) is positive. Vernon also reports that MNCs appear to use home-country (capital-intensive) technology in their core production, because they fear the risks of innovation, but that they tend to adapt to more labor-intensive techniques in peripheral activities, such as material inputs and transportation.

THE MANAGEMENT OF MONEY AND DEBT

In the international monetary system, the NIEO hangs on to the coattails of a problem that MDC governments have long perceived as entirely their own. During the 1920s, when the quantity of gold became no longer sufficient to finance expanding world trade, governments looked for new ways of creating international reserves. The gold exchange standard became a temporary expedient, with the dollar as the key currency. As foreign-held dollars came to exceed U.S. gold reserves, the European nations became fearful for U.S. creditworthiness and less willing to submit to U.S. money management. Their answer was the Special Drawing Right (SDR), an international reserve currency to be issued by the International Monetary Fund.

Under present rules, new SDRs are divided among countries in accordance with their relative quotas in the IMF. Since rich countries have the highest quotas, they receive more SDRs than poor countries. They justify this result by its neutrality. Suppose some country should double its national money supply, by giving each person or institution an extra peso for each peso already held. Each one would have twice as much money, but *relative* quantities held would be unchanged. If prices were doubled by this action, real purchasing powers would remain unchanged. The same principle (affluent countries aver) should hold for world reserves. New SDRs should be distributed in rough proportion to reserves already held.

LDC governments argue differently. New international reserves are an opportunity to improve world distribution, as well as to redress the perceived wrongs of the past. They therefore propose that SDRs should be distributed primarily to poor countries. Because it would unite two worldwide problems (money and development), this method has become known as "the link." Furthermore, the NIEO calls for "full and effective participation of developing countries in all phases of decision-making for the formulation of an equitable and durable monetary system . . ."

For two reasons, MDC governments are unwilling to comply. First, they see "the link" as a way of taking foreign aid out of their control. It would supply LDCs with claims on the products of MDCs, spendable anywhere and for whatever purpose. Second, they do not trust LDC governments to manage the international monetary system prudently, and they tie their own economic survival to its prudent management. The major inflations of postwar years have taken place in LDCs, because (MDC officials believe) of governmental mismanagement. They do not want these inflations to be transmitted to the international economy.[4] One will not find these reasons in transcripts of the dialogues, for it would not be diplomatic for MDC governments to state them officially. But between the lines, they are present.

An adverse evaluation of LDC management is also reflected in the reluctance of MDCs to cancel debts. In the past decade, LDCs have borrowed increasing amounts from international institutions and private banks in MDCs. From 1970 to 1976, the external debt of 96 LDCs approximately tripled, from $54 thousand million to $161 thousand million (World Bank, 1978:38).[5] Part of this borrowing

---

[4]Ironically, the NIEO suggests precisely the *opposite* reasons for its proposed reforms. It calls for "measures to check the inflation already experienced by the developed countries, to prevent it from being transferred to developing countries . . ."

[5]Some have argued that the debt problem, with the exception of some cases, is not overly alarming (see the special issue of *World Development*, February 1979), or that the real debt has been sharply reduced by inflation in the currencies in which the debt is specified, usually U.S. dollars (Smith, 1979).

financed the higher price of oil, surely not the fault of the NOPEC group. In the NIEO, they have therefore asked for "debt renegotiation on a case-by-case basis with a view to concluding agreements on debt cancellation, moratorium, rescheduling, or interest subsidization."

There are two ways to assess the burden of debt. One is by the debt-service ratio (payments of principal and interest as a percentage of exports of goods and services), and the other is by the terms (the length of maturity and the interest rate). The debt-service ratios for selected LDCs from 1970 to 1976 are shown in Table 13–4, while the average terms of commitments (for official and private loans separately) are shown in Table 13–5. Here it is seen that for many of the major borrowers, debt-service ratios have been increasing, and terms have been hardening (shorter maturities and higher rates).

With some exceptions, the MDC response has been disappointing to LDCs. In debt almost to the point of bankruptcy, Turkey was granted a multilateral rescheduling in May, 1978; Zaire and Sierra Leone had achieved the same in 1977. Canada, the Netherlands, and Sweden have forgiven about $600 million of the debt of the poorest countries, and Germany and the United Kingdom have announced similar intentions.

Yet the bulk of the debt remains. One explanation for creditor reluctance is that debt forgiveness is not the normal practice of creditors. But there are

TABLE 13–4
Service Payments on External Public Debts as a Percentage of Exports of Goods and Services, Selected LDCs, 1970 and 1976

	1970	1976
AFRICA SOUTH OF THE SAHARA		
Burundi	2.3	4.6
Chad	3.9	4.1
Ethiopia	11.3	6.3
Ghana	4.9	4.6
Kenya	5.5	5.0
Madagascar	3.5	4.7
Mauritania	3.2	37.0
Nigeria	4.1	2.3
Sierra Leone	10.0	21.4
Swaziland	4.7	0.8
Uganda	3.2	2.5
Zambia	5.4	8.9
Average for countries in this area	5.3	6.9

SOURCE: World Bank (1978:212–13). In order to condense the table, only every third country (for which data are available for 1976) has been shown, together with the average ratios of all countries (taken country by country) for each area. In order to show the countries with the greatest debt ratios, all countries not included in the selection but with debt ratios of 10 percent or more in 1976, were included in a final section. Reprinted by permission.

NOTE: Debt-service ratios are based on debt service actually paid and not on contractual service due. Further information on sources, definitions, and interpretation is given by World Bank (1978:15–20).

TABLE 13—4
(continued)

	1970	1976
EAST ASIA AND THE PACIFIC		
Indonesia	6.4	11.2
Papua New Guinea	0.6	4.8
Thailand	3.3	2.4
Average for countries in this area	4.8	5.0
LATIN AMERICA AND THE CARIBBEAN		
Bolivia	10.9	16.4
Colombia	11.6	9.4
Ecuador	9.0	5.8
Guyana	3.6	10.4
Jamaica	2.9	11.1
Panama	7.7	8.1
Trinidad and Tobago	2.0	2.6
Average for countries in this area	9.5	15.1
NORTH AFRICA AND THE MIDDLE EAST		
Algeria	3.2	14.1
Iraq	2.2	0.9
Syrian Arab Republic	11.0	7.9
Average for countries in this area	9.6	7.9
SOUTH ASIA		
Bangladesh	—	13.4
Nepal	10.7	2.3
Average for countries in this area	15.3	15.7
MORE ADVANCED MEDITERRANEAN COUNTRIES		
Cyprus	2.2	2.9
Malta	1.7	0.4
Turkey	16.3	7.1
Average for countries in this area	7.7	5.7
REMAINING COUNTRIES WITH DEBT RATIOS (1976) OF 10 PERCENT OR MORE		
Guinea	28.7	20.8
Sudan	10.3	16.7
Zaire	4.4	11.7
Argentina	21.4	18.3
Brazil	14.1	14.8
Mexico	23.6	32.3
Nicaragua	10.4	12.2
Peru	13.6	21.6
Uruguay	21.5	29.2
Egypt, Arab Republic of	28.7	17.6
Burma	16.1	16.3
India	22.0	12.0
Pakistan	23.6	18.2
Sri Lanka	9.6	20.1
Greece	10.1	11.2
Israel	12.7	12.1
Chile	18.9	32.9

TABLE 13–5
**Average Terms of Loan Commitments Made by Official and Private Creditors,
96 LDCs, 1970 and 1976**

	1970	1976
OFFICIAL		
Amount ($ − 000,000,000)	8.13	23.35
Interest rate (percent)	4.0	5.6
Maturity (years)	26.4	22.8
Grant element (percent)	45	31
PRIVATE		
Amount ($ − 000,000,000)	5.96	28.78
Interest rate (percent)	7.2	7.9
Maturity (years)	9.5	7.7
Grant element (percent)	12	7

SOURCE: World Bank (1978:217). Reprinted by permission.

NOTE: The grant element refers to concessionary loans. It is the face value of the commitment minus the discounted (at 10 percent) present value of the future flow of payments of principal and interest, expressed as percentage of the face value.

deeper reasons as well. If we again read between the lines, we find MDC officials suspicious that LDC governments have not managed their budgets wisely, have spent on projects that were not carefully considered, or have used funds for patronage. There is no direct evidence of this judgment; rather, it is surmised from the assumption that properly-managed projects would have yielded revenues for their own servicing, just as any prudently-managed company would. If bad luck intervenes (such as anchovies disappearing from the Peruvian coast and projected oil finds in Peru not materializing), it is assumed that this should have been allowed for in prudent calculations. A more severe adversity, such as the oil price increase, may take more time to overcome, but it must be managed nevertheless.

We shall add one further reason for not acceding to this request. If once again we divide the world into rich and poor *people* or *units*, and not rich and poor *countries*, we find that only the rich or the moderately-rich have the capacity to borrow. The very poor—even the very poor *countries*—are not among the principal debtors. Out of a $15.6 billion debt for Africa south of the Sahara in 1976, that of Burundi was only $23.7 million, that of Lesotho was $15.4 million, and that of Upper Volta was $84.4 million (World Bank, 1978:38). Within countries, we do not immediately presume that the proceeds of debt are spent for the benefit of the poor; indeed, in the absence of evidence, we presume the opposite. Debt cancellation is foreign aid, since the debt is incurred to buy real resources. Foreign aid is scarce, and we would prefer to see it spent on the poorest of the poor.

How, on balance, do we make an assessment? Have LDCs been drawn hopelessly into debt by circumstances beyond their control (the oil price increase)? Or is their debt the product of mismanagement? We cannot tell, for the two are intermixed. Adversity is the harsh tester of management skills. Whatever our judgment, the MDCs have not been willing to relieve LDCs of their burden. The oil facility established by the International Monetary Fund, plus loans by foreign governments and banks, will allow more time for adjustment. But there is some evidence that these may be reaching their limit, and in any event, the loss in real terms must ultimately be faced by every oil consumer individually.

THE GENERALIZED SYSTEM OF PREFERENCES

Through the United Nations Conference on Trade and Development (UNCTAD, begun in 1954), LDC governments had been requesting preferential access to markets of MDCs, long before the NIEO was proposed. In 1963, the European Economic Community (EEC) signed the Yaoundé Agreement with 18 French-speaking countries from West and Central Africa, providing for reciprocal preferences, financial and technical cooperation, investment and financial aid, and the right of companies from EEC countries to operate in African member territories. This agreement was extended in 1969. In 1973, Kenya, Uganda, and Tanzania entered into the Arusha Agreement, by which EEC countries granted *nonreciprocal* trade preferences (with a few minor exceptions). But the Arusha Agreement contained none of the nontrade features of the Yaoundé Agreement. All talk of combining the two agreements early foundered on the question of reciprocity; the East African countries would not give up their nonreciprocal privileges in exchange for the wider financial advantages (Republic of Kenya, 1974:32). In 1974, the NIEO called for expansion of a Generalized System of Preferences (GSP) to cover more of the exports of LDCs and to include other MDCs such as the United States and Canada.

GSP had long been accepted in principle by the United States, which nevertheless was holding out for an accord with the European countries. The United States wanted a global agreement, covering all the MDCs and all the LDCs, whereas the EEC wanted to confine its preferences to former European colonies, leaving Latin America in the orbit of the United States. By 1974, it became clear that no agreement could be reached between European countries and the United States, so each implemented GSP in its own way.

Britain's entry into the EEC in 1972 paved the way for joint action by EEC countries with all former colonies. During 18 months of negotiations (1973–1974), the EEC at first demanded reciprocal preferences, while the African countries insisted on one-way preferences. The Europeans finally gave in, and the Lomé Convention (1975) spelled out an entire set of relationships between 9 members of the EEC and 46 former colonies, which became known as the ACP countries (for Africa-Caribbean-Pacific). The main features of the Lomé Convention (Commission of the European Communities, 1975:22) are free access without reciprocity to the European market for goods exported from the ACP, a stabilization fund to compensate the ACP in case of reductions in receipts from exports of basic products, financial aid for the ÁCP, industrial and technical cooperation, and joint institutions to supervise the agreement.

The American response was more limited than the European in goods covered, but it was broader geographically. The Trade Act of 1974 (United States, 1975:35) authorizes duty-free entry for certain "eligible" products from all LDCs. These include goods for which the U.S. Government predicts no harm to domestic producers. In principle, domestic producers will yield a greater relative share of *expanding* domestic markets to imports from LDCs, but they will not reduce their sales absolutely. In case sales should fall off, escape clauses would protect them.

While the intentions for GSP have been good (and probably sincere), results have been disappointing. The "Tokyo round" of multilateral trade negotiations (MTN) started with high hopes in 1973. In addition to mutual reductions of duties covered by the usual practices of the Reciprocal Trade Agreements Program (initiated in 1934), the Trade Act of 1974 authorized United States representatives to negotiate mutual reduction of nontariff barriers (NTB) to multilateral trade. These barriers include restrictive government purchasing procedures, the setting of high standards ostensibly for health or safety but actually to limit trade, and the red tape of licensing (U.S. Department of State, 1979). The Tokyo round was concluded in 1979, with tariff reductions of approximately one-third of remaining U.S.duties (NYT, 1–16–79). Because of the general business stagnation of preceding years, however, the ardor of major countries for cutting has been seriously dampened, and even as some NTBs were being reduced, others were being initiated (Balassa, 1978, and Helleiner, 1979). The EEC was initiating a program to regulate prices of domestic and foreign steel and to conclude bilateral agreements with foreign suppliers, while the United States was negotiating antidumping limits on the exports of foreign steel (IMF Survey, 4–9–79:101, 108).

Not all LDCs belong to the General Agreement on Tariffs and Trade (GATT), and therefore they did not all participate in the Tokyo round. Those that did, however, boycotted the signing of the final agreement (Lewis, N.Y.T., 4–13–79). They argued that key documents were drafted without an input from them, that the major powers did not take them into account when planning timetables, and that they were consulted only with respect to the special preference clauses (NYT, 7–4–78). But their greatest disappointment was the meager expansion of GSP.

LDC strategy appears to presume that LDCs need special preferences to expand exports, while generalized tariff reductions within GATT are relevant only for MDCs. Empirical studies of both the Dillon (completed 1961) and Kennedy (completed 1972) rounds of tariff concessions (Finger, 1974; 1976) reveal this as a mistaken impression. In the earlier round, traditional LDC exports receiving concessions[6] expanded no faster than those without concessions, presumably due to original cost advantages so great that tariff reductions could not improve their competitiveness. Untraditional exports, similar to goods

---

[6]"Concessions" are normally received through spillovers, since tariff cuts are usually negotiated between principal suppliers (MDCs) and accrue to LDCs via most-favored-nation treatment.

traded between MDCs, did expand when concessions were received, and in about the same way as they expanded among MDCs. During the later round of tariff cuts, LDC exports in all categories were affected by at least the same degree as those among MDCs.

Given the relative responses of LDC exports, the policy to push for preferences may be wrong (Finger, 1976:95). In the Kennedy Round LDCs benefited more than the MDCs from general most-favored-nation tariff cuts. Empirical comparisons show that in the unlikely event that the GSP is expanded to include textiles and shoes, *and* all value limits are removed, only then would the GSP yield greater benefit than a 50 percent across-the-board tariff cut within GATT (Baldwin and Murray, 1977). This conclusion holds even if textiles and shoes are not favored by tariff reduction. Diverting attention from generalized tariff reductions to concentrate on the GSP may therefore waste effort on the least useful of the current alternatives.[7]

MORALITY, REFORM, AND THE NIEO

The NIEO is both a petition for redress of grievances and a declaration for reform. Since such petitions and declarations are not unique in history, we must examine similar occurrences to judge the probability of success. In doing so, we formulate a theory of reform and morality.

LDC governments have asked MDC governments to make concessions with no quid pro quo. MDCs would willingly pay higher prices for primary products than they have to; they would voluntarily curb practices of multinational corporations whose countenance is advantageous to them; they would share with LDCs the management of the international monetary system when it would be more comfortable for them not to; and they would grant LDCs preferential access to their markets without receiving the same in return. The LDCs do not threaten sanctions if the MDCs refuse; they will not invade MDC territories; and except for OPEC, they cannot withhold anything the MDCs want. The appeal is entirely moral. MDCs should consent to the NIEO because to do so is deemed right, and because their behavior in the past is wrong.

How extraordinary! And yet, is it? We have already seen (Chapter 11) that agrarian reform has occurred, and slavery has ended, by the voluntary action of landlords and slave-owners. We have also seen (Chapter 12) that free education, hospitals, and health services have gradually been extended to relatively poorer social groups. In the twentieth century, virtually all industrialized countries have adopted income and inheritance taxes and effective systems of social

---

[7]Baldwin and Murray (1977) indicate that the higher-income LDCs are the current beneficiaries of the GSP but that they would benefit even more from most-favored-nation tariff cuts. The world's poorest countries may indeed benefit more by GSP, since their total affected exports are so small that they do not feel value limitations and since most-favored-nation tariff cuts would not aid them as much. A constructive policy position would therefore be for high-income LDCs to give up GSP in exchange for general trade-barrier reductions in MDCs, while both groups might extend GSP to the poorest countries.

security, unemployment insurance, and welfare assistance. LDCs are following suit, although their systems are often more effective on paper than they are in fact. These and similar events have caused Boulding (1973) to study the "grants economy." Why do people give?

We would like to believe that reforms occur because of moral sentiment. But that would be wishful thinking. Widespread acceptance of all the reforms mentioned came only after the reforms had occurred, and sometimes not until two or three generations had passed.

So it was with slavery. Little can be found in Roman or Greek literature to confirm any moral abhorrence of slavery. In medieval times, the villein-serf-master relationship was universally accepted. The Church frequently pressed to alleviate the suffering of the poor, but there was little belief in the rightness of freedom. European literature of the eighteenth century reveals a belief that Africans were inferiors, akin to beasts, to be treated as chattel. Yet, twenty centuries after Roman times, six centuries after medieval Europe, but only one century after emancipation in the Western world, there is hardly a soul who would not strongly condemn slavery.

What brought about this change? And what brought about changes in education, health, social security, child labor, and all the rest? Our suggested theory of reform and morality runs as follows. Humans are born with no culture whatsoever; only the self is esteemed. Over time, some individuals pressure others into a more social relationship. The pressure may be military or economic. The mentality shifts from individualism and private goods to cooperation and a mixture of private and public goods. Certain codes of conduct become good for all, and each one participates in the "all." Whatever conduct is generally practiced becomes moral.

This process may lead to feudalism and slavery, or to a relatively equitable distribution of skills and power, or—as happened in Western history—first to the former, then to the latter. How it develops depends on how evenly leverage (the capacity to exert pressure) is distributed along the way.

Every reform entails risk. The present situation is known, but the reformed one is only probable. Three kinds of discount are applied: time preference, probability, and risk aversion. The first reflects preference for present goods over future ones; the second measures the individual's subjective assessment of the probability of outcome; and the third expresses a greater or lesser preference for certainty even where the expected values of high- and low-probability alternatives may be the same. Suppose an individual discounts by 10 percent for time preference and he guesses that an investment of $80 today has an 80 percent probability of yielding $114 a year hence. The present expected value of that event is about $80 (a discount of 10 percent for time preference and a further discount of 20 percent for risk), or the same as the initial investment. If he is a risk-averter, however, he discounts further, for he prefers the certainty of $80 now to an equal, discounted expected value in the future.

Risk-taking is learned. Primitive societies are strongly risk-averting, as witnessed by the belief in early African cultures that strangers are not to be trusted (Bozeman, 1976:98–9). As the pressures of some force others to take risks, the latter learn that prediction is less hazardous than they had believed, and they become more risk-inclined.

Reforms that promote development and equitable distribution require some leverage on the part of the poor that will force the rich to take risks. Feudalism ended in Europe when the supervision of serfs became too costly; the same was true for slavery in nineteenth-century Europe and the Americas (Chapter 11). Health services were extended to the poor in medieval Lombard towns because diseases were contagious, and the rich might become exposed (Chapter 10). Free compulsory education reached the common labororer (also Chapter 10) not only because he would be more useful if skilled, but also because his skills had given him the clout to demand suffrage and then more education. All these reforms were accompanied by small but vocal minorities who lobbied for them on moral grounds. But widespread acceptance—hence morality—came only after the reforms had been put into effect, and after those who lived with them realized that their fears of the reforms were unfounded.

But are we not in a vicious circle? Leverage engenders reforms in one's favor, but only after the reforms does one achieve leverage. The process is indeed cumulative. But very few (if any at all) in the world today possess no leverage whatsoever, or are unable to achieve any. Leverage may spring from the most surprising of sources (as when the Black Death brought it to European laborers in the fourteenth century). Since leverage comes first, reform next, and morality last, those who demand reform must seek their leverage first. To rely first on appeals to morality is futile. This convolution of LDC strategy is a principal reason why their NIEO demands go largely unanswered.

In searching for leverage, the first consideration is the principle of progression. LDC governments may choose among many reforms. With NIEO, they prepared a list of all the reforms they could think of and appeared to be demanding them all at once. Their probabilities would be improved if they would first seek those reforms for which they have greatest leverage, hoping that achievement of these would enhance their leverage for the next priorities.

The more efficient a reform, the greater the leverage for it *(ceteris paribus)*. We have seen that feudalism and slavery ended when other forms of economic organization became more profitable. Universal education was introduced when communities in need of greater skills found it the most effective way to compel parents to enroll their children. Social security and unemployment insurance followed the demise of the extended family in MDCs. The need for the mobility of nuclear families shifted care of the elderly and unemployed to the State, and serendipitously extended it to the poor. Efficient reforms are more likely to be accepted if only because more people are likely to benefit from them.

As a reform is linked increasingly to other economic and social events, the leverage for it increases (again *ceteris paribus*). A self-sufficient family need not care whether its neighbor's children are educated and healthy, or even whether they are enslaved. But a family dependent on others for raw materials or markets is likely to care how efficient the others are.

Let us now apply the principles of efficiency and linkage to the four provisions of NIEO that we have already encountered.

PRICE SUPPORTS FOR COMMODITY EXPORTS OF LDCs

We have already shown that proposals for commodity price supports involve two reforms: one to damp the fluctuations and the other to increase the overall price level. Euphemistically, only stabilization is mentioned in the NIEO; in negotiations, however, "stabilization" also means "support."

Stabilization alone is efficient; both buyers and sellers benefit from the improved future vision that it brings. But artificially higher prices are not efficient. They lead to surplus production and to costly and oppressive methods of control. Licenses to produce the restricted quantities become patronage plums. Price distortions are extended backward to the factors of production, which yield more in the protected areas than elsewhere; therefore, nonprotected areas are discriminated against. The protected areas lose the competitive incentives for improved efficiency. Finally, all purchasers pay the higher prices, not just the rich ones. If the two reforms could be delinked, it is probable that stablization by itself would be universally welcomed, but supports would not be.

Since primary products have high linkage with industry, they are a matter of concern to MDCs. If supports were accepted, however, this very linkage would ultimately cause them to be reversed. As LDCs industrialize, their ardor for paying higher prices themselves for the exports of their less advanced (and less efficient) neighbors would quickly cool.

It is possible to force a reform, even when it is inefficient, if the activity in question has high linkage with something desired by whoever must yield the reform, and if the proponents of reform have other leverage. Such appears to be the case with petroleum. But the appearance may be deceptive. Higher prices for depletable resources are efficient if the increase reflects future scarcity, and if conservation equalizes the present price with the time-discounted values of annual quantities to be released in the future (Williams, 1978). Some argue that the price of oil is now what it "should" be by that calculation. If so, the increase is efficient. We do not wish to join this debate, but we will make the comment that in general such calculations may be made by the market and that no monopoly or artificial support is needed.

MULTINATIONAL CORPORATIONS

The NIEO would like the MNCs to be placed under international control. An evaluation of this proposed reform depends on what kinds of controls are foreseen and how they would be implemented. The vagueness of the question increases the risk and thus decreases the likelihood of action. The fact that Latin American countries rejected World Bank intervention in their disputes with MNCs also indicates that perhaps LDCs would not be happy to yield an area of sovereignty to international supervision. Their support for international control must indicate that they envisage LDC control over the international agency, but the prospect for this is also doubtful. Although an intergovernmental commission was appointed to study international controls, the NIEO and the Charter of Economic Rights and Obligations of States imply that most controls will be national.

Four decades ago, MNCs exerted great leverage over their host governments. Military intervention was deemed moral; ignorant and sometimes illiterate dictators in host countries could sell privileges wholesale without being called to task; MNCs operated mainly in enclave-type, extractive industries; and frequently they could write their own terms.

But the balance of leverage has shifted dramatically since that time, both politically and economically. The East-West conflict enhanced for MDCs the value of alliances with LDCs. The British and French discovered that colonialism was costly, and (as with the demise of feudalism) they sought more efficient ways of maintaining trade relationships and political affiliations. The United States sought to strengthen its own "special relationship" in the Western Hemisphere and its naval influence in the Pacific. All these events curtailed the crudity with which MDC governments might intervene in LDC affairs, and as a spinoff, they shifted the balance of political leverage away from MNCs and in favor of host governments. Further leverage for LDCs occurred as economic development made their markets more attractive to MNCs engaged in manufacturing.

This increased leverage has enabled LDC governments to increase taxes on MNCs, to regulate their wages and often their prices, to restrict their repatriations of capital and earnings, and finally, to expropriate companies completely, often with compensation that is less than the book or market value of net assets. Probably these actions represent the extent of the new leverage. LDC governments have not been able to compel MNCs to share technology except on the terms of the latter, nor have they succeeded in controlling transfer prices. Because of the laxity in their own administrations, they have not been able to eliminate bribery by MNCs. Finally, expropriations have not always proceeded smoothly; sometimes postexpropriation exports are boycotted, or shipping is denied, or the MDC government attempts to influence compensation, with whatever retaliatory measures it can muster. It is doubtless in these areas that LDC governments look to the NIEO to redress grievances. Let us examine proposed reforms in terms of their efficiency.

If transfer prices occur to avoid controls on capital repatriation, they are efficient on a worldwide basis. It is the LDC-imposed controls themselves that are inefficient, for they prevent capital from moving to the point of its greatest earnings. There will be little sympathy on the part of MDCs for limiting the use of transfer prices to repatriate earnings. If, however, prices are manipulated to shift profits from one country to another, then the degree of sympathy will depend on the direction of the shift. Vernon (1971:139) argues that in terms of relative tax rates, there is usually little incentive to shift profits in either direction between MDCs and LDCs; therefore, he doubts that such shifts are significant. Kopits (1976) has surveyed the literature on the impact of taxation on MNC behavior; he concludes that there is evidence MNCs are induced to shift investments and profits in order to minimize taxes, but the quantitative studies are inconclusive.

There remains the possibility of the tax haven. Suppose a MNC wishes to export from Country X to Country Y, and suppose taxes are the same in both countries. The MNC may still export to a third country, and by underpricing may transfer its profits there. If it then reexports to Country Y, this time overpricing, it retains its profits in the third country, where the tax may be low. Reforms to prevent such transfers would be probable on an efficiency basis; both Countries X and Y would benefit. Whether they would occur then depends on the significance of this kind of subterfuge. Is there sufficient linkage so that X and Y would be concerned? Since we know of no research on this matter, we cannot offer any opinions.

The argument sometimes heard (Vaitsos, 1972), that technology should be transferred free because the marginal cost of so doing would be zero, is not accepted by MNCs. Their officials would answer that the licensing of patents is costly to them, for it diminishes their markets. There is also some doubt about the efficiency of wholesale technology transfer, since we believe (Chapter 8) that most technology is sensitive to time and place; that it needs to be adapted when moved elsewhere; and that research and development capabilities are sorely needed in LDCs. For most efficient deployment, therefore, we feel that technology should be invented (at some cost) or purchased (at some price). The East Asian countries, and particularly Japan, have received their technology mostly in this way. Ever since the wave of nationalizations in the sixties and seventies, MNCs have been seeking new relationships in LDCs, including cooperative ventures and licensing. Technology is being purchased; there is no reason to believe that instead it will soon be given away.

Should bribery be controlled by an international agency? Whether bribery is inefficient or not depends on the alternative. If a tax system and government services are otherwise lacking, bribery may be a crude but effective way to bring them into being. It may also be effective where taxes and services exist but are themselves inefficient. On the other had, bribery is not the most efficient system possible. Nor do we have ways of determining conclusively whether it fulfils its functions tolerably well or not. If bribery is *believed* by MDC governments to be more efficient than the alternatives, they will do little to control it through the home offices or parent companies of the MNCs.

In discussions of international control, LDC representatives to the intergovernmental commission have argued that controls on MNCs should be mandatory, but those on LDC governments should be voluntary (Rolston, 1979). Who, then, will bell the cat? Effective control always requires sovereignty; if it is to be undertaken by an international organization, then LDCs will have to surrender sovereignty to that organization. The U.S. government has passed laws requiring full disclosure of bribery, but it cannot on its own territory police actions that occur on another.

For all the above reasons, it appears to us unlikely that the international community can be persuaded to provide the leverage upon MNCs that LDC governments have failed to achieve at home.

THE INTERNATIONAL MONETARY SYSTEM

LDC governments will not be granted a significant (as opposed to a token) role in shaping the international monetary system in the foreseeable future, since this sytem is the keystone for MDC economic survival. Indeed, the slowness and partial nature of reform to date is explained in part by risk. But it is also risky *not* to reform the system in the face of new economic circumstances.

Although no diplomat will say so, the main reason for not expanding LDC participation is the judgment that LDC governments have not run their own monetary systems efficiently. Like a national monetary system, the international system operates efficiently if it is not overly used to deflect resources in one direction or another. Anyone suspected of wanting to change that rule will not be allowed in the game.

LDC leverage is also low because of low linkage. The world is not sufficiently integrated, nor LDC economies sufficiently strong, for MDC governments to care much about what happens to LDC currencies. Any Latin American peso may explode out of bounds, and New York will scarcely murmur. The U.S. Government has been known to bolster LDC currencies when the alternative was believed to be a vacuum susceptible of being filled by communists, as in Guatemala and Bolivia in the 1950s. France supports the currencies of certain West African countries in order to maintain her political link. Aside from these cases, MDC governments are concerned only with bolstering the currencies of one another.

THE GENERALIZED SYSTEM OF PREFERENCES

Whether GSP is efficient, compared to its alternative, depends on whether it is trade-creating or trade-diverting. The analysis is the familiar one of Viner (1950). Suppose a U.S. consumer would previously buy a product in the United States at a cost of $1. If a LDC can produce the same product for $0.90, and the duty is 20 percent, the U.S. consumer would buy at home (for $1) if no GSP is granted. With GSP, he would shift to the LDC source (and buy for $0.90), thus reducing the social cost of consumption by $0.10. This trade *creation* is efficient, compared to its alternative. But if some European country can produce the same product for $0.80 (the cost with duty is then $0.96), and if GSP causes the U.S. consumer to shift from a European source (at a social cost of $0.80) to a LDC source (at a social cost of $0.90), then the trade *diversion* has entailed an inefficiency. Baldwin and Murray (1977) have made estimates of 1971 trade diversion and trade creation caused by GSP, and these estimates have been updated to 1974–1975 by Birnberg (1979). Of the total LDC expansion of exports to the United States,[8] EEC, and Japan, 86 percent ($957 million) was attributed to trade creation, with slightly higher proportions of creation in manufacturing categories than in agricultural ones. Thus, in all likelihood, the establishment of GSP is an efficient reform.

But social efficiency alone will not cause GSP to be accepted. Leverage and linkage play their parts as well. Leverage reflects the relative influence of the gainers (LDC exporters) and losers (MDC competitors). But there are also gainers in MDCs. The same exporters who have supported reciprocal tariff reductions since the 1930s will also benefit from the international trade multiplier, as

---

[8]The U.S. GSP did not go into effect until 1976. Birnberg's estimates apply the structure of the U.S. scheme to 1974–1975 trade flows.

increased exports provide LDCs with the foreign exchange to buy more imports. In additions to all these interests, the political concerns of MDC governments must be considered. To the Europeans, these include maintenance of relationships with their former colonies. To both European countries and the United States, they include keeping LDCs in the Western alliance.

No one has measured these various efficiencies, leverages, and linkages exactly. But the fact that GSP has been accepted by both Europe and the United States would indicate that in the subjective judgment of decision-makers, they balance out positively. If concessions have not gone further than they have, it can only be that this net positive judgment also has its limits.

DEPENDENCY AND REALÖKONOMIE

We have suggested the determinants of probability of a proposed reform. Reforms do not occur because of a previous finding that they are moral; morality emerges later. The question now arises: Why do LDC governments make moral appeals for reforms that will likely fail because they are inefficient, or are insufficiently linked to the interests of those who would concede them, or which LDC governments lack the leverage to effect?

There are three possible answers. One is that they do not accept our theory of reform and morality. They may believe that on the contrary, morality comes first and reform follows. The second is that, accepting our theory, they make different assessments of efficiency, linkage, and leverage. They may believe that controls on the repatriation of capital are efficient, and bribery is not. The third—to which we subscribe—is that they are only now learning how the international system works. Having been excluded from it for so many years by colonial status, distance, or lack of development, their government officials have much to learn on what will succeed and what will not. They do not know how to assess their own leverage; they sometimes underestimate and sometimes overestimate it.

For many years, LDC economists and diplomats have been proclaiming the weaknesses of their countries. During the 1950s and 60s, the Economic Commission for Latin America (ECLA) formulated a number of theories demonstrating how the development of Latin America depends on forces outside Latin American control. The alleged secular decline in terms of trade is the best known of these theories. Both demand and supply of Latin American exports were declared (without much empirical support) to be inelastic and factor mobility low; hence, it was argued, there was little domestic influence over prices. Inflation was believed to be caused by unchangeable structures (Chapter 14). According to the theories, development could not occur without inflation; inflation engendered balance-of-payments deficits; and thus development was dependent on foreign aid. LDCs were referred to as "peripheral" to "the center." A selection of articles covering these theories is published in UNECLA, 1970.

The linear descendent of the ECLA theories is doubtless *dependency* theory, which emerged during the 1960s. Dos Santos (1968:7; 1970:231) defined dependence as follows:

> By dependence we mean a situation in which the economy of certain coun-
> tries is conditioned by the development and expansion of another economy
> to which the former is subjected. The relation of interdependence between
> two or more economies, and between these and world trade, assumes the
> form of dependence when some countries (the dominant ones) can expand
> and can be self-sustaining, while other countries (the dependent ones) can
> do this only as a reflection of that expansion, which can have either a
> positive or negative effect on their immediate development.

We believe we understand the essence of dependency theory, which is that
MDCs have considerable economic and political leverage over LDCs. But we
have difficulty with the dependency literature. Often we wade through pages
of rhetoric, full of pejorative terms such as capitalists, bourgeoisie, imperialists,
serfs, and subjugation, but precise definitions escape us. Sometimes dependence
seems to mean that a large portion of GDP is marketed abroad or that many
goods must be imported. Sometimes it means an undue reliance on primary-
product exports, at other times a high ratio of foreign to domestic investment.
At all times, one senses the feeling of despair, behind which somewhere lurks
the proposition that violent revolution may be the only way out.

We recognize that leverages cannot be measured precisely. However, they
can be described and subjectively evaluated. We find little in the dependency
literature to hint that LDC governments possess any leverages at all, or any
influence whatsoever over their fates. While we can accept that MDCs have
more leverages over LDCs than vice versa, nevertheless the increasing abilities
of LDC governments to manage their economies, to save and to invest, to
determine their priorities, and to expropriate, control, or set terms for MNCs
leads us to believe that certain leverages are on their side. Since small countries
such as Belgium import and export large percentages of GDP; since some exporters of primary products are rich, such as Australia and New Zealand; and
since some rich countries depend vitally on decisions made elsewhere, such as
the United States vis-à-vis OPEC, it is hard for us to draw the line between who
is dependent and who is not.

Our own preference is to examine the efficiency of whatever reforms may
be proposed, the linkages of these reforms to the economies of MDCs, and the
leverages of LDCs required for their implementation, as well as ways to increase
efficiency, linkages, and leverages. Such *Realökonomie* appears to us to be a
more promising strategy than declaring one's weaknesses before international
tribunals, or proclaiming that "I am poor because you are rich." It is in this
context that we will examine the economic policies of LDCs (Chapter 14).

BIBLIOGRAPHY

American Friends Service Committee, 1976:
   The United States and Latin America Today, Philadelphia, Pennsylvania.
Bairoch, Paul, 1975:
   The Economic Development of the Third World Since 1900, Berkeley, California,
   University of California Press.

Balassa, B., 1978:
"The 'New Protectionism' and the International Economy," *Journal of World Trade Law*, 12:5, September/October, 409–36.

Baldwin, R. E., and Murray, T., 1977:
"MFN Tariff Reductions and LDC Benefits under GSP," *Economic Journal*, 87:345, March, 30–46.

Barnet, Richard J., and Müller, Ronald E., 1974:
Global Reach: The Power of the Multinational Corporations, New York, Simon and Schuster.

Birnberg, T. B., 1979:
"Trade Reform Options: Economic Effects on Developing and Developed Countries," in Cline, W. R., ed., *Policy Alternatives for a New International Economic Order*, New York, Praeger, 215–83.

Boulding, Kenneth E., 1973:
The Economy of Love and Fear: A Preface to Grants Economics, Belmont, California, Wadsworth.

Bozeman, Adda B., 1976:
Conflict in Africa, Princeton, N.J., Princeton University Press.

Cline, W. R., 1980:
"International Economic Reform and Income Distribution," *CEPAL Review*, April.

Commission of the European Communities, 1975:
"APC-EEC Convention of Lomé" (text of the Lomé Convention), *The Courier*, No. 31, special issue, Brussels.

Dos Santos, Theotonio, 1968:
"La Crisis de la Teoría del Desarrollo y las Relaciones de Dependencia en América Latina," Boletín del CESO, Santiago, Chile.

Dos Santos, Theotonio, 1970:
"The Structure of Dependence," *American Economic Review*, vol. 60, No. 2, May.

Ellsworth, P. T., 1956:
"The Terms of Trade Between Primary Producing and Industrial Countries," *Inter-American Economic Affairs*, Summer.

Finger, J. M., 1974:
"GATT Tariff Concessions and the Exports of Developing Countries," *Economic Journal*, 84:335, September, 566–75.

Finger, J. M., 1976:
"Effects of the Kennedy Round Tariff Concessions on the Exports of Developing Countries," *Economic Journal*, 86:341, March, 87–95.

Garnier, G.; Osborn, T. N.; Arias, F.; and Lecón, R., 1979:
The Decision-Making Relationships Between U.S. Multinationals and Their Mexican Affiliates," in Poulson, B. W., and Osborn, T. N., eds., *U.S.–Mexico Economic Relations*, Boulder, Colorado, Westview Press.

Helleiner, G. K., 1979.
"The New Industrial Protectionism and the Developing Countries," *Trade and Development* No. 1, Spring, 15–37.

ILO, 1976:
Wages and Working Conditions in Multinational Enterprises, Geneva, International Labor Organization (ISBN 92-2-101475-4).

International Monetary Fund, 1977a:
Annual Report, 1977, Washington, D.C.

International Monetary Fund, 1977b:
IMF Survey, September 19.

International Monetary Fund, various dates:
International Financial Statistics, tables of financial data on countries reporting to IMF, published monthly, Washington, D.C.

IMF Survey, 4–9–79:
  "Retreat from Liberal Trade Becomes Clearer as More Restrictive Practices Take Effect," Washington, D.C., International Monetary Fund.
Jain, Shail, 1975:
  Size Distribution of Income: A Compilation of Data, Washington, D.C., World Bank.
Jaksch, H. J., 1977:
  "Export and Import Prices of the Developing Areas of the Sixties," Weltwirtschaftliches Archiv, 113:3, 501–15.
Kindleberger, Charles P., 1956:
  The Terms of Trade: A European Case Study, Cambridge, Mass., Technology Press (M.I.T.) and Wiley.
Kopits, George F., 1976:
  "Taxation and Multinational Firm Behavior: A Critical Survey," IMF Staff Papers, November.
Kravis, I.B.; Heston, A.; and Summers, R., 1978:
  International Comparisons of Real Product and Purchasing Power, Baltimore, Md., Johns Hopkins University for the World Bank.
Lewis, Paul, NYT, 4–13–79:
  "Trade Pact Ceremony Boycotted," New York Times.
Lewis, W. Arthur, 1952:
  "World Production, Prices, and Trade, 1870–1950," The Manchester School of Economic and Social Studies, Vol. XX.
Meier, Gerald, 1968:
  The International Economics of Development, New York, Harper and Row.
Mill, John Stuart, 1844:
  "Essays on Some Unsettled Questions of Political Economy," written 1829–30 but not published until 1844; reprinted (with extensions) in Principles of Political Economy, Book 3, Chapter 18.
NYT, 1–16–79:
  "Moving Toward Freer Trade" (editorial), New York Times.
NYT, 7–4–78
  "Developing Bloc Irked on Trade," New York Times.
Nurkse, Ragnar, 1961:
  Equilibrium and Growth in the World Economy: Economic Essays, edited by Gottfried Haberler and Robert M. Stern, Cambridge, Mass., Harvard University Press.
Nyerere, Julius K., 1976:
  "The Economic Challenge: Dialogue or Confrontation?" International Development Review, Vol. 18, No. 1.
Pinto, Anibal, and Kñakal, Jan, 1973:
  América Latina y el Cambio en la Economía Mundial, Lima Peru: Instituto de Estudios Peruanos.
Powelson, John P., 1979:
  A Select Bibliography on Economic Development, Boulder, Colorado, Westview Press.
Powelson, John P., 1978:
  "The LDCs and the Terms of Trade," Economic Impact, No. 22, (Published by U.S. International Communications Agency, Washington, D.C.).
Powelson, John P., 1977a:
  "The Balance Sheet on Multinational Corporations in Less Developed Countries," Cultures et Developpement (University of Louvain, Belgium), vol. 9, No. 3.
Powelson, John P., 1977b:
  "The Oil-Price Increase: Impacts on Industrialized and Less Developed Countries," Journal of Energy and Development, Autumn.
Powelson, John P., 1970:
  "The Terms of Trade Again," Inter-American Economic Affairs, Spring.

Prebisch, Raúl, 1962:
  "The Economic Development of Latin America and its Principal Problems," *Economic Bulletin for Latin America*, Vol. VII, No. 1, February.
Republic of Kenya, 1974:
  Development Plan, 1974–78, Nairobi, Government Printing Office.
Rolston, Rick, 1979:
  "Code of Conduct for TNCs?" *In and Around the U.N.*, New York, Quaker Office at the United Nations, March.
Schlote, W., 1962:
  Entwicklung und Struckturnwandlungen des englischen Aussenhandels von 1700 bis zur Gegenwart, Jena, 1938. English translation by W. O. Henderson and W. H. Chaloner, *British Overseas Trade from 1700 to the 1930s*, Oxford.
Smith, G. W., 1979:
  "The External Debt Prospects of the Non-Oil Exporting Developing Countries," in Cline, W. R., ed., *Policy Alternatives for A New International Economic Order*, New York, Praeger, for Overseas Development Council.
Stern, E., and Tims, W., 1975:
  "The Relative Bargaining Strength of the Developing Countries," *American Journal of Agricultural Economics*, 57:2, May, 225–32.
UNECLA, 1970:
  Development Problems in Latin America, Santiago and New York, United Nations Economic Commission for Latin America.
United Nations, 1950:
  The Economic Development of Latin America and its Principal Problems, New York, Economic Commission for Latin America.
United Nations, 1974a:
  Declaration of the Establishment of a New International Economic Order, U.N. Resolution 3201 (S–VI), 1 May, 1974.
United Nations, 1974b:
  Charter of Economic Rights and Duties of States, U.N. Resolution 3281 (XXIX), 12 December, 1974.
United States, 1975:
  International Economic Report of the President, Washington, D.C., Government Printing Office, March.
U.S. Department of State, 1979:
  Multinational Trade Negotiations, Current Policy Statement No. 56, Bureau of Public Affairs, Office of Public Communication, Washington, D.C., February.
Vaitsos, Constantino, 1972:
  "Patents Revisited: Their Functions in Developing Countries," *Journal of Development Studies*, Vol. 9.
Vernon, Raymond, 1971:
  Sovereignty at Bay: The Multinatinal Spread of U.S. Enterprises, New York, Basic Books.
Viner, Jacob, 1950:
  The Customs Union Issue, New York, Carnegie Endowment for International Peace.
Weintraub, S., 1979:
  "The New International Economic Order: The Beneficiaries," *World Development*, 7:3, 247–58.
Williams, Stephen F., 1978:
  "Running Out: The Problem of Exhaustible Resources," University of Chicago Law School, *Journal of Legal Studies*, January.
World Bank, 1976:
  World Tables, 1976, Washington, D.C.
World Bank, 1978:
  World Debt Tables, Washington, D.C.

14

GOVERNMENT AND ECONOMIC POLICY

According to the doctrines of benevolent despotism ... the chief instrumentality for the improvement of society was not private philanthropy but the state. The government had primary responsibility for preparing the way for that golden age which, in the opinion of many intellectuals, awaited mankind.
"HISTORY OF GERMANY: ERA OF FREDERICK THE GREAT," ENCYCLOPEDIA BRITANNICA, 1974, MACROPEDIA, 8:100.

His overriding concern today ... is with the suffocating power of the state, not only in Mexico, where one party had been in power for 50 years, and in the Communist countries, but also in the Western nations, where he sees "bureaucratic capitalism" adopting the vices of "bureaucratic socialism."
ALAN RIDING, REFERRING TO MEXICAN POET OCTAVIO PAZ, NEW YORK TIMES, MAY 3, 1979

Government's impact on economic development has never, to our knowledge, been examined in a scientific manner. On the one hand, it has been treated ideologically by those who view intervention as desirable or undesirable per se. On the other hand, it has been assumed without question by modern economists, who routinely enter policy variables into their calculus. But we do not know of anyone who has related the degree of *overall* government intervention with the rate of growth or the distribution of income for any significant period.

"Degree" of government intervention is at once a difficult and a subjective concept. We think of all the ways in which the government may influence the economic process, such as through number, type, and total amount of taxes; regulation of the money supply and exchange rates; restrictions on foreign trade; control over prices and wages; direct ownership and operation of productive assets; licensing; legal capacity to make direct decisions on production by non-government units; or the sheer weight of government spending (in proportion to the GDP). Long before the nation-state, all these interventions had been practiced by tribal chiefs, emperors, tyrants, kings, nobles, and military officials.

"Degree of government intervention" is a vague-bordered set, for three reasons. One is that its elements (among them policy) can only be weighted subjectively. The second is that many instruments cannot themselves be adequately measured: licensing, for example, where one license is more restrictive than another. The third—and most problematic of all—is that intervention is differentially enforced. Some instruments may be on the books only; others may be applied against political adversaries but not against friends; and still others may affect all alike. Nevertheless, the fact that one control can be substituted for another, and that they combine to effect the government's leverage on other sectors, make "overall degree of intervention" a useful concept.

Over the centuries, the degree of intervention has fluctuated widely, geographically and temporally. After a period of "relative liberalism" in the nineteenth century, it has increased in Western nations—sporadically, irregularly, but also dramatically. At first, the reason was bigness. Some enterprises, such as utilities and railroads, found economies in bigness. Where bigness meant monopoly, it became public policy to require that economies be shared with the general public through regulated prices. As big units began to impinge on one another—such as labor versus industry—the government became arbiter, balancer, and protector of the public. Finally, with the great depression, government regulation was extended to the macroeconomy, to promote its stability.

Government intervention was historically derived in the Western world for numerous reasons. Even as intervention was emerging, Western countries were applying controls so that government power might not be abused. Although these controls have not been completely effective, each new control has been subject to review, by being spread among different agencies, by beig audited, or by passing political tests in elected parliaments. The slow emergence of these institutions, combined with the growing productivity (hence economic leverage) of poorer units, has thus provided a certain redressing of political imbalance.

The same has not been so with LDCs. Nations have burst forth over decades rather than over centuries. Many possess trappings of the parliamentary democracy that the Western world worked out by bitter compromise. But the suddenness of their creation, in the face of pervasive poverty and low productivity of poorer units, has created an elite possessed of modern instruments of political control with few checks on their ability to use them. It is almost as if Richard II had overnight acquired a twentieth-century army, electronic communications, and a modern banking structure with which to face the Peasant's Revolt of 1381!

But the picture is not really so bleak. Modern equipment does not ensure the loyalty of the army; the instancy of communication does not guarantee that the "right" messages will be sent; and the central bank has little impact on non-monetized sectors. The most effective defense of the poor may well be the same as it was in Richard II's time: their ability to evade governmental regulations.

Yet the problem is not so simply dissected. Often elites are genuinely concerned for their nations' development, are benevolent toward the poor, and put forth their policies in good faith. Even though the policies may not cater to special interests, however, they may still reflect the inexperience of the leaders, who—not able to predict well what will work and what will not—jump from one experiment to another. Their ability to do so is enhanced by their lack of need to consult disparate interests. Both capriciousness and differential enforcement increase uncertainty and hence risk; they may thus retard new enterprise and investment.

IMPORT-SUBSTITUTION INDUSTRIALIZATION[1]

In the early post-World War II years, development was usually equated with industrialization and infrastructure. The World Bank specialized in loans for electric power. Planning departments in search of projects would study the list of imports, for here were goods for which the local market had been tested. Policies to protect and promote the new industries were formulated. We have already referred to the impact of these policies on technological dualism (Chapter 8). Now we will consider them in greater detail.

Thirty years of experience have mellowed the enthusiasm for import-substitution industrialization (ISI). During the mid-seventies, observers began to suspect that ISI was leading not only to dualism, but to selection of the wrong industries: those in which industrial countries had a comparative advantage. Once firms reached a certain size, they would have to export in order to capture further economies of scale. With little or no comparative advantage, and having been protected and subsidized, they were socially inefficient, and they could not compete abroad unless their protection were continued—an action by which LDCs would subsidize the rest of the world.

These results were largely confirmed by a study conducted by the National Bureau of Economic Research (NBER) and summarized by Bhagwati (1978) and Kreuger (1978). The major conclusion was that economic distortions of ISI have been a principal cause of slow growth in LDCs. A ten-country comparison shows that periods of import liberalization are associated with export expansion and accelerated growth. ISI distortions harm exports, slow agriculture, and reduce overall economic efficiency.

INTEREST AND CREDIT

The bias toward ISI affects the credit market in two demonstrable ways (Tun Wai, 1977). First, lending institutions are often unavailable to small-scale producers, both farm and nonfarm. Second, interest rates are kept lower in the

---

[1]Richard Stock, graduate student at the University of Colorado, contributed information on ISI to this and succeeding sections (Stock, 1980).

"formal" sector (where ISI occurs) than in the "informal" one. Sometimes real rates (nominal rates less inflation rates) are negative. We will add a third way. With rates artificially low, scarce funds must be rationed. The rationing system is often informal; both personal relationships and government policy may lead to credit being differentially extended in favor of ISI producers. This third way cannot be demonstrated, but our informal information holds that it operates frequently.

In studying the organized credit markets in all countries, Tun Wai (1972) found the nominal rates in LDCs to be about the same or only slightly higher than those in MDCs (Table 14–1); prime or secured loans would be in the neighborhood of 6 to 9 percent. Higher rates for Latin America probably reflect those few countries with exceptionally high rates of inflation. Tun Wai (1977) also found much higher rates in the unorganized (or "informal") money markets—in the neighborhood of 25 to 50 percent (Table 14–2). Credit in the unorganized market is usually supplied by "money lenders," or rich local persons who have some personal relationship with the borrowers; they are sometimes called "patrons," a term harking back to its feudal ancestry. In suggesting reasons for the differential, Tun Wai cited those by Bottomley (1975)—the opportunity cost of funds, the premium for administering the loan, the premium for risk, and monopoly profit—and those by Long (1973)—the scarcity of capital, high administrative costs, a high default rate, and the seasonal character of demand for agricultural credit. Tun Wai saw only weak links between the unorganized and organized markets, the former operating on supply-demand principles and the latter by administrative fiat.

The discount rates (Table 14–1) offered by LDC central banks do not serve as credit rationers where loans are made more ad hoc than impartially on demand. Arbitrary lending decisions may explain the low mean rate (4.84) for African countries in 1970, compared to the world mean (5.89).

A low interest rate is a way of subsidizing capital. Combined with differential access, this policy promotes ISI and discriminates against more employment-creating types of investment. It also explains why multinational corporations may prefer local sources of funds. Why bring money from London, which can earn (say) 10 percent there, if loans are locally available for (say) 6 percent? Those who criticize MNCs for their failure to bring in more funds from abroad might well direct their attention to LDC credit policies.

TRADE POLICY

ISI has also been promoted through the trade policies of LDCs. The general pattern, observed by several authors (Balassa and Associates, 1971 and Williams College, various dates), includes heavy protection for consumer goods, intermediate protection for raw materials or semiprocessed goods, and low protection for capital goods. These tariff policies are often reinforced by quantitative or exchange restrictions on imports, and by licensing.

Earlier methods of measuring the height of tariffs become no longer appro-

TABLE 14–1
Selected Median and Mean Interest Rates, 1963 and 1970
(percent per annum)

Area	Year	Discount Rate	Government Bond Yield	One-Year Deposit Rate	Prime or Secured Loans
WORLD MARKETS[a]					
Median	1963	3.50	4.49	3.77	5.30
	1970	6.00	7.56	6.15	8.00
Mean	1963	3.69	4.67	3.80	5.05
	1970	5.89	7.49	6.00	8.08
AFRICA					
Median	1963	3.50	5.38[b]	3.00	6.00
	1970	3.50	5.88[c]	3.69	6.50
Mean	1963	3.88	5.38[b]	3.21	6.07
	1970	4.84	6.06	3.76	6.52
LATIN AMERICA					
Median	1963	5.50	6.95[d]	5.50[e]	7.50[f]
	1970	6.30	8.25	7.00	10.50
Mean	1963	6.12	6.70[d]	6.25[e]	8.88[f]
	1970	8.21	9.79	10.29	15.33
ASIA					
Median	1963	4.75	4.68[g]	4.00	7.50
	1970	5.75	5.50	7.00	8.30
Mean	1963	6.28	5.13[g]	5.66	7.98
	1970	8.04	5.73	9.38	10.54
MIDDLE EAST					
Median	1963	5.00	4.64[h]	4.50	7.00[i]
	1970	6.00	4.84	4.75	8.00
Mean	1963	5.00	4.64[h]	4.31	8.00[i]
	1970	6.28	5.28	5.35	8.27

[a]Seven countries: United States, United Kingdom, France, West Germany, Japan, Netherlands, and Switzerland.
[b]Only two countries: Sudan and Mauritius.
[c]Four countries: Sudan, Nigeria, Mauritius, and Ethiopia.
[d]Five countries: Costa Rica, Jamaica, Paraguay, Peru, and Uruguay.
[e]Eight countries: Costa Rica, El Salvador, Honduras, Jamaica, Mexico, Paraguay, Peru, and Uruguay.
[f]Seven countries: Costa Rica, El Salvador, Guatemala, Guyana, Jamaica, Mexico, and Peru.
[g]Five countries: Ceylon (now Sri Lanka), India, Malaysia, Pakistan, and Thailand.
[h]Only one country: Turkey.
[i]Only three countries: Iraq, Turkey, and Yemen.

SOURCE: Tun Wai (1972). From *Fiscal Intermediaries and National Savings in Developing Countries* by U Tun Wai. Copyright © 1972 by Praeger Publishers, Inc. Reprinted by permission of Praeger Publishers.

priate. Even these methods had been imprecise, for reasons cited by Kindleberger (1963:324):

> It is evidently a mistake to compare customs revenues with total imports, as is frequently done, because prohibitive tariffs eliminate all imports in given categories, and produce no revenue . . . For comparison of the tariffs of two countries, one can either weight by free-trade values, which must

TABLE 14–2
Excess of Noninstitutional Over Institutional Rates of Interest in Certain Countries (percentage points), 1948–1951 and 1968–1971

Region and Country	1948–1951	1968–1971
AFRICA		
Nigeria	41.50	23.50
ASIA		
India	25.00	18.75
Indonesia	38.00	25.00
Pakistan	24.75	18.50
Philippines	52.50	19.20
South Vietnam	67.00	15.00
Sri Lanka	11.75	8.00
Thailand	27.50	16.00
LATIN AMERICA		
Colombia	14.00	11.50
Honduras	25.00	31.00
Mexico	49.00	43.00
MIDDLE EAST		
Jordan	38.00	11.60
Lebanon	18.20	6.00
Average for all countries	33.24	19.00

SOURCE: Tun Wai (1977:307). Reprinted by permission of the Banca Nazionale del Lavoro.

be hypothetical since there is no free trade, or average ad valorem tariffs on an unweighted basis, which means assigning equal weights to each tariff category.

Balassa and Associates (1971) noted a further reason why measures of this nature do not give a reasonable picture of the amount of protection. Effective protection, they argued, should be related to *value added*; duties paid on import components should be subtracted from the *nominal* duties on the final product. Effective Protection is defined as ". . . the percentage excess of domestic value added . . . over . . . world market value added," (Balassa *et al.*, 1971:4). Suppose raw material imports with a value of 20 and a duty of 50 percent (or 10) are used to produce a finished good that sells for 180. If the finished good is protected by a tariff of 80 percent, so that competing imports would cost 100 in the world market, effective protection would be calculated as follows:

	At home (with protection)	Abroad (without protection)
Sales price of finished good	180	100
Less cost of imported materials	30	20
Value added	150	80

The rate of effective protection is (150–80)/80, or 87.5 percent of value added abroad. In this example, the domestic price is presumed to exceed the world price by the amount of nominal tariff. If, however, the rate is so high that local demand does not "use it all up," then the nominal tariff is not a good measure. In the example, the nominal duty might be 100 percent instead of 80 percent, but demand might not be sufficient to raise the domestic price to 200; the product might still sell for 180. If so, the effective protection remains the same as calculated above.

Balassa and Associates also adjust for exchange rate. Any tariff restricts imports. The decreased demand for imports causes the exchange rate to appreciate (compared to free trade) in whatever amount is necessary to reduce exports and balance the international accounts. *Net* effective protection is effective protection in which currency is converted at a shadow (hypothetical) exchange rate that would be simulated in a free-trade model.

Protection of imports discriminates against exports. First, it may be necessary to pay duties on the import components of exportable goods, which (not offset by duties on the final product) yield *negative* effective-protection rates. Second, the positive effective protection of imports acts as a subsidy, enabling ISI products to bid factors of production away from exportables. This bidding increases factor prices, thus increasing the cost of exportables.

All the "successful" countries of Europe and East Asia (Chapters 15 and 16), except the People's Republic of China, have developed their economies through strong export encouragement, and even P.R. China is now shifting to an export orientation. Not only does ISI violate comparative advantage by causing LDCs to produce at home those goods whose factor requirements (much capital, little labor) correspond to the factor availabilities of industrialized countries, but as the other of the coin, it discriminates against those goods (exportables) whose factor requirements conform to domestic availabilities.

Balassa's associates studied effective protection in six LDCs (Brazil, Chile, Mexico, West Malaysia, Pakistan, and the Philippines) and one MDC (Norway). In all the LDCs, they found conditions similar to those described above. Bueno (pp. 199–200) reached the following conclusions for Mexico: (1) "there is relatively little correspondence between the levels of nominal and effective protection;" (2) "a large diversity of rates of both nominal and effective tariff protection (provides) . . . evidence for a lack of a consistent set of criteria in setting tariff rates;" and (3) "effective rates of protection are higher than nominal rates on manufactured goods but lower on primary products, (reflecting) escalation in nominal tariffs from lower to higher degrees of fabrication." Even so, Bueno found that (4) "net effective protection is on the average lower than in most other developing countries and there is less discrimination against exports." He found a "growing concern for the high cost of . . . import-substituting industrialization . . . and the limits to which it is subject." When one of the present authors discussed this situation with a senior official in the Bank of Mexico (who does not want to be named), we found the same concern, compounded by a certain despair over the political probabilities of dislodging the protected from their vested positions.

For West Malaysia, Power (p. 219) found "little discrimination among the principal sectors of the Malayan economy . . . (but) a bias in favor of import substitution and against exporting in the individual sectors." For Brazil, Bergsman and Malan reported (p. 130) that protection "strongly favored production for the domestic market, and discriminated against exports during the postwar period." Jeanneret summed up Chile as entailing "a substantial degree of discrimination among economic activities, against exporting, as well as against imports" (p. 167). In Pakistan, Lewis and Guisinger discovered (p. 258) that "the average net effective protection of manufacturing industries was about 100 percent," and in the Philippines, Power reported that exports were "the most heavily penalized group" (p. 284).

Only in Norway did the results differ significantly from these. Balassa and Munthe found that for 57 production categories in 1954, nominal import duties averaged only 9.84 percent, while effective protection averaged 16.46 percent (p. 305). After studying the products individually, they concluded that "the results show little discrimination among economic activities, in favor of import substitution, or against exports. The adoption of a liberal trade policy has in turn had beneficial effects on the development of an efficient manufacturing sector in Norway" (p. 311).

INFLATION

The potential of inflation for diverting real resources from one use to another makes it a candidate policy for ISI. Either by direct control over lending or by concessionary terms, LDC governments may make credit differentially available to ISI industries. Obviously, those with preferential access to credit are the gainers from inflation. Since these policies belong to a "grey" (semilegitimate) area, their use cannot be confirmed. But the fact that credit has been directly or differentially allocated, and that ISI has been widespread, would make the link likely.

The proposition that LDCs have been more inflationary than MDCs does not go undisputed. Taking *average* rates of inflation over countries, Adekunle (1968:531) found that the annual rate for LDCs, 1949–1965, was 9.89 percent, compared to 3.70 percent for MDCs. However, by removing six high-inflation LDCs (Korea, 53.81 percent; Bolivia, 44.00 percent; Chile, 32.57 percent; Brazil, 31.57 percent; Argentina, 28.28 percent; and Uruguay, 19.24 percent), he lowered the rate for the remaining LDCs to 3.63 percent, which approximately equals that of MDCs. Before 1965, therefore, it would seem that the reputation of LDCs for monetary "irresponsibility" was the product of only a few countries, the remainder being as "responsible" as the MDCs.

The mid-fifties and early sixties were a period of relative price stability in most industrialized countries. The worldwide acceleration of inflation began in the late sixties and continued throughout the seventies and on into the eighties. Using data from *International Financial Statistics* (May, 1978), we calculated the annual average rates of inflation for all countries with consumer-price indices available for a recent ten-year period (for most, 1967–1977). Of these, 27 LDCs (or 34 percent of the total of 79) had rates of inflation less than

10 percent, while 17 out of 20 (or 85 percent) of MDCs performed similarly. The remaining 52 LDCs (66 percent), but only three MDCs (15 percent), exceeded 10 percent. No countries showed rates between 30 and 50 percent during the period, but three LDCs had rates above 50 percent (Argentina, 55.96 percent; Chile, 112.30 percent; and Uruguay, 62.09 percent). It would appear, therefore, that the inflation of the seventies accelerated more in LDCs than in MDCs.

The structuralist theory, which emerged during the fifties, no doubt reinforced the reputation of LDCs for inflation. It is perhaps no coincidence that this theory originated in Chile, which has been persistently in the high-inflation group. But it caught on in other Latin American countries and has been associated with ECLA doctrine (Economic Commission for Latin America).

This theory is best expounded by Sunkel (1958) and Pinto (1960, 1973); an explanation in English is found in Grunwald (1961). Briefly, it runs as follows. Suppose a LDC possesses unemployed factors of production, which might increase industrial output by (say) 10 percent, provided bank loans are made to appropriate firms. Because of rigidities in feudal agriculture, it is impossible to increase the output of foodstuffs. As urban industrial workers receive wages based on the new credit, they demand more food. With the food supply inelastic, farm prices rise. Higher food prices lead to demands for higher wages, which in turn increase the costs of industry. If the central bank refuses to supply the necessary credit, the inflation will of course be stopped, but so will the opportunity for increased industrial output. Thus development that is physically possible would be arbitrarily stopped by central banks insisting on monetary stability.

In addition to agriculture, the supply of exports is cited as inelastic. Most Latin American exports are foodstuffs or minerals. Mines cannot be excavated quickly nor without great cost. Even if they were, the foreign demand is perceived to be inelastic. As the new urban industries require imported inputs, exports cannot be expanded sufficiently to acquire additional foreign exchange. Hence a balance-of-payments deficit is unavoidable.

The imbalance would stop only as development occurs (the structuralists continue). "Only through economic development can the economy be made more flexible and strengthened, so that it becomes less prone to inflation. If growth were slowed down in an attempt to avoid inflation, the day would be postponed when the economy could be developed with less strain and thus less danger of inflation" (ECLA 1962:26).

The structuralist theory was at once opposed by the monetarist school (Campos, 1961), which was frequently associated with the International Monetary Fund because of its advocacy of stabilization. This school argued that excessive inflation would cause investment to be distorted into inflation-protected areas, such as luxury construction, rather than the nitty-gritty of development, such as textile mills. The inevitable balance-of-payments deficits could not be financed forever, and the development solution forseen by the structuralists would not be realized. There is no dispute with the concept of bottlenecks, but they must be resolved in other ways than inflation.

As more data were accumulated during the fifties, the relationship between inflation and development became empirical. Comparing rates of growth (GDP per capita) with rates of inflation for 44 LDCs, for varying periods, Tun Wai (1959) found that "the rate of growth was higher when the rate of inflation was lower." To this finding, he attached the usual statistical qualifications associated with the small number of countries and the scattered years for which data were available. No further comparisons have to our knowledge been made, perhaps because they are not necessary. An informal scan of many countries would yield so many different combinations of inflation with and without growth that the case for no consistent pattern could easily be made.

Concerns about elasticities of supply and demand for LDC exports have been shown to be unfounded. Cohen and Sisler (1971) have examined the growth rate and composition of LDC exports to the EEC, US, Japan, and USSR during the 1960s. They discovered that the export earnings of nonpetroleum exporting LDCs rose at a rate of over 5 percent annually in real terms, led by manufacturing exports, which grew at 15 percent. These trends have continued through the 1970s (Yeats, 1979), with manufactured exports increasingly in the forefront despite the constraints of the energy crisis (Loehr, 1980). The structuralist idea that supply inelasticities limit export expansion does not appear well founded. Indeed, the NBER studies (Krueger 1978, and Bhagwati 1978) give the distinct impression that supply rigidities were self imposed.

The structuralist-monetarist controversy was never resolved; it simply vanished from the literature. Possibly it is no more than a historical oddity in the evolution of development thought. It is now generally accepted that inflation is associated with pathological events whose roots run far deeper than the need for economic development.

While we do not wish to join the debate on the causes of inflation, we offer a few comments. Inflation *always* originates because some unit (with monetary access) diverts resources from the channels that would be chosen by the market or by "legitimate" taxes. Many rulers of preindustrial times (such as the later Roman emperors, Henry VIII, and Suleyman I) debased their currencies when they were unable to persuade or coerce their subjects to pay the taxes to finance their wars. Present-day LDC governments have looked upon credit creation as a means to finance development projects in the public sector. The diversion may not be successful, for discriminated groups sometimes have their defenses (they may go to the bank, too).

Let us define the market, plus taxes (with the consent of the taxed), subsidies, and public goods, as the "legitimate" means of allocating resources. To qualify inflation as "illegitimate" then reflects its uncertain nature. Resources are "legitimately" allocated to those who produce them, according to the laws of marginal productivity; these allocations are adjusted by socially-approved redistributions. "Illegitimate" redistributions occur through administrative fiat, which favors those who have greater access to credit than others.

Only as the future price index is predictable equally by all, only as all have equal access to the bank (in proportion to their previous asset holdings), only as financial assets and liabilities are indexed to a representative price index (if there is one) as prices rise daily (and not at the end of the month) can we project that inflation will have no effect on the distribution of resources. If these rare events had all occurred, there would have been no inflation in the first place. If we agree, for classical reasons, that the market is an efficient allocator of resources (subject to socially-approved redistributions), then inflation can only lead to inefficiencies.

EXCHANGE POLICY

Exchange policies of LDCs are multimotivated. In the postwar period, LDCs have adjusted these policies more frequently and more abruptly than have MDCs. They have introduced multiple rates and quantity restrictions and have devalued in answer to inflation and reserve shortages, in cases where MDCs might more readily employ monetary and fiscal policies (de Vries 1968:571). One even detects a certain ad hoc nature, in that LDC policies have responded more to immediate exigencies than to any long-term program such as ISI. The country studies in the NBER project mentioned above indicate that multiple exchange rates and quantitative restrictions in most cases were originally responses to balance of payments crises. Only later were they perceived as tools for ISI.

The following strategy to promote ISI appears to apply to many LDCs. A government allows ISI industries to buy exchange more easily than others; at the same time it overvalues the currency so that those same industries may import their supplies and capital goods more cheaply.

It is impossible objectively to determine whether a currency is overvalued or not. Purchasing power parity comparisons are not valid because of transportation costs and nontradable goods (including services). De Vries (1968) has argued against the "conventional wisdom" that LDC currencies are generally overvalued, by demonstrating that over a nineteen-year period (1948–1967) their devaluations have been as great as their internal inflations. The NBER studies indicate that restriction and liberalization move in phases, where phases are initiated by a need to respond to specific problems such as balance of payments difficulties, or by changes in governments of different philosophies.

But the conventional wisdom may yet be right if the devaluations always lag behind the price increases. Bhagwat and Onitsuka (1974:426) show that "especially in large, discrete exchange rate changes, the currency is apt to have been overvalued in the immediate predevaluation period." Let us project the following scenario. A LDC sets an exchange rate that clears the international accounts (neither overvalued nor undervalued); a subsequent inflation leads to a balance-of-payments deficit (the rate is therefore overvalued); the currency is devalued so that the international accounts again clear; and the process starts anew. The rate is therefore neither overvalued nor undervalued only after the devaluations; at all other times it is overvalued. A spot comparison at the beginning and end of the period (taken right after devaluations) would not reveal that the currency was overvalued, but at most dates chosen randomly during the period, it would have been.

In an earlier study, de Vries (1965) found that multiple exchange rates had been used by LDCs for a variety of purposes, such as "holding down external deficits, redistributing internal income, and checking inflation" (p. 310). Since multiple exchange rates act as alternatives to tariffs, they have also protected favored industries, possibly for patronage and possibly for genuine ISI.[2] But de Vries concluded that they could rarely achieve all these objectives simultaneously, and that under conditions of inflation, the following unfavorable effects are noted (p. 311):

> . . . Discouragement of basic export industries through maintenance of penalty export rates at overvalued levels; insufficient stimulation of new export industries even where there have been special rates for minor exports; distortions in domestic production and investment from multiple import rates; local currency losses, rather than revenue, from the exchange system; and rigidity of rate structure so that overvalued rates emerge or, alternatively, the country tends to meet balance of payments difficulties by depreciating the rate structure instead of adopting appropriate domestic policies.

The proportions of MDCs and LDCs adopting Article VIII status with the International Monetary Fund may give some indication of their comparative uses of exchange (as opposed to monetary and fiscal) policy. In the euphoric optimism of the postwar forties, the IMF divided the world into two groups: "Article VIII" countries, which renounced the sovereign right to restrict foreign exchange purchases for current transactions, and "Article XIV" countries, which would retain that right during the (undefined) "postwar transitional period". As of the end of 1978, 82 out of 107 non-oil-exporting LDCs still enjoyed Article XIV status, whereas 14 out of 15 MDCs had adopted Article VIII (IMF, 1978). We should not overdo the distinction. The IMF may permit Article VIII countries to impose restrictions, and sometimes it ignores their violations. On the other hand, the Article XIV list includes countries with a wide variety of restrictions and substantial reliance upon them.

WAGES POLICY

In wage policy, LDCs face an intractable contradiction. On the one hand, the morality imported from the West calls for the protection of labor through unionism and high wages, which are possible in the modern sector that ISI has generated. On the other hand, high wages throughout the country are incompatible with the low productivity of labor in the traditional sectors. Most LDCs settle for an uneasy compromise. A small number of laborers succeeds in entering the modern sector; their earnings are bolstered by bargaining and minimum wage laws. Most laborers, however, are in the traditional sector or unemployed, and their earnings are not protected at all.

In the preindustrial Western World, wages were forever low, usually the minimum for subsistence or even less. As the integrative process worked historically downward (kings made peace with nobles, both of them made peace with the bourgeoisie, and so on), laborers were the last to share in the bounties

---

[2]The latter observation is our own, not necessarily attributable to de Vries.

of increased productivity. The reason (we believe) was their excessive numbers: low productivity applied to factors of production generally, but low *marginal* productivity applied to the most abundant factor. Only as science, industry, and capital made labor relatively scarce did its marginal productivity rise, and hence its wage. We see no reason to believe the process will be otherwise with LDCs. Premature minimum wages promote dualism, unemployment, and income disparity, improving the lot of a few and deteriorating that of many.

Union activity in LDCs is considerably different from that in MDCs. Let us set forth two polar constructs, each of them an abstraction. At one extreme, the union faces the employer, with no government intervention. Wage bargaining depends on relative strengths, which in turn depend on productivity of labor, relative monopolies (union and company), demand for product, relative abilities to survive a long strike, and so on. At the other extreme, the union acts entirely through the political process. The Ministry of Labor is forever present in the bargaining process, and in final analysis, government determines the settlement. Even outside of bargaining, the two parties press government for regulations concerning wages and employment conditions. In a strike, the government may swing its weight one way or another: against labor by declaring the strike illegal, arresting its leaders, and withdrawing all protection, or against management by ruling that workers must be paid while on strike, or by threatening arrests.

Now, consider a continuum between the two poles. Starting at the nongovernment end, we gradually add intervention. At first there are labor laws (such as the Taft-Hartley in the United States) to equalize perceived disparities in bargaining position. If we start from the other end, we introduce certain types of direct contact between labor and management. Negotiation may occur before the Ministry of Labor is called.

We find all countries arrayed along the continuum, but MDCs (Europe and North America) cluster toward the nongovernment end, while LDCs cluster around government intervention. In fact, they are quite close to that pole, so that in most cases labor can do virtually nothing without government protection. The reason is not difficult to see. On the one hand, other government policies (favoring ISI) have created a modern sector, highly protected and subsidized, with opportunities for high profits. With the aid of university-trained leaders, labor organizes itself into a countervailing power (in a Galbraithian sense; see Galbraith, 1952) that demands its share of government protection, similar to that of industry. On the other hand, the vast numbers of unemployed would threaten labor's privileges if the government did not regulate strictly, making it possible for labor's new elite to keep the others out.

This emerging morality is consonant with our theory of morality (Chapter 13). The protection of labor becomes a social value once it has been institutionalized; unless and until the outsiders worm their way in, the same law protecting the labor elite excludes the others.

We go further. The distinction between "rural" and "urban" is too gross. In fact, varying degrees of labor protection apply to sectors that may be more or less "modern." Nelson, Schultz and Slighton (1971:132) found highly disparate wage increases in urban Colombia. From 1951 to 1964, wages in public utilities increased to a factor of 15.1, while modern manufacturing increased to 5.64 and craft manufacturing to 5.60. Personal services (mostly domestic) increased to only 3.45. Compare these contrasts with similar data from the United States, where average earnings of domestic workers increased to a factor of 1.61, from 1951 to 1964, and those of manufacturing employees to 1.38 (United States, 1975:166–67). In general, and apart from initial differences, wages in LDCs probably increase with greater intersectoral disparities than in MDCs.

These disparities are so severe that it is hard to attribute them to differential productivity increase. Rather, in many LDCs it is customary (or legal) for the government to set minimum wages, sector by sector, and often by type of employment within a sector. Not only that, but the government may set minimum education requirements for particular jobs. These requirements (like the nontariff barriers of Chapter 13) may have little to do with the technical requirements of the job. Indeed, the Ministry of Labor does not ordinarily possess a staff skilled in all the diverse technical needs of every employment in the modern sector. Because decisions are made under varying political pressures and without technical knowledge, they tend to be capricious.

In sum, government intervention in the labor market reinforces the strategy of ISI, whose major characteristic is the creation of a small, modern sector, replicating industries in MDCs. Counterpart to this sector are labor unions, whose leaders come from the universities rather than the ranks. Possessed of the education and other resources with which to gain the necessary political leverage, they divert to themselves and to their workers what they consider to be their share of the gains of the modern sector. By the same token, they limit the access of others.

TAXATION

ISI has also been promoted by tax concessions in favor of investment. Almost universal in the tax laws of LDCs is some kind of exemption for new enterprises from duties on imported capital goods. In addition, tax holidays are often granted them; the most frequent is 5 years, but they range up to 25 years (in Togo). Taxes may also be reduced as specific investments are made, and sometimes reinvested earnings are exempt. Lent (1967) provides a full review of these procedures.

The incentive in favor of capital is often compounded by payroll taxes, which are disincentives for employment. Sometimes payroll taxes finance social security, but often they contribute to the government's general budget as well. Even where they are paid to the social security agency, this agency may be reputed to be the "slush fund," with informal complaints that it does not return to workers what it has taken in. Unless independently-audited reports are published (and these are rare), it is not possible to judge the accuracy of these rumors.

In principle, a tax holiday is neutral with respect to capital- or labor-intensive technology and therefore is preferred to an investment allowance. Lent

(1971:408) reported, however, that tax holidays often require a minimum investment, and in a minority of cases their length depends on the amount of investment. They are therefore biased toward capital-intensive technologies.

A more subtle (and perhaps unintended) way of favoring ISI lies in the overall structure of taxes. Where tax-collection methods are underdeveloped (with scant audit control and high evasion opportunity) the system must rely heavily on those taxes that are collectible, instead of those that may optimize welfare or promote equity or efficiency. Income and profit taxes are difficult to collect; import and export taxes, payroll taxes, and sales taxes are easier. Both import and export taxes discriminate against exports, compared to import substitutes (Goode, Lent, and Ohja, 1966), and of course *any* measure to reduce international trade promotes ISI.

The regressive nature of payroll and sales taxes (Kaldor, 1963) discriminates against the kinds of goods consumed by the low-income community. Tun Wai (1962:431) reported that in 1959, direct taxes represented 43 percent of total central government income for the median high-income country (GDP per capita of $500 or more), but only 29 percent for the median middle-income country ($200–$500), and only 20 percent for the median low-income country (below $200). Chelliah (1971) found that the average ratio of tax revenue to GNP increased from about 11 percent in 1953–1955 to 14 percent in 1966–1968 for a sample of 30 LDCs. During this period, he reported a relative shift away from taxes on international trade and toward production and internal taxes. Average elasticity of taxes to GNP was 1.4. Despite their regressive nature, sales taxes and excises reflected the highest income elasticity of all, probably because the rates themselves were increasing. During the same period, however, the ratio of direct to total taxes declined slightly, from 31.1 to 30.2 percent.

All the above fiscal effects on ISI and income distribution have been indirect. There are also direct effects, through taxation that burdens particular groups and spending that benefits other groups. In earlier chapters (for example, 6 and 10), we have questioned whether the direct effects do in fact redistribute income in favor of the poor.

Considering the tax side alone, we find no convincing evidence of progressivity in LDCs taken as a whole.[3] Most LDC tax laws stress progressive principles, but in practice come out proportional (FitzGerald, 1978, Cline, 1972, and Harberger, 1977). Tax evasion, loopholes, and poor administration may well be more weighty in determining tax incidence than is the legal structure.

The experience of MDCs may not be greatly different. All have basically progressive tax legislation, but once again underreporting, loopholes, and exceptions may offset the progressive nature (Sawyer, 1976). Rather, in MDCs progressivity is restored on the expenditure side. In the United States, Reynolds and Smolensky (1977) found taxes to be roughly proportional but expenditures progressive.

---

[3]Estimating tax incidence in LDCs is a crude science; most studies do not convincingly account for the indirect effects of tax-distorted prices on income. In the present section, therefore, we refer mainly to taxes paid and expenditures received by different groups, but not to market-reallocation effects.

Even if it should occur, major tax reform in LDCs is not likely to improve equity substantially. When Harberger (1977) simulated the "legal" U.S. tax structure on a "typical" LDC, post-tax income distribution was little changed. However, expenditures did make a difference. An assumption of equal expenditures per capita in the Harberger model caused a significant redistribution toward lower-income groups. The powerful effect of expenditures has also been demonstrated by others (Cline, 1972, de Wulf, 1974, Berry and Urrutia, 1976: Ch. 7, and McClure, 1975).

PRICE CONTROL AND LICENSING

A cynical piece of "humor" circulating among development economists suggests the following distinction between MDCs and LDCs: "In a MDC you can do anything that isn't forbidden, but in a LDC you can do nothing unless it is specifically approved." This barb doubtless comes closest to its mark in the areas of licensing and price control. In most LDCs, almost all kinds of business activity, even down to small family enterprise and street vending, require licenses. Often these licenses are locally and routinely issued. Our informal questioning in rural Kenya revealed that bribes are ordinarily not required for "little" people in routine cases. But wherever a special privilege can be accorded, some "compensation" is usually needed. Special licenses are required for selling sugar (a state-controlled commodity in Kenya); these might call for delays of a year or more unless greater speed was "facilitated." In many LDCs, drivers' licenses allegedly require a "fee" for the tester, which is widely reported to compensate for deficiencies in driving ability.

In many countries, price control is pervasive. Often the justification is that "articles of prime necessity" (a term frequently heard in Latin American countries) must be sold cheaply enough so that the urban poor will be fed. Such controls work reasonably well if the government contributes a subsidy. For example, the Mexican government buys corn through a government corporation known as CONASUPO, selling it at a loss to the *tortillerías* of the city. Similarly, the government of South Korea purchases rice at subsidized prices from farmers, selling at a loss in the cities. Subsidies of this nature add to the difficulties of budget and inflation control, and if they must be removed in response to a stablization program mandated by the IMF, street rioting may ensue (as in Egypt in 1979).

Provided the budget is adequate, subsidies for "articles of prime necessity" may constitute a socially-approved way of transferring resources from rich to poor. Except where they engender inflation, they cannot be labeled inefficient. But price controls without subsidies are another matter. Governments attempting to turn the terms of trade against farmers in favor of the urban poor do so at peril to agricultural output. Such was the case in Perón's Argentina (Chapter 16). Our own informal questions in rural Kenya showed us that family enterprises selling price-controlled merchandise earned less than others. Many enterprises would shy away from these items; if controls were too onerous, the controlled goods would disappear from the shelves. Often price-controlled articles are smuggled into other countries, where they are sold on the black market.

MARKETING BOARDS
AND GOVERNMENT CORPORATIONS

In addition to the regulations we have just discussed, LDC governments have intervened directly in the economies either by buying and selling commodities or by producing commodities themselves. The former has been done through marketing boards, and the latter through government corporations.

Marketing boards were established in Asia and Africa during World War II and in the immediate postwar years (Goode, Lent, and Ohja, 1966:455). They are less common in Latin America, although several countries use them for coffee. To ensure an uninterrupted supply of exports during the war, the British government set up a cocoa marketing board in Ghana in 1939 (Bauer, 1972:390); other boards followed in West Africa for ground nuts, palm products, and cotton. After the war, they were continued by colonial and then by independent governments, ostensibly to smooth out the price fluctuations inherent in primary production.

When granted monopoly powers over purchase and sale of the commodities concerned, the boards turned into convenient taxing devices. Marketing board profits are similar to export taxes; both are among the more easily collected. Bauer (1972:400) reported that exports of cocoa, ground nuts, palm kernels, and palm oil from Gold Coast and Nigeria, 1939–1951, carried duties ranging from 4 to 16 percent, but if the surpluses of the marketing boards are added, the effective levies were increased to a range of 32.3 to 255.0 percent, with a mode between 50 and 80 percent. He concluded (p. 405) that "the terms of trade of the producers were depressed far below what they would have been without this system and well below those of their principal competitors." Goode, Lent, and Ohja (1966:456) reported that "in Nigeria, the marketing boards served from their inception as instruments for the mobilization of savings for government-sponsored projects; after the reorganization of the boards in 1954 on a regional, rather than a commodity, basis the regional governments explicitly stated that the surpluses provided an important source of revenue for their development budgets."

Once they had been successful with respect to export products, it was not a difficult move to extend marketing boards to products for domestic consumption. In Kenya, all private producers of maize were for a time (late sixties and early seventies) required to sell their total output to the Maize and Produce Board, which set prices and controlled distributions. But the prices were set more on the basis of ephemeral political exigency than on the basis of reasoned economic strategy. Sometimes they were high in order to placate farmers, and at other times they were low in order to feed government budgets. Naturally, such changes have affected farm output (Government of Kenya, 1974:233).

How do we assess marketing boards? Clearly, storing products and damping price fluctuations are useful objectives, which may be performed equally well by the private or the public sector. The government may even lend to private storage firms or subsidize them if necessary.

We are less sanguine about marketing boards when they are used to tax agriculture, or when their pricing policies appear capricious. We have seen (Chapter 11) that development theory of the fifties and sixties (Lewis, 1955, and Fei and Ranis, 1961) tended to approve the taxing of agriculture (or turning the terms of trade against it) in order to extract investment funds from what was believed to be the major available source. Owen (1966) warned of the squeeze on agriculture, from taxing it and then failing to reinvest adequately in it. Another 15 years of experience reveal that Owen was right: agriculture *has* lagged in most of the developing world, and the discrimination against it, in which marketing boards have played a role, is doubtless a cause.

Government corporations are another form of direct intervention. Railroads, airlines, communications, and public utilities are government-owned in virtually all LDCs. So also are certain basic industries, such as mining, petroleum, and possibly steel. Beyond these, some governments have elected to extend themselves deeply into production. Virtually every conceivable corporate form has been used: mixed private-government corporations; holding companies; development corporations that buy and sell shares of subsidiaries; enterprises owned by and responsible to specific ministries; or autonomous (parastatal) enterprises, financed by government capital but leading an independent life.

Any study of the efficiency of such corporations encounters enormous obstacles. Statements for many of them are not available, or if they are, they may come unaudited. Accounting practices differ widely; there is no standard way of taking depreciation; and book values of assets lag behind inflation to differing degrees (Gantt and Dutto, 1968:104). Pricing policies vary from monopoly pricing to subsidies of consumers. To record whether government corporations earn profits or not tells little. Sometimes the companies are tariff-protected monopolies in basic sectors, so that they cannot help being profitable if they wish. Often they are charged with being havens for patronage, paying higher salaries than even government officials can command.

The only study we know of, which attempted to combine all information available for all countries, is that of Gantt and Dutto (1968). Because of variations in depreciation practices, they based their measures on "flow-of-funds," which they defined as net profit without depreciation deduction, and they calculated ratios of flow-of-funds to investment. They reported their findings as follows (p. 108):

> A wide divergence existed in the sample between areas and between different types of industries. For the areas, there are broadly two groups of corporations: the European and the Latin American corporations in one group, and the African and the Asian corporations in the other. The European and the Latin American corporations barely covered their current costs, not including depreciation, whereas the African corporations had a

flow-of-funds ratio of 20 percent. Asia can also be considered a high-profit area, as the average return on activity was 16 percent. These results were statistically significant, at the 90 percent level or above.

Gantt and Dutto went on to ask whether government corporations could be counted on to raise (through their profits) funds for further development investment. Their conclusion was negative, if investment is taken as a cost (through depreciation allowances). "Government-owned corporations, rather than serving as a focal point for collecting financial resources for their own investment or for other purposes, have generally placed a financial burden on parent governments" (p. 126).

THE INTERNATIONAL LABOR ORGANIZATION

Concerned for widespread unemployment in LDCs, the International Labor Organization (ILO) has conducted major surveys and made policy recommendations in Colombia, Sri Lanka, Kenya, Iran, the Philippines, and Sudan. In addition, the ILO has undertaken studies of specific development problems, such as agrarian reform and multinational corporations. Their recommendations generally propose a retreat from ISI and a movement toward export orientation, along with greater stress on agriculture, rural development, appropriate technology, and small-scale industry.

In the Philippines, for example, the ILO (1974) proposed "a policy of shared restraint." Their package included mobilization of the rural sector, continued pursuit of agrarian reform, more irrigation, incentives for medium- and small-scale industry, decentralization of industry, a realistic or somewhat undervalued exchange rate, higher interest rates, liberalization of import restrictions and lowering of tariffs, a unified technical assistance and adaptive technology effort, and dismantling of the system of investment incentives. All these recommendations would be consonant with the critiques of these policies that we have made in this chapter.

On wages, the ILO treads delicately. On the one hand, higher wages have long been the political thrust of labor, which ILO represents. On the other hand, one senses a recognition, on the part of ILO missions, of the relationship between high wages and unemployment. In its Kenya report, the ILO (1972) criticized the policy of "paper qualifications" for employment and the discrimination among industries with respect to minimum wages. In the Colombia report (1970), the ILO suggests (p. 185) that "it would be desirable . . . to avoid increases in wages that would cause opportunities of exports (or import substitution) to be missed." In the Iran report (ILO 1973), the mission justifies increases in minimum wages, especially for lower-income groups, as indispensable for improving the distribution of income (p. 81). For Ceylon (Sri Lanka), the mission stresses the perverse incentives of the wage structure—"perverse in the sense of over-encouraging the search (or waiting) for certain types of work, so that the numbers are well beyond those the occupation can absorb" (p. 118). They characterize the union structure, organized on the basis of political affiliations, as "far from satisfactory in terms of either good labor relations and effective bargaining or the needs of a national strategy for full employment" (p. 125). In the context of full employment versus high wages, the mission to the Philippines (ILO 974:45) wrote that the ILO "fully agree(s) with those who have called unemployment the worst exploitation of the working man."

PROJECT ANALYSIS

As governments have increasingly distorted the allocation of resources, economists have sought ways to offset these distortions in the actual selection of projects. Under classical principles, the project with the highest rate of return on capital would be chosen, then the next highest, and so on until the capital runs out.

The use of classical principles implies that the government has a certain amount of available capital, which it will invest directly or whose investment it will control or lever through an agency such as a development bank. If the costs of a project are true opportunity costs, and the revenue represents the true social value of its output, then profit (being the excess of revenue over cost) measures net social value added. Nothing is implied about the distribution of profit (paid to government, paid to private sector, or earmarked for social uses). A socialist government has as much reason to use profit as its criterion as does the government in a capitalist country.

Suppose, however, the cost of capital is low because of free imports of capital goods and because of investment incentives. Suppose further that borrowing is facilitated by interest rates unrepresentative of the scarcity of capital and that wages are higher than the marginal productivity of labor in alternative employment. Then the costs of a project reflect a lower social value for capital than the market would have assigned it from its scarcity. If this situation is combined with a higher-than-world-market price for output because of protection or subsidy, then profit will be a doubly distorted reflection of "true social value."

Economists have drawn on benefit-cost principles to reverse these distortions. Benefit-cost analysis has been developed, since the 1930s, largely for the assessment of water projects in the United States (Dorfman, 1965:2). It has two distinguishing features. First, it substitutes "benefit" instead of "revenue." Benefit includes not only the revenue from sale of output, but economies (accruing to others) as well. "Benefit" thus equals "social revenue." Similarly, "costs" include all social costs (such as pollution) that deteriorate the welfare of others and are not necessarily costs to the project agency. Second, benefit-cost analysis is based on discounted lifetime streams for all benefits and costs. Given an appropriate discount rate, these streams (benefits minus costs) can be reduced to the present value of a capital sum, which is then compared to the necessary investment. Alternatively, given the amount of investment but no preselected discount rate, it is possible to solve for the "internal rate of return" of the project, which can then be compared with the going interest rate.

Benefit-cost techniques have been extended to development project analysis by the introduction of shadow prices. A shadow price is substituted instead of the market price when the latter is believed to have been distorted. For example, the world price of imports may be substituted instead of the cost of imports including duty; this price may be further adjusted to reflect a "realistic" instead of an overvalued exchange rate. A shadow wage would be one representing the marginal productivity of labor in its alternative employment. In short, shadow prices are applied to benefit-cost analysis in order to simulate the market as it would be, were it not for all the policy distortions we have cited earlier in this chapter.

We do not discuss the techniques of benefit-cost analysis, but we cite the works where they are covered. Shadow prices are usually attributed to Tinbergen (1958:82); the concept also appeared in the United Nations (1958). Bryce (1960) integrated them into the principles of industrial development. The OECD (1968) prepared a more extended manual, which for many years served as the basic set of procedures. Reutlinger (1970) showed how the system could be adapted to take uncertainty into account. A collection of papers by Harberger (1973) outlines essential principles, and Lal (1974) has reviewed alternative project-selection procedures for the World Bank. Probably the most widely-used system is that of Little and Mirrlees (1974), in which world prices are suggested as shadows. The shadow wage is made dependent on income distribution, and more sophisticated ways are proposed for determining shadow prices of non-traded goods and services. Van Delft and Nijkamp (1977) extended the system to multidimensional projects with trade-offs among goals. UNIDO (1978) also prepared a manual for social benefit-cost analysis.

Shadow prices and benefit-cost analysis are sometimes used by international lending agencies, more so (we understand) for heavy infrastructure projects than for lighter ones. Various case studies are available, by King (1967), Little and Scott (1976), Misham (1976), Rondinelli (1977), and others. But we know of no general assessment of the extent of their use, or of the overall results.

To us, it is a marvelous thought that those very people who created the panoply of distortions on a macro-level should behave on a micro-level as if they hadn't done it at all! Once again we touch the area of our ignorance about development. *Why* are the macro-distortions created? *Why* would anyone use shadow prices for project selection, who is able but unwilling to dismantle the structure that made them necessary? No one can answer these questions. But we suspect a mixture of two of the qualities cited in Chapter 1—propensity for power and shortness of vision—along with a lack of experience in understanding how the economy functions. Combine these with the prospects of individual gain on the part of those who select the projects.

Support for benefit-cost analysis with shadow prices implies a belief that the government is indeed the farseeing representative of social welfare and the arbiter of conflicting interests, instead of (as we would suspect) a set of indi-viduals motivated in part by these noble instincts, but also seeking to maximize their individual, private welfares, and subject to a very high margin of error.

We have now reviewed all the policies by which a government can promote ISI. The supposition that these policies are in fact motivated by ISI, or that their implementation promotes ISI, may be overly charitable. For *the same panoply of powers may be used to discriminate in favor of preferred interests. Whenever one group is benefited, another must pay the cost. In LDCs, where the structure of countervailing powers and protective institutions has not fully blossomed, and where vast numbers are ignorant of how controlled policy will affect them, the probability that government may indeed so discriminate becomes fearful.*

ECONOMIC INTEGRATION

LDC governments have not ignored the possibilities of gain through the economic integration of neighboring countries. But they have also not been very eager for it, and they have sometimes acceded only at the behest of former colonial powers such as Britain and France, or (for Latin America) the United States. The success of LDC integration ranges from none to little.

The greatest potential for improved income would lie in trade creation among participating countries, with new opportunities for division of labor and economies of scale. International flows of capital and labor might lead to their more rational allocation. The classic conditions of Viner (1950), which set limits to these opportunities, still form the core of integration theory, which has been fleshed out and extended by Balassa (1961).

No serious integration plan has been launched in Asia.[4] The most promising one in Africa—the East African Community (formed in 1967)—was defunct by 1977 because of intractable political problems among the participating powers[5] (Chapter 16). We shall therefore turn to Latin America, where four integration programs have been put into operation: the Latin American Free Trade Area (LAFTA), the Central American Common Market (CACM), the Caribbean Community and Common Market (CARICOM), and the Andean Group.[6]

LAFTA started with high hopes in 1961: a plan to eliminate all duties in ten years (with only a few exceptions) among member countries (all of South America, plus Mexico). The early years saw the appearance of progress, with duties lowered or eliminated on 18,000 items (Banks, 1978:541). But these were the "easy" ones, for they wrought little hardship on producers in participating countries. The difficult reductions resisted like a stone wall, and by 1967 negotiations had all but stalled, causing Banks (1978) to comment that the annual meeting "has become a parody of itself."

CACM initially made the greatest progress of all, with a firm schedule for eliminating most duties and (unlike LAFTA) establishing a common tariff vis-

---

[4]Possible reasons are: the sour taste of the Japanese-dominated "Greater East Asian Co-prosperity Sphere" of World War II, the communist-capitalist ideological split among nations, and the geographic distances.

[5]Other African arrangements include the Central African Customs and Economic Union (UDEAC), the Common African and Mauritian Organization (OCAM), and the Economic Community of West African States (ECOWAS). These are all described in Banks (1978).

[6]These are also described in Banks(1978).

à-vis outsiders (Cohen Orantes, 1972). Intraregional trade increased. But war between Honduras and El Salvador (1969), a coup in Honduras (1978), and civil wars in Nicaragua (1978–79) and El Salvador (1980) blocked the single artery connecting all Central American countries. Politics was not all, however. Facing economic crisis, Nicaragua unilaterally imposed duties on the other countries, and Honduras withdrew because it found its industries uncompetitive (LAER, 8–25–78:261).

The Andean Group (Venezuela, Colombia, Ecuador, Bolivia, Peru, and Chile) also showed early progress, with significant reductions in duties, far-reaching plans for integrated investment, and great increases in intraregional trade (LAER, 6–16–78:178). But a quarrel over the degree of controls on multinational corporations led to Chile's withdrawal (LAER, 9–24–76:145). Progress was slowed thereafter by the inability of governments to reach basic agreements (LAER, 8–11–78:242).

CARICOM has made plans for a common market among former British colonies in the Caribbean, but disagreements among negotiators, and balance of payments difficulties, have led to unexpected restrictions and slow progress (LAER, 2–11–77:23, and 9–23–77:146).

Why such persistent failure in LDC integration schemes? Perhaps we can shed some light by comparison with the European Economic Community (EEC), which was established by the Rome Treaty in 1957–1958.

First, the European countries were willing to bury animosities in the interests of trade. The bitterness between France and Germany was surely no less than that between Kenya and Tanzania, or between Honduras and El Salvador, yet somehow it could be overcome.

Second, business enterprises in Europe seemed far more committed to integration than were their counterparts in LDCs. One possible reason is that major LDC enterprises were largely government-controlled and therefore reflected political uncertainties more than did those of Europe. Another might be the lesser propensity of LDC business leaders to take risks. Still another may be the greater fluidity of European politics, which permitted potential gainers from exports to gain a political edge over principal losers from foreign competition—while the advantage was still held by the latter in LDCs. Whatever the cause, once integration had been decided upon, previously-recalcitrant European businesses insisted on accelerating the schedule (Benoit, 1961:88). LAFTA negotiators, on the other hand, continually found ways to thwart it.

Third, and possibly the most serious of all, Latin American integration was monopoly-*creating*, whereas European was monopoly-*reducing*. In LAFTA, CACM, and the Andean bloc, treaties all provided for "integration industries," to be divided by agreement among member countries, each of which would have a monopoly for regional sales. But negotiation turned out to be extraordinarily difficult; time and again negotiators felt they were getting the short end, with the advantage "always" going to the other countries. Not only were few integration industries established, but the possibility of them would have deterred entrepreneurial initiative in other countries. In the Rome treaty, on the other hand, enterprises from other countries within EEC were accorded the same privileges as national companies (Frank, 1961:92–123).

CONCLUSION: IS GOVERNMENT "TOO BIG?"

We return to the words attributed to Octavio Paz at the beginning of this chapter, and we ask whether the net impact of government on development is positive or negative.

We distinguish MDCs from LDCs. In MDCs (for the most part), government intervention has developed through three stages (to be elaborated in Chapter 15). The first was one of despotism and serfdom, in which kings, nobles, or town patricians attempted to control all production and prices within their jurisdictions. This era gradually gave way to one of liberalism and humanism, with government in retreat. The third stage occurred when government again intervened, this time to offset libertine imbalances and to promote full employment in complex economies. Each new intervention, however, was accompanied by safeguards against its abuse. None of these is a "pure" stage; the safeguards have not matched the potential abuses exactly, and the characteristics of a stage are taken only "on the average."

In LDCs, the first and the third stages become blurred. Expatriate advisors (representing international agencies, foreign-aid agencies, foundations, or on direct hire by governments) often confuse the third stage in the countries from which they come with the first stage in the countries where they serve. Modern instruments of government control are transmitted to countries where the appropriate checks and balances have not been forged.

Some would believe that the LDC "policy package"—low interest rates, overvalued exchange rates, high effective protection for consumer goods and sometimes negative effective protection for exports, investment incentives, and high wages—represents a conscious, well-thought-out strategy for ISI. Others look upon it as "conspiracy" in which government elites form dualism-promoting policies so that they and their colleagues may skim the cream of the modern sector. Still others view government intervention as a genuine effort to promote development.

Our own view is at once none of these and all of these. We do not know the mix of government motives. At one time, policy stems from ISI strategy. At another time, policies may be formed for individual gain, although we believe the government elite do not possess the unity attributed to them in conspiracy theory. Our own experience is that many officials in LDCs act out of a genuine concern for their nations' progress.

We join ILO in recommending a shift away from ISI and toward export orientation, small-scale production, and labor-intensive technology, to promote employment and to counter dualism. But we doubt that sophisticated techniques of project analysis will persuade planners (except those from MDCs and international agencies) to negate the effect of macro-distortions. Even so, these are not our major concerns. The common feature of all the policies cited in this chapter is their inconsistency and capriciousness. These are manifest in the diverse protection structures uncovered by Balassa and Associates (1971), the frequent changes in exchange policy referred to by de Vries (1968), the great disparities in wages found by Nelson, Schultz and Slighton (1971), the ad hoc applications of price controls and licensing, and others.

We also sense a communality between tight and pervasive internal controls on the one hand and the failure of economic integration on the other. Both reflect an aversion to risk. Pervasive controls imply that it would be risky to decentralize, ceding decision-making powers to local communities and the poor. (We are reminded of the benevolent despots of eighteenth-century Europe.) Similarly, the risk of regional integration without centralized management has been too great. Yet centralized management internationally, with its implied loss of sovereignty, has also been elusive.

When the bureaucracy is so thin that individuals make decisions without review, when key individuals cannot agree among themselves, when overall policy can be set aside in its many individual applications, when officials make decisions from which they can gain personally, when risks are unpopular because of a suspicion that someone else will gain too much, and when well-meaning officials do not have the experience to trace out the full impact of their decisions on the economy, then (we believe) the government does not necessarily redress imbalances among the people nor adequately protect the general welfare.

BIBLIOGRAPHY

Adekunle, Joseph O., 1968:
   "Rates of Inflation in Industrial, Other Developed and Less Developed Countries, 1949–1965," *IMF Staff Papers*, Vol. XV, No. 3, November.
Balassa, Bela, 1961:
   The Theory of Economic Integration, Homewood, Illinois, Irwin.
Balassa, Bela, and Associates, 1971:
   The Structure of Protection in Developing Countries, Baltimore, Md., Johns Hopkins University Press, for the World Bank.
Balassa, Bela, and Munthe, Preben, 1971:
   "The Structure of Protection in Norway," in Balassa and Associates, 1971, op. cit.
Banks, Arthur S., ed., 1978:
   Political Handbook of the World, New York, McGraw-Hill.
Bauer, P. T. 1972:
   Dissent on Development: Studies and Debates in Developing Economies, Cambridge, Mass., Harvard University Press.
Benoit, Emile, 1961:
   Europe at Sixes and Sevens: The Common Market, the Free Trade Association, and the United States, New York, Columbia University Press.
Berry, A. and Urrutia, M., 1976:
   Income Distribution in Colombia, New Haven, Ct., Yale University Press.
Bhagwat, Avinash, and Onitsuka, Yusuke, 1974:
   "Export-Import Responses to Devaluation: Experience of the Nonindustrial Countries in the 1960s," *IMF Staff Papers*, Vol. XXI, No. 2, July.
Bhagwati, J. (1978):
   Anatomy and Consequences of Exchange Control Regimes, (Cambridge, Mass.: Ballinger Publishing Co. for the NBER).
Bottomley, Anthony, 1975:
   "Interest Rate Determinations in Underdeveloped Rural Areas," *American Journal of Agricultural Economics*, Vol. 57.

Bryce, Murray, 1960:
   Industrial Development: A Guide for Accelerating Economic Growth, New York, McGraw-Hill.
Bueno, Gerardo, 1971:
   "The Structure of Protection in Mexico," in Balassa and Associates, 1971, op. cit.
Campos, Roberto, 1961:
   "Two Views on Inflation in Latin America," in Hirschman, Albert O., ed., *Latin American Issues*, New York, Twentieth Century Fund.
Chelliah, Raja J., 1971:
   "Trends in Taxation in Developing Countries," *IMF Staff Papers*, Vol. XVIII, No. 2, July.
Cline, W. R., 1972:
   Potential Effects of Income Redistribution on Economic Growth, New York, Praeger.
Cohen, B. and Sisler, D. (1971):
   "Exports of Developing Countries in the 1960's," *Review of Economics and Statistics* Vol. 53, 354–61.
Cohen Orantes, Isaac, 1972:
   Regional Integration in Central America, Lexington, Mass., Lexington Books, D.C. Heath.
de Vries, Margaret G., 1965:
   "Multiple Exchange Rates: Expectations and Experiences," *IMF Staff Papers*, Vol. XII, No. 2, July.
de Vries, Margaret G., 1968:
   "Exchange Depreciation in Developing Countries," *IMF Staff Papers*, Vol. XV, No. 3, November.
de Wulf, L., 1974:
   "Do Public Expenditures Reduce Inequality?" *Finance and Development*, September, 20–3.
Dorfman, Robert, Ed., 1965:
   Measuring Benefits of Government Investments, Washington, D.C., The Brookings Institution.
ECLA, 1962:
   "Inflation and Growth: A Summary of Experience in Latin America," *Economic Bulletin for Latin America*, Santiago, February.
Fei, John C. H., and Ranis, Gustav, 1961:
   "A Theory of Economic Development," *American Economic Review*, September.
FitzGerald, E.V.K., 1978:
   "The Fiscal Crisis of the Latin American State," in J.F.J. Toye, ed., *Taxation and Economic Development*, London, Frank Cass, 125–60.
Frank, Isaiah, 1961:
   The European Common Market, New York, Praeger.
Galbraith, John Kenneth, 1952:
   American Capitalism: The Concept of Countervailing Power, Boston, Houghton Mifflin.
Gantt, Andrew H., and Dutto, Giuseppe, 1968:
   "Financial Performance of Government-Owned Corporations in Less Developed Countries," *IMF Staff Papers*, Vol. XV, No. 1, March.
Goode, Richard; Lent, George E.; and Ohja, P. D., 1966:
   "Role of Export Taxes in Developing Countries," *IMF Staff Papers*, Vol. XIII, No. 3, November.
Government of Kenya, 1974:
   Development Plan, 1974–78, Nairobi, Government Printing Office.
Grunwald, Joseph, 1961:
   "The 'Structuralist' School on Price Stability and Development: The Chilean Case," in Hirschman, Albert O., ed., *Latin American Issues*, New York, Twentieth Century Fund.

Harberger, A.C., 1977:
"Fiscal Policy and Income Redistribution," in C. R. Frank and R. C. Webb, eds., *Income Distribution and Growth in the Less-Developed Countries*, Washington, D.C., Brookings Institution.

Harberger, Arnold C., 1973:
Project Evaluation, Chicago, Illinois, Markham.

ILO, 1971:
Matching Employment Opportunities and Expectations: A Programme of Action for Ceylon, Geneva, International Labor Office.

ILO, 1970:
Towards Full Employment: A Programme for Colombia, Geneva, International Labor Office.

ILO, 1972:
Employment, Incomes, and Equality: A Strategy for Increasing Productive Employment in Kenya, Geneva, International Labor Office.

ILO, 1974:
Sharing in Development: A Programme of Employment, Equity, and Growth for the Philippines, Geneva, International Labor Office.

ILO, 1973:
Employment and Income Policies for Iran, Geneva, International Labor Office.

IMF, 1978:
Twenty-Ninth Annual Report on Exchange Restrictions, Washington, D.C.

Jeanneret, Teresa:
"The Structure of Protection in Chile," in Balassa and Associates, 1971, op. cit.

Kaldor, Nicholas, 1963:
"Will Underdeveloped Countries Learn to Tax?" *Foreign Affairs*, January.

Kindleberger, Charles P., 1963:
International Economics, Third Edition, Homewood, Illinois, Irwin.

King, John A., 1967:
Economic Development Projects and Their Appraisal, Baltimore, Md., Johns Hopkins University Press, for the World Bank.

Krueger, A. (1978):
Liberalization Attempts and Consequences (NY: NBER).

LAER, 1976–1978:
Latin American Economic Report, a weekly newsletter published by Latin American Newsletters, Ltd., London.

Lal, Deepak, 1974:
Methods of Project Analysis, Baltimore, Johns Hopkins University Press, for the World Bank.

Lent, George E., 1971:
"Tax Incentives for the Promotion of Industrial Employment in Developing Countries," *IMF Staff Papers*, Vol. XVIII, No. 2, July.

Lewis, W. Arthur, 1955:
The Theory of Economic Growth, Homewood, Illinois, Irwin.

Lewis, Stephen R., and Guisinger, 1971:
"The Structure of Protection in Pakistan," in Balassa and Associates, 1971, op. cit.

Little, I. M. D., and Mirrlees, James A., 1974:
Project Appraisal and Planning for Developing Countries, New York, Basic Books.

Little, I. M. D., and Scott, M., 1976:
Using Shadow Prices, New York, Homes and Meier.

Loehr, W. (1980):
"Post-1973 Adjustment Problems of Oil-Importing Latin American Countries," in Muñoz, H. and Orrego, F. (eds) *Factores Internacionales y el Dessarrollo Energético* (Santiago: University of Chile).

Long, Millard F., 1973:
"Credit for Small Farmers: Indonesia, Malaysia, Thailand," U.S. AID, *Spring Review of Small Farmer Credit*, Vol. XV, February.

McClure, Jr., C. E., 1975:
"The Incidence of Colombian Taxes," *Economic Development and Cultural Change*, Vol. 24, No. 1, October.

Misham, E. J., 1976:
Cost-Benefit Analysis, New York, Praeger.

Nelson, Richard R.; Schulz, T. Paul; and Slighton, Robert L., 1971:
Structural Change in a Developing Economy: Colombia's Problems and Prospects, Princeton, N.J., Princeton University Press.

OECD, 1968:
Manual of Industrial Project Analysis, Paris.

Owen, Wyn F., 1966:
"The Development Squeeze on Agriculture," *American Economic Review*, March.

Pinto, Aníbal, 1960:
Ni Estabilidad ni Desarrollo: La Política del Fondo Monetario Internacional, Santiago.

Pinto, Aníbal, 1960:
Inflación: Raices Estructurales, Mexico City, Fondo de Cultura Económica.

Pinto, Aníbal, 1973:
"Inflación: Raices Estructurales," *Ensayos*, No. 3, Mexico City, Fondo de Cultura Económica.

Power, John H., 1971:
"The Structure of Protection in Mexico," in Balassa and Associates, 1971, op. cit.

Reutlinger, Shlomo, 1970:
Techniques for Project Appraisal Under Uncertainty, Baltimore, Md., Johns Hopkins University Press, for the World Bank.

Reynolds, M., and Smolensky, E., 1977:
Public Expenditures, Taxes and the Distribution of Income: The United States, 1950, 1961, 1970, New York, Academic Press.

Rondinelli, Dennis A., ed., 1977:
Planning Developing Projects, Stroudsberg, PA., Dowden, Hutchinson, and Ross.

Sawyer, M., 1976:
"Income Distribution in OECD Countries," *OECD Occasional Studies*, Paris.

Stock, R., 1980:
"An Analysis of the Costs of Import Substitution Policies and the Benefits of Export Expansion," (Boulder, University of Colorado, unpublished).

Sunkel, Osvaldo, 1958:
"La Inflación Chilena: Un Enfoque Heterodoxo," *Trimestre Económico*, No. 100, October/December.

Tinbergen, Jan, 1958:
The Design of Development, Baltimore, Johns Hopkins University Press, for the World Bank.

Tun Wai, U, 1959:
"The Relation Between Inflation and Economic Developmetn: A Statistical Inductive Study," *IMF Staff Papers*, Vol. VII, No. 2, October.

Tun Wai, U, 1962:
"Taxation Problems and Policies of Underdeveloped Countries," *IMF Staff Papers*, Vol. IX, No. 3, November.

Tun Wai, U, 1972:
Financial Intermediate and National Savings in Developing Countries, New York, Praeger.

Tun Wai, U, 1977:
"A Revisit to Interest Rates Outside the Organized Money Markets of Underdeveloped Countries," Banca Nazionale del Lavoro (Rome) *Quarterly Review*, No. 122, September.

UNIDO, 1978:
Guide to Practical Project Appraisal, New York, United Nations, 1978.
United Nations, 1958:
Manual on Economic Development Projects, New York.
United States, 1975:
Historical Statistics of the United States: Colonial Times to 1970, Washington, D.C.,
Department of Commerce.
Van Delft, Ad, and Nijkamp, Peter, 1977:
Multi-Criteria Analysis and Regional Decision-Making, Leiden, Martinus, Nijhoff.
Viner, Jacob, 1950:
The Customs Union Issue, New York, Carnegie Endowment for International Peace.
Williams College, Department of Economics, various dates:
Research Memoranda on International Trade and Development, xeroxed.
Yeats, A. J. (1979)
"Recent Changes in Developing Country Exports," *Weltwirtschlaftliches Archiv* 115:1,
149–65.

A
NEW LOOK
AT
ECONOMIC
DEVELOPMENT

15[1]

EUROPE

*"The economic problem must be fundamentally the
same in all ages."*
HECKSCHER (1926:525–34).

Almost invariably, theorists have approached development as a study in
inputs and outputs. The output is growth (or development, however defined, and/or income distribution), while the inputs are capital, technology,
and economic policy that may affect them. Suppose we narrowed the output
to growth of GDP per capita (hereafter, called *economic growth*), dropping all
preconceived notions of the inputs. Suppose further we surveyed the entire range
of human history, to examine events (economic or otherwise) that appear to
be repeatedly related to growth. Would we end up with the same set of inputs
now commonly used by development economists?

The general philosophy of this quest is described by Wilson (1977:13) as
follows:

> In short, the study of prices, wages, and profits provides an endless series
> of problems in the social development of early modern society, comprising
> saving, investment, private and public borrowing, and the consequences of
> all these on production and consumption. To assess the interaction of such
> variables we are likely to have to rely on data which an economist would
> dismiss as flimsy and unreliable. There must remain a large area of history
> where the historian has to rely on his general "feel" of the times and use
> his intuition as well as his techniques of exact measurement.

---

[1]The authors are indebted to historian Stephen Fisher-Galati for his review of this chapter.

Our present ambition is more modest than such a wide-ranging study, but it is in the same direction. We seek intuitively a plausible set of explanations of the economic growth of Europe that conforms to classical economic theory. By classical theory, we mean the laws of supply and demand and of comparative advantage. These appear to us logically compelling, and prior acceptance of them limits our search considerably. We do not hope for a *unique* set of explanations; no one will ever explain conclusively why (for example) the industrial revolution occurred first in England. Rather, we seek similarities and contrasts within Europe, and in the next chapter we will examine whether the same explanations might apply to today's LDCs.

THE MAJOR QUESTIONS

In addition to the industrial revolution and England, nine other conundrums dominate.

FIRST: What explains the contraction of growth in the fourth to sixth centuries? Was it the collapse of Roman institutions of government? Was it the overbearing restrictions imposed by the later emperors on their people, tying them to the soil and forcing them into hereditary jobs? Was it the impossible burden of conscription and taxation, necessary to implement the barbarian wars? Was it the consolidation of large landholdings and the enserfment of peasants, who sought protection through *patrocinium*? Was it the lack of education for the masses? Was it the physical destruction of the wars? Was it the new legal, political, and landholding systems imposed by the barbarian governments?

SECOND: Why did the medieval renaissance occur? Recent historians have contested the concept of the "Dark Ages," pointing rather to the continuity of trade, industry, and landholding structures, and to the development of Roman law by the Visigoths, Franks, and others. Nevertheless, growth slowed in the fifth century and revived with a "commercial revolution" in the tenth to thirteenth centuries. This new growth was reflected in rising output and population, new institutions of trade and finance, and increases in consumption. The old explanation of the Crusades as the initiator of trade is no longer tenable; clearly they stimulated it, but the "revolution" was under way before the Council of Clermont (1095), which launched the first Crusade.

THIRD: Why did this commercial revolution come to an end, in approximately 1300? The explanation that the Black Plague (1348) and the Hundred Years War (1337–1453) were the villains is no longer acceptable. Surely they reinforced its demise, but historians of late have uncovered evidence of agricultural contraction (including abandoned lands), growing poverty, and industrial and trading decline even before 1300.

FOURTH: Why did the cities of Northern Italy lead the medieval commercial revolution? Why were they the dominant economic force in Europe in the ensuing centuries, surviving the catastrophes of the fourteenth? And why did

Italy decline as a major financial and commercial power in the seventeenth century?

FIFTH: How does one account for the economic vigor of Flanders and Holland, from the twelfth century onward, as opposed to England and other regions of Europe? Why did Holland rise to surpass Italy as the leading commercial power of Europe in the sixteenth century? Why did Holland, like Italy, decline (relatively) in the seventeenth century, to be overtaken and finally surpassed by the "johnny-come-lately," England?

SIXTH: Why did Spain, with its great colonial wealth, fail so miserably in economic growth in the sixteenth and seventeenth centuries? Was it perhaps *because of* its riches in metallic money?

SEVENTH: Why did Central Europe (Germany, Poland, Russia, and smaller principalities) not only turn the clock backward in the sixteenth century, but set it running in reverse? These countries, whose standard of living and freedom (from enserfment) may have been greater in the twelfth century than those of Western Europe, *intensified* feudalism in the seventeenth century, restricting those very economic liberties that were being strengthened in the West. Even Peter the Great's imitation of the West did not delay the process. Did the fault lie in the Thirty Years War (1618–1648)—perhaps the most destructive since the Hundred Years War? Or was it the grain trade, through which Central Europe became the principal supplier of this major raw material to the West? Was the evolving feudalism of Germany—so dependent on primary-product exports to the more-developed West—perhaps similar to that of Latin America in the twentieth century?

EIGHTH: Why did Germany reverse its clock again in the eighteenth century, and set it running so fast in the nineteenth that by the turn of the twentieth it had overtaken England, to become the leading industrial power of Europe? Why did the nineteenth century agrarian reforms of Stein and Hardenberg, which reversed feudalism, occur when they did? Why was Germany so far ahead of England in mass education at the beginning of the nineteenth century? Is this the explanation for the German successes later on? Russia appeared to be following Germany with only a few decades of lag (the freeing of serfs occurred in 1861 and the great industrial advance was in 1910–1914). Would Russia have achieved industrial dominance similar to that of Germany had it not been set back by its revolution (with its conjectured GDP per capita attaining in 1928 only the level it had reached by 1911)?

NINTH: Why did France—perhaps the richest and most promising country of Europe at the time of Louis XIV (ruled 1643–1715)—always run in slower gear than England? Was it because of the absolutist policies of the three Louis (XIV, XV, and XVI), for which Colbert set the tone? Was it the alliance between the monarchy and the nobility, contrasting with an England in which the monarchy relied more on the bourgeoisie, while the nobility disintegrated?

We do not hope to answer these questions, any more than those who have posed them before us. Our "plausible explanation," however, takes the form of a set of propositions with which we hope to address the questions. We will list the propositions in the next section and discuss them in turn; then, in the next chapter, we will speculate on whether the same propositions might be applicable to the third world today.

PROPOSITIONS ABOUT EUROPEAN DEVELOPMENT

FIRST: The history of Europe from the late Roman Empire on consists of a protracted struggle for liberalism—freedom *from* serfdom, *from* monopoly, and *from* privilege, and freedom *of* trade. But it was "three steps forward and two back" all the way. Restrictions were intensified in times of troubles, caused by depression, plague, warfare, and rivalries with other countries. Liberalization occurred because of hard bargaining, by powerful people addressing themselves to other powerful people whose acquiescence was necessary to their own aspirations and was achievable only through concessions. Progress in the struggle is prodigious, but it has not yet been won.

SECOND: European development has been accompanied by an increasing balance of leverage, both political and economic (defined on page 16). Balance (which is never fully achieved) is increased when a powerful group is required (usually for its own benefit) to make concessions to a weaker one. In the European experience, progress is more likely in "pluralistic" societies, or those containing many identifiable groups (such as kings, nobles, clerics, town patricians, bourgeoisie, artisans, workers, and different minority or ethnic groups), who see momentary advantage in temporary coalitions. Flexibility in coalition-forming makes it possible for weaker groups to make their advantages secure by shifting from one strong partner (becoming oppressive) to another. In Europe, kings, nobles, and the Church made their bargains with one another first; as these coalitions broke, one or the other group allied itself with town patricians and/or bourgeoisie. Over time, artisans joined the process; workers followed in the nineteenth and twentieth centuries. Minority groups and recent immigrants are only now joining; their entry into "the system" is not yet complete.

THIRD: By its introduction of more complex means of production, economic development requires increasingly complex institutions of trust. Institutions of trust depend on the keeping of promises, whether to preserve one's own creditworthiness or to prevent social or legal sanction if they are broken. Each such institution is formed when its marginal utility to the group having power to form it is greater than the marginal cost that the same group would suffer for *not* having formed it. In Europe, these institutions grew *very* slowly (by modern perceptions), and with many reverses. On the economic side, they include the banking system, the promissory note, legal business forms such as partnership and corporation (with limited liability), stock exchanges, and many more. On the political side, they include parliaments, courts, and other instruments to resolve conflicts in a predictable fashion. Adam Smith pointed out that the division of labor is limited by the size of the market, but he lived in an era in which the basic institutions were already in place.

Had he lived earlier, he might have commented that the division of labor is limited by the extent of the institutions of trust.

FOURTH: Europe's economic development depended on the elimination of endemic warfare. Endemic (as opposed to institutionalized) warfare breaks out spontaneously; in medieval Europe it was a daily affair for knights, nobility, and kings. Its endemic nature was reinforced by the existence of private armies and by the custom that anyone could make war who could afford to do so. A king (or prince) might finance a war from his own treasury or by borrowing from allies, bypassing whatever legislature might otherwise encumber him. Institutionalized warfare (which occurred increasingly from the sixteenth century on) required parliamentary approval and financing. The shift from one to the other was gradual, and the border between them was vague. Though institutionalized warfare may be more lethal, it appears to interfere less with economic development—possibly because it has definite dates of beginning and end, thus promoting predictability, or possibly because parliamentary approval may take into account economic interests as well as those of power.

FIFTH: Europe's economic development appears to be associated with a shift, among the rulers, away from a "propensity for power" and toward a "propensity for material wealth." The shift has not been complete, and probably never will be. There is little evidence that Roman rulers (either the Senate or the Emperors) were concerned with economic development (except for agriculture). Although the Romans traded, despoliation of neighbors was a principal means of obtaining wealth. By contrast, Henry VII and Elizabeth I of England, and Henry IV and Louis XIV of France, took strong measures for the development of their countries at least a century before the industrial revolution occurred.

The first evidence of shift came when economic development was recognized as a *means* to power. In this first enlightening, neighbor-despoliation and tribute (such as Danegeld) on the one hand, and production on the other, were equally legitimate means of achieving income, choices being made (we suppose) along benefit-cost principles. The mercantile age was the product of this reasoning. Only with the Physiocrats, and then Adam Smith (helped by David Hume), did rulers become conscious that one's own well-being was enhanced by the prosperity of one's neighbors. This new enlightenment (we speculate) reinforced the propensity for wealth and also may have diminished the likelihood of endemic war, while promoting liberalism, bargaining, and the creation of institutions of trust.

THE FIVE PROPOSITIONS AND THE THREE PATHS

For Europe, these five propositions largely mirror the three paths of development (personal, political, and economic) which we set forth in Chapter 1. In many ways, the relationship between these two chapters is obvious, but a few comments may be necessary to complete it.

We take as self-evident that economic development requires an ever-expanding production-possibility curve (moving outward), as well as efficient positions (along the curve) rather than inefficient ones (below and to the left of the curve). However, we do not envisage the curve as a single line (as in classical economics) but as a vague band (see Figure 15–1). Assume a society at point A. Different individuals see the remaining curve differently, according to their differing future visions, time horizons, and propensities for risk. No point other than A is *known*; every other point can be achieved only at some risk. All points except A bear a discount, which differs among individuals according to time horizon. Some points (achievable in the more distant future, but with technology known now) are visible to some but not to others. The density (darkness) of the band reflects the number of people who "see" a given point as a maximizing alternative to A. Thus there are many curves, as seen by different individuals that pass through A. Some curves even pass *above* A, for individuals who envisage A itself as inefficient, but presumably no curve passes through the ray from the origin to A (not drawn).

Economic growth consists in the outward movement of A. At first, A moves from its location to some point within the band (already perceived by some people). As A moves, and more persons become aware that its new position is possible, further positions become perceived by some. Whether such people do propel A outward depends on their capacity and incentive to do so. The greater the risk-propensity, future vision, and time horizons of individuals

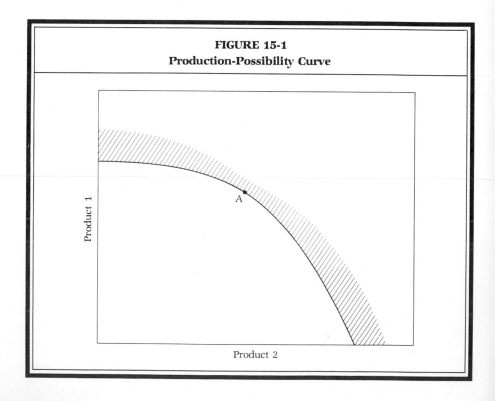

FIGURE 15-1
Production-Possibility Curve

Product 1

A

Product 2

with the political and material clout to make choices, the wider the band, and the more likely A (and thus the entire band) will move.

For reasons well known to economic theory, efficiency requires that factor prices be proportional to marginal productivities; only thus will they reflect relative scarcities. Classical economists have devised a theory (depending on the free market) to explain how such efficient positions are reached. But most propositions of that theory were violated endlessly throughout European history, through concentrations of power in which private goals and incentives differed from those of economic growth. Progress in our five propositions, which depends as much on the decisions by key people as on the millions of individuals functioning in markets, is therefore jerky.

Certain situational reasons partially explain the early progress by some areas: Venice's relationship with the Byzantine Empire and her position on the eastern trade routes, Champagne at the crossroads of Europe's north-south and east-west routes, Flanders and Holland on the North Sea, and England's ability to produce wool. But these reasons do not explain why Venice, Flanders, and Holland declined relatively in the seventeenth century, or why others in similar situations (Constantinople or Alexandria instead of Venice, Denmark on the North Sea, and Spain with the ability to produce wool) did not compete more effectively than they did.

We claim no prophetic judgment or even originality in the five propositions, for we view them with hindsight and with the help of economic historians. It was far different for the decision-makers who took the risks as history unfolded! We submit (as a hypothesis) that the differential development of Europe occurred primarily because critical individuals made different judgments, sometimes advancing their countries along the paths and sometimes retarding them. These individuals had different perceptions of risk, future, and time, and different propensities for power and for material wealth. We neither prove nor measure the propensities, but only infer them from the decisions. We have carried our reductionism as far as it will go.

Let us turn now to specific examples of the five propositions.

FIRST PROPOSITION: THE STRUGGLE FOR LIBERALISM

Rome at the time of Augustus (27 B.C.–14 A.D.) had few restrictions on commerce. Roman citizens were free to move or trade as they wished. Taxes, primarily on land and people, were suspended in periods when booty was sufficient. There were also modest port taxes. Though most products were consumed locally, nevertheless sailing vessels traveled as far as China and throughout the Mediterranean, visiting European, Asian, and African ports. Fairs were frequent and vigorous. No one measured gross domestic product, but surely it was increasing.

By the time of Diocletian (284–305 A.D.) and Constantine (311–337), the Empire was under severe military pressure. Earlier wars had caused heavy population decline. In response, peasants were tied to the soil, branded if they

escaped and were caught; merchants and producers were frozen in their occupations, which their sons were forced to continue; prices were rigidly fixed
to control inflation (under penalty of death, although it was not frequently
exercised); professional corporations were held to their duties by the State; and
tasks (such as fire or police protection) that had earlier been honorific became
onerous. Taxes were increasingly severe. In defense, peasants put themselves
under the patrocinium of the powerful, and some fled to the barbarians (more
so in later years).

As the Empire crumbled nonetheless, these restrictions were eased. Both
production and trade declined, as evidenced by the retraction of city walls, by
the wasting-away of towns and roads, by the replacement of merchants by
clerics as the principal townspeople, and by the decreased references to shipping. Most persons lived on self-sufficient and self-defending estates. Neither
commerce nor fairs were extinguished; salt and products of the Far East continued to be brought to the estates, principally by Jews and Syrians. But variety
and volume had declined enormously (although we have no secure data). Domain lords exerted monopolies (banal rights) over grist mills and courts; except
for these, potential traders were inhibited mainly by lawlessness outside their
protected areas, or by the time-consuming performance of feudal obligations.

With the commercial revolution of the tenth to thirteenth centuries, trade
restrictions took a new turn. The growth of towns *freed* workers of their servile
obligations (whoever lived in a town for a year and a day became free). The
trading axis (luxury goods from Northern Italy, wool from England, cloth from
Flanders, and grain from Central Europe) centered on Champagne, where the
great fairs were held in the twelfth and thirteenth centuries. Merchants "gelded"
together to provide common services, protection, and quality control, as well
as for taxation. Town governments were soon controlled by these merchant
guilds; thus they resembled corporate states where the common weal was not
distinct from the welfare of the governors. In the tenth century, entry into the
guilds was easy, regulations were flexible, and trade was almost unrestricted,
although guilds often had to bargain with feudal lords for town privileges.

By the thirteenth century—when population had expanded, land was scarce,
and Europe was therefore "saturated"—towns, guilds, and principalities had
become a mosaic of restrictions: on prices, on kinds of goods produced, on
entry into occupations, on currency transactions, on trading in specified places.
Aliens were discriminated against; Jews were expelled; and townsmen were
classified according to rank and privilege. Towns and merchants preserved their
monopolies by dirty tricks (such as by waylaying competitors, silting rival
harbors, or sinking ships). They also used piracy, embargoes, contentious di-
plomacy, and often outright war (van Werveke, 1971:14). Restrictions on wages
and labor movement were intensified in Europe's "time of troubles" (the fourteenth century, marked by famines, plagues, and warfare).

Europe's commercial history from the thirteenth century on is one of hard
bargaining to soften the restrictions on one's own trade, while reimposing them
to finance wars, beleaguer enemies, promote companies, and strengthen temporary monopolies. England vascillated between taxing wool exports (to promote the domestic cloth industry) and encouraging the exports of both cloth

and wool (to bolster the exchequer). European towns entered into agreements (of which the Hanseatic League is the most famous) for reciprocal privileges, creating a set of discriminating duties so complex that errors (and corruption) must have been fearful.

By the fourteenth century, inter-town agreements were numerous. Lombardy, Flanders, and Holland in particular bargained their way into markets of other principalities, took stands against monopolies, and extended their trading as far as eastern Europe, the Ottoman Empire, and the Far East (Glamann, 1977:224, and Cipolla, 1963:425). Philip of Alsace, who ruled from 1168 to 1191, bargained strongly for Flemish merchants. Later Flemish counts were not so effective, and leadership in trade negotiations passed to the dukes of Brabant, especially Henry I, who ruled from 1190–1235, and John I, who ruled from 1268–1294 (van Werweke; 1963:334–6). One explanation for the success of the Low Countries and Italian cities may be that they were small, ruled by liberal counts and dukes (Flanders and Brabant) or town councils (Italy) that could overcome internal tolls. England, France, and Germany on the other hand, were crowded with tolls imposed by domain lords—frequent in England (until the eighteenth century), overwhelming in France (until the Revolution), and strangling in Germany (until the Zollverein, 1833).

The rise of Northern Italy, Holland, and Flanders was thus associated with bargaining for freer trade and with emphasis on exports (major question numbers 4 and 5). By analyzing tolls collected in Genoa, Lopez (1976:100) showed that free access to markets was more important in Italy's advance than any political controls. With virtual free-trade policies in the sixteenth century, Amsterdam became the commercial and banking center for Europe, which Gresham used as a model for England. The Dutch designed vessels far in advance of other European countries (cheaper to build and operate, with a multipurpose design) and captured the grain trade between Central Europe and the West. Finally Italy's decline in the seventeenth century was associated with increasing inflexibility: trade restrictions and adherence to monopolistic guilds existed long after their counterparts had been overcome in England.

Advocates of protection for development often point out that the industrial revolution in England occurred after a protectionist and mercantilist thrust. This thrust included the Navigation Act (1651); commercial wars with France, Holland, and Spain; the theory that "trade follows the flag;" and numerous restrictions on exports such as the Cokayne Plan (1614). Similarly, Germany's development in the late nineteenth century occurred in a period of increasing protectionism, following the doctrines of List. But this view neglects the observation that these events were but countercurrents in a dominant trend toward dismantling the enormous number and kinds of restrictions inherited from the Middle Ages. Europe's rapid development occurred as internal barriers were swept away (in the eighteenth and nineteenth centuries). Finally, the nineteenth century—when development was most rapid—was one of unprecedented freedom in international trade. A temporary backlash, however, occurred at the end of the century, but it was reversed with reciprocal bargaining in the 1930s followed by the General Agreement on Tariffs and Trade in the 1940s.

SECOND PROPOSITION: BALANCE OF LEVERAGE

Commercial liberalism could only have been possible with increasing balance of leverage, in which coalitions bargained to obtain mutual privileges and to break down the monopolies of others. No better weapon was available to town burgesses than their ability to throw weight to one side or another in the rivalry between barons and king, or between king and Church. It was largely as counterweight to his barons that Edward I (who ruled 1272–1307) called knights and burgesses into the first English parliaments and instituted land laws favoring tenants (as opposed to barons), which (though Edward hardly had intended it) promoted the ultimate demise of feudalism. The economic superiority of the towns of North Italy may be explained, in part, by their intermediate location, in which the political gravities of the Holy Roman Empire, the Pope, Norman Sicily, and the Byzantine Empire exerted mutual counter-pulls. Although pledging fealty to Frederick I (Peace of Constance, 1183) and paying taxes, the towns remained virtually autonomous in economic management. The dispersion of Hanseatic power, from Novgorod to the Teutonic Order, on through Lübeck and into Norway, Flanders, and even England, enabled the League to play one monarch against another, taking its business where the greatest privileges were offered.

New activities would open gates to new groups. The growth of commerce shifted wealth relatively away from kings and nobles and toward merchants. As financial systems emerged, merchants and financiers became separate groups, each with its separate leverage on the other. The merchants had leverage because they created time and place utility, the financiers had it because they organized and manipulated credit. The leverage of kings lay in their ability to tax, to farm taxes, to pledge future revenues against current borrowing, to sell titles to nobility, and to debase the currency. By the thirteenth century, the domainal revenues of kings were insufficient to finance their wars and the profligate spending of some of them; hence their leverage decreased. The greater financiers, of course, had more leverage against kings than the lesser ones, so they could bargain for better terms—not only better rates of interest, but also privilege and monopoly.

Town and country distinctions further contributed to Europe's pluralism. Flemish counts and countesses of the twelfth and thirteenth centuries vascillated between their favor of cities for their infrastructure and their fear of the growing power of guilds. When the latter became too great, they would shift encouragement to rural industry. The same effect occurred spontaneously in eighteenth-century England. To escape the restrictions of urban guilds, many merchants "put out" their materials to rural craftsmen, thus strengthening rural industry as a counter-weight to urban.

Balance of leverage may be very delicate, easily upset. By the fourteenth century in France, artisans' guilds were beginning to challenge the dominance of merchant guilds in town government. They may have done so too soon; this dissention may have weakened the towns in their struggle with the monarchy. By issuing titles and privileges to the artisans' guilds. Charles VII and Louis IX established the custom of royal control over these matters (Miskimin, 1975:107).

The same events appear not to have happened in England; merchant power gradually gave way without royal intervention in every city except London. Could this difference be one reason for the relative backwardness of France during this period (major question number 9)?

The granting of privileges could also be a force *toward* balance. Charlemagne and his sons granted fiefs, and in return the lords supplied the emperor's army. The emperor *had* to buy his defense; yet the more land he paid out, the less was his remaining leverage over the lords. By similar token, kings who granted tax farms (common in the sixteenth and seventeenth centuries) promoted administrative decentralization (van der Wee, 1977:359).

Always, groups acquiring leverage (even the poorest of the poor) had goods or services to offer. As Central Europe regressed into feudalism in the sixteenth century, some princes (in Habsburg lands, Prussia, and Saxony) took an increasing interest in the welfare of the peasantry—sometimes for humanitarian reasons, but more often because they saw in them taxpayers and soldiers (Slichter van Bath, 1977:177).

Leverage of the previously unprivileged advanced significantly in the nineteenth century. Greater access to land and political institutions came with the French Revolution, the wave of reforms in Britain during the 1830s, the freeing of slaves in all of Europe (England in 1833), the agrarian and administrative reforms of Central Europe (including the end of Russian feudalism), and above all, the spread of education. The rivalry between Gladstone and Disraeli resulted in each trying to outdo the other in electoral and educational reforms. All these reforms occurred in the wake of an increasing shortage of labor. The leverage of workers had been established earlier, through the industrial revolution; the reforms only made it manifest. Population was growing, but technology was advancing more than apace. A skilled citizenry was needed to operate the machines and increase the supply of foodstuffs. Education, political access, unionism, and higher wages were both the means to obtain these skilled workers and the price that had to be paid.

Balance of leverage is a *condition*, to be distinguished from the *institutions* through which it operates. The ideal condition is that no unit (private or government) shall exercise more economic or political control than is necessary for its efficient functioning and that each unit shall have enough political or economic power to defend itself reasonably well (adequate defense being a matter for interpretation). The free market, on the other hand, is an institution for exercising leverage, but not the only one. Industry- or government-administered allocations of resources have also proved efficient (for example, Germany in the 1860s and Russia in the 1890s). Gerschenkron (1962:23) shows how the private banking system in France redistributed resources away from archaic enterprises and toward progressive ones in the mid-nineteenth century. But no institution—free market, government, industrial corporation, or bank—will prove effective unless the underlying condition of balance in leverage is present to some reasonable degree.

In summary, all incomes are derived directly or indirectly from production. Therefore the share of *everyone* depends on how factor incomes are initially apportioned or subsequently redistributed. Any unit (sector) with excessive influence over the pricing process may distort income in its favor, thus upsetting the market efficiency of Smithian economics. These distortions can be lessened (hardly eliminated) *only* in societies where competing units exert enough force against one another to prevent undue monopoly by any one. Weaker units may leverage their force with appropriate alliances. Full balance has never existed completely and probably never will. The closer a society comes to it, however, the less distorted will be its factor prices. Since efficiency is an ingredient in development, we would suggest that a tolerable balance of leverage, historically derived, *may* explain (in part) the association of both commercial liberalism and more equitable income distribution on the one hand, with the economic development of Europe and its North American descendants on the other.

THIRD PROPOSITION: INSTITUTIONS OF TRUST

It took almost four hundred years for the "writings obligatory" (extension of commercial credit), common in the thirteenth century, to evolve into the endorsable promissory note. Why? In the thirteenth century, cumbersome formalities were necessary to protect all parties against fraud. Only by formal *cessio*, sworn before a notary, could the writing obligatory be transferred to another individual. To sue a defaulting debtor, the holder had to have permission of the original writer. Naturally, the bills did not circulate freely. In the sixteenth century, most of these cumbersome formalities remained in France, but they had been loosened in Flanders (major question numbers 5 and 9). A verdict in Antwerp gave the bearer the same rights as the original creditor. In Holland, these rights were later written into law, and a similar set was included in the English Promissory Notes Act of 1704.

Institutions of trust (of which the promissory note is but an example) are required to assure a smooth flow of transactions, with appropriate protection for all parties. Northern Italy's lead over the rest of Europe in such instruments in the high Middle Ages reflected the trust of investors for venturers who carried their merchandise to distant shores. A small, close-knit society, where important people knew one another, facilitated the trust. These instruments may have been both a result and a cause of Northern Italy's advanced position by the twelfth century (major question number 4).

The number of such institutions is legion. Included are the monetary system, parliamentary democracy, the business corporation (with limited liability), the division of powers between central and local governments, the contract (and means of its enforcement), and on and on. Like the promissory note, these institutions developed step by step, over centuries. The great limited companies of the seventeenth century (of which the East India Company is most famous) resembled feudalism more than they did the modern corporation with limited liability; they were the lords over colonial territories. Public finance experimented with innumerable instruments and procedures as it evolved from the borrowings of kings in the thirteenth century to a flexible process by which—

with a limited number of instruments—a government now bridges the gap between its receipts and expenditures and capitalizes on future receipts.

An examination of the full history of such institutions would reveal that they often lag far behind the first instances of need for them. The lag (we suppose) comes from the risk of anything new (who will suffer from it?) and the jockeying for maximum protection and advantage. De Vries (1976:41) cites "institutional inflexibility" as a major reason for delaying agricultural reform in the seventeenth century. "Noble, clerical, and bourgeois landowners who leased so much of their land to peasants were eager to protect (it) from tenants who might deplete the soil by overcropping. Their leases frequently stipulated conservative practices and frequent fallows."

Trial, error, and reversals occurred over and again. Elizabeth I established a highly efficient system of public finance under Gresham's tutelage, but the Stuarts destroyed it with their profligacy (van der Wee, 1977:380–1). It had to be restructured under William and Mary. Sometimes a system that was basically sound would be destroyed when subjected to excesses at a tender age, such as John Law's *Banque Royale*, which failed to withstand the stock speculations of 1720. The British, on the other hand, did not destroy their public finance system because of the South Sea bubble, also in 1720. Partly as a result, the English system of banking and finance was more modern than the French in the eighteenth century (major question number 9).

An institution of economic growth must promote efficient allocation of factors of production; therefore, it must enforce decisions adverse to those groups (even the wealthy and powerful) whose activities have become obsolete. The free market is such an institution, provided it is not encumbered by too much monopoly or privilege. Parliamentary democracy is another, provided it is not manipulated by powerful groups. Such institutions must therefore be sufficiently valuable to the powerful that they will not destroy them to avoid adverse decisions. The demise of feudalism and the gradual freeing of serfs and villeins indicate that institutions for efficient allocation were evolving in Europe (however imperfectly) in the Middle Ages. These included towns, new land distributions, the relinquishing of banal rights, rent payments instead of feudal obligations, as well as banks, commercial instruments, and new types of companies.

Yet institutions of trust may not always have emerged fast enough. In major question number 3, we asked why the commercial revolution ended about 1300. North and Thomas (1973) have proposed a Malthusian answer: the earlier rise in population had outstripped known technology. Without contesting this hypothesis, we add a complementary one: that production had outstripped medieval institutions, which did not adapt sharply enough to handle the higher volume of trade. The new forms were often resisted by feudal lords, monarchies, and tradesmen unwilling to cede monopolies or vaguely fearful that they would be "done in" by devils other than those they knew.

We now see a relationship among the first three of our five propositions. Relative balance of leverage is essential to the growth of liberalism, while institutions make secure whatever leverage has been achieved. Possibly long-range cycles occur because of relative *imbalance* among these three—for example, the recession of the fourteenth century might have occurred (in part) because institutional development had not kept pace with the degree of liberalism and balance in leverage achieved before 1250.

The retreat of liberalism may have been the result: guilds and towns restricted trade far more in 1300 than they did in 1100. The leverage of persons not in guilds or holding other privileged positions was thereby diminished. Many starved; population declined. Further restrictions occurred in the fourteenth century (such as the Statute of Laborers), which together with the general discontent led to the *Jacquerie* revolt (France, 1358) and the Peasants' Revolt (England, 1381).

Then came the reversal. Further loss of life by famine, plaque, and warfare increased the marginal productivity of the surviving unprivileged. This increase in their leverage, along with the new institutions, restored relative balance (approximately 1450), and economic growth continued.

An even longer cycle is seen in Central Europe (major question number 7). East of Elbe, the decline of feudalism was arrested and reversed in approximately the sixteenth century; serfdom and other obligations were not dismantled until the nineteenth century, and then abruptly. From the sixteenth to the nineteenth century, they were becoming *more* severe, in contrast to the liberalization of the West. Why? Some historians have suggested the "primary-product syndrome," or "exploitation" by the West, with arguments resembling those of the New International Economic Order today. Others rely on situational factors: sheer distance from the center of the growth axis, difficulties of overland transport (roads were usually tracks, and journeys were therefore arduous and time consuming), and good natural conditions in Centural Europe for crops.

We see no reason to join this debate now. While both sides may be partly right, neither of their reasonings is compelling. The "colonization" of East by West had been largely overcome after the defeat of the Teutonic Order at Tannenberg (1410), and those estates situated close to the Elbe were not without access to the sea. So we add a further set of reasonings. The German Empire, previously one of the most efficient, progressive, and unified states of Europe, disintegrated (after 1250) into a number of warring principalities, just in the age when France and England were emerging as nation-states. The institutions promoting trade in the West were (we have suggested) evolving out of a tug-and-pull among kings, nobles, and merchants. The "beggar kings" of Germany were too weak to exert any such pull. Many of the German princes were profligate in their borrowing and personal consumption, and there was no counterforce to stop them. Often they mediatized their towns to secure their debts. Against this power, the towns could not grow. Without the same leverage that they had in the West, traders could not bargain for liberalization; oppressive river tolls prohibited long-distance trade for anything except those goods (such as grain exports) on which the princes depended. In exchange, they imported manufactures, mainly from England and Holland.

One final word on European feudalism. For all its ultimate limitations, it was constantly evolving. Unlike his Japanese, Chinese, Ottoman, and other counterparts, the European lord did not have life-or-death power over his subjects, and after Charlemagne, European feudalism was *not* (as it was in China) destroyed and recreated by periodic overthrows. It was marked by clearly-defined mutual obligations: the lord had the duty to protect and defend those entrusted to him. Perhaps the coexistence of Church and lay properties, and the "parallel government" of the Church (Chapter 1) helped create this mutality and adaptability. With some hesitation, we suggest that perhaps the European ability to compromise, so important to institutional flexibility in the high Middle Ages, had some of its roots in Carolingian feudalism.

FOURTH PROPOSITION: WARFARE

"The typical (tenth-century) lord lived by and for constant fighting . . . Villages with no châteaux were often ruined, and wide stretches of land became waste" (Koebner, 1966:69). "The feudal order . . . gave birth to a military nobility whose industry *par excellence* was warfare. The very prospect of the campaigning season brought joy . . ." (Miller, 1963:299).

In early medieval Europe, war was continuous; there was no day in which any person might be reasonably secure that his assets would not be despoiled by nightfall. This fact alone increased the risk of trade enormously and is probably the major reason why so little of it occurred.

War was twice devastating: first, it destroyed real capital, and second, it drained away the financial assets that might have promoted investment. The literature is replete with examples; we have space for only a few.

On the financial side, the large amounts of royal, ducal, and comital borrowing in the Middle Ages were primarily for war and consumption, and only secondarily for productive investment (Fryde and Fryde, 1963). Postan (1971:588) writes how 120 years of war in the eleventh and twelfth centuries damaged English landowners financially, especially Edward III's war taxes and purveyances on wool. In France, royal expenditures on war would inevitably work their way down to the towns. Fryde and Fryde (1963:534) cite reports submitted to Louis IX in 1260 on how communes attributed their financial weaknesses to the costs of the Crusade of 1248. The treaty with France (1305) imposed a crushing burden on Flanders, and the Hundred Years War had disastrous effects on town finances throughout France (Fryde and Fryde, 1963:537), in addition to helping drive Edward III of England into bankruptcy. If we (very reasonably) assume that town finances might have gone primarily for production, and royal finances primarily for war, we can—even without exact figures—surmise that the adverse effects on trade and production were enormous.

The Italian Wars (1494–1517), the French-Habsburg Wars (1519–1559), the sporadic wars with the Ottoman Empire, the Revolt of the Netherlands (1567–1579), and the Thirty Years War (1618–1648) mopped up Europe's available resources in swift succession. Henry VIII's war with France nearly bankrupt the English exchequer and led to major currency debasement (whose silver lining was a dramatic increase in exports). The Great Northern War and its predecessors in the Baltic left Swedish kings in great debt throughout the seventeenth century and on up to 1720 (Wilson, 1967:565). The seventeenth century saw only three years in which Europe was not at war. The War of the League of Augsburg (1689–1697) drove even Louis XIV to the brink of bankruptcy. The wars of the Spanish Succession (1701–1714) and Austrian Succession (1740–1748) also drained the treasuries of the leading continental powers. The cost of war with the Portuguese was so high that the Dutch West India Company ran serious losses despite the profitable slave trade of the seventeenth century (Rich, 1967:337). Indeed, commercial wars were the single, prime cause of the decline of Holland (major question number 5). Crushing taxes were imposed on Dutch businesses, which were simply too few in number to match such formidable opponents as France, England, and Spain.

Physical destruction was also enormous and frequent. The Roman Empire collapsed in the midst of war on all sides (major question number 1). Clark (1968:85) reports that "several historians would put the epoch of greatest confusion and destruction, and consequently maximum depopulation, about the ninth century," the period of Saracen, Viking, and Magyar invasions. Farms were laid waste, and agriculture had to be reorganized in concentrated plots around castles (Koebner, 1966:57–64); lands had to be repopulated afterward.

Some writers have, however, suggested that premodern war was often less than devastating. First, it was not clear whether armies belonged to kings or to political entities such as countries, principalities, and towns. Trade with the "enemy" might go on almost undisturbed. Second, armies were small, advanced overland slowly, fed themselves from the farms, but may have left little damage. These accounts must be balanced against others of great devastation and widespread burning and looting of farms, villages, and castles. No doubt both types of warfare occurred. In either case, however, the physical destruction of the battle was probably the least of the harmful effects. Wars spread plague; they caused famine as crops were destroyed or not sown; many more died from these effects than from battle.

In a world of continuous fighting, shifting alliances, and vague boundaries between brigandage and war, it is impossible to quantify war. Yet there *seems* to have been some lessening of hostilities in Western Europe at the time of the commercial revolution (*c* 950 to 1300). (The campaigns of the Eastern emperors against the German princes, the popes, and rival dynasties continued, however.) We except the Crusades from this suggestion: they may even have diverted or united the West, shifting the stage of warfare to the Mediterranean.

Five bits of evidence on the lessening of warfare in the High Middle Ages are: *first*, the Cluniac reforms and concerns of the Church for peace, which culminated in the Truce of God, limiting warfare to certain days; *second*, the safe-conduct passes for traders, issued by princes and town patricians, and especially by the Count of Champagne; *third*, increasing centralization in later Capetian France and England (in contrast to early Capetian times and to Germany after 1250), which led to royal protection for trade; *fourth*, the decline in the number of castles; and *fifth*, greater safety on roads and the decline of armed caravans in the thirteenth century.

The administrative efficiency of the Teutonic Order in its territory and the naval force of the Hanseatic League may also have protected the peace. There were even occasional, local periods of peace for several years. The reign of Henry I of England (1100–1135) brought thirty years of peace, which coincided with a strengthened economy and the development of political institutions such as itinerant justice. Much was lost in the subsequent civil war between Stephen and Mathilda, however.

All this came to an end in the fourteenth century. The Hundred Years War wrought physical destruction on France, while sapping the resources of England as well. Cipolla (1976:236) believes the Italian Wars (1494–1517) marked the beginning of the decline of Italy (major question number 4). The dynastic wars between Lancaster and York (ending in 1485) laid waste much of England. But from that point on, the only wars waged on British territory were either civil wars or battles involving Ireland, Scotland, and Wales.

Wars continued unabated on the Continent, however. The Thirty Years War (1618–1648) was enormously destructive, causing population losses of up to 50 percent in several German principalities. The subsequent consolidation of farms may have been a factor in resurgent feudalism (major question number 7).

Nevertheless, the sixteenth century would seem to be a turning point for Western Europe. First, nation-states were gaining stature, along with national finances and national armies. Kings and princes could enforce peace *within* their territories as never before. As a result, wars increasingly had beginning and ending dates; less and less did they burst out spontaneously. Second, warfare shifted more to the sea. While it was still destructive, some of its effects were removed from the land. Third, the financial exhaustions had a silver lining. Peace treaties were increasingly compromises; less and less was there a clear victor and a clear vanquished. The Italian Wars ended when Francis I, Maximilian, and Charles V negotiated away all remaining differences. Louis XIV was contained time and again, yet his France remained the richest country on the Continent, with secure borders. The Treaty of Utrecht (1714) was a masterpiece of balancing of interests. The doctrine of balance of power emerged, as each sovereign became aware that his nation could not dominate.

The process was carried a step further by the Peace of Paris, ending the Seven Years War (1756–1763). England was the clear victor and had the opportunity of humbling France into a second-rate power. Yet she did not do so (much to the annoyance of William Pitt, who was out of office at the time). Aware that the conquest of North America and India brought her empire to its economic limit, England returned territories conquered in the Caribbean and Africa to France. Physiocratic ideas were increasingly heard, that benefits are mutual and good is not limited; Adam Smith was not long off. The loss of the American Revolution (1775–1783), followed by England's greatest commercial activity to date, taught her that empire and military victory do not always promote trade and prosperity—a lesson that had to be learned again, in Africa and Asia, in the twentieth century.

The Congress of Vienna (1815) marked another step in Europe's ability to compromise. The negotiating skill of Tallyrand, who divided his opponents, again assured that France would not be overly weakened. The resulting "century of peace" (with but a few interruptions) coincided with Europe's greatest economic advance to date.

We begin—albeit dimly—to see a pattern in. European development. The greatest eras of economic advance (950–1300; 1815–1914; and the sixteenth century in England) are precisely those in which both endemic warfare decreased and artificial restrictions on trade and industry were loosened, while the periods of major retraction (the decline of the Roman Empire and the fourteenth and early fifteenth centuries in the West) were those of pervasive warfare and more centralized control. Our sample is far too small to satisfy a statistician, but it is the only one we have.

We do not, however, see any evidence that warfare slowed the development of institutions, nor the evolution of science or education. These appear to have their own explanations. While the institutionalized warfare of the nineteenth and twentieth centuries destroyed capital and thereby slowed growth, nevertheless Europe appeared to have passed a threshold, and early economic recuperation from war would now seem possible. Janossy (1971) has shown how Europe's "economic miracles" of the twentieth century were no more than returns to the trend line of economic growth established before each war. It would be dangerous to extrapolate this "happy finding," however, for nuclear war may again change all the parameters.

FIFTH PROPOSITION: PROPENSITY FOR POWER VERSUS PROPENSITY FOR WEALTH

The persistent and pervasive role of warfare, from the dawn of history to the sixteenth century, leads us to infer that the propensity for power (among the rulers) dominated that for material wealth. Caesar did not conquer Gaul for its mineral resources or even for its foodstuffs. Roman imports of grain were a byproduct of the African conquest, not a reason for it. The constant offensive to control the lives of others was matched by a neglect of one's own production potential. The Romans did care about agriculture and ranching, for these were the occupations of patricians. Cato called agriculture the citizen's "most honorable profession." But he contrasted it with usury, which he considered the most shameful (Koebner, 1966:14). The Senate showed little interest in commerce or industry; it closed the Macedonian mines (167 B.C.) and destroyed the fine harbors of Corinth and Carthage.

Yet the two propensities are never completely separate; in the Middle Ages, they reinforced each other. There have always been two ways to obtain wealth: by production and by despoiling one's neighbor. The Vikings appear to have made a deliberate calculation. The forests of Scandinavia were difficult to cut down in the tenth century, and the climate was harsh for farming. It was less costly to raid the coasts of Europe and to settle there. Frederick II of the Holy Roman Empire (who ruled 1208–1250) became one of the wealthiest kings of Europe by taxing Lombardy, not by cultivating his domain.

If one were to offset the fortunes squandered for war against those gained from it, however, the balance would lie heavily with the former. (The calculation is not worth making, for the "benefits" are always difficult to determine and subject to ideological interpretation.) The literature on medieval wars does not give even an inkling that economic advantage was a major motive of the generals. Trade was a byproduct of the Crusades, while the power to dictate religion was the moving force. The Burgundian dynasty in Flanders borrowed excessively in its quest to be equals to the major powers of Europe, and the Emperors of Germany (after 1250) pledged lands, mediatized towns, and borrowed to buy the favor of electors (Fryde and Fryde, 1963:501, 507).

For some centuries (say, the tenth to the eighteenth), war and trade were opposite sides of the coin. A German poetic dictum of the seventeenth century holds that war, trade, and piracy are one-in-three, not be sundered *(Krieg, Handel, and Piraterie; Dreieinig sind Sie, nicht zu trennen)* (Glamann, 1977:265). Mercantilism was the child of this marriage.

It is difficult to say when the balance shifted. Rich (1967:323) suggests that "in the fifteenth and sixteenth centuries, statesmen, secular and ecclesiastical, thought more of economic factors than they had previously done." Gold and silver, which had been a means to territorial expansion in earlier centuries, had become ends in themselves. The business-like manner with which the great chartered companies were outfitted and managed and the scant attention paid by kings to territory per se would suggest that the colonization of the New World was primarily for economic profit (Coornaert, 1967:228). Lands were for plantations and for the religiously persecuted. Caribbean Indians, who would not be slaves, were a "bother," not a prize such as the Habsburgs saw in the Magyars or the Ottomans in the Arabs and the Berbers.

Smith criticized mercantilism for its inconsistency with economic maximization. But mercantilism made good sense in its formative years, when territorial aggrandizement was the major goal, and gold and silver the means to achieve it. By the eighteenth century, when the goal had shifted, the inconsistencies of mercantilism would soon have become obvious—an observation that does not diminish the geniuses of the Physiocrats and Smith for pointing them out.

The values we have attributed to statesmen in general, with respect to national power, can also be attributed to individuals, with respect to personal power. On the one hand are men like Pericles, Alcibiades, Caesar, Pompey, and Sulla, whose object was to rule, and who struck down their enemies mercilessly (Caesar was planning a war of revenge for Crassus when he was killed in the Senate). Among such men also was Selim I (who ruled 1512–1520). In accordance with Ottoman custom, he killed all his brothers and four of his five sons, so there would be no quarrels over succession. Francis I of France (who ruled 1515–1547) showed by his shifting alliances with Protestants, Catholics, and even the Turks, and by his scorched-earth policy in Burgundy, that his supreme interest was personal power; both religion and economics were secondary. At the other extreme, we have Walpole, who resigned as Prime Minister of Britain in 1742 because he had lost a majority in Parliament. He was the first of this tradition. From 1750 on, there were no more dynastic wars in Europe.

We are left to ponder the relationship, if any, between the decline of the power motive and the industrialization of Europe. There may be none whatsoever, but if not their coincidence is indeed most curious.

CONCLUSION

We have sought a plausible explanation for the economic growth of Europe—why it foundered after its first two promising starts, at the time of Augustus and again in the tenth to thirteenth centuries, and why it finally succeeded in its third try, in the eighteenth and nineteenth centuries. Our explanation must be consistent with classical economic theory, especially comparative advantage and the proposition that growth requires high efficiency. It must also help explain why some geographic areas of Europe either led others or fell into relative decline, at different threshold dates.

The usual explanations of economic growth are entrepreneurship, a high rate of saving, and employment of efficient technology (reflecting factor scarcities). These would indeed appear to be the explanations each time growth occurred, while absence of entrepreneurship or saving (or destruction of capital), and use of inappropriate technology, are invariably associated with periods of retrogression. Yet they seem not to be the ultimate explanations; something else in turn explains *them.*

We have suggested that the ultimate explanations are a relative success in the constant struggle for liberalism; an emerging balance of leverage among participating groups in a pluralistic society; the generation of institutions of trust; the decline of endemic warfare; and a relative shift (among the leaders) away from the propensity for power and toward a propensity for material wealth. In specifying these elements, we believe we have carried our reductionism to its limit.

The Roman Empire at the time of Augustus (*d.* 14 A.D.) showed the first promise of generating an industrial revolution. *Pax Romana* everywhere (except on the borders) supplied a vast trading area with relatively few restrictions and little burdensome taxation. Capital was supplied by both agriculture and trading; it was invested in aqueducts, irrigation, ships, and horses. A large portion of the population was literate and numerate; mathematics and astronomy were relatively well advanced; craftsmen were skilled in metallurgy; and the properties of steam power were known by at least 100 A.D. A sophisticated public administration was capable of providing infrastructure, especially roads, and an efficient postal service existed. Corporations were formed for certain kinds of industrial production and state services. Yet obvious inventions such as the rudder and the compass were not made; capital was not concentrated into great trading companies such as those of the seventeenth century; and no industrial revolution occurred.

No one, of course, can offer an unimpeachable explanation, but with the hindsight of the Middle Ages, a few observations can be made. Slavery did not decline as serfdom did in the fourteenth and fifteenth centuries. The "equites" ("horsemen," or civil servants) did not gain enough power, vis-à-vis the generals, to be a balancing force to which lower classes might become allied. Drawn into *patrocinium*, the lower classes thus never attained leverage against their "superiors." The constant fighting of later centuries, the crushing restrictions on personal liberty, and the enormous burden of taxation are sufficient themselves to explain why no threshold was reached. The generals never relinquished their obsession for power.

Europe's second opportunity came with the commercial revolution of the tenth to thirteenth centuries. Once again, trade routes were expanded, wars declined, and merchants were protected. New towns provided freedom from feudal obligations; trading institutions emerged, such as fairs and money exchanges. Yet again the process slowed at the end of the thirteenth century.

Once again no one can say why. North and Thomas (1973) have suggested excessive population growth. We add the possibility that institutions of trust (such as the banking system, promissory notes, and limited-liability companies) had not evolved sufficiently to service the new volume of trade, and what was achieved began to be lost. This decline, in turn, brought about renewed warfare—endemic and persistent—accompanied by plagues and famine.

The cities of Northern Italy (Genoa, Milan, Venice, and Florence) seized the vanguard in the tenth to thirteenth centuries and did not lose it even in the general decline of the fourteenth. Their fortunate positions on the Mediterranean trade routes helped, but did not explain everything. The Italian success in institutional development—banking, financial instruments, accounting, and rules for associations and partnerships—may also explain in part their lead over northern Europe. Their relative freedom from overlords and their skill in bargaining for reciprocal trading privileges may be further explanations.

Their ultimate decline is more complex. In the sixteenth and seventeenth centuries, they lost ground first to the Dutch and eventually to the English. One reason may have been that Italy was Europe's battlefield during the Italian (1494–1517) and the French-Habsburg (1519–1559) wars. Still another may have been the close association of Genoese bankers with Spain and the Habsburgs, which brought great wealth during the heyday of Spanish colonialism but failed to provide a solid base when Spain itself declined. Italy did *not* decline—as some have supposed—because overland trade routes to the East were cut off. Both the Egyptians and the Arabs were eager to maintain that trade, and all ruptures were temporary. However, the Italians did not withstand Dutch competition in grain and shipping. In the sixteenth century, it was the Dutch that were developing the most advanced financial institutions (for example, the Amsterdam Exchange Bank), as well as the most efficient ships. The final blow, however, was that guild power, restrictions, and monopoly persisted in seventeenth-century Italy, just when they were being overcome by the English and the Dutch. The struggle for liberalism was not won in Italy.

The Dutch decline, on the other hand, appears to be the aftermath of war and its financing. The Dutch waged several trade wars against the English, and they fought the Spanish in the war of Dutch independence (1567–1579). They were greatly feared by Colbert, whose perception of them as one of France's most serious threats led to the lengthy warfare between Louis XIV and Holland. Holland was too small a state to finance wars against these powers, and the crushing tax burden made their industries, and ultimately their touted banking systems, noncompetitive with the rising English ones.

To state that the French were late in their development should be tempered by pointing out that until the nineteenth century, they were never very far behind the English, and in some periods they were probably ahead. Their administrative and tax machinery developed almost on a par with the English. Still, several factors stand out. The first is that almost continuous warfare plagued the Continent for over two centuries after the English had—with a few exceptions—rid themselves of it on their soil. The second is that the sociopolitical groupings through which balance of leverage improved in England turned out a bit differently in France. The merchant-craftsman classes did not play off the nobility against the monarchy so effectively in France as they had in England, and therefore in the seventeenth century they did not enjoy the same leverage for parliamentary action as did their English counterparts. Landholding became more "democratized" in England as Henry VIII sold lands confiscated from the Church and (through attainders) from his and his father's enemies. The increase of nonnoble landed and merchant effectiveness in Parliament may have led to the more liberal trade and enclosure laws of Elizabeth's time, as well as to Gresham's financial reforms, just when the Wars of Religion were paralyzing France. Finally, although the Stuarts in England and Louis XIV in France were probably of equal mind for absolute monarchy, Louis was able to implement it more effectively. His minister, Colbert, promoted French economic development through a powerful statism whose efficiency many historians have questioned. Though French and English per capita incomes may have been similar in the fifteenth century, the English was probably higher and rising faster by the seventeenth, for at least a century before the "industrial revolution" (by its most limited definition) began. The isolation of France (and the rest of the Continent) by the Napoleonic wars left England free to develop the world's trade routes, a not insignificant advantage.

There is little disagreement about Spain's backwardness. Inundated by gold and silver from the New World in the sixteenth century, she devoted herself almost single-mindedly to keeping her treasure, and as a result she lost it over the centuries. Her economy was the most restricted and monopolized in Europe. She did not develop popular institutions like those of the English, French, and Dutch, and she built no infrastructure. Instead of creating a banking system, she relied on the Genoese. She could not even manage the lucrative slave trade to her own colonies, which she farmed out to the Portuguese. Philip II's insistence on maintaining political hold on the Netherlands, his marriage to Mary I of England, and his attempts to make his daughter the Queen of France, and then of England, reflect his narrow pursuit of power. The decline of the Flemish (with respect to the Dutch) may also be associated with the continuation, for a time, of Spanish power in the Southern Netherlands. (It was shortly after the revolt of the United Provinces of the North that Amsterdam replaced Antwerp as the principal financial center of the Continent, because the River Schelde was arbitrarily closed to international trade.)

The rise of Germany at the end of the nineteenth century is perhaps the most-frequently explained and yet the most unexplained phenomenon of European development. Gerschenkron's (1962) thesis that "latecomers develop fast" was intended as an explanation; but not all latecomers have done so well.

Germany was an enigma as far back as the thirteenth and fourteenth centuries, when the administrative efficiency of the Teutonic Order contrasted starkly with the political disintegration of Germany as a whole. We have earlier suggested that the outcomes of wars and other political decisions in Germany led away from the pluralistic society, with its improving balance of leverage, that was evolving in the West. When did the reversal occur?

It probably began about the time of Frederick II the Great (who ruled 1740–1786) in Prussia. Frederick was as absolutist, as mercantilist, and as warlike as Louis XIV had been before him. Although Louis (primed by Colbert) might have agreed with Frederick that economics was the key to military strength, only Frederick recognized that material power required the counsel of a broad-based bourgeoisie (the "Cameralists"). In that respect, he compared more with Edward I of England.

The development of Germany was thereafter compacted, with little of the see-saw progress-cum-retrogression that had characterized the West. The highly-touted "Prussian efficiency" evolved in the time of Frederick, as a clearly-defined, tightly-run administrative hierarchy. The ruling powers recognized that freeing the serfs would promote agricultural efficiency; the agrarian reform occurred quickly and cleanly (under Stein and Hardenberg) after the Napoleonic defeats in 1806–1807. Elementary education was recognized as a national need earlier than in England; German schools were the most advanced of the Continent in the early nineteenth century. Scientific schools and universities came later in the century (in an "appropriate" relationship to the elementary schools). Internal free trade was brought about over a few decades, as the Zollverein (1833) expanded. In the late nineteenth century, the masterful strategy of Bismarck created a unified nation. The temporary return to protectionism may have corresponded to the nationalist policies of the Tudors in England; surely it helped establish Germany as a major producer of chemicals, metals, and scientific instruments. Protectionism was not so great as to preserve inefficient enterprises, however, for the same industries survived and were strengthened in the returning era of liberalism under GATT.

Gerschenkron (1962:123–124; 1965:717–762) explains the slowness of Russian development, relative to that of Germany, partially by the fact that Russian peasants remained heavily encumbered long after the liberation of serfs in 1861. It was difficult for them to establish businesses (even though they were a principal entrepreneurial force), and they did not begin to become a mass purchasing sector until after the Stolypin reforms that began in 1906.

Our brief synopsis of the relative development of European countries is not original, and we have not defended it as we would have to if it were. We have assembled it only to illustrate the five propositions made in this chapter. We will again test them, in the next chapter, as they apply to the LDCs of today.

BIBLIOGRAPHY

In the following references, *CEHE* refers to the *Cambridge Economic History of Europe*, published by the Cambridge University Press, which consists of the following volumes:

I. *The Agrarian Life of the Middle Ages*, Second Edition, 1966, M. M. Postan, editor.

II. *Trade and Industry in the Middle Ages*, new volume in preparation.

III. *Economic Organization and Policies in the Middle Ages*, 1963, M. .M. Postan; E. E. Rich; and Edward Miller, editors.

IV. *The Economy of Expanding Europe in the 16th and 17th Centuries*, 1967, E. E. Rich and C. H. Wilson, editors.

V. *The Economic Organization of Early Modern Europe*, 1977, E. E. Rich and C. H. Wilson, editors.

VI. *The Industrial Revolutions and After* (in two volumes), 1965, H. J. Habakkuk and M. M. Postan, editors.

VII. *The Industrial Economies: Capital, Labor, and Enterprise*, (in two volumes), 1978, Peter Mathias and M. M. Postan, editors.

Cipolla, Carlo M., 1963:
"The Economic Policies of Governments: The Italian and Iberian Peninsulas," *CEHE* 3, ch. 6, part 5.

Cipolla, Carlo M., 1976:
Before the Industrial Revolution: European Society and Economy, 1000–1700, London, Methuen and Co.

Clark, Colin, 1968:
Population Growth and Land Use, New York, Macmillan, St. Martin's Press.

Coornaert, E. L. J., 1967:
"European Economic Institutions and the New World; the Chartered Companies," *CEHE* 4, ch. 4.

De Vries, Jan, 1976:
The Economy of Europe in an Age of Crisis, 1600–1750, New York, Cambridge University Press.

Fryde, E. B., and Fryde, M. M., 1963:
"Public Credit, with Special Reference to Northwestern Europe," *CEHE* 3, ch. 7.

Gerschenkron, Alexander, 1962:
Economic Backwardness in Historical Perspective, Cambridge, Mass., the Belknap Press of Harvard University Press.

Gerschenkron, Alexander, 1965:
"Agrarian Policies and Industrialization: Russia 1861–1917," *CEHE* 6, ch. 8.

Glamann, Kristoff, 1977:
"The Changing Patterns of Trade," *CEHE* 5, ch. 4.

Heckscher, Eli, 1926:
"A Plea for Theory in Economic History," in *Economic History*, supplement to *Economic Journal*, no. 9, pp. 525–34.

Janossy, Ferenc, 1971:
The End of the Economic Miracle: Appearance and Reality in Economic Development, White Plains, NY., International Arts and Science Press (originally in German, 1966).

Koebner, Richard, 1966:
"The Settlement and Colonization of Europe," *CEHE* 1, ch. 1.

Lopez, Robert S., 1976:
The Commercial Revolution of the Middle Ages, New York, Cambridge University Press.

Miller, Edward, 1963:
"The Economic Policies of Governments: France and England," *CEHE* 3, ch. 6, part 2.

Miskimin, Harry A., 1975:
The Economy of Early Renaissance Europe, 1300–1460, New York, Cambridge University Press.

North, Douglas C., and Thomas, Robert Paul, 1973:
The Rise of the Western World: A New Economic History, Cambridge University Press.

Postan, M. M., 1971:
"Medieval Agrarian Society in its Prime: England," *CEHE* 1, ch. 7.
Rich E. E., 1967:
"Colonial Settlement and its Labor Problems," *CEHE* 4, ch. 6.
Slichter van Bath, B. H., 1977:
"Agriculture in the Vital Revolution," *CEHE* 5, ch. 2.
van der Wee, Herman, 1977:
"Monetary, Credit, and Banking Systems," *CEHE* 5, ch. 5.
van Werveke, H., 1963:
"The Rise of the Towns," *CEHE* 3, ch. 1.
Wilson, C. H., 1967:
"Trade, Society and the State," *CEHE* 4, ch. 8.
Wilson, C. H., 1977:
"The Historical Study of Economic Growth and Decline in Early Modern History," *CEHE* 5, ch. 1.

16

ASIA, AFRICA, AND LATIN AMERICA

Whether development in the third world is similar to or different from that of Europe is a sterile debate. The real questions are: In what ways is it similar? In what ways is it different?

THE AUTHORS

Is there any common thread in the principles of economic development for Europe, East Asia, and for today's third world? We suggest there may be. Once again, however, our ambitions are modest: plausible explanations rather than proofs. We select certain countries as illustrations; they are not a cross-section of the third world. We believe they present enough evidence, however, that we may hazard the suggestion that the five propositions of Chapter 15 *might* also apply to the third world. But all countries must be examined meticulously (and we hope to do this in the future) before we can be reasonably well assured.

The third world is widely heterogeneous; some authors refer also to the fourth and fifth worlds, and who knows how many more? To lump together countries of such diverse political and economic structures and distributions of income and wealth would be a travesty were it not a necessity. It is justified only by the wide economic gap between this group on the one hand and all the MDCs on the other.

One group bridges that gap. Japan, a LDC only 50 years ago, is a MDC today; Taiwan, Hong Kong, and Singapore are not far behind. The People's Republic of China, South Korea, and possibly North Korea, will doubtless be MDCs by the end of the century. In this chapter, we have space only for Japan, Taiwan, and P.R. China, as "representatives" of all of East Asia.

What do these countries have in common? Most notably, they are all historically associated with the Chinese and Confucianism. But this helps us little,
for the rest of the world cannot be told that it must become Chinese in order
to develop. Rather, they share the following experiences. Each has undertaken
an agrarian reform that has effectively put decision-making in the hands of the
peasants or peasant-run institutions (except North Korea, where reform has
occurred but decisions are still centralized). Each has ended endemic warfare
(though occasional violence occurs, as it does everywhere). Each has used labor-
intensive technology where labor is abundant, shifting to capital-intensive only
where it is unavoidable. Each has low unemployment. Except for North Korea,
each has effectively controlled population growth. Each has emphasized both
small-scale industry and small farms, though large units have emerged where
necessary (as in iron and steel, communications, and certain crops). Above all,
each has been *export-oriented* (in contrast to the ISI policies of most LDCs),
except P.R. China, which is now moving in that direction.

JAPAN

Slightly over 100 years ago, Japan's economy closely resembled thirteenth-cen-
tury Europe, in feudal structure, intense poverty of the many, and wealth of
the few—an agrarian society with little industry. Today, it is a modern nation,
with average wages higher than those in several European countries. Japan's
income distribution is one of the most egalitarian of the world (Gini = .3106,
compared to .4171 for the United States; see Table 4–2). Among OECD countries, Japan has the highest income accruing to the lowest two deciles of households, according to Sawyer's (1976) data, and her distribution is becoming
increasingly egalitarian. As recently as 1952, Japan's per capita GNP was below
that of Brazil, Chile, or Malaysia. But from then until 1978, GNP at 1975 prices
grew an average of 8.3 percent per year, or 7.1 percent per capita, thus multiplying eightfold in total and sixfold per capita (IFS Yearbook, 1979). From
1952 to 1973, the growth rate was 9.6 percent; thereafter it slowed because of
the petroleum crisis. By 1976, Japan's PQLI index stood at 96, one point higher
than the United States and exceeded only by Iceland, Norway, and Sweden, tied
at 97 (McLaughlin, 1979:164). Her GNP per capita in 1978 was $7,082, com-
pared to $9,738 for the United States (IFS Yearbook, 1979).

Japan's postwar "miracle" can be understood only in historical terms. In
1637, the shogun (who exercised power in the name of the emperor) closed the
country to all foreigners, except for limited privileges granted to the Chinese
and Dutch. Japanese were not allowed to travel abroad; those who escaped
would be executed if they returned. The feudal structure was as clearly-defined
as that of medieval Europe, but there was less reciprocity of obligations; the
daimyos (feudal lords) had life-and-death power over their peasants. Occupations were by caste and were hereditary; social or economic mobility was
zero.

The outer daimyos (those living far from the capital, Edo, now Tokyo) were
required to spend several months each year in Edo, and to leave their families

there as hostages for the remaining months; their periodic travel led to passable roads, inns, and other commercial services. Possibly because of Confucian traditions introduced as early as the seventh century, education had long been valued; in the mid-nineteenth century, 40 to 50 percent of all males had some formal schooling (Ohkawa and Rosovsky, 1978:141). Houses were well-engineered; dress was functional and beautiful. The highly-structured Japanese society of 1868 already fulfilled two of our propositions for development: little or no endemic warfare and a high degree of discipline through institutions of trust.

What did it lack? Most of all, it lacked freedom; everyone except the shogun was subject to severe restriction of movement. Certainly economic and political leverages were highly unbalanced; peasants and craftsmen had no power over themselves or their products. Among the daimyos and the shogun, there was little evidence that accretions of wealth counted highly, except as a way to conserve power.

As Japan was opened to foreign trade (1853) and the shogun gave way to the emperor (1868), the big question was: would the enormity of the transformation from feudal to modern nation destroy the institutions of trust that had carefully been elaborated over the centuries, and would internal warfare erupt, as it did when European feudalism decayed? The answer was no. In about half a century, the Japanese *peacefully* reconstructed their nation in ways that took Europe six to eight centuries of great destruction and bloodshed. We know of no other country that has accomplished as much.

The secret (we believe) lay first in the Japanese style of saving the face of those who had to yield and of compensating them. Pensions replaced the stipends that daimyos had received from the shogun, and they were assured of high prestige and position to compensate for loss of titles and lands. Second, the Japanese were aware (as some LDC governments today have not been) that improved agriculture lay at the foundation of a strong nation; this required land to be turned over to the peasants and taxes to be paid at uniform rates on assessed valuation rather than (as before) on the harvest.

Third, foreign trade was based on comparative advantage. Since the Japanese had no "absolute" advantages, they specialized for many years in labor-intensive, low-cost goods whose production richer nations were abdicating, such as dishware and trinkets.

The emperor's prime incentive for material wealth was national prestige and power, just as it had been for Peter the Great, for Frederick the Great, for Louis XIV, and for other European rulers during the trend away from propensity-for-power and toward propensity-for-wealth. Model factories were established and foreign experts hired. There was no call for multinational corporations, direct investment, or foreign aid. Japanese investment was financed mostly by private saving; the small amount needed from abroad was borrowed in the market; and interest was paid at market rates. Technology was copied where that was feasible and bought where it was not; Japanese innovators adapted foreign technology to local conditions.

Who knows which of these characteristics led the others? Certainly we do not. But as we contemplate Japanese history compared to both those that precede it and those that follow it, we venture that face-saving is the most likely feature. It not only insured internal peace, but time and again, it smoothed decisions as management systems, financial institutions, and labor relations evolved. *Ringi* (*rin*, submitting a proposal to one's superior, and *gi*, to discuss) is a system of decision-making used during the Tokugawa shogunate, which continued as a modern management principle (Yamamura, 1978:258). A worker suggests a new measure by discussion with his peers; it is modified and submitted upward with no name attached; and the chief consults others at his level before adopting it or passing it on for higher, similar discussion. If it is rejected, no face is lost; if it is accepted, no honor is attached, for it would not be proper to receive credit personally. Yamamura criticized this system for being slow and cumbersome, but it is also effective.

In a local version of the putting-out system, early Japanese factories hired group managers (*oyakata*), who independently commanded teams of workers and contracted for their products; thus the factory was a large village of many workshops (Taira, 1978:189). When it became necessary to consolidate these units into a single administrative hierarchy, the *oyakata* were "bought off" with money or management positions, just as the daimyos had been compensated before them. When elementary education was first needed (to train factory workers), but families resisted with riots (because children were needed on the farms), government strategy quickly changed (school ordinances of 1886): financing became national rather than local, with vocational and professional training subsidized.

But the transition was not easy. Labor unions were suppressed; wages were at subsistence level; factories were prisons where employees lived under guard, so that they would not escape until their contracts had expired; and personal behavior was supervised paternalistically, to the last detail. Early studies show that Japanese workers had a negative self-image. They took factory jobs to stave off family poverty, not to better themselves, and there was no class consciousness or worker solidarity (Taira, 1978:199). At least two generations of workers were thus sacrificed to slave-like conditions, and for this reason we do not tout the Japanese model as example for the world to imitate holistically.

Labor conditions eased in time, but only as labor became scarce and marginal productivity rose. The Factory Act (1911) regulated child labor, and hours and conditions for adults. Employers opposed it at first, but they were quickly converted when they grasped that improved working conditions led to increased productivity. Other factory legislation followed in the twenties. The government opposed outright unionization most of the way, but it yielded during the twenties and thirties, and wages rose.

Other works on Japanese development emphasize the relationship between family conglomerates (*zaibatsu*) and government, and the planning undertaken by private sector and government jointly. These were, however, only the forms taken by a special kind of cooperation among groups. More importantly, the proliferation of identifiable economic interests has led to a process of shifting alliances for improved distribution of political and economic leverage, in much the same way it happened in Europe over a longer period. Patrick and Rosovsky (1976:51) sum it up as follows:

So we must conclude that a pluralist interpretation of the distribution of power in economic decision making—an interpretation that takes into account the competition among big business, small business, farmers, labor, the government bureaucracy, the media, consumers, urban residents, environmentalists—is more useful in understanding Japan's contemporary political economy. The group-oriented and highly competitive behavior of Japanese, together with conflicts of interest on concrete issues, is reflected in the multitude of factions and interest groups within the government bureaucracy, big business, and the Liberal Democratic Party, and expressed in the dealings of each group with the others. Pluralism is reinforced by the power of outside interest groups to influence and shape certain government policy decisions. Furthermore, alliances of interest are not static: various interest groups compete in some areas, on some problems, under some circumstances, and cooperate on others.

CHINA

Chinese history may be viewed in two interlocking patterns. One is of cycles, the other of continuity. Certain events occurred over and again, each time in a new context with contemporary variations, but with an essential sameness nonetheless. Other events were cumulative, always with some direction. But the cycles were heavy drags on the continuity, cutting short all likely opportunities for an industrial revolution, until the twentieth century.

The dynastic cycle dominated the first pattern. A new dynasty would sweep clean the corruption of the old. Lands would be confiscated, redistributed among the new emperor's favorites, and sometimes even among the peasants. Economic growth would be vigorous; ever-normal granaries established; commercial routes constructed (roads, canals, and bridges); new crops planted and agricultural research undertaken; science promoted; and firm administrative structures and credit and financial institutions founded (sometimes amazingly similar to modern ones). Civil service examinations would be restored. Ultimately, however, corruption and greed in the imperial court and nobility would lead to overtaxation of peasantry and abuse of craftsmen; court in-fighting and intrigue would exhaust resources; formal government structures would be evaded or ignored; opposing nobility would call on outsiders (adjacent northern tribes such as Hsiung-nu, Mongols, or Ju-Chen) for military assistance against other Chinese; and rebellions would break out, until some new person consolidated power and started the cycle anew. With appropriate variations, this description fits the early Han dynasty (206 B.C.–9 A.D.), the later Han (23–220 A.D.), the Sui (580–618), the T'ang (618–906), the Sung (960–1279), the Yüan (1280–1368), the Ming (1368–1644), and the Ch'ing (1644–1912). Among these dynasties, the T'ang, Sung, and Ming were long-lasting and vigorous, with extended periods of internal peace and population growth, and conditions bordering on breakthrough to modern society. In other dynasties, however, warfare was endemic and continuous, both internally and on the borders, and population declined. During dynastic interregnums (220–580 and 906–960), China would be divided into competing, warring groups.

As these scenes were repeatedly played, income, wealth, and power were all highly skewed; peasants were insecure and impoverished, often seeking protection of the powerful, to whom they committed their lands and bodies. Few were "free" in any sense; towns of the European style were not formed at least until modern times; and peasants over centuries paid 40 or 50 percent of their produce, sometimes more, as rent. By the nineteenth century, China stood weak, a prey to foreign powers.

Yet the continuous pattern persisted as well. From Confucian times (*c.* 500 B.C.) on, scholarship was highly valued (among the elites). Loyalty and respect for elders, ancestors, and persons of higher rank were deeply ingrained: the son to the father, the father to the head of the clan, the latter to the feudal lord, the lord to the emperor, and the emperor to God. That these loyalties could be so betrayed and yet remain so firm constitutes one of the "contradictions" that have become entrenched in Chinese tradition (and to which we will return later). Institutions (such as civil service examinations) might be destroyed in dynastic overthrows, but they lived on in the mind, and they were restored intact when the new moment was propitious. Agricultural knowledge built upon itself; new crops and new methods survived and were extended, slowly in time of trouble, but without being forgotten. Once discovered, scientific knowledge (such as metallurgy, printing, gunpowder, and ceramics) was never lost, but compounded itself cumulatively.

Let us suggest that the continuous pattern made an industrial revolution inevitable, but the cyclical pattern time and again constrained it. A third force may have been the foreign interventions of the nineteenth century (Opium War and extraterritorial privileges), both for their demonstration effect and for the nationalism they engendered. The parameters in these three equations—which we do not try to disentangle—were such that our own century was selected for the transformation.

The continuities had indeed built up.. Perkins (1975:3) credits the Chinese with *"a prior accumulation of experience with complex organizations or institutions"*(italics his), such as the following:

(1) A high degree of commercialization; most farmers produced for the market.
(2) A bimetallic currency and premodern banks.
(3) Cities with populations of 500,000 to a million, with commercial networks.
(4) Land tenure based on private ownership and sale and rental by formal contract.
(5) A high man-land ratio, complex farm technology, and a high yield per acre.
(6) A modern political system, with positions filled by examination.
(7) A high value on education and literacy.

In 1949, China split into two, and the warring ended. Modern writers, prejudiced by contemporary obsession with capitalism versus communism, often see these political systems as significantly different. But we see such a strong common force in historical momentum, that greater similarities than differences have emerged in the recent development of the two Chinas.

TAIWAN (REPUBLIC OF CHINA)

Taiwan's economic growth, both per capita and overall, has been impressive since 1949. But the period falls into two parts, the first until 1963–1965 and the second thereafter. During the first period, Taiwan was distinguishable from many LDCs only by the amount of aid she was receiving from the United States (Jacoby, 1966). Gross national product per capita grew at an average of 3.65 percent per year, 1953–1963 (Ho, 1978:122). Her trade balance was in heavy deficit, and her average inflation rate was 17.8 percent, 1950–1955 (IFS Yearbook, 1979). The inflation and balance-of-payments deficit led to controls on foreign exchange and imports, rationing, hidden subsidies, and price administration that resembled the ISI policies of many LDCs (Ho, 1978:106, 119). Much of the increase in GNP represented only the recuperation of a wartorn economy; much of it satisfied heavy military demand. The foundations for further growth had not yet been laid.

Toward the end of the decade, largely under United States pressure, a general rethinking occurred. Price and exchange controls were dismantled; military expenditure was reduced in proportion to both GNP and total government expenditure; the inflation was brought down to an average of 1.2 percent per year, 1961–1966. Officials turned away from government initiative as the spearhead for development and relied more on private sources. With prices again reflecting factor scarcities, small-scale enterprise flourished and exports were encouraged. Government funds were directed more toward agriculture, in the form of extension services and infrastructure for the small farms and cooperatives created under the agrarian reform (Chapter 11).

The policies worked. Trade deficits that had averaged $121 million, 1958–1962, were reduced immediately, to an average of $38 million, 1963–1969, and then to a surplus averaging $445 million, 1970–1973. (Deficits followed thereafter on account of the petroleum crisis, but the balance of trade has again been in surplus since 1976.) U.S. foreign aid was terminated in 1965.

No special effort has been made to encourage enterprise of any particular size; for the most part, the market has been the determiner. Some large-scale enterprises have emerged, and foreign firms (multinationals) are welcome. Often small scale enterprises supply the inputs for large-scale enterprises, and it is likely (though not clear) that the latter have in this way promoted the former more than they have replaced them.

The adoption of labor-intensive technology is manifest in the unemployment rate, which dropped from 5.2 percent in October 1963 to 1.1 percent in October 1973 (Ho, 1978:145) and has remained low thereafter. The growth rate of gross national product per capita increased to an annual average of 8.84 percent, 1964–1973 (Ho, 1978:122), one of the highest in the world. It declined absolutely, 1974–1975, on account of the petroleum crisis, and grew again at 5.1

percent, 1975–1977 (GOC, 1978). Income distribution has become more equitable. The inflation of the early fifties confiscated much of the compensation
to former landlords (Chapter 11); the Gini coefficient (based on household
shares) dropped from 0.56 in 1953 to 0.28 in 1972 (Ho, 1978:141). Taiwan
therefore possesses one of the most equitable recorded distributions of income
in the world. Its PQLI stood at 87 in 1976, compared to 62 average for the
upper-middle-income Asian group to which it belongs (McLaughlin, 1979:162).
Per capita GNP was $1,124 in 1978 (IFS Yearbook, 1979).

PEOPLE'S REPUBLIC

P.R. China stopped publishing economic data in 1958, and from then until
1979, our information came mainly from outside observers ("China watchers"),
who have meticulously compared scattered bits from publications and radio
broadcasts. The U.S. Central Intelligence Agency has summarized these findings
and added some of its own, in periodic reports. Then, in 1979, the veil of secrecy
was lifted, as the Chinese government issued a comprehensive report on the
state of the economy. This report showed that the China watchers and C.I.A.
were largely on track except that their estimates of electrical output were low
(Shabad, NYT, 7-12-79).

In what ways (economically) are P.R. China and Taiwan similar? First, both
economies are decentralized; decisions on most prices and production are taken
locally. Second, both have favored labor-intensive technology and small-scale
enterprise. Third, both have encouraged agriculture and have undertaken agrarian reform. Fourth, both have decreased their population growth through family
planning, to the neighborhood of 2 percent per year (U.S. Department of Commerce, 1978:155–7). Fifth, both have reduced their unemployment to very low
levels. Some China watchers, comparing the amount of output with working
population, believe there is some unemployment (or underemployment) in P.R.
China (for example, Karcher, 1975). If so, its burden is lessened by communal
sharing of incomes. In the only in-depth study that we know of on employment
in P.R. China, however, Rawski (1979, for the World Bank) concluded that
although "unemployment certainly exists in the cities," China has been basically
successful in providing employment for a growing work force, mainly by keeping
most of it on the farm. The age-old hunger problem is "mostly" solved, although
some China watchers calculate (on the basis of food production-population
comparisons, as well as occasional reports of protests) that local famine does
occur from time to time (London and London, 1979).

In P.R. China, the central government controls amounts of output sold by
provinces to cities, from one province to another, as well as prices of these
goods. It also controls transport and communication, heavy industry (such as
iron and steel) and other infrastructure, and State investment in these sectors.
Until 1979, the central government controlled exports and imports completely;
in that year, however, it began to grant autonomy in some foreign trade to
provincial governments (Butterfield, NYT, 12–27–79). The central government
does *not* control either prices or quantities of goods sold and/or consumed in

the province of origin, *which account for the bulk of Chinese GNP* (Donnithorne, 1971:119–32). Outside cities, the country is divided into approximately 70,000 communes, which contained (in 1970) an average of 2,900 households each, or 13,000 persons, or 5,400 labor force units (Crook, 1975:375). Each commune is divided into a number of production brigades, averaging a little over ten per commune, but with wide variance depending on commune size. Brigades engage in larger-scale farm activities (such as orchards, fish ponds, and timber) and medium-sized industry (such as grain, edible oil processing, and equipment repairs). They in turn are divided into teams, which are the basic production unit. In the past 15 years, however, there has been a slight tendency toward more activity at the brigade and commune levels, as economies of scale become feasible. A production team has approximately 33 households (on the average), or 145 persons, and cultivates 20 hectares (Crook, 1975:395). Communes, brigades, and teams own their own productive assets (lands, buildings, and equipment), each at its own level; sometimes the higher level owns common-service equipment, which it rents to lower levels. Unlike the Soviet Union, the central government does *not* own most industry.

The central government formulates an economic plan, stipulating quantities of products to be delivered from communes to cities, and their prices. The communes control totally the ways in which the goods will be produced and delivered. Normally, the commune decides what portion of the quota will be produced at commune level, but the bulk will be reassigned to brigades, which may in turn pass it on to teams. Thus planning is done at all levels. Over time, the tradition has grown that all quotas will be exceeded. Incomes are distributed at the same level at which they are produced, some being retained as working capital or for reinvestment, some allocated to social or educational purposes, and the rest paid to individuals according to work points assigned in group meetings on the basis of effort, need, or political coloring (although the latter has been deemphasized since the death of Mao).

Prices are determined by the appropriate administrative authority (centralized or decentralized) and not by the market (Prybla, 1978:97). "Essential" goods are priced low, possibly below cost and with rationing. "Everyday necessities" are priced at or above average cost, to create a "social surplus," while "secondary consumer needs" (luxuries) may be priced well above cost. Although this system may appear to violate "invisible-hand" principles, the fact that major consumer needs are met, and that "appropriate" technologies are for the most part used, would indicate that it does not grossly distort the rational allocation of resources. This is probably so because it is decentralized, and local authorities are aware of local needs and capabilities. Furthermore, the guidelines require that prices on the whole be set so as to absorb consumer incomes. The implied subsidies and taxation may not be greatly different from their overt counterparts in market economies, in which such necessities as New York subway rides are subsidized by local authorities, while unfavored goods, such as liquor and cigarettes, may be taxed. The Chinese experience raises the hypothesis, therefore, that the efficiency of a pricing system may not depend so much on whether it operates by market rules (adjusted by taxes and subsidies) as it does on whether it is sufficiently decentralized, so that price-makers may take into account the full micro-impacts of their decisions on factors, final goods, and consumer incomes within their geographic regions.

Furthermore, the Chinese have announced plans for more decentralization and greater dependence on profit, beginning in 1981. State-owned industries will be charged interest and taxed, small-scale businesses ("mom and pop stores") will be permitted, and private farm plots extended. In a comment reflective of both increased balance of leverage and greater risk propensity, Sterba (NYT, 9–1–80) reports that Chinese leaders believe "the political risks of dispersing economic power would be greatly offset by positive economic results welcomed by the people."

How well has the Chinese economy performed? The consensus of China watchers is that the record is impressive, in both growth and equity. The first four years (1949–1953) were a period of rehabilitation from war, in which reconstruction alone would show high percentage increases: 400 percent for industry (Field, 1971:79) and 40 to 45 percent for agriculture (Chao, 1970:227). From then on, strong growth has been upset by periodic political upheavals,[1] like the dynastic cycle in microcosm. The increase in producers goods averaged 13 percent per year, 1954–1957; it jumped to 45 percent from 1957 to 1958 and 22 percent from 1958 to 1959. It began to level off (4 percent from 1959 to 1960), then fall sharply after the Great Leap Forward, and by 1961 it was only slightly above the level of 1957 (Field, 1975:149). From 1961 to 1966 it grew at an average rate of 16 percent per year. With the Great Cultural Revolution, it dropped by 13 percent in one year (1966–1967), but from them on it grew steadily, averaging 11 percent per year until 1974. Over the entire period (1953–1974), the average growth rate for producer goods was 9.8 percent per year; it probably was higher from then until 1978 (NYT, 7–5–79).

Grain output increased by between 4 and 5 percent per year, 1953–1958. It fell sharply, by over 25 percent during the Great Leap Forward, 1959–1961, which also coincided with bad weather. From 1960/61 to 1966/67, it increased again, at an average of 6 percent per year (Chao, 1970:250). From 1967 to 1968 (the Great Cultural Revolution), grain output decreased by only about 9 percent, after which it steadily increased, by 2.9 percent per year, 1968–1974 (Erisman, 1975:328) and by 4.5 percent, 1974–1978 (NYT 7–5–79). Total output of grains thus approximately doubled, from about 154 million tons in 1952 to 304 million in 1978, at an average rate of 2.7 percent per year. Overall growth rates have thus been less than for Taiwan, but they rank alongside the faster-growing third world countries, such as India, Kenya, and Mexico.

Nevertheless, the aggregates show China to be still very much a third world country: the per capita income of her 800 million peasants was only $49 in 1978, while that of industrial workers was $415, less than their average income of 1958 ($423). This failure of the latter to increase may be caused by China's redistributive policies—urban to agricultural—as well as by the great increase in numbers of industrial workers.

---

[1]The major upheavals of the period were the Great Leap Forward (1959–1960) and the Great Cultural Revolution (1967), each accompanied by a sharp reduction in output. We do not describe these upheavals, since they are amply reported elsewhere; see, for example, MacFarquhar (1974).

Has China's policy toward equity interfered with economic efficiency? Lardy (1978) addressed this question, pointing out that China (unlike Taiwan, although like South Korea) has turned the terms of trade in favor of agriculture and rural areas through those prices that are centrally administered. The terms of trade for agriculture were 163.9 in 1974 (1952 = 100) (Lardy, 1978:177). Agriculture prices were again increased in 1979 as incentives for increased food production were needed (Butterfield, NYT, 4–26–79). Although income distributions within provinces are matters for local control, the central government has redistributed from more productive to less productive provinces. Our guess (along with Lardy's) is that efficiency has been minimally affected. Although we do not have percentile distributions or Gini coefficients, the available data suggest that P.R. China's income distribution may be about as equitable as that of Taiwan.

Instead, we raise a different question. Have these impressive results been achieved *because* central government leaders (like Mao Tse-tung, Chou En-lai, and Liu Shiao-chi) have been oriented toward socialism? Or have they been achieved because of an understanding that national strength depends on growth with reasonable distribution, peacefully achieved, while the precise path for accomplishing this may be secondary? No one, of course, can answer these questions definitively. Our belief that only the second merits an affirmative stems from comparison with Taiwan, South Korea, Hong Kong, and Singapore, where similar results were achieved without socialism, and from another comparison with Tanzania, Zambia, and Ethiopia, where the leadership is just as dedicated as the Chinese, but where the results have fallen short.

The virtue of the Chinese (it appears to us) is that *the leaders understand the degree of leverage they possess*, and they do not behave as if they had more than they do. They decentralized because they had to. The peasants had high leverage, enhanced by their distance, and the leaders knew it. The decision did not come easy. The early option (in the fifties) was for centralized socialism on the Soviet model. Great dissention among government and party leaders accompanied the switch to peasant- and agriculture-orientation, during which time there was much talk of "contradictions" between profits and socialism, between agriculture and industry, between small-scale and large-scale production, between seaports and the interior, and of "walking on two legs," which meant living with (not resolving) the contradictions. Whereas Western econo-mists might talk of "dynamic equilibrium," Mao felt economic progress depended on a widening of contradictions, offset by periodic upheavals to release the tension. Capitalist attributes would naturally increase with development (Mao thought), so abrupt adjustments back to socialism would be required. Thus he did not wince at the damage wrought by the Great Leap Forward or the Great Cultural Revolution. It was in this convulsive way that the Chinese shifted direction.

The party ("parallel government") has played an enormous role in keeping the situation under control. While specific decisions may lie in local hands, the ideology underlying them is handed down through party channels, centrally controlled. Often party officials and government officials are the same at local levels.

Our "plausible explanation" of the achievements of P.R. China is summarized as follows. Since 1949, the diverse interest-groups have settled into an institutional cooperation in which each implicitly respects the leverages of the others; each no longer tries to enhance its own power militarily or through repressive, economically-distortionary controls. Although prices are not of the market, nevertheless the local (decentralized) technique for determining most of them results in an efficiency comparable to that of market-economies-*cum*-subsidies-and-taxation. Terms of trade shifted in favor of agriculture through centralized decision but in response to an excess of demand over supply of foodstuffs. P.R. China's slow rate of growth and lower per capita incomes, compared to those of Taiwan, may have two explanations: that Taiwan is a compact island, to which an enormous amount of refugee talent flowed in 1949, and that the periodic convulsions of P.R. China took their toll on its economy. The change of leadership after Mao's death (suppression of the "gang of four") appears not to have been convulsive; 12 years of peace have led to higher rates of growth in the seventies than ever before.

IRAN

The uprising, which started in January 1978 and ended February 11, 1979, was by far the most massive, broad-based and sustained popular agitation in history. Some 20,000 demonstrators died in the years of protest, while the economic institutions and the public services were virtually shut down.
AHMAD, NEW YORK TIMES MAY 25, 1979

What was the object of the *massive, broad-based, popular uprising* that Ahmad exaggerated into one of the superlatives of history? Was it to overthrow an oligarchy that had monopolized land, enslaved the peasantry, confined education to the elite, neglected its nation's health, concentrated wealth in the hands of a few, and suppressed all social reform? Nothing of the sort. It was directed against a Shah (Mohammed Reza Pahlavi) who had accomplished one of the most daring, all-inclusive land reforms in history, giving the peasants not only his own lands but those of all large landowners (purchased at low, tax-declared values); who had revamped the educational system, opening it to all, building new universities and increasing the number of students in all schools from 74,000 in 1925 when his father became Shah to 4,820,000 in 1972; who had westernized the legal system, taking justice out of the hands of the Church (the *olama*) and establishing secular courts; who had emancipated women, removing the veil and opening equal opportunities in employment (some had become members of Parliament); who had initiated a Literacy Corps that had reduced the number who could not read from about 80 percent of the population in the early sixties to about 60 percent by the mid-seventies; who had greatly increased the number of hospitals and doctors, providing free medical care for the poor; who had professionalized the civil service and the army; who had promoted farming cooperatives and had provided technical assistance and funds for small farmers; who had caused agricultural value-added to increase by an average of 9 percent per year for the 15 years ended 1974/1975, an almost unbelievable rate, while the corresponding rate for industry was 16.8 percent; and who had overseen an increase in private consumption per capita from $131 in 1959/1960 to $416 only 15 years later. (We use private consumption as our measure because GNP per capita, which increased from $179 to $1,099 in the same period, is affected by the increase in oil prices in 1973). We do not have data on income distribution, but there is no doubt that it became more equitable during the Shah's reign, since the 43 percent of the employed population engaged in agriculture in 1972 (down from 56 percent in 1956) had been relieved of feudal rents while their productivity was increasing, and since more jobs opened up in mining and industry (up from 20 percent of all workers in 1956 to 30 percent in 1972), while wages rose.[2]

Three reasons usually explain why the "ungrateful" nation turned on its Shah. First, although called "the revolution of the Shah and the people," nevertheless the Shah imposed it virtually by himself, backed by an army equipped through the revenues of oil. Parliament was a rubber stamp. Second, the Shah rode rough over political opponents, jailing, executing, and (it is alleged) torturing them. Third, perhaps most serious of all, he crossed swords with the religious authorities, who had owned much of the appropriated land. When these authorities took power, they charged that the Shah had stolen some $17 to $30 billion from his people. But "few distinctions were made between State funds and the Shah's own resources" (Crittenden and Telsch, NYT, 11–25–79), a condition that had always existed in Iran and that resembles all of Europe before the English revolution of 1688. Had he lived in the eighteenth century, alongside Frederick the Great, Catherine the Great, and Maria Theresa, the Shah would have fit gracefully with these enlightened despots, who did so much for their people while despising them.

We detect a fourth reason as well. None of the Shah-favored groups had the political or economic leverage, or alliances with more powerful interests, to stand on their own feet without him. Small farmers were weakened by the nation's ability to buy imported foodstuffs with oil money. Indeed, the poor, and the students whom the Shah so lavishly sent abroad, became the most suspect for subversion. Their best bet was to join the mobs and save their skins, and thus they gave credence to Ahmad's exaggeration, that the Iranian revolution of 1979 would go down as the most popular in history, surpassing (it must be supposed) the French, the Russian, and the English Peasant's Revolt of 1381. But we see it instead as one more support to our proposition that successful economic development depends on a "reasonable" balance in political and economic leverages within a pluralistic society.

---

[2]The quantitative data in this paragraph are taken from Lenczowski (1978), with exchange-rate conversions and population figures from IFS Yearbook (1979).

EAST AFRICA

KENYA

When the World Bank (1975) issued its country report on Kenya, the diagnosis was that the country's development is progressing very well, but that the going will be harder in the future. The "easy" stage has ended. Not only has the economy "come much nearer to the limit of resources available for development" (p. xi), but the possibilities for import substitution in manufacturing are largely exhausted. Kenya is thus "at a turning point."

How odd! Surely Europe and the Far East found the *initial* stages of development difficult; the "easy" stage came *later*. Surely the resources for development are never "limited," for capital can always be found if reasonable projects exist and if the institutional framework is appropriate. The Bank's hypothesis stems (we believe) from too little attention to historical analogy, too little belief in continuity, and too much faith in an econometric model whose parameters the Bank had prewritten.

Kenya's record since independence has been unusually good, compared to most LDCs. Her real GDP has increased by an average of 6.8 percent, 1965–1978 (GOK,[3] *Economic Survey*, 1979 and 1970). Even with population growth as high as 3.5 percent a year, per capita GDP has been growing by 3.3 percent. Income distribution is very inequitable (Gini = .6368 for income recipients in 1969; Jain, 1975:64), and it may not have been improving. While middle-group incomes have indeed been growing in number and amount, nevertheless the poorest of the poor (for example, nomadic tribes in desert-like Turkana or the northeast) have benefited little, so that relatively the flows may have been from the rich and poor ends into the middle (with perhaps no net effect on the Gini). But the increase in modern-sector employment from 563,600 in 1964 to 1,085,000 in 1978 (4.3 percent per year) and the doubling of agricultural output in 20 years (GOK, Plan IV:207) are healthy. Is there any reason to believe these successes will not continue?

Probably not. Nevertheless, we do share the Bank's concerns. For many years, the Bank has been advising the GOK to emphasize agriculture; to moderate the share of the central government in direct development expenditures; and to dismantle its elaborate restrictions and price controls. All these suggestions are good. Agricultural development historically precedes and underlies that of industry. The Bank found that government investment not only had little direct impact on employment, but that its incremental capital-output ratio was too high already and was still rising. Finally, restrictions and price controls are prejudicing resources toward urban, capital-intensive manufacturing. Indeed, Kenya is a prime example of the "ISI" policy package we referred to in Chapters 8 and 14. All these recommendations by the Bank had also been made by the International Labor Organization (1972).

Except perhaps for agriculture, there is little evidence that the GOK is disposed to follow the Bank/ILO advice.

---

[3]GOK = Government of Kenya.

Plan IV (1979–1983) promises more resources to agriculture than ever before. Plan III (1974–78:171) had proposed that 8.5 percent of government budget be allocated to agriculture for the five-year period; the outcome was 9.3 percent (Plan IV:116), even though the real value of expenditures turned out to be less than projected because of inflation. For Plan IV, the government promises 11.1 percent of its expenditure for agriculture. There is, however, no indication of how much of this will reach small farms or poor farmers. Kenya has many large-scale farms inherited from British colonists. Some were divided up in a land reform, but some are still large, owned by wealthy Africans. Much of the credit and extension services go to them. Heyer, Maitha, and Senga (1976:30) have complained that "it is the Ministry of Finance and Planning and the Ministry of Agriculture, *but not the President's office* that pushes rural development." (Italics added) They imply that the planners do not have the power of decision.

On public expenditures, the GOK will do the opposite of the Bank's counsel. While total government expenditure was 22.5 percent of GDP in 1975/1976, Plan IV calls for it to be increased to 36.3 percent by 1982/1983. Government expenditures are thus projected to increase at 13.72 percent per year, compared to 6.12 percent for GDP.

On price controls and restrictions, Plan IV speaks equivocally. The *general* statement is clear: foodstuffs will be sold at international prices, and "it is not possible to control inflation by an even stricter imposition of price controls" (p. 32). But a number of other statements suggest that exceptions will be numerous. Indeed, it is difficult to conclude that the GOK will backtrack much on price controls and trade restrictions.

Why not? Is not the GOK committed to development and equitable income distribution? Do not the World Bank staff hold the expertise on these? Both are true. We suggest two hypotheses for the apparent contradiction.

The first is that expenditures on the rural poor, and policies in their favor, both depend on the leverage of those poor, relative to competing interests. The poor do have leverage: they can vote, they can riot, and they can interfere with government sovereignty in their regions. They provide some of the food needed for industrialization, and most of the food needed for rural tranquility. But the parliament for which they vote is weak compared to the presidency, riots can be put down, and food is also produced by rich farmers. We hypothesize that policies favoring the poor depend on the government's assessment of these relative forces. If the Bank (or other foreign aid agency) provides funds earmarked for the rural poor, it merely relieves the GOK of the political necessity to provide those funds itself.

The second hypothesis is that the amount of government's expenditure on development and its exercise of price controls and restrictions depend in part on the propensity of government officials to power, compared with competing propensities. There is a certain exhilaration in telling 13 million people what they can import and how much they will pay for matches, especially when one has led oneself to believe that these decisions are in the interest of those who are restricted. It is also a heady feeling to manipulate a government budget and to watch the computer churn out one's projections of GDP.

Propensity for power depends not only on personal exhilaration, but also on what power can do. In Kenya, as in many other countries, urban interests compete with farmers on the price of foodstuffs. If the former provide more staying-power to the government than the latter, the prices may be controlled low. If vice versa, they may be controlled high. "National interest" is only demagoguery.

Propensity for power does not (we believe) die a natural death. It ends (with respect to food-price controls) when the political leverages of farmers and urban interests become balanced, and/or when these groups come to believe that freedom of pricing is in their mutual interests. This has not yet happened in Kenya (nor entirely in the United States). We doubt that the World Bank's admonishments will have much effect.

Kenya's growth is inefficient, inequitable, and strong. But we know too much of the growth of earlier countries to believe that it is at a "turning point" merely because of its deficiencies.

KENYA AND TANZANIA

Kenya and Tanzania are frequently contrasted because of the capitalist ethic in the former and the socialist in the latter. Like the two Chinas, however, we find the difference exaggerated, for once again, similar historical forces are at play. The Kenya and Tanzania interiors were both populated through Bantu migrations, although Kenya alone felt the influence of Nilo-Hamitic tribes from the North. Both countries have long had Arab trading and imperial pressures on their common coast; both have been penetrated by Christian missionaries; and both have been colonized by the British, though Tanganyika was German before World War I.

The divergence in ideology seems to stem, not from historical or ethnic differences, nor from the chances of war, nor from religious or educational training, but from the personalities of two men: Jomo Kenyatta, first President of Kenya, and Julius Nyerere, first President of Tanzania.

There are, to be sure, geographic differences. Kenya's climate, in the former "white highlands" of the Center and West, is more propitious for agriculture than anything in Tanzania, except the watered plains around Kilimanjaro. The British preferred Kenya for settlement, not only for its climate but because of its strategic location in the defense of the Upper Nile, leading to the Uganda railroad which also linked the principal producing areas of Kenya. Upon independence, Kenya had a stronger infrastructure left by the British, in schools, hospitals, urban electricity, farm services, and transport.

TANZANIA

Tanzania's growth rate has been slower than that of Kenya, only 4.8 percent average, 1965–1978 (IFS Yearbook, 1979). Her population has grown more slowly also (2.7 percent), and per capita GDP has been increasing at only 2.1 percent. Whether the differences are due to geographic settings, to Kenya's head start, or to differing policies are questions that ideologues delight in discussing, but we do not.

The socialist direction was not clear at independence (1961). The first five-year plan (1964–1970) proposed that three-fourths of industrial investment should be private; both public and private foreign finance were sought. Strongly influenced by Nyerere, however, the political leadership became displeased by the socio-economic results of these policies: the widening rural-urban gap, growth of an urban elite, and class formation even among peasants. The Arusha Declaration (1967) marked the policy change toward socialism, broad-based rural development, and self-reliance in national and local affairs. All these objectives took their place alongside economic growth.

Yet the results on all scores have been disappointing. With his characteristic honesty, Nyerere (1977) issued a report, *The Arusha Declaration Ten Years After*, which confesses that the growth rate of GDP declined from 6.4 percent, 1964–1967, to 4.2 percent, 1967–1975 (p. 32); in particular, agricultural production has been deficient; political corruption has not been overcome (pp. 23–24); although investment has been high, in many years over 20 percent of GDP (IFS Yearbook 1979), resources have not been used efficiently: and parastatal enterprises have prohibitively high costs and are not earning enough profits (pp. 33–34). Since 1967, government has been the fastest-growing sector: 80 percent of recurrent revenue allocated to the regions has gone into wages of government officials, whose productivity (it is implied) may not have been high (p. 38).[4]

Tanzanian socialism has four distinguishing characteristics. First is a Leadership Code, requiring that government officials live simply (they do not draw high salaries, and they own only the home in which they live). No one in Tanzania will live on "unearned income." Second, no enterprise shall grow above a certain size without being nationalized or becoming parastatal. A parastatal enterprise is owned by the government, operates autonomously, but reports to a specific ministry. Third, peasants shall live in *Ujamaa* villages. *Ujamaa*, which means "familyhood" in Swahili, also denotes socialism. Families scattered over the countryside have been concentrated into villages, so they may efficiently be supplied with education and infrastructure. Fourth, planning shall be done on a local level, and the national plan shall (somehow) be a sum of the local plans.

The results on all four are sadly deficient. While government salaries for specific ranks are stipulated, modest living can be averted through promotion to higher-ranking jobs; this has happened significantly for high government officials. Although parastatals publish financial statements, these are neither controlled nor fully audited and are reputed to be the source of high salaries and other perquisites for their officials. Parastatals have tended toward modern technologies with high capital-output ratios, therefore not contributing sufficiently to national employment. Macro-data certainly support the case for inefficiency: the high rate of investment should have yielded a greater return than

---

[4]Page numbers in this paragraph all refer to Nyerere (1977).

it has. The Barton gap (p. 28) has appeared as small-scale manufacturers do not expand into the sizes where they risk being nationalized, yet nationalized and parastatal enterprises have neither the resources nor the skills to fill the void.

There has been much opposition to *Ujamaa* villages. The "villagization" took place largely from 1973 to 1977, with about 11 million people settled in over 7,000 villages within three years (Nyerere, 1977:41). Some movement was by military force (Nyerere has apologized for this); there were some rebellions, and much discontent. Forced villagization coincided with a drought (1974) and depression from the increased price of oil. Intent on reinstating their subsistence crops, farmers failed to provide adequately for the market. Local planning has not succeeded. The national plan due in January 1976 had to be postponed several months (and was redone in Dar es Salaam) because the sum of village demands on the central Treasury far exceeded financial availabilities. (Most of the information in these two paragraphs comes from our conversations with Tanzanian government officials in Dar es Salaam. We believe they were telling the truth, but we cannot quantify more than we have.)

TANZANIA AND KENYA: AGAIN THE COMPARISON

We find, therefore, the following common points. Both Kenya and Tanzania have centralized their planning and policy. We cannot help believe that exhilaration from exercise of power and enjoyment of its perquisites affect high civil servants and municipal officials in the two countries similarly. This belief is reinforced by the complaints of Nyerere (1977:40) himself, who wrote:

> Yet in practice leaders at all levels seem to delight in saying "no" in response to even the most reasonable requests. Ask them why they have said something can be done in six days, or six months, but not now, and they have no answer; the truth is that by giving that decision they have demonstrated their authority. And in some cases they are also indicating that if a little "chai" is passed over, the matter can be speeded up!

We have no recent information on the distribution of income in either country, but one might guess that both remain highly unequal. The slow rate of rural development in Tanzania has surely widened the income gap, especially if the perquisites from high office in parastatals are counted as personal income. In each country, we believe the political attention given to the rural poor depends not on the ideology of the leaders, but on the extent to which the rural poor can threaten the existence of the government. Such use of negative (rather than positive) reinforcements is (to our mind) a sign of underdevelopment.

Each country depends heavily on price control and quantity restrictions on imports; in each case the controls have harmed the farmers. The explanation is in both cases the same: that articles of prime necessity for the urban poor must be provided at reasonable prices. In each case, the urban rich benefit as well, except to the extent that price-controlled goods are driven from the market.

Economic growth in Kenya will probably continue, because it has too much going for it. But we remain concerned about Tanzania—not solely because

because of government policies, but because of the slow start that the unfortunate policies are compounding. It would appear that Nyerere is trying to order his country to behave as if the morality of "socialist man" were already on earth. Such morality (according to our own theory) will come about only when the income, hence the leverage, of the rural poor has already increased. In the meantime, economic incentives alone work.

Finally, we are saddened by the demise of the East African Community. In the euphoria of independence, the three East African states (Kenya, Tanzania, and Uganda) unified their monetary and exchange policies; endorsed the Common Services Organization to coordinate post office, communications, and other services; and continued joint operation of railways, harbors, and air transport. Trade was to be liberalized. There would be an East African investment bank, and integrated development projects were expected. Surely the wider market would be auspicious for advantages of scale and trade.

As Kenyan productivity increased more than Tanzanian and Ugandan, and the latter currencies began to depreciate (in the "informal" market) with respect to the Kenyan, currency and trade restrictions were introduced, generally aimed against Kenya. The ideological conflict between Kenya and Tanzania widened. A dictatorial government in Uganda became alienated from Tanzania because the latter was harboring the deposed Ugandan president, and eventually the two countries went to war.

In 1977, the border between Tanzania and Kenya was closed, and it is still closed three years later. The quarrel, initially over the amount of taxes Kenyan vehicles would pay for using Tanzanian roads, erupted with Tanzania collecting a number of Kenyan vehicles within its territory as the border closed. The railroad stopped functioning across the border and cars were not returned. Kenya retaliated by collecting all the East African aircraft in the Nairobi airport before the Tanzanians had grasped what was going on. The impact was felt as far as Zambia, whose copper exports, unable to use the Kenyan port of Mombasa, overtaxed and eventually clogged the port of Dar es Salaam.

The quarrel is a childish one, not befitting great statesmen of great countries. But it may be more the stuff of which economic development is made or unmade than are capital-output and savings ratios.

ARGENTINA

An economist observing the Western Hemisphere in the 1880s might have recorded an optimistic impression of Argentina. Here was a country only about 40 years behind the United States. Unified and with a new constitution in 1862, her interior finally freed of customs duties, she put behind her the interprovincial rivalries, wars, and extravagant land policies of the early part of the century, and settled into strong industrialization. She was geographically-favored: fertile soil and abundant rainfall in the large Province of Buenos Aires, easy routes for internal transport, and a good harbor. Under the newly-centralized government, a modern banking system had formed; skilled laborers were immigrating from Europe in vast numbers as a national policy; and manufacturing grew under protection not overly strong to make it inefficient. Credit standing was good in international markets. British companies invested heavily, building the country's railroads and other infrastructure. Loans were obtained easily from British banking houses. Yet growth was still spearheaded by exports, principally beef; policies were export-oriented, and cattle ranchers provided capital for industry.[5]

Only a century later, Argentina is virtually a military camp, rent asunder internally, industry all but stopped, growth of GDP slow and in some years falling, persistent inflation the worst in the world, and beef still the principal export but lagging in both quantity and efficiency. Time seemed to stop for Argentina about 1920. What happened?

Of course, no one knows for sure, but we do have a potential explanation. In retrospect, we can see the seeds of decline as far back as 1900. Toward the end of the nineteenth century, with the Indians brutally conquered, the nation was dividing into distinct groups, at odds with each other, and uncompromising. These qualities are not among those that social scientists can measure (they are vague-bordered sets). Yet if they have interfered with consistency and stability, not only in national policy but also within individual enterprises, they may be the principal explanations of Argentine inefficiency and backwardness.

The first groups to emerge were three: the traditional oligarchic families, who had owned land and dominated Argentine politics from independence; the middle- and lower-class natives; and the immigrants, who did not hold Argentine nationality. Many authors have cited the low political participation of immigrant groups (Cornblit, 1967, Imaz, 1964, and Hunt, 1968); they could not vote until they were nationalized as citizens, and few applied for that status. Middle- and lower-class natives, many of whom had immigrant parents, became strongly xenophobic, competing fiercely with immigrants for jobs and other places in industry. At the turn of the century, these mainly supported the Radical Party.

This party, personified by its presidential candidate, Hipólito Yrigoyen, refused to negotiate politically with any of the opposition, including the oligarchy. It refused to enunciate any policy except its goal for a compulsory, secret ballot with universal male suffrage (finally achieved in 1912). Revolution, not compromise, was believed the major political weapon; one rebellion was attempted, in 1905. Yrigoyen coined the term "intransigent," which he applied to both himself and his wing of the party. After achieving power in 1916, the party was unprepared with any reform-oriented development policies but spent itself on personal feuds, which resulted in its split, with the "anti-personalist" faction in power, 1922–1928.

The twenties to the mid-forties were a period with bitter infighting; the now-senile Yrigoyen returning to power (1928–30); the military take-over and world economic crisis (1930s); and then World War II, which led into the populist, charismatic regime of Juan Domingo Perón (1946). Perón's approach was inflammatory and divisive; he played to the class-consciousness of the workers, promising them higher wages and more social benefits than he would

---

[5]Randall (1977a) provides quantitative information on all these events.

have been able to deliver had he remained in power. He financed them for a time through inflation, loss of international reserves, and internal decapitalization (especially loss of reproductive cattle), until the military—alarmed by impending bankruptcy—overthrew him (1955). The unavoidable austerity that followed left the working classes with strong nostalgia for Peronist bounty, and the belief that it had been taken from them not by exhaustion of resources but by some plot of the ever-powerful elite.

From that point on until the present, Argentina has vacillated between political regimes (military and civilian) and a wide range of policies, sometimes leaping from one set to its polar opposite. Randall (1977b) has argued that frequent changes in Argentine policy account for desultory economic performance. One student (Perez-Blanco, 1966) described the situation as follows:

> Argentina has tried all kinds of financial policies. Free exchange, official exchange, control of imports, industrialization plans that diverted most resources from agriculture to industry, plans of defense of agriculture that ruined new industries, and a tremendous inflation with control of certain prices, and rents, and salaries, that distorted completely the play of economic factors, creating enormous injustices in the distribution of wealth.

Argentina is by no means a primitive economy, but it is hard to measure how far advanced she really is. The Ministry of Economy (1979) reported GDP per capita in 1978 at $2,100 in 1960 dollars (adjusted by the consumer price index in the United States, this would be $5,345 in dollars of 1979). However, McLaughlin (1979), for the Overseas Development Council, reports Argentine per capita GDP at $1,550 in 1976,[6] and PQLI at 85. Per capita growth rates of GDP were 2.1 percent (1950–1960); 2.5 percent (1960–1970); and 3.7 percent (1970–1975). Thereafter, however, production spluttered. GDP, both overall and per capita, and industrial production, were less in 1978 than in 1974 (IFS Yearbook, 1979). Inflation (based on the consumer price index) averaged 117 percent per year, 1970–1978, reaching a rate of 175 percent, 1977–1978 (IFS Yearbook, 1979). Because of both the widely-shifting policies and the difficulties of measuring results, it appears to us impossible to perform any meaningful statistical analysis of the impacts of different policies.

The model of the Argentine political economy that most suggests itself to us is outlined in Figure 16–1.

Let us assume two products, military services and education, each with some objective measure other than money expenditure. The production possibility curve is divided into three segments. *BC* represents the "normal" range, showing substitutability of military for education in ways familiar to economists. If, however, students are deprived of education, to a point less than *OE*, they will riot. Resources necessary to suppress them subtract from *both* education and military effectiveness, so that the production possibility curve declines as one moves back from *B* toward *A*. Similarly, if the military is deprived

---

[6]GDP per capita depends on the exchange rate and the price index; defensible alternative rates yield widely divergent results. GDP per capita therefore becomes a very crude measure.

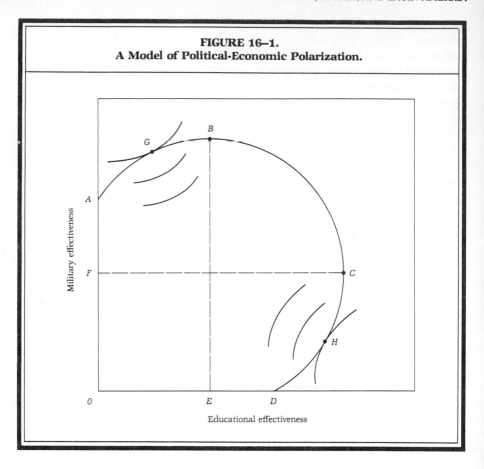

FIGURE 16–1.
A Model of Political-Economic Polarization.

Military effectiveness

Educational effectiveness

(less than *OF*), they will attack the students or close the university; this waste of resources causes the production possibility curve to decline again, as one moves from *C* toward *D*.

On the demand side, the military and the students so dislike each other that each has a positive indifference curve, rather than the usual negative. The military not only want to increase their own resources, but they delight in reducing those of the students, by ordering the schools to close. The students for their part would willingly harm themselves (through strikes) if they thought they could do more damage to the military. The military indifference curves are the ones that are convex upward. If the military are in power, the equilibrium is at *G*. The student indifference curves are convex downward, and if they are in power, the equilibrium is at *H*. A shift in power, from one group to the other, therefore leads to a pole-to-pole jump in national policy. Compromise within the "normal" range *(BC)* is not conceived of by either party.

This model, if applied to a number of other controversies as well, "explains" the endemic warfare that has been smouldering in Argentina for over two decades. The present "peace," in which the government has presumably defeated the guerrillas, represents only a more effective (and more expensive) lid than earlier, not a real reduction in pressure. As the rest of the world has condemned the official use of kidnapping and torture, the government has replied that similar tactics are employed by the guerrillas. It thus demotes itself to one of the contending parties, on the same level as the guerrillas. By its own choosing, it is no longer the superior power, whose duty would be to set the tone of national morality, moderation, and compromise.

CHILE[7]

In studying eighty-odd years of inflation in Chile, Hirschman (1963:209) makes a pregnant observation. Persistent inflation was the result of many controversies, each one different, strung out over the entire period, which nevertheless had one common characteristic: the inability of groups to make the compromises necessary for sound money. Hirschman suggested that a militant stance in and of itself had intrinsic value to each group, and that inflation was its cost. As inflation quickened, the intergroup hostilities became increasingly "expensive." Because no one side could concede gracefully, it was necessary to bring in foreign experts, who suggested no options that Chileans had not previously recognized. Rather, they supplied the "excuse" for otherwise embarrassing concessions, and they served as scapegoat for the inevitable austerity. These expert missions were a precursor to the International Monetary Fund, which has now institutionalized the excuse/scapegoat role.

Chile in the 1880s displayed many of the same promises as Argentina: the central valley was fertile and well irrigated by melting snows from the Andes. Like the English in the sixteenth century, the landowning aristocracy had incorporated nontraditional, bourgeois farmers who experimented with new methods. Capitalized by mineral exports as well as by agriculture, Chilean manufacturing grew strongly until the 1880s, bringing the country the strength to win the War of the Pacific in 1879 (Pike, 1968:61). From the late 1880s on, however, growth slowed, inflation persisted and occasionally intensified, and an earlier tendency toward income equality was reversed. In the twentieth century, income and wealth were very inequitably divided; industrial growth languished; the large farms (*fundos*) were notorious for their inefficiency; food production lagged; and Chile began to import the grains it should have exported. With peaceful and strongly constitutionalist traditions, the Chileans attempted many reforms through legislation, for which other Latin American countries resorted to violence. But none seemed to work.[8]

Let us consider one such attempt at reform, and its tragic consequences. In 1970, Salvador Allende was elected president through a coalition known as

---

[7]Much of the material in the present section, with additional data, was published in Powelson (1974).

[8]Some critics explain the Chilean turnabout by the overthrow of President Balmaceda in one of Chile's exceptional revolutions (1891). Balmaceda was an advocate of socialist-type reforms, expansion through paper money, and centralized government controls. This explanation appears to us simplistic, if only because we do not see how the Balmaceda conditions could continue to affect the country over half a century later.

Popular Unity, on a platform of radical land reform, nationalization of industry, expropriation of foreign companies, and central direction of the economy. One of his two opponents (Radomiro Tomic of the Christian Democrats) proposed substantially the same platform. Although Allende won by a plurality, his votes added to those of Tomic constituted a clear majority; hence a mandate for reform.

When Allende took office, Chile was divided into three distinct constituencies. In clear minority were the Conservatives, advocating the status quo. At the opposite extreme were the reformists, also a minority, many of them revolutionary, favoring the Popular Unity platform. In between was a large number of "middle class" voters, who might be persuaded either way. It was the support of this group (mainly Christian Democrat) that swung the election to Allende.

At first, Allende tried to steer a constitutionalist course, which might have kept the affection of the middle group. His reforms would be radical, but his methods legal. But the personnel of his own coalition would not permit this. Prophesying that reform could occur *only* through extralegal or illegal means, the left-wing groups within Popular Unity occupied farms without Allende's consent. Unwilling to alienate his supporters, Allende could only endorse their actions.

The prophesy was self-fulfilling. Through strict controls, the government diverted income to the poorer classes. Factories were required to hire more workers and pay them higher wages than could be afforded in the market. When management demurred, workers (unauthorized by government) would occupy the plant (without Allende's consent), forcing nationalization. Once nationalized, the factories had to be supported by subsidy. The ensuing government deficit led to both inflation and balance of payments deficit. To protect workers against the higher cost of living, the government subsidized commissaries in the factories. The balance of payments deficit led to import restrictions, which—together with diversion of domestic output to the workers' commissaries—emptied the ordinary shops patronized by the middle classes. These then defected to the Conservatives. Two years after he had taken office, Allende's country was polarized into his supporters and detractors, each of them feeling the case very strongly. Mass demonstrations were held in Santiago, one time by supporters and another by opposition. The other side would stay home behind shuttered windows while the streets would fill, giving the illusion of unanimity and great strength—each time for a different side.

The Christian Democrats held the balance of power in Congress; had they voted with Popular Unity (as many were at first inclined to do), the reforms could have occurred legally. Each time both groups were in basic agreement on a reform, however, minor discrepancies would bog them down. At one point (early 1973), they agreed on a list of companies to be nationalized, with the exception of one, representing the newsprint industry: Christian Democrats feared that its nationalization would lead to government control of the press; Popular Unity countered that nationalization was opposed because the company in question was owned by "favored" interests. Instead of accepting the bulk of the list and postponing the difficult decision, Parliament scrapped the whole matter, so "of course" the reform could not proceed legally.

The agrarian reform was undertaken with all deliberate speed. The previous government had expropriated 1,400 of the 5,350 farms above 80 hectares, and Popular Unity quickly expropriated the rest. During a visit to a reformed farm in 1972, the director of the Agrarian Reform Corporation (David Baytelman) explained to one of the present authors that the central valley of Chile is equal to California in both size and potential for fruit growing, and in addition it equals New Zealand in cattle possibilities. Whereas only 70,000 hectares were planted in fruit trees in 1970, it would be possible to have 500,000. Whereas New Zealand, with less pastoral land, had approximately 8 million head of cows and 70 million sheep, Chile had only 2.5 million cows and 6 million sheep. Not only was agricultural output low, but it was neither growing rapidly nor employing much labor. Reasons for this have been discussed in Chapter 11. Popular Unity recognized the situation and had high hopes of correcting it. But during their three years of power, agricultural output declined. When a nation has to be fed, three years may be all that a government is allowed.

In October, 1972, truck owners in the South went on strike to protest the government's ban on importing spare parts, one of the general restrictions caused by the balance of payments deficit.[9] Instead of gracefully acknowledging that spare parts were necessary to national transport and granting an exception, Allende retorted that the truck owners were "imperialist enemies" and threatened to nationalize them. This infuriated them, for they envisaged themselves as honest working men, not as "exploiters" in the same category as (say) the *fundo* owners.

Personal insults were traded with the Christian Democrat leaders as well. Once this threshold had been crossed, restoration of personal relations was impossible. The government could no longer finance itself by parliamentary sanction, only by printing money. Inflation ran at 19 percent during the first year of Popular Unity, 79 percent during the second, and 352 percent the third. (It continued high for several years after the regime had fallen). Manufacturing output increased by 15 percent during the first year, tapered to 2.7 percent during the second, and then fell by 4 percent during the third.

Some have argued that intervention by the United States was responsible for the overthrow. The Central Intelligence Agency is known to have supported the truckers' strike as well as to have financed opposition newspapers. But more likely explanations are the depth of the economic damage, wrought by dissention within Popular Unity, the inability to cooperate with the Christian Democrats, and above all the inflation that distorted resource allocations; the declining production; and the balance-of-payments shortages. It was indeed a Greek tragedy. Inexorable human impulses, including a belief in class struggle and martyrdom, made impossible those things that most Chileans had wanted.

---

[9]In various publications, slide shows, and movies prepared by Allende supporters in the United States after the overthrow, it has been alleged that U.S. automakers caused the shortage of spare parts by boycotting exports to Chile. After careful search, including the sources of information of some of those making the allegation, we have been unable to substantiate this belief. We followed the events closely as they occurred; the news explanations at the time were that shortages were caused by the balance-of-payments deficit, which led to a wide range of import restrictions.

CONCLUSION

The countries we have selected have not been random, and we have "proved" nothing. We have, however, attempted to show the likelihood that strong forces other than those normally considered by economists *may* underlie a country's rate of economic development. Economists familiar with LDCs will quickly recognize that the characteristics we have attributed to our selection are also found in other countries. Zambia's experience with inefficient parastatals parallels that of Tanzania; Uruguay's great promise at the turn of the century, and then her decline, reflect the experience of Chile and Argentina; Ethiopia's endemic warfare has slowed or stopped her growth, as warfare has also in Guatemala and El Salvador half way around the world; and intertribal warfare in Rwanda, Burundi, and Chad probably slows the growth of these countries as much as their geographical isolation. But no one yet knows how extensive these forces are or how well or poorly they correlate with development.

Let us now apply the five propositions of Chapter 15 to the countries we have discussed in the present chapter. The first, *freedom from restrictions*, requires qualification and interpretation. We do *not* mean a totally free market, which could be abused by those with financial power, either private corporations or government. We *do* mean decentralization of decisions, so that power over production and prices resides primarily with producers or their immediate agents. We have seen, in P.R. China, that such power can be efficiently exercised by local authorities. With this qualification, we find that relative freedom from restrictions applies to the three East Asian countries. We also find that the period of relative liberalism in Chile and Argentina in the nineteenth century corresponded to the period of their most rapid growth, just as it did in Europe.

In all our countries except Iran, the *leverage* of workers and peasants is indeed increasing. Only Iran has been able to offset it by importing sufficient foods (with revenues from oil). For the others, the increasing need for foodstuffs in the cities, and the capacity of peasants to evade controls, have been constraints on central government authority. The contrast lies mainly in the propensity of the East Asian governments to yield to this leverage, but of others to fight it. In both Chinas and in Japan, the governments have given the peasants wide range. In Kenya, the government is giving in grudgingly, retaining its control over food prices, but supplying more technical and financial assistance to farmers. The leverage of the *poor* farmers, however, is reduced by the existence of rich ones. If Kenyan authorities remain perceptive of their own degree of leverage, they will in the future give in to the poorer farmers as their products are more and more needed.

In other countries, the leverage of farmers has been recognized only slowly and inconsistently. Despite Tanzania's rhetoric, her central government has maintained a firm hand over both rural planning and the pricing of foodstuffs. The resulting tension may help explain Tanzania's slowness. Because food is needed in the cities, the farmers *have* leverage; ultimately, this fact *must* be recognized. The rate of economic growth may therefore depend on how long it takes the authorities in Dar es Salaam to allow farmers free rein over production, prices, and allocation of resources. This is a question of their own future vision.

In both Chinas and Japan, *institutions of trust* are strongly developed. They have been for years, even centuries. Revolutions have interrupted them, but they have always been restored. In the other countries, *there is a tendency to suspend or destroy the institution if it yields a decision unfavorable to some group with the power to suspend or destroy.* Thus Parliament was prorogued in Kenya when (in 1976) it voted to investigate the mysterious death of one of its members who happened to have presidential ambitions and strong popular support. Planning in Tanzania, although local in the rhetoric has been centralized de facto. Allende of Chile tried to abolish Parliament and establish a one-house Assembly when Parliament would not pass his proposals into law. In Argentina as well as in Chile, the entire government was set aside because the military decided it was not functioning "properly." The ability to change, suspend, or abolish institutions at will enhances the capriciousness and volatility of policy, which we observed in Chapter 14 and again here, thus increasing the risks for development projects, whoever may undertake them. We therefore suggest that economic development requires a high value to be placed on institutions per se, such that the loss of one would be a greater cost than that of any unfavorable decision it might make. Parallel governments, such as the party in P.R. China, often sustain national ideology in favor of the country's institutions.

Certain personal qualities enhance or detract from the probability of firm institutions. We saw, for Europe, how the ability of governments to compromise evolved very slowly, along with the concept of balance of power. There is much evidence that in today's LDCs this ability also does not come easily. To force one's opponent to yield in disgrace appears to supply personal satisfaction. In 1979–1980, the most important objective of the Islamic government in Iran was not anything related to economic development or relief from want; it was to bring a cancer-ridden Shah home from exile so they could shoot him. Instead, he died abroad. In Japan, by contrast, the *protection* of one's opponent from disgrace is recognized as a principal ingredient in achieving a satisfactory compromise, so that one can get on with one's business. Institutions are needed for compromise; they do not serve well for confrontation.

Endemic warfare ended in East Asia in 1949. Japan had a bit of guerrilla action with the opening of a new airport in 1979, but it has been limited. The Chinese have shown an uncanny capability to turn on criticism, and then turn it off when it becomes excessive, with an obedience on the part of its people which would be unheard-of in most countries. This happened in the Hundred Flowers campaign (1957) and again with Democracy Wall (1979). This degree of restraint may be attributable to the Confucian ethic for loyalty, or to the effectiveness of the party in dispensing ideology, or to the police. Whichever it may be, endemic violence is under control. There is virtually no endemic violence in Kenya or Tanzania, but there are strong pressures for it in Argentina and Chile, which at the time of writing are being kept under lid. But they might explode at any time.

Finally, the shift from *propensity-for-power* to *propensity-for-material-wealth* is as elusive here as it was in Europe. We do not argue that Chinese and Japanese leaders do not like power for its own sake; certainly they wield it strongly, and there is much political repression in each part of China. But political power in these countries depends on material wealth; if development should stop, the government would fall. The same may also be so in Kenya, but it is probably not true for Iran, Tanzania, Argentina, or Chile. Other forces than economic growth appear to determine who will hold power in these countries.

In all these propositions, our critics will note the risk of circular reasoning, and we are also aware of it. First, we cannot measure any of the qualities we have observed (they are all vague-bordered sets). But more importantly, we may tend to confuse the results of (say) leverage with leverage itself. If we say that peasant leverage leads to decentralized decision-making, and if we infer the former from the latter, we have reasoned circularly.

The problem is not insoluble; it is just that we have not solved it. There may well be independent measures of peasant leverage on which social scientists could agree, so that the effects in different countries could be compared rigorously. We do not pretend that this does not need to be done; on the contrary, we hope to draw the attention of social scientists to the need.

BIBLIOGRAPHY

Ahmad, Eqbal, 4–25–79:
    "Iran: A Possible Landmark," *New York Times.*
Butterfield, Fox, 4–26–79:
    "China is Trying New Incentives for its Farmers," *New York Times.*
Butterfield, Fox, 12–27–79:
    "China's Trade Plan Has Capitalist Tinge," *New York Times.*
Chao, Kang, 1970:
    Agricultural Production in Communist China, 1949–1965, Madison, Wisconsin, University of Wisconsin Press.
CIA, 1978:
    China: Gross Value of Industrial Output, 1965–77, document no. ER78–103555, Langley, Va., Central Intelligence Agency (Xerox).
Cornblit, Oscar, 1967:
    "European Immigrants in Argentine Industry and Politics," in Véliz, Claudio, ed., *The Politics of Conformity in Latin America,* New York, Oxford University Press.
Crittenden, Ann, and Telsch, Kathleen, 11–25–79:
    "Shah's Disputed Wealth: A Key Issue in U.S.- Iran Conflict," *New York Times.*
Crook, Frederick W., 1975:
    "The Commune System in the People's Republic of China," in U.S. Congress Joint Economic Committee, *China: A Re-Assessment of the Economy,* Washington, D.C., Government Printing Office, pp. 366–410.
Donnithorne, Audrey, 1971:
    "Central Economic Control," in Chen, Kuan-I and Uppal, J.S., *Comparative Development of India and China,* New York, Collier-Macmillan (Free Press), pp. 119–32.
Erisman, Alva L., 1975:
    "China: Agriculture in the 1970s," in U.S. Congress, Joint Economic Committee, *China: A Reassessment of the Economy,* pp. 324–49.
Field, Robert M., 1971:
    "Chinese Communist Industrial Production," in Chen, Kuan-I and Uppal, J.S., *Comparative Development of India and China,* New York, Collier-Macmillan (Free Press), pp. 78–84.

Field, Robert M., 1975:
"Civilian Industrial Production in the People's Republic of China, 1949–74," in U.S. Congress, Joint Economic Committee, *China: A Reassessment of the Economy*.

GOC (Government of China/Taiwan), 1978:
Taiwan Statistical Yearbook, 1978, Taipei, Government of the Republic of China, Council for Economic Planning and Development.

GOK (Government of Kenya), various dates:
Plan I (1964–70); Plan II (1970–74); Plan III (1974–78); Plan IV (1979–83). Each plan is entitled *Development Plan;* each was issued in its initial year, Nairobi, Government Printing Office.

GOK (Government of Kenya), various dates:
Economic Survey, issued annually; Nairobi, Government Printing Office.

Heyer, Judith; Maitha, J.K.; and Senga, W.M., 1976:
Agricultural Development in Kenya: An Economic Assessment, Nairobi, Oxford University Press.

Hirschman, Albert O., 1963:
Journeys Toward Progress, New York, Twentieth Century Fund.

Ho, Samuel P. S., 1978:
Economic Development of Taiwan, 1860–1970, New Haven, Yale University Press.

Hunt, James C., 1968:
"Argentina," in Véliz, Claudio, *Latin America and the Caribbean: A Handbook*, New York, Praeger.

IFS Yearbook, 1979:
International Monetary Fund, *International Financial Statistics*.

Imaz, José Luis, 1964:
Los que Mandan (Those Who Rule), Buenos Aires, Editorial Universitaria, translated into English (1970) by Carlos Astiz, published by State University of New York Press, Albany, N.Y.

International Labor Organization, 1972:
Employment, Incomes, and Equality: A Strategy for Increasing Productive Employment in Kenya, Geneva.

Jacoby, Neil, 1966:
U.S. Aid to Taiwan, New York, Praeger.

Jain, Shail, 1975:
Size Distribution of Income: A Compilation of Data, Washington, D.C., World Bank.

Karcher, Martin, 1975:
"Unemployment and Underemployment in the People's Republic of China," *China Report*, Vol. XI, Nos. 5 and 6, September-December. Also, World Bank reprint series, No. 25 (1975).

Lardy, Nicholas R., 1978:
Economic Growth and Distribution in China, New York, Cambridge University Press.

Lenczowski, George, 1978:
Iran Under the Pahlavis, Stanford, California, Hoover Institution Press, Stanford University.

London, Miriam, and London, Ivan D., 1979:
"Hunger in China: The Failure of a System?" *Worldview*, Vol. 22, No. 10, October.

MacFarquhar, Roderick, 1974:
The Origins of the Cultural Revolution, New York, Columbia University.

McLaughlin, Martin M., 1979:
The United States and World Development, Agenda 1979, New York, Praeger.

Ministry of Economy of Argentina, 1979:
"Argentina in Figures," in *Economic Information on Argentina*, No. 100, September-October.

New York Times, 7–5–79:
"China Acts to Slow its Rate of Growth," *New York Times*.

Nyerere, Julius K., 1977:
  The Arusha Declaration Ten Years After, Dar es Salaam, Government Printing Office.
Ohkawa, Kazushi, and Rosovsky, Henry, 1973:
  Japanese Economic Growth, Stanford University Press.
Ohkawa, Kazushi, and Rosovsky, Henry, 1978:
  "Capital Formation in Japan," in Mathias, Peter, and Postan, M. M., *The Cambridge Economic History of Europe*, Vol. VII, Part 2, New York, Cambridge University Press.
Patrick Hugh, and Rosovsky, Henry, eds., 1976:
  Asia's New Giant: How the Japanese Economy Works, Washington, D.C., Brookings Institution.
Pérez-Blanco, Irma, 1966:
  "Analysis of Argentina's Finances," unpublished paper written for graduate seminar at the University of Pittsburgh.
Perkins, Dwight, H., 1975:
  China's Modern Economy in Historical Perspective, Palo Alto, Ca., Stanford University Press.
Pike, Frederick B., 1968:
  "Chile," in Véliz, Claudio, *Latin America and the Caribbean: A Handbook*, New York, Praeger.
Powelson, John P., 1974:
  "What Went Wrong in Chile," in *Cultures et Développement* (Belgium: University of Louvain), Vol. IV, No. 3.
Prybla, Jan S., 1978:
  The Chinese Economy: Problems and Policies, Columbia, S.C., University of South Carolina Press.
Randall, Laura, 1977a:
  A Comparative Economic History of Latin America, 1500–1914, Vol. 2: Argentina, Ann Arbor, Michigan, University Microfilms International, for the Institute of Latin American Studies, Columbia University.
Randall, Laura, 1977b:
  An Economic History of Argentina in the Twentieth Century, New York, Columbia University Press.
Rawski, Thomas G., 1979:
  Economic Growth and Employment in China, New York, Oxford University Press, for the World Bank.
Sawyer, M., 1976:
  "Income Distribution in OECD Countries," *OECD Occasional Studies*, Paris, July.
Shabad, Theodore, 7–12–79:
  "Peking Gives First Details of Economy in 20 Years," *New York Times*.
Sterba, James P., 9–1–80:
  "New Chinese Policy Emphasizes Profit and Local Control," *New York Times*.
Taira, Koji, 1978:
  "Factory Labor and the Industrial Revolution in Japan," in Mathias, Peter, and Postan, M. M., *The Cambridge Economic History of Europe*, Vol. VII, Part 2, New York, Cambridge University Press.
U.S. Department of Commerce, 1978:
  World Population, 1977, Washington, D.C.
World Bank, 1975:
  Kenya into the Second Decade, Washington, D.C., World Bank.
Yamamura, Kozo, 1978:
  "Entrepreneurship, Ownership, and Management in Japan," in Mathias, Peter and Postan, M. M., *The Cambridge Economic History of Europe*, Vol. VII, Part 2, New York, Cambridge University Press.

EPILOGUE

(Continued from the Prologue, on the assumption that the book has been read in between.)

"But wait!" one may object. Another difference is that the universe of astrophysicists operates by laws of its own, beyond the control of those who study it. Do not economists at least influence the development of our universe?

Do we? Would it not be shattering to discover that economic development also operates by laws of its own, which we cannot control? Physicists do know ways to improve human welfare. They tell us how to keep warm, how to have light without sun or fire, and how to conserve energy. Perhaps economists can do nothing more than the analogues of these.

Let us settle for an in-between position. Economic development is not quite so uncontrollable as the physical universe. The Japanese did it later and faster than the Europeans. The differences were not preordained from a big bang but depended on the choices of the Europeans and the Japanese, on economic, political, and other policies. But all of these choices appear to us to depend on reasons that are primarily noneconomic. For example, the Japanese preference for compromises and face-saving decisions may have accelerated development (after 1868), which was so retarded by endemic violence in Europe.

Revolutionaries will disagree with us, for they may believe that equitable development is impossible without confrontation and violence. They will criticize us for allowing our ethical judgment against war to interfere with our objective reasoning. We admit the ethical judgment, but we also believe there is strong evidence that endemic violence has eaten away capital, both financial and real, that it has increased objective risk, and that it has clouded the visions of persons who might otherwise have perceived economic opportunities through cooperation with adversaries.

We further believe that revolutionaries rely on violence in part because they do not understand leverage. Believing the powerful elites to be monolithic, revolutionaries may not seek fissures among them by which the poor, through strategic alliances, might lever their minimal power. We also wonder if the revolutionaries' belief in the powerlessness of the poor is similar to the disdain for the poor expressed by Europe's "enlightened" despots.

So, how does one decide whose judgment is correct, the revolutionaries' or ours? We have tried to argue our case on historical evidence: the power (however little) that the poor have exercised in the past, the ways they have manipulated their alliances, the fissures among the powerful groups, and the ways slavery has ended and agrarian reform has occurred without violence in some places. Let the revolutionaries argue their case on the same grounds, and it is not impossible that an impartial jury might be found.

We have also argued that, in the long term, economic development occurs only with increasing equity. The evidence lies in the more equitable distribution of income in MDCs than in LDCs and the increasing use of leverage by the poor to obtain social reforms such as universal free education, effective unemployment insurance, hospitalization, and old-age benefits.

The underlying leverages do not depend on whether the regime is capitalist or socialist, but on whether the poor posses the requisite skills and organization. The same leverage that gave rise to labor unions in the North German Federation in 1869 before an unwilling, autocratic Bismarck, did so in Poland in 1980 before an equally recalcitrant Gierek. Development is also bestowing leverage on black workers in South Africa. In the long run, the South African question is the same as in any country—not whether development will occur with equity but whether both will or will not be sustained at all, and whether they will be delayed by violence. These are the human questions whose answers do not lie in economics.

Having said that, we descend from outer space into the world where economists mainly function. Here we meet the problems of technological choice, investment, employment, population, human capital, and policy and planning, which occupy the minds of most development economists. We have reviewed the literature in all these fields. We have suggested that "proper" choices (such as technology that takes factor endowments into account) and decisions to save adequately and to invest ("the poor will save when they see a valid opportunity to invest") depend on pluralism and relative balance of leverage. The ability to shift alliances leads to more efficient allocation of factors, because efficient alliances have the greatest pay-off (by definition).

Our schema are explained in Figure E–1. The lower third of this figure is the area of growth theory, centering on land, labor, capital, technology, and GDP. We move upward into government policies and individual decisions that affect these variables and are affected by them. The top line of the lower half portrays the kinds of institutions that evolve with economic development. It is here that large numbers of micro-studies are being done, which (we suggest) are making the most insightful contributions to economic development today.

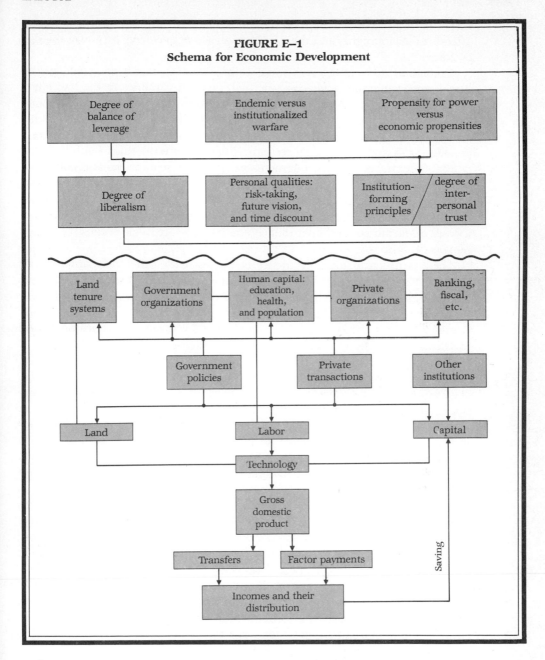

FIGURE E–1
Schema for Economic Development

Above this area is a wavy line; above that line are the softest variables of all (vague-bordered sets). Not only do we not know how to define them clearly, but we do not know precisely how they influence those in the lower half. The upper area consists of qualities of people and institutions, generally taken as *certeris paribus* in economic models, or else considered to be the unknown reasons why parameters differ in different cultures. Would we not be surprised some day to discover that these *cetera paria* were indeed the major forces affecting development, and that we have all along been trying to wag the dog by its tail?

In Chapter 1, we suggested three paths of development: personal, institutional, and economic. The economic path deals in variables in the lower half of Figure E–1; in number of pages, it constitutes the bulk of this book. Our venture into the upper part (personal and institutional) is inferential. We cannot as yet isolate individuals with greater time discount, future vision, and propensity to risk and show that these individuals prefer economic wealth to power or that they make superior judgments on economic institutions and policy. All we can do is show (by historical example, not proof) that development is likely to be associated with the three items at the top of the chart (balance of leverage, decline in endemic warfare, and shift of propensities away from power and toward materialism) and infer that choices on these are made because of certain personal qualities.

There is much historical evidence to suggest wide differences among both national leaders and humbler people in the four personal characteristics we have mentioned. Intuitively, we attribute differences in development outcomes to differences in these characteristics. Medieval rulers in Europe persistently passed regulations that they had no hope of enforcing. Since we see no motive for them knowingly to do so, we assume shortness of vision. The volatility of economic policies in many LDCs today (Chapter 14) also implies shortness of vision. Frequent, sudden shifts by the same government to diametric opposites suggest that the full implication of at least one of the policy sets was not understood. Volatility in government behavior must also cloud the vision of those whose decisions depend on what the government does. The tendency toward extreme measures—such as a cut-off of all imports to solve a balance of payments deficit (which Kenya and Argentina have done within the past decade)—suggests incomplete understanding of the effect on industrial output and employment.

Sometimes it is difficult to tell what mix of the four personal characteristics affects a particular case, although we sense their influence in the aggregate. In Chapter 14, we observed the alacrity with which European countries constructed their economic community, whereas every experiment in economic integration in the less-developed world was persistently delayed until it largely failed. Since few would question the powerful academic arguments for integration, and since the failures have all been of political will rather than of inappropriate economics, one must attribute these failures to deficiences in the personal characteristics mentioned—possibly among the rulers, but just as likely among the businesses and laborers whom they represent.

The pervasive restrictions imposed by LDC governments may also reflect an unwillingness to risk economic failures by entrusting outcomes to the citizens (disdain for the poor). The unwillingness of many LDCs to join the General Agreement on Tariffs and Trade (GATT) may also reflect risk aversion, representing in part a belief that whatever MDCs "connive" to do is not in LDC interests and in part a lack of confidence in their own negotiating ability.

Excessive promises by politicians not only reflect their own weak vision but also may impair the vision of their constituents. The administrations of Perón in Argentina, Goulart in Brazil, Arosemena in Ecuador, Paz Estenssoro in Bolivia, Sukarno in Indonesia, and Allende in Chile promised their constituents far more than they could deliver, given any objective assessment of their resources. These were not the usual superlatives touted by politicians everywhere; they were vastly excessive commitments which both the candidates and the constituents genuinely believed could be performed. In Allende's Chile, workers or farmers occupying factories or farms believed that public programs would provide them with inputs whose aggregate demand clearly exceeded the government's capacity to supply.

We have selected the four personal characteristics in order to condense the many variables that other social scientists have described: overall modernity, anomie, limited good, culture of poverty, and the like. The models of these social scientists do not easily integrate with one another, much less with economic models. But our personal characteristics, if quantified, might represent all of them and be compatible with economic models, taking their place alongside technology and factors of production as explanations of growth.

Since the four characteristics have not been quantified, we have contented ourselves with historical inferences. Our ambition was only to present a plausible description of the development process, through the five propositions of Chapter 15, which depend on the three paths of Chapter 1. We cannot at this stage prove that this description is correct, nor can anyone prove it is wrong. Yet policy decisions depend on beliefs about these propositions, one way or another.

Let us see how this is so. Suppose (for argument) that the quantity and allocation of investible funds in any country are determined by the soft variables at the top of Figure E–1. In that case, they are not primarily influenced by the availability of funds from international institutions or foreign-aid programs. These institutions may only replace funds (in both quantity and allocation) that would otherwise have been supplied from other sources, causing private or public funds to be diverted to consumption or to acquisition of foreign assets. But the way the international-aid programs operate must reflect a belief that this is not so, that instead, economic explanations dominate development.

Suppose, alternatively, the international financial institutions and administrators of aid programs did believe our propositions. In that case, they might make their aid depend not on a national economic plan, but on the government's ability to compromise with its adversaries or to end endemic warfare (by other means than putting a military lid on it). They might also experiment with ways to increase the propensity for risk-taking or to decrease the future discount of decision-makers in client countries. Since (in one way or another) the behavior of lending institutions must depend on their beliefs about the development process, any serious propositions should not be cast aside merely because they cannot be proved.

International institutions and foreign-aid administrators are often referred to as advocates of development. But if our description of development is valid, no one advocates it. Rather, development happens or fails to happen as non-development objectives are specified and achieved. Each so-called advocate of development can be no more than an advocate of a specific person or group. Missionaries advocate those whom they help; philanthropic agencies working in rural areas may advocate the rural poor; the World Bank advocates its member governments; and foreign-aid agencies advocate their home governments.

We demonstrate the above by making a contrary assumption. Suppose the World Bank were an advocate of development. Its most rational behavior, then, would be to define its product (development) and to buy it. Suppose development were measured by an increase in per capita GDP and an improved distribution of income, with a specified trade-off (perhaps through a GAD index). The distribution part might be difficult to measure without bias (for Gini coefficients can be faked), but it could be estimated by proxy. The Bank could infer that income distribution is improved if the earnings of a random sample of small farmers or inhabitants of urban slums are increased. It might make its own measures, unannounced, just as an auditor makes a surprise visit to count his client's cash. If its loans were made only to creditworthy governments to reward measured achievements, the Bank would no longer have to analyze projects, prepare models, or suggest policy. Surely its work would be more efficient, and it might "buy" a greater increment in human welfare than it does now.

If the Bank were only an advocate of development, it would probably do something of this sort. Because it does not, we infer that instead, it advocates its member governments. To survive, it must make a certain number of loans to a certain number of countries (both numbers not formally specified). If it "bought" development where the quantity was greatest and the price cheapest, it might confine its activities to only a few countries.

If economic consultants and purveyors of funds do not advocate development, what do they do? They enhance the leverages of their client groups, and whether or not development is promoted depends on whether this enhancement promotes overall balance, as well as on the policies of those groups. By enhancing the leverage of LDC governments, quite possibly the World Bank promotes *im*balance of leverage. Much depends on how leverage is already distributed. If LDC government officials believe their own political futures are advanced by advocacy of small-scale farming, then development may be promoted (because we know, from history, that widespread agricultural development precedes industrial development). But if they believe their own futures are best ensured by investing in enterprises from which they gain personally, then development may not be advanced significantly. The degree of organization among small-scale farmers, the needs of urban industry for food, the alternative possibility of buying from "efficient" large-scale farmers or from foreigners, and the forward vision, risk-propensity, and time discount of the government officials and farmers—all affect the leverages that determine the outcome. It is in these areas that further study is needed.

If our four personal characteristics were quantified for a number of countries, we might not have to rely primarily on historical inferences. It would seem reasonable that social psychologists could devise measures of all of them. Aggregates (averages and dispersions) could then be estimated for different populations, for nations as a whole and for subgroups within them.

Why has this not happened? We see five possible reasons, all of which relate to the human interaction between researcher and subject. First is our reluctance to "blame" people. It is easier to attribute underdevelopment to "things," such as lack of capital. President Mobutu of Zaire refers to "underequipped nations." Second, MDC social scientists are still smarting from nineteenth-century ethnocentricism and racism and from the now-discredited belief in cultural evolution from "lower" to "higher" orders.[1] Third, there is always the temptation to call others "short-sighted" merely because they disagree with us. This cannot be avoided if (as in the present book) the schema are intuitive. But it could be avoided if measurements were made. Any measure of shortness of vision (and the other characteristics as well) must be objective. Fourth, we economists do not wish to offend our clients or their institutions. We prefer to make recommendations for economic policy, and if those recommendations are not accepted, it is not our fault. (Ours not to reason why). A fifth reason may be that some LDC governments require official approval of all social research done in their countries, whether by nationals or by foreigners. The bureaucrats may fear research whose findings might threaten them. These five inhibitions are all part of Mannheim's (1929) Paradox, that we social scientists try "objectively" to study ourselves.

In the quotation introducing Chapter 3, Etzioni and Etzioni (1964) suggested that one day there might be a theory of history which, upon empirical investigation, would be found true. We do not see any sign of such a theory. Our own attention has been directed to history only as it might explain economic development. We have also examined numerous micro-studies, each one relating to development in some specific way. While we have generalized upon these studies and upon history, we despair of combining them into a single, provable grand design. For the foreseeable future, therefore, there will be alternative paradigms for development, of which ours is one.

Consciously or not, economists do select among such paradigms in setting the frameworks for their policy decisions. It has been our modest hope that we might, in this book, make more explicit some of the assumptions that economists have been wont to make, implicitly, one way or another.

BIBLIOGRAPHY

Etzioni, Amatai, and Etzioni, Eva, 1964:
  Social Change: Sources, Patterns, and Consequences, New York, Basic Books.
Mannheim, Karl, 1929:
  Ideology and Utopia, translated by Louis Worth and Edward Shils, New York, Harcourt, Brace, and Co., 1946.

---

[1]One of the pre-publication reviews of the present manuscript suggested racism in our own reasoning—a charge we deny emphatically, for our personal characteristics are individual. We do suggest they may not be randomly distributed over the world, but differentially among cultures and historical eras (within western as well as other cultures). Nothing hints at a racial distribution.

AUTHOR INDEX

This index contains all authors cited in the book, both persons and institutions. Page numbers following the letter *T* refer to citations within the text. Page numbers following *B* indicate where an author is listed in an end-of-chapter bibliography. These bibliographies are presented in alphabetical order, but authors whose names appear second or later in a citation will be found in the alphabetical order of the author first mentioned. Persons cited in a capacity other than as an author are found in the subject index.

SUBJECT INDEX

This index includes names of all persons cited in the text in a capacity other than as author.

A

Abaluhya tribe, 280
Abassid caliphate, 237
Abélard, Peter, 238
Absenteeism, 224
Absolute income level, 135, 137
Absolute poverty, 82, 116
Accounting, 71
Accounting unit, 99
Achievement need, 62
ACP Countries, 309
Adullamites, 29
Advocacy, 415
African kingdoms, hierarchy in, 29
Age Gini, 115
Aggregate output, 164
Agrarian reform:
    and mechanization, 259
    and productivity, 257
    and violence, 255–57
Agricultural mechanization, 143
Agricultural productivity, 137
Agricultural sector, 141
Agriculture, size and efficiency, 29–30

Alexander the Great, 55
Allende, Salvador, 403–405
Amoral familism, 63–64
Amsterdam Exchange Bank, 375
Andean Group, 344
Anomie, 57–58
Appropriate technology, 169, 170, 187
APRA, 12
Argentina, economic development, 399–403
Aristotle, 3
Arusha Agreement, 309
Arusha Declaration, 397
Asoka, 236
Assets, 156
Augustus, 28, 195, 361
Austrian Succession, War of, 370

B

Backward-sloping supply curve, 70
Balance of leverage:
    definition, 16–17
    theory, 364–66